Lathyrus

The complete guide

Greg Kenicer & Roger Parsons

RHS Horticultural Monograph

Inspiring everyone to grow

First published in 2021 by the Royal Horticultural Society:
RHS Media, Churchgate, New Road, Peterborough PE1 1TT, UK

Registered office:
Royal Horticultural Society, 80 Vincent Square, London SW1P 2PE, UK

Registered charity number 222879 / SC038262

rhs.org.uk

10 9 8 7 6 5 4 3 2 1

ISBN 9781911666127

A CIP catalogue record for this book is available from the British Library.

Specialist Publications Editors: Mike Grant & Rosalyn Marshall
Specialist Production Editor: Ally Page
Art Editor: Mark Timothy
Designer: Fiona Hood
Colour reproduction: Anthony Masi
Books Publisher: Rae Spencer-Jones
Head of Editorial: Chris Young, Tom Howard

Printed and bound by Bell & Bain Ltd, Glasgow, UK

Front jacket: *Lathyrus belinensis*

Rear jacket: *Lathyrus odoratus* 'Gwendoline' (left), *Lathyrus rotundifolius* (top right), *Lathyrus multiceps* (bottom right)

Half-title page: *Lathyrus latifolius* from Pierre-Joseph Redouté's *Choix des Plus Belles Fleurs* (1827–1833)

Opposite title page, left to right: *Lathyrus rotundifolius, Lathyrus nervosus, Lathyrus pratensis*

Opposite: *Lathyrus aureus*

Contents

Foreword

This monograph is unquestionably a monumental work that will be quoted for decades to come. It is especially pleasing to see the fusion of botanical and horticultural knowledge in one volume.

As a sweet pea breeder myself, I know that an understanding of the botany, distribution and ecology of a genus is fundamental to the successful cultivation and breeding of a plant. While sweet pea (*Lathyrus odoratus*) is the best known garden plant in the genus, it is important to be alerted to the virtues and uses of other members of the genus provided by the comprehensive 'Species' chapter.

Many garden plants owe their variability to hybridisation between species brought together in cultivation. In contrast, the sweet pea and probably most of the other *Lathyrus* species are obligate inbreeders where pollination occurs several days before each individual flower opens. For this reason, each taxon brought into cultivation has remained as a self-perpetuating pure species, with substantial breeding barriers between each. This explains the limited variability of species other than *L. odoratus*, which until recently has relied entirely on mutation for variation.

The 'Breeding and Selection' chapter alone reflects decades of disciplined historical research reaching worldwide. It provides a balanced and comprehensive account of the development of the sweet pea in cultivation while disabusing a few myths and misconceptions on the way.

This publication is a worthy addition to the series of monographs devoted to individual genera, published by the Royal Horticultural Society, thereby further adding to the Society's reputation as the world leader in promoting science-based horticulture to all gardeners and plant enthusiasts.

Dr Keith Hammett QSM
President of the Royal New Zealand Institute of Horticulture
April 2021

Widespread in South America, *Lathyrus nervosus* is a beautiful species that will thrive in a mild garden.

Acknowledgements

Greg Kenicer would like to thank his wife Kim for her huge support through many years, and also Joe and Sam for their patience with a dad who wanders off to look at *Lathyrus*. It must be said that he is delighted at their interest and knowledge on the topic. He would also like to thank friends and supervisors of his *Lathyrus* studies, particularly Toby Pennington, Gwil Lewis, Steve Broich, Jin Murata, Tadashi Kajita, Janet Sprent, and Euan James as well as the late Philip Smith, each of whom was inspirational. Similarly, Colin Hughes and the immensely supportive global community of legume specialists. Research and care of collections would be impossible without the support of David Knott and the superb horticulture team at RBGE; Michelle Hart, Laura Forrest and Ruth Hollands in the labs; and Lesley Scott, Elspeth Haston and David Harris among many others in the herbarium. Thank you also to the many hundreds of students who have enjoyed and endured learning about these fascinating plants.

Greg's greatest debt of thanks is to the late Sylvia Norton, former Plant Heritage National Plant Collection holder for *Lathyrus*. Her knowledge and passion for the genus were always a delight to experience, and it is hoped that this book can in some measure pass that on to others.

Roger Parsons would like to thank his wife, Alison, who has been with him through everything since their marriage in 1977 and without whose support and understanding he would have achieved little in his life. He would also like to thank his many friends in the National Sweet Pea Society and elsewhere, especially those raising new cultivars, who have helped with bits of information and pictures for use in this book. It is always risky to highlight outstanding support, but two people deserve particular thanks: Dr Keith Hammett of Auckland, New Zealand, who has been a friend, guide and inspiration for about 25 years; and Dr Kaoru Nakamura from the Miyazaki Agricultural Research Institute, Japan, has always cheerfully helped with information relating to sweet peas in Japan.

For Roger, the work represents a culmination of about 35 years growing and learning about sweet peas. He has relied on a more detailed account of the cultivation of sweet peas which appears in his book *Sweet Peas: An Essential Guide* (2011), and is grateful to Crowood Press for their support in enabling this current RHS book to be published. He is still learning about the genus and cannot speak too highly of the friendship and good will that exists among *Lathyrus* enthusiasts, especially all those he has met along the way at flower shows.

Greg Kenicer Royal Botanic Garden Edinburgh
Roger Parsons Chichester, West Sussex
April 2021

Lathyrus odoratus 'America' is an Old-fashioned Grandiflora cultivar from 1896 and is still considered good enough to hold the RHS Award of Garden Merit.

Introduction

Lathyrus have had a connection with humans for nearly 10,000 years. They were almost certainly used as food in the early days of agriculture, and still are to the present day. In modern times they are subjects for agronomic, ecological and genetic research. Of more relevance to readers of this book will be their significant ornamental value in gardens. The sweet pea (*Lathyrus odoratus*) in all its colourful and scented diversity is the best known example, and regularly tops surveys of favourite garden plants. However, many other species are also appreciated in gardens, and we highlight others here that we hope will become more widely grown.

There has never been a monograph of the entire genus, although sweet peas themselves have been covered by two books for gardeners in the past two decades (Rice 2002, Parsons 2011). This book comes at a time when there has been a resurgence of interest in *Lathyrus*. This interest is not only in sweet peas, where a wider range of types than ever before is now available to gardeners, particularly in the semi-dwarf types suitable for smaller gardens. It also extends to species such as *L. vernus* and its expanding range of cultivars, as well as more unusual subjects such as *L. magellanicus* and *L. nervosus*. In addition, *Lathyrus* is a genus where new species continue to be described, such as *L. belinensis*, discovered in Turkey in 1987, and now contributing in a major way to sweet pea breeding.

Seed companies have also increased their range of cultivars and mixtures. Much of the credit for this, and for better quality stocks of cultivars, goes to wholesale suppliers such as

LEFT **The genus *Lathyrus* contains much diversity in flower colour and form. Clockwise from top: *L. sativus*, *L. tingitanus* 'Roseus', *L. pratensis*, *L. aphaca*, *L. pratensis*, *L. tingitanus*, *L. chloranthus*, *L. sativus*, *L. latifolius*, *L. grandiflorus*, *L.rotundifolius*, *L. tuberosus*, *L. nervosus*.**

RIGHT **Discovered as recently as 1987, *Lathyrus belinensis* from Turkey is already contributing to sweet pea breeding.**

Lathyrus belinensis

Seedlynx of Maldon in Essex, and to Dr Keith Hammett in New Zealand. Public awareness in the UK has also been supported by the many National Sweet Pea Society displays at RHS flower shows and other major shows. These exhibits, mostly led by Tom Atherton, tell the story of the whole genus, not just sweet peas, and introduce gardeners to the diversity across this exquisite group of plants.

The recent revival in interest in growing sweet peas for cut flowers has been part of a broader movement to return to the cutting garden, inspired by ambassadors such as Sarah Raven and Georgie Newbery in the UK, and Erin Benzakein and Bailey Hale in the USA. This combination of home-grown produce and innovative floristry has created enormous interest in artisan growing, where locally-sourced flowers contribute to a richer and more sustainable lifestyle. Plant breeders such as Keith Hammett and author Roger Parsons were quick to support this emerging market by conserving good stocks of existing cultivars for cut-flower purposes and improving the choice of cultivars available.

The nursery owned by author Roger Parsons is a hub for sweet pea breeding and the conservation of cultivars.

Above all, this book has come about through the recognition by Plant Heritage of two National Plant Collections of *Lathyrus* in the UK. They are each held by the authors, and each with a different but complementary focus. Roger Parsons recalls growing sweet peas as a child along with other easy and delightful annuals such as stocks, marigolds and pansies. He started work as a professional horticulturist in 1970 and began growing sweet peas as a hobby in 1984. In 1993, as Head of Parks, he created a *Lathyrus* garden in Hotham Park, Bognor Regis, to house a National Plant Collection of *Lathyrus* species. At that time he was becoming alarmed at the loss of good sweet peas in the seed trade and the narrowing of the gene pool. He therefore began a seedbank in 1998 with the aim of conserving all *Lathyrus* in cultivation, which now contains around 1,300 cultivars stored in freezers. In 2005 he took early retirement and created the Roger Parsons Sweet Peas company. He was able to transfer the National Plant Collection from Hotham Park, having the time and space to extend this to include *L. odoratus* cultivars. His main interests are in the maintenance of cultivars and the breeding of new ones, in improving the quality of seed available to gardeners, and in recording the history of the sweet pea. His book *Sweet Peas: An Essential Guide* was published in 2011. From 2017 to 2020 he was Chairman of the National Sweet Pea Society, formed in 1900 with the objects 'to disseminate knowledge of sweet peas and other *Lathyrus* species, to encourage, improve and extend the cultivation of these flowers by means of scientific trials, the holding of exhibitions and displays, by publications and other activities'. The Society has an international membership. In 2012 he received the Henry Eckford Gold Memorial Medal, the National Sweet Pea Society's highest award, and in 2019 he received the Brickell Award for excellence in cultivated plant conservation from Plant Heritage.

Gregory Kenicer is a specialist in wild *Lathyrus* diversity. With interests in their evolution and biogeography, Greg was first inspired by the native UK species and their traditional uses. However, his PhD focussed on section *Notolathyrus*, the South American species that were largely unknown to horticulture. He investigated their biogeography and evolution and revised the taxonomy of the section as a whole. With many international collaborators, Greg has helped to unravel the underlying genetic relationships in *Lathyrus* and its allies, showing how the pea (*Pisum*) and the rare near-eastern alpine genus *Vavilovia* should be included in *Lathyrus*. This book adopts these recent findings. The wild species are found throughout most of the temperate regions of the world and have diversified into many forms and evolutionary niches. Some species are widespread and others very locally endemic and threatened in the wild. Some species are unmistakable, while others form complexes that can prove difficult to distinguish from each other, giving us fascinating snapshots of 'evolution in action'. Their huge popular appeal and potential to humanity as crops for the future means this book is hopefully a valuable first attempt to capture the diversity of this fascinating genus.

Lathyrus macropus from South America is one of the many species studied by author Greg Kenicer at Royal Botanic Garden Edinburgh.

Pois de senteur. *Lathyrus odoratus.*

History

As well as desirable ornamental plants, the genus *Lathyrus* includes species of prehistoric, historic and modern importance. This includes food crops, fodder plants, medicines, environmental improvers and weeds. Although a full discussion of its agronomy is beyond the scope of this book, *Lathyrus oleraceus* (previously *Pisum sativum*), garden pea, is considered one of the 'founder crops' of agriculture (Zohary *et al.* 2012). The genus also includes other important species for agronomic, ecological and genetic research, and several offer excellent potential for food security for arid lands.

For parts of the developing world, certain species of *Lathyrus* are critical sources of dietary protein, act as important fodder crops and are more widely used as ornamentals. The importance of the group as a whole was recognised in the United Nations International Year of the Pulse, celebrated in 2016. *Lathyrus* and its relatives offer huge potential for the future in this respect. Many have large, easily stored, nutritious, protein-rich seeds, and there are many drought-tolerant species in the group, such as *L. sativus* (grass pea) and *L. cicera* (red-flowered chickling vetch). They are not without their downside, as some of the otherwise edible species produce amino acids that act as neurotoxins if they form too high a proportion of the diet. Efforts to breed tasty, completely non-toxic cultivars are under way.

In this chapter the use of *Lathyrus* species as crops and garden plants through history is discussed.

PREHISTORIC USES

Humanity's relationship with *Lathyrus* is ancient. It goes back to the earliest days of agriculture, and almost certainly before. There is evidence that species were important crops, grown both for human consumption and as animal fodder, and were agricultural weed plants throughout the earliest Middle Eastern cultures (Riehl 2008).

LEFT *Lathyrus odoratus* (sweet pea) from Pierre-Joseph Redouté's *Choix des Plus Belle Fleurs* (1827-1833).

RIGHT *Lathyrus cicera* (red-flowered chickling vetch) was widely grown as a food crop in prehistoric times.

Seeds of unidentifiable *Lathyrus* species have been found in food stores in Çatalhöyük, a Neolithic urban settlement, now in modern Turkey (Fairbairn 2007). Similar finds have also been made in Egypt, long before the time of the Pharaohs (Van Zeist & de Roller 1992). At Jarmo in modern Iraq, another Neolithic site, evidence has been found of the use of *L. sativus* from about 8,750 years ago (Stearn 1996). Finds from two sites in Iran suggest that *L. sativus* was quite a common food there in the early Neolithic, between 11,500 and 7,700 years ago (Jackson & Yunus 1984). Remains of this species have also been found in early Neolithic sites in Cyprus, Hungary, Palestine and Switzerland (Stearn 1996). There is no direct evidence of cultivation at these sites, but the widespread distribution suggests people were moving the species around. Evidence from the Balkan Peninsula led Kislev (1989) to suggest annuals, including *L. sativus*, were cultivated there about 8,000 years ago. Remains from India from 3,500–4,000 years ago may indicate that the crop was being spread by people eastwards as well as westwards from western Asia (Campbell 1997).

After *L. oleraceus* and *L. sativus*, *L. cicera* was probably the third most cultivated species in prehistory. It has been grown in Spain since the early Neolithic (Peña-Chocarro & Peña 1999), and remains from the archaeological site of Azmaska Moghila in Bulgaria, dating to a similar time, about 8,000 years ago, are thought to be *L. cicera* (Renfrew 1969). It is morphologically similar to *L. sativus*, with wings on the upper edge of the pods. This has led to speculation that they may share a recent common ancestry, or that *L. cicera* has a hybrid origin (Jackson & Yunus 1984, Campbell 1997). More recent DNA evidence (Schaefer *et al.* 2012) suggests they are clearly distinct species, but an ancient hybridisation event cannot be completely ruled out.

In classical times, all three of the above species appeared in the writings of Dioscorides, Theophrastus and Pliny as both medicines and foods.

USES IN THE MODERN ERA

Seeds of *L. japonicus* were eaten, without recorded toxic effects, in Suffolk, England, during a famine period in 1555 (Miller 1768). More recently, the same species was recorded

LEFT **Evidence of the consumption of *Lathyrus sativus* goes back at least 11,500 years.**

BELOW ***Lathyrus cicera* growing as an arable weed in Crete.**

BOTTOM **The edible seeds of *Lathyrus cicera* (left), *L. gorgonei* (right) and *L. sativus* (front). The different colours of *L. sativus* seed can reflect geographical origin.**

ABOVE LEFT **The pods of *Lathyrus japonicus* (sea pea) yield seeds that have been eaten in times of famine.**

ABOVE RIGHT **The tubers of *Lathyrus linifolius* have been chewed as a stimulant or added to spirits.**

as an impromptu snack from 20th-century Kent (Phillips 1983). In reality, the entire plants were probably eaten during the 16th century, as they would have been nutritious and fairly palatable. The effort required to collect the seeds that are smaller, harder and less tasty than peas would have been considerable.

Other species have also been used as foodstuffs by humans and may offer potential for revival as crop species. *Lathyrus tuberosus* is cultivated for its edible tubers (swollen rhizomes) throughout northern Europe, albeit on a far smaller scale than in the past. The tubers were particularly popular in 19th-century Holland, where they were eaten roasted (Lawson 1852, Johnson & Sowerby 1862, Norton 1996). The species also appears in Fuchs's *Herbal* (1542).

Another species with edible tubers is *L. linifolius*. The rhizomes were collected from the wild in Scotland and chewed as a stimulant, particularly by crofters in the Gaelic-speaking west and north of the country. Martin Martin, a Gaelic speaker writing in 1695 (Martin 2014), described it:

> 'The plant itself is not used, but the root is eaten to expel wind and they say it prevents drunkenness by frequent chewing of it; and being so used, gives a good relish to all liquors, milk only excepted. It is aromatic and the natives prefer it to spice for brewing aquavitae [whisky]. The root will keep for many years; some say that it is cordial, and allays hunger.'

Writing more than 70 years later, James Robertson, recording his tour of the Highlands of 1767–1771 (Henderson & Dickson 1994) said:

> 'The natives eat the root of the *Orobus Tuberosus*, or as they call it Charmelic,

it is said to be aromatic and is eaten before drinking Strong Liquors to prevent intoxication.'

Seeds of *Lathyrus sativus* for sale in Greece, where they are typically made into various types of fava dish.

Within a century, *L. linifolius* had become quasimythical – Thomas Pennant (1774) suggested that when infused in whisky it produced an agreeable beverage, which, 'like the Nepenthe of the Greeks, exhilarates the mind'.

John Lightfoot, in his *Flora Scotica* (1777), explained that:

'The Highlanders have great esteem for the tubercles of the roots of this plant; they dry and chew them in general to give better relish to their liquor; they also affirm them to be good against most disorders of the thorax, and that by the use of them they are able to repel hunger and thirst for a long time. In Breadalbane and Ross-shire they sometimes bruise and steep them in water and make an agreeable fermented liquor with them. They have a sweet taste, something like the root of liquorice, and when boiled, we are told, are well flavoured and nutrative, and in times of scarcity have served as a substitute for bread.'

Many of the larger species have been used as fodder for livestock (Fedchenko 1948) and several species, including *L. ochrus*, *L. sativus* and *L. tingitanus*, are grown in large quantities for this purpose. The drought tolerance of these species makes them suitable for cultivation in arid areas. *Lathyrus sativus* in particular is a significant crop in Ethiopia, Sudan and India, with 1.6 million hectares producing around 0.5 million tonnes of seed annually in India (van der Maesen & Somaatmadja 1989, Mathur *et al.* 1999). The seeds form an important part of the human diet in these areas, too, and are particularly important during times of famine. *Lathyrus sativus* flour is also made into various regional dishes, usually of a paste-like consistency, such as gachas manchegas in La Mancha, Spain. *Lathyrus clymenum* flour is mixed with chopped onion to make fava santorinis on the island of Santorini, Greece, typically served with olive oil, pine nuts and lemon. Also in Greece, the shoots and leaves of *L. ochrus* are a spring delicacy.

TOXICITY AND LATHYRISM

Several toxic, non-protein amino acids are present in *Lathyrus*, and are found in the seeds, roots and stems (Bell 1962a, Bell 1962b, Simola 1968b, Lambein *et al.* 1999). These give rise to a group of conditions termed lathyrism, which falls into two classes – neurolathyrism which causes paralysis, and osteolathyrism which causes skeletal deformations.

Both forms of lathyrism appear to be caused by metabolites of heterocyclic isoxazolin-5-one non-protein amino acids. One of these toxins, β -(isoxazolin-5-on-2-yl)-l-alanine, has been shown to be a broad-spectrum antifungal and is toxic to other eukaryotes, including plants and unicellular green algae. It is exuded from the roots of *L. odoratus* and *L. oleraceus* and may play an allelopathic role (Bell & Foster 1962, Lambein *et al.* 1999), helping to kill off neighbouring competitive seedlings, although this has not been demonstrated conclusively.

The main component causing neurolathyrism is β-N-oxalyl-L-α,β-diamino-propionic acid (β-ODAP) and is present in the seeds of many species, including *L. sativus*. β-ODAP is toxic when consumed as more than 40% of the total diet over extended periods, causing leg paralysis and muscle wastage. However, this level of consumption is rare and it is generally considered safe as part of a normal diet.

In order to improve it as an ideal famine food, a vast body of work has been devoted to research on *L. sativus* and closely related species in efforts to breed less toxic cultivars and document genetic diversity (discussed in Mathur *et al.* 1999). Although low-toxicity strains have been produced in the past, uptake was relatively limited in the areas where the plant is traditionally cultivated as local growers tend to regard seeds with an unfamiliar look or taste with suspicion. Recently developed Syrian strains are said to be very close in taste and appearance to traditional cultivars (Raloff 2000). However, these improved germlines will not breed true for low toxicity unless they are grown in isolation from high toxicity strains to reduce the risk of cross pollination.

Francisco de Goya's *Gracias á la Almorta* (1812–1814) is often translated as 'Thanks to the millet', but actually refers to grass pea, *L. sativus*. It depicts a real conflict between starvation and disability. The refugees of war survive thanks to the resilient grass pea crop, but at a cost to their mobility – the woman in the foreground is suffering from neurolathyrism.

A case of neurolathyrism is depicted in Goya's *Gracias á la Almorta.*

EARLY CULTIVATION

Interest in cultivating *Lathyrus* in gardens arose for possible food, fodder and medicinal uses. Of species not native to the UK, the first to be introduced was probably *L. sativus*. It is likely to be the 'Aegyptian common narrow-leaved wilde chickling' in John Tradescant's *Garden Catalogue* (1656) and was probably introduced to Britain and mainland Europe much earlier than 1656. *Lathyrus latifolius* is thought to have been introduced to Britain in the 16th century.

Gerard's Latin name	Gerard's common name	Modern interpretation
Lathyrus major latifolius	Pease everlasting	The illustration and description appear to depict *L. sylvestris*.
Lathyrus angustifolius flore albo	White floured chichlings	The illustration and description appear to depict *L. sativus* f. *albus*.
Lathyrus angustifol. flo. purp	Purple floured chichlings	The illustration and description appear to depict *L. sativus* var. *cyaneus*.
Lathyrus Aegyptiacus	Egyptian chichlings	The illustration and description appear to depict *L. sativus* f. *azureus*.
Lathyrus annuus siliquis Orobi	Party coloured chichling	The illustration and description appear to depict *L. articulatus*.
Lathyrus sylvestris flo. luteo.	Tare everlasting	The illustration and description appear to depict *L. pratensis*.
Terraglandes	Pease earth-nut	The illustration and description appear to depict *L. tuberosus*.
Astragalus sylvaticus	Wood pease, heath pease	The illustration and description appear to depict *L. linifolius*.
Orobus Venetus	Venice pease	The illustration and description appear to depict *L. venetus*.
Orobus sylvaticus vernus	Spring pease	The illustration and description appear to depict *L. vernus*.
Orobus montanus angustifolius	Narrow leafed mountaine pease	The illustration and description appear to depict *L. pannonicus*.
Ochrus, sine Ervilia	Birds pease	The illustration and description appear to depict *L. ochrus*.
Aphaca	Small yellow fetch	The illustration and description appear to depict *L. aphaca*.
Ervum sylvestre	Crimson grass fetch	The illustration and description appear to depict *L. nissolia*.
No Latin name given	A certaine pulse or pease … in Suffolk at a place by the sea side all of hard stone and pibble	A plant discussed under *Aphaca* of which the locals ate the seeds and roots, which appears to be *L. japonicus*.

Plants now in *Lathyrus* discussed in *The Herball* by John Gerard, revised by Thomas Johnson (1636)

RIGHT **Native to Mediterranean regions,** *Lathyrus amphicarpos* **was mentioned by Bauhin in 1650.**

Gerard's *Herball*, first published in 1597, contains descriptions, images and medicinal uses of a wide range of plants. It was the first herbal to be written in English and to include North American native species. The *Lathyrus* species included in the later 1636 edition revised by Thomas Johnson are detailed in the table (left).

Further *Lathyrus* species were either introduced or recorded in the 17th century. *Lathyrus aureus* was first seen by Bauhin in 1608 (Bauhin 1650). *Lathyrus annuus* is sometimes grown for fodder but its Iraqi name, *habb adh-dharāt* (meaning fart seed), may hold a clue why it is not more widely grown (Townsend 1974). It was introduced to Britain in 1621. *Lathyrus vernus* is said to have been introduced in 1629 and *L. articulatus* in 1640 (Chittenden & Synge 1956). *Lathyrus amphicarpos* is listed by Bauhin (1650), along with *L. hirsutus*. Fedchenko (1948) recommended *L. hirsutus* as a fodder crop. Yielding an abundant mass of foliage and remaining green for a long time, it has had recent favour for this purpose in Alabama, Georgia, Louisiana and Mississippi. *Lathyrus ochrus* is another long-established fodder crop. *Lathyrus tingitanus* was introduced to Britain in 1680 (Chittenden & Synge 1956). *Lathyrus laxiflorus* was known to Hermann Boerhaave and to Linnaeus in the early 18th century (Linnaeus 1753).

RIGHT **From eastern Europe,** *Lathyrus aureus* **was recorded by Bauhin when he saw it in 1608.**

FAR RIGHT *Lathyrus hirsutus* **is finding favour again as a fodder crop.**

FAR LEFT **Highly desirable in gardens, *Lathyrus nervosus* was introduced to England in 1744.**

LEFT TOP *Lathyrus pannonicus* **arrived from Europe in 1794.**

LEFT BOTTOM **The leaves of *Lathyrus pubescens*, which was introduced in 1840, distinguish it from *L. nervosus*.**

THE PLANT-HUNTING ERA

Around half of *Lathyrus* species have rarely, if ever, been introduced to cultivation. Many of those that are cultivated are limited to botanic gardens or specialist plant collections. The number of species in wider cultivation for their decorative or economic value is probably no more than 30. Several species in section *Lathyrostylis*, such as *L. cyaneus* and *L. digitatus*, are gardenworthy but have rarely been introduced, a situation that needs to be remedied.

From South America, *L. nervosus* was brought to England by Lord Anson in 1744. His sailors were said to have survived on its seeds while shipwrecked near Cape Horn (Gorer *et al.* 1991). There is a superbly accurate illustration of the species by Georg Ehret, dated June 1748, in the Natural History Museum, London. It was first mentioned in Philip Miller's *Gardener's Dictionary*, originally published between 1756 and 1759, and had been growing at Chelsea Physic Garden. He thought it was a biennial and says it is called Cape Horn pea, suggesting knowledge of the species was widespread among gardeners. He later named it *Pisum americanum* (Miller 1768) but this epithet could not be used in *Lathyrus* as Miller had named another plant *L. americanus* which is now a *Rhynchosia* (Gorer *et al.* 1991). Known now under Lamarck's 1788 name, *L. nervosus*, it has been reintroduced several times since and is commonly known as Lord Anson's pea. It was frequently listed in catalogues throughout the 19th century but there is good evidence that seed sellers were actually supplying *L. sativus* f. *azureus* under this name. To add to the confusion, illustrations of the true species were often incorrectly labelled as *L. magellanicus*, a completely distinct species, a practice which persisted until the middle of the 20th century (Gorer *et al.* 1991). A problem that then arose for those introducing true *L. magellanicus* in the late 20th century was a persistent belief that this was simply an outdated synonym of *L. nervosus*.

Also from South America, *L. pubescens* was introduced to Britain in 1840 when John Tweedie sent seeds from Buenos Aires (Brickell & Sharman 1986). It has similar fragrant flowers to *L. nervosus*, but the flowers of *L. pubescens* are paler, and this species deserves to be more popular. The two are easily distinguished by their very different leaves.

North American introductions have proved difficult to cultivate, even in North America, and are rarely encountered. *Lathyrus polyphyllus* is currently available and is similar to *L. japonicus*. *Lathyrus vestitus* is sometimes encountered and works well scrambling through other plants. *Lathyrus splendens* has been frequently introduced, first in 1881, but fails to survive. Its cultivation requirements are thought to include a complete absence of summer irrigation (Connelly 1993).

Of a few other widely grown species, European *L. pannonicus* was introduced to Britain in 1794, Mediterranean *L. grandiflorus* was introduced in 1814, Pyrenean *L. cirrhosus* in 1870 and East Asian *L. davidii* in 1883 (Chittenden & Synge 1956).

INTRODUCTION OF THE SWEET PEA

The sweet pea was first described in 1696 when Franciscus Cupani included it in his *Hortus Catholicus* (Cupani 1696) as *Lathyrus distoplatyphylos, hirsutus, mollis, magno & peramœno, flore, odoro*. Claims of earlier references have occasionally arisen but these have actually described other *Lathyrus* species.

BELOW LEFT **With its cane-like stems, *Lathyrus davidii* from East Asian woodlands was introduced to Britain 1883.**

BELOW RIGHT ***Lathyrus vestitus* is one of the few species from North America that do well in gardens.**

In 1699, Cupani sent seeds from Palermo, Sicily, to Robert Uvedale in Enfield, UK, and Caspar Commelin in Amsterdam, the Netherlands (Commelin 1701). A pressed specimen from 1700 is deposited at the Natural History Museum in London. Sweet peas have been in cultivation ever since, although representatives of the wild species had been lost by the end of the 19th century and were subsequently reintroduced (Parsons 2000). The first illustration, a drawing by Jan Mominckx, appeared in 1701 in Commelin's *Horti Medici Amstelodamensis*.

Sweet peas quickly became popular. James Petiver (1713) described what is now known as *Lathyrus odoratus* and said: 'This elegant sweet-flowered plant I first observed with Dr Plukenet in Dr Uvedale's most curious garden at Enfield, and since at Chelsea and elsewhere'. The colour was described as 'purple' but it is likely this refers to the maroon and violet bicoloured flower of the type species (Parsons 2011).

Lathyrus odoratus was introduced to Europe in 1699 but wild sweet pea is rarely seen in cultivation.

Other colour forms quickly arose by gene mutation from the dominant to the recessive condition. Heinrich Bernhard Rupp (1718) says of the sweet pea: 'Sometimes it varies with a white flower'. It is not clear when the pink and white bicoloured form (now called 'Painted Lady') arose but Linnaeus listed it in 1737 as *Lathyrus zeylanica* (Linnaeus 1753). It may predate the white form, since a pink and white bicolour is only one mutation removed from the wild type, whereas it takes two mutations to produce a pure white flower. In the 1730s, a seed catalogue from Robert Furber lists purple, white and 'variegated or Painted Lady sweet-scented pea' (Parsons 2011).

Weston's *Flora Anglicana* of 1775 includes *Lathyrus odoratus coccineus*, the scarlet sweet pea (Wright 1912). This is thought to be the colour now described as carmine. The first truly scarlet sweet pea was 'Queen Alexandra', announced in 1905 (Anon. 1905) and introduced in 1906. In 1782, Thomas Barnes of Leeds sold seed of scarlet, white, purple and 'Painted Lady' to Edwin Lascelles of Harewood House in West Yorkshire (Harvey 1974).

In 1788, William Curtis said: 'There is scarcely a plant more generally cultivated than the sweet pea... Several varieties of this plant are enumerated by authors, but general cultivation extends to two only. The one with blossoms perfectly white, the other white and rose-coloured, commonly called the Painted Lady Pea' (Curtis 1788).

In 1793, a seedsman named John Mason of Fleet Street, London, listed five sweet peas: black, purple, scarlet, white and 'Painted Lady', and a black-purple is mentioned in 1800 (Curtis & Eckford 1900), presumably the same as Mason's black. This may be the colour now seen in 'Purple Prince' (Parsons 2000).

EVOLUTION OF COLOURS IN THE 19TH CENTURY

In 1807 Thomas Martyn described the 'New Painted Lady pea', with red standards and pink wings (Miller & Martyn 1807, Parsons 2011). Beal (1912) thought this may have been the earlier 'Scarlet', which is elsewhere described as *Lathyrus odoratus rosea*. The two are never seen listed together. Page (1818) lists white, purple, black, scarlet 'Painted Lady' and striped, all grown at Southampton Botanic Garden. References from the 19th century to striped colouring describe what is now called flaked colouring. Modern use of the term 'striped' refers to a mutation first seen in the 1925 cultivar 'Lady Gay'.

Carter's 1838–1839 seed catalogue lists seven colours (Martin 2017). Mrs Loudon's *Ladies' Flower Garden of Ornamental Annuals* of 1840 includes the purple wild type, New Painted Lady, white, Old Painted Lady, blue ('which has the wings and keel a pale blue and the standard a dark bluish purple') and violet ('which has the keel a pale violet, the wings a deep violet and the standard a dark reddish purple'). Violet appears to be the earlier black or black-purple. In the second half of the 19th century a huge number of new colours and types arose through intentional crosses, and these are discussed in the 'Breeding and selection' chapter.

RIGHT **An illustration of *Lathyrus odoratus* in *The Botanical Magazine* (Curtis 1788).**

FAR RIGHT ***Lathyrus odoratus* 'Painted Lady' was one of the first sweet pea cultivars.**

INTRODUCTION TO OTHER COUNTRIES

It is not known exactly when the sweet pea was introduced into North America. It is reported to have been growing in the Governor's garden at Williamsburg by 1750 (Haughton 1978). At that point it was still a European novelty but was much admired, and soon became more widespread. In 1760 a Boston newspaper carried an advert from an enterprising milliner announcing that packets of sweet peas would be exhibited in her shop window along with the latest in spring bonnets (Haughton 1978). An 1804 seed list from Bernard McMahon of Philadelphia includes purple, white, blue, scarlet and 'Painted Lady'. The blue may be *L. sativus* f. *azureus*.

By 1870, James Vick of Rochester, New York, was offering nine colours. His cultivar named 'Black' is described as 'very dark, brownish purple' and his cultivar named 'Black with Light Blue' is described as 'brownish purple and light blue' (Vick 1871).

The 1890s saw an explosion of interest in sweet peas in North America, outstripping their popularity in the UK. This was fuelled by the writings of Revd. William Tucker Hutchins (1849–1917) and the importation of Henry Eckford's new Grandiflora cultivars. The first American cultivar was D.M. Ferry's 'Blanche Ferry' in 1889, and from then on American plant breeders were every bit as successful and innovative as those in Europe. American seed production utterly dominated the world from the 1890s onwards and is only now, in the 21st century, starting to lose that dominance.

Wherever British colonialists went, they seem to have taken sweet peas with them. In 1823, Mrs John Busby brought 'Painted Lady' into New South Wales, Australia, although the species may have been introduced into Australia earlier. The Busby family maintained this stock through many generations so that it remains in cultivation today (Pockley 1983). Winter-flowering cultivars are preferred in Australia because of the hot summers, and cultivation is mostly limited to the cooler states where keen competition still exists among the many exhibitors at local flower shows. The distinctive Gawler cultivars were developed in South Australia from the 1930s onwards. They tend to have characters such as hairless vegetative parts, multiple petals and exceptionally strong fragrance.

Sweet peas were grown in the Dunedin area of New Zealand by the 1880s, perhaps earlier, and Dunedin remained an important area for decades. George J. Errington (1878–1960) was an active exhibitor, breeder and judge of new varieties from Edwardian times until his death. Charles Trevethick (1854–1928) of Lower Hutt, Wellington, was a notable exhibitor, breeder and seedsman. In 1957, Patricia Unwin moved to the Gisborne area and started producing seeds for her father's UK seed business. The quality of these was soon recognised and Gisborne remains today the area where arguably the world's best sweet pea seed is produced.

A reference to the sweet pea in Chile in Gay's *Flora Chilena* (Clos 1846) may be the first record of its cultivation in South America (Burkart 1935). Its

The seed produced at Gisborne in New Zealand is regarded by some as the best quality in the world.

appearance in Gay's *Flora* suggests that the species had escaped from earlier introduction. However, speculation that the sweet pea was introduced to South America in the 16th century by Spanish conquistadors does not appear have any basis in evidence (Turral 1965).

In Africa, sweet peas grow well at altitude, such as the Kenyan highlands, or in parts of South Africa. The distinctive Télemly Series of winter-flowering cultivars, now lost, was developed in Algiers during the Edwardian period by Revd. Edwyn Arkwright (1839–1922), who was presumably there as a Christian missionary (Jacob 1911). Sweet peas have even made it to St Helena, where the uniform day length and cooling sea breezes mean sweet peas can be flowered almost throughout the year (Thomas 1971).

Sweet peas also grow well at altitude in northern India and Sri Lanka. They are now grown in China and are especially popular as a cut flower crop in Japan. Inoue (2007) states that sweet peas were introduced to the Japanese cut-flower industry from 1929. However, amateur gardeners there were growing them as early as 1900 (Hammett 2000) and the Imperial Horticultural Society of Japan held a sweet pea show at Tokyo in 1913, reported to be the first in the country (Motoyama 1914). Competitive showing of sweet peas, where they may also be dyed, remains popular among cut-flower growers in Japan and commercial production is an important industry there. Around 50% of blooms produced in Japan are produced in Miyazaki prefecture, where Kaoru Nakamura is employed as a plant breeder and is actively working on new cut-flower cultivars.

USE AS A MODEL ORGANISM

Lathyrus species have been used as model organisms for scientific research in a broad range of areas. Many wild species are common in Europe and North America and are easy to cultivate. Furthermore, the widespread distribution and diverse, but manageable, size of the group makes it ideal for research into evolutionary and biogeographical patterns at the genus level. At the specific level, the cultivars of *L. odoratus* and *L. sativus* are readily propagated, fast-growing annuals so they can be maintained as experimental populations. Of course, with *Pisum* moving into *Lathyrus*, it could be argued that Mendel's peas, the original model organism for genetics, were a *Lathyrus* all along.

During the 1960s and 1970s the chromatographic techniques developed for research into lathyrism were applied to the seeds of *Lathyrus*, *Vicia* (vetches) and the two genera that have been recently moved into them, *Pisum* (peas) and *Lens* (lentils) respectively. These genera are among the plant groups in which protein and amino acid chemistry has been most intensively investigated. During this period research focussed on the phylogenetic significance of seed non-protein amino acids (Bell 1962a, Bell 1962b, Bell *et al.* 1978, Simola 1966, Simola 1968b, Lambein *et al.* 1999). These studies also suggested that non-protein amino acids might act as feeding deterrents to insect pests (Jansen 1969, Waterman 1994). Simola (1968b) provided a detailed comparison of the development of amino acid pools in *L. japonicus*, *L. niger* and *L. sylvestris* as the individual organisms developed through their life cycle.

Lathyrus has also been an important genus in genetic research. Narayan (1982) and Rees & Narayan (1989) investigated chromosome evolution, Gutiérez *et al.* (1994) investigated the process of polyploidy in the genus, and Nandini *et al.*

(1997) demonstrated discontinuous variation in DNA sizes across the entire genus. The karyology of *Lathyrus* is generally well understood, with chromosome counts available for the majority of species. Kenneth Wolfe (pers. comm.) and his research team at Trinity College Dublin has investigated rates of evolution in the chloroplast genome of *L. latifolius*. They have found that it possesses a highly localised gene region that is one of the fastest evolving regions so far discovered in angiosperms.

Ecological studies also use *Lathyrus* as model organisms, such as the analyses of phenological and community behaviour in *L. vernus* by Ehrlen (1992, 1995a, 1995b; Ehrlen & Eriksson, 1995) and Ritchie & Tilman (1995). Matthias Schlee (pers. comm.) at the University of Tübingen in Germany has investigated evolutionary patterns in *L. pannonicus* and *Oxytropis pilosa*, concluding that ancestral populations of *L. pannonicus* were reliant on regularly grazed, open grasslands. On an autecological level, Bal & Khetmalas (1996) investigated seasonal behaviour of root nodules in *L. japonicus*, noting their importance as starch storage organs. At the University of British Columbia, Quentin Cronk (pers. comm.) and his team have uncovered the role of the CYCLOIDEA gene in flower architecture and have conducted extensive research on the chloroplast evolution of the group.

Throughout Europe, interest in *L. cicera*, *L. sativus* and other traditional crop species is resurging across agricultural research institutes. Their low antifeedant properties for livestock, and low toxicity when eaten as a small portion of the diet, combined with their tolerance of a huge range of conditions, make them superb candidates as future crops. As part of this research, a complete reading of the *L. sativus* genome, led by research teams at the John Innes Centre, is imminent at the time of writing.

One of the gene regions of *Lathyrus latifolius* has been discovered to be particularly fast-evolving.

Classification

Lathyrus is a member of the pea family, *Fabaceae*, also known as *Leguminosae*. Within this huge family of more than 19,000 species, *Lathyrus* belongs in the subfamily *Papilionoideae* – again, a huge group, containing all the pea-flowered members of the family. In this group sits a subgroup called tribe *Fabeae*, which contains around 350 species of herbaceous, pea- and vetch-like plants from temperate areas (Kupicha 1983).

LATHYRUS AND TRIBE *FABEAE*

Tribe *Fabeae* is one of our most important groups of plants, both economically and culturally. As well as *Lathyrus*, it includes the vetches (*Vicia*), lentils (now in *Vicia*, previously *Lens*) and peas (now in *Lathyrus*, previously *Pisum*). The group includes many species that were among our ancestors' earliest domesticated plants, such as faba bean (*Vicia faba*), lentil (*Vicia lens*, previously *Lens culinaris*), and chickling vetch (*Lathyrus sativus*).

All members of the tribe are herbaceous with the intricate papilionoid flowers found in much of the wider pea family. The leaves have one to many pairs of leaflets and in more than half of the species, the leaves are tipped with tendrils to aid in climbing. Traditionally, the genera in the group were separated on the basis of the vein patterns in the leaves, the way leaves open, and the patterns of hairs on the styles.

Inevitably, recent DNA evidence (Schaefer *et al.* 2012) has shaken up this traditional view, and means the names and groupings in tribe *Fabeae* are changing to reflect this more natural classification. *Lens* is now contained within a larger *Vicia*, and becomes section *Lens* within *Vicia*, including lentil species such as *Vicia lens* and *Vicia nigricans*. *Pisum* is now

LEFT With tendrils and usuallly a single pair of leaflets, *Lathyrus sylvestris*, here painted by Lilian Snelling, shows some of the characteristics of the genus.

RIGHT With some of the largest flowers in the genus, *Lathyrus grandiflorus* illustrates well the papilionoid flower form.

contained within a larger *Lathyrus*, and garden pea, *Pisum sativum*, becomes *Lathyrus oleraceus*, resurrecting an old name from 1779 (Coulot & Rabaute 2016). The attractive central Asian *Vavilovia*, previously containing just one species, *V. formosa*, is also now contained within *Lathyrus*, becoming *Lathyrus formosus*. There are other new name combinations that will need to be made, but the work of Coulot & Rabaute has made a systematic start to the process.

When the morphology of *Lathyrus* is looked at again in the light of the DNA evidence, some anomalies and doubts that botanists had in the past about classification will be cleared up and many fascinating new questions will be prompted.

More widely in tribe *Fabeae*, the genus *Lens* (lentils) has been subsumed into the larger genus *Vicia* (vetches), as the clade the lentils belong to sits well inside the bulk of *Vicia*. In addition, two other groups formerly considered part of *Vicia* have been shown to sit outside it (Schaefer *et al.* 2012). Both correspond fairly closely to old sections in *Vicia*, and have previously been regarded as individual genera by various authors They have now been raised to genus status again. Of the two, *Ervum* is closer to *Lathyrus*, and is a group of small, often ruderal species. The other genus, *Ervilia*, is a more mixed group of annuals and perennials, and is basal to tribe *Fabeae*, representing the earliest diverging lineages.

BELOW LEFT **Only recently assigned to the genus,** *Lathyrus formosus* **was previously known as** *Vavilovia formosa***.**

BELOW RIGHT **Garden pea, previously** *Pisum sativum***, is now** *Lathyrus oleraceus***.**

	Lathyrus (incl. Pisum & Vavilovia)	Ervilia	Ervum	Vicia (incl. Lens)
Common names	Chickling vetch, sweet pea, garden pea	Four-seeded vetch and allies	Hairy vetch, wood vetch, tare	Vetch, lentil
Distribution	Northern hemisphere, South America, introduced worldwide as crops and weeds	Western Eurasia	Europe	Northern hemisphere, South America, introduced worldwide as crops and weeds
Lifecycle	c. 75% perennial, 25% annual	Annuals	Annuals & one perennial	c. 50% perennial, 50% annual
Stipules	Variable, some semi-sagittate	Semi-sagittate	Semi-sagittate	Semi-sagittate
Leaf venation	Often parallel main veins, reticulate between	Reticulate	Reticulate	Reticulate
Style pubescence	Hairs on inside (adaxial)	Hairs all round style	Hairs all round style	Various: hairs all round style; in a slender ring; tufted; v-shaped and on inside (adaxial) in former members of Lens

Summary of the characteristics of the genera in tribe *Fabeae*

EVOLUTIONARY ORIGINS

It is almost impossible in modern botany to understand a group of plants without an evolutionary context, and *Lathyrus* certainly has an interesting one. The genus evolved in the Mediterranean region around 12 million years ago. The Mediterranean, and the eastern Mediterranean in particular, remains its stronghold, with the majority of species in Turkey, the Caucasus and Iran. Although botanists can tell relatively little about their early evolution, they suspect that the majority of species were annuals, adapted to the hot and arid conditions of the Mediterranean that are seen today.

Evidence for this comes from DNA, which tells us that most of the annual lineages appear to be ancestral to the newer, perennial lineages. This is not an uncommon occurrence in other herbaceous plant groups, with perennials being derived from annuals. The timing for this big shift to perennial lineages is interesting, as many of the big diversification events happen just after a critical event in the history of the Mediterranean. Around 6.3 million years ago, the Mediterranean almost entirely dried out, having lost its connection to the Atlantic. The basin became a series of extremely saline lakes, much like the Dead Sea today, and extremely challenging for plant life. Indeed, only specialised annuals would be able to cope with the conditions.

When the connection with the Atlantic was re-established just after 6 million years ago, the Mediterranean reflooded. At some time around that period several lines of *Lathyrus* may have escaped into more forgiving temperate climates, and

made the shift to perenniality, *L. tuberosus* being a modern descendant of such a group. These went on to become the lineages that colonised eastwards to Asia, and ultimately North America.

The South American species, however, have a surprising origin. They appear to have colonised directly from western Eurasia or Africa, implying a long-distance dispersal all the way to modern South America sometime between 5 and 2.5 million years ago. Botanists cannot be certain of exact timing and movements, as intermediate species have undoubtedly gone extinct, and whole floras will have moved, but *Lathyrus* is certainly a very mobile group. One can only speculate as to where it will end up in the next 12 million years!

TAXONOMY FROM CLASSICAL TO LINNAEAN TIMES

The name *Lathyrus* appears in classical texts, but there is some ambiguity over its meaning. The name, which was ultimately adopted by Linnaeus, comes from the Greek medical writers, Dioscorides and Theophrastus, who discuss a plant called λα-τουρισ (*la-thyris*). The *thyris* element of the name is usually interpreted as powerful or vigorous, with the *la* prefix indicating the diminutive form, so, little powerful one.

Interestingly, this means much the same in Greek as the word *potentilla* does in Latin, although *Lathyrus* and *Potentilla* are not closely related. It is unclear from the classical writers whether the powerful element of the name refers to some powerful medical quality of the plant, or a vigorous growth habit. Unfortunately, there is more potential confusion as both writers may have been referring to *Euphorbia lathyris*, a member of the spurge family used as a powerful medical purgative.

In the classical and later mediaeval herbals, discussion of names, plants and uses swaps around, which adds further to the confusion. For example, Dioscorides describes the fruit of lathyris (i.e. the *Euphorbia*) as 'about the size of an *ervum* seed'. Although the word *ervum* was later applied to some members of *Vicia*, it appears from Dioscorides's descriptions to have been *Lathyrus sativus*.

In classical times, Dioscorides records *ervum* as being used to make *ervina*, or *farina ervi*, a medicinal flour used as a purgative. Not only were the medicinal actions of *ervum* (possibly *Lathyrus*) and *lathyris* (*Euphorbia*) plants comparable, but Pliny records *ervina* flour being mixed with the juice of *tithymallus* (a coastal spurge) to make a purgative (Jones & Andrews 1956).

There is also an intriguing mention of the plant in the nickname for an Egyptian King. Ptolemy Soter (∏τολεμα ος Σωτήρ, or Ptolemy the Saviour) was the 8th or 9th Ptolemy in the dynasty following Alexander the Great. Also known as Πτολεμα ος Λάθυρος (Ptolemy Lathyrus), this nickname is often interpreted in recent times as Ptolemy Chickpea, although again, it is not certain what plant is being referred to, let alone why he should have such an interesting nickname. Born in the early 140s BCE, he died in 81 BCE, having ruled twice, being deposed from 107 to 88 BCE.

Following on from the rediscovery of Dioscorides and the work of other classical writers in the Middle Ages, many of the late mediaeval and Renaissance European accounts are somewhat vague as to the identity of *lathyris* or *lathyrus*. This might be because they were referring to such a commonplace medicinal substance, or because, like us, no one was sure what the Classical writers meant.

The beautifully illustrated *De Historia Stirpium* of Leonhart Fuchs (1542) follows the classical authors closely. He applied the name *lathyris* solely to *Euphorbia*, and used the name *Ervum sativum* for the modern *Lathyrus sativus*. Turner's herbal (1551) gives the first discussion of some confusion between the two names. He stated that the plant known as *fichlynge* (vetchling) or *cicercula* in English (Chapman & Tweddle 1995) 'is called in Greke *lathyros*'. John Gerard (1597) appeared to be aware of the confusion, explaining about *Lathyrus sylvestris* in his *Herball* that the plant is 'called *Lathyrus*, to make a difference betweene it and and

ERVVM
SATIVVM.
Weiß Eruen.

bb 4

Lathyris, or Spurge'.

In spite of Johnson's attempt in his revised edition of Gerard (1636) to straighten this problem out, the name *Lathyrus* had stuck and was being used by botanists for the tendril-bearing plants of today. Indeed, this was the name chosen by Linnaeus for his genus *Lathyrus* (Linnaeus 1753), and it remains in use. Of course, taxonomists need to tweak definitions of genera to better reflect their real diversity and relationships, so the *Lathyrus* of Linnaeus is somewhat different to the modern understanding of the genus. The names *Orobus* and *Aphaca* were also applied to species of *Lathyrus* in pre-Linnaean times and both have been adopted as taxa in the modern *Lathyrus*.

The definition of the genus given by Linnaeus was wide enough to include *Lathyrus pratensis*.

THE MODERN BOTANICAL VIEW

The original Linnaean definition of the genus corresponds quite well with section *Lathyrus* of more recent authorities. It included many of the sprawling and climbing plants with tendrils and a single pair of leaflets, such as *L. odoratus*. Linnaeus's definition did also include some similar species now treated in different sections, such as *L. pratensis*, now considered part of section *Pratensis*. He also established another genus, *Orobus*. These were the upright species lacking tendrils, often from temperate woodland areas, and included species such as *Orobus vernus* (now *L. vernus*). Doll's later (1843) version of *Orobus* brought in all the species without a twisted style in the flower.

As it turns out, neither interpretation was quite right, and both *Lathyrus* and *Orobus* contained a mix of the species now regarded as belonging to *Lathyrus* and *Vicia*. The current view has between 140 and 160 species each in *Lathyrus* and *Vicia*, with *Orobus* relegated to a section inside modern *Lathyrus*. Sections have been used in *Lathyrus* to make the diversity in this large genus more easy to understand.

The most recent revision of the whole group that looked at section level is Kupicha's excellent 1983 account. She recognised 13 sections, and with the good sense of a balanced taxonomist her interpretation was workable, based on sound evidence, and with clear explanations of any ambiguities. It is fortunate that in *Lathyrus* the species do fall into relatively clear groups. In contrast, the related *Vicia* (vetches) are far more challenging to tell apart.

Some earlier workers, such as Bässler (1966, 1971, 1973), split the large sections

Linnaeus (1753)	Godron (1848)	Boissier (1872)	Czefranova (1971b)	Kupicha (1983)	Asmussen & Liston (1998)	Kenicer (2007)	Coulot & Rabaute (2016), modified
				Notolathyrus	Orobus	Notolathyrus	Notolathyrus
Orobus	Orobus	*Orobus*	Lathyrobus	Orobus		Orobus	Orobus
		Orobastrum	Orobus	Lathyrostylis	Lathyrostylis	Lathyrostylis	Lathyrostylis
			Pratensis	Pratensis	Pratensis	Pratensis	Pratensis
			Eurytrichon				
Lathyrus	Aphaca	Aphaca	Aphaca	Aphaca	Aphaca	Aphaca	Aphaca
	Orobus	Orobastrum	Neurolobus	Neurolobus	Neurolobus	Neurolobus*	Neurolobus
			Orobon	Orobon			
	Eulathyrus	Eulathyrus	Lathyrus	Lathyrus	Lathyrus	Lathyrus	Lathyrus
Lathyrus	Cicercula	Cicercula	Cicercula		Cicercula		
Orobus	Orobus	Orobastrum	Orobastrum	Orobastrum	Orobastrum		
					L. sphaericus	*L. sphaericus*	Lathyrostylis
				Linearicarpus	*L. angulatus*	*L. angulatus*	Angulati (here, sect. Lathyrus)
						Linearicarpus	Linearicarpus
				Viciopsis		*Vicia*	*Vicia*
Lathyrus	Nissolia	Nissolia	Nissolia	Nissolia	Nissolia	Nissolia*	Nissolia
	Clymenum	Clymenum	Clymenum	Clymenum	Clymenum	Clymenum	Clymenum
					L. gloeosperma	*L. gloeosperma*	
						Pisum	Lophotropis
						Vavilovia	Alophotropis

Comparison of the main classifications of *Lathyrus* over the past 250 years.
Text in bold indicates genera, other text indicates sections within *Lathyrus* or species.

such as section *Orobus* into series. Until the mid 1990s, taxonomists trying to understand *Lathyrus* diversity and relationships were reliant on the structure of the plants (including microscopic features), as well as some characters of shared chemistry and geography.

The DNA revolution has changed all that, allowing taxonomists to look at hundreds of thousands of characters across the whole group at the same time, giving a clearer picture of the underlying relationships. DNA shows quite clearly that two similar-looking species may not be closely related, while very different-seeming ones may in fact be close. One example is the slender, pink and

white-flowered *L. pannonicus*. Once placed in section *Lathyrostylis*, DNA reveals that it is more closely related to *L. vernus* in section *Orobus*. DNA evidence also confirms Kupicha's (1983) suspicions about *L. saxatilis* – it is not a *Lathyrus* at all, but a *Vicia* (vetch). Botanists had assumed it was a *Lathyrus* because the style was only hairy on the inside (adaxial) edge, as in every other species of *Lathyrus*. *Vicia* species usually have styles with hairs all round, or in quite elaborate tufts. It turns out to be coincidence that '*Lathyrus*' *saxatilis* has the same hair pattern as true *Lathyrus* species, perhaps driven by a particular shared pollinator, or simply because the flower is too small to fit much hair inside it. Perceptive as always, Kupicha explained that she 'would be glad of more evidence to support its position in *Lathyrus*!' There is now excellent evidence in the form of the DNA that it is a *Vicia*.

This DNA evidence suggests that some changes are required to clean up the classification of *Lathyrus* and there is still a big job involved in assigning each species into workable sections according to standard taxonomic rules.

That said, most of the groups recognised over the last 200 years still hold up fairly well. Botanists have an excellent 'roadmap' to the diversity of the genus and its relatives in the form of Schaefer *et al.* (2012) who give a phylogenetic tree of relationships. Most of the future changes will involve moving several species between sections, and perhaps establishing or reviving one or two old sections. Species currently treated as *Vicia* appear in many places on the tree, so will need

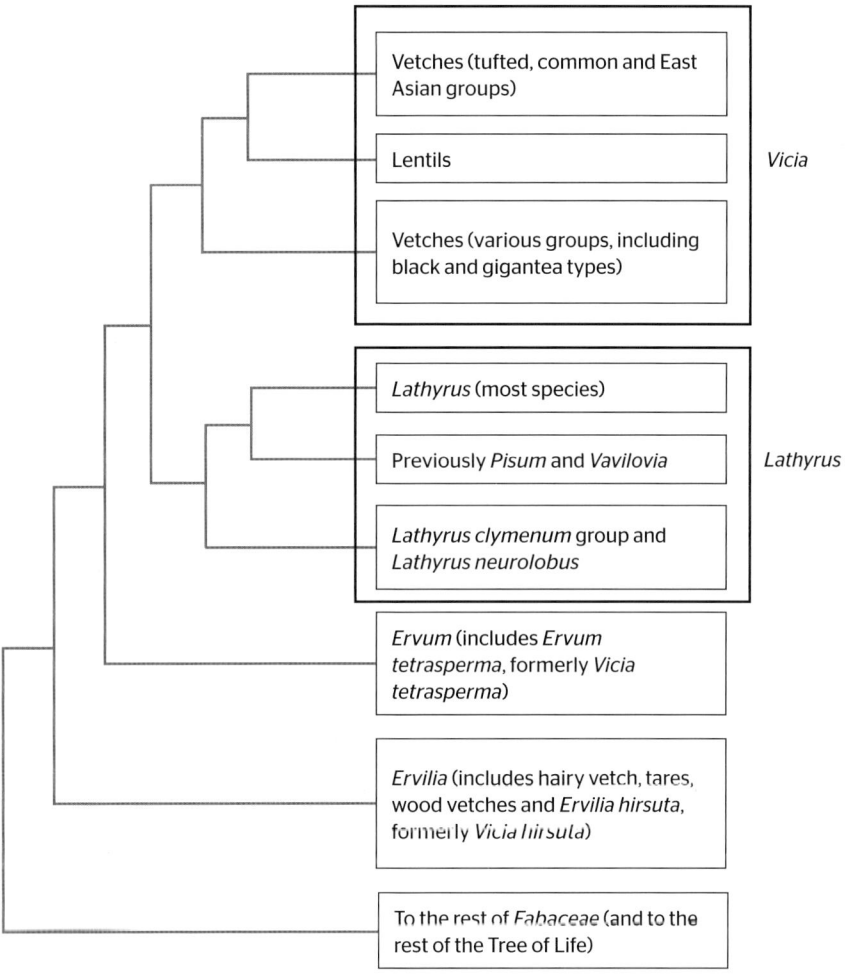

Vetches (tufted, common and East Asian groups)

Lentils

Vetches (various groups, including black and gigantea types)

Vicia

Lathyrus (most species)

Previously *Pisum* and *Vavilovia*

Lathyrus clymenum group and *Lathyrus neurolobus*

Lathyrus

Ervum (includes *Ervum tetrasperma*, formerly *Vicia tetrasperma*)

Ervilia (includes hairy vetch, tares, wood vetches and *Ervilia hirsuta*, formerly *Vicia hirsula*)

To the rest of *Fabaceae* (and to the rest of the Tree of Life)

Simplified diagram of relationships in tribe *Fabeae* based on modern DNA classification

to be included in several genera, including at least the resurrected *Ervilia* and *Ervum* as well as *Vicia*. A major change is that *Pisum* and *Vavilovia* are now included in *Lathyrus*. If an alternative approach had been taken with *Pisum* and *Vavilovia*, maintaining them as separate genera, then *Lathyrus* would have to lose *L. clymenum*, *L. neurolobus* and *L. ochrus*. On balance, the inclusion of *Pisum* and *Vavilovia* in *Lathyrus* entails fewer name changes and more accurately reflects the morphology of the group, meaning the inwardly hairy style is a defining character for the genus (Coulot & Rabaute 2016).

The accounts of the species in this book are laid out to reflect current knowledge of the relationships between species, but the names for these groups remain largely informal. In fact, they are probably more useful for the horticulturist than the classic section names are.

Morphology

The incredible diversity of *Lathyrus* reflects the wide range of habitats and niches they are adapted to. Their wild environments have shaped the morphology and behaviour of the plants into the 150 species known today. Although the species grown in gardens are generally well known, botanists are still just getting to know the genus to understand the reasons behind their structure, and their place in the plant communities that they live in. Species such as *L. japonicus*, *L. pratensis* and *L. vernus* have been studied by ecologists, but there are many that are less well known. This chapter covers the diversity of form and structure in *Lathyrus*.

LIFECYCLE

All *Lathyrus* species are herbaceous, with around 30 annuals and 120 perennials. The majority of annual *Lathyrus* species are relatively delicate. However some annual species, such as *L. odoratus* and *L. paranensis*, are robust and can only be recognised as annuals by their feeble, non-perennating rootstocks. Because *Lathyrus* is mainly restricted to seasonal environments (cool temperate or Mediterranean), the above-ground stems of perennial species die back during the non-growing season.

In traditional classifications of *Lathyrus*, habit and lifecycle were often interpreted as a general indication of relationships. To some extent this still holds up; all members of section *Orobus* are perennial, for example. Some *Lathyrus* lineages, such as in section *Lathyrus*, have switched from annual to perennial, and in some cases back again, several times through their existence. Fluctuating climate has undoubtedly played a major

LEFT **Of the perennial species, *Lathyrus latifolius* is one of the largest and most robust.**

RIGHT **Annual species, such as *Lathyrus tingitanus*, make up a smaller proportion of the genus than perennials.**

part in the evolution of *Lathyrus* lifecycles. The earliest lineages were probably annual Mediterranean species, suited to hot summers but some lines branched out into more temperate cold-winter climates, typically becoming perennial in the process. This shift to perenniality seemingly gave these species a great advantage, allowing them to colonise new corners of the globe. However, whether they are annual or perennial, the main structures in *Lathyrus* species remain fundamentally the same.

ROOTS

As with most annual plants, annual species of *Lathyrus* have small, superficial roots, and are thus sensitive to root disturbance. The few biennial species, such as *L. nigrivalvis* from eastern South America, tend not to have large storage tap roots. Instead, these biennials overwinter above ground and die back somewhat, returning from basal buds.

The perennial species have creeping, or thickened rhizomes or tubers and may form extensive clumps or patches, even when the above-ground stems themselves are relatively short. In plants from favourable mesotrophic conditions, the roots are usually fibrous, as in many of the clump-forming or running rhizomatous species such as *L. niger*, *L. roseus* and *L. vernus* from western Eurasia, or *L. quinquenervius* from east Asia. Larger tap roots are seen in some perennial species and seem to be mostly for anchorage. Such roots can also be water-searching and play a storage role, as in *L. tomentosus*, a near-xerophyte from seasonally dry areas of southern Brazil, Uruguay and Argentina. True root tubers for carbon storage are relatively uncommon in the genus, but the long, thickened, finger-like roots of *L. pannonicus* and swollen rhizomes of *L. tuberosus* certainly do this job. It is usually rhizomes that act as the main perennating organs in most longer lived species. The rhizomes probably afford the plants a quick response to clement conditions and allow them to mobilise resources straight into the neighbouring buds. In gardens this translates to relatively easy propagation by division across most perennials.

The slender, creeping rhizome of *Lathyrus quinquenervius*, a species of wet riverside meadows.

As with many legumes, *Lathyrus* species form root nodules in conditions where they can benefit from additional nitrogen. The nodules are modified root hairs that play host to *Rhizobium* bacteria, with each nodule about 5mm in diameter and usually clustered into irregular masses. The bacteria capture atmospheric nitrogen, making it available to the plant in exchange for nutrients and the security of a protective nodule (Sprent *et al.*

Root nodules in *Lathyrus* contain bacteria that capture atmospheric nitrogen for nutrition. The pink colour is due to leghaemoglobin.

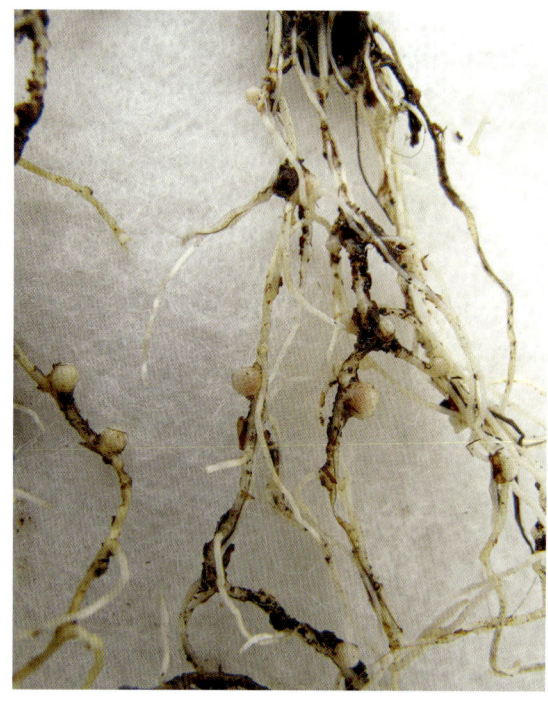

2017). In areas where nitrogen-rich fertilisers are added, the plants may not form as many, if any, root nodules. They are not essential for the plants to thrive, and their presence does not indicate nitrogen stress, but is undoubtedly one of the reasons for the success of *Lathyrus* in colonising challenging soils. The nodules tend to be seasonal, being at their largest and most active during the growing season. Many of them shrivel and die over winter in perennial species, with new ones being formed the following spring. Some nodules persist through winter and there is some evidence that they have a role in overwinter storage in species such as *L. japonicus* (Bal & Khetmalas 1996).

If you find nodules on roots, you can break one open with a fingernail and, if pink or red inside, the bacteria are active. They use leghaemoglobin, structurally similar to mammalian haemoglobin, to store and transport nitrogen and oxygen. So far, each of the species of *Lathyrus* that have been closely studied show a close association with one bacterial variety, *Rhizobium leguminosarum* biovar. *viceae*. However, there are still many species that have not been assessed, and given the importance of nitrogen in producing sustainable crops to feed the world, this is a fascinating area for further study. Currently, it is a focus of work by the James Hutton Institute in Scotland.

STEMS

All *Lathyrus* species have herbaceous stems, although in most of the longer-lived, clump-forming species these can become fibrous and near-woody at the perennating base, as in *L. latifolius* or *L. roseus*. None are shrubs, but *L. davidii* from East Asia approaches being shrubby. It is part way between upright and climbing, with thick, cylindrical, cane-like stems, but has tendrils. It is one of the few members of the genus with stems that become thick enough to be hollow.

Stems in other species are occasionally cylindrical, and may be round, square or intermediate in cross section, but this has little value for identification or classification. The stems in a wide range of seemingly unrelated species are often winged, with wings reaching almost a centimetre across in the larger species of section *Lathyrus*, such as *L. latifolius*, *L. odoratus*, *L. sativus* and *L. sylvestris*. Winged species from other groups include *L. linifolius*, *L. pannonicus* and *L. quinquenervius*, all from the perennial widespread section *Orobus*, and several South American members of section *Notolathyrus*, such as *L. macrostachys* and *L. paranensis*. In all winged species the stem wings are green and thus increase the photosynthetic area of the plant.

LEAVES

Leaves in *Lathyrus* are very variable. They are typically compound, with multiple leaflets, and many species have tendrils which have evolved to support a climbing habit. Tendrils are usually at the tip of the leaf, although any leaflet can manifest as a tendril. The petiole is flanked at the base by a pair of leafy stipules. These stipules protect the curled leaf and growing tip of the plant in bud. The stipules are green and photosynthetic so, once the leaf emerges, they increase the overall area of the leaf for catching sunlight. In species such as *L. nervosus* and *L. pisiformis* the stipules can be the same size as a leaflet, so must contribute significantly to photosynthesis. In some species of *Vicia* the stipules have nectar-producing glands to attract ants as defenders, but these are not present on *Lathyrus*.

The leaves are almost always paripinnate in basic plan. This means they have a pair, or up to 10 pairs of leaflets, but no solitary leaflet at the tip as found in many other legume species. Instead, the terminal leaflet has become a tendril that may

Winged stems are a feature seen in many species across the genus, such as here in *Lathyrus sativus*.

FAR LEFT Stipules, which subtend leaves, vary greatly in size from species to species, but are relatively large and broad here in *Lathyrus davidii* where they can be seen prior to the leaflets unfurling.

LEFT In contrast, *Lathyrus quinquenervius* has small, narrow stipules.

be robust and much branched, as in *L. nervosus* and *L. odoratus*, or reduced to a simple arista, as in *L. aureus* and *L. vernus*. Beware though, as aberrations are very common, particularly in early-season leaves, so some leaves on an individual plant may have an uneven number of leaflets, with a leaflet at the tip. These may also have a tendril or arista besides.

Leaves almost always have one to 10 pairs of leaflets. The only exceptions are *L. aphaca*, *L. nissolia* and young specimens of *L. articulatus*, *L. clymenum*, *L. gloeosperma* and *L. ochrus*. In *L. aphaca* the leaflets are completely absent and the leaves are reduced to a simple tendril with large, arrowhead-shaped stipules at the base of the tendril doing the job of photosynthesis. In *L. nissolia* the leaves are simplified to a single, long, narrow blade that is so grass-like that the plants can be almost impossible to spot in their meadow habitats. Only the tiny pea flowers or pods nodding among the grass can pick it out as a legume. It almost appears to be mimicking the grasses of its typical habitat, but quite why this would be remains a mystery. The stipules in this species are reduced to spurs. *Lathyrus articulatus*, *L. clymenum*, *L. gloeosperma* and *L. ochrus* are all annuals that begin life with blade-like leaves on the lower nodes, but as they age the newer leaves higher up the plant produce leaflets and tendrils from the side of a large central blade.

Leaves in many species of *Lathyrus* have several parallel primary and secondary veins, which can be a useful character to distinguish them from *Vicia*,

but other species have a reticulate network of veins, as in *L. vaniotii*. If reticulate veins are present, however, they tend not to collect together and loop back from the edges in the characteristic pattern seen in many *Vicia* species.

Other leaf characters, such has cell shapes and numbers of stomata on the surfaces, have been investigated by researchers such as Bässler (1966, 1973, 1981), Simola (1968a) and Kupicha (1976, 1983), but these tend not to show any distinct patterns useful for identification.

FLOWERS

Flowers can be solitary or in racemes of up to 30 flowers. Flower numbers are usually lower in annual species, such that the members of section *Lathyrostylis* are defined by their annual habit and solitary flowers. Each flower has a slender pedicel and a small floral bract at the base. The pedicel often thickens considerably after pollination, raising the fruit horizontally or upright, as in *L. macropus*.

Several species, mainly in section *Orobus*, have a distinctive inflorescence type with many (15–30) small, somewhat waxy flowers that begin white and darken to yellow, and then orange as they mature. Perhaps in order to fit this high number of flowers into a dense display, these taxa share relatively narrow, oblong standard petals. Examples include *L. laevigatus* and its allies (western and central Eurasia), *L. davidii* (East Asia), and *L. sulphureus* and *L. ochroleucus* (North America). This same inflorescence type is also seen in *L. hasslerianus* (South America) and *Vicia pisiformis* (western Eurasia).

It is important to note that small, relatively few flowers are the norm among smaller annual species in particular, so in the garden they may not be as striking

Some species, such as *Lathyrus vaniotii*, have reticulate leaflet venation.

The flowers of *Lathyrus* can be solitary, as in *L. sphaericus* (FAR LEFT), or in racemes of up to 30, as in *L. venosus* (LEFT).

as larger annuals or perennials. This is probably because the small annuals do not waste resources on overly showy flowers or scents. Indeed, it is thought that the majority of flowers in *Lathyrus* species self-pollinate, with less than 20% of a given plant's seed coming from successful cross-pollination. This is an excellent thing for the grower, as it means most species give a ready supply of seed, even without external pollinators. This behaviour is taken to the extreme in *L. gloeosperma* which is cleistogamous; its flowers never truly open and it is apparently purely self-pollinating.

The flowers themselves are typical of a papilionoid legume – the classic pea flower. The calyx is bell-shaped with five teeth that may be equal in length (as in *L. annuus*), or very unequal, with the lowest tooth longest, the side teeth shorter, and upper teeth shortest (as in *L. macrostachys*). These teeth are clearly the tips of five fused sepals.

The corolla consists of five petals; the upper standard (also known as the banner or vexillum), two lateral wings (ala), and a keel at the bottom, made from two fused keel petals (carina). Each petal has a claw that attaches it to the flower, and a main blade that does the job of attracting pollinators. It is worthwhile pulling a flower or two apart, as they are little wonders of natural mechanical engineering.

Standard petals can be broad, as in *L. grandiflorus* (typically 6cm across), or narrow, as in *L. neurolobus* (0.5cm across). The wing and keel petals have a simple system of bumps and pouches that acts as a spring, holding the flower closed. This ensures only an insect of the right weight or strength can push the flower open to get at the nectar inside, and receive a dusting of pollen in the process. The keel petals are strongly fused along the lower edge, so appear to be a single folded over petal, but the presence of two claws at the base shows it is two petals.

10mm

K

S W1 W2

G Ke1

A Ke2

A dissected flower of *Lathyrus cabrerianus* showing the parts typical of most of the genus
K = calyx
S = standard petal
W1, W2 = wing petals
Ke1, Ke2 = keel petals
G = gynoecium
A = androecium
Note the distinction between blade and claw on the wing and keel petals.

Petal colour varies widely across the genus. Purples, pinks and blues are the most common, but reds, including brick red, yellow and white are also found. Colour is variable within species and changes, usually deepening as a flower ages, although the lilac and pink flowers of *L. niger* become parchment-coloured then brown after pollination. In several species the standard petal is darker than the wings and keels, presumably providing a contrast between the upper part and the lower part that acts as a landing pad.

The venation on the standard can often be darker than the surrounding tissue, appearing as darker traceries, which may act as nectar guides. In species such as *L. tingitanus* there is a distinctive flush of colour at the base of the standard, where pollinators access the nectar – a very distinctive nectar guide.

Investigations by Pecket (1960) showed that among the anthocyanin pigments, the red flowers (such as *L. cicera* and *L. rotundifolius*) contain delphinidin, pink flowers (*L. sylvestris* and allies) had malvidin, and the bicoloured or deep purple flowers (*L. clymenum*, *L. tingitanus*) had both these compounds as well as petunidin. Yellow flavonol compounds are also found in some of these anthocyanin-dominated species, and appear with malvidin in blue- and purple-flowered species such as *L. sativus* and *L. vernus*. Yellow-flowered species such as *L. aphaca* and *L. pratensis* do not have anthocyanins, but flavonols are, unsurprisingly present.

What can be seen, of course, is only part of the story. A great undergraduate study by Sarah Mitchell and Jane Wishart of the University of St Andrews, carried out at Royal Botanic Garden Edinburgh, looked at many aspects of pollinator appeal in detail (Mitchell 2016). Using scanning electron microscopy they discovered patches of conical cells on the wings of *L. pratensis*. It is suspected that these provide a better grip for visiting pollinators, as seems to be the case in members of the unrelated *Solanaceae*. As well as this, the study looked at flower patterns in the ultraviolet spectrum that insect pollinators will see, and they found a surprising array of different flower types.

They also confirmed previous knowledge that the main glandular scent-producing cells in *L. odoratus* are found on the standard petals. These are the

Pattern examples and species	Normal light	Ultraviolet light

Banner reflecting, wings absorbing

Lathyrus articulatus

Both banner and wings absorbing

Lathyrus chrysanthus

Both banner and wings reflecting

Lathyrus linifolius

No distinct areas of reflection or absorption

Lathyrus odoratus white cultivar

Nectar guide absorbing, rest reflecting

Lathyrus tingitanus

Patterns of ultraviolet absorbance and reflectance in *Lathyrus* flowers
Each pair of images shows an example of a species or cultivar which exhibits that particular pattern (Mitchell 2016)

petals held up in the air, so scent can be carried readily away. Only very few species of *Lathyrus* are scented. *Lathyrus odoratus* is undoubtedly the strongest, and the wild-type Sicilian plants have a glorious fragrance. The closely related *L. belinensis*, *L. chloranthus* and *L. chrysanthus* have fainter scents, but few others have anything detectable by the human nose. *Lathyrus cabrerianus*, from temperate Chile and Argentina, is an

exception. Despite its geographical and genetic distance from the Mediterranean *L. odoratus*, this large perennial climber has beautiful primrose yellow flowers with a scent only slightly weaker than that of *L. odoratus*.

The androecium is diadelphous, with nine stamens fused into a tube, and a tenth sitting mostly free from the others above. As the fruit matures, it pushes this top stamen easily out of the way without the developing fruit being damaged.

Styles are all hairy on the adaxial edge, forming what is known as an introrse pollen brush, and most are slender and linear. However, members of section *Clymenum*, many members of section *Linearicarpus* and a few in section *Notolathyrus* have spathulate styles, broadening towards the tip. In the case of *L. clymenum* and *L. ochrus*, this spathulate shape strongly hints at the close relationship with *L. formosus* and *L. oleraceus* (formerly in *Vavilovia* and *Pisum* respectively). There are many intermediate style widths in species throughout the genus. Many species in section *Lathyrus* have distinctly twisted styles. This almost certainly ensures the pollen and stigma contact the side of the visiting bee, reducing competition for the top and bottom of the pollinator's body, where most other flowers deposit their pollen.

As the anthers usually dehisce before the flower opens, the pollen brush holds the pollen in place so it is picked up by the pollinator. The stiff hairs may also play a role in splitting the anthers open (Gunn & Kluve 1976).

Stigmas are usually a simple strip of receptive tissue on the tip of the style, but in *L. clymenum*, *L. ochrus* and species in the former *Pisum* and *Vavilovia*, the stigma has a central point. In contrast, some of the South American species have two small flaps at the tip, a feature characteristic of xerophytic species such as *L. pubescens* and *L. tomentosus*.

Clearly, the visual appeal across the spectrum, scent, timing, size and mechanics of the flowers in *Lathyrus* make for such an elaborate diversity across the genus.

The seeds of *Lathyrus tingitanus* are ellipsoid and there are typically six to seven per pod.

FRUITS

Fruits are always a legume – a pea pod. The two halves of the pod (valves) can be simple and completely hairless as in *L. vernus*, or quite elaborate, with dense, woolly hairs as in *L. tomentosus*. Species such as *L. japonicus* and *L. palustris* have some populations with hairy pods and others not. This has been the basis for some hotly debated subspecies and varieties, but tends to be a relatively fluid trait across populations. Other species have wings on the fruits either side of the suture, the line of weakness down which the pod splits. These are particularly prominent in *L. ochrus* and *L. sativus*. *Lathyrus neurolobus* has raised veins across the fruit, as its name suggests, while *L. gloeosperma* has raised veins along the fruit. The beautifully named *L. blepharicarpus* – literally 'eyelash-fruited lathyrus' – has a fringe of eyelash-like hairs around the suture.

It is not clear what purpose any of these elaborate appendages on the fruit serve, but one possibility is that the ridges, wings and hairs may prevent oviposition by beetles whose larvae eat the seed. Bruchid beetles are particular culprits here, with one or a few grubs making their way into a pod then eating sequentially through the seeds before pupating and emerging as adults. Perhaps to counter this kind of predation, South American species often have a fluffy internal pith between each seed.

Fruits contain between two and 15 seeds ranging in size from 3 to 8mm in diameter. They can be rounded cuboids (*L. sativus*), to ellipsoid (*L. linifolius*), to spherical (*L. annuus*). Seeds may be smooth through to echinate and have variable lengths of hilum – a feature traditionally used to aid in identification.

Germination appears to be hypogeal in all species so far observed. Upon germination, leaves are usually produced in a sequence, with simple leaves, or one pair of leaflets only, for the first few nodes, then an increasing number of leaflets up to the maximum. Tendrils, and later, flowers, only appear on leaves arising from later nodes.

Lathyrus pods come in a range of shapes, sizes and ornamentation.

RIGHT to FAR RIGHT
The hairy pods of *L. tomentosus*, the winged pods of *L. ochrus* and the prominently veined pods of *L. gloeosperma*.

Distribution and habitats

Lathyrus is a well-travelled genus. The nodules on the roots give them access to nitrogen, even in difficult soils. Hairs and thick cuticles allow species to survive in near-desert conditions, or on salt-laden sandy beaches. The climbing habit of many species gives them an advantage in accessing light by scrambling over neighbouring plants. The tough seed coats, and a good balance between dormancy for emergencies and quick-response germination (particularly in the annuals), allows them to get going when conditions are right. They made their way from their probable origin in what is now the eastern Mediterranean to cover the Eurasian continent. They then crossed what was the Bering land bridge to colonise North America. Perhaps more impressively, it is suspected that a lone seed from Europe or West Africa drifted across the Atlantic to South America, establishing a new lineage there. It is impossible not to admire the adaptability, opportunism and success of this wonderful group of plants.

ORIGIN OF THE GENUS

Lathyrus species are native throughout the temperate regions of the world with the exception of Australia and New Zealand, although *L. japonicus* has been introduced to New Zealand. They originated in the northern hemisphere, and over 85% of the modern species are found there.

Most species are from temperate or Mediterranean habitats, with a strong tendency towards perennials in cool-winter temperate areas and annuals in hot-summer

LEFT **Field margins, roadsides and open ground are the habitats of *Lathyrus clymenum* in the Mediterranean.**

RIGHT **From southern Europe to western Asia, *Lathyrus digitatus* is found in open woodland.**

Distribution of the genus *Lathyrus*

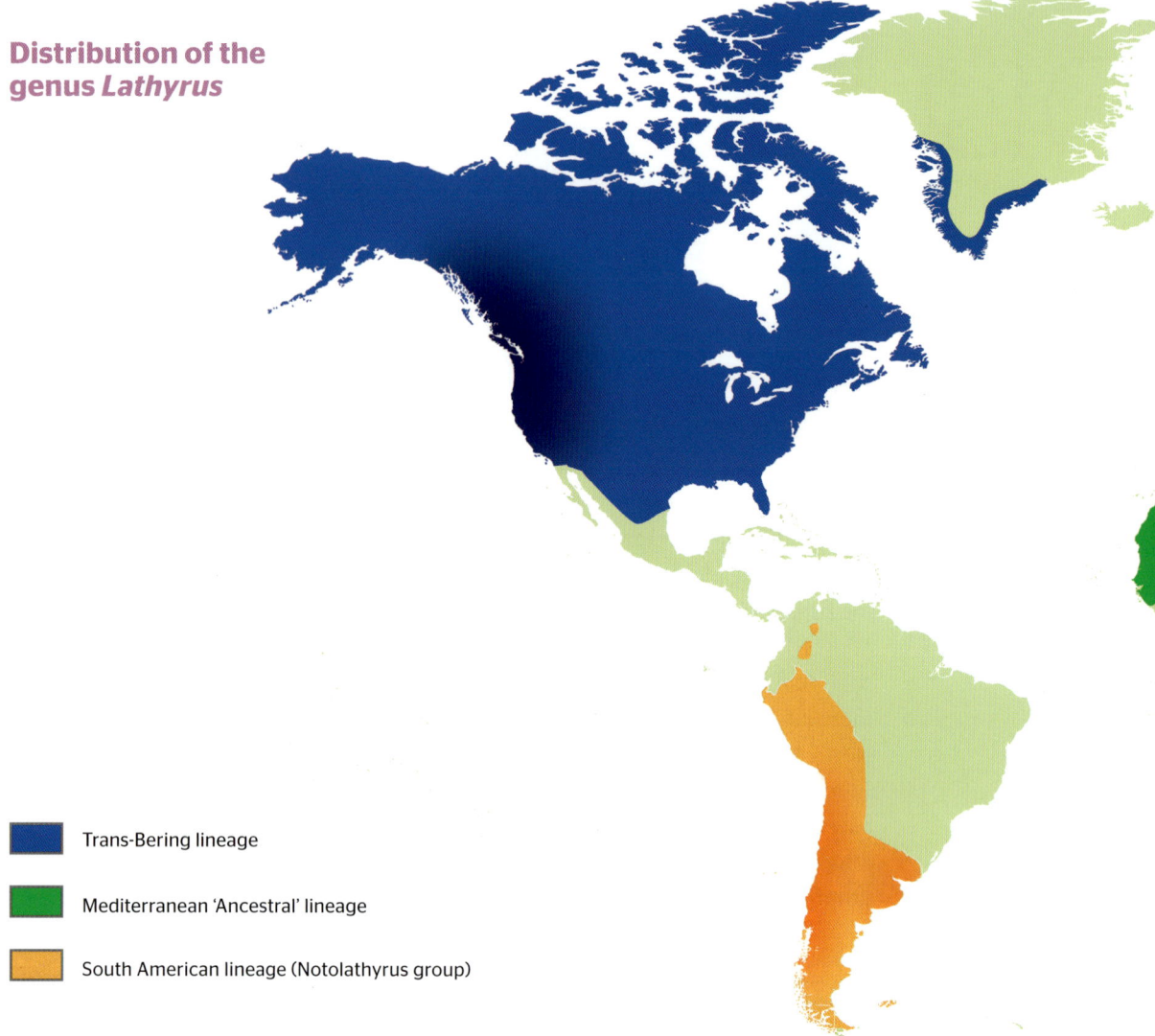

■ Trans-Bering lineage

■ Mediterranean 'Ancestral' lineage

■ South American lineage (Notolathyrus group)

Mediterranean habitats. Some species make it into tropical Africa, mostly the eastern part, with *L. hygrophilus* the only endemic and certain native (ILDIS 2002) there. The remainder inhabit South America and belong to the Notolathyrus group that spans the continent from Tierra del Fuego to the high cloud forest and páramo of Colombia. The subtropical and tropical species are typically found higher up mountains in cooler, temperate habitats, so *Lathyrus* species increase in altitude as you approach the Equator.

Some species have found their way around the globe with the aid of humans. These include crop and fodder species that have been in cultivation since the first farmers were domesticating plants in the Near East. Examples include *L. cicera*, *L. sativus* and *L. tuberosus*. The same is true of ornamental species, such as *L. odoratus* and *L. latifolius*, which have been moved worldwide into gardens and have sometimes escaped. The latter has become an invasive species in

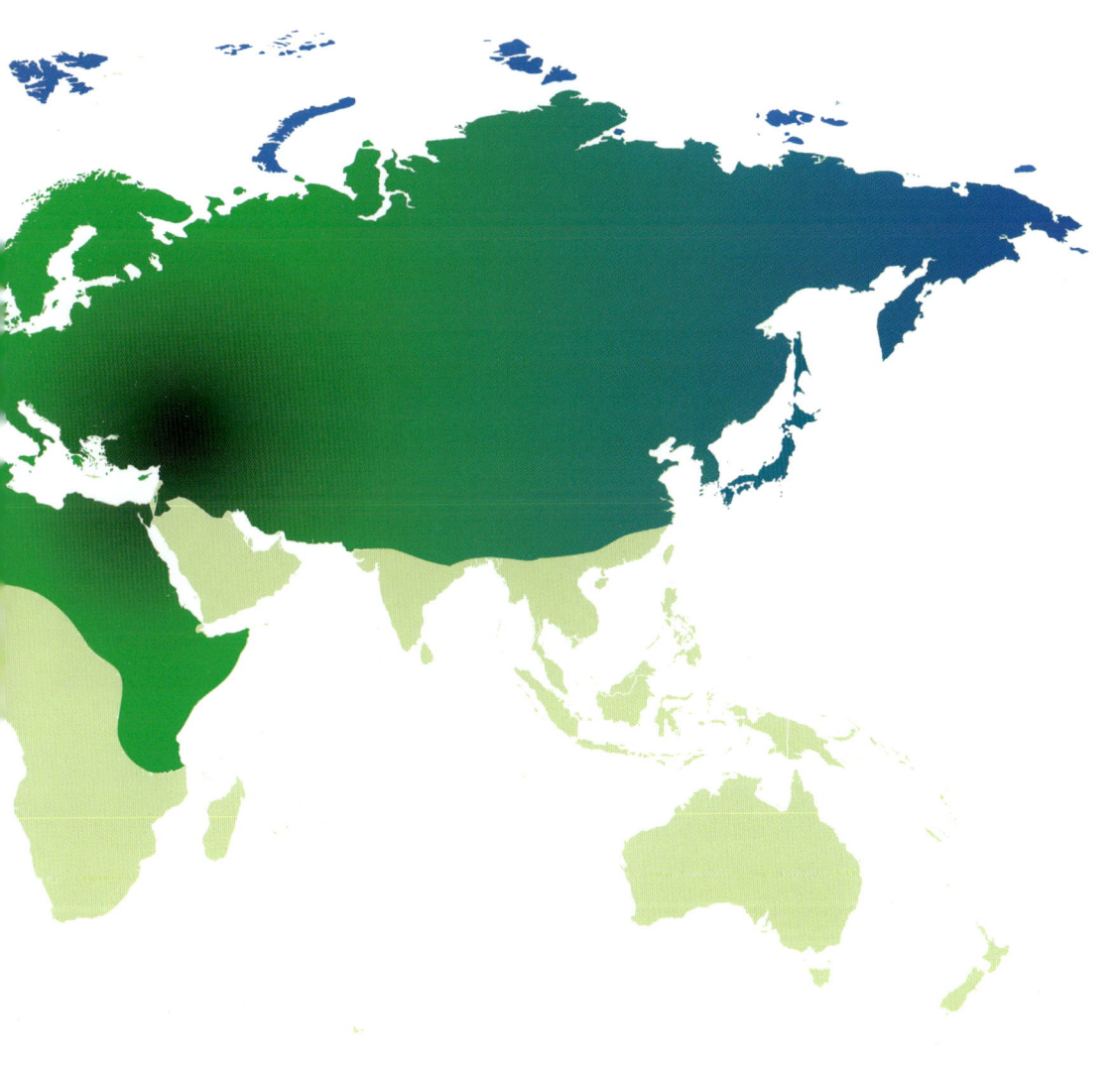

Mediterranean habitats throughout the world. Less ornamental species, such as *L. aphaca*, *L. clymenum* and *L. pratensis*, can also behave as weedy invasives in many habitats outside the hot tropics.

CENTRES OF DIVERSITY

The real stronghold of *Lathyrus* is western Eurasia, particularly around the eastern Mediterranean with over a third of the species being native to Turkey (Davis 1970). Secondary centres of diversity are in East Asia and North and South America. There are few *Lathyrus* species in Central Asia, with perhaps only five truly native to the Himalayas (Ohashi 1979, Tsui 1998) and even fewer on the Indian subcontinent east of Pakistan. In Central Asia and further north, in spite of the low diversity, there are some interesting species such as *L. pisiformis* and *L. humilis* in section *Orobus*, and the lovely *L. mulkak*, a relative of *L. latifolius*.

CONTINENTAL DISTRIBUTIONS

Almost all the East Asian and North American species belong to the very diverse section *Orobus*. All of them are perennial and they form what appears to be recently evolved set of species. Although the species are distinct from each other, and hold up as very good species, botanists are still trying to unravel their relationships, as the 40 or so species in the group evidently evolved in relatively recent times. East Asia has its own group of native species, found from the far east of Russia into Mongolia and much of China (excluding the subtropical south), and in Japan from Hokkaido to Kyushu (Bässler 1973, Kupicha 1983). It may be that the dry steppe of central Russia and the altitude of the Himalayas presents too much of a modern barrier for eastern and western Eurasian species to cross. The only species in East Asia that are not in section *Orobus* are introduced ones consisting of crops, ornamentals and weeds, and the possibly native *L. pratensis*.

One of the few species native to central Asia, *Lathyrus mulkak* is among the most beautiful in the genus.

Only two species, *L. palustris* and sea-dispersed *L. japonicus*, naturally straddle the Old and New Worlds, being distributed across the whole of the temperate northern hemisphere. The area around the Bering Strait has periodically been a temperate land-bridge through the past 3 million years, so would easily allow plants to shift back and forward between the continents. These two, and almost all the native North American species, belong to section *Orobus*. In North America there are 25 species, with the greatest diversity in the west, particularly on the shoulders of the Rocky Mountains and in coastal Oregon and California. This

Only two *Lathyrus* species are naturally found in both the Old World and the New World, *L. palustris* (FAR LEFT) and *L. japonicus* (LEFT).

western distribution, and the similarity in structure and DNA to the East Asian species all adds weight to the theory of a Bering Straits migration.

Lathyrus pusillus is the oddity of the North American species. It is found in the southeastern states of the USA, from Texas to Florida and South Carolina. There is strong DNA evidence that it is distinct from the other North American section *Orobus* species and is, in fact a part of the South American *Notolathyrus* section. Indeed, the species is also found in South America. Section *Notolathyrus* was first established by Kupicha in 1983, and contains around 23 species. It is represented by five species in the tropical Andes, which are actually separated by more than 2,500m of altitude. The group is more diverse in the subtropical and temperate lowlands of South America, where they spread to coastal regions as far south as Tierra del Fuego. For instance, *L. nervosus* forms drifts on the coast and *L. magellanicus* is found more widely inland. The real centre for diversity in South America is Argentina and southern Brazil. Arturo Burkart, one of the giants of Argentine botany, reviewed the indigenous species (Burkart 1937), listing 20 species he believed to be native to Argentina. These live in a wide range of habitats such as subtropical forest, the swamps of the Paraná River delta, the Mediterranean climate zone (pampa) and the slopes of the central Andes.

Lathyrus japonicus is the only Eurasian species that extends as far as South America, ranging from the east coast of North America, through Greenland, Iceland, Atlantic Europe and the Barents Sea to Kamchatka, Korea, northern China and Japan. It is common on the Aleutian chain and down as far as coastal Oregon, and has some isolated freshwater populations on the Great Lakes of Canada and the USA. These Great Lakes populations were trapped on the shores of the newly formed lakes when the land between Hudson Bay and the lakes rose. In addition, it is found in both New Zealand and Chile. The plants of the isolated Chilean localities were believed by Burkart (1937) to be introduced, potentially in the ballast of ships. The consensus is the same for the New Zealand plants. Although this opinion has gained general acceptance, there is no conclusive evidence and *L. japonicus* is certainly capable of long-distance dispersal by sea. Indeed, this species was a favourite of Charles Darwin and his contemporaries when testing the viability of sea-

Lathyrus magellanicus is found in the far south of South America.

drifted seeds. The seeds are known to remain viable in seawater for up to five years (Nelson 2000). If these southern hemisphere populations prove to be natural dispersals, without the help of humans, it would make this one of the greatest seed-sailors in the plant kingdom.

Below are the numbers of species of unequivocal natives taken from some standard Floras of major regions of the world. The numbers of species cited agree largely with the treatment in this book.

- *Flora Europaea* (Ball 1968): 54
- *Flora of Turkey* (Davis 1970): 58
- *Flora of the USSR* (Fedchenko 1948): 50
- *Flora Iranica* (Rechinger 1979): 25
- *Flora of China* (Bao & Kenicer 2010): 14
- *Flora of North America* (Broich, in press): 31
- *South America*, several Floras (see Kenicer 2007): 26

ECOLOGY IN THE WILD

Throughout their vast range, and given the 150 species, it may be no surprise that *Lathyrus* grow in a great diversity of habitats. There are examples from each of the classic triad of competitive, weedy and specialised lifestyles.

Perhaps the majority of species are mesophytes – growing in what seems to us like forgiving conditions in open habitats or forest margins, often on apparently good soils in mild climates. Although these may seem benevolent habitats, they can often be subtly challenging for species, and there can be significant competition for light, nutrients and pollinators. Needless to say, *Lathyrus* species have developed many adaptations to cope, and these make for some interesting options for gardeners.

Lathyrus pratensis is able to compete with other plants by climbing through them.

Sprawlers and climbers

Among the mesophytic species of *Lathyrus*, there are two primary life forms: sprawling, or tall-climbing, species usually with tendrils; and shorter, upright, free-standing species with very reduced or absent tendrils.

The sprawlers such as *L. clymenum* and *L. hirsutus*, and the grassland climbers such as *L. pratensis* and *L. pubescens*, are quite good competitors in the wild. Filling a surprising area or volume from a few slender stems at ground level, they can shade out neighbours. By nitrifying the soil they can

make conditions challenging for neighbouring plants that favour low nutrient levels.

The smaller, tendril-bearing species from sections *Lathyrus* and *Orobus* and members of section *Pratensis* typically cling to surrounding vegetation, often with their own stems forming clumped masses for support. Such species are therefore common in grassland and ungrazed verges and meadows.

Climbers from the woodland edges tend to be leggier, larger species, and often have larger flowers, or more, smaller flowers per inflorescence. Although they can act as specialists, climbing through shrubs and smaller trees to reach the light, they can just as easily shift to become competitive sprawlers in more open habitats. Thus, species such as *L. grandiflorus* (eastern Mediterranean) and *L. vestitus* (North America) can scramble to heights of 3m or more in the right conditions, or switch to form a dense carpet on scrubby hillside habitats. This approach allows them to cope well with long-term changes in the balance between woodland or neighbouring grassland, and adapt to either. Of course, for gardeners it gives the option of using the plants as ground cover or climbers. This ability is one that Gertrude Jekyll exploited when growing *L. latifolius* up cones in herbaceous borders then 'pulling them down' as infill when neighbouring plants had gone over.

Non-climbers

Perhaps unsurprisingly, the upright, often tendril-lacking species favour areas without much to climb on. This can be quite a range of habitats, such as flat, open scrubland and rock, alpine meadows without large grasses, or forest understories without a tall herb layer. In open habitats, species such as *L. laevigatus* and *L. luteus* are found in the alpine meadows of Europe, often near the edges of woodland. These are members of section *Orobus*, and about a dozen further Eurasian members of this section are similar perennials from open or woodland habitats lacking tendrils. Species from section *Orobus* are mostly gardenworthy, such as *L. niger* which is tolerant of moderate shade, and *L. pannonicus* and *L. linifolius* which are equally content in light shade or open situations.

Members of section *Lathyrostylis* have a remarkably similar habit and habitat preferences to the above and also offer potential for gardens. *Lathyrus macropus* is found in hard-baked sandy clays around 2,000m in the dry central Andes of

Argentina, and some of the very variable *L. magellanicus* are found in the bleak, volcanic ash fields or glacier edges of Chile. Although these two species do have tendrils, they are only used in habitats with vegetation up which to climb. If such props are not available, the plants are shorter and more spreading – an excellent adaptation for coping with changing vegetation and habitats.

Ruderals

Annual species with a somewhat weedy lifestyle are represented by *L. aphaca* and *L. clymenum* and their close relatives, as well as some of the South American species and a few members of section *Lathyrus*. These species are generally classic ruderals, doing well in a range of disturbed habitats such as cultivated fields and roadsides. Agriculturally significant weedy species include *L. aphaca* and *L. ochrus*, both of which are drought-tolerant (Holm *et al.* 1979). Species such as *L. hirsutus* and *L. pratensis* are often found as non-natives in seed mixes, and so have a widespread temperate distribution. Both of these species are naturalised in East Asia, Australia and North America, and *L. hirsutus* is occasionally found in Argentina and Chile (Burkart 1937). Escapes from cultivation include *L. tuberosus*, a former food crop, and ornamentals such as *L. latifolius*, *L. grandiflorus* and *L. odoratus*. The last three species are very widely cultivated and commonly escape, sometimes establishing significant populations. Indeed, one of the authors (GK) has seen *L. latifolius* naturalised, presumably as a garden escape, in South Africa, Japan, western North America and Argentina, with extensive patches in the latter two areas, reflecting its potential as an invasive plant.

The annuals are often very fast to reproduce and species such as *L. annuus*, *L. inconspicuus* and *L. setifolius* can readily manage two generations in a long, warm season. This is clearly an adaptation to dry summers in Mediterranean climates, where the seeds will over-summer, and germinate opportunistically in mild winter- or spring-like conditions whenever they might occur. Germinating these Mediterranean annual species is often very easy, with an overnight soak mimicking winter rain, and perhaps a nick with a knife or a rub on sandpaper just to break the seed coat to simulate natural abrasion.

TOLERATING EXTREMES

The range of tolerance of the genus as a whole reveals members surviving from the coasts of Greenland to the Galápagos Islands, dealing with extremes of cold, heat, dry and wet, low and high light intensities, and year-round to three-month growing seasons.

Species such as *L. palustris* in the northern hemisphere and species such as *L. macrostachys*, *L. nigrivalvis* and *L. paranensis* from wet areas of northern Argentina and around the Uruguay and Paraná rivers of South America are adapted to inundated marshlands. At the other extreme are arid-loving species such as *L. hitchcockianus* from Death Valley, USA, the lovely silvery *L. tomentosus* from

Lathyrus magellanicus survives in extreme habitats, such as the cold lava fields of Tronador, an extinct volcano in the southern Andes on the border between Argentina and Chile.

arid regions of the Argentine Pampas, *L. macropus* from the high, dry Andes, and *L. magellanicus* from the volcanic ash fields of Chile.

The widespread *L. japonicus* and west-coast US species *L. littoralis* are classic patch-forming species from beaches. Both have creeping, sand-catching rhizomes and semi-succulent leaves. *Lathyrus japonicus* is almost hairless, with a waxy bloom, while *L. littoralis* has dense, silky hairs throughout. Both are adaptations to the drying effect of salt-laden coastal winds. Perhaps the most similar species to *L. littoralis* morphologically is *L. tomentosus*, from semi-arid inland areas of South America. Where *L. littoralis* has running rhizomes to cope with shifting sand, *L. tomentosus* and others from similar inland habitats have deep tap roots for accessing water, and for nutrient storage.

There are also several small, prostrate species, as well as intermediate types. Some, such as *L. davidii*, hint at becoming shrubs, with slightly woodier tissues and a robust upright habit. Such species are invariably from woodlands and can tolerate a considerable degree of shade. In the case of *L. davidii*, it grows at the margin of extremely dense *Cryptomeria japonica* forest and large leaflets can exploit the light, even where narrow roads cut through the gloom. *Lathyrus aureus* and *L. roseus* are the equivalent in the forests of the southern and eastern Black Sea region. None of these species are evergreen or particularly early flowering, but the smaller *L. vernus*, the aptly named spring vetch, escapes shade by flushing and flowering early in spring before the tree canopy closes over.

The greatest asset in colonising such a range of habitats is undoubtedly the diversity of the genus. The default pattern for many species, that of climbing with tendrils or sprawling, makes them highly versatile, so this genus is certainly 'one to watch' in the face of climate change..

Breeding and selection

Since the middle of the 19th century, plant breeders have given considerable attention to the production of new *L. odoratus* (sweet pea) cultivars. However, work on the rest of the genus has been quite minimal, with fewer than 10 species being subject to the selection of cultivars. This chapter is mainly concerned with selection and breeding of sweet peas, but includes sections on other species, particularly *L. vernus*, and on interspecific hybrids.

EARLY SWEET PEA SELECTION

It is not clear how new sweet pea colours in the 18th and early 19th centuries were being introduced. Mutation and accidental cross-pollination are most likely to have played a role. There is no evidence that the size of flowers, number of flowers per raceme, or vigour of the plants were increasing. However, some changes were occurring by small increments over the generations of the annual life cycle.

James Carter (1797–1855) of Holborn, London, opened his first shop selling seeds in 1834. Around 1838 he bought the older business of Dunnett & Beale and formed James Carter & Co. His 1838–1839 seed catalogue lists seven sweet pea colours. Between 1845 and 1849 he introduced 'New Large Purple', 'New Striped' and 'Painted Lady', suggesting seed sellers had started

LEFT **A selection of *Lathyrus odoratus* cultivars displayed by Eagle Sweet Peas in 2009.**

RIGHT **James Carter opened his first seed shop in London in 1834.**

to consciously improve the flower form, size and plant vigour.

The firm continued to thrive after Carter's death, run by the Dunnett and Beale families. Edward John Beale (1835–1902) was a partner and vice-president of the Sweet Pea Bicentenary Committee. This was set up by prominent horticulturists in 1899 to celebrate its 1699 introduction and to hold an exhibition in 1900 at Crystal Palace, London. In 1860, H.N. Dunnett also became a partner in the business, which had two distinct sides. The wholesale side was known as Carter, Dunnett and Beale while the retail side became Carters Tested Seeds. Dunnett had three children, Norman, Jack and Daisy, and in the last quarter of the 19th century, a William Herbert Dunnett was a partner with three Beale brothers, Gilbert Charles, Reginald and Harold (Taylor 2014). Harold was in charge and is the one remembered in the sweet pea world. He was president of the National Sweet Pea Society (NSPS) in 1929 and in 1937 was awarded their Henry Eckford Gold Memorial Medal. In 1927 or 1929 the firm appointed John Ness (1877–1955), who had previously raised sweet peas for Thomas Cullen & Sons of Witham, Essex. Ness's novelties for Carters included 'Carlotta', which remains popular, 'Swan Lake', 'Cream Delight' and other influential Spencer cultivars of their day (Davis 1965). In 1966, both the wholesale and retail businesses of Carters were absorbed into the R. & G. Cuthbert Group (Roper 1989). Prior to this they had introduced at least 140 sweet pea cultivars. The firm's archives, dating from the 1830s, are deposited at Lewisham Local History and Archives Centre, London (ref. A/78/28).

In 1860, a picotee cultivar was introduced by Carters and named 'Blue Edged'. It was raised by Major Trevor Clarke and received a First Class Certificate (FCC) from the RHS in 1883 under the name 'Blue Hybrid'. Other reports of people consciously crossing sweet peas soon followed, the result of increasing interest in the flower from commercial seed sellers. Between 1860 and 1870 many new sweet peas were introduced. In 1867, 'Scarlet Invincible' became the first to be recognised for an award, receiving an FCC from the RHS. This was raised by Steven Brown of Sudbury, Suffolk, and introduced by Carters.

1253	Palma Christi	*Ricinus major*	21	49	94	hha	gr.
1254	Pea, Tangier, 2 var.	*Láthyrus tingitànus*	17	45	106	ha	r.&s.
1255	Lord Anson's	*magellánicus*	...	...	...	...	bl.
1256	winged, 2 var.	*Lòtus tetragonólobus*	...	...	...	...	y & r
1257	Pea, sweet, per lb. 4s.	*Láthyrus odoràtus*	...	...	...	...	div.
1258	black	— *niger*	...	...	...	...	bla.
1259	painted Lady	— *pictus*	...	...	...	...	var.
1260	purple	— *purpùreus*	...	...	...	...	pur.
1261	new large purple	— *atropurpùreus*	...	...	...	...	...
1262	scarlet	— *coccíneus*	...	...	...	...	sc.
1263	striped	— *striàtus*	...	...	...	...	stri.
1264	— new striped	— *striàtus nòvus*	...	...	...	...	...
1265	white	— *albus*	...	...	...	...	wh.
1266	Persicaria, red	*Poly'gonum orientàle*	8	28	128	...	red
1267	white						

Sweet peas offered by James Carter between 1845 and 1849 show that selection was being undertaken.

RIGHT **German seed company Haage & Schmidt raised 'Kronprinzessin von Preussen' in 1868.**

FAR RIGHT **Raised by John Ness in 1937, 'Carlotta' remains popular today.**

BELOW **Worcestershire breeder Hilda Hemus raised many cultivars in the early 1900s, but none survive.**

Haage & Schmidt of Erfut, Germany, a firm founded in 1823 to specialise in vegetable seeds, were also active in the 1860s. They raised new cultivars such as 'Kronprinzessin von Preussen' (Crown Princess of Prussia) in 1868, 'Feenkönigin' (Fairy Queen) in 1873, and 'Bronze King' in 1894. Carl Schmidt represented the business on the Bicentenary Committee in 1899.

From 1877, Thomas Laxton (1830–1893) of Bedford, Bedfordshire, began to improve sweet peas, receiving an FCC in 1883 for his 'Invincible Carmine'. He raised 10 excellent cultivars but is barely remembered among sweet pea enthusiasts because he came up against Henry Eckford. As Henry Eckford's son, John, reported: 'Mr Laxton was too good a florist to create confusion by distributing similar varieties under different names and so his work was to a large extent discounted' (Curtis & Eckford 1900). His last introduction was 'Princess May' in 1893. Two of his sons, William and Edward, went into partnership in 1888 to form Laxton Brothers.

Hilda Hemus (1874–1954) of Upton-on-Severn, Worcestershire, was the sister-in-law of pioneer geneticist Sir Rowland Biffen

(1874–1949). Biffen produced a few new sweet peas himself during the Edwardian era but Hemus was the sweet pea specialist and raised at least 138 cultivars, introduced between 1906 and 1914. None of her introductions have survived. The Hemus business struggled with labour during the First World War so Hilda sold it to Samuel Ryder (1858–1936) of St Albans, Hertfordshire (Taylor 2014).

OLD-FASHIONED GRANDIFLORA SWEET PEAS

Henry Eckford (1823–1905) of Wem, Shropshire, is remembered as the father of the sweet pea. A Scot by birth, a detailed biography of him was written by Martin (2017). His name more than others is associated with the development of the sweet pea in the 1880s and 1890s. Up until that time there had been little improvement in the vigour of cultivars, the length of racemes, the number of flowers per raceme or the size of petals. Eckford coined the term Grandiflora for his new cultivars on account of their flower size. Eventually, Frank Cuthbertson (1916) noted: 'the name of Grandiflora has become a decided misnomer'. Nowadays, cultivars from the Eckford era have the smallest flowers of sweet peas, so the term Old-fashioned Grandiflora is more appropriate for them.

A profusion of new colours belonging to this type arose during the 1890s

ABOVE LEFT **Henry Eckford was a major breeder of sweet peas who introduced many improvements.**

ABOVE RIGHT **A sweet pea catalogue issued in 1908, three years after Henry Eckford's death.**

and 1900s, together with improvements on existing colours, with much breeding activity in the UK and USA. Eckford was 65 when he started his sweet pea business and most of the running of it fell to his son, John Stainer Eckford, who continued trading until around 1939. John was no longer raising new sweet peas after his father's death and by 1906 he was assisted by a John Jones.

Old-fashioned Grandifloras were eventually considered obsolete by seed sellers, and the fact that some have survived at all is mainly thanks to the Ferry Morse Seed Co. in California, USA, who maintained 13 cultivars and enabled their reintroduction into the UK in 1950. They were maintained by Major John F. Turral (d. 1967) of Farnley in North Yorkshire. On his death they passed to Keith Hammett (b. 1942) in New Zealand and Ron Bailey (d. 1993) of Abergavenny in Wales, later of Hereford, so we have good provenance for most of these (Parsons 2014). Others which purport to be Old-fashioned Grandifloras are 're-creations' by Peter Grayson (d.2013) of Chesterfield, Derbyshire. Grayson was successful in bringing *Lathyrus* species and Grandiflora sweet peas to a wider audience (Buchan 1999). He caused confusion, however, when he found something new and gave it the name of an Old-fashioned Grandiflora cultivar which he imagined might have looked the same. He then sold it as a re-discovery of the old original.

SPENCER SWEET PEAS

The big change in sweet pea flower development came in 1901 when a cultivar called 'Countess Spencer' was displayed for the first time at the first exhibition of the new National Sweet Pea Society. It was raised in 1900 by Silas Cole (1866–1939), head gardener to John Spencer (5th Earl Spencer, 1835–1910) at Althorp, Northamptonshire. This cultivar had much longer racemes than previously seen and reliably produced four flowers per raceme, each floret with much larger, wavy petals. Cole was equivocal about the origin of his cultivar, but there is no doubt it was enormously influential. Cultivars with long stems and large wavy petals are to this day

Introduced in 1901, 'Countess Spencer' was a major improvement due to its longer racemes reliably bearing four flowers.

New Sweet Pea
GYPSY QUEEN

known as Spencer sweet peas.

There was an explosion of interest in sweet peas during the Edwardian era, fuelled by this new type. In 1911, the *Daily Mail* ran a competition inviting readers to submit a bunch of sweet peas by post that received around 39,000 entries. Amateurs and professionals alike turned their hand to breeding new Spencer sweet peas. Although most of these new cultivars did not survive the First World War, improvements were being made and considerable activity continued during the interwar period to improve flower size, raceme length, frilliness of flowers and number of florets per raceme.

The demand for novelty was mostly driven by florists and amateur exhibitors who wanted clear colours and uniformity, leading to a decline in interest in fancy colour patterns. By the mid 20th century, a good Spencer cultivar produced five florets and was suitable for cut-flower sales or exhibition.

After 1945 there was a shift away in the UK from most new cultivars being raised by packet-seed companies. The focus moved towards amateur raisers whose primary interest was growing for exhibition. Most amateur raisers were keen exhibitors who required cultivars to uniformly produce four florets per raceme. Supreme among them was Bernard Rees Jones (1906–1996) of Warwick, Warwickshire, whose influence was enormous. A pharmacist by profession, he was a prolific writer and breeder of many successful Spencer cultivars, and known to all as The Maestro. In 1958 he was awarded the NSPS Henry Eckford Gold Memorial Medal. Rees Jones raised at least 24 novelties which were introduced by various seed sellers between 1951 and 2009.

LEFT TOP **Introduced in 1964, 'Gypsy Queen' is a Spencer that reliably produces five florets.**

LEFT BOTTOM Active in the second half of the 20th century, **Bernard Rees Jones raised many successful Spencers.**

SEMI-GRANDIFLORA (UNWIN) SWEET PEAS

When cut-flower grower William James Unwin first saw 'Countess Spencer' in 1901, he remarked: 'I have that variety at home' (Curtis 1905). Where 'Countess Spencer' was unstable, Unwin's cultivar, 'Gladys Unwin', had the distinct advantage of being completely fixed and more free-flowering. Its reliability meant that it was initially far more popular than 'Countess Spencer'. Other cultivars were bred from 'Gladys Unwin' to produce what became known as the Unwin type. These were very similar to the Spencer type but the florets were not quite as large. More definitively, they had the closed (or clamped) keel of the Old-fashioned Grandifloras rather than the open keel of the Spencer type.

The Unwin type did not survive long. Frank Cuthbertson (1916) said 'The name Unwin [...] has been dropped by common consent'. He illustrated the three flower forms and described:

1. Grandiflora type showing clamped keel
2. Waved Grandiflora showing clamped keel
3. Waved Spencer showing open keel.

Elsewhere, Morse described the Waved Grandiflora cultivars as Rogue Spencers. In 1926, Charles Unwin named the type as Semi-grandiflora and said they were obsolete. They may have been consigned to history if not for the introduction in 1999 of 'Albutt Blue', raised by Harvey Albutt. This very free-flowering cultivar has waved petals and a clamped keel, florets that are not quite as large as the Spencers, and the wonderful fragrance of the Old-fashioned Grandifloras. A number of cultivars with this form have followed, including some which originated as Spencers but have reverted to clamped-keel form.

Three popular sweet peas illustrated in *The Garden* in 1909. Mauve 'Frank Dolby' and white 'Nora Unwin' are Semi-grandiflora types whereas red 'King Edward VII' is a Grandiflora.

THREE POPULAR SWEET PEAS.
MAUVE, FRANK DOLBY.
WHITE, NORA UNWIN.
CRIMSON, KING EDWARD VII.

DWARF SWEET PEAS

In 1893, at Lester Morse's ranch in Santa Clara, California, USA, the first dwarf sweet pea arose and was named 'Cupid'. It had white flowers and was saved from among plants of the white-flowered, tall-growing cultivar 'Emily Henderson'. Morse sold 'Cupid' to Atlee Burpee in 1894. At the same time, a similar sport was identified and saved by Ernst Benary (1819–1893) of Erfurt, Germany, who named his 'Tom Thumb White', which was either identical to 'Cupid' or a little taller, according to different reports. Both 'Cupid'

and 'Tom Thumb White' bred true from the start, but Burpee Seeds published Morse's name first, so 'Cupid' was established as the name for this cultivar. Other colours followed, such as 'Pink Cupid' in 1898, followed by 'Primrose Cupid' (Parsons 2000). Frank Cuthbertson (1916) lists 29 dwarf cultivars, all apparently with Old-fashioned Grandiflora flower form.

This dwarf type almost died out, but was again maintained by Ferry Morse Seed Co. where in 1958 Frank Cuthbertson introduced his 'Cuthbertson Cupid' mixture. It is not clear to what extent these arose from hybridisation or simply reselection of old material. Ferry Morse Seed Co. described them as 'our own development'. Ten colours had been submitted for trial in 1957 at RHS Garden Wisley and all were Highly Commended. The individual colours were given names such as 'White Carpet' and 'Pink Carpet' but were only sold as a mixture. Existing cultivars such as 'White Cupid' appear to be the Cuthbertson Cupid material, but 'Pink Cupid' may be the original material. Recent developments of this type include Fantasia Series from Farmen of Naples, Italy, Cherub Series from Mark Rowland (b. 1947) at Owl's Acre Sweet Peas in Lincolnshire, and others from Andrew Beane (b. 1949) of Leeds.

There was little interest in the dwarf cultivars, but a few with Spencer form are recorded prior to the introduction of Little Sweetheart Series in 1957. Hemus introduced a few in 1912 and there was 'Little Nell', a winter-flowering dwarf, introduced in 1922 by Yates, Australia. All have an erect, bushy habit rather than the trailing habit of the Cupid Series. Many dwarf series were developed around the 1960s, particularly in the US. Patio Series from Burpee Seeds was an improvement on Little Sweetheart Series and flowers earlier. Bijou Series was originally Semi-multiflora but has nowadays lost this character. More recently, the Sprite Series of early-flowering dwarf Spencers was developed by Mark Rowland of Owl's Acre Sweet Peas at Spalding, Lincolnshire (Rowland subsequently sold the retail seed side of the business to Elizabeth Crawford in East Yorkshire). Bijou Series and Sprite Series both have a trailing habit.

EARLY-FLOWERING SWEET PEAS

The early-flowering character was first recorded in the US in 'Blanche Ferry', introduced by D.M. Ferry & Co. in 1889. This cultivar arose from unconscious selection of 'Painted Lady' by a quarryman's wife over 40 years, when saving only the earliest seeds each year. The cultivar currently in commerce as 'Blanche Ferry' was 'rediscovered' in the 1980s by Ron Bailey of Hereford, but the colour may be wrong and it is not early-flowering.

Work to produce new early-flowering cultivars, in which flowering initiates on a shorter daylength, was carried out by Carl Gustav Engelmann of Saffron Walden, Essex, and by Revd. Edwyn Arkwright (1839–1922) in Algiers, where he found the summers too hot for summer-flowering cultivars (Parsons 2011). Engelmann said his winter-flowering material had arisen from a sport of 'Captain of the Blues'.

Development of the early-flowering character also took place in the US where the name of Anton Zvolanek (1878–1958) is most associated with them. He grew cut flowers for market and one year noticed in a row of 'Lottie Eckford' a plant that

Dwarf sweet peas flowering in a trial at RHS Garden Wisley in 2013.

flowered two weeks earlier. He saved this and crossed it with 'Blanche Ferry' to produce 'Zvolanek's Christmas', introduced in 1899. A series of early cultivars followed. In 1907, Lester Morse noted these as: 'Really a distinct class. Planted in October they will give cut flowers all winter, and until the following June' (Beal 1912). In 1902 Zvolanek received seeds of 'Countess Spencer', and many more crosses led to his Early Spencer Series.

The Late Spencer type must have been imported early into Australia because an Early Spencer cultivar, 'Yarrawa', had arisen by 1909 in the Sydney garden of a Mr James

Young. It was introduced in 1912 by Arthur Yates & Co. of Sydney, New South Wales. From this, many new Australian cultivars were raised by crossing 'Yarrawa' with American cultivars. At the same time, American raisers imported 'Yarrawa' and other Australian cultivars for their own breeding work. Selection for earliness meant that, in time, seed sellers began to distinguish between winter-flowering and spring-flowering cultivars.

Cuthbertson Series was a popular spring-flowering type. It originated in 1930 when Frank Cuthbertson, working at Ferry Morse Seed Co. in California, selected a particularly strong plant with long racemes. The material was not fixed so various colours arose from this plant and were crossed with early-flowering cultivars to produce a range of hues. This series flowered several weeks earlier than Spencers and had some heat resistance so was considered to be late spring-flowering. It was introduced in the 1940s and later crossed with multifloras raised by William Zvolanek, son of Anton, to create the Cuthbertson Floribunda Series. Royal Series, introduced by Ferry Morse Seed Co. in 1968, is a later evolution of this type.

In 1912–1913, Lionel D. Waller (1882–1940) and Dr. John Henry Franklin (1880–1934) established the L.D. Waller Seed Co. at Guadalupe, California. Waller had learned his trade working for Louis Routzahn at Arroyo Grande and was reckoned to have an aggressive management style. Franklin served in the medical department during the First World War but returned to the company in 1919 and took charge of the plant breeding work. In 1926 they became the Waller-Franklin Seed Co. The company raised around 80 cultivars, among which the early-flowering type dominated. Later, they became the Waller Flowerseed Co. that then became part of the Ball Group of PanAmerican Seed.

In 1921, William Macdonald (1883–1955) joined L.D. Waller Seed Co. and later formed the Macdonald Seed Co. at Bonita near San Diego. He too is most noted in sweet pea terms for his early-flowering cultivars. The company introduced at least 98 cultivars between 1929 and 1951. His three children continued the business after his death but it was dissolved in 1963. This firm should not be confused with D.J. McDonald (b. 1941) of Stockbridge, Hampshire, who has recently introduced some Late Spencer cultivars.

GAWLER SWEET PEAS

Just as American breeders used 'Yarrawa' in their work on early Spencer cultivars, so Australian breeders were working with American material to produce new and improved Australian cultivars. Arthur Yates & Co. started to specialise in early-flowering sweet peas from 1908. Its founder had emigrated from the UK to New Zealand in 1879 and he later moved to Australia in 1887, founding seed companies in both countries. However, the interest in novel cultivars did not continue after Yates's death in 1926. His firm remains one of the most notable names in Australian and New Zealand gardening. In the 1990s it introduced innovative late Spencers from New Zealand breeder Keith Hammett.

Hot summers meant that early cultivars quickly became more popular with Australian gardeners than the summer-flowering cultivars imported from the UK. Otherwise, sweet pea growing in Australia developed along UK lines with keen competition at flower shows between exhibitors. This was primarily restricted to the cooler states, particularly New South Wales, Victoria and South Australia. As well as Arthur Yates & Co., notable seed sellers included Anderson & Co., Sydney, and Searle, later Gill & Searle, of Melbourne. Amateur raisers of early-flowering cultivars in early decades included newspaper proprietor Hamilton Charnock Mott (1871–1963) of Albury, New South Wales, and W.H. Hatcher of Sydney who developed the Zyris strain.

Leading exhibitors around Sydney in the 1930s included Hatcher's son, Charles Hatcher, and W. Steward whose cultivars were sold by George L. Gallatly of Sydney up to the early 1960s. Gradually there was a shift away from New South Wales, and t he Adelaide area became recognised as the area for producing new sweet peas. In the 1930s E. & W. Hackett Ltd of Adelaide sold the Karkoo strain,

A packet of sweet pea seed supplied by Anderson & Co. in the 1920s.

499

SWEET PEAS, Early Flowering Spencer
The Allan Strain, Extra Choice-Mixed.

Anderson & Co Ltd.
SEED MERCHANTS, SYDNEY.

PRINTED BY JOHN SANDS LTD SYDNEY

Gawler cultivars are classified as Spencers and are favoured for their frilliness. Examples include 'Gawler Cerise' (ABOVE LEFT), 'Gawler Louise' (ABOVE TOP) and flaked 'Gawler Margaret' (ABOVE).

and Harris Scarfe Ltd of Adelaide sold what they termed 'Invincible cultivars raised by Harkness, well-known exhibitor' under the heading 'Gawler Sweet Peas'. These took their name from a town near Adelaide and included cultivars such as 'Gladys Harkness'. Leading growers from the Adelaide area in the 1940s included James Harkness of Willaston and Eric C.A. Carter, trading in 1947 as Carter Bros. of Woodville and in 1955 as Eric Carter of Broadview. A later generation of breeders included Fred Martin of Gawler South, who was still alive in 1980.

The town of Gawler in South Australia became a centre for growing and raising new cultivars from the late 1930s onwards. Here, flaked cultivars remained popular. As new cultivars were developed, emphasis was placed on fragrance and frilliness so that nowadays Gawler sweet peas are highly distinct due to their very wavy petals, often duplex or triplex florets, and wonderful fragrance. Many also have smooth or hairless vegetative parts, including the seed pods. In a letter of 1980 to Keith Hammett, Richard F. Bennett of Willaston, South Australia, explained that the extreme frilliness of the Gawler strain was developed by a Mr Pengilly who took 13 years to produce this character in 'Athol Pearl Pink'. This cultivar was then used by Harkness in his breeding work. In a letter to Hammett in 1971, Fred Martin explained that the Elfin Series consisted of early Spencers developed in the 1920s by a Mr E. Fidge of Adelaide Hills. 'Elfin White' was used by

Gawler sweet peas being cultivated by Brad McDougall in Evanston, near the town of Gawler in Australia.

J. Harkness, when producing his first cultivar in 1926.

Most of these strains are now lost. Gawler sweet peas have been maintained by the McDougall family. They are Malcolm McDougall of Meadows, his brother Barry McDougall of Gawler South, and Barry's son, Brad McDougall, of Evanston. The unique characteristics of this strain are a great resource for plant breeders. However, for most of the world, the development of early multiflora Spencer cultivars by US breeders meant that interest in early non-multifloras disappeared.

MULTIFLORA SWEET PEAS

The term multiflora refers to racemes with more than five florets per raceme. Early

multiflora Spencer cultivars arose in parallel with the multiflora character that was first developed in summer-flowering or late Spencers. The first multiflora cultivar appears to be summer-flowering 'Sextet Queen', introduced by Suttons of the UK in 1931. This had white flowers making it very suitable for crossing with other colours. Further cultivars with a Sextet prefix were introduced by Suttons during the 1930s. In the first few years, 'Sextet Queen' was popular for exhibition because it retained all six flowers fresh at the same time. However, this quality was lost and did not reappear in later cultivars. Flower size also quickly reduced, so the type lost favour. To distinguish types with fewer flowers, Keith Hammett has informally coined the term pauciflora to refer to blooms with four or fewer flowers.

Interest in having more flowers per stem remained, particularly for cut-flower growers who get a longer vase life when new florets open as the lower ones fade. In 1958, Burpee Seeds in the US introduced the first of their summer-flowering Galaxy Series which produced up to eight flowers per raceme. These were later offered by companies such as Samuel Dobie & Son in the UK. Mass seed production led to a gradual reduction in the number of florets, which also reduced in size. In 1998, Denholm Seeds in the US introduced their Bouquet Series to supersede Galaxy Series. Current breeding work is focussed on improving these for raceme length, floret size and placement. Good placement is achieved with five or six florets per raceme, but above this the placement of florets along a stem becomes irregular and florets can develop as a whorl, rather than all facing forward. Recent developments have resulted in up to 15 florets per raceme in cultivars such as 'Aphrodite' and 'Chelsea Centenary'.

In 1947, William Zvolanek (1892–1979), son of Anton, selected a plant with six flowers per raceme among 'Early Zvolanek Rose'. After many crosses, he produced a hybrid that usually produced six to eight flowers, but anything up to 11 per raceme. He named this 'Whirlwind' and other early multifloras soon appeared. All had Spencer form but had relatively poor placement and relatively small flowers. An improved series appeared in 1960 when Denholm Seeds introduced their early multiflora Gigantea Series. These proved extremely popular with cut-flower growers in many parts of the world. They have been periodically renewed by reselection and crossing. William Zvolanek continued to work on them until his retirement in 1975 when he sold the business to Denholm Seeds (Christensen 2006). In 1973, David Lemon (b. 1934) joined Denholm Seeds and started working on this type, creating the Mammoth Series introduced in 1982. These are more early spring-flowering rather than winter-flowering, but in 1984 Lemon moved to Bodger Seeds of El Monte, California, where he created the Winter Elegance Series introduced in 1992. Lemon continued to work on this type, producing for PanAmerican Seeds material that was subsequently refined for the UK by Mark Rowland of Owl's Acre Sweet Peas and introduced as part of the Winter Sunshine Series. Lemon's final evolution of the type is Solstice Series, introduced in 2009.

DUPLEX FORM SWEET PEAS

Reference has already been made to duplex form, often seen in Gawler cultivars. This term refers to the presence of two standard petals instead of one, giving a more frilly appearance. Triplex florets are also sometimes seen. The character is sometimes confused with malformation of florets, which is when petals fail to develop in the normal way and may be tucked into each other, or extra wings may be present or the wings ticked into keels. The duplex form has not been welcomed by most sweet pea

Double Sweet Pea
Bride of Niagara.

enthusiasts since it robs the floret of its symmetry. However, cut-flower growers saw it as a step towards fully double florets that in other genera are associated with longer vase life. This could lead to increased commercial cut-flower production, so development of the duplex form was keenly pursued by some breeders early in the 20th century.

The first appearance of duplex standard petals was recorded in 'Bride of Niagara', introduced by Vick in 1896 before the advent of wavy petals. Both Morse and Burpee Seeds were very active in trying to fix the duplex character in early-flowering cultivars and these started to appear in the late 1920s. 'Fluffy Ruffles', introduced by Burpee Seeds in 1928, was very frilly and often produced duplex florets. It was the first of what became popular in the USA as the summer-flowering Ruffled Series. Although frilly, the racemes in this series were not as long as cut-flower growers would wish.

In 1934, Robert Bolton introduced 'Gigantic' in the UK with huge, densely frilled blooms, often duplex, that became widely used by breeders to improve the Spencer type. The presence of the duplex character in modern Spencer cultivars is primarily due to the genetic influence of 'Gigantic'. While cut-flower growers remain happy to see duplex florets, they have had few champions since the death of Charles Unwin in 1986, but strong frilliness remains popular with general gardeners.

The term 'duplex flowers' should not be confused with 'twin flowers', which is used when two racemes emerge from a single leaf axil. This can give up to double the number of flowers per plant, improving the decorative effect. It is rare, but most frequently seen in semi-dwarf Spencer cultivars raised by Dickson Place.

FLAKED AND BICOLOURED SWEET PEAS

Flaked and bicoloured flowers were initially not popular and mostly ignored. The new striped colours, developed by Unwins Seeds in the 1920s and 1930s, were never popular. It is only in recent decades that these fancy colour patterns have seen a surge in popularity, when interest in growing for cut-flower sales and exhibition waned. Gardeners now predominantly want cultivars for garden decoration and cutting for the house. Much of this improvement has come from Charles Andrew Beane, an amateur raiser from Leeds, who is still active.

LEFT TOP **Although Galaxy Series originated in the US in 1958, Dobies were quick to offer these multifloras in the UK.**

LEFT **Mammoth Series was a later multiflora from 1982 and includes cultivars such as 'Mammoth Cream Pink'.**

ABOVE **The first sweet pea with double standard petals was 'Bride of Niagara, first offered by Vick in 1896.**

Improvement of bicolours has been led by Keith Hammett in New Zealand from the 1970s onwards. This includes the creation of the distinct 'reverse bicolours', such as 'Erewhon', where the darker colour is in the wings rather than in the standard petal.

SEMI-DWARF SWEET PEAS

Semi-dwarf cultivars are intermediate in height between tall sweet peas and dwarf sweet peas, attaining between 0.6m and 1.2m. Some prefer the name intermediate type to semi-dwarf on the basis that semi-tall is equally valid. Objectors to intermediate dislike the lack of reference to height. They are also sometimes called bush-type, although this refers to a specific 'bush' gene that can be seen in both semi-dwarf and dwarf cultivars. The gene, as a heritable character, was identified before 1905 but the first semi-dwarf cultivar in commerce appears to be 'Marjorie Hemus Intermediate', introduced by Hemus in 1912.

The semi-dwarf character seems to have been largely ignored until the introduction by Ferry Morse Seed Co. of Knee-Hi Series in 1965. These arose from crossing William Zvolanek's dwarf Pygmy Series with Cuthbertson Floribunda Series. As with both parents, Knee-Hi Series originally had multiflora Spencer racemes on semi-dwarf plants although the Knee-Hi mixture sold nowadays has mostly lost its multiflora character. Jet Set Series is a later evolution of this type, introduced by Ferry Morse in 1973, but again the mixture still in commerce has deteriorated. It arose from work by David Lemon to cross Knee-Hi Series with Royal Series. Good stocks of both Knee-Hi and Jet Set have now been re-introduced by Roger Parsons. Both series have distinctively short internodes compared with tall cultivars.

More recent semi-dwarf cultivars clearly have reduced height because of the bush gene, seen in their prolific side-shoots and erect habit. These were primarily developed by Joseph Dickson Place (1929–2007) in Cumbria and often have a 'Solway' prefix. Some of his semi-dwarf cultivars have Old-fashioned flower form and some have Spencer form. These have only recently come into commerce so are not well known, but are excellent for smaller gardens because of their prolific flowering and decorative effect. They have good fragrance but the racemes are quite short compared with earlier series from Ferry Morse Seed Co. His semi-dwarf Spencer cultivars are very frilly and many have a 'Minuet' prefix.

TOP 'Erewhon' is a reverse bicolour, where the wings are darker than the standard.

ABOVE Semi-dwarf Knee-Hi Series was first marketed in 1965.

RIGHT **Jet Set is a later semi-dwarf series, dating from 1973.**

FAR RIGHT **More recent cultivars from semi-dwarf series include 'Minuet Orange Pink Splash'** (TOP) **and 'Solway Sapphire'** (BOTTOM).

NON-TENDRIL-LEAVED SWEET PEAS

Among the semi-dwarf series are several that bear leaves without tendrils. These have the tendrils replaced by extra leaflets, a character caused by the 'acacia' gene, and are sometimes known as acacia-leaved. The term 'non-tendril' is preferred because the leaves do not closely resemble acacia leaves. The gene has been known since about 1889, as a heritable character, in tall cultivars. These originally had rather weak racemes and poor flowers but George Burt, working for E.W. King & Co. of Essex, produced a series of tall, non-tendril cultivars with Spencer flower form in the 1930s and 1940s. These did not prove popular, possibly because for garden decoration they are not self-supporting, and perhaps the flowers were still not as good as tendril cultivars.

Later, amateur hybridisers such as Harvey Albutt, Joseph Dickson Place and his son Richard Place (b. 1953), produced non-tendril cultivars with exhibition-quality blooms. In 1999, E.W. King & Co. introduced the Heavenly Series, which have zodiac-sign names, but initially they did not find favour. Only now are cut-flower growers becoming aware that there is a significant saving of time not having to remove the tendrils from cordon-grown plants. There are now winter-flowering, multiflora, non-tendril cultivars, particularly Musica Series from Kaoru Nakamura of Miyazaki prefecture, Japan, which are favoured by cut-flower growers.

In 1957, Jim Tandy, working for E.W. King & Co., crossed George Burt's tall, non-tendril cultivars with the tall Spencer 'Geranium Pink' in order to increase their flower size to contemporary standards. By 1962 he was able to cross the resulting progeny with William Zvolanek's dwarf multiflora Pygmy Series to produce dwarf, non-tendril, multiflora types named Snoopea Series. Supersnoop Series and

NEW NON-TENDRIL WAVED SWEET PEAS
1945

E. W. KING & CO. LTD., ("The Sweet Pea King")
COGGESHALL, ESSEX.

Explorer Series are later evolutions of this material, raised in California. All can usually only be bought as mixtures.

MODERN GRANDIFLORA SWEET PEAS

Such has been the interest in old-fashioned sweet peas during recent decades that people have wanted more of them. A few recently introduced cultivars, such as 'Bramdean' and 'Dave R', have genuine old-fashioned characteristics. These have all the vigour, flower size, flower number and raceme length of the old-fashioned type.

Others have small plain flowers but have one or more characteristics that betray Spencer ancestry. These characteristics are: four or more flowers produced regularly, larger flowers, longer racemes, and taller and more vigorous growth. Sweet peas with these characters are known as Modern Grandifloras. Some have been raised while others are reverted Spencer cultivars. As mentioned above, a few were marketed by Peter Grayson of Chesterfield, Derbyshire, as being 're-creations' of old cultivars and given the original cultivar names, so there is now confusion over whether some old cultivars are genuine or not. This practice was quickly stopped, so that most of Grayson's introductions are clearly Modern Grandifloras. Unwins Seeds have also been very active in introducing new cultivars of this type. Some, such as 'Romeo' from Unwins, 'High Scent' from Hammett, and 'Matucana' from Harland, are among the most fragrant of all sweet peas. This, and their prolific flowering, means they are likely to become even more popular for garden use.

SNAPDRAGON SWEET PEAS

This type is mentioned simply as a botanical curiosity. In 1897, the Sunset Seed and Plant Co. of California introduced 'Red Riding Hood'. It was the first of a type known as Snapdragon because of their alleged similarity to an *Antirrhinum*. The standard petal is undeveloped and folds down to form a hood over the wings. Further introductions followed over the following five years, but the type was never popular and died out within 10 years.

Similar mutations have since arisen on at least two other occasions. In 2003 Peter Grayson introduced 'Lady's Bonnet' which has superficially similar form. It has also arisen on winter-flowering material in Japan. It originated there in the cream-flowered 'Stella' and a series of crosses have been made to widen the range of colours. They remain restricted to a few cut-flower growers in Japan who do not wish competitors to have access to this material. Most enthusiasts consider this form to be unattractive.

AMATEURS TURN PROFESSIONAL

Some amateur raisers have converted to become professional sweet pea specialists. Many have also exhibited at Chelsea and other RHS flower shows. Those who have become professional include Bill Maishman (1913–1995) of Reigate, Surrey, until 1983, then of Stowmarket, Suffolk. He introduced three cultivars for Kershaw from 1972 to 1980, and others for Hammett. Maishman's business was taken over by Diane Sewell (b. 1945) of Over, Cambridge, and she retired in 2005. Norman Peter Thomas Brackley (1926–2016) of Aylesbury, Buckinghamshire, was active between 1974 and 2001.

Eagle Sweet Peas of Stafford was formed by Derek Heathcote (b. 1947) in around 1994 and continues in partnership with his son, Andrew. Eagle Sweet Peas introduced many cultivars raised by Harvey Albutt as well as their own and other raisers' novelties.

Sydney Harrod (b. 1933) of Londonderry, Northern Ireland, had been raising new cultivars since the 1960s but started trading as Cooltonagh Irish Sweet Peas in 2005. He has won many awards for these and in recent years has been working with Chris McAleer and Thomas Butterly, both of Co. Dublin. His seeds are now sold through Roger Parsons Sweet Peas of Chichester, West Sussex.

Roger Parsons (b. 1953) is co-author of this book and currently Chairman of the National Sweet Pea Society. He started a seedbank in 1998 to conserve *Lathyrus* species and cultivars and is a UK National Plant Collection holder for *Lathyrus*. In 2012 he received the NSPS Henry Eckford Gold Memorial Medal.

Sydney Harrod started raising new cultivars in the 1960s and subsequently traded as Cooltonagh Irish Sweet Peas.

Phil Kerton (b. 1947) of Bridgwater, Somerset, formed Kerton Sweet Peas with his wife Joyce in 1990. They introduced many cultivars raised by amateur exhibitors as well as over 30 of their own raisings. Kerton Sweet Peas is still very active.

Pip Tremewan (1919–1994) of St Austell, Cornwall, was another West Country raiser turned seed seller. Tremewan raised at least 14 cultivars introduced between 1984 and 1999. These were initially introduced by Marchant but later he retailed directly to the public. On his death, his F2 material was passed to Mike Carr who raised a further three cultivars introduced by Parsons.

David Matthewman (b. 1948) of Pontefract, West Yorkshire, started trading in 1993. Matthewman Sweet Peas are now sold from Solihull, West Midlands.

BRITISH SWEET PEA BREEDERS

Several well-known businesses specialising in breeding sweet peas developed in the UK. Sweet peas were the mainstay for William James Unwin (1872–1947) who founded his general seed business in 1903. He was a general cut-flower grower at Histon, Cambridgeshire, who was a friend of pioneer geneticist Sir Rowland Biffen and had access to the findings of early geneticists. His son Charles Unwin (1895–1986) produced very many cultivars and Unwins Seeds remained as raisers of new cultivars until the family sold the Unwins Seeds business in 2005. In 2001 to 2002 they had bought out Robert Bolton and Sons of Birdbrook, Halstead, Essex.

E. W. King & Co. of Coggeshall, Essex, was formed by Ernest William King

(1869–1930) in 1888, initially retailing seeds but later he bought land and started to produce his own seeds, mostly vegetables, for which they remain well known. His father William King was an illegitimate son of John Kemp King of J.K. King & Sons. Ernest King was awarded the NSPS Henry Eckford Gold Memorial Medal in 1928. Although he introduced cultivars, it is not clear that Ernest King raised any himself in the early days. In 1912, George H. Burt (1886–1959) moved to E.W. King & Co. and was an active raiser of new cultivars. Burt was succeeded by Thomas Campbell Baines (1920–1985). In 1955, Jim Tandy (1914–1989) replaced Baines. Jim Tandy is perhaps best remembered for developing the Snoopea Series (Jones 1986, 1990). The company still trades from Coggeshall, Essex, as Kings Seeds.

Dobbie & Co. was founded by James Dobbie (1817–1905) in 1865. The company was active in sweet peas from early days and between 1900 and 1967 they introduced over 160 cultivars, including 'Mrs Collier' in 1907. They were based at Rothesay from 1900 to 1908 but then moved to Edinburgh. Their seed ground at this time was at Marks Tey, Essex. William Cuthbertson (1859–1934) bought Dobbie & Co. from James Dobbie (1817–1905) in 1887. They employed Donald Allan (d. c.1956) from 1919 to 1953. In 1969, Dobbies was acquired by Waterers and continues as Dobbies Garden Centres. It should not be confused with Samuel Dobie & Sons Ltd of Chester. The latter was founded in 1881 and introduced 'Edd Fincham' in 1994. Dobies is now part of the same group as Suttons Seeds.

Suttons Seeds of Reading, now based in Paignton, Devon, was very active in sweet peas in the early 20th century. In recent decades it continued to introduce new cultivars from amateur raisers, such as Alan Williams of Leamington Spa,

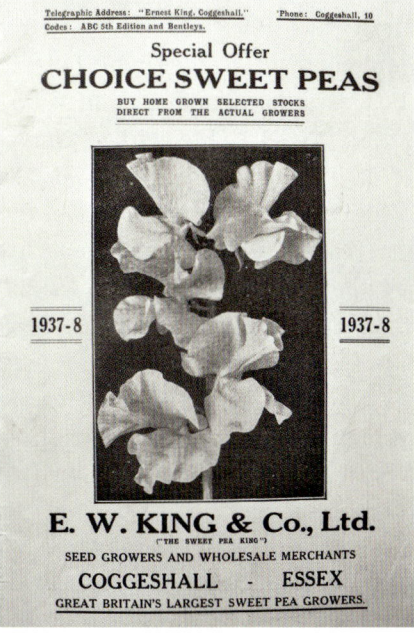

RIGHT **Unwins Seeds was a family business for more than a century.**

FAR RIGHT **E.W. King & Co. was founded in 1888.**

Warwickshire. Bill Sutton (d. 2015) of Southport, Lancashire, raiser of 'Patricia Anne', has no connection with this business.

Thompson & Morgan of Ipswich, Suffolk, were not active in sweet peas until recent years but have introduced some interesting cultivars. Until recently they employed Charles Valin (b. 1978) as their plant breeder and he actively worked on new sweet peas and interspecific hybrids. The firm was founded in 1855 by William Thompson (1833–1903), later to be joined by John Morgan (d. 1921).

Fothergills of Newmarket, Suffolk, have become more active in introducing new sweet pea cultivars in the 21st century.

AMERICAN SWEET PEA BREEDERS

The Ferry Morse Seed Co. of San Francisco was formed in 1930 as a merger of D.M. Ferry & Co. and C.C. Morse & Co. Dexter Mason Ferry (1833–1907) formed D.M. Ferry & Co. in 1879 in Detroit as a seed merchant. The firm does not appear to have introduced new sweet peas after 1907. Charles Copeland Morse (1842–1900), who was a successful businessman, not a plantsman, moved to Santa Clara, California, and founded C.C. Morse & Co. He had five children including Lester L. Morse (1871–1953) who succeeded him. Lester was a horticulturist and noted in 1884 that sweet peas were the newest vogue, adding them to the firm's list. He was succeeded by his own son, Charles Pierce Morse (1907–1970). The firm had moved to San Francisco before 1906 and was devastated by the earthquake of that year but recovered and rebuilt. Its headquarters are now at Fulton, Kentucky (Taylor 2008). In the early years Morse usually sold their new cultivars on to other seed sellers, such as Burpee Seeds and Vaughan's Seed Store of Chicago. The latter was founded in 1876 by John Charles Vaughan and was merged into Novartis which later was subsumed into Syngenta.

Frank Cuthbertson (d. 1973), stepson of William Cuthbertson (who bought Dobbie & Co. in 1887), joined C.C. Morse & Co. in 1911. His major achievements include the conservation of

Sutton's Giant Frilled Sweet Peas.

old-fashioned cultivars, and creating the spring-flowering Cuthbertson Series, Cuthbertson Floribunda Series and Dwarf Cuthbertson Cupid Series. Cuthbertson was succeeded by Harry Joy, who worked for Ferry Morse Seed Co. from 1930 until 1968, then Elmer Twedt (d. 1976) until 1972, then David Lemon.

The Buckman, Denholm & Holden Seed Co. was formed in 1939 by Harry Buckman (1879–1947), who had worked for Burpee Seeds at Lompoc since 1910, and David S. Denholm. Denholm was a Scot who worked for Dobbie & Co. in 1924, then joined C.C. Morse & Co. working at their trial grounds in Salinas, California. In 1937 Denholm had moved to Bodger Seeds. Ted Holden was their hybridiser, having previously also worked for Bodger Seeds. Denholm became sole owner of the company in 1945. In 1973 Denholm Seeds became part of the Ball Group of PanAmerican Seeds (Christensen 2006). Notable introductions include early multiflora Gigantea Series in 1960, Mammoth Series in 1982, Supersnoop Series around 1983 and Bouquet Series in 1998.

Washington Atlee Burpee (1858–1915) started his business, W. Atlee Burpee & Co., Philadelphia, USA, in 1875 and introduced his first sweet pea novelty in 1896. The business, also known as Burpee Seeds, went on to raise and introduce hundreds of cultivars. In 1909 Burpee Seeds bought land at Lompoc, California, for seed production. Following Atlee's death the business was continued by his son, David Burpee (1893–1980), responsible for introducing Ruffled Series, Galaxy Series and Bijou Series (Davis 1965). David Burpee received the NSPS Henry Eckford Gold Memorial Medal in 1964. Much of the breeding work for Burpee Seeds was done by George W. Kerr (1865–1930), a Scot who migrated to the USA in about 1908 and was president of the short-lived American Sweet Pea Society.

John Bodger (d. 1924) was an Englishman who moved to California in 1891 and set up a plant nursery, trading as John Bodger & Sons. He handed over to his sons in 1909 and, following his death, the business also bought land in Lompoc in 1924 to produce, among other things, sweet pea seeds. Walter Bodger (1876–1931) succeeded his father as president of the company in 1924. In 1930 the business became Bodger Seeds Ltd with Walter's brother John Charles (Jack) Bodger (1880–1950) in charge. Walter's son, John Francis Bodger (1905–1970), next took control in 1950 and was succeeded in 1970 by Jack's son, Howard Stanton Bodger (1921–2003). Although the world's largest producer of sweet pea seeds, they only started to breed new cultivars in 1984 when David Lemon joined them. They introduced Explorer Series and Winter Elegance Series in 1992. In 2009 the part of their business including sweet pea seed production was sold to Hem Zaden of the Netherlands (Bodger Whitman 1981).

INTERSPECIFIC HYBRIDS IN COMMERCE

Where hybridisation within *Lathyrus* has been successful, the resulting material segregates over a few generations to adopt the morphological characteristics of one or other parent. *Lathyrus rotundifolius* × *L. tuberosus* was reported by Eric Marsden-Jones (1920). He exhibited a plant from this cross at an RHS show in July 1957 where it won an award (Norton 2008). Two plants of the cross obtained by Norton, although not directly traced back to the Marsden-Jones crosses (Turrill

1962, Norton 2008), have the form of *L. rotundifolius* but with purple-pink instead of brick-red flowers (Norton 1994). Both remain in cultivation under the names *L.* 'Tubro' and *L.* 'Tillyperone'. DNA testing supports their hybrid origin (Kenicer, unpublished). Norton regarded them as different to each other, with 'Tillyperone' having slightly larger flowers of a more intense colour. However, they are both propagated by seed that has caused variation which blurs these differences.

Working at the Long Ashton Research Station in Bristol, Barker (1916) reported *Lathyrus odoratus* × *L. hirsutus* and this, together with its reciprocal cross, has been replicated several times since. Such material raised by Keith Hammett is available as *L.* 'Little Gems'. It has segregated to adopt the form of *L. hirsutus* but its flowers have paler shades than the type. Keith R.W. Hammett (b. 1942) worked for the Horticulture and Food Research Institute of New Zealand Ltd, Auckland, but is now an independent plant breeder in Auckland. He has had a lifelong passion for *Lathyrus* and remains the most innovative of plant breeders. More than anyone else he has worked to diversify the gene pool in sweet peas.

Lathyrus odoratus × *L. chloranthus* was reported by Khawaja (1988a) but the same cross was unsuccessful for Murray & Hammett (1989). They did however cross *L. chloranthus* with *L. chrysanthus*. Other crosses are reported by Davies (1957) but material from these types of experiments rarely enter horticulture.

Lathyrus odoratus 'Mrs Collier' × *L. belinensis* is an exception. This cross was achieved using embryo rescue technology (Hammett *et al.* 1994), a technique for taking the immature seed embryo and growing it on in a laboratory. The F1 generation was self-infertile but produced pollen that was backcrossed to produce

fertile seeds. The F1 hybrid has been named as *L.* × *hammettii* (Edwards 2014). It is named for Keith Hammett who would be the first to proclaim that his interspecific hybridisation was carried out as part of a larger team. The contribution of Brian G. Murray (b. 1949), among others, is of particular importance in their achievements. Brian Murray worked at the University of Auckland's School of Biological Sciences. Some cultivars developed from *L.* × *hammettii* through subsequent crossing are now in commerce and are morphologically identical to *L. odoratus*. Other material from

'Little Gems' is a hybrid between *Lathyrus odoratus* and *L. hirsutus*.

Lathyrus x *hammettii* (centre) is a cross between *L. odoratus* 'Mrs Collier' (left) and *L. belinensis* (right).

L. × *hammettii* has segregated to be morphologically identical to *L. belinensis*. The parentage of most new *L. odoratus* cultivars is undeclared by breeders and a small proportion of these may include *L.* × *hammettii*. Without the co-operation of the raiser there is usually no way to distinguish them. This lack of distinction means that *L.* × *hammettii* hybrids are usually listed in commerce as *L. odoratus*.

Hammett has carried out further work using these hybrids. *Lathyrus* 'Little Gems' has been crossed with *L.* × *hammettii* and the resulting material has the working name of HOOB Series, after the initials of the parent species: (*L. hirsutus* × *L. odoratus*) × (*L. odoratus* × *L. belinensis*).

GENETICS OF SWEET PEAS

In 1900, Mendel's long-forgotten treatise on his experiments in plant hybridization was rediscovered (Bateson 1909). This sets out the fundamental laws of heredity. Gregor Mendel (1822–1884) worked with edible garden peas but work to verify his laws was done using sweet peas. We are fortunate that early genetics researchers continued to use sweet peas, among other species, in order to more fully understand heredity. By 1939 a good knowledge of characters had been published, by, for example, Beale *et al.* (1939) and Crane & Lawrence (1947). However, in later decades researchers switched to fruit flies (*Drosophila*) and then to yeasts to give increased numbers of generations in a shorter period.

Tall-growing plants with procumbent habit form the vast majority of cultivars. They are said to have indeterminate growth because they just keep growing upwards when supported. Plants showing bush habit are said to be determinate in growth because shoots reach a certain length and then side shoots are formed. Some dwarf cultivars have procumbent habit, such as Cherub Series, while others have erect habit, such as Patio Series. Semi-dwarf cultivars are tall plants with shorter internodes expressing determinate growth

Factors that affect flower form are not always clear. With standard petals, there are degrees of waviness from very frilly through to almost plain. With keels, a varying amount of clamping may be evident in open-keel cultivars.

Old-fashioned, plain, typical and normal Grandiflora flowers have a plain standard and a clamped keel, whereas Semi-grandiflora flowers have a waved standard and a clamped keel. Spencer flowers have a waved standard and an open keel. There is instability in the Spencer form which is not fully understood, but means that over many generations the recessive characters will revert to the dominant characters. This is also associated with a reduction in petal size. Some flower colours arise from more than one gene. Modifications to how these colours are displayed also show patterns of dominance.

It is not the purpose of this book to explain Mendel's laws or other aspects such as linkage. There are, however, certain factors known to be dominant or recessive to each other that are very useful for those wishing to raise new sweet pea cultivars (Parsons 2011). These factors are listed below.

Vegetative characters

- Tall plant height is dominant to dwarf plant height.
- Procumbent habit is dominant to bush (erect) habit.
- Hairy plants are dominant to smooth (hairless) plants.
- Tendril form is dominant to non-tendril form.

Flower production and morphology

- Summer-flowering is dominant to early-flowering.
- Pauciflora racemes are dominant to multiflora racemes.
- Plain standard is dominant to waved standard.
- Clamped keel is dominant to open keel.

RIGHT **'Crimson Cherub'** belongs to a dwarf series that is procumbent, a habit that is dominant in breeding to being erect.

FAR RIGHT **Semi-dwarf** cultivars are tall plants with short internodes.

Flower colour

- Purple is dominant to maroon.
- Maroon is dominant to mauve and lavender.
- Lavender (and mauve?) is dominant to blue.
- Blue is dominant to red.
- Magenta is dominant to scarlet.
- Crimson is dominant to pink.
- Pink is dominant to orange and salmon.
- Orange and salmon are dominant to white.
- White is dominant to cream.
- Bicolour is dominant to self-colour (all one colour).
- Self-colour is dominant to flaked.
- Flaked is dominant to striped and marbled.
- Full colour (deep) is dominant to picotee.
- Pale wing colour is dominant to dark wing colour.
- Normal is dominant to dull (dull has more blueness, so that red is dominant to red tinged with blue).
- Normal is dominant to bright (bright deepens colour, and it has more redness on forms that are mauve or flaked).
- Bright is dominant to dull.

There is no data available on the modifying factors contributing to modern cultivars. It should be possible to identify these through research but for practical plant breeding the benefit would not justify the time involved. The flower colour factors are a simplification useful to breeders but in truth hide a more complex situation. Colour factors rely on differences in plant pigments based on varying levels of anthocyanins and anthoxanthins, and these are affected by differences in pH and sugar levels. However, plant breeders do not need an understanding of cytochemistry to be successful.

Polyploidy, where the number of genes exceeds the normal diploid form, has been identified in a number of naturally occurring or experimentally created *Lathyrus* taxa. Polyploidy has been observed in *Lathyrus odoratus*, *L. pratensis* and *L. venosus*. There do not seem to be any polyploid forms in general cultivation. They have so far been limited to research collections. Wild-collected specimens of *L. pratensis* from Albania grown at Royal Botanic Garden Edinburgh are suspected polyploids and are larger and more vigorous than native British specimens grown in similar conditions. This polyploid vigour is a common phenomenon across all plants.

BARRIERS TO HYBRISATION

The earliest report of a *Lathyrus* hybrid was in 1860 when Major Trevor Clarke (1813–1897) of Daventry, Northamptonshire, claimed that the origin of his sweet pea 'Blue Edged' was by crossing a white sweet pea with *Lathyrus nervosus* (Curtis & Eckford 1900). Anton Zvolanek later claimed that crosses with a *Vicia* species were in the origins of his first winter-flowering sweet peas. Neither of these are plausible claims but they enabled the raisers at the time to avoid having to reveal the real origin of their new cultivars. Similarly, a claim by George Morrison Taylor in 1916 to have crossed *L. odoratus* with *L. pratensis* (Taylor 1916) has never been replicated and no new cultivar was introduced. Taylor was a gardener in Midlothian who knew William Cuthbertson, owner of Dobbie & Co. from 1887. Many attempts to introduce yellow pigment into sweet peas have continued but remain unfulfilled (Edwards 2014).

Barriers to interspecific hybridisation have long been known and investigated. Differences between species in how the pollen tube grows down the style of a flower creates different degrees of compatibility. Successful hybridisation has sometimes involved stylar amputation, where the length of the style is reduced. This can increase the success of a pollen tube growing to the opening in the ovule of the flower ovary. Pollen tube penetration still does not necessarily result in the generation of viable embryos. In such cases, defective endosperm development appears to be the problem (Murray & Hammett 1989, Herrick *et al.* 1993)).

Intermediate populations between species are sometimes reported from the wild. These include intermediates between *Lathyrus laevigatus* and *L. occidentalis*, along with *L. binatus* × *L. pratensis* and *L. hallersteinii* × *L. pratensis* (Ball 1968). Such reports support a case that these pairs may not be distinct species. In addition, other reported crosses involve species that some botanists already consider to be a single species, such as in the following examples. *Lathyrus articulatus* × *L. clymenum* and its reciprocal have been reported several times. *Lathyrus annuus* × *L. hierosolymitanus* was reported by Hammett *et al.* (1996). *Lathyrus sylvestris* × *L. latifolius* was reported by Davies (1957) and successful reciprocal crosses were reported between these two and *L. heterophyllus* by Nandini *et al.* (1999).

Jackson & Yunus (1984) suggested the close morphological affinity of *L. sativus*, *L. cicera* and *L. gorgonei* may arise from a common ancestry or even hybridisation. *Lathyrus sativus* and *L. cicera* were crossed independently by Lwin (1956) and Burton (1956), and Davies (1958). All three worked at the University of Manchester where Stephen Cross Harland (1891–1982) was Professor of Botany from 1950 to 1958. Khawaja (1988b) reported crossing *L. amphicarpos* with both *L. sativus* and *L. cicera* while he was based at the National Agricultural Research Station, Islamabad, Pakistan.

BREEDING AND SELECTION OF OTHER SPECIES

There is every likelihood that not a single cultivar from any species, other than *L. odoratus*, has arisen through deliberate crossing of individuals within a species. All are likely to have arisen through selection of plants in cultivation or from variation in wild populations. Although selections within species have occasionally been crossed, there is no record of a named cultivar arising from this method. The one possible exception to this, which has not been verified, is that the late Peter Grayson's *L. annuus* 'Mrs R. Penney' may have arisen by crossing *L. annuus* 'Hotham Red' with typical *L. annuus* var. *annuus*. Grayson also claimed to have created *L. tingitanus* 'Harmony' by crossing *L. tingitanus* with *L. tingitanus* 'Roseus', but 'Harmony' cannot actually be distinguished from *L. tingitanus* 'Roseus'. Crossing individuals within species uses the same techniques as in sweet peas, but is considerably more difficult because of the smaller flower sizes.

Many cultivars of *Lathyrus vernus* have been selected, differing mainly in flower colour and leaflet width.

The species showing most variation is *L. vernus* (Colborn 2006). The starting point for this is the many named infraspecific taxa that were described by Bässler (1973) and others. Variation within this species occurs in flower colour (mauve, blue-mauve, mauve and lavender bicolour, pink, pink and white bicolour, very pale pink, and white). It also occurs in the width of the leaflets, where the narrowest leaflets provide a hazy background for the flowers.

A sweet pea flower in which the stigma is ready to receive pollen and the anthers can be removed before they reveal their own pollen.

PRACTICALITIES OF HYBRIDISATION

The structure of the flower means that sweet peas are naturally self-pollinating, although the following comments perhaps also apply to other *Lathyrus* species. By the time the flower opens, it has already self-pollinated. In order to make a cross between two sweet peas, the petals of the seed-bearing (pistillate) parent must be unfurled while still in bud and the anthers removed before they have developed pollen. The flower bud must be sufficiently developed for the stigma to be mature enough to receive pollen, but not so developed that pollen has started to arise. Initially, it requires trial and error to identify the optimum size of flower bud. Start with the lowest (oldest) bud on a raceme, perhaps one starting to show colour, and see if the anthers show pollen. If they do, move on to the next flower up. If this has no pollen, it is at the right stage of maturity for crossing. Before going further, loosely attach a label to the raceme naming the cultivars being crossed and a reference number if necessary.

Different raisers have slightly different methods of preparing a flower for hand pollination before pollen is introduced from the pollen-bearing (staminate) parent onto the stigma. One method is to pluck the staminate flower, remove its standard and wing petals, fold back the keel petals of the pistillate flower, and invert the keel of the plucked flower over the style of the pistillate flower so that the pollen can be tapped onto its stigma. The keel petals of the pistillate flower can then be folded back so that the flower develops naturally. Rather than folding back, or cutting a slit into the keel of the pistillate parent, some like to remove the keel altogether. This raises the risk of other pollen accidently being introduced, but this can be avoided if the flower is protected within a fine muslin bag. Making your cross on a warm, still day will increase the chances of success. If the cross has been successful, a seed pod will form and develop and can then be harvested when ripe.

The seed from this cross forms the F1 generation, which should be allowed to self-pollinate and set seed. The resulting seed will form the F2 generation that, when it flowers, will segregate according to the genetic composition of the parents. One of the joys of breeding sweet peas is that when crossing a tall with a dwarf cultivar, or a summer-flowering with a winter-flowering cultivar, the F2 offspring really will segregate along classic Mendelian lines and 25% of the F2 generation will be double recessive. Considerable care should be taken in choosing which cultivars to cross because other characters, such as raceme length or seeding quality, will also be inherited. On very rare occasions a desirable plant may be self-infertile, in which case it will either be lost, or there may be pollen that can be back-crossed or transferred to another cultivar.

Cultivation

The huge diversity of *Lathyrus* species and the robust, competitive growth habits that many of them show is generally excellent news for gardeners in temperate climates. As with all genera, having a good understanding of how the species grow in the wild makes it much easier to understand their needs and ensure success in cultivation. Information about the native habitats of all species can be found in the Species chapter. By far the most widely grown species is *Lathyrus odoratus*, sweet pea, so the majority of this chapter concerns that. However, the other widely grown species are covered in the early parts of this chapter.

SOILS

Most of the species are usually happy in a wide range of soils. As a legume, the roots of *Lathyrus* contain root nodules of *Rhizobium* bacteria that fix nitrogen, so application of nitrogen fertiliser is not needed on most soils. *Lathyrus* have long been known to have mycorrhizal fungi associated with them, and this includes sweet peas (Jones 1924).

As with most plants, the perennial species perform better in heavier soils than the annuals do. Generally speaking, *Lathyrus* species prefer an open-structured soil, although there is still much work to be done on understanding the detail of soil preferences. Some of the alpine species from Europe, such as *L. laevigatus*, do well on neutral or alkaline soils, while *L. linifolius*, from acid grasslands of northern Europe, is tolerant of soils with a very low pH.

Lathyrus magellanicus is a highly variable species with a broad distribution in South America, tolerating anything from relatively rich woodland

LEFT **Sweet peas can be attractively integrated into herbaceous borders, as here at Raveningham Hall in Norfolk.**

RIGHT **In the wild *Lathyrus linifolius* thrives in acid soils.**

A medium loam that has been lightly cultivated is ideal for sweet peas.

soils to bare volcanic ash of the central Chilean volcanoes. The South American perennial species seem to behave in an interesting way in cultivation. When grown in pots in conventional, non-loam-based media, they will grow reasonably happily. However, when transferred to grow directly in the ground in rich, northern-temperate garden soils, the plants often go through a wonderfully showy mass-flowering, expend much of their vigour in one year but then deteriorate markedly in subsequent years. This is still anecdotal, and quite what is going on here still needs further investigation. It seems their adaptation to the relatively low-phosphate soils of their native habitats may have something to do with it. Interestingly, we see less obvious, and less frequent, nodulation on the roots of the South American species in their native habitat. The partnership between bacteria and plant undoubtedly changed in the species that evolved away from the northern hemisphere.

For sweet peas, a good medium loam that has received light cultivation is best. They will also benefit from a little well-rotted manure or garden compost, but avoid making the soil too rich. Unbroken clay soil needs to be more deeply cultivated with the addition of humus. Light soils, such as on chalk or sand, will need more humus and nutrients. Some growers like to incorporate slow-release fertiliser at planting out, which is beneficial. Light soils may also benefit from incorporating moisture-retaining granules. Addition of kieserite to chalk soils, prior to planting out, helps reduce the effects of high calcium levels. Other specific nutrient requirements will vary with the soil, but sweet peas will also benefit from additional potassium as sulphate of potash.

PLANTING POSITION

Choice of position in the garden depends on the species and its natural requirements. Some species are woodland-edge plants. For example, *L, vernus* flowers in spring when full light is available but is then happiest if located where it gets light shade during the hotter days of summer. Some species, such as *L. latifolius*, will cope with a little shade but are at their best in full sun.

Shorter annual and perennial species are suited to meadow planting, this being their natural habitat. These tend to have a more lax habit than the self-supporting species and rely on companion plants in the meadow mixture for support. Species such as *L. pratensis* are excellent inclusions in perennial plantings, and *L. annuus*, *L. clymenum* and *L. hirsutus* are good for annual plantings.

Many perennial species are self-supporting, so make excellent specimen plants or groups in a mixed border. They retain attractive foliage and, generally, the later they flower the taller they grow. These self-supporting species fall into two groups. The first has cream flowers that turn brownish orange, and includes *L. aureus*, *L. davidii*, *L. laevigatus*, *L. occidentalis* and *L. transsylvanicus*. The former is the first to flower out of the group, in late spring. It has been popular since Victorian times because of its early flowers, yellowish foliage and ease of cultivation. The second group has mauve-blue or purple flowers. *Lathyrus vernus* is the earliest of these to flower, in spring, and there is a range of cultivars with different flower colours, including the lovely pink and white 'Alboroseus'. The cultivars with finer leaflets are also particularly attractive. If the dead flowerheads are removed, a smaller, second flush of flowers can occur in summer and, on rare occasions, it may flower again in autumn. Also flowering relatively early, but not belonging to the above groups, *L. venetus* flowers about a month later than *L. vernus*, in late spring, around the same time as *L. aureus* and at a similar height, and *L. niger* flowers in early summer and is taller.

Lathyrus japonicus was once widely cultivated, often under the synonym *L. maritimus*, when rock gardens were more fashionable. Its natural habitat of maritime shingle made it suitable for such well-drained situations but its sprawling habit mean it is best suited to larger rock gardens. More suited to smaller rock gardens is *L. linifolius*, often found in old books and catalogues as *L. montanus*. *Lathyrus palustris*, *L. paranensis*, *L. macrostachys* and *L. nigrivalvis* are plants for wet ground, although their

One of the earliest species to flower is *Lathyrus vernus* which thrives in an open position or under deciduous trees or shrubs.

crowns do not like being waterlogged. These four can be very challenging to grow in the UK, but are satisfying pond marginals in warmer areas when placed among other vegetation to support them. If grown in a pot, they should be stood in a saucer of water during summer. *Lathyrus mulkak* has never been easy to cultivate in the West but Fedchenko (1948) reported that this handsome perennial was a garden favourite in Russia.

North American species have proved difficult to cultivate, even in North America, and are rarely seen in gardens. All require good drainage. Two rhizomatous species that are sometimes encountered are *L. polyphyllus* from the Pacific Northwest, which is similar to *L. japonicus*, and *L. vestitus* from the West Coast. *Lathyrus splendens*, known as pride of California, has been frequently introduced to gardens but fails to survive. It is hardly known, even in California. Out of 1,200 plants set out at Rancho Santa Ana Botanic Garden in California between 1927 and 1950, only about 12 survived to the end of the period. One plant lived for 10 years. Excessive water was the main cause of their demise. Easily started from seed, summer drought and very free-draining soil such as gravel appear to be essential to maintain this perennial from one season to another. A note in *Gardeners' Chronicle* said 'it is one of those plants which seem to be benefited by the ordeal of fire, which renders the vine more prolific, and adds brilliancy to the blossoms' (W.W. 1894).

The taller-growing perennial species usually need some form of support. They can be grown against a wall, but can also be allowed to scramble over fences, hedges or other plants in less formal situations. The most successful are *L. latifolius*, *L. rotundifolius* and *L. sylvestris*.

Sweet peas (*L. odoratus*) are commonly thought to require full sun but actually do not like temperatures above 30°C. In areas with hot summer days they are best in a site that gets full sun in the morning and evening but with shade from a tree or building during the hottest part of the day. However, if grown with a plentiful supply of water, such as in a hydroponic situation, they will cope well with temperatures above 30°C.

PLANT SUPPORTS

Where supports are needed, such as for sweet peas, then old-fashioned pea sticks are particularly attractive. These consist of small, twiggy branches cut from trees such as birch or hazel. More substantial, longer branches can also be woven to form arches and tunnels. Plants can also be trained into all sorts of striking situations by training the stems along swags of rope, or even over a suitable *Clematis* (Hull 1994). A wigwam of bamboo canes is often a popular choice for sweet peas, but has the disadvantage of plants trying to crowd into too small a space once they reach the top. Instead, a circle of vertical canes linked by large-diameter mesh, pig netting or string provides a support column with as much space at the top as at the bottom. Lines of plants can also be grown against a wall or trellis, or netting can be strung between wooden posts.

Branches woven together into arches or tunnels make a sturdy support for sweet peas.

Sweet peas and taller annual species such as *L. chloranthus* and *L. tingitanus* can be allowed to develop naturally by leaving all side shoots and tendrils in place. This can provide greater decorative effect, utilising the full height of the plants, and sweet peas grown this way will still provide stems long enough for cutting. Both the above species have attractive foliage too, downy in *L. chloranthus* and greyish and purple-tinged in *L. tingitanus*. The annuals can also be allowed to self-seed without becoming a nuisance.

It is worth getting to know some of the other species and explore their decorative uses. *Lathyrus neurolobus*, for example, is an adaptable perennial and reveals remarkably different habits depending on garden location. It will grow as a tight clump in a gravel path, a short trailing plant in good garden soil, or a taller sparse climber among pond-margin plants. It also has the benefit of self-seeding readily.

FAR LEFT **Cordons should be set out in two rows that are 30–50cm apart.**

LEFT **In this cordon the stems that have reached the top of each cane have been laid down and tied up four canes away.**

THE CORDON METHOD

Sweet peas grown for cut flowers and exhibition have long been grown using the cordon method. Sweet peas were first grown as cordons from around 1906 by 'Old' Tom Jones (d. 1940) of Ruabon in North Wales. The method involves growing a single stem from each plant, letting it grow to the top of a cane while harvesting the flowers, then lowering the stem to the ground and training the tip up another cane to carry on producing more flowers. Start by setting out two rows of 2.4m canes with the canes in each row 20cm apart. The two rows can be as long as you need but should be 30–50cm apart. Plant a sweet pea at the base of each cane and select a single stem to train up, ensuring all the plant's energy is put into the growth of this one shoot. Tie it on with string, rings or tape and remove side shoots as they develop. It will grow to the top quickly and flower readily. However, deadheading is essential in order to prevent plants setting seed and to prolong the flowering season.

When it reaches the top, untie the stem (sometimes called a haulm) from its cane and lay it along the row on the ground so the tip can be tied into a new cane further along. The stem will continue to grow upwards, producing flowers at a manageable height. The lowering can sometimes be done more than once in a season. The double row means that plants near the end can have their horizontal stems turned round to continue in the opposite direction. Tendrils are usually removed in cordon cultivation to aid the production of straight flower stems. They are not required to support the plant but they may twist around the flower stems, thereby causing them to bend. Alternatively, non-tendril cultivars can be grown.

A double-cordon system is sometimes used in very favourable growing conditions, where two stems are grown from each plant. In the past, growers used

RIGHT **'Old' Tom Jones, the inventor of the cordon system, tending to tall canes.**

RIGHT BOTTOM **The black winter structure of *Lathyrus niger* can be used to striking effect.**

very tall canes and tended their plants from high step-ladders, but this is less common now. In a protected environment, such as a glasshouse, where there is no wind, strings can be used instead of canes.

Lathyrus latifolius can also be grown for cut-flower production, but are so bushy that cordon culture is not necessary to produce saleable blooms. In 2016, one of the authors (Roger Parsons) saw a trial crop of cordon-grown *L. nervosus* in Japan.

PROLONGING FLOWERING AND SAVING SEED

All species benefit from the removal of flower stems once the flowers fade, in order to prolong the flowering period. This needs to be done quite diligently with annual species, as it prevents them from running to seed and ending of the plant's life cycle. There is a fallacy that sweet pea blooms need to be cut as soon as the flowers open in order to prolong flowering. However, this then deprives the plants of any decorative value in the garden. So, leave the flowers on the plants if you wish, but remove the fading blooms before they even start to form seed pods. Some gardeners like to let sweet pea plants run to seed at the end of the season with the specific aim of producing the next season's seed. Such seed often fails to store well if harvested late, so it is better to grow a few plants in a quiet corner that are allowed to form seeds early.

Lathyrus niger is commonly known as black pea because all parts of the plant turn black in autumn, with the seed pods turning first. This gives a striking and statuesque presence, especially in snow, if plants are left to stand for the winter.

Seed provides a ready means of propagating *Lathyrus*, but ripe pods spring open when ripe to disperse their seeds. Gardeners wishing to harvest seeds should put seed pods into a paper bag just before they are fully ripe. The bag should be left somewhere

warm and dry to finish ripening and for the pods to open. Seeds of all species are best stored in the bottom of a fridge where they should remain viable for two or three years. Longer term storage can be achieved by putting seeds in an airtight container in a domestic freezer where they remain viable for at least 40 years.

CONTAINER CULTIVATION

All *Lathyrus* can be grown in containers, although for many an unrestricted root run in open ground is preferred. Those that are particularly suited to cultivation in containers include species that require better drainage or a specific growing medium, and those shorter species that form more compact plants. The roots of plants in containers tend to be warmer than those in the open ground and this is particularly beneficial for dwarf and semi-dwarf sweet peas.

There are a few basic rules to consider in choosing a container for your plants. Firstly, sweet peas require a minimum of 5 litres of growing medium per plant. For a longer display, the larger the container the better. So three or four plants in a 20-litre tub should make a suitable display. Secondly, the growing medium needs to be coarse and aerated, with good moisture retention. Incorporation of moisture-retaining granules may be helpful. Thirdly, the plants will need feeding more than in the open ground. A slow-release fertiliser could be incorporated into the growing medium, or alternatively feed weekly with a high-potassium fertiliser, such as tomato feed. The choice of container is not significant. Baskets, troughs and pots might all be appropriate but in general having a greater depth than width is useful. The deep pots in which container roses and clematis are sold in the UK are very good for individual plants.

It is generally best to start plants off as described under the Propagation section below, but direct sowing into the final container is another option. Sow more seeds than the final number of plants required. Reduce this number as the plants develop to the appropriate density for the container.

PROPAGATION

Propagation is normally by seed or division, though propagation using softwood cuttings is also possible. Division is useful for those perennial species that spread by stolons. In fact,

Sweet peas can be grown in containers, but they need at least 5 litres of potting compost and regular watering and feeding.

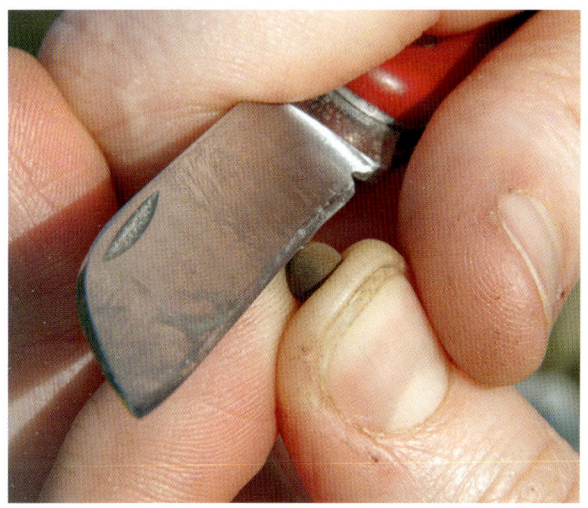 

ABOVE **Chipping involves removing a small area of seed coat to allow water uptake.**

ABOVE RIGHT **Chitting encourages germination before sowing, by leaving seeds on damp tissue in a warm environment.**

L. grandiflorus rarely sets seed so is most commonly propagated by division or cuttings. As with many other herbaceous plants, division of the crown simply means breaking off a part of the plant with the capacity for root and shoot regeneration. This is best done in spring when new vegetative growth is starting to emerge.

All *Lathyrus* species, including annuals, seem to root readily as softwood cuttings. These may be taken from side shoots of an established perennial or from the young growth of an annual plant. Some sweet pea growers use the growing tip as a cutting, obtained when pinching out primary growth to encourage side-shoot development.

Preparing seed

Seed is the most popular propagation method, even for perennial species. Seeds vary enormously in size, colour and shape. There can be wide variation in seed colour within a single species, although any one cultivar should have consistently uniform seed. Seed normally germinates in two or three weeks at ambient temperatures. Some perennials can be slower and more erratic, which may be due to an unnaturally hard seed coat arising during seed production. Also, some may benefit from vernalisation, such as *L. davidii*, and some from 'baking', such as *L. laxiflorus*. Vernalisation consists of giving the seeds a short period of sub-zero temperatures in a freezer, or in colder climates sowing them in autumn in a cold frame so they experience freezing temperatures. Baking is achieved by sowing the seeds normally, watering them, and then allowing them to fully dry out before further watering.

Pre-sowing treatments are popular with many sweet pea growers. These include chipping, chitting, soaking in water or soaking in acid. Chipping is where the seed coat is broken on the side away from the hilum (that part must be left intact) using a knife or razor blade or gently rubbing with sandpaper. Where seed has been produced in a temperate climate, it should germinate naturally so chipping is not necessary, but it does no harm.

A chemical method of chipping that remains popular in Japan is to soak the seeds for about 5 seconds in concentrated sulphuric acid. The seed is then thoroughly rinsed prior to sowing. Another technique popular with Japanese cut-flower growers is to chit the seeds and then refrigerate them for up to 4 weeks prior to planting. This induces earlier flowering but several attempts by different UK growers have been unable to replicate this.

Chitting is where seed is placed on damp tissue or vermiculite in a warm environment for up to a few days, so that germination begins before the seed is sown. Any seeds that have not swollen can then be chipped to encourage germination. Soaking in water for a few hours, overnight or up to 24 hours, is frequently practised, but trials have always shown subsequent germination to be either worse or no better.

Sowing seed

Good drainage is essential to the germination of all *Lathyrus*, even species requiring a moist soil such as *L. palustris*. Fine grit as a pure growing medium suits species naturally found on shingle, such as *L. littoralis*. Seeds can be sown in shallow trays or pots and then pricked out once germinated. However, as most *Lathyrus* seeds are quite large, the pricking out stage can be avoided if seeds are sown straight into deeper containers suitable for growing on. Rootrainers, a cellular system of deep modules, are popular in the UK with sweet-pea growers and work well.

Seeds should be sown onto the surface of an open growing medium, best created using multipurpose compost to which perlite, vermiculite or fine grit has been added. They should then be thinly covered with the medium. Very fine seeds, such as those of *L. angulatus* and *L. neurolobus*, are best left uncovered. These small-seeded species give a better display if a few seeds

BELOW LEFT **Pricking out can be avoided if sweet peas are sown into deep containers such as newspaper tubes.**

BELOW **Rootrainers are an alternative to homemade containers.**

Autumn-sown sweet peas ready for sale in early spring.

are sown together, forming a small clump of plants, as traditionally done with bedding lobelia. The seeds should then be watered from above, which settles the growing medium and initiates germination. Keep them at a temperature of 10–15°C. Perennials are best sown in spring so that they have time to produce large enough plants to survive their first winter. Most annual species do well from a spring sowing, but *L. chloranthus* and *L. paranensis* need an autumn sowing to provide a long growing period prior to flowering. Most annual species can be sown successively to provide an extended period of flowering.

Sweet peas are popularly sown in October in the southern half of the UK, where it is mild enough for them to germinate outdoors or in a cold frame or cold glasshouse. This means they grow slowly and by mid January they are about 75mm tall. In northern England and Scotland, sowing of sweet peas should be delayed until January or February because the winter light levels are too poor, unless supplementary lighting is provided. At the same time a little warmth should be provided at night, to ensure the seeds are not held for too long in cold, damp conditions. Some growers like to use a heated bench, but avoid using a propagator as its enclosed, warm, moist conditions, can encourage seeds to rot. Later sowing is possible, even desirable, if late summer and autumn flowers are wanted, but the longest stems for cutting arise from seeds sown in February or earlier.

Sweet peas happily tolerate frost down to -10°C but need shelter from strong winds. In colder climates sowing should be done indoors six weeks before the last

hard frost is expected. For commercial cut-flower production, in heated glasshouses or polytunnels, sowing of winter-flowering cultivars is done from midsummer onwards. In parts of the USA and Japan this enables flowers to be produced from mid November onwards. Similar results are achieved in Australia, New Zealand and South Africa using the corresponding season.

Growing on

Seeds should not be watered after their initial soaking, in order to reduce the risk of fungal infection. Once germinated, watering can be gradually introduced. Some growers may wish to use a fungicidal treatment. Lack of success from an early sowing is usually because the plants are not grown cold enough or they are eaten by mice.

You can pinch out the tops of sweet peas and other *Lathyrus* to encourage more bushy plants with side shoots. Autumn-sown sweet peas should not be pinched out. This is because in a mild winter side-shoot development will be premature, and will mean plants are ready to go outdoors too early. If growth has got long and straggly it can be cut back at the end of January, and then side shoots will develop at the right time.

Plants will be ready to go into their flowering position in March, so they get several months of vegetative growth to build up strength prior to flowering. Late-winter-sown sweet peas will be ready to plant out in April. There should be no concern about late frosts if plants have been grown slow and cold prior to planting out. However, some temporary shelter may be beneficial if growing in a location exposed to northern and easterly gales. Even if roots have been disturbed during planting, plants should establish and start new growth after a week or so.

PLANT ASSOCIATIONS

Many prefer to grow sweet peas on their own, such as up canes, pea sticks, woven twigs, netting, trellises or fences. However, taller sweet peas enjoy scrambling through shrubs and other robust plants. Shrubs should have an open habit, such as *Hibiscus syriacus* or *Fatsia japonica*, or a framework such as that provided by *Lophomyrtus obcordata*. The sweet peas will need their own space away from the shrub's roots to establish, before they are encouraged to grow through the crown of the shrub. *Lathyrus* also look well against finer leaves or smaller flowers so that the *Lathyrus* flowers are not dominated by larger companions.

LEFT **Plant out young sweet peas in March or April.**

OPPOSITE
TOP LEFT **Even small-flowered sweet peas such as 'Cupani' will look good growing through open shrubs such as *Acer negundo* 'Flamingo'.**

TOP RIGHT **In an informal arrangement, sweet peas have been allowed to scramble up a pergola and over nearby herbaceous perennials.**

BOTTOM LEFT **Low-growing sweet peas such as Cupid Series complement colourful bedding plants such as coleus.**

BOTTOM RIGHT **Perennial species of *Lathyrus* such as *L. rotundifolius* are often best supported by shrubs – here *Cotinus coggygria* 'Royal Purple' provides an attractive colour combination too.**

The foliage of some *Lathyrus*, and particularly sweet peas, is not particularly decorative. Shorter annual *Lathyrus* species, including shorter sweet peas, can be associated with airy plants and flowers that help mask the foliage. Suitable subjects include *Lobelia*, *Gypsophila*, *Asarina*, *Nemophila* and *Geranium* (Hull 1994). Smaller flowers such as *Alchemilla mollis*, *Ammi majus* and other umbels, *Thalictrum* species and *Verbena bonariensis* are also valuable for associating with sweet peas cut for the house in a vase, in addition to being useful associate plants in the garden.

Spring-flowering *L. vernus* is a fine plant for borders where it can add variety to a succession of spring bulbs. This might involve starting with *Eranthis hyemalis*, *Galanthus* and dwarf *Iris*, followed by *Tulipa* species and *Lathyrus vernus* itself. It generally flowers around the same time as Dutch *Crocus* and some miniature daffodils such as *Narcissus* 'Baby Moon'. The succession could be completed by later daffodils such as *N. poeticus* hybrids. *Lathyrus laxiflorus* can form an attractive undercarpet for Dutch tulips.

Cultivars of *Lathyrus vernus* such as 'Alboroseus' associate well with other early-flowering woodland plants such as *Brunnera macrophylla* 'Jack Frost' and *Myosotis*.

PESTS AND DISEASES

The perennial species of *Lathyrus* are remarkably resilient to pests and diseases, the main concern being powdery mildew in hot, dry seasons. In the annual species, intensively grown sweet peas are the most susceptible to problems. What follows are the most commonly encountered pests and diseases, but most growers will probably never experience the majority of disorders discussed here.

Aphids and viruses

These sap-sucking insects can carry viral diseases so should not be tolerated on sweet peas. By the time you see aphids, your plants may already be infected. There are many viruses that can affect sweet peas, and symptoms include mottled foliage, a distorted growing point, or breakdown of colour in the petals.

Aphids can be controlled by squashing the colonies with your fingers. There are also organic and non-organic chemicals available for use on ornamental plants.

Pollen beetles

Pollen beetles (*Meligethes* species) are tiny black or dark-coloured insects that reside within the keel petals of pea flowers, making them difficult to control.

They are attracted by the pollen, which they eat, and can reduce seed yield if plants are being grown for seed. They are more abundant in areas where oil seed rape is grown, where they develop in the flower buds. They can be a problem for gardeners who cut blooms for the house, because the insects leave the flowers and head for the windows. Reduce their impact by placing cut blooms in a dark corner of an outbuilding, opposite a window or open door. After a few hours most of the pollen beetles will be attracted away from the flowers towards the light source.

Pea weevil

Feeding damage from pea weevil (*Sitona lineatus*) or other weevils can be seen as scalloped edges on the leaflets of young plants. This does reduce the leaf area for photosynthesis. However, plants usually outgrow the damage quite quickly, so control is not normally required.

Pea moth

Growers who save their own seed may occasionally encounter the larvae of pea moth (*Cydia nigricana*) which appear as creamy white grubs in the pods feasting on the seeds. The adult moths are active in mid-summer when they lay eggs on the flowers, and the emerging larvae find their way into developing seeds. This pest is more of a problem on later flowering species such as L. *latifolius*, but as it just affects the seeds then there is little need to control it. For commercial seed production, spraying insecticide against the adult moths is effective, but most sweet pea seed producers prefer to rely on early cropping.

RIGHT TOP **Virus** symptoms on sweet pea are revealed as yellow mottling.

FAR RIGHT TOP **Pea** weevil typically eats the edges of sweet pea leaflets.

RIGHT BOTTOM **Aphids** are easy to spot, but they also transmit viruses.

FAR RIGHT BOTTOM **Pea** moth larvae, seen here on *Lathyrus tingitanus*, eat the seeds and leave deposits of frass.

Molluscs

As with many garden plants, slugs and snails can damage young or newly emerging leaves and stems, so need to be guarded against. Damage is usually seen as pale leaf blotches, with or without holes, and most often weakens rather than destroys young plants.

Birds

In some areas woodpigeons will attack young plants, eating the tender young shoots and killing the plants. Protect plants using chicken wire until they are large enough, usually about six weeks after planting out.

A different problem faced by growers in some areas is when open flowers are attacked by small birds such as tits. It is not clear what initiates this behaviour, but it may be that they are eating pollen beetles. Some growers have had to resort to growing sweet peas in fruit cages to avoid such damage.

Mice and other mammals

Mice love to eat sweet pea seeds. Even when plants have germinated and are growing on, mice may destroy them by eating the residue of the seed. It is more of a problem with autumn- and winter-sown seed when there is little other food around. One solution is to present mice with an overhang. If the seeds are growing on a board which overhangs its support, any mice climbing the support cannot reach the seeds. Alternatively, carefully placed wire mesh will help.

If rabbits and deer are a problem, then suitable fencing will be required. Of course, the threat from these will apply to many garden plants, not just *Lathyrus*.

Powdery mildew

The most significant fungal disease, which can disfigure a wide range of *Lathyrus*, is powdery mildew (*Erysiphe pisi*). It forms a white, dusty coating on the foliage of sweet peas and *L. nervosus*, and is most prevalent during hot, dry conditions.

The incidence can be reduced by planting in areas where there is good air movement and space between plants, and avoiding intermittent drought stress. There are fungicides available to control powdery mildew on ornamental plants.

Root and foot rots

Root and foot rots can develop in sweet peas, especially in wet years on heavy soils. Above-ground symptoms are stunting and yellowing of leaves, and below ground the roots will be rotted, often with black lesions at the base of the stem. These rots are mostly caused by *Fusarium solani, Pythium ultimum, Rhizoctonia solani* and *Thielaviopsis basicola*. Growing sweet peas in well-drained soil and avoiding deep planting and overcrowding will minimise the risk. Also, try to use crop rotation, as with peas in a vegetable garden

Other problems

Some leaf-spot fungi such as *Ramularia deusta* affect *Lathyrus* and can be disfiguring. These can sometimes be avoided by using crop rotation, and controlled by removing and destroying affected leaves. There are fungicides available to

gardeners to control fungal leaf spots on ornamentals.

Symptoms that look like infections can arise from physiological conditions. These include an imbalance of nutrients in the soil or a nutrient deficiency, and are generally only encountered on chalk or very sandy soils.

When immature flower buds on the raceme fall off, this is known as bud drop and is a response by plants to changes in temperature. It is associated with high day and low night temperatures, which may occur early in the flowering season during periods of high pressure, or when warm weather is followed by colder conditions. It ceases to be a problem once the season warms up or plants adapt to the new, colder conditions. A few sweet peas have a reputation for resisting bud drop, notably 'Marion', while many are thought to be more prone.

NATIONAL PLANT COLLECTIONS

In the UK, National Plant Collections (NPCs) are administered by Plant Heritage, a cultivated plant conservation charity. The first NPC of *Lathyrus* was held by Sylvia Norton (c.1926–2015) in Cambridgeshire, from 1991 to 2015. At its peak she held 82 species (Norton 1996, 2008), sourced from individuals such as Steve Broich in the US, Keith Hammett in New Zealand, Tomoaki Inoue in Japan, and Greg Kenicer and Roger Parsons in the UK. There are two current NPCs, one held by Roger Parsons at his nursery in West Sussex, and one held at Royal Botanic Garden Edinburgh (RBGE) curated by Greg Kenicer.

Roger Parsons has held his NPC since 1993. The emphasis of the collection is on annual species and on good garden selections. It includes more than 1,300 sweet pea cultivars that are used as a resource for breeding new cultivars. Conserving the original qualities of cultivars forms a key aspect of his work. By growing a small number of plants of each cultivar, Parsons tries to ensure that seed is only saved from plants having the cultivar's original qualities. This seedbank is then available to major seed producers wishing to replace the degenerated stock of a cultivar. Degeneration is a particular problem in Spencer cultivars that revert to Old-fashioned form. This is a problem for major packet-seed companies who need to produce large volumes of each cultivar they sell. In large-scale commercial seed production, deterioration of Spencer cultivars is inevitable over a period

Part of the National Plant Collection held by author Roger Parsons near Chichester in Sussex.

of time. Degeneration also happens with Multifloras reverting to pauciflora form, early-flowering cultivars losing their earliness if not reselected regularly, and semi-dwarf cultivars becoming taller over many generations.

The collection at RBGE was given NPC status in 2015. It started as a resource for Greg Kenicer's taxonomic studies of South American *Lathyrus* in the early 2000s. In 2008 it was supplemented by numerous accessions from Sylvia Norton's NPC, and more arrived after she died in 2015. The collection is curated by Greg Kenicer and now places particular emphasis on perennial species and the wild provenance of taxa. A great driver for this was collaboration with Sylvia Norton and her passion for the wild species in particular. Her collection gained NPC scientific status and a great many of her accessions were the first to have their DNA sequenced, as she gifted seed to RBGE. Indeed, we would not have the understanding of wild *Lathyrus* species we have today if it were not for Sylvia's drive to make her collection useful. Nowadays, the collection is used to investigate morphology and genetics, it supports conservation, and it helps uncover the mysteries of partnerships with nitrogen-fixing *Rhizobium* bacteria. For public display, *Lathyrus* at RBGE are grown in ecological plantings throughout the garden and are a critical teaching aid for horticulture students. A display bed is developed every year by a student team, and they attempt to make some of the smaller flowered and more obscure species as attractive to the public as they are to the collection's curator..

OTHER PLANT COLLECTIONS

Other gardens that have good collections of *Lathyrus* species include RHS Garden Wisley in Surrey and Bramdean House in Bramdean, Hampshire. Gardens that usually display a broad selection of sweet peas include Aberglasney Gardens, Carmarthenshire; Baronscourt, Co Tyrone; Beaumaris Castle, Anglesey; Chatsworth, Derbyshire; Dyffryn Gardens, Vale of Glamorgan; Easton Walled Gardens, Lincolnshire; Eden Project, Cornwall; Florence Court, Co Fermanagh; Forde Abbey, Somerset; Gresgarth Hall, Lancashire; Highgrove, Gloucestershire; Kingston Lacy, Dorset; Melbourne Hall, Derbyshire; Saumarez Park, Guernsey; and Woburn Abbey, Bedfordshire.

Sweet peas are demonstrated in many different ways at Easton Walled Gardens in Lincolnshire.

RHS AND NSPS TRIALS

In order to monitor the quality of their seed stocks, responsible seed suppliers will conduct their own trials of cultivars to ensure they remain pure and true. Such trials are not normally open to the public, so the RHS and the National Sweet Pea Society (NSPS) have long held trials and made awards where appropriate. In fact, the holding of trials is one of the charitable objectives of the NSPS.

The first sweet pea trial by the RHS was conducted in London in 1894 when 59 cultivars were grown. The next RHS trial of sweet peas was at RHS Garden Wisley in 1911 when 70 cultivars were assessed, a tiny proportion of the number in commerce at that time. From 1906 to 1916 the NSPS also carried out annual trials.

In 1911 there were two distinct NSPS trials, both held near Guildford in Surrey. NSPS trials were larger than RHS ones because they included stocks of each cultivar from various suppliers to help gardeners see which firms carried the best stocks. Annual NSPS trials resumed after the First World War in 1920 but very many cultivars had been lost or deteriorated during wartime. Each year from 1921 to 1925, the RHS also resumed trials at Wisley and extended these to include stocks of a cultivar from different suppliers. A cultivar might achieve an award based on a quality stock while other suppliers held inferior stocks of the same cultivar. There was some confusion that both societies were making independent awards so that a cultivar might achieve, for example, an Award of Merit with one society but not the other.

In order to address this confusion, in December 1926 the RHS approved a joint trials committee of the two societies. However, it took until 1932 for the rules of the joint committee to be adopted and the first joint trials to be held at Wisley. The joint committee remained in place until disbanded at the end of 2015. Awards were made for exhibition or for garden decoration. The joint committee went into abeyance during the Second World War and trials from 1946 were held at non-RHS sites until they returned to Wisley in 1950 (Parsons 2002). Duplicate trials assessed by a separate panel were grown by the Northern Horticultural Society at Harlow Carr garden in Yorkshire from 1987 so that performance could be assessed in a different environment. These duplicate trials ended after 2004, once the RHS had acquired Harlow Carr.

As a result of the RHS withdrawing from the joint committee in 2015, the NSPS now holds duplicate annual trials at Sparsholt College, Hampshire, and Askham Bryan College, Yorkshire, where awards are made for garden decoration or for exhibition. These are First Class Certificate, Award of Merit or Highly Commended. Similarly, the Scottish National Sweet Pea, Rose and Carnation Society was formed in 1919 and has run trials of sweet peas in most years since 1925. In recent decades these have been grown at Bellahouston Park in Glasgow. Awards made can include Silver Medal, First Class Certificate or Certificate of Merit. All these trials are for new cultivars not yet introduced into commerce.

Although no longer holding annual sweet pea trials at Wisley, the RHS holds occasional trials of new cultivars and these are considered for the Award of Garden Merit (AGM). The next sweet pea trial is expected to take place in 2022 and 2023. The RHS also periodically reviews existing AGM awards, including those to perennial *Lathyrus*.

The impressive sweet pea trials at RHS Garden Wisley were jointly administered by the RHS and the NSPS.

Species

For the purposes of this account we have broken *Lathyrus* into seven groups based on the current DNA evidence (Asmussen & Liston 1998, Kenicer *et al.* 2005, Schaefer *et al.* 2012, Oskoueiyan *et al.* 2014). These correspond fairly well with traditional sections, but this is a fast-evolving, dynamic and adaptable genus, spread across a huge range of habitats throughout the temperate areas of the world, so there are always exceptions. The seven groups are:

- Lathyrus group (p126). These are often climbers with tendrils and a single pair of leaflets, and may be annual or perennial. Many members have twisted styles, giving a contorted keel in the flower. The section includes members of Kupicha's (1983) sections *Lathyrus*, *Orobastrum* and *Orobon*. It includes *L. odoratus* (sweet pea) and *L. latifolius* (broad-leaved everlasting pea), as well as several other highly gardenworthy species. They are native to western Eurasia.

- Lathyrostylis group (p158). Perennial and upright, these have leaves with several pairs of leaflets but the tendrils are reduced to a bristle-like arista. They are often fairly small or medium-sized plants from open, woodland and rocky habitats and offer some lovely species for the garden. Their distribution is centred on the eastern Mediterranean.

- Lincaricarpus group (p170). A group of little, upright annual species, these are often small-flowered and with limited garden appeal. They are native to western Eurasia.

- Notolathyrus group (p176). A diverse group of species, almost all have a single pair of leaflets, and the majority are perennial. It includes some superb plants for gardens. They are native to a wide range of habitats across temperate and subtropical South America.

- Orobus group (p198). Almost exclusively perennial, these usually have multiple pairs of leaflets with or without tendrils. They are native to temperate areas of the northern hemisphere in western Eurasia and North America. All native North American species belong to section *Orobus*, with the exception of *L. pusillus* in section *Notolathyrus*. The Orobus group is divided here into an Old World subgroup (p199) and a New World subgroup (p227). The Old World subgroup is further divided into the Vernus clade (p200), containing *L. vernus* and allies, and the Luteus clade (p205), containing many of the yellow-flowered species. These groups correspond roughly with the series of Bässler (1973). The remainder of the Old World species are treated as the Eurasian grade

Native throughout much of Europe, *Lathyrus niger* is in the Eurasian grade of the Orobus group.

(p212) pending greater resolution from DNA data.

- Pratensis group (includes sections *Pratensis* and *Aphaca*) (p244). Distinctive for their large, sagittate stipules, this group includes some superb garden species. They are native to western Eurasia, with one species extending to China.
- Oddities (members of sections *Clymenum*, *Neurolobus* and *Nissolia*, and species previously in *Pisum* and *Vavilovia*) (p254). These species have notable characteristics that set them apart from the other main groups. All are native to areas around the Mediterranean in Europe, western Eurasia and North Africa.

Species in this chapter are described in varying degrees of detail. Those with longer accounts, including extensive morphological descriptions, are usually those species that are best known in cultivation, have horticultural potential, or are valued as crops. Those species that are less well known in cultivation, or which are at the more weedy end of the spectrum, have shorter accounts. Where debated species are mentioned, these accounts do not claim to make a definitive taxonomic decision. Two species recently described from Turkey, *L. cirpicii* and *L. tefennicus*, are not covered as we have not had the opportunity to verify them, but from the protologue descriptions they are likely to be distinct species. Only a few synonyms are given for each species in these accounts. A more complete synonymy can be found in the 'Checklist of botanical epithets' chapter.

Infraspecific taxa are not treated in great depth, given the huge range of subspecies, varieties and formas proposed across the genus. There is a continuing need for closer investigation of all of them. However, they are mentioned if they give significant insight into variation within a species. Botanical authorities for infraspecific taxa are not given in the text but can be found in the 'Checklist of botanical epithets' chapter.

The diagnostic character for *Lathyrus* is a style with adaxial hairs, pointing inwards towards the stem, and can readily be seen with a ×10 hand lens. The various groups within *Vicia* (now including *Lens*) all have variations of hairs surrounding the styles, with tufts, forward-pointing hairs and similar. Of course, as with most things in nature, there is an exception – the only other species in this group that has this adaxial hairs on the style character is *Vicia saxatilis* (formerly *Lathyrus saxatilis*), which is a small annual with unwinged stems, one or two pairs of leaflets per leaf and a mucro or simple tendril. Kupicha (1983) placed this in its own section of *Lathyrus*, *Viciopsis*, aware that it was a fairly suspect member of the genus. Recent DNA evidence (Schaefer *et al.* 2012) has confirmed her suspicion and it has been moved into the genus *Vicia*.

KEY TO THE GROUPS OF *LATHYRUS*

Given the size and complexity of *Lathyrus*, a key to every species would be very challenging to produce, and we have not attempted to do so. This is because the same character states have evolved again and again. This is in part because of the fundamental palette of genes available, but also because different lineages tend to 'solve' the same challenges thrown up by the niches they inhabit using the same structures (e.g. tendrils to help climbing in vegetated areas). For instance, species in the Notolathyrus group of South America, while closely related to one another, have a diversity of form that rivals that seen across all the Eurasian species. And the diverse and widespread Orobus group has considerable overlap with other groups, in particular the Lathyrostylis group. Therefore, the key given here directs you to the different groups and to some of the more distinctive species within the groups. Sources of further keys to geographical and taxonomic groups are given at the end.

1a Plants with no leaflets – only phyllodes or modified stipules   **2**

1b Plants with one or more pair of leaflets in the upper leaves   **3**

2a Plant grass-like with leaves appearing as slender phyllodes – stipules a pair of tiny spurs at the base of the phyllode, and no tendrils, corollas pink to orange(note young specimens of *L. articulatus, L. clymenum, L. gloeosperma* and *L. ochrus* have phyllodic leaves, but usually tipped with a tendril)   **L. nissolia**

2b Stipules broad, triangular or hastate, either side of a simple tendril   **L. aphaca**

3a Annual plants of the Mediterranean region with lower leaves phyllodic, the upper with two or more pairs of leaflets arising from a broad phyllodic, or winged rachis   **4**

3b Annual or perennial plants from throughout the range with leaflets on lower leaves, and with rachis winged or unwinged   **7**

4a Flowers very small (standard <8mm broad) seldom opening fully

                                           L. gloeosperma

4b Flowers large (1cm broad, or wider), opening fully   **5**

5a Corolla white or pale yellow, phyllodic rachis >1.5cm broad, leaflets ovate

                                           L. ochrus

5b Corolla pink, purple or bicoloured (with pink standard, white wings and keel), rachis ≤1cm broad, leaflets linear to lanceolate   **6**

6a Fruit straight, wall of pod not adhering closely to the seeds, leaflets 8mm or broader, corolla typically single-coloured   **L. clymenum** (this species and *L. articulatus* are notoriously inconsistent in morphological characters and are usually distinguished on the basis of genetics)

6b Fruit slightly upcurving and 'bumpy' (wall of pod following contour of seeds closely), leaflets <11mm broad (usually <8mm), corolla two-toned or bicoloured

                                         L. articulatus

7a Plants with 1 pair of leaflets   **8**

7b Plants with more than 1 pair of leaflets on upper leaves   **13**

8a Small, glabrous creeping perennial, leaflets <2cm long with solitary purple flowers (endemic to moist mountain areas of western Crete)   *L. neurolobus*

8b Plant not as above   **9**

9a Small, running-rhizomatous, perennial tendril-less plant from high montane screes of eastern Mediterranean (Taurus and Caucasus)   *L. formosus*

9b Plant not as above   **10**

10a Plants from South America or southeastern USA, mostly perennial (*L. berteroanus, L. campestris, L. crassipes, L. paranensis* and *L. pusillus* are annual, *L. nigrivalvis* is annual or biennial) with sagittate or semisagittate stipules and often drying black, others densely pubescent (*L. pusillus*, from southeastern USA, is largely hairless, but has semisagittate stipules)   **Notolathyrus group**

10b Plants from the northern hemisphere (although *L. cicera, L. hirsutus, L. latifolius, L. odoratus, L. tingitanus* and *L. tuberosus* – all Lathyrus group – are known from South America as aliens)   **11**

11a Plants perennial with sagittate stipules   **Pratensis group**

11b Plants annual or perennial with semi-sagittate stipules   **12**

12a Plants always annual, small, stems unwinged, leaves with usually unbranched tendrils, inflorescence with one (rarely two) flowers and a slender filament extending beyond the flower at the tip of the inflorescence; corollas crimson to purple, styles not contorted (*L. sphaericus* belongs to Lathyrostylis group)   **Linearicarpus group**

12b Plants annual or perennial, stems often winged, usually with branched tendrils, inflorescence with 1–12 flowers and a slender filament extending beyond the tip of the inflorescence rachis; corollas variously coloured, style often contorted (note *L. cirrhosus, L. heterophyllus* and *L. mulkak* of Lathyrus group have two pairs of leaflets and key out below)   **Lathyrus group**

13a Plants annual   **14**

13b Plants perennial   **15**

14a Leaflets broadly elliptical to ovate, stems round (unwinged), flowers variously white, pinks, purples or ochre-yellow (although see also *L. ochrus*, which is superficially similar)   *Lathyrus oleraceus* & *L. fulvus*

14b Leaflets lanceolate, stems winged, flowers blue or rarely pure white   **L. sativus** (only some individuals have multiple pairs of leaflets)

15a South American plants (montane areas of west-central Argentina and neighbouring Chile) with >5 sky-blue to purple flowers   **L. macropus** and some individuals of **L. pubescens (var. monticola)**

15 Plants from Eurasia or North America, not as above   **16**

16a Sprawling / clambering plants from western or central Eurasia, style contorted (curving to the right, when flower is viewed face-on)   **17**

16b Sprawling, erect or climbing plants from throughout the northern hemisphere, style not contorted   **19**

17a Upper leaves one pair, plants of northern Europe   *L. heterophyllus*

17b Upper leaves with more than two pairs of leaflets   **18**

18a Flowers medium -sized (wings <2.5cm long, standard <2.5cm wide), Iberian peninsula   *L. cirrhosus*

18b Flowers very large (wings >3cm long, standard >3cm wide), Central Asia (Western Pamirs of Afghanistan and Tajikistan)   *L. mulkak*

19a Plants erect, stems unwinged, leaves without tendrils, leaflets typically with major veins parallel, style often flared at the tip, western Eurasia and north Africa, Turkey and upland areas of the Near East   **Lathyrostylis group**

19b Plants highly variable, sprawling, erect or climbing, stems winged or unwinged, with or without tendrils, leaflets usually with reticulate venation, styles usually linear, Eurasia or North America   **20 (Orobus group)**

20a Plants sprawling or climbing, with simple or branched tendrils, Eurasia or North America   **Orobus group (including New World subgroup)**

20b Plants erect, without tendrils, Eurasia only   **21**

21a Plants of montane forests, woodlands and meadows, stems unwinged, leaflets with reticulate veins, corollas white, yellow or orange   **Luteus clade**

21b Plants of lowland forests, stems slightly winged or unwinged, leaflets with reticulate veins, but three primary veins parallel in the leaflet, corollas pink to purple (*L. niger* and *L. venetus* are similar, but do not technically belong in this group – both have corollas with dark purple veins)   **Vernus clade**

KEYS IN OTHER WORKS

If you know the geographical origin of an unidentified plant, then the following keys from particular regions will be helpful.

Ornamental species in European gardens

Hibberd, F.K. (2011) *Lathyrus*. In Cullen, J., Knees, S.G. & Cubey, H.S. (eds) *The European Garden Flora, Volume 3*. 2nd edition. Cambridge University Press, Cambridge. Covers 15 mostly Eurasian species.

Europe and Mediterranean region

Ball, P.W. (1968) *Lathyrus*. In: Tutin, T.G., Heywood, V.H., Burgess, N.A., Moore, D.M., Valentine, D.H., Walters, S.M. & Webb, D.A. (eds.) *Flora Europaea, Volume 2*. Cambridge University Press, Cambridge. Although somewhat outdated, this is an excellent overview of 54 species in Europe and the Mediterranean islands.

Coulot, P. & Rabaute, P. (2016) *Monographie des Leguminosae de France. Tome 4. Tribus des Fabeae, des Cicereae et des Genisteae*. Societe Botanique du Centre-Ouest, Jarnac (in French). A superbly comprehensive account of the species in France, and the first in recent times to include *Pisum* in *Lathyrus* on the basis of DNA evidence.

Davis, P.H. (1970) *Lathyrus*. In: Davis, P.H. (ed.) *Flora of Turkey and East Aegean Islands, Volume 3*. Edinburgh University Press, Edinburgh. When published this was the definitive guide to the 58 species of *Lathyrus* in its centre of diversity, including fairly short descriptions, a good key and maps for many species.

Gallego, M. J. (1999) *Lathyrus*. In: Talavera, S., Aedo, C., Castroviejo, S., Romero Zarco, C., Sáez,L., Salgueiro, F.J. & Velayos, M. (eds.) *Flora Iberica, Volume 7*. Real Jardín Botánico, Madrid. Excellent and considered coverage, in Spanish, of the 35 species on the Iberian peninsula.

Plitmann, U. (1972) *Lathyrus*. In: Zohary, M. (ed.) *Flora Palaestina, Volume 2*. Jerusalem Academy of Sciences and Humanities, Jerusalem. An excellent account covering the 15 eastern Mediterranean species outside the *Flora of Turkey* area.

East Asia and Russia

Bao, B. & Kenicer, G.J. (2010) *Lathyrus*. In: Wu, Z.Y., Raven, P.H. & Hong, D.Y. (eds.) *Flora of China, Volume 10*. Science Press, Beijing, and Missouri Botanical Garden Press, St. Louis. This covers the 18 species of China, Japan and Korea.

Fedchenko, B.A. (1948) *Lathyrus*. In: Komarov V.L., Shishkin B.K. & Bobrov E.G. (eds) *Flora of the USSR, Vol. 13*. 1972 translation by the Israeli Program for Scientific Translation, Jerusalem.

Africa

There are relatively few species in Africa but the numerous regional floras are all helpful. Gallego's (1999) *Flora Iberica* account highlights Iberian species shared with nearby countries of north Africa.

North America

Broich, S.J. (in press) *Lathyrus*. In Flora of North America Editorial Committee (eds.) *Flora of North America*, New York & Oxford.

South America

Neubert, E.E. & Miotto, S.T.S. (2001) O gênero *Lathyrus* L. (*Leguminosae – Faboideae*) no Brasil. *Iheringia, Série Botânica* 56: 51–114. This Brazilian revision is useful. For the wider continent there are numerous regional floras, with those of Argentina being particularly valuable.

Kenicer, G.J. (2007) Systematics and biogeography of *Lathyrus* L. (*Leguminosae*), *Papilionoideae*. PhD thesis, University of Edinburgh. This contains an account of the South American species, plus *L. pusillus* from North America. It also has a continent-wide revision of section *Notolathyrus*, but does not include introduced species that are predominantly from section *Lathyrus*.

Lathyrus group

**Includes most members of section *Lathyrus* Medik., *Vorles. Churpf. Phys. Ges.*
2: 358 (1787), as interpreted by Kupicha (1983)**
Number of species: 35

This group is the classic model of the genus and contains *L. odoratus* (sweet pea),
the most familiar garden species. Typical members have a single pair of leaflets
and grasping tendrils, with semisagittate stipules. They may be annual or
perennial, with annual plants being anything from small ruderals to relatively
large climbers, the latter being exemplified by *L. odoratus*. The perennials are all
medium to large in size. Many members have a distinctly twisted style, giving an
S-shaped contortion to the keel petals when viewed from the front. Winged
stems and rough seed coats are also common features in the group, with the
latter being uncommon in the rest of the genus.

There are a few exceptions to this general ground plan, which many authorities
have wrestled with, but are included in this group. For instance, Frances
Kupicha's seminal work of 1983 pulled out two species as distinct. One is
L. setifolius, a very small, annual plant with slender leaflets, sometimes regarded
as the sole member of section *Orobastrum* Boiss. (*Flora Orientalis* 2: 601 (1872)).
She retained it as distinct from section *Lathyrus* on the basis of its violin-shaped
standard petal and a few other features that were reminiscent of other groups,
resulting in it being classed as a bit of an orphan species. The other odd species
in this group is *L. roseus*, a highly gardenworthy perennial from the Black Sea
region that formerly belonged to its own section *Orobon* Tamamschjan (*Flora
Armenii* 4: 316 (1962)). It is upright, clump-forming, and lacks tendrils, somewhat
like members of section *Orobus*. It does, however, share the twisted style of
many other members of section *Lathyrus*. Both of these species were known
by Kupicha to be close to her section *Lathyrus*, and she was reticent to pull them
off as separate. However, DNA evidence ((Asmussen & Liston 1998, Kenicer *et al.*
2005, Schaefer *et al.* 2012) now shows that they are clearly true members of this
section, so Kupicha's hunch about the relationships was right. The other species
included here is *L. angulatus*, previously in section *Linearicarpus* Kupicha
(1983).

Members of this group often have relatively large seeds and many have a
distinctive rough surface to the seeds, which can be an aid to placing them in
the group. The annuals in particular retain seed viability well, as many are from
Mediterranean habitats where harsh summer conditions require responsive
germination. They will germinate readily, even if poorly stored.

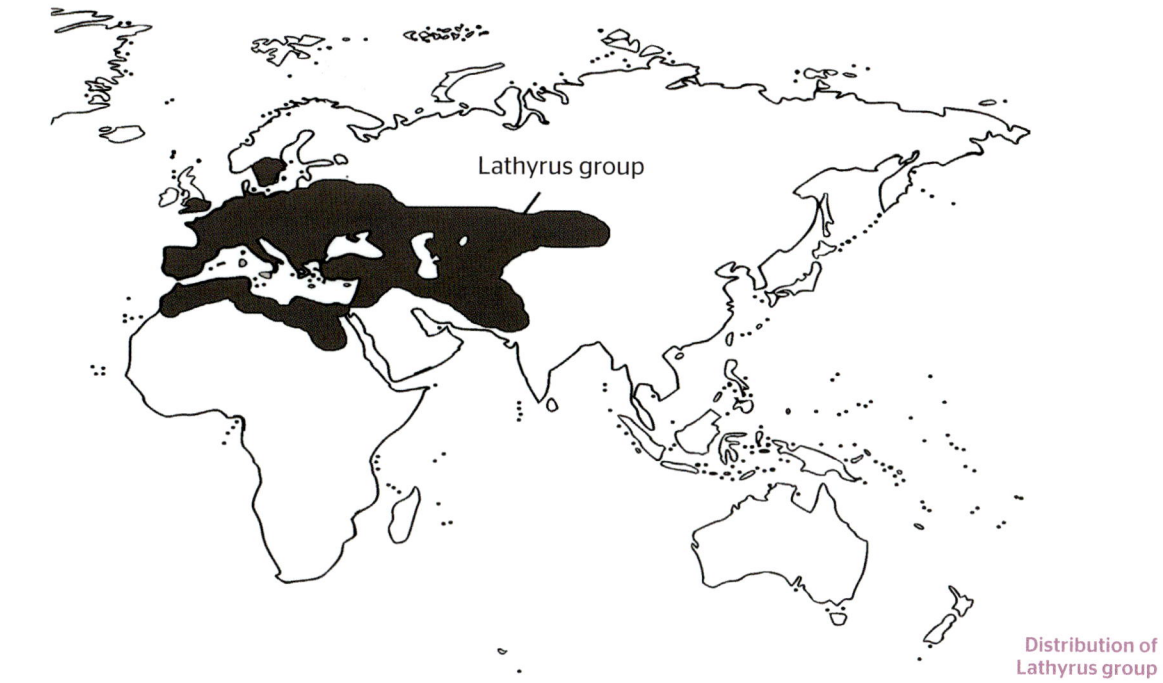

Lathyrus group

Lathyrus amphicarpos

Lathyrus amphicarpos L., *Sp. Pl.* 2: 729 (**1753**)
Syn. *L. quadrimarginatus* Bory & Chaub.

Habitat: Open ground, as a ruderal
Distribution: North-coastal Mediterranean region,
particularly in the Iberian peninsula.

A sprawling and scrambling annual, this species
produces many small-winged stems to 50cm high, but
usually shorter. The stipules are semisagittate, the leaflets
are elliptic, to 40mm long, and less than 10mm wide. The
tendrils are usually simple and only in the upper leaves.
The corollas are orange to red and the fruits are
somewhat inflated with a pair of wings running around
the suture. This places *L. amphicarpos* in the same group
as *L. cicera* and *L. sativus*. What sets this species apart,
however, is its habit of having some cleistogamous
flowers pushed below the ground, which ultimately
produces some aerial and some underground fruits.
Specific epithet origin: with two types of fruit, above
and below ground.

Lathyrus angulatus

Lathyrus angulatus L., *Sp. Pl.* 2: 731 **(1753)**
Brown vetchling, angled pea

Habitat: Open ground, field margins, as a ruderal
Distribution: Western and central Mediterranean

This species has only recently been returned to section *Lathyrus* from the similar section *Linearicarpus*. Like members of the latter group it is a delicate little annual and a common weedy species. The lack of wings on the stems is one feature that previously separated it from the other members of section *Lathyrus*.
Specific epithet origin: angled, referring to the unwinged stem.

Lathyrus annuus

Lathyrus annuus L., *Demonstr. Pl.*: 20 **(1753)**
Syn. *Pisum flavum* E.H.L. Krause
Annual vetchling, fodder pea

Habitat: Open and semi-open areas, often as a ruderal in disturbed ground, field margins and roadsides
Distribution: Widespread throughout the Mediterranean region

A medium-sized sprawling and climbing annual, this can reach 2m in height but is often much less. The plant is usually glabrous with narrow, linear stipules. The flowers are typically solitary (up to three per peduncle), fairly small, with a standard up to 15mm wide, and pale yellow through peach to pale red. The fruits are oblong and not particularly inflated.

Allied species include *L. hierosolymitanus* and *L. gorgoni*, which are distinguished on the basis of flower colour, stipule shape and overall size. The recently described *L. cirpicii* (2019) from Turkey is almost certainly a distinct and related species. It has slightly larger and more numerous red flowers (4–6 per raceme). *Lathyrus cassius*, sometimes treated as a synonym of *L. annuus*, is very similar, but has a lilac standard and white wings and keel.

   Lathyrus annuus and the above relatives may be suitable for mixed-meadow plantings in warm areas. Specific epithet origin: annual.

Lathyrus basalticus

Lathyrus basalticus Rech. f., *Ark. Bot. ser. 2, 1: 511* (1952)

Habitat: Open, stony ground
Distribution: Lebanon, Syria

Very closely related to *L. cicera*, this species overlaps it in range but is distinguished by the tuberculate hairs on the fruit. The fruit, as in *L. cicera* and its allies, including *L. amphicarpos*, is somewhat inflated. It could be treated as a geographical (i.e. subspecific) variant of *L. cicera*. Specific epithet origin: (growing on) basalt.

Lathyrus belinensis

Lathyrus belinensis N. Maxted & Goyder, *Kew Bull.* 43(4): 711 (1988)

Belin pea

Lifecycle: Annual
Habit: Sprawling or clambering
Height: 200cm
Pubescence: Scattered tuberculate hairs on young organs and ovaries
Stem wings: Present
Stipules: Semisagittate, upper part to 15mm
Leaflet number: 1 pair
Leaflet shape: Ovate to oblanceolate
Leaflet length x width: 15-65 x 5-20mm
Tendril: Present
Flowers per raceme: 3-5
Peduncle or pedicel length: 16-30cm
Calyx teeth: Subequal, about the same length as the tube
Standard width: 20-25mm
Petal colour: Orange blending to yellow at the base with red venation
Style: Contorted
Fruit size: 20-40mm
Fruit shape: Falcate, curving upwards
Fruit features: Tuberculate hairs
Number of seeds: 2-8
Wild flowering period: April-June
Habitat: Stony areas and field margins on limestone; 500-750m
Distribution: Southern Turkey

A relatively recent find, this was first described in 1988 from Antalya and is endemic to that region. It is one of relatively few species in *Lathyrus* to have a scent. Genetic evidence shows it is closely allied to *L. chloranthus*, *L. hirsutus*, *L. lycius* and *L. odoratus*, all of which have hairs arising from swollen tubercles, and some degree of scent. This closeness has led to *L. belinensis* being used in breeding experiments to introduce yellow colour to *L. odoratus*. However, it makes for a handsome garden plant in its own right.

The proportion of orange to yellow in the standard petal varies in individuals, although we are not yet sure if this is due to soil, seasonal growing conditions or some other factor. The fruits are somewhat small and twisted, and are indehiscent, which is highly unusual in the genus.

Specific epithet origin: from the type locality of Belin, southern Turkey.

Lathyrus blepharicarpus

Lathyrus blepharicarpus Boiss., *Diagn. Pl. Orient.* ser. 1, 9: 126 (1849)
Eyelash pea, ciliate vetchling

Habitat: Dry to moist, stony habitats and field margins
Distribution: Eastern Mediterranean

One of the group of small annuals with inflated fruits containing few seeds, this is allied to *L. amphicarpos*, *L. cicera* and *L. sativus*. It has a distinctive fringe of hairs around the suture of the fruit that looks somewhat like eyelashes.

Specific epithet origin: eyelash-fruited, referring to ciliate hairs on the margin of the fruit.

Lathyrus chloranthus

Lathyrus chloranthus Boiss. & Balansa, *Diagn. Pl. Orient.* ser. 2, 6: 67 (1856)
Yellow-green pea, yellow-green sweet pea

Lifecycle: Annual
Habit: Sprawling or clambering
Height: 50-100cm
Pubescence: Densely pilose-tomentose

Stem wings: Present
Stipules: Semi-sagittate
Leaflet number: 1 pair
Leaflet length: 20-60mm
Leaflet width: 5-25mm
Leaflet shape: Elliptic
Tendril: Present, branched
Flowers per raceme: 1-2
Peduncle or pedicel length: 3-8cm (as long as or longer than leaflets)
Calyx teeth: Subequal, longer than the tube
Standard width: 15-25mm (pubescent on upper surface)
Petal colour: Yellow, with faint green tinge throughout, and occasionally some red on the standard.
Style: Contorted

Fruit size: c.50mm long
Fruit shape: Oblong
Fruit features: Covered in long, tuberculate hairs
Number of seeds: 5–9
Wild flowering period: June–July
Habitat: Scrubland and streamsides; 500–2,000m
Distribution: Central Turkey to Caucasus, Iran, Iraq, Lebanon, Syria

This attractive species is closely allied to *L. belinensis* and *L. odoratus*, and almost certainly to *L. chrysanthus*, all of which are scented to a degree, and have tuberculate hairs. In the field it is perhaps most difficult to distinguish from *L. chrysanthus*, although *L. chloranthus* is a larger plant, typically from further north and east in the Irano-Turanian region than *L. chrysanthus*. The flower is much more of a green, sulphurous yellow than the vivid golden yellow of *L. chrysanthus*, and the standard petal has distinctive hairs on the adaxial surface and can sometimes show a bit of red colouring.

This species does well in temperate gardens in similar conditions to *L. odoratus*, but tends not to grow to such a size as sweet pea cultivars.
Specific epithet origin: yellow-green, from the colour of the corolla.

Lathyrus chrysanthus

Lathyrus chrysanthus Boiss., *Diagn. Pl. Orient.* ser. 1, 6: 46 (1846)
Golden pea, golden sweet pea

Habitat: Open rocky ground and the margins of cultivated land
Distribution: Syria, Lebanon and Israel

This species is similar to *L. chloranthus* and is likely to be a close relative, although its genetic relationship has not yet been researched. *Lathyrus chrysanthus* is typically a smaller plant, with golden rather than greenish-yellow flowers and without the hairs on the back of the standard found in *L. chloranthus*. It is found

further south and west in the Irano-Turanian region than
L. chloranthus, with a more limited range.

This is a very attractive plant because of the dense grey pubescence and striking yellow flowers, and performs well in similar conditions to sweet peas.
Specific epithet origin: gold-flowered.

Lathyrus cicera

Lathyrus cicera L., *Sp. Pl.* 2: 730 (1753)
Red-flowered chickling vetch

Habitat: Open, disturbed ground and field margins
Distribution: Throughout Mediterranean region, extending possibly as far as Afghanistan

This is a medium-sized annual species that sprawls or scrambles. The flowers are a distinctive brick-red to crimson. Like other closely related species such as *L. amphicarpos* and *L. sativus* the fruits are short, broad and somewhat inflated with relatively few, large seeds.

It is occasionally cultivated as a fodder and food crop.
Specific epithet origin: chick-pea like.

Lathyrus ciliolatus

Lathyrus ciliolatus Sam. ex Rech. f., *Ark. Bot.* ser. 2, 1: 311 (1950)
Ciliolate chickling vetch

Habitat: Open areas, fields, as a ruderal
Distribution: Syria

Although treated as a separate species here, this is very similar to *L. amphicarpos*. Many specimens, including the type, have subterranean, long-pedunculate fruit, a significant feature shared with *L. amphicarpos*.
Specific epithet origin: with ciliate hairs

Lathyrus cirrhosus

Lathyrus cirrhosus Ser., *Prodr.* [A.P. de Candolle] 2: 374 (1825)
Syn. *L. sylvestris* var. *cirrhosus* (Ser.) P. Fourn.

Habitat: Fertile banks and roadsides; 300–1,600m
Distribution: Catalonia and eastern Pyrenees

This species appears superficially similar to *L. sylvestris*, which is more widespread in Iberia and throughout Europe, but differs in having 2–4 pairs of leaflets. In this respect it is more like *L. heterophyllus*, which DNA evidence (Schaefer *et al.* 20102) suggests is its closest relative. The 4–8 flowers per raceme have pink corollas with a standard 20–30mm broad, so this is a highly striking and attractive plant, certainly worthy of more attention for garden use.
Specific epithet origin: equipped with tendrils.

Lathyrus gorgoni

Lathyrus gorgoni Parl., *Giorn. Sci. Sicilia* 62 (184–185): 3(–4) (1838)
Syn. *L. amoenus* Fenzl

Habitat: Open areas, road and field margins, as a ruderal
Distribution: Mediterranean region, Asia Minor

Along with *L. annuus* (including *L. cassius*) and *L. hierosolymitanus*, this is one of the small annuals in section *Lathyrus* that have oblong, not inflated, pods. They probably represent a species complex as there is not much difference between them. *Lathyrus gorgoni* is the most distinct genetically and has larger (2cm across), solitary flowers with orange petals and pods with a 'beak' (where the tip attenuates towards the style). Interestingly, this feature is more typical of the group with inflated pods that includes *L. cicera* and its allies.
Specific epithet origin: named for Giovanni Gorgone (1801–1868), a professor of anatomy at Palermo. The name is often corrected to *L. gorgonei* or *L. gorgonii*, but *L. gorgoni* is how it was originally published.

Lathyrus grandiflorus

Lathyrus grandiflorus Sm., *Fl. Graec. Prodr.* 2(1): 67 (1813)

Syn. *L brutius* Ten.

Large-flowered everlasting pea, two-flowered everlasting pea

Lifecycle: Perennial
Habit: Climbing
Height: 200cm
Hair: Present, although variable on individuals
Stem wings: Absent
Stipules: Semi-sagittate, rarely sagittate, upper lobe to 10mm
Leaflet number: 1 pair
Leaflet length: 20-50mm
Leaflet width: 10-40mm
Leaflet shape: ovate to rotund
Tendril: Present, branched
Flowers per raceme: 1-4
Peduncle or pedicel length: 50-80mm
Calyx teeth: Shorter than the tube
Standard width: 25-40mm
Petal colour: Standard pink, wings maroon, keel pink
Style: Contorted
Fruit size: 60-90mm
Fruit shape: Oblong
Fruit features: Glabrous
Number of seeds: 15-20
Wild flowering period: May-June
Habitat: Woodland and shady banks; 500-1,400m
Distribution: European Mediterranean (Greece, Albania, southern Italy, southern France). Introduced as an ornamental and naturalised in temperate areas such as the UK, New Zealand, Pacific North West of USA and Canada

The slender, terete stems and tiny stipules combined with the broad, rounded leaflets make this unlike others in section *Lathyrus*. One of the few producing running rhizomes, it is also a vigorous climber and sprawls over vegetation or open ground. As the name suggests, it has some of the largest flowers in the genus, with broad standards and maroon wings making it particularly attractive.

In the warm areas in which it is found, it lives in cool woodlands and gullies, so is adapted to cooler temperate gardens. It can be quite vigorous, so removing unwanted rhizomes can be a challenge. However, it is a striking perennial and, in a suitable spot, can cover a considerable area, or cover medium-sized shrubs. Specific epithet origin: large-flowered.

Lathyrus heterophyllus

Lathyrus heterophyllus L., *Sp. Pl.* 2: 733 **(1753)**
Syns. *L. sylvestris* subsp. *heterophyllus* (L.) Bonnier &
Layens, *Pisum heterophyllum* (L.) E.H.L. Krause
Norfolk everlasting pea

Habitat: Scrub, woodland margins and clearings
Distribution: Throughout central Europe

Very like *L. latifolius* in overall appearance, this is
sometimes treated as a central European variant of it.
Although the ranges of the two species overlap, the DNA
evidence (Schaefer *et al.* 2012) suggests that they are
quite distinct. This species is readily distinguished by its
multijugate leaves – many of the upper leaves have two
pairs of leaflets, which is a condition seen in only a few
other members of section *Lathyrus*, such as *L. cirrhosus*
and *L. mulkak*.

As a garden plant it performs similarly to *L. latifolius*,
although it is perhaps a little less tolerant of very
oceanic, wet conditions.

Specific epithet: different leaved, referring to its one
or two pairs of leaflets.

Lathyrus hierosolymitanus

Lathyrus hierosolymitanus Boiss., *Diagn. Pl. Orient.*
ser. 1, 9: 127 **(1849)**
Syns. *L. annuus* var. *hierosolymitanus* Post, *L. chius*
Boiss. & Orph.
Jerusalem vetchling

Habitat: Open areas, field margins, as a ruderal
Distribution: Eastern Mediterranean mainland
and Cyprus

This species is related to *L. annuus* but is distinguished
by being more consistently small, having slightly

narrower pods, and more flowers per raceme (up to six) that are pale pink. Consequently, it might be appropriate to treat it as a variety within *L. annuus*.

That said, two varieties, *L. hierosolymitanus* var. *amphicarpus* and yellow-flowered *L. hierosolymitanus* var. *luteus* have been recognised (Plitmann 1972). These taxa, along with *L. annuus* (including *L. cassius*) and *L. gorgoni*, probably represent a complex of allied species, although they are more genetically distinct than their morphology would suggest, and are closely related to perennials in this section such as *L. sylvestris*.
Specific epithet origin: of Jerusalem

Lathyrus hirsutus

Lathyrus hirsutus L., *Sp. Pl.* 2: 732 (1753)
Syn. *Pisum hirsutum* (L.) E.H.L. Krause
Hairy vetchling, singletary pea, Caley pea, rough pea

Habitat: Grasslands, meadows, fields
Distribution: Throughout much of western Eurasia, but mostly temperate Europe, north and east coasts of the Mediterranean and into the Caucasus. Introduced as a fodder crop or seed alien in North America.

A medium to large sprawling annual, this tends to be more cool-tolerant in the wild than similar annuals such as *L. annuus*. The racemes consist of 1–3 flowers that are two-tone blue and pink with paler or white wings and keel. It is hairy throughout with tuberculate hairs on the pods. These tubercles at the base of each hair are distinctive for the subset of species allied to *L. odoratus*, which DNA evidence (Schaefer *et al.* 2012) suggests is the case for *L. hirsutus*.

This species may be a UK native, having been known from neutral clay grasslands of the Thames estuary since at least the 17th century (Rumsey 2019), although it is a casual elsewhere in the UK. It is occasionally grown as a fodder crop in some parts of the world.
Specific epithet origin: hairy.

Lathyrus hirticarpus

Lathyrus hirticarpus Mattatia & Heyn, *Israel J. Bot.* 25(3-4): 216 (1976)

Habitat: Open, rocky areas
Distribution: Israel, Syria

This species has brick-red flowers and fruits with tuberculate hairs and two narrow ridges on the upper suture. These characters are intermediate between two of the main groups in section *Lathyrus* – the *L. cicera*-like and *L. odoratus*-like species. Maxted (1993) suggests a close relationship of *L. hirticarpus* to *L. basalticus*, which also shares both these features and has a close, but not overlapping range. He also interprets both of these species as limited nowadays to basaltic habitats. Specific epithet origin: hairy-fruited.

Lathyrus latifolius

Lathyrus latifolius L., *Sp. Pl.* 2: 733 (1753)
Syns. *L. sylvestris* subsp. *latifolius* (L.) Bonnier & Layens, *L. sylvestris* subsp. *latifolius* (L.) Arcang., *L. megalanthus* Steud., *L. membranaceus* C. Presl
Broad-leaved everlasting pea, perennial pea

Lifecycle: Perennial
Habit: Climbing or sprawling
Height: 300cm
Hair: Glabrous or sparsely pubescent
Stem wings: Present, broad
Stipules: Semi-sagittate, lanceolate to ovate, upper lobe to 50mm
Leaflet number: 1 pair
Leaflet length: 40-200mm (usually c. 120mm)
Leaflet width: 5-50mm
Leaflet shape: Narrow-lanceolate to ovate
Tendril: Present, branched and robust
Flowers per raceme: 5-15
Peduncle or pedicel length: 5-30cm
Calyx teeth: Usually shorter than the tube
Standard width: 15-30mm

Petal colour: Various shades of pink, or white
Style: Contorted
Fruit size: 70-100mm
Fruit shape: Oblong
Fruit features: Thickened margins to the suture, pale faun colour
Number of seeds: 10-20
Wild flowering period: June–August
Habitat: Open ground, woodland, field margins; to 1,800m
Distribution: Throughout temperate Europe. Where introduced it can be invasive, particularly in the cooler edges of Mediterranean habitats

This species, *L. heterophyllus* and *L. sylvestris* share many characters and are sometimes treated as a single species. However, DNA evidence (Schaefer *et al.* 2012) suggests they are distinct, with *L. latifolius* relatively distant from the other two. In comparison to *L. sylvestris*, *L. latifolius* is larger throughout with broader stipules and leaflets with a matt surface and reticulate venation, as well as more, and larger flowers. *Lathyrus sylvestris* has glossier, narrow leaflets with some parallel venation. *Lathyrus heterophyllus* is most readily distinguished by having multiple pairs of leaflets on the upper leaves.

Cultivars are mainly variants in flower colour, from reds through pinks to white. All of these can be found in natural populations, with the majority being vivid pink. Moldenke (1973, 1974) treated wild, white-flowered plants as *L. latifolius* f. *albiflorus* and red-flowered ones as *L. latifolius* f. *rubicundus*.

Although unscented, the flowers provide a good garden display. It was one of Gertrude Jekyll's favoured plants for 'pulling down' to cover unsightly gaps in late-season herbaceous plantings. This takes advantage of the mixed strategy of the species in the wild – in open ground it sprawls extensively, but in forest areas clambers over shrubs and low trees. Multiple annual stems arise from a thickened, tuberous rhizome. Although the plant does not run, it can seed freely.

Specific epithet origin: broad-leaved, referring to the leaflets.

Lathyrus lentiformis

Lathyrus lentiformis Plitm., *Israel J. Bot.* 14: 90 (1965)
Lentil vetchling

Habitat: Slightly wet, basaltic soils in open ground
Distribution: Israel

The overall habit and small purple flowers of this species are reminiscent of the Cretan endemic *L. neurolobus*. However, the very small pods are borne on short stipes that hold them down and away from the remnants of the calyx, a feature also seen in *L. setifolius*. As a result, it is an interesting little plant, although not especially gardenworthy.
Specific epithet origin: shaped like *Lens*, the related lentil genus.

Lathyrus lycius

Lathyrus lycius Boiss. & Heldr., *Diagn. Pl. Orient.* ser. 1, 9: 128 (1849)
Syn. *L. phaselitanus* Huber-Mor. & P.H. Davis
Lycian vetchling

Habitat: Open rocky areas; sea level to 500m
Distribution: Turkey (Anatolia)

This medium-sized species, reaching a height of about 80cm, is similar to *L. chrysanthus* and *L. hirsutus*. The petiolate leaves have elliptic to oblanceolate leaflets and racemes of 1–4 flowers in the axils. These are larger than in *L. hirsutus*, with corollas to 2.5cm across and pink. The adaxial (upper) surface of the standard petal has hairs, a feature also seen in *L. chrysanthus*. The fruits have the distinctive tuberculate hairs found in *L. chrysanthus*, *L. hirsutus*, *L. odoratus* and a few other species.
Specific epithet origin: from Lycia.

Lathyrus marmoratus

Lathyrus marmoratus Boiss. & Balansa ex Boiss., *Fl. Orient.* [Boissier] 2: 606 (1872 or 1873)

Habitat: Open sandy and rocky ground, open woodlands

Distribution: Eastern Mediterranean (from Turkey round to Egypt) and the Middle East

This widespread species has red flowers and fruits that are somewhat inflated, both features shared with *L. blepharicarpus* and *L. cicera*, to which it is undoubtedly related. In *L. marmoratus*, however, the calyx does not have a fringe of hairs, the fruits are less inflated and the wings on the upper suture are smaller. Flowers are a pale red or red-violet rather than bright red, and darker veins are usually apparent.

Specific epithet origin: streaked, possibly referring to the veins in the flower.

Lathyrus mulkak

Lathyrus mulkak Lipsky, *Trudy Imp. S.-Peterburgsk. Bot. Sada* 18: 49 (1900)

Habitat: Stony ground; 1,500–2,500m

Distribution: Afghanistan, Tajikistan and Uzbekistan

This is a beautiful species, reminiscent of *L. grandiflorus*, a relationship supported by DNA evidence (Schaefer *et al.* 2012). However, it is one of the few species in this section, along with *L. cirrhosus* and *L. heterophyllus*, that is multijugate. It consistently has 2–3 pairs of leaflets rather than a single pair. Although fairly closely related, they are not especially close. The leaves consist of elliptic leaflets, 25–70 x 10–40mm, and have a robust tendril. The racemes bear 3–12 large, scented flowers, to 35mm across the standard, with pink to deep maroon petals.

It is poorly known in horticulture but deserves wider cultivation.

Specific epithet origin: from a local name for the plant.

Lathyrus odoratus

Lathyrus odoratus L., *Sp. Pl.* 2: 732 (**1753**)

Sweet pea

Lifecycle: Annual
Habit: Climbing or sprawling
Height: 3m
Pubescence: Pubescent throughout with tubercles at base of hairs
Stem wings: Present
Stipules: Semi-sagittate, upper part lanceolate
Leaflet number: 1 pair
Leaflet length: 25-80mm
Leaflet width: 20-50mm
Leaflet shape: Ovate to broadly elliptic
Tendril: Robust and branched
Flowers per raceme: 2-4
Peduncle or pedicel length: 4-30cm
Calyx teeth: Unequal, the lowest as long as the tube
Standard width: 18-30mm
Petal colour: Standard maroon, wings and keel lilac to pale violet
Style: Contorted
Fruit size: 6-140mm
Fruit shape: Oblong
Fruit features: Covered with tuberculate hairs
Number of seeds: 5-12
Wild flowering period: April-June
Habitat: Open areas near cultivated fields, grassland and scrub
Distribution: Sicily and neighbouring parts of southern Italy, but also recorded from Corsica, Sardinia and nearby Mediterranean Islands

This large, climbing species belongs to the clade of section *Lathyrus* that includes the tuberculate-haired species such as *L. belinensis, L. chloranthus* and *L. hirsutus*, as well as several smaller species. In the wild the flowers are smaller than most cultivars and the petals typically have a non-wavy edge. In addition, *L. odoratus* in the wild often has the stigma curving to the right, when viewed front-on, as is the case in many other members of this tuberculate-haired group.

Lathyrus odoratus is the wild ancestor of all garden sweet peas. Relatively undeveloped cultivars such as 'Cupani' are closest to the wild species and share the strong fragrance found in the wild species as well as a bicoloured corolla. Electron microscopy studies (e.g. Mitchell 2016) have shown scent is produced by specialised glandular cells (osmophores) borne on the standard and wing petals. Specific epithet origin: smelly, in this case scented.

Lathyrus pseudocicera

Lathyrus pseudocicera Pampan., *Nuovo Giorn. Bot.*
Ital. n.s. 31: 213, 214 (1924)
False chickpea vetchling

Habitat: Open ground; sea level to 1,000m
Distribution: Eastern Mediterranean from Turkey to Iraq

Similar to *L. cicera* and *L. gorgoni*, this species also has
a somewhat inflated fruit. It is distinguished from the
former by having reddish orange rather than red flowers,
sepals not recurving in fruit, and a line down the side of
the fruit valve. These three species and subsp. *negevensis*
blend into each other and need further investigation.
Specific epithet origin: false chickpea.

Lathyrus pulcher

Lathyrus pulcher J. Gay, *Ann. Sci. Nat., Bot.* sér. 4, 8:
311 (1857)
Syns. *L. tremolsianus* Pau, *L. elegans* Porta & Rigo

Habitat: Scrubland, field edges; sea level to 1,200m
Distribution: Southern and eastern Spain, North Africa

This elegant species has long, slender leaflets in single
pairs and few, large, pink flowers to 25mm across the
standard, borne on long pedicels. The fruits are oblong
and slender, quite unlike the inflated pods of *L. cicera*
and *L. sativus*, which DNA evidence (Schaefer *et al.*
2012) suggests are close relatives.
Specific epithet origin: beautiful

Lathyrus roseus

Lathyrus roseus Steven, *Mém. Soc. Imp.*
Naturalistes Moscou 4: 92 (1813)
Syn. *Orobus roseus* Ledebour
Rose-flowered pea

Lifecycle: Perennial

Habit: Erect

Height: 60cm, very rarely to 1.2m

Hair: Glabrous

Stem wings: Absent , stems terete

Stipules: Semi-sagittate, lanceolate to 15mm

Leaflet number: 1 pair

Leaflet length: 15–50mm

Leaflet width: 10–35mm

Leaflet shape: Orbicular

Tendril: Absent

Flowers per raceme: 1–5

Peduncle or pedicel length: 2–7cm (longer than the leaflets)

Calyx teeth: Unequal, shorter than the tube

Standard width: 12–20mm

Petal colour: Pinkish purple, usually single-coloured

Style: Contorted

Fruit size: 30–55mm

Fruit shape: Broad-linear

Fruit features: Pale brown

Number of seeds: 4–10

Wild flowering period: May–July

Habitat: Pine and spruce forests, oak and hazel maquis and garrigue; sea level to 2000m

Distribution: Throughout the Black Sea Region, central and northern Caucasus

With its single pair of rounded leaflets and no tendril, coupled with a clump-forming, upright habit, almost forming canes, this species is atypical for related members of section *Lathyrus*. Indeed, it looks much more like members of section *Orobus* in its habit and has been placed in its own section *Orobon* in the past. The style is contorted, however, which is a trait exclusive to section *Lathyrus*, so it clearly belongs here, and this has been confirmed by DNA evidence (Asmussen & Liston 1998).

A highly gardenworthy species for warmer areas, this is a classic woodland plant. It can be tricky to establish but does well in light shade and a deep, rich, moist soil with mulch to prevent water loss, but it can be fairly tolerant of a wide range of woodland conditions.

Specific epithet origin: rose-coloured, referring to the petals.

Lathyrus rotundifolius

Lathyrus rotundifolius Willd., *Sp. Pl.*, ed. 4 [Willdenow] 3(2): 1088 (1802)
Syn. *L. litvinovii* Iljin
Vermilion everlasting pea, round-leaved everlasting pea

Lifecycle: Perennial
Habit: Sprawling or clambering
Height: 1m
Hair: Glabrous
Stem wings: Present
Stipules: Semi-sagittate to unevenly hastate, upper part lanceolate to 25mm
Leaflet number: 1 pair
Leaflet length: 25-65mm
Leaflet width: 10-45mm
Leaflet shape: Ovate to orbicular
Tendril: Present, branched
Flowers per raceme: 3-13
Peduncle or pedicel length: 6-15cm
Calyx teeth: Unequal, slightly shorter than the tube
Standard width: 15-25mm
Petal colour: Deep reddish-pink (vermilion)
Style: Contorted
Fruit size: 40-70mm
Fruit shape: Linear-oblong
Fruit features: Glabrous, drying pale yellow-brown
Number of seeds: 6-10
Wild flowering period: June-July
Habitat: Scrub and open agricultural areas, 1,000-2,200m (subsp. *rotundifolius*);
pine and spruce forest, 1,000-2,200m (subsp. *miniatus*); deciduous forest and
open margins, roadsides, sea level to 600m (subsp. *undulatus*)
Distribution: North-east Turkey and Caucasus (subsp. rotundifolius); Crimea,
(subsp. miniatus); European part of Turkey (subsp. undulatus)

The three subspecies occupy different areas and habitats, as outlined above.
Lathyrus rotundifolius subsp. *miniatus* differs from the type in being more
robust in the stem, and having longer leaflets and more flowers per raceme with
a larger calyx. *Lathyrus rotundifolius* subsp. *undulatus* is distinguished by its
wavy leaflet margin and the lowest calyx tooth being longer than the calyx tube.

All are attractive plants with vermilion flowers. Annual stems arise from a
tuberous rhizome that can become almost woody at ground level. They are
tolerant of well-drained soils and will perform well in dappled shade.
Specific epithet origin: round-leaved, referring to the leaflets.

Lathyrus sativus

Lathyrus sativus L., *Sp. Pl.* 2: 730 (1753)
Syns. *L. asiaticus* (Zalkind) Kudr., *L. sativus* subsp. *asiaticus* Zalkind
Chickling vetch, Indian pea, blue pea, azure pea

Lifecycle: Annual
Habit: Climbing
Height: 1m, sometimes more
Hair: Glabrous
Stem wings: Present
Stipules: Semi-sagittate
Leaflet number: 1 pair
Leaflet length: 25-150mm
Leaflet width: 3-10mm
Leaflet shape: Narrow-lanceolate
Tendril: Present, branched
Flowers per raceme: 1
Peduncle/Pedicel: 3-10cm (shorter than leaflets)
Calyx teeth: Equal, much longer than the tube
Standard width: 15-25mm
Petal colour: Blue, often with pink markings at base of standard
Style: Contorted
Fruit size: 20-40mm, plump
Fruit shape: Oblong
Fruit features: Two wings either side of the upper suture
Number of seeds: 2-4
Wild flowering period: March–August
Habitat: Open ground, field margins
Distribution: Throughout warm areas of western Eurasia, particularly the Mediterranean, as far as western Himalaya ; sea level to 1,600m. Moved widely as a crop since ancient times, its original range is not known, but it is also found as an introduced casual in eastern India, Bangladesh, East Asia, the Americas and Oceania

As well as the species related to *L. odoratus* characterised by tuberculate hairs and scent, there are two other large groups of annuals in section *Lathyrus*. One of these is allied to the perennials and includes *L. annuus*, while the other includes *L. sativus* and *L. cicera* among others. There are no strong diagnostic characters to distinguish these two groups, although fruits in the latter group are often inflated.

This is an elegant, relatively small, climbing species, and one of the most widely cultivated in the genus. It is typically grown as a fodder crop, but is a

worthy annual ornamental in its own right. The striking blue flowers with broad standards, and the inflated fruits with two wings on top, are distinctive for this species. The large seeds, which are somewhat like chickpeas, have long been used in various porridges throughout the Mediterranean region, northern Africa and India. However, they can cause lathyrism if consumed as a high proportion of the diet.

This plant does well in a wide range of climates, being one of the most drought-tolerant crops known. It will flower and seed readily in latitudes ranging from Scotland to Kenya. The flowers are typically blue, but variants bearing white (f. *albus*), azure blue (f. *azureus*), cyan blue (var. *cyaneus*) and violet blue (f. *violascens*) flowers are widely cultivated.

Specific epithet origin: cultivated, as a pulse and fodder crop.

Lathyrus setifolius

Lathyrus setifolius L., *Sp. Pl.* 2: 731 (1753)

Habitat: A ruderal in disturbed habitats, roadsides and open ground
Distribution: Southern Europe, Mediterranean region

This is a delicate annual with tendrils and red flowers that appears superficially similar to members of section *Linearicarpus* and the smaller annuals of section *Lathyrus*. Kupicha (1983) separated this species from both these sections on the basis of its characteristic stipitate pods (i.e. narrowing towards the calyx). However, DNA analysis by Asmussen & Liston (1998), Kenicer *et al.* (2005) and Schaefer *et al.* (2012) show it to be a member of section *Lathyrus*.

Lathyrus setifolius var. *sharonensis* from wetlands on the Sharon plain in Israel has longer leaflets and only unbranched tendrils, but may be extinct.
Specific epithet origin: bristle-leaved, referring to the very narrow leaflets.

Lathyrus stenophyllus

Lathyrus stenophyllus Boiss. & Heldr., *Diagn. Pl. Orient.* ser. 1, 9: 126 (1849)
Syn. *L. egirdiricus* H. Genç & A. Sahin

Habitat: Disturbed habitats, roadsides, open ground, open pine forests; sea level to 800m
Distribution: Mediterranean Turkey, northern Syria, Iraq, and recorded from Crete

With its elegant narrow leaflets and narrow stipules this species looks similar to *L. setifolius*. However, the slightly paler flowers help distinguish it. A third species, *L. egirdiricus*, was described in 2008 from Turkey and is morphologically very similar. Its darker flowers and slightly narrower fruits are not sufficient to warrant separate recognition, hence its synonymous status here. Specific epithet origin: narrow-leaved, referring to the leaflets.

Lathyrus sylvestris

Lathyrus sylvestris L., *Sp. Pl.* 2: 733 (1753)
Syn. *L. platyphyllus* Retz.
Narrow-leaved everlasting pea, flat pea

Habitat: Scrub, woodland margins, clearings
Distribution: Throughout central Europe

Filling a similar niche as *L. latifolius*, this is a smaller, more slender species, although it does reach 2m in height. It is actually more closely related to *L. heterophyllus*, and individuals with two pairs of leaflets on the upper leaves are common in this species.

It can establish itself readily as a colony with shortly creeping rhizomes or short stems behaving like stolons, but most reproduction is by seed. It is vigorous and potentially slightly invasive in gardens through self-seeding, but easy to control by pulling or digging out. Specific epithet origin: of woodlands.

Lathyrus tingitanus

Lathyrus tingitanus L., *Sp. Pl.* 2: 732 (**1753**)

Syns. *L. coruscans* Emb. & Maire, *L. mexicanus* Schlecht.

Tangier pea

Lifecycle: Annual
Habit: Climbing
Height: 1.5m
Hair: Glabrous
Stem wings: Present
Stipules: Semi-sagittate, upper part ovate to lanceolate to 35mm long
Leaflet number: 1 pair
Leaflet length: 15-90mm
Leaflet width: 5-35mm
Leaflet shape: Elliptic to obovate
Tendril: Present, branched
Flowers per raceme: 1-3
Peduncle or pedicel length: 3-17cm
Calyx teeth: Unequal, usually shorter than the tube
Standard width: 20-30mm
Petal colour: Pink and deep magenta
Style: Not contorted
Fruit size: 70-120mm
Fruit shape: Oblong-elliptic
Fruit features: Densely glandular-hairy
Number of seeds: 6-10
Wild flowering period: April-June
Habitat: Scrubland and forest margins, roadsides; 100-1,000m
Distribution: Throughout the western Mediterranean, north Africa, southern Iberian peninsula and Sardinia

This distinctive species has strikingly coloured flowers, somewhat glaucous-grey stems and leaves, and is largely hairless. In habit and size it is similar to *L. odoratus*, and perhaps fills a similar ecological niche to that species and its allies. However, DNA evidence (Kenicer *et al.* 2005, Schaefer *et al.* 2012) suggests that *L. tingitanus* is not particularly closely related to any of the other groups in section *Lathyrus*, and comes from a relatively early-diverging lineage.

It is perhaps the second most commonly grown and commercially available annual from the genus, and performs very well in comparable conditions to *L. odoratus*.

Specific epithet origin: from Mauretania Tingitana, an ancient Roman province in north Africa.

Lathyrus trachycarpus

Lathyrus trachycarpus (Boiss.) Boiss., *Fl. Orient.*
[Boissier] 2: 608 (1872)
Syn. *Orobus trachycarpus* Boiss.

Habitat: Scrub, open forest
Distribution: Turkey

Known largely from 19th-century herbarium collections, this species is endemic to the area around Diyarbakır, Turkey. Erect and without tendrils, it is perhaps most reminiscent of some members of section *Lathyrostylis*, particularly *L. boissieri*, although most of these have multiple pairs of leaflets. The flowers are relatively large (standard over 2cm across), but the fruits are very short (to about 2cm) with only one or two seeds, rarely more. The fruit is densely covered with the tuberculate hairs, typical of species allied to *L. odoratus*, although the rest of the plant is glabrous.
Specific epithet origin: rough-fruited, referring to the tubercles at the base of the hairs on the pod.

Lathyrus tuberosus

Lathyrus tuberosus L., *Sp. Pl.* 2: 732 (1753)
Tuberous pea, earth-nut pea, earth chestnut

Lifecycle: Perennial
Habit: Sprawling or clambering
Height: 30–100cm, rarely larger
Hair: Glabrous, or occasionally sparsely hairy
Stem wings: Absent
Stipules: Semi-sagittate, rarely sagittate, upper part 5–20mm long
Leaflet number: 1 pair
Leaflet length: 15–45mm
Leaflet width: 5–15mm
Leaflet shape: Elliptic, oblanceolate
Tendril: Present, branched
Flowers per raceme: 2-8

Peduncle or pedicel length: 5-12cm

Calyx teeth: Unequal, usually slightly shorter than the tube

Standard width: 10-15mm

Petal colour: Magenta

Style: Slightly contorted

Fruit size: 20-40mm

Fruit shape: Oblong

Fruit features: Some glandular hairs

Number of seeds: 2-6

Wild flowering period: April-August

Habitat: Meadows, fields and roadsides; sea level to 1,500m

Distribution: Much of central and western Eurasia, from cool temperate regions to the Mediterranean

In overall appearance this species is perhaps most reminiscent of some of the South American species, such as *L. magellanicus*, but it is very distant both geographically and in terms of evolution. The stipules are relatively large and broad, and can sometimes be sagittate, which is a feature much more typical of the South American species. Its range in Eurasia is mostly continuous, but some of its distribution can probably be attributed to humans.

A very attractive species ornamentally, the racemes of vivid pink flowers stand out well against the clean, green foliage. The perennating tubers that give the plant its name are a particularly distinctive feature, as such structures are relatively rare in the genus. These teardrop-shaped tubers were widely cultivated in northern Europe and roasted as a starchy, nut-flavoured food. The tubers have led to confusion between it and *L. linifolius*, the other European species from which the tubers were sometimes eaten, as *L. linifolius* was formerly known as *Orobus tuberosus*.

Specific epithet origin: tuberous.

Lathyrostylis group

Includes most members of section *Lathyrostylis* (Griseb.) Bässler, *Feddes Repert.* 82(6): 433 (1971)

Number of species: 17

This is a fairly uniform group of small to medium-sized, erect plants, all of which are perennials. The exception is annual *L. sphaericus*, which was formerly placed in section *Lathyrus* but which DNA evidence now places here. Perennation is by running rhizomes or thickened, tuberous rhizomes. The leaves have 2–5 pairs of narrowly lanceolate leaflets. These often have no petiole and a very short rachis, making them appear digitate (almost compound-palmate), and they lack tendrils – the leaves usually terminating in an arista. This overall ground plan was typical of the now defunct genus *Orobus*, and many of these species were originally in that genus. The racemes have several to many, medium-sized (c. 1.5cm) flowers, with shades of violet, blue and white on the petals. The styles are broadly spathulate towards the tip – the source of the section's name.

Most of these species are from forest, open woodland, rock or grassland habitats in the eastern Mediterranean, with the greatest diversity in and around Turkey.

The section includes many species that might be gardenworthy if better known and more widely trialled. *Lathyrus pannonicus*, which is sometimes grown in gardens, was for a long time a member of section *Lathyrostylis* until DNA evidence (Schaefer *et al.* 2012) placed it in section *Orobus*. This is very telling, as it suggests the 'oroboid' habit may have arisen more than once. The same DNA study also showed *L. sphaericus*, previously in section *Linearicarpus*, belongs to section *Lathyrostylis*, making it the sole known annual member of the section. Many of the other species have yet to be assessed to determine their genetic relationships in detail.

Although all of the accounts below are relatively short, this should not be taken as a lack of endorsement for a lovely group of plants.

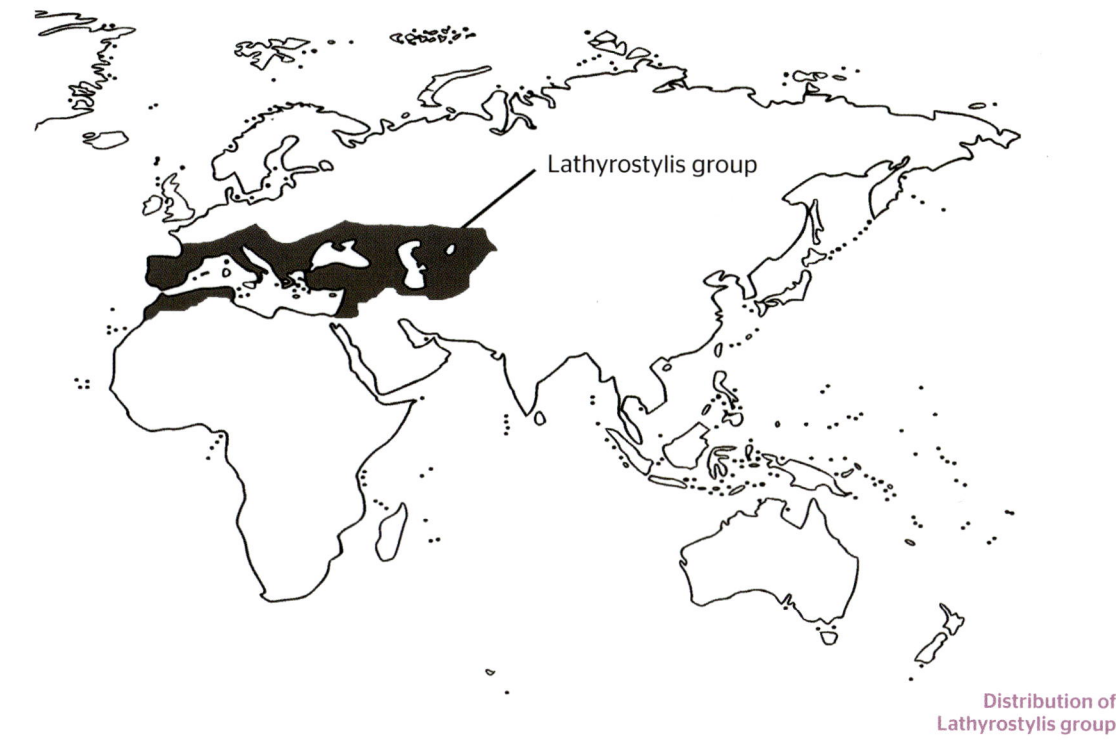

Lathyrostylis group

Distribution of
Lathyrostylis group

Lathyrus armenus

Lathyrus armenus (Boiss. & A. Huet) Čelak.,
Oesterr. Bot. Z. 38: 85 **(1888)**
Syn. *Orobus armenus* Boiss. & A. Huet

Habitat: Meadows, open areas, woodland margins
Distribution: Turkey (central Anatolia through to
neighbouring regions in the Caucasus)

A patch-forming perennial, this tends not to run.
It is akin to the more widespread *L. cyaneus*, but
the peduncles are relatively short and stout, usually
shorter than the leaflets. The flowers are small to
medium-sized with violet petals.
Specific epithet origin: from Armenia.

Lathyrus bauhinii

Lathyrus bauhinii P.A. Genty, *Bull. Soc. Dauphin. Échange Pl. ser. 2, 3: 90* **(1892)**
Syns. *L. filiformis* subsp. *ensifolius* (Lapeyr.) Gams, *Orobus ensifolius* Lapeyr.

Habitat: Alpine meadows; 1,000–2,000m
Distribution: Throughout southern and central European mountains – Pyrenees, Alps and Jura

A slender species with narrow, digitate leaflets 50–80mm long. Flowers are borne on long peduncles (twice as long as the leaflets), medium-sized (standard 18–24mm across), and have petals from lilac to blue. Specific epithet origin: named for Swiss botanist Gaspard Bauhin (1560–1624).

Lathyrus boissieri

Lathyrus boissieri Širj., *Izv. Bulg. Bot. Druzh. 6: 62* **(1934)**

Habitat: Oak woodlands, stream margins, on calcareous soils
Distribution: Eastern Turkey and western Iran

This is an interesting member of this section as it is highly reminiscent of some members of section *Lathyrus*. It often has only a single pair of leaflets per leaf, and the style is relatively narrow throughout whereas most members of this group have spathulate styles that broaden towards the tips. The corolla is relatively small (c. 15mm wide) and pink or purple. It may be relatively close to members of section *Lathyrus* such as *L. mulkak* or *L. cirrhosus*, or to *L. cilicicus* in section *Lathyrostylis*.
Specific epithet origin: named for Swiss botanist and explorer Pierre Edmond Boissier (1810–1885).

Lathyrus brachypterus

Lathyrus brachypterus Čelak., *Oesterr. Bot. Z.* 38: 47 **(1888)**

Syn. *Orobus speciosus* Hausskn. ex Širj.

Habitat: Pastures and rocky slopes; 1,500-2,500m
Distribution: Turkey

An attractive little plant, this has 2–3 pairs of leaflets per leaf and the 4–7 flowers per raceme are relatively large, 20–25mm across, with pale sulphur-yellow corollas.

A variety, *L. brachypterus* var. *hausknechtii*, is recognised on the basis of its shorter leaf rachis giving a more digitate appearance to the leaf.
Specific epithet origin: broadly-winged, possibly referring to the leaflets that look like spreading wings.

Lathyrus cilicicus

Lathyrus cilicicus Hayek & Siehe, *Ann. Nat. Hofmus. Wien* 28: 164 **(1914)**

Habitat: Scrubland, open areas, rocky ground, disturbed ground, field margins; 500-1,500m
Distribution: Turkey (Asia Minor)

A particularly tall and elegant member of the section, *L. cilicicus* is an erect plant to 60cm or more in height. It has long, slender leaflets to 20cm long and tall racemes bearing 8–12 very large flowers with purple corollas. In overall appearance it is reminiscent of some members of section *Lathyrus* such as *L. mulkak* and *L. cirrhosus*, or to other members of section *Lathyrostylis* such as *L. boissieri*. However, the very narrow leaflets distinguish it readily from all of these.
Specific epithet origin: from Cilicia

Lathyrus cyaneus

Lathyrus cyaneus (Steven) K. Koch, *Linnaea* 15(6): 723 (1842)
Synonym: *Orobus cyaneus* Steven

Habitat: Woodland, scrub, rocky areas; 500–2,500m
Distribution: Throughout much of eastern Europe, the Black Sea region and eastern Mediterranean

A widespread species, *L. cyaneus* has thickened, running rhizomes and is quite variable. It is relatively small for a member of section *Lathyrostylis*, reaching a maximum of 50cm in height. The leaves are digitate or pinnate, with pinnate individuals sometimes separated as *L. cyaneus* subsp. *pinnatus*. The flowers are fairly small (15–20mm wide), and the typical variety, var. *cyaneus*, has a linear, non-spathulate style, which is relatively uncommon in this section, although var. *pinnatus* has a more typical broader style than var. *cyaneus*.
Specific epithet origin: cyan blue, referring to the corolla colour.

Lathyrus digitatus

Lathyrus digitatus (M. Bieb.) Fiori, *Fl. Italia* 2: 105 (1900)
Syns *L. cyaneus* subsp. *digitatus* (M. Bieb.) Ponert, *Orobus digitatus* M. Bieb., *Orobus sessilifolius* Sibt.

Habitat: Pine and other open woodland; 200–2,300m
Distribution: South-central Europe, from Italy through to western Asia

This species is a typical small member of section *Lathyrostylis*, being erect, with no tendril and 2–6 narrow leaflets held stiffly upright from a short rachis, giving a digitate effect. The flowers are small to medium, 15–20mm across the standard and violet to blue in colour. It is close to *L. cyaneus*.

Specific epithet origin: with fingers, referring to the apparent arrangement of the leaflets on the short rachis, making the blade appear almost compound-palmate

Lathyrus filiformis

Lathyrus filiformis (Lam.) J. Gay, *Ann. Sci. Nat., Bot. sér. 4*, 8: 315 (1857)
Syns. *L. canescens* (L. fil.) Gren. & Godron, *Orobus filiformis* Lam.

Habitat: Rocky areas and alpine meadows, preferring calcareous or silicaceous soils; 500-2,000m
Distribution: Southern Europe (Iberian Peninsula, France, Italy), Algeria, Morocco

A creeping, rhizomatous species, this reaches 50cm in height, bearing leaves with 1 to 3 pairs of slender leaflets that are 25–70mm long and 2–6mm wide. Its racemes of 3–9 lilac to purple-blue flowers are borne on long peduncles. Similar to *L. digitatus* and allied species, its closest molecular relationship is to *L. pallescens* and it may represent a more westerly element of that species. Specific epithet origin: thread-like form, referring to the leaflets.

Lathyrus karsianus

Lathyrus karsianus P.H. Davis, *Notes Roy. Bot. Gard. Edinburgh* 24: 19 (1962)

Habitat: Open rocky areas, often near streams; 1,350–2,500m
Distribution: Endemic to Turkey (eastern area around Kars)

A medium-sized member of the section, this arises from a woody rhizome that is slightly thickened, and tends not to run. The leaves have 2 to 3 pairs of fairly short, narrowly elliptic leaflets to 6cm long, and subtend racemes with a dense head of 5–10 medium-sized, lilac-blue flowers.

Specific epithet origin: from the town of Kars, the type locality.

Lathyrus nivalis

Lathyrus nivalis Hand.-Mazz., *Ann. Nat. Hofmus. Wien* 27: 80 (1912)

Habitat: Rocky alpine meadows, and open oak woodlands; 2,400–3,200m
Distribution: Eastern Turkey and Azerbaijan

A small, high-altitude species, this much-branched plant emerges from a woody rhizome. It has short leaflets to 4cm long, and 2–4 medium-sized flowers that may be lilac, mauve, or violet, often with paler wings and keel. The fruits are short and broadly oblong with a slight upcurve.

   In contrast to the glabrous subsp. *nivalis*, specimens from Azerbaijan have a dense, appressed pubescence and are sometimes treated as *L. nivalis* subsp. *atropatanus*. Plants with smaller, darker flowers from the central Taurus mountains are referred to *L. nivalis* subsp. *sahinii*.

Specific epithet origin: snowy, referring to the habitat.

Lathyrus pallescens

Lathyrus pallescens (M. Bieb.) K. Koch, *Linnaea* 15(6): 723 (1842)
Syns. *L. angustifolius* (L.) D. Litw., *Orobus angustifolius* L., *O. pallescens* M. Bieb.

Habitat: Upland grassland and rocky areas; 1,600–2,400m
Distribution: Southeastern Europe, Anatolian Turkey and the Caucasus mountains

A slender, upright species to 40cm high, this has leaves with 2–4 pairs of leaflets and its 3–8 flowers are borne on long racemes. The corollas are sulphur-yellow to cream-coloured, often with a flush of pink. It is highly reminiscent of *L. pannonicus*, a species that was long considered a member of section *Lathyrostylis* but is now placed in section *Orobus* and DNA evidence (Kenicer *et al.* 2005) confirms they are distinct. *Lathyrus pallescens* can be distinguished from *L. pannonicus* by its broadly flaring style and longer calyx teeth that are all roughly equal in length. The DNA evidence actually suggests a close relationship to the much more westerly *L. filiformis*. Specific epithet origin: pale, referring to the corolla colour.

Lathyrus pancicii

Lathyrus pancicii (Jurišić) Adamović, *Prosv. Glasn.* 22(9): 1246(–1247) (1901)
Syn. *Orobus pancicii* Jurišić

Habitat: Upland grassland, woodland margins
Distribution: Northern Balkan region (Serbia, Republic of North Macedonia and Bulgaria)

A very distinctive species, this has upright stems to 70cm tall. The leaves, which appear quite uniform, are 2–6cm long, tipped with a short arista, and are densely and evenly spaced up the stem. They bear 3–5 pairs of leaflets that are 2–6cm long and 0.3–0.5cm wide. The racemes are very dense, containing 6–12 medium-sized, pale yellow flowers.

DNA relationships have not yet been established for this species, but the petal colour and venation in the leaflets (3 distinct parallel veins) hint that it may be allied to *L. pannonicus*, which would place it outside section *Lathyrostylis* and in section *Orobus*.
Specific epithet origin: named for Serbian botanist J osif Pančić (1814–1888).

Lathyrus satdaghensis

Lathyrus satdaghensis P.H. Davis, *Notes Roy. Bot. Gard. Edinburgh* 29: 317 **(1969)**

Habitat: Rocky areas; 1,900–2,200m
Distribution: South-eastern Turkey, possibly endemic

A tall, robust species reaching 70cm in height, this has rounded stems that are slightly angled on two sides and is finely pubescent throughout. The leaves have 3–6 pairs of leaflets and the racemes are dense, with 4–8 medium-sized flowers that are up to 2cm wide across the standard.
Specific epithet origin: from Sat Dagh mountain in south-eastern Turkey.

Lathyrus spathulatus

Lathyrus spathulatus Čelak., *Oesterr. Bot. Z.* 38: 6 **(1888)**

Habitat: Open woodland, scrub, rocky areas; 300–1,700m
Distribution: Turkey and further south in the eastern Mediterranean

A small- to medium-sized member of the section, this species reaches 40cm in height. The upper leaves have two pairs of very close leaflets that are slender and up to 10cm long, making them appear digitate. The 4–7 lilac to deeper purple flowers have long pedicels and are spaced across a long raceme. The standard petals are tall and broad, to 2.4cm across.

Lathyrus spathulatus subsp. *elongatus* (Bornm.) Ponert always has a single pair of leaflets per leaf, relatively longer leaflets (to 14cm), and larger, more floriferous racemes (up to 20 flowers rather than up to 7 in subsp. *spathulatus*). *Lathyrus variabilis* is undoubtedly close to *L. spathulatus*, and Davis (1970) speculated that the two may hybridise. The recently described *L. tefennicus* from Turkey may be conspecific, but requires further investigation and molecular data. Specific epithet origin: spathulate, referring to the style.

Lathyrus sphaericus

Lathyrus sphaericus Retz., *Observ. Bot.* 3: 39 **(1783)**
Syn. *L. angulatus* subsp. *sphaericus* (Retz.) Mateo & Figuerola

Habitat: Open areas as a ruderal, open woodland
Distribution: Widespread through much of southern Europe and Asia Minor

A small annual to 30cm in height, this has a single pair of leaflets that are 40–120mm long and usually very slender, about 3mm wide. The flowers are solitary, small, to 15mm across, and nearly sessile. The petals are brick red to crimson, so it may be mistaken for *L. cicera*, but the latter is larger and has longer pedicels, tendrils and inflated fruits.

Lathyrus sphaericus is the sole known annual member of the Lathyrostylis group. Until DNA evidence (Schaefer *et al.* 2012) placed it here, it was considered a part of section *Linearicarpus*. As with the wider genus, and indeed tribe *Fabeae*, it sits on an early-diverging lineage, implying the Lathyrostylis group began as annuals before evolving perenniality.
Specific epithet origin: spherical, referring to the seeds.

Lathyrus tukhtensis

Lathyrus tukhtensis Czeczott, *Acta Soc. Bot. Polon.* **9: 36 (1932)**

Habitat: Open pine and oak forest and scrub, grasslands, limestone areas; 700-2,500m
Distribution: Western Turkey, possibly endemic

This small member of the group stands around 30cm tall. The individual stems are unwinged and run for up to 40cm underground from a thickened, tuberous rhizome. The petioles are very short, giving a digitate appearance to the glaucous, grey leaves. Indeed, Davis (1970) suggests it is most similar to L. *digitatus*. The flowers are typically magenta to lavender-blue or true blue.
Specific epithet origin: from the village of Tukht, the type locality in the central Black Sea region of Turkey.

Lathyrus variabilis

Lathyrus variabilis (Boiss. & Kotschy) Čelak., *Oesterr. Bot. Z. 38: 46 (1888)*
Syn. Orobus variabilis Boiss. & Kotschy

Habitat: Open forest, oak scrub, rocky slopes; 1,000-1,700m
Distribution: Southeastern Turkey to Lebanon

A glabrous perennial with running rhizomes, the aerial stems of this species reach 40cm high. The elliptic leaflets are relatively short and broad for the group, and are usually in two pairs, very closely arranged on a sessile leaf, so it appears digitate. The 4–7 flowers, borne on long, loose racemes, are medium-sized with lilac to purple petals. Davis (1970) suggests it may hybridise with L. *spathulatus*, which has more slender leaflets.
Specific epithet origin: variable, referring to the leaflet shape.

Linearicarpus group

Includes some members of section *Linearicarpus* Kupicha, *Notes Roy. Bot. Gard. Edinburgh* 41(2): 238 (1983)
Number of species: 6

This group consists of small, annual, upright species from western Eurasia, particularly from around the Mediterranean, with one species from subtropical and tropical Africa. Most are well-adapted to dry climates as annuals, so they are frequently ruderal with short, fast, weedy lifestyles. Consequently, they invest relatively little in size and flowers. The flowers are usually fairly small, borne on a short peduncle and solitary, but begin low down the plant, on early nodes. Some of the species have an arista on the tip of the peduncle, appearing as a bristle that extends beyond the flower. This was thought to be a useful character for the group by Kupicha (1983). However, *L. angulatus*, which is more closely allied to section *Lathyrus*, shares this trait, while *L. tauricola* and *L. woronowii* do not. Only the upper leaves have tendrils in some species, and these are almost exclusively simple and unbranched. On the whole, members of the group have little horticultural merit, but are fascinating from an evolutionary perspective.

Kupicha (1983) recognised seven species in section *Linearicarpus*. However, recent studies (Kenicer *et al.* 2005, Schaefer *et al.* 2012) show that *L. angulatus* and *L. sphaericus*, both once members of the section according to Kupicha (1983), are actually members of section *Lathyrus* and section *Lathyrostylis* respectively. Kupicha (1983) did not consider *L. brachyodus* in her treatment, but we have included it here. *Lathyrus hygrophilus* and *L. inconspicuus* form a grouping within the section, but the true relationships of the remaining four species are not known. Several authors (Davis 1970, Czefranova 1971) have treated members of this group as section *Orobastrum*. The exact number of species that may eventually be assigned to the section is uncertain, as not all likely members have had their DNA studied. Ultimately, the position of all these species will need to be revised.

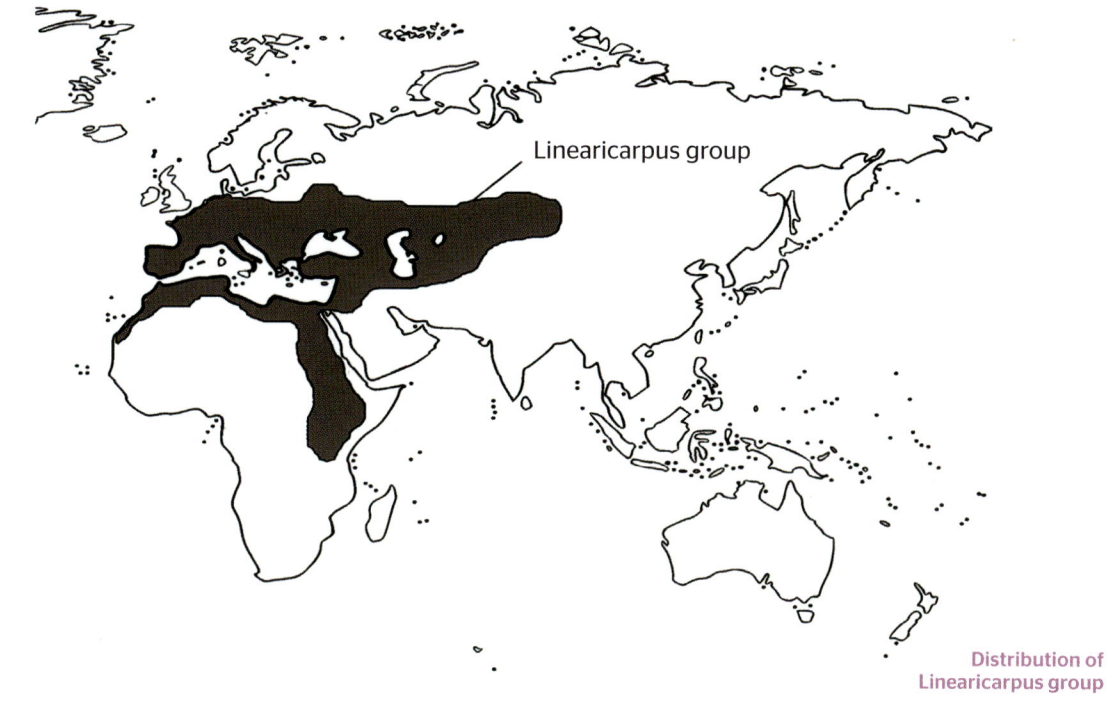

Linearicarpus group

Lathyrus brachyodus

Lathyrus brachyodus Murb. & Murb., *Contrib. Fl.
Nord-Ouest Afr.* ser 2: 44 (1905) [amended from
L. brachyodon Murb., *Acta Univ. Lund.* 33(12): 77
(1897)]

Habitat: Disturbed, open habitats, as a ruderal
Distribution: Tunisia

Endemic to Tunisia and poorly known, this species is
distinguished by its very short, blunt calyx lobes and
oblanceolate leaflets. It is believed to be closely allied
to *L. angulatus* or *L. sphaericus*. This may mean it is
best placed in sections *Lathyrus* or *Lathyrostylis*,
but it has been traditionally placed here in section
Linearicarpus. The rough seeds and slightly contorted
style would suggest section *Lathyrus*, but more
convincing evidence from DNA is required.
Specific epithet origin: broad-toothed, referring to
the calyx lobes.

Lathyrus hygrophilus

Lathyrus hygrophilus Taub., *Pflanzenw. Ost-Afrikas C*: 219 (1895)

Syn. *L. kilimandscharicus* Taub.

Habitat: Disturbed areas in moist soils
Distribution: Tropical Africa (Democratic Republic of Congo, Ethiopia, Kenya, Malawi, Sudan and Uganda)

This small annual with a single pair of elliptic leaflets to 25mm long has a simple tendril on each leaf. The flowers are solitary on short peduncles to about 5cm long and the fruits are relatively large, oblong pods to 8cm long. DNA evidence (Schaefer *et al.* 2012) shows a close relationship to *L. inconspicuus*, but morphologically it is reminiscent of two New World species, *L. crassipes* and *L. pusillus* from section *Notolathyrus*. It is perhaps too tempting to see this similarity as reflecting a once common ancestor, but further DNA evidence is required.
Specific epithet origin: moisture-loving

Lathyrus inconspicuus

Lathyrus inconspicuus L., *Sp. Pl.* 2: 730 (1753)
Syn. *L. erectus* Lag.

Habitat: Disturbed, open ground; sea level to 1,800m
Distribution: Eastern Mediterranean and western Asia

This small annual to 40cm in height has many branches and paired leaflets without tendrils. The flowers start low down by node four, are borne on short petioles of less than 1cm, and are small (standard to 1cm across) and pale blue to lavender, sometimes with white wings and keel. The erect pods are strangely reminiscent of those of *L. crassipes* from South America, suggesting either a genuine relationship or convergence driven by their shared ruderal niche.
Specific epithet origin: inconspicuous, referring to its small and unassuming habit.

Lathyrus tauricola

Lathyrus tauricola P.H. Davis, *Notes Roy. Bot. Gard. Edinburgh* 29: 318 (1969)

Habitat: Open conifer forest
Distribution: Turkey (Anatolia)

This little-known species is a small plant, without an apparent arista on the peduncle, and the flowers are pale violet to lilac.

It may eventually be placed in section *Lathyrus* as it is akin to *L. angulatus*, and perhaps even *L. amphicarpos* as the fruits are believed to be amphicarpic, with some forming above ground and some below ground.
Specific epithet origin: from the Taurus mountains.

Lathyrus vinealis

Lathyrus vinealis Boiss. & Noë, *Diagn. Pl. Orient.* scr. 2, 2: 42 (1856)

Habitat: Heavy or stony soils in vineyards, open grassland and disturbed areas
Distribution: Turkey to Armenia, Iran and Iraq

One of the larger members of section *Linearicarpus*, this species looks like it belongs in section *Lathyrus* and would move there if DNA evidence supports the morphological similarities. Reaching 40cm in height, the stems are lightly angled. The leaves have one or two pairs of linear leaflets that are 50–90 × 5mm and are tipped with a simple tendril in upper parts of the plant. The brick-red flowers are solitary and borne on a peduncle about 5cm long which is tipped with a distinctive arista that is 1–3cm long.
Specific epithet origin: relating to vineyards, referring to the habitat from which it was originally described.

Lathyrus woronowii

Lathyrus woronowii Bornm., *Věstn. Tiflissk. Bot. Sada* 26: 2 (1912)
Syns. *L. furtivus* Woronow, *Ervum woronowii* (Bornm.) Stank.

Habitat: Schist scree
Distribution: Endemic to the eastern Pontic region of Turkey

A poorly-known species, this is said to be related to *L. vinealis*, but it has two or three pairs of shorter, broader, elliptic leaflets to 15 × 7mm. The flowers are pale yellow, with long wings and keel, and a strongly reflexed standard. It appears to lack the characteristic arista on the peduncle of the flowerhead seen in some other members of section *Linearicarpus*.

Specific epithet origin: named for Russian botanist Jurij Woronow (1874–1931).

Notolathyrus group

Includes all members of section *Notolathyrus* Kupicha, *Notes Roy. Bot. Gard. Edinburgh* 41(2): 240 (1983)
Number of species: 25

This group corresponds to Kupicha's (1983) section *Notolathyrus*, a diverse collection of species from a wide range of habitats across temperate, subtropical and upland tropical South America. A single species, *L. pusillus*, is found only in the southeastern states of the USA. Almost all have a single pair of leaflets, sagittate stipules are common, and the majority are perennial. Around a third of the species dry to grey, or partially or wholly black, and these species are all thought to be closely allied. Of the non-black-drying species, several, including *L. acutifolius*, *L. linearifolius*, *L. macropus*, *L. nitens*, *L. pubescens*, *L. subulatus* and *L. tomentosus* are densely pubescent and have a stigma with two distinct flaps, so may readily represent another natural grouping. Although relationships among these suggested species groups are not yet clear, current DNA evidence (Kenicer *et al.* 2005, Schaefer *et al.* 2012) does show the *Notolathyrus* group to be monophyletic, suggesting a single long-distance colonisation event from western Eurasia or Africa.

This group contains many potentially gardenworthy species. However, substrates in temperate South America, particularly Chile, can be challenging to replicate for smaller herbaceous species in phosphorus- and potassium-rich northern hemisphere soils. A curious side-effect of this is that some of these perennials thrive wonderfully in their first year or two, flowering profusely, but then exhaust themselves and die.

Notolathyrus
group

Lathyrus acutifolius

Lathyrus acutifolius Vogel, *Linnaea* 13: 27 **(1839)**

Habitat: Open grassland, but very susceptible to grazing
Distribution: Southern Brazil and Uruguay

This attractive perennial grassland species reaches 70cm
tall and has pubescent, unwinged stems. The narrowly
elliptic leaflets to 8cm long are subtended by
semisagittate stipules with a basal spur and the 8–14,
pale purple flowers are borne in racemes.

This species can be confused with *L. nitens*, which
does not have winged stems, has simple stipules without
a basal spur, and has rounded, rather than acute, apices
to the leaflets. Many specimens labelled *L. nitens* in
herbaria are actually *L. acutifolius*.
Specific epithet origin: pointed leaves, referring to the
slender leaflets.

Lathyrus berteroanus

Lathyrus berteroanus Colla, *Mem. Reale Accad. Sci. Torino* 37: 61 (1834)
Syns. *L. debilis* var. *berteroanus* (Colla ex Savi) Reiche, *L. gracilis* Phil.

Habitat: Lomas (areas of fog-watered vegetation in coastal deserts of western South America)
Distribution: Chile (around Valparaiso and northwards)

One of the few annual, or sometimes biennial, species in the group, this has stems to a height of 40cm and it does not blacken on drying. The leaflets are lanceolate to narrowly elliptic and to 5cm, or rarely 7.5cm long, with semisagittate stipules. The pale lilac flowers are fairly small, around 15mm long, and 13mm across the standard which is often darker with red venation. They have equal calyx teeth and two are borne on each peduncle. Specific epithet origin: named for Italian botanist Carlo Giuseppe Bertero (1789–1831).

Lathyrus cabrerianus

Lathyrus cabrerianus Burkart, *Darwiniana* 6: 14 (1942)
Syns. *L. dumetorum* Burkart, *L. pubescens* Clos. Cabrera's pea

Lifecycle: Perennial
Habit: Climbing
Height: 300cm, rarely to 500cm
Hair: Present
Stem wings: Absent
Stipules: Semi-sagittate, ovate, upper part 7-15mm long,
Leaflet number: 1 pair
Leaflet length: 45-75mm
Leaflet width: 10-30mm
Leaflet shape: Lanceolate to narrow-ovate
Tendril: Present, branched and robust
Flowers per raceme: 6-15
Peduncle or pedicel length: 7-20cm

Calyx teeth: Unequal, shorter than the tube

Standard width: 15-18mm

Petal colour: Creamy white maturing to pale primrose yellow

Style: Not contorted

Fruit size: 60-70mm

Fruit shape: Linear-oblong

Fruit features: Densely hairy

Number of seeds: 7-11

Wild flowering period: October–December

Habitat: Open *Nothofagus* and other broadleaved woodland and forest margins, roadsides; 50-900m

Distribution: Northern areas of the temperate rainforest zone in Argentina (Neuquen, Río Negro) and Chile (Bío-Bío, Araucanía, Los Lagos)

This attractive species is one of the few, apart from *L. odoratus*, with any scent, although it is faint. The pale yellow flowers are robust and particularly attractive, borne in dense, umbel-like racemes. It is densely pubescent and does not dry black

The type specimens of *L. pubescens* appear to be morphologically very similar to *L. cabrerianus* – indeed, they are closer to it than the plants typically recognised as *L. pubescens*. Furthermore, these types are from Chile, where the blue-flowered plant currently known as *L. pubescens* is not thought to grow. All these *L. pubescens* specimens are from the early 1800s, and lack colour in the flowers, or any notes as to their original colour. All this means that a change of name may be required, with the yellow-flowered Chilean species becoming *L. pubescens* and the blue-flowered plant currently known as *L. pubescens* requiring an alternative name.

Lathyrus cabrerianus is a large plant in the wild and climbs vigorously on robust tendrils, so would make an attractive climber in cultivation. However, it has proven very challenging to cultivate in European soils, even in climates that are similar to its native range.

Specific epithet origin: named for Argentinian botanist Ángel Lulio Cabrera (1908–1999).

Lathyrus campestris

Lathyrus campestris Phil., *Linnaea* 28(5): 626 (1857) Syns. *L. debilis* var. *campestris* (Phil.) Reiche, *L. gracillimus* Reiche

Habitat: Coastal mist forests
Distribution: Central Chile (Valparaiso and southwards)

A small annual species to 20cm in height, this is densely tomentose. The leaflets are narrowly lanceolate, reaching 2cm long, on leaves tipped with an arista or feeble tendril, and subtended by semisagittate stipules. The blue-purple flowers are solitary, with equal calyx teeth.

This species is like a small *L. berteroanus*, but can be distinguished by its pubescent ovary. It is poorly known, so may be extinct, threatened, or merely overlooked. Specific epithet origin: of fields or open plains.

Lathyrus crassipes

Lathyrus crassipes Gillies, *Bot. Misc.* 3(8): 198 (1833) Syns. *L. arvensis* Philippi, *L. cicera* var. *patagonica* Speg., *L. dicirrhus* Clos, *L. guaraniticus* Hassler, *L. montevidensis* Vogel

Habitat: Roadsides, disturbed areas, grassland
Distribution: Argentina, Brazil, Paraguay, Uruguay, Bolivia, Peru, Ecuador, including the Galápagos Islands

A widespread species, this is medium-sized and usually annual. The leaves have a feeble tendril, linear to elliptic leaflets and sagittate stipules. The thickened peduncle bears one to three, but usually two, fairly small flowers. These are pale lilac to purple, sometimes with paler or white wings and keel, and have equal calyx teeth.

The inclusion of *L. crassipes* in the morphologically similar *L. pusillus* in Kenicer (2007) does not reflect recent DNA evidence (Schaefer *et al.* 2012), so they are kept separate in this book.
Specific epithet origin: thick-stemmed, referring to the thickened peduncle.

Lathyrus elegans

Lathyrus elegans Vogel, *Linnaea* 13: 30 (1839)

Habitat: Moist, subtropical forests
Distribution: Southern Brazil, north-east Argentina, northern Uruguay

A robust, climbing or sprawling perennial reaching 4m in height, this species resembles a sturdier *L. nervosus*. It has relatively thick, hollow stems, lanceolate leaflets with rounded apices, and racemes of 11–20 medium-sized blue flowers.
Specific epithet origin: elegant.

Lathyrus hasslerianus

Lathyrus hasslerianus Burkart, *Revista Fac. Agron. Veterin.* 8: 100, figs. 16c & 17r (1935)

Habitat: Deep shade beside rivers and streams and in moist *Araucaria angustifolia* forest
Distribution: Argentina (Misiones) and southern Brazil

This glabrous perennial climbs through vegetation to a height of 3m using robust, branching tendrils. The leaflets are ovate to broadly lanceolate and up to 5.5cm long, subtended by broad, semisagittate stipules. The creamy white flowers that age through yellows to orange are up to 17mm long and borne on racemes of 10–17.

A very distinctive species for South America, the numerous yellow flowers are far more reminiscent of species in the Old World Orobus group, or *L. ochroleucus* or *L. sulphureus* from North America.

The red, iron-rich, subtropical soils on which it grows means this species is perhaps unsuited to garden cultivation.
Specific epithet origin: named for Swiss botanist Emil Hassler (1864–1937) who specialised in the plants of Paraguay and neighbouring Argentina.

Lathyrus linearifolius

Lathyrus linearifolius Vogel, *Linnaea* 13: 28 (1839)

Habitat: Grassland
Distribution: Southern Brazil and Uruguay

Perennial with shortly-running rhizomes, this erect species reaches 90cm in height. It is pubescent throughout and distinctive for its long, linear leaflets to 15cm long. The leaves have an arista or occasionally a short, unbranched tendril and are subtended by semisagittate stipules. The small, lilac flowers are borne in racemes of 8–20. This is one of a group of similar species that includes *L. acutifolius* and *L. nitens*. Specific epithet origin: linear-leaved, referring to the long, slender leaflets.

Lathyrus lomanus

Lathyrus lomanus I.M. Johnst., *J. Arnold Arbor.* 19: 250 (1938)

Habitat: Margins of aguadas
Distribution: Northern Chile (Antofagasta)

This medium-sized perennial is known only from the type collection. It was discovered at Aguada de Panul, a watercourse in the southern Atacama desert, and does not seem to have been collected since, in spite of return visits. It was found at the side of the aguada, a permanently wet area in an otherwise extremely arid zone, and may have gone extinct during an extended dry period. It is most reminiscent of *L. cabrerianus*, but shorter and with purple flowers.
Specific epithet origin: unknown.

Lathyrus macropus

Lathyrus macropus Gillies, *Bot. Misc.* 3: 198 **(1833)**
Syn. *L. linearifolius* Griseb.

Habitat: Sunny slopes on gravel and scree; 1,500–3,000m
Distribution: Western Argentina (Sierras de Cordoba and Andes), possibly into neighbouring Chile

An attractive species, this upright or sprawling, medium-sized perennial grows from a thickened rhizome. The arching leaves have grasping tendrils and 3–5 pairs of erect, lanceolate or elliptic leaflets to 10cm long. It is the only species of section *Notolathyrus* with consistently more than one pair of leaflets per leaf. The blue-purple, slightly fragrant flowers are up to 18mm long and held in erect racemes of 7–15, occasionally up to 20. At least one herbarium specimen is notated as having orange flowers. Specific epithet origin: large-footed, referring to the rhizome.

Lathyrus macrostachys

Lathyrus macrostachys Vogel, *Linnaea* 13: 23 **(1839)**

Habitat: Seasonally inundated wet chaco grasslands
Distribution: Northern Argentina, Paraguay, Uruguay

This medium-sized, sprawling perennial dries jet black when picked. The leaves have very robust, much-branched tendrils and usually long, narrowly elliptic, acutely pointed leaflets to 17cm long, all subtended by sagittate, acute stipules. The large, sky blue to deep purple flowers are up to 19mm long with long, slender calyx teeth and borne in inflorescences of up to 17. The fruits are slender and black, held horizontally and upcurved at the tips, with up to 13 seeds.

This is a very attractive plant and is most likely to be confused with *L. magellanicus*, but the acute tips to the stipules, very long lower calyx teeth and wetland habitat are distinctive for this species.
Specific epithet origin: large spike, referring to the racemes.

Lathyrus magellanicus

Lathyrus magellanicus Lam., *Encycl.* [J. Lamarck *et al.*] 2(2): 708 (1788)

Syns. *L. hookeri* G. Don, *L. hookeri* var. *trichocalyx* (Phil.) Burkart, *L. patagonicus* Hauman, *L. pterocaulos* Phil., *L. sessilifolius* Hook & Arn.

Lifecycle: Perennial
Habit: Sprawling or clambering
Height: 10–150cm
Hair: Glabrous, or sparsely hairy in some geographical areas
Stem wings: Present
Stipules: Sagittate, upper part ovate to linear, very variable
Leaflet number: 1 pair, very rarely 2 pairs
Leaflet length: 20–150mm
Leaflet width: 2.5–35mm
Leaflet shape: Rotund to linear-lanceolate
Tendril: Present, simple or branched
Flowers per raceme: 2–12
Peduncle or pedicel length: 3–20cm
Calyx teeth: Unequal, same as or longer than the tube
Standard width: 14–20mm
Petal colour: Pale pink to violet, wings and keel often paler
Style: Not contorted
Fruit size: 35–70mm
Fruit shape: Linear
Fruit features: Glabrous, black
Number of seeds: 9–15
Wild flowering period: November–February
Habitat: A wide range of habitats, from Patagonian steppe to tropical cloud forest margins; sea level to 3,700m
Distribution: Argentina, Bolivia, Chile, Colombia, Ecuador, Peru

One of the most variable species in the genus, this shows an intricate mosaic of diversity of form and habitat preferences across its range. It is undoubtedly adapting to a variety of temperate areas throughout South America. The sagittate stipules and black-drying vegetative parts often used to identify it are not even consistent across the whole species, and are shared by several distinct, but allied, species.

The taxonomy is difficult, and it synonymy is extensive. Various elements have been treated as different species or infraspecific taxa. *Lathyrus magellanicus* var. *glaucescens* is a small, greyish-leaved variety from the Magellanic areas of southern Chile and Argentina, whereas *L. magellanicus* var. *gladiatus* is an

elegant, slender-leaved plant found from Andean north Argentina to Colombia. *Lathyrus magellanicus* f. *albiflorus* has white flowers. Although any of them might have their place in gardens, the largest, and perhaps most generally gardenworthy plants, are from temperate regions of Chile. We do not separate these off as species here, but they have been referred to as *L. hookeri* and *L. sessilifolius*, with particularly robust specimens placed under *L. pterocaulos*. However, all of these entities blend into each other, so they do not readily justify separate status.

The species is often confused with *L. nervosus*, which is invariably more glaucous blue in its foliage, utterly glabrous and does not blacken on drying.

Specific epithet origin: from the Magellanic area at the southern tip of South America.

Lathyrus multiceps

Lathyrus multiceps D. Clos, *Fl. Chil.* [Gay] 2(2): 149 (1847)

Syns. *L. ecirrhosus* Phil., *L. eurypetalus* Phil., *L. pastorei* (Burkart) Rossow, *L. setiger* Phil.

Habitat: Open woodland and sunny forest margins and banks; 1,000–2,000m
Distribution: Temperate Andes of Chile and Argentina

An attractive perennial species, this ranges in habit from a leggy, forest understory herb with running rhizomes to a clump-forming rock plant. Often pubescent, it does not blacken on drying. It has leaves with semisagittate stipules, an arista or simple tendril, and leaflets up to 7cm long that are narrowly lanceolate to elliptic. The medium to large flowers are magenta, lilac or blue, with white wings and keel petals. They are up to 22mm long with a standard 20mm across and borne in racemes of 3–6.

It can be confused with *L. subandinus*, which is densely pubescent with silvery hairs throughout, erect racemes with two or three whorls of relatively small bicoloured deep purple and white flowers, with a standard to 16mm across. There are several morphotypes in *L. multiceps*, but they are poorly separated, with many intermediates. The clump-forming types typically have large, showy flowers with a strongly contrasting violet standard and white wings and keel.

When grown in garden soils in the northern hemisphere the species is short-lived, typically two to four years, but flowers profusely.
Specific epithet origin: many-headed, referring to the several flowers per inflorescence.

Lathyrus nervosus

Lathyrus nervosus Lam., *Encycl.* [J. Lamarck *et al.*] 2(2): 708 (1788)

Lord Anson's pea

Lifecycle: Perennial
Habit: Sprawling or clambering
Height: 50cm, sometimes more
Hair: Glabrous
Stem wings: Absent
Stipules: Sagittate, upper part ovate to lanceolate
Leaflet number: 1 pair
Leaflet length: 20-40mm
Leaflet width: 12-25mm
Leaflet shape: Orbiculate to broadly elliptic
Tendril: Present, branched and often robust
Flowers per raceme: 3-8
Peduncle or pedicel length: 4-12cm
Calyx teeth: Unequal, the lower teeth longer than the tube
Standard width: 6-12mm
Petal colour: Pink to violet, often with white wings and keel if standard is violet
Style: Not contorted
Fruit size: 65-80mm
Fruit shape: Linear
Fruit features: Glabrous, red-brown to dark brown
Number of seeds: 11-15
Wild flowering period: September to March
Habitat: Beaches, steppe, pampas, forest margins in north; sea level to 500m
Distribution: Argentina, Brazil, Chile, Uruguay

This widespread species is relatively uniform throughout much of its range, albeit more spreading and short in the south. Only in the subtropical forests of northern Argentina and Brazil does it become a much taller, more robust, climbing plant, where it merges with the closely related *L. elegans*. The latter is similar, but larger throughout and with more flowers per raceme, as well as having longer, more slender leaflets. It may warrant treatment as a subspecies of *L. nervosus*.

It is a highly attractive, short-lived perennial with glaucous-grey foliage and strikingly coloured flowers. In the UK it seems to prefer a mild, maritime climate with plenty of rain and is easily raised from seed (Teesdale 2006). It is probably the South American species most commonly grown in northern hemisphere gardens, although historical misidentifications sometimes see it sold as *L. magellanicus* or vice-versa.

Specific epithet origin: with comspicuous nerves, referring to the leaflets.

Lathyrus nigrivalvis

Lathyrus nigrivalvis Burkart, *Revista Fac. Agron. Veterin.* 8: 68, figs. 6 & 17b (1935)

Habitat: Wetland margins
Distribution: Northern Argentina and Paraguay, in the watershed of the Parana river

This annual or biennial has slightly winged stems and climbs using simple or few-branched tendrils. It is glabrous and glaucous-grey, but the whole plant darkens a bit on drying, with the fruits and calyces turning black. The leaflets are narrowly ovate to lanceolate and 40–75mm long, while the stipules are sagittate and ovate and up to 20mm long. The small flowers, to 13mm long, are sky blue to mauve, often with a paler wings and keel, and borne in racemes of 1–4 but usually just two. Specific epithet origin: black valves, referring to the fruit.

Lathyrus nitens

Lathyrus nitens Vogel, *Linnaea* 13: 25 (1839)
Syn. *L. ibicuiensis* M.L.A. Abruzzi de Oliveira

Habitat: Rocky grasslands
Distribution: Southern Brazil, and possibly Uruguay

A perennial, pubescent species with wingless stems, this reaches 70cm in height and does not blacken on drying. The leaves have some simple tendrils and leaflets with rounded tips reaching 75mm long, while the small stipules are long-deltoid to 15mm long. The pale purple flowers, to 15mm long, are arranged in whorls of 6–16 on erect racemes. It can be distinguished from *L. acutifolius* by the lack of stem wings, no basal spur on the stipule and rounded leaflet tips.

For many years this species was known only from herbarium specimens of the early 1800s. However, collections in the 1980s and 2010s were described as *L. ibicuiensis*, now recognised as a synonym. It is possibly critically endangered.
Specific epithet origin: shining.

Lathyrus paraguariensis

Lathyrus paraguariensis Hassl., *Repert. Spec. Nov. Regni Veg.* **16: 224 (1919)**

Habitat: Moist subtropical forests and forest margins
Distribution: Argentina, southern Brazil and Paraguay

A robust, glabrous perennial without stem wings, this species climbs to 1m with very strong, branched tendrils. The sessile, narrow leaflets are elliptic-lanceolate, reach 15cm long and are tucked in close to the large, hastate stipules that are 35mm long in the upper lobe. The small flowers, to 12mm long, are pale purple-blue and borne in racemes of 16–30. It appears to have affinities to *L. nervosus* and perhaps *L. magellanicus* and is known from only a few collections.
Specific epithet origin: from Paraguay.

Lathyrus parodii

Lathyrus parodii Burkart, *Revista Fac. Agron. Veterin.* **8: 100 (1935)**

Habitat: Inundated areas and other very wet soils near forest margins
Distribution: Argentina (Buenos Aires province) and Brazil (Paraná).

A perennial species that does not blacken on drying, this has stems with narrow wings and perpendicular lines of hairs that lead to pubescent nodes. The leaves have a branching tendril and narrowly lanceolate leaflets to 11cm long, subtended by sagittate stipules with lanceolate upper lobes to 35mm long. The small purple flowers to 13mm long are borne in racemes of 8–12.

The similar *L. paranensis* is an annual or biennial that has larger flowers, to 21mm long, and which blackens somewhat on drying. It has a white-flowered form, *L. paranensis* f. *albiflorus*.
Specific epithet origin: named for Argentinian botanist, Lorenzo Raimundo Parodi (1895–1966).

Lathyrus pubescens

Lathyrus pubescens Hook. & Arn., *Bot. Beechey Voy.* 21 (1830)

Syns: *L. dumetorum* Phil., *Orobus pubescens* Alef.

Lifecycle: Perennial

Habit: Sprawling or clambering

Height: 1m, or 2m if supported

Hair: Pubescent

Stem wings: Absent

Stipules: Semi-sagittate, ovate, to 25mm long

Leaflet number: 1 pair

Leaflet length: 20–65mm

Leaflet width: 5–20mm

Leaflet shape: Elliptic to lanceolate

Tendril: Present, branched and often robust

Flowers per raceme: 7–15

Peduncle or pedicel length: 3–25cm

Calyx teeth: Unequal, lower 3 teeth much longer than the upper 2

Standard width: 15–20mm

Petal colour: Blue to mauve, often with white wings and keel

Style: Not contorted, stigma with two flaps at tip

Fruit size: 65–80mm

Fruit shape: Linear, bumpy and lomentose

Fruit features: Densely pubescent, olive-brown, to chestnut when maturer

Number of seeds: 6-10

Wild flowering period: August–February

Habitat: Open campo, woodland margins, riversides, upland banks and screes; sea level to 3,200m

Distribution: Argentina, Bolivia, Brazil, Uruguay and possibly Chile

This species is easily distinguished from *L. nervosus* by its different leaves. Plants recognised as *L. pubescens* var. *monticola* from the Andes of Argentina and Bolivia are less branched and more slender-leafleted, and the fruits are held upright. In addition, the upper leaves tend to have three or four leaflets.

The exact identity of Hooker and Arnott's original *L. pubescens* specimens from the early 1800s is uncertain. Several that they mention in later works are apparently from Valparaiso in Chile, and look more like *L. cabrerianus*. If they were from Chile, then they have not been collected since. All recent specimens are from the eastern slopes of the Andes and are less robust than the Chilean specimens. It may be that the labels for these early specimens refer to where they were shipped to Europe from, rather than where they were collected. Specific epithet origin: pubescent.

Lathyrus pusillus

Lathyrus pusillus Elliott, *Sketch Bot. S. Carolina* 2: 223 (1923)

Tiny pea, singletary vetchling

Habitat: Open grassland, roadsides; 50–150m
Distribution: Southeast USA (Alabama, Arkansas, Louisiana, Mississippi, Missouri, Oklahoma, Texas)

An annual species to 50cm in height, this has slightly winged stems in its upper parts and does not blacken on drying. The leaves have a simple, often feeble, tendril and narrow-elliptic leaflets to 65mm long, subtended by stipules that are somewhat falcate and semisagittate, reaching 20mm long. The small, pale lilac to purple flowers to 14mm long often have darker veins and are borne in racemes of two. The seed coat is rough, a feature not seen in South American members of section *Notolathyrus*, but reminiscent of some Eurasian species.

The only member of the Notolathyrus group from outside South America, it most closely resembles *L. crassipes*, and is sometimes treated as a synonym. DNA evidence (Schaefer *et al.* 2012) suggests it may belong to the base of the Notolathyrus group, and be distinct from *L. crassipes*. It is also similar to *L. hygrophyllus* from central Africa in section *Linearicarpus*, which suggests an intriguing, but purely speculative, connection.
Specific epithet origin: small.

Lathyrus subandinus

Lathyrus subandinus Phil., *Linnaea* 33(1): 52 (1864)
Syn. *L. prostratus* Lam.

Habitat: Alpine rocky areas; 1,500–2,500m
Distribution: Andes of central Chile above Santiago, both slightly north and southwards

A densely pubescent perennial, this species creeps and branches underground producing a clump with many aerial stems. The stems can reach a height of 70cm, but usually less, are unwinged and do not blacken on drying. The leaves have usually simple, occasionally branched tendrils, and leaflets up to 50mm long but occasionally longer. The stipules are semisagittate, the upper lobes reaching 20mm and are somewhat falcate. The medium-sized flowers to 14mm long are pleasantly scented and have a purple standard, usually with white wings and a keel, and are borne in racemes of two or three separate whorls.

This attractive species has clear affinities with *L. multiceps* but is found further north in Chile. It can be distinguished by the dense silvery hairs and smaller flowers in two or three separate whorls on the raceme. Specific epithet origin: sub-Andean, referring to the montane areas in which it grows.

Lathyrus subulatus

Lathyrus subulatus Lam., *Encycl.* [J. Lamarck *et al.*] 2(2): 707 (1788)
Syns. *L. debilis* Vogel, *L. missionum* Hassl.

Habitat: Open dry grassland and scrub; 100–2,200m
Distribution: Argentina, Uruguay and possibly southern Brazil

A small, silvery-pubescent, prostrate perennial, this produces several stems from a shortly creeping rhizome and does not blacken on drying. The leaves have an arista or fine, simple tendril (rarely branched) and linear leaflets to 40mm long, occasionally to 65mm. The stipules are small, subulate and to 15mm long. The small, sky-blue to pale mauve flowers to 15mm long are borne in racemes of 2–4. Like *L. pubescens*, *L. tomentosus* and a few other pubescent species, this has two receptive flaps on the stigma tip.
Specific epithet origin: awl-shaped, referring to the stipules.

Lathyrus tomentosus

Lathyrus tomentosus Lam., *Encycl.* [J. Lamarck et al.] 2(2): 709 (1788)
Syn. *L. sericeus* Lam.

Habitat: Dry scrub and rocky Mediterranean-type vegetation; sea level to 300m
Distribution: Northeastern Argentina, southern Brazil, Uruguay

A rhizomatous perennial with a thickened taproot, this has unwinged stems reaching 40cm high. It is densely tomentose, giving a woolly, silvery appearance and does not dry black. The leaves have lanceolate leaflets to 6cm long, a sometimes branched tendril, and medium-sized, semisagittate stipules of which the upper lobe reaches 25mm long. The medium-sized flowers are pale cream or white with strongly contrasting purple veins and are borne 3–8 per raceme. The stigma has two receptive flaps on the tip, as in *L. pubescens*, *L. subulatus* and several other pubescent species.

In the past, more upright specimens with unbranched tendrils were separated off as *L. sericeus*, but this distinction is unwarranted, as there are many intermediates. It is one of several pampas species that have undoubtedly been heavily impacted by grazing over the past two centuries.

This species is unmistakable, with its long tap root, spreading habit, and dense silky hairs which also suggest it is one of the most xerophytic species. In cultivation in colder temperate areas it grows well in a very free-draining, gravelly compost in a terracotta pot under glass, where it can be relied on to flower and set fruit readily. Specific epithet origin: tomentose, referring to its thick, woolly pubescence.

Lathyrus tropicalandinus

Lathyrus tropicalandinus Burkart, *Darwiniana* 6: 16 (1942)

Syn. *L. longipes* var. *peruvianus* J.F. MacBride

Habitat: Upland and cloud forests; 2,800–3,900m
Distribution: Andes of Argentina, Bolivia and Peru

This medium to large perennial species climbs to 2m or more from a thickened, rhizomatous rootstock. Its stems are unwinged, or occasionally very slightly winged, and it does not dry black. The leaves have a slender, simple or branched tendril and lanceolate to elliptic leaflets reaching 65mm, occasionally 73mm, in length, with rounded tips. The stipules, to 30mm long in total, are usually semisagittate with upper lobes lanceolate or long-triangular. The medium to large flowers to 20mm long are deep purple to blue, often with white wings and keel, and with darker tracery of veins. The lower calyx teeth are long, to 8mm, and narrow, and the flowers hang quite loosely from relatively long pedicels, to 5mm, in racemes of 6–15.

Quite variable across its range, and with no clear affinities to other members of section *Notolathyrus*, it is perhaps most like *L. hasslerianus*, a yellow-flowered lowland species.

Specific epithet origin: from the tropical Andes.

Orobus group

Includes members of section *Orobus* (L.) Baker, *Flora of British India*: 180 (1879)
Number of species: 51

Eurasia: 24
North America: 25
Circumboreal: 2 (*L. japonicus* and *L. palustris*)

The Orobus group represents the largest and most widespread section in the genus. The current DNA evidence (Schaefer *et al.* 2012) suggests it is a true group, appearing monophyletic on phylogenetic trees. All of the species in this group are perennial, which could represent an 'escape' from the annual habit more typical of Mediterranean species. This may have been a factor in their success at colonising much of the temperate northern hemisphere. Indeed, they are found throughout Eurasia and, with the exception of *L. pusillus* (in the Notolathyrus group), all native North American species belong to section *Orobus*.

Most species in this group have multiple pairs of leaflets per leaf and some lack tendrils. This was the combination of characters most commonly used to define the old genus *Orobus*, which also included several species that are now in *Vicia*. The current definition of the group, as defined by Kupicha (1983), covers a broad range of morphological diversity and is seemingly stable and monophyletic. This circumscription is supported by DNA evidence (Kenicer *et al.* 2005, Schaefer *et al.* 2012). The North American species alone range from scrambling climbers of woodland margins in the wet Pacific northwest to xerophytes from near Death Valley, and foreshore dune species as well as the sole bird-pollinated species in the genus, *L. splendens*. Fortunately there are distinct subgroups in here as well.

In the accounts below we have split the species into an Old World (Eurasia) subgroup and a New World (North America) subgroup. Within the Old World subgroup we have divided the species into a Vernus clade, a Luteus clade and a Eurasian grade, which are explained in more detail in the next section.

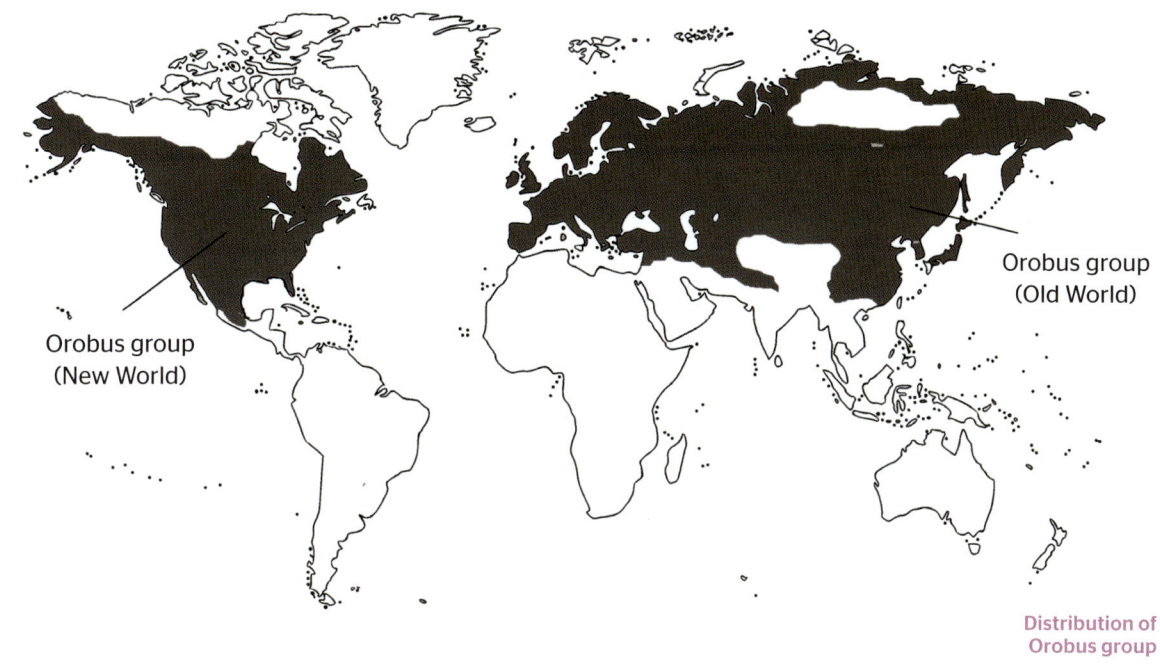

Distribution of
Orobus group

Old World subgroup

The members of the Old World subgroup of the Orobus group are widespread, ranging almost throughout Europe and Asia. However, the classification within the subgroup is somewhat fragmentary. Among the species lacking tendrils, a group of mostly purple-flowered plants with three veins in the leaflets were recognised as series *Verni* by Bässler (1973), while others lacking tendrils, but with cream-to yellow flowers, he recognised as series *Lutei*. Here, we call them the Vernus clade and the Luteus clade, based loosely on the molecular groupings of Schaefer *et al.* (2012). We have retained *L. aureus* in the Luteus clade due to its morphological similarity to other members, although the DNA suggests it is more distant. It should be stressed that these are not formal taxonomic proposals, as further detailed DNA evidence is necessary.

Most, but not all, other members of the Old World subgroup have tendrils and were placed in five smaller series by Bässler, reflecting their varied morphologies. They form a disparate group of species or pairs of species, leading towards the more derived New World subgroup. Such a succession of lineages branching off like this is usually termed a grade, so we call this group the Eurasian grade. Each species in this grade has several unique features and is distinct from the others, so at present, DNA and morphological evidence for organising them into series is lacking. Species represented in this Eurasian grade include several from western Eurasia, such as *L. incurvus* and *L. pisiformis*, the widespread, circumboreal

L. japonicus and *L. palustris*, as well as almost all of the East Asian species such as *L. davidii*, *L. quinqenervius* and *L. vaniotii*. Some of the Chinese species, such as *L. anhuiensis*, *L. caudatus* and *L. dielsianus*, are still poorly understood and need further research to understand their status and relationships.

Vernus clade

This clade includes *L. vernus* (spring vetchling), which is perhaps the most popular species in horticulture after *L. odoratus* (sweet pea) and *L. latifolius* (broad-leaved everlasting pea). Species in the Vernus clade all have several pairs of leaflets per leaf and at most have only a simple tendril, with many lacking tendrils altogether. Most have three distinct major veins running through the leaflet. They are distributed from the Iberian peninsula to the Korean peninsula, typically in mesophytic woodlands and the margins of woodland scrub. DNA evidence (Schaefer *et al.* 2012) suggests *L. linifolius* belongs in this clade, although it was not included in Bässler's (1973) series *Verni*.

Lathyrus alpestris

Lathyrus alpestris (Waldst. & Kit.) Kit. ex Reichb.,
Ic. Fl. Germ. Helv. 22: t. 219 (1886)
Syn. *Orobus alpestris* Waldst. & Kit.

Habitat: Relatively low alpine meadows, woodland margins, rocky spots
Distribution: Montane southern Europe (Italy, Austria, and Slovenia to Bulgaria)

A compact and robust alpine perennial species, this has thickened rhizomes that sometimes run short distances, but without the distinct tubers seen in *L. linifolius*. There are 2–3 pairs of elliptic to lanceolate leaflets per leaf and the flowers range from mauve to purple to blue.

It is similar to the typically northern *L. linifolius*, but distinguished by having rounded tips to the leaflets and a rhizome rather than tubers. DNA evidence (Schaefer *et al.* 2012) certainly suggests a close relationship. A slightly more eastern subspecies from Bulgaria, *L. alpestris* subsp. *friedrichsthalii*, has been recognised.
Specific epithet origin: from the Alps.

Lathyrus frolovii

Lathyrus frolovii Fisch. ex Rupr., *Fl. Ingrica*: 290
(1860)
Syn. *L. vernus* var. *frolovii* (Fisch. ex Rupr.) Trautv.

Habitat: Open woodlands, meadows
Distribution: Central Siberia

Similar to *L. komarovii*, this species differs in having
faint wings on the stems, slightly larger flowers, to 25mm
long, and a more westerly distribution, around the Altai
Mountains.
Specific epithet origin: named for botanist Y. Frolov.

Lathyrus komarovii

Lathyrus komarovii Ohwi, *J. Jap. Bot.* 12: 329 (1936)
Syns. *L. alatus* (Maxim.) Komar., *L. vernus* var. *alatus*
Maxim., *Orobus alatus* Maxim., *O. komarovii* (Ohwi)
Stank. & Roskov

Habitat: Open woodlands, grassland
Distribution: Eastern Siberia, Far Eastern Russia,
Mongolia, northern China, North Korea

The easternmost representative of the Vernus clade, this
species is akin to *L. frolovii* and *L. alpestris* in overall
form, with thickened and somewhat running (not
clump-forming) rhizomes giving rise to individual stems.
It lacks stem wings and the flowers are just 20mm long.
Specific epithet origin: named for Russian botanist
Vladimir Leontyevich Komarov (1869–1945).

Lathyrus linifolius

Lathyrus linifolius (Reichard) Bässler, *Feddes Repert.* 82(6): 434 (1971)
Syns. *L. macrorrhizus* Wimm., *L. montanus* Bernh., *Orobus linifolius* Reichard, *O. tuberosus* L.
Bitter vetch, heath pea

Habitat: Acid grassland and heath, woodland margins and among rocks, more typically upland; sea level to 1,500m
Distribution: Throughout much of northern Europe

This is one of the few species with distinctive tubers. The rhizomes are slender and running, but form tubers along their length, manifesting as swellings up to 5cm across. The 2–3 pairs of leaflets can be broad and elliptic, or very narrow and linear. The pink to blue flowers are borne in racemes of 4–6.

This species has many synonyms which can cause confusion. Although they are very different plants, records for this species can sometimes be listed as *L. tuberosus*. In addition, *L. appeninus* is allied to *L. linifolius* but its status needs further investigation.

The tubers are recorded as being eaten in several parts of Europe, but most famously in Gaelic-speaking areas of Scotland, where they were believed to suppress the appetite and enhance energy as well as being used to flavour spirits in a similar way to liquorice. Much research still remains to be done to determine if there is any validity to these claims, or if the plant is dangerous to consume. In any case, it is an interesting little plant for the garden in small-scale plantings such as troughs, and naturalises well in meadows of short grass.
Specific epithet origin: flax-leaved, referring to the narrow leaflets, although many have quite broad leaflets.

Lathyrus vernus

Lathyrus vernus (L.) Bernh., *Syst. Verz.*: 248 (1800)
Syn. *Orobus vernus* L.
Spring vetch, spring vetchling, spring pea

Lifecycle: Perennial
Habit: Erect
Height: 40cm
Hair: Glabrous, or very sparsely hairy
Stem wings: Absent
Stipules: Semi-sagittate, upper part ovate to lanceolate
Leaflet number: 2–5 pairs
Leaflet length: 25–80mm
Leaflet width: 10–30mm, 2mm in some forms
Leaflet shape: Ovate to lanceolate
Tendril: Absent
Flowers per raceme: 3–10
Peduncle or pedicel length: 3–8cm
Calyx teeth: Unequal, the lowest as long as the tube
Standard width: 12–18mm, rarely to 21mm
Petal colour: Pink, lilac to violet, with white or pale pink variants common
Style: Not contorted
Fruit size: 35–70mm
Fruit shape: Linear-oblong
Fruit features: Glabrous
Number of seeds: 7–14
Wild flowering period: April–May
Habitat: Forest clearings and margins, sometimes in rocky areas away from grazing; sea level to 2,000m
Distribution: Throughout much of temperate Eurasia, as far as Siberia

A widespread and variable perennial species, this often forms dense clumps rather than the more scattered tufts or individual stems of other members of the series. Plants in the north of the range are considered typical *L. vernus*, with 2–4 pairs of ovate to lanceolate leaflets. Those in the south of the range, from Romania to southern France, can often have 2–3 pairs of much more slender leaflets, and have been treated as *L. vernus* subsp. *flaccidus*. Flower colour is also variable, and has been exploited in the many cultivated selections, but much of this variation seems to arise repeatedly in isolation rather than having a geographical component. For a thorough overview, Bässler's (1973) account of section *Orobus* in German is useful.

These combinations of leaflet and flower colour traits can readily be maintained in breeding lines, and have found their way into cultivation as a range of cultivars. The two main variables that distinguish cultivars are flower colour and leaflet size. Leaflets may have the typical width of subsp. *vernus* which contains f. *vernus* (leaflets 30–100mm wide) and f. *angustifolius* (15–30mm), while plants with narrow leaflets belong to subsp. *flaccidus* which contains f. *flaccidus* (4–12mm) and f. *gracilis* (1–2mm). Cultivars with a pink standard and white wings and keel are derived from f. *variegatus*.

A clump-forming, fairly compact perennial, it is equally at home in woodland, rock or more formal border settings, and provides welcome colour in mid spring, the flowers often slightly preceding the leaves. Specific epithet origin: of spring, referring to flowering time.

Lathyrus vivantii

Lathyrus vivantii P. Monts., *Bull. Soc. Bot. France, Lett. Bot.* 127(5): 517 (1981)
Syn. *Orobus tournefortii* Lapeyr.

Habitat: Calcareous and other basic soils in moist areas of woodland margins, meadows, on rocks; 1,200–1,800m
Distribution: Pyrenees

A robust but compact species akin to *L. alpestris*, this is distinguished by its ciliate margins to the leaflets and calyx. In *L. alpestris* the calyx is more densely pubescent throughout. These are minor differences, so subspecific status under *L. alpestris* may be warranted. It is separated from *L. linifolius* by being a larger plant, more commonly reaching 50cm in height, having ciliate leaflet margins, and perennating with thickened rhizomes, some of which run, but without the distinctive tubers of *L. linifolius*.

Specific epithet origin: named for the collector of the type specimen, French botanist Jean Vivant (1923–2010).

Luteus clade

This is a slightly artificial grouping, based on the plants being erect, lacking tendrils and having racemes of several to many, orange and yellow flowers. Although they do not form a single clade in DNA analyses (Kenicer *et al.* 2005, Schaefer *et al.* 2012), they are all quite closely related. These flower characteristics are also seen in more distantly related species outside series *Lutei*, such as in *L. davidii* from East Asia, *L. ochroleucus* from North America, and *L. hasslerianus* from South America. However, these other species all have shorter flowers with more waxy petals, with the standard more erect and flaring out to a broader tip. It is likely that this is a convergence to attract similar guilds of pollinators.

Although the clade takes its name from *L. luteus* Baker, a synonym of *L. emodi*, the key species pulled out in the fuller description that follows is *L. aureus*, a relatively common plant in gardens. It is a bit of an outlier, as the rest of the group are much more morphologically uniform and more closely related. The remaining five have potentially complex classifications and nomenclature, as taxonomists have been unable to decide whether they represent subspecies within a very widespread, but disjunct species, or if each of the five entities is a species in its own right. Distinctions among the species are based mainly on overall size of the plant, with larger species in the east, and on the distribution and types of hairs. These entities correspond to groups of plants from Siberia (*L. gmelinii*-type), western Himalaya (*L. emodi*-type), eastern Mediterranean (*L. libani*-type), Romania-Hungary (*L. transsylvanicus*-type), and Alps-Pyrenees (*L. laevigatus*- / *L. ochraceus*-type).

This clade probably represents remnants of a once far greater range for some ancestral species, or multiple colonisations of areas by such a species. All are attractive for gardens, but each will have particular preferences for conditions. Flowering can be sporadic and brief.

Lathyrus aureus

Lathyrus aureus (G. Lodd. ex Drapiez) D. Brândză, *Prodr. Fl. Romane*: 546 (1883)

Syn. *Orobus aureus* G. Lodd. ex Drapiez

Golden-flowered wood pea

Lifecycle: Perennial

Habit: Erect

Height: 80cm

Hair: Present, often sparse, and with glandular hairs

Stem wings: Absent

Stipules: Semisagittate, the upper part lanceolate

Leaflet number: 3-5 pairs

Leaflet length: 40-120mm

Leaflet width: 15-50mm

Leaflet shape: Ovate

Tendril: Absent, an arista

Flowers per raceme: 10-25

Peduncle or pedicel length: 5-15cm

Calyx teeth: Unequal, lower tooth longer than the tube

Standard width: 10-15mm

Petal colour: Golden-orange

Style: Not contorted

Fruit size: 50-70mm

Fruit shape: Linear

Fruit features: Chestnut brown, with sparse glandular hairs

Number of seeds: 6-12

Wild flowering period: May to July

Habitat: Broadleaved forest and more open scrubland; sea level to 2,000m

Distribution: Bulgaria, Romania, Turkey, Ukraine (Crimea), Georgia (Caucasus)

This species forms loose clumps and can spread to cover considerable patches on running rhizomes. It overlaps somewhat in appearance with the members of the core series *Lutei*, all of which share its lack of tendrils and many-flowered racemes with cream, golden and orange petals. However, *L. aureus* is a bit of an outlier genetically. It is a larger, looser plant from woodland habitats, the flowers are smaller than the others in the series and the petals are usually a deeper orange.

It is a highly gardenworthy species, quite hardy and does well in

mixed plantings under shade or in open woodland, ultimately filling some considerable space, but without being invasive. *Lathyrus aureus* is sometimes confused in cultivation with the other five species in this clade. Originally named as *Orobus aureus*, it is often listed in old books and catalogues as *Orobus luteus*, or *Lathyrus luteus* or *L. luteus* subsp. *aureus*.

Specific epithet origin: golden, referring to the flowers.

Lathyrus emodi

Lathyrus emodi (Wall. in Fritsch) Fritsch, *Sitzungsber. Akad. Wiss. Wien* 104: 516 (1895)
Syns. *L. laevigatus* subsp. *emodi* (Wall.) Breistroffer, *L. luteus* Baker, *Orobus emodi* Fritsch
Himalayan golden pea

Habitat: Open, mixed woodland; 1,500–2,500m
Distribution: Southern slopes of the Himalaya in Afghanistan, Pakistan, India, Nepal

Perhaps the most robust species in this clade, this is quite upright and the aerial stems do not spread as much as those of *L. aureus*. It is erect, to 80cm in height, with thick, cylindrical stems and 3–4 pairs of large, lanceolate leaflets to 9cm long, but usually shorter. The flowers are similarly large, to 28mm long with standards 10–14mm across, and are cream to golden, fading to orange.

  Lathyrus emodi is most likely to be closer to *L. gmelinii* than others in the clade, implying a dispersal through the Tajikistan–Afghanistan corridor of the Pamir mountains.

Specific epithet origin: from Emodi Montes, the Greek name for the Himalaya.

Lathyrus gmelinii

Lathyrus gmelinii (Fisch. ex DC) Fritsch, *Sitzungsber. Akad. Wiss. Wien* 104: 516 (1895) Syns. *L. laevigatus* subsp. *gmelinii* (Fisch. ex DC) Hendrych, *L. luteus* var. *gmelinii* (Fisch. ex DC) Rchb., *Orobus gmelinii* Fisch. ex DC, *O. luteus* L.

Habitat: Upland meadows, margins of steppe woodlands
Distribution: The Pamirs of Tajikistan through central Siberia, the Altai and Balkhash regions, and Kyrgyzstan to Xinjiang in China, and records from Afghanistan

The most easterly species of the clade, this is a fairly large plant, to 60 or 70cm high, but compact and not widely branching. The leaves have 3–4 pairs of large, lanceolate leaflets to 90mm long, and the large flowers are 30mm long, although still relatively narrow across the standard. It can be confused with *L. aureus* but is slightly later to flower, a little taller, has longer petioles and flowers, and less obvious veins on the leaflets.

Plants with very slender, narrowly lanceolate leaflets of 70–100 × 6–12mm from the east of the range have been treated variously as *L. gmelinii* var. *angustifolius*, *L. krylovii* or *L. laevigatus* subsp. *krylovii* but their status is currently uncertain.

Specific epithet origin: named for German botanist Johann Georg Gmelin (1709–1755).

Lathyrus laevigatus

Lathyrus laevigatus (Waldst. & Kit.) Gren., *Grenier Fl. Chain Jurass.*: 193 (1865)
Syns. *L. subalpinus* Beck, *Orobus laevigatus* Waldst. & Kit.

Habitat: Alpine meadows, woodland margins
Distribution: Pyrenees and alpine areas of Europe

The most westerly species of the Luteus clade, this is smaller than the steppe and montane species to the east. It reaches 50cm in height, the leaves have 3–4 pairs of lanceolate leaflets, up to 60mm long, and there are about 12 flowers per raceme. It is quite variable across its range, mostly in the distribution of hairs, with specimens from the Pyrenees having been separated off as *L. occidentalis*, although these are perhaps better treated as *L. laevigatus* subsp. *occidentalis*. Indeed, all western and central European plants might best be treated under another name, *L. ochraceus*.

Lathyrus laevigatus is sometimes encountered in cultivation and deserves to be more popular. It is later flowering than *L. gmelinii* which is taller and has longer leaflets and narrower legumes.
Specific epithet origin: smooth, referring to the fruits.

Lathyrus libani

Lathyrus libani Fritsch., *Sitzungsber. Akad. Wiss. Wien* 104: 517 (1895)
Lebanon vetchling

Habitat: Open upland forests, cedar woodland
Distribution: Eastern Mediterranean (south-eastern Turkey, Syria, Lebanon)

This is another of the relatively large-flowered eastern species in the Luteus clade, with flowers to 28mm long.
Specific epithet origin: from Lebanon.

Lathyrus transsylvanicus

Lathyrus transsylvanicus (Spreng.) Rchb. f.,
Sitzungsber. Akad. Wiss. Wien 104: 517 (1895)
Syn. *Orobus transsylvanicus* Spreng.

Habitat: Beech and hornbeam forests
Distribution: Eastern central Europe (Hungary, Romania)

A fairly compact member of the clade, this is
distinguished by its dense pubescence on the calyx,
and many scattered glandular hairs on the stems,
leaflet undersides and calyces. The stems are often
dark purple throughout.
Specific epithet origin: from Transylvania.

Eurasian grade

The remaining Old World members of the Orobus group that are not in the Vernus clade or Luteus clade form a fairly disparate group. DNA evidence (Schaefer *et al.* 2012) currently does not resolve their relationships, although they are evidently close. For simplicity, we treat it as a grade, a term derived from phylogenetic analysis of DNA. It consists of seven eastern species (*L. anhuiensis*, *L. caudatus*, *L. davidii*, *L. dielsianus*, *L. humilis*, *L. quinquenervius*, *L. vaniotii*), five western species (*L. incurvus*, *L. niger*, *L. pannonicus*, *L. pisiformis*, *L. venetus*) and two circumboreal species (*L. japonicus*, *L. palustris*).

Lathyrus anhuiensis

Lathyrus anhuiensis Y.J. Zhu & R.X. Meng, *Acta Phytotax. Sin.* 24(5): 402 (1986)
Syn. *L. henanensis* S.Y. Wang

Habitat: Open woodland
Distribution: China (Anhui, Hupeh)

This species is perhaps a southerly relative of *L. davidii*, but it remains poorly known. It has up to seven pairs of leaflets per leaf, and in some individuals either a simple or absent tendril. Described in 1988, *L. henanensis* differs only in its branching tendrils and a glabrous ovary.
Specific epithet origin: from Anhui province, China.

Lathyrus caudatus

Lathyrus caudatus Wei & H.P. Tsui, *Bull. Bot. Res., Harbin* 4(1): 49 (1984)

Habitat: Open, mixed woodland
Distribution: China (Zhejiang)

Somewhat like *L. davidii*, this differs in being pubescent and having narrower, lanceolate leaflets, narrow stipules and fewer flowers. There is overlap in its morphology with members of the Luteus clade as well. This species is known only from very few collections.
Specific epithet origin: caudate, referring to the leaflets.

Lathyrus davidii

Lathyrus davidii Hance, *J. Bot.* 9: 130 (1871)
Père David's pea

Lifecycle: Perennial
Habit: Erect
Height: 200cm
Hair: Glabrous
Stem wings: Absent
Stipules: Semisagittate, the upper lobe large and ovate
Leaflet number: 3–5 pairs
Leaflet length: 60–150mm
Leaflet width: 30–80mm
Leaflet shape: Ovate
Tendril: Present, robust
Flowers per raceme: 10–40
Peduncle or pedicel length: 5–20cm
Calyx teeth: Equal, very short
Standard width: 12–15mm
Petal colour: Cream, maturing yellow to orange
Style: Not contorted
Fruit size: 80–150mm
Fruit shape: Linear
Fruit features: Glabrous, chestnut brown
Number of seeds: 8–15
Wild flowering period: June–September
Habitat: Forest margins with moist substrate, mid-age *Cryptomeria* plantations;, 350–1,500m
Distribution: East Asia (extreme Russian Far East, China, Korean peninsula, Japan)

One of the tallest and most robust species, this has cane-like primary stems and is as close as *Lathyrus* come to being shrubby. The large leaflets and stipules contribute to photosynthesis in its shady habitats. It is one of several species in unrelated parts of tribe *Fabeae* that have many small, clustered, yellowish flowers.

In the wild and in gardens it appreciates semi-shade and moist soil, and is the last to flower in this grade. The seeds require cold stratification before germination. Specific epithet origin: named for Père Armand David (1826–1900), a French missionary to China.

Lathyrus dielsianus

Lathyrus dielsianus Harms, *Bot. Jahrb. Syst.* 29(3–4): 417 (1900)

Syns. *L. hupehensis* (Pamp.) E. Peter, *L. wilsonii* Craib

Habitat: Mixed woodland
Distribution: China (Hubei, Shaanxi, Shanxi, Sichuan)

A poorly understood species from western China, this purple-flowered plant looks similar to *L. incurvus* and *L. palustris*, although it has small, narrowly-triangular stipules similar to those seen in *L. vaniotii*.
Specific epithet origin: named for German botanist Ludwig Diels (1874–1945).

Lathyrus humilis

Lathyrus humilis (Ser.) Fisch ex Spreng., *Syst. Veg.* 3: 263 (1826)

Syns. *L. altaicus* Ledeb., *L. dominianus* Litv., *Orobus humilis* Ser.

Habitat: Steppes and forest margins
Distribution: Eastern Russia, Mongolia, northern China (Xinjiang) through Kyrgyzstan and the Pamirs (Tajikistan) to Pakistan, Kashmir and India (Himachal Pradesh)

Upright, and reaching 70cm in height, although usually less in the north and east of the range, this has 3–5 pairs of leaflets and an often feeble tendril. The flowers are purple to blue, sometimes with white wings and keel. It might be confused with *L. pisiformis* in some areas, but it is smaller, the stipules are much smaller than the leaflets, and the petals are a more uniform colour (not densely veined). A taxon that has seldom been collected, *L. dominianus*, appears to represent individuals of *L. humilis* with very small leaflets.

Although later, *L. altaicus* (1831) may be the valid name for this species as *L. humilis* is not confidently stated as being a *Lathyrus* by Fischer.
Specific epithet origin: humble, small.

Lathyrus incurvus

Lathyrus incurvus (Roth) Willd., *Sp. Pl.* ed. 4
[Willdenow] 3(2): 1091 (1802)
Syns. *Orobus incurvus* (Roth) A. Braun, *Vicia incurva*
Roth

Habitat: Open grassland, woodland margins; sea level
to 500m
Distribution: Widespread through southern central
Eurasia

This handsome plant has 3–5 pairs of elliptic-lanceolate leaflets with rounded apices and 7–15 flowers per raceme. Related to *L. niger*, *L. palustris* and *L. pisiformis*, it dries dark like *L. niger*. It also has quite large stipules, but these are not as big as the leaflets, like they are in *L. pisiformis*. The flowers are more like those of *L. palustris*, being medium-sized and with corollas that are uniform purple, or purple with white wings and keel, unlike the small, much-veined, red-purple corollas of *L. niger* and *L. pisiformis*. Willdenow's original protologue described it as 'Similis *L. palustri*, des omnibus partibus major', meaning 'resembling *L. palustris*, but with all parts larger'.

Mainly inhabiting the Black Sea and Caucasus regions, there it replaces *L. niger* from eastern Europe and it occurs generally further south than *L. pisiformis*. Specific epithet origin: incurved, referring to the upcurving legume.

Lathyrus japonicus

Lathyrus japonicus Willd., *Sp. Pl.*, ed. 4 [Willdenow] 3(2): 1091
(1802)

Sea pea, beach pea, circumpolar pea

Lifecycle: Perennial
Habit: Sprawling or clambering
Height: 40cm
Hair: Glabrous or pubescent
Stem wings: Absent, or very slight
Stipules: Sagittate, the upper lobe lanceolate to ovate
Leaflet number: 3-5 pairs
Leaflet length: 25-45mm
Leaflet width: 6-20mm
Leaflet shape: Elliptic, lanceolate to ovate
Tendril: Present
Flowers per raceme: 2-6
Peduncle or pedicel length: 3-10cm
Calyx teeth: Subequal, longer than the tube
Standard width: 15-20mm
Petal colour: Pale pink to violet, often with white wings and keel
Style: Not contorted
Fruit size: 40-70mm
Fruit shape: Oblong
Fruit features: Glabrous
Number of seeds: 4-11
Wild flowering period: April –July
Habitat: Sand and pebble beaches on the foreshore; sea level to
100m in some inland areas
Distribution: Circumboreal - throughout coastal areas of the
temperate northern hemisphere, from Greenland to China and as far
south as northern California

This is a very attractive plant indeed, and in terms of distribution
is the most widespread species of the genus. The foliage is green
to glaucous grey, but with green and pink flushes throughout. The
leaves are arching, and although they possess tendrils, the plant
tends to sprawl in its typical beach habitat where there is plenty of
space. Indeed, there are few sights more striking than a beach-front
massed with L. japonicus in flower. Forms with narrow leaflets are
considered to be the type, but the leaflets range from ovate to
linear-lanceolate. Although some plants are glabrous, the degree

and distribution of pubescence has also been a character for distinguishing subspecies or varieties. *Lathyrus japonicus* subsp. *maritimus* (syn. *L. maritimus*) has larger leaflets, to 50mm, and, if pubescent, tends to have slightly more hair than subsp. *japonicus*.

This is the classic sea-drifted plant, which Charles Darwin and his 19th-century contemporaries studied by dunking seeds in salt water and giving them a shake every so often. From these experiments, *L. japonicus* was shown to be highly resilient to sea water and retains viability after more than six weeks. Interestingly, several genetic studies (e.g. Barrington & Schmitz 2013) have shown that the genes of this species are not strongly segregated into geographical groups. This indicates that active long-distance dispersal may be keeping the populations quite mixed throughout the huge range, with dispersal around the Arctic allowing exchange between Atlantic and Pacific populations. There are also populations on Chiloe Island, Chile, and in New Zealand, both of which suggest the intriguing possibility of long-distance dispersal from the northern hemisphere. However, they might just as easily have arrived in the ballast of ships or by other human-mediated dispersals.

The plant can be grown readily in gardens if given the right conditions of an extremely free-draining soil. It is particularly well-suited to coastal gardens or plantings.

Specific epithet origin: from Japan, as Willdenow, who named it while working in Berlin, had received specimens from Japan.

Lathyrus niger

Lathyrus niger (L.) Bernh., *Syst. Verz.* [Bernhardi]: 248 (1800)

Syn. *Orobus niger* L.

Black pea

Lifecycle: Perennial

Habit: Erect

Height: 80cm

Hair: Glabrous, or very sparsely hairy

Stem wings: Absent

Stipules: Semi-sagittate, upper part lanceolate

Leaflet number: 3-5 pairs

Leaflet length: 10-30mm

Leaflet width: 4-13mm

Leaflet shape: Elliptic to ovate

Tendril: Absent

Flowers per raceme: 3-8

Peduncle or pedicel length: 4-10cm

Calyx teeth: Unequal, the lowest shorter than the tube

Standard width: 10-14mm

Petal colour: Pink ageing to blue, often with darker veins

Style: Not contorted

Fruit size: 40-50mm

Fruit shape: Linear

Fruit features: Glabrous, black

Number of seeds: 6-10

Wild flowering period: May–July

Habitat: Open forests and woodland margins; sea level to 1,500m

Distribution: Widespread throughout much of Europe

This is an erect, fairly shade-tolerant species with annual stems arising from a woody, thickened, perennating rhizome. The dense racemes of relatively small flowers are similar to those found in *L. pisiformis* and *L. venetus*, which are closely allied. The flowers are an interesting range of colours, being reddish pink darkening to blue, or muddy cream with strong violet venation and an orange flush at the base, again turning blue as they age.

Although several species of *Lathyrus* dry black to varying degrees, this one is perhaps the most extreme. The stems turn jet black as they senesce and allow easy identification if any aerial parts can be found in suspected locations. Several other members of nearby groups such as *L. linifolius* and *L. incurvus* also dry dark or patchily

black, but *L. niger* does still remain distinct from them in its many, relatively small flowers, and drying completely black throughout. It is on an isolated lineage with no very close sister species.

In gardens this is a reliable species, and although the flowers are not spectacular, it works nicely in woodland or similar shady spots.
Specific epithet origin: black, referring to the colour when dry.

Lathyrus palustris

Lathyrus palustris L., *Sp. Pl.* 2: 733 (1753)
Syns. *L. incurvus* Rchb., *L. linearifolius* Nyman, *L. myrtifolius* Muhl. ex Willd., *L. occidentalis* Nutt. ex Torr. & A. Gray, *L. pilosus* Cham., *Orobus myrtifolius* (Muhl. ex. Willd.) Hall, *O. palustris* (L.) Rchb.
Marsh pea

Habitat: Marshes, bogs, fens, including brackish dune-slack marshes
Distribution: Throughout the cool-temperate northern hemisphere

The species is an upright but climbing perennial with 3–4 pairs of leaflets per leaf, and with simple or branching tendrils. It clings to reeds or other grasses in its marshy habitat. The racemes consist of 3–7 lilac, violet or blue flowers, sometimes with white wings and keel.

Plants with wingless stems and deep red-purple corollas are referred to *L. palustris* subsp. *nudicaulis*, which may warrant distinction at species level. East Asian *L. pilosus* has been distinguished from this species on the basis of greater pubescence. However, there is considerable variability in this character in *L. palustris* as a whole so the former is regarded as a synonym here.
Specific epithet origin: of marshes.

Lathyrus pannonicus

Lathyrus pannonicus (Jacq.) Garcke, *Fl. N. Mitt.-Deutschland* ed. 6: 112 (1863)

Syns. *L. albus* (L. f.) Kitt., *L. ledebourii* Trautv., *Orobus albus* L. f., *O. ledebourii* (Trautv.) Roldugin, *O. pannonicus* Jacq., *O. versicolor* J.F. Gmel.

Pannonian vetchling

Lifecycle: Perennial

Habit: Erect

Height: 50cm

Hair: Glabrous, or very sparse

Stem wings: Absent

Stipules: Semi-sagittate, upper part narrow-lanceolate

Leaflet number: 1-4 pairs

Leaflet length: 15-75mm

Leaflet width: 2-10mm

Leaflet shape: Linear to lanceolate or elliptic

Tendril: Absent

Flowers per raceme: 3-10

Peduncle or pedicel length: 3-7cm

Calyx teeth: Unequal, as long as the calyx

Standard width: 12-18mm

Petal colour: White or pale yellow, often tinged pink

Style: Not contorted

Fruit size: 30-70mm

Fruit shape: Linear-oblong

Fruit features: Glabrous

Number of seeds: 12-20

Wild flowering period: April-July

Habitat: Open grassland, upland meadows, forest margins; 50-2,000m

Distribution: Central and southern Europe (Spain to western Russia)

This is one of the species that produces distinctive underground tubers. In this case they are finger-length and slender, and brown or chestnut-coloured. It was long thought to belong to section *Lathyrostylis*, but recent DNA evidence (Kenicer *et al.* 2005, Schaefer *et al.* 2012) places it firmly in section *Orobus*.

A number of subspecies are recognised. In Spain there is subsp. *longestipulatus* (syn. subsp. *hispanicus*) which has winged stems. From western Europe, subsp. *asphodeloides* is shorter than subsp. *pannonicus* and has broader leaflets that are elliptic-lanceolate rather than linear. From eastern Europe, subsp. *collinus*, along with subsp. *pannonicus* and subsp. *multijugus*, consistently has 5–6 pairs of leaflets, as opposed to 4–5. These subspecies may be better recognised at varietal level, as their geography is not clear cut, as one might like to see for subspecies. Indeed, the whole species needs researching across its range.

This is a highly gardenworthy plant, being upright and with attractive racemes of flowers ranging from white through cream to pale pink, with yellow flushes. Specific epithet origin: of Pannonia, a Roman province south of the middle and upper Danube.

Lathyrus pisiformis

Lathyrus pisiformis L., *Sp. Pl.* 2: 734 (**1753**)

Habitat: Open woodland, woodland margins
Distribution: Throughout much of central Eurasia, from eastern Europe to Xinjiang in China

A large species, this has stems to 1.5m long. The leaves have 3–5 pairs of ovate leaflets and tendrils. Very large stipules are similar in size to the leaflets and give the plant its specific epithet. The flowers are relatively small, with a standard to 16mm across, and have petals that are deep reddish purple, fading to cream and blue. The petals have strong purple veins on them.
Specific epithet origin: pea-shaped, referring to the large stipules reminiscent of *Pisum* (now in *Lathyrus*).

Lathyrus quinquenervius

Lathyrus quinquenervius (Miq.) Litv., *Opred. Rast. Dal'nevost. Kraia* 2: 683 (1932)
Syns. *L. palustris* var. *sericea* Franch., *Vicia quinquenervia* Miq.

Habitat: Marshlands, river margins
Distribution: Eastern Russia, north-eastern China, Korean peninsula, Japan

Reaching 80cm in height, although usually about 50cm, this species is elegant and stiffly upright. The leaves have 3–5 pairs of slender, lanceolate leaflets and tendrils. It is most reminiscent of *L. palustris*, but the stiffer leaflets with five distinct parallel veins are diagnostic. The flower colour is typical for this group, being purple to violet. Specific epithet origin: five-nerved, referring to the leaflet venation.

Lathyrus vaniotii

Lathyrus vaniotii H. Lév., *Repert. Spec. Nov. Regni Veg.* 7: 230 (1909)
Syn. *Vicia venosa* var. *willdenowiana* Miura
Korean mountain vetchling

Habitat: Woodland margins, scrub; 500–1,200m
Distribution: Far eastern Russia, northeast China, Korean peninsula

An attractive little upright species, this reaches 50cm in height. The leaves have 3–4 pairs of broadly lanceolate leaflets, 30–70mm long, with rounded, mucronate tips, dark green above and pale, with distinctive reticulate veins, beneath. The racemes bear 4–8 flowers in various shades of purple, sometimes with white wings and keel. Specific epithet origin: named for French botanist Eugène Vaniot (1845–1913).

Lathyrus venetus

Lathyrus venetus (Mill.) Wohlf. ex Koch, *Syn. Deut. Schweiz. Fl. ed. 3: 714*
Syns. *L. variegatus* (Ten.) Gren. & Godr., *Orobus venetus* Mill.
Venetian vetchling

Habitat: Woodlands, woodland margins
Distribution: Eastern and southern Europe

A robust, upright, clump-forming plant with no tendrils, this has leaves with 3–5 pairs of leaflets. The racemes consist of 8–16 small flowers, similar to those of *L. niger* and *L. pisiformis*, with petals that have deep red or purple venation on a paler reddish purple background.

It is grown in gardens and can be mistaken for *L. vernus*. However, the leaflets of *L. venetus* are more broadly ovate, and have reticulate venation throughout, so they lack the three major parallel veins of *L. vernus* and its allies. The flowers of this species are also smaller, with distinctive strong red venation. Flowering in late spring, this is about a month later than *L. vernus*, so makes for an attractive successional display in conjunction with it.

Specific epithet origin: possibly named for the Veneti, ancient inhabitants of northeastern Italy, or a Latin term referring to the bluishness of the flowers.

New World subgroup

Section *Orobus* made its way into North America almost certainly through the Bering land bridge, or by seeds that drifted over the North Pacific, probably within the last 2 million years. Given the relatively young age of the group, they have produced an impressive diversity of form and ecology. All but one of the native species of North America are from section *Orobus*, and all of these are endemic. The exception is *L. pusillus* from the southeastern United States, which is a member of the predominantly South American section *Notolathyrus*.

The endemic members of section *Orobus* cover a huge geographic and climatic range, from *L. ochroleucus* in USDA plant hardiness zones 2 and 3, through to *L. splendens* in zone 10. Habitats include coastal foredunes, marsh, woodlands, prairie step and badlands. Around half are climbing and sprawling herbaceous plants of various sizes. All species have multiple pairs of leaflets on each leaf, but these are seldom truly paired, being offset somewhat from each other. They are most reminiscent of the purple-flowered Old World species such as *L. humilis*, *L. incurvus*, some of the central Chinese species and *L. palustris*. Further south and inland from the Pacific Ocean they are typically more variable, and one finds small, erect species without tendrils.

The recent work by Steven Broich for the *Flora of North America* (in press) is very well-considered, drawing on extensive research over three decades, so provides the basis for much of the account outlined below. Some parts of the group are particularly challenging, with species complexes manifesting as slight regional variations as one moves up the West Coast or inland from there.

Lathyrus biflorus

Lathyrus biflorus T.W. Nelson & J.P. Nelson,
Brittonia 35: 183 and fig. (1983)
Two-flower pea

Habitat: Pine woodlands on serpentine rock; 1,300–1,400m
Distribution: Northern California (Humboldt county).

This is a small species to 20cm in height with 3–5 pairs of lanceolate leaflets and tendrils reduced to an arista. The flowers, which appear from June to August, are white and are held as one or two per raceme.
Specific epithet origin: two-flowered.

Lathyrus brachycalyx

Lathyrus brachycalyx Rydb., *Bull. Torrey Bot. Club* 34: 425 (1907)
Bonneville vetchling, Rydberg's sweet pea

Habitat: Sagebrush, juniper and pine scrub, woodland; 1,300–2,300m
Distribution: Southwestern USA, on and east of the Rockies (Arizona, Colorado, Nevada, New Mexico, Utah)

This scrambling plant can reach 50cm, but is often shorter, and has 3–6 pairs of lanceolate leaflets, although they are not truly opposite. The racemes consist of 2–5 medium-sized flowers with pink- to blue-purple standards.

Relatively large, glabrous plants with larger leaflets and emarginate standard petals are sometimes separated as *L. brachycalyx* var. *zionis*, which is found further south and east in Arizona, Colorado, New Mexico and Utah. The typical var. *brachycalyx* is shorter, villous, with smaller leaflets and shallowly emarginate standard petals.
Specific epithet origin: broad calyx.

Lathyrus delnorticus

Lathyrus delnorticus C. Hitchc., *Univ. Wash. Publ. Biol.* 15: 30 (1952)
Del Norte pea

Habitat: Forest margins; sea level to 1,000m
Distribution: California (Del Norte and Siskiyou counties), Oregon (Josephine and Curry counties)

This sprawling species reaches about 1m. The leaves have 4–6 pairs of lanceolate leaflets and tendrils. The racemes consist of 8–12 cream or white flowers, borne from May to June.
Specific epithet origin: from Del Norte County, California.

Lathyrus eucosmus

Lathyrus eucosmus Butters & H. St. John, *Rhodora* 19: 160 (1917)
Syn. *L. brachycalyx* subsp. *eucosmus* (Butters & H. St. John) S.L. Welsh
Seemly vetchling, bush vetchling

Habitat: Pine woodland, scrub, open grassland-prairie; 1,200-2,500m
Distribution: Northern Mexico and the USA (Arizona, Colorado, New Mexico and Utah)

A short, upright species, this can reach 50cm tall, but is usually less. The leaves have 3–4 pairs of non-opposite, ovate to lanceolate leaflets, each to 45mm long, and terminate in a tendril. The racemes bear 2–4 relatively large, purple flowers, each to 20mm long.
Specific epithet origin: in perfect order, hence the common name too.

Lathyrus glandulosus

Lathyrus glandulosus Broich, *Madroño* 33: 136 (1986)
Sticky pea, redwood pea

Habitat: Roadsides, open oak woodlands; 1,200-2,500m
Distribution: California (Humboldt and Mendocino counties)

An upright species, climbing with the aid of tendrils. Leaves are very long, with 7–9 pairs of ovate to lanceolate leaflets, which are often not truly opposite. Racemes bear 7–12 fairly small flowers (to 15mm long) with purple corollas.
Specific epithet origin: glandular – of the sticky glandular hairs on the leaflets and ovary.

Lathyrus graminifolius

Lathyrus graminifolius (S. Watson) T.G. White, *Bull. Torrey Bot. Club* 21(10): 454 (1894)
Syn. *L palustris* var. *graminifolius* S. Wats., *Orobus dissitifolius* Alef.
Grassleaf pea

Habitat: Open pine and other conifer woodland, oak-juniper forest; 1,000-2,800m
Distribution: Northern Mexico (Sonora, Chihuahua) and neighbouring southern USA (Arizona, New Mexico, Texas)

A fairly short, upright species to 60cm, but usually shorter, this arises from a woody or slightly creeping rhizome. The leaves have 2–4 pairs of linear leaflets, each to 80mm long, and usually less than 10mm wide. The leaflets can be narrowly lanceolate if greater than 10mm, and rarely up to 20mm, wide. The upper leaves have a tendril. The racemes consist of 5–8 small flowers to 15mm long which are white, often with a pale purple-blue flush particularly on the standard.
Specific epithet origin: grass-leaved.

Lathyrus grimesii

Lathyrus grimesii Barneby, *Intermount. Fl.* [Cronquist *et al.*] 3(B): 208 (1989)
Grimes's pea

Habitat: Sagebrush habitat on slopes; 2,200-2,350m
Distribution: Nevada (Independence Mountains in Elko County)

This very short plant, to 20cm, has 2–3 pairs of lanceolate to linear leaflets per leaf and no tendril. The flowers are fairly small, to 17mm long, with white petals tinged purple on the standard.
Specific epithet origin: named for US botanist James Grimes (b. 1953).

Lathyrus hitchcockianus

Lathyrus hitchcockianus Barneby & Reveal, *Aliso* 7: 362 (1971)
Hitchcock's pea, Bullfrog Mountain pea

Habitat: Sagebrush habitats, pine-juniper woodlands; 1,400–1,600m
Distribution: Death Valley areas of Nye County, Nevada, and Inyo County, California

A small plant, this has leaves with 2–3 pairs of leaflets, each to 50mm long and 5mm wide, that are tipped with branching tendrils. The racemes consist of 2–3 small, blunt, purple-pink flowers.
Specific epithet origin: named for US botanist Charles Leo Hitchcock (1902–1986).

Lathyrus holochlorus

Lathyrus holochlorus (Piper) C.L. Hitchc., *Univ. Wash. Publ. Biol.* 15: 31 (1952)
Syn. *L ochropetalus* subsp. *holochlorus* Piper
Thinleaf pea

Habitat: Open oak woodlands, roadsides; sea level to 150m
Distribution: Oregon

A medium-sized, scrambling plant, this can reach 1m long. The leaves have 4–6 pairs of loosely paired leaflets that are ovate to lanceolate and up to 45mm long, along with branched tendrils. The racemes consist of 5–15 fairly small, creamy white flowers to 15mm long.
Specific epithet origin: wholly greenish yellow, referring to the corolla colour.

Lathyrus jepsonii

Lathyrus jepsonii Greene, *Pittonia* 2(9): 158 (1890)
Jepson's pea, delta tule pea

Habitat: Wetlands near sea level (var. *jepsonii*), streams in woodlands and in open meadow areas (var. *californicus*);, sea level to 1,500m
Distribution: California

A medium-sized plant to about 1m, this has 4–6 pairs of leaflets, the pairs often not opposite, and a robust tendril. The racemes consist of 5–15, pale pink to pinkish purple flowers, each up to 20mm long.

Lathyrus jepsonii var. *jepsonii* is glabrous and is restricted to wetlands in the San Francisco Bay area, whereas the pubescent var. *californicus* is found across California by streams in woodlands and in meadows. Specific epithet origin: named for US botanist Willis Linn Jepson (1867–1946).

Lathyrus lanszwertii

Lathyrus lanszwertii Kellogg, *Proc. Calif. Acad. Sci.* 2: 150 (1863)
Syns. *L. arizonicus* Britton, *L. bijugatus* T.G. White, *L. brownii* Eastw., *L. coriaceus* T.G. White, *L. laetivirens* Greene ex Rydb., *L. leucanthus* Rydb., *L, goldsteiniae* Eastw., *L. oregonensis* T.G. White, *L. tracyi* Bradshaw
Lanszwert's pea, Nevada pea, thick-leaved pea

Habitat: Open pine woodlands, scrub; 600-3,200m
Distribution: Western North America

This is a variable species, with several varieties recognised across its range, which covers Texas and a broad swathe of western states up to British Columbia.

Larger plants, with 3–5 pairs of leaflets, climb with tendrils (var. *lanszwertii* in the west and east, and var. *pallescens* to the east). Smaller plants have one or two pairs of leaflets in the northern part of the range (var. *sandbergii*), and two or three pairs in the Cascades range to the west (var. *aridus*) and Utah, Colorado and Arizona to the east (var. *leucanthus*). The 2–6 flowers are relatively small and snub-nosed (to 15mm long, 10mm in some varieties), and the petals are white in most of the varieties, but purple in var. *lanszwertii*.

Lathyrus brownii and *L. laetivirens*, listed as synonyms here, will both be treated as distinct by Broich (in press). Specific epithet origin: named for a Dr Lanszwert who sent it to Kellogg from Washoe County, Nevada.

Lathyrus littoralis

Lathyrus littoralis (Nutt.) Endl. ex Walp., *Repert. Bot. Syst.* 1: 722 (1842)
Syns. *Astrophia littoralis* Nutt., *Orobus littoralis* (Nutt.) A. Gray
Silky beach pea, silky peavine

Habitat: Foreshore dunes
Distribution: Canada (southern British Columbia), USA (Oregon, Washington)

This species, despite its apt common name, is similar to *L. japonicus* in having relatively large stipules and a foreshore habit. Furthermore, DNA evidence (Schaefer *et al.* 2012) suggests a close relationship. The two differ in *L. littoralis* being a smaller plant overall, with smaller, inrolled leaflets (to 20mm long), the stipules are not quite sagittate (in *L. japonicus* they are), and the whole plant is densely covered in silvery tomentose hair. The flowers are borne in racemes of 4–7 and are usually bicoloured, with a dark purple standard and white wings and keel.

Overall, this plant is most reminiscent of some of the South American members of section *Notolathyrus*, with the habit of *L. tomentosus* and flowers akin to those of *L. subandinus*, but this is evidently a convergence of form.

Specific epithet origin: littoral, referring to its habitat.

Lathyrus nevadensis

Lathyrus nevadensis S. Watson, *Proc. Amer. Acad. Arts* 11: 133(–135) (1876)
Syns. *L. cusickii* S. Watson, *L. parkeri* H. St. John.
Sierra pea

Habitat: Mixed woodland
Distribution: Canada (British Columbia), USA (Alaska, California, Oregon, Washington)

This is a highly variable, small to medium, erect or climbing species to 60cm. It has 2–5 pairs of ovate to lanceolate leaflets and the 2–8 purplish pink flowers are 12–22mm long.

Broich (in press) notes three varieties (including var. *cusickii* and var. *parkeri*) and several forms within these that show variation in overall size, number and shape of leaflets, strength of tendril, and flower size. These intergrade over its range, and intermediates are found in areas where they overlap. Like several other species on the Pacific west coast of North America, this is a complex and challenging species to understand, so one that requires further study.
Specific epithet origin: of the Sierra Nevada range in California.

Lathyrus ochroleucus

Lathyrus ochroleucus Hook., *Fl. Bor.-Amer.* 1(3): 159 (1831)
Syns. *L. albidus* Aikin ex Eaton, *L. glaucifolius* Beck, *Orobus ochroleucus* (Hook.) Brown
Cream pea

Habitat: Woodlands
Distribution: Northern USA, Canada (except far northeast), Alaska

This scrambling plant grows to around 1m and has leaves with large stipules to 35mm and 3 pairs of ovate to lanceolate leaflets to 65mm long. The racemes have 4–10 fairly small flowers, each to 15cm long, with pale cream-coloured petals.

It is reminiscent of *L. davidii* from the other side of the Pacific and seems to fill a similar niche. Although current DNA evidence (Schaefer *et al.* 2012) suggests they are in the same broad group, they do not appear to be direct neighbouring sister species in evolutionary terms. In fact, *L. ochroleucus* may be relatively close to the other yellow-flowered North American species, *L. sulphureus*. Specific epithet origin: yellowish white, referring to the corolla colour.

Lathyrus parvifolius

Lathyrus parvifolius S. Watson, *Proc. Amer. Acad. Arts* 17: 345 (1881–82)
Syn. *L. schaffneri* Rydb.

Habitat: Open scrub and grassland in upland areas; 1,800–2,500m
Distribution: Central Mexico

This erect, glabrous species supports itself with tendrils and the leaves have 4–6 pairs of lanceolate to ovate leaflets. The racemes are quite loose, bearing 6–12 fairly small, purple flowers. Although a poorly known species, it is the most southerly member of the Orobus group in the New World, except for *L. japonicus* populations in Chile and New Zealand whose provenance is uncertain. Specific epithet origin: small-leaved.

Lathyrus pauciflorus

Lathyrus pauciflorus Fern., *Bot. Gaz.* 19: 335 **(1894)**
Syns. *L. bradfieldianus* A. Nelson, *L. parvifolius* var.
tenuior Piper, *L. utahensis* M.E. Jones
Fewflower pea, few-flowered vetchling

Habitat: Sagebrush, prairie steppe, pine woodlands at
500–2,000m (var. *pauciflorus*) and similar habitat at
higher altitudes of 1,300–2,900m (var. *utahensis*)
Distribution: USA (Colorado, Oregon, Idaho, Utah,
Washington)

A medium to tall herbaceous species, this reaches
80cm but is often sprawling as it clings to surrounding
vegetation. The leaves have 4–10 pairs of ovate to
lanceolate leaflets, although these are not opposite,
and a tendril. The racemes consist of 4–15 medium
to large flowers, each 12–20mm long, with pale purple
or pale blue to white petals.

The typical variety has lanceolate leaflets and is
native to eastern Oregon, Washington and Idaho.
Plants with broader, ovate leaflets have been assigned
to *L. pauciflorus* var. *utahensis* and are found in the
southeast of the range, in Colorado, Idaho and Utah.
Specific epithet origin: few-flowered.

Lathyrus polymorphus

Lathyrus polymorphus Nutt., *Gen. N. Amer. Pl.* 2:
96(–97) **(1818)**
Syn. *Orobus polymorphus* (Nutt.) Alef.
Manystem pea, variable peavine

Habitat: Open wooded areas and sandy soils of the
prairies of the Great Plains; 1,200–2,200m
Distribution: USA (Colorado, Kansas, Nebraska,
Oklahoma, South Dakota, Wyoming)

A small, rhizomatous plant, this is sprawling or upright
to 30cm. The leaves have 4–6 pairs of lanceolate to linear
leaflets, which are usually opposite, and the leaf

terminates in a short awn-like bristle rather than a tendril. The racemes consist of 2–6 large, often bicolored flowers, each 16–22mm long, with pale purple, pink or white petals. It is distinct among the American species for its stipitate fruits – the pod has a short, narrow 'neck' at its base before broadening out.

The typical variety is glabrous, whereas var. *incanus*, from slightly higher altitudes, is pubescent.
Specific epithet origin: polymorphic, referring to the leaflet shape.

Lathyrus polyphyllus

Lathyrus polyphyllus Nutt., *Fl. N. Amer.* [Torr. & A. Gray] 1(2): 274 (1838)
Syn. *L. ecirrhosus* A. Heller
Leafy pea, Oregon pea

Habitat: Clearings in coastal conifer forests; sea level to 1,300m
Distribution: Canada (British Columbia) and USA (northern California, Oregon)

A medium-sized species, this clambers to about 80cm. It has large stipules, almost the same size as the leaflets, and 5–8 pairs of ovate to lanceolate leaflets which are seldom opposite each other on the leaf. Each leaf is tipped with a grasping tendril. The racemes consist of 8–12 medium-sized flowers, about 18mm long, with purple petals.
Specific epithet origin: many-leaved, referring to the leaflets.

Lathyrus rigidus

Lathyrus rigidus T. White, *Bull. Torrey Bot. Club*
21(10): 455 (1894)
Syn. *L. albus* A. Gray
Stiff pea, stiff vetchling, Modoc pea, bushy pea

Habitat: Sagebrush steppelands; 800-1,700m
Distribution: USA (California, Idaho, Nevada, Oregon)

A compact, very upright species, this has short leaves
with 4–5 pairs of lanceolate leaflets, each about 30mm
long, with the leaves terminating in an awn-like bristle
rather than a tendril. The racemes consist of 2–3
medium-sized flowers, each to 18mm long.
Specific epithet origin: rigid, referring to the upright
habit.

Lathyrus splendens

Lathyrus splendens Kellogg, *Proc. Calif. Acad. Sci.* 7: 90 (1876)
Pride of California, Campo pea

Lifecycle: Perennial
Habit: Climbing
Height: 40-300cm
Hair: Present, sparsely pubescent
Stem wings: Absent
Stipules: Semisagittate, upper part lanceolate to linear
Leaflet number: 6-10 leaflets, often not directly paired
Leaflet length: 20-40mm
Leaflet width: 3-15mm
Leaflet shape: Ovate to linear
Tendril: Present
Flowers per raceme: 5-10
Peduncle or pedicel length: 4-16cm
Calyx teeth: Unequal, shorter than the tube
Standard width: 25mm
Petal colour: Scarlet to magenta
Style: not contorted
Fruit size: 50-80mm
Fruit shape: Linear
Fruit features: Glandular hairy
Number of seeds: 5-10
Wild flowering period: March–May
Habitat: Open chaparral; 50-150m
Distribution: Mexico (Baja California), USA (California)

This species is unique in the genus as it is bird-pollinated, hence the crimson flowers with a strongly reflexed standard petal that allows access for hummingbirds. The leaves have 6–8 pairs of non-opposite, oval leaflets and a tendril. It is closely allied to *L. vestitus* var. *alefeldii*, which shares many characters including the reflexed standard, but its flowers are smaller, deep pink and largely pollinated by butterflies.

Cultivation of this species can be challenging as it is half-hardy (USDA Hardiness Zone 10) and in cooler temperate areas it needs to be grown under glass. Specific epithet origin: splendid, beautiful.

Lathyrus sulphureus

Lathyrus sulphureus W.H. Brewer ex A. Gray, *Proc. Amer. Acad. Arts* 7: 399 **(1868)**
Snub pea, Brewer's pea, sulfur pea

Habitat: Oak woodlands; 100–800m
Distribution: USA (California)

This species sprawls and climbs to 150cm, using branched tendrils. The leaves have fairly large stipules, to 25mm long, and 4–6 pairs of non-opposite, ovate leaflets about 50mm long. The dense racemes have 9–15 short, snub-nosed flowers, each to 13mm long. These are creamy yellow, turning more orange as they age.

Akin to *L. davidii* from eastern Asia, this is one of the only North American species with yellow to orange, snub-nosed flowers. *Lathyrus ochroleucus* is similar but typically has paler flowers.

The typical variety is glabrous, but the rare and poorly known *L. sulphureus* var. *argillaceus* is recognised on the basis of dense, velvety pubescence over the entire plant.

Specific epithet origin: sulphur-yellow, referring to the flower colour.

Lathyrus torreyi

Lathyrus torreyi A. Gray, *Proc. Amer. Acad. Arts* 7: 337 **(1868)**
Syn. *L. villosus* Torr.
Torrey's pea, redwood pea

Habitat: Open coastal conifer woodland; 50-150m
Distribution: Pacific coast of the USA (California, Oregon, Washington)

An upright or sprawling species, this is densely velvet-pubescent throughout. The leaves have 4–8 pairs of small, ovate to lanceolate, non-opposite leaflets to 15mm long. The racemes have just 1–2 small flowers, each only 12mm long, and with purple petals.
Specific epithet origin: named for US botanist John Torrey (1796–1873).

Lathyrus venosus

Lathyrus venosus Muhl. ex Willd., *Sp. Pl.* [Willdenow] ed. 4, 3(2): 1092 **(1802)**
Veiny pea, bushy vetchling

Habitat: Open woodlands, woodland margins; sea level to 1,000m
Distribution: Central and eastern North America

This medium-sized, clambering species reaches 1m. The leaves have 4–7 pairs of leaflets, often not opposite each other, and branched tendrils. The dense racemes consist of 5–20 flower, each 10–15mm long, with purple, bluish or pink petals. It is one of the most easterly distributed of the New World subgroup.

Pubescent plants, usually from the northwest of the range, have been recognised as *L. venosus* var. *intonsus*. Glabrous plants with calyx teeth shorter than the tube (usually from the east of the range) are *L. venosus* var. *venosus*. Those with long calyx teeth (from the south of the range) are *L. venosus* var *arkansanus*.
Specific epithet origin: veined, referring to the leaflets.

Lathyrus vestitus

Lathyrus vestitus Nutt., *Fl. N. Amer.* (Torr. & A. Gray) 1(2): 276 (1838)

Pacific pea, hairy peavine

Lifecycle: Perennial
Habit: Climbing
Height: 20-200cm
Hair: Glabrous (in north of range) to densely pubescent (south)
Stem wings: Absent
Stipules: Semi-sagittate, upper part lanceolate to linear
Leaflet number: 3-5 pairs, often not opposite
Leaflet length: 15-40mm
Leaflet width: 5-25mm
Leaflet shape: Ovate to linear
Tendril: Present
Flowers per raceme: 5-20
Peduncle or pedicel length: 5-25cm
Calyx teeth: Unequal, shorter or longer than the tube
Standard width: 12-25mm
Petal colour: White to deep maroon
Style: Not contorted
Fruit size: 40-60mm
Fruit shape: Linear to slightly falcate
Fruit features: May be pubescent
Number of seeds: 5-9
Wild flowering period: February-May
Habitat: Chapparal in the south to open woodland in the north; sea level to 1,200m
Distribution: Mexico (Baja California), USA (California, Oregon, Washington)

This species has a complex taxonomic history because of its broad range up the Pacific coast of North America. It transitions from relatively small-flowered plants in the north, to large-flowered ones in the south that have strongly reflexed standards. Ovary pubescence and style size are also variable and have been used to separate off distinct species in the past, in conjunction with geography. Broich (in press) recognises three varieties. *Lathyrus vestitus* var. *vestitus* is centred around

California and Mexico and has bluish purple, upright standard petals, while var. *ochropetalus* has white flowers with upright standards and is in the northern, more temperate areas of its range. *Lathyrus vestitus* var. *alefeldii* is found in the south of the range, where it overlaps with *L. splendens*, and is evidently closely related to it, as suggested by the larger, deep pink flowers with reflexed standard petals.

Although perhaps a little tender for more northern climates, this is one of the most attractive North American species for the garden. It is a vigorous herbaceous scrambler, producing large volumes of dead matter each year in the woodlands in which it grows, which can be a significant fire risk.

Specific epithet origin: clothed, referring to the pubescence.

Lathyrus whitei

Lathyrus whitei Kupicha, *Notes Roy. Bot. Gard. Edinburgh* **41(2): 226 (1983)**
Syn. *L. longipes* T.G. White

Habitat: Dry, open woodland, scrub
Distribution: Mexico (possibly Nuevo Leon)

This small, poorly known species has leaves with 2–3 pairs of ovate leaflets, each 20–40mm long and 10–25mm wide, with branched tendrils. The racemes consist of 4–6 purple flowers.

Originally described by White as *L. longipes*, it was later discovered that name had already been used for the species now called *L. tropicalandinus*.

Specific epithet origin: Named for US botanist Theodore White (1872–1901), who first recognised the species.

Pratensis group

Includes members of sections:
Pratensis Bässler, *Feddes Repert.* 72: 90 (1966)
Aphaca (Miller) Dumort., *Fl. Belg.*: 103 (1827)
Number of species: 8

Members of the Pratensis group are distinctive for their relatively large, sagittate stipules – a feature usually restricted to the coastal *L. japonicus* in section *Orobus* and members of the exclusively New World section *Notolathyrus*. Members are found throughout western and central Eurasia, although both *L. pratensis* and *L. aphaca* have spread further afield as introduced aliens.

This group consists of three elements:

- *Lathyrus aphaca* and *L. stenolobus* – both annual species, which are usually treated as a section *Aphaca*. They are distinctive in their lack of leaflets – the stipules are the main photosynthetic surface
- Yellow-flowered members of section *Pratensis* – all perennial, and including *L. pratensis*, *L. binatus* and *L. hallersteinii*. The latter two species are only doubtfully distinct from *L. pratensis* itself.
- Purple- or blue-flowered members of section *Pratensis* – all perennial. *Lathyrus laxiflorus* is widespread, while *L. czeczottianus* and *L. layardii* are from more limited areas of eastern Turkey and neighbouring areas.

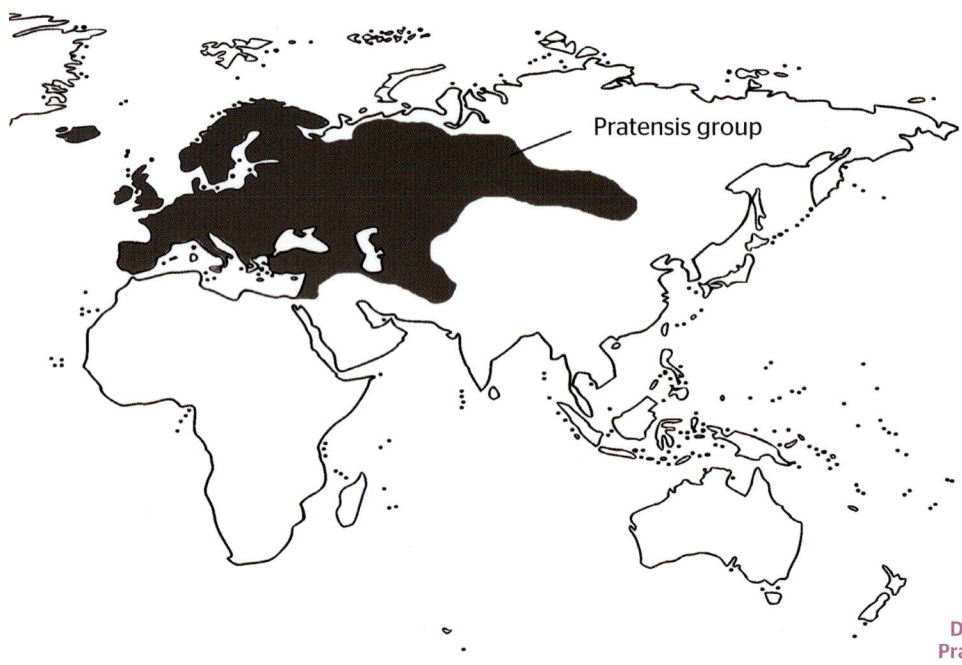

Pratensis group

Distribution of Pratensis group

Lathyrus aphaca

Lathyrus aphaca L., *Sp. Pl.* 2: 729 (1753)
Syns. *L. affinis* Guss., *L. floribundus* Velen.
Yellow vetchling

Lifecycle: Annual
Habit: Sprawling or clambering
Height: 30cm, usually less
Hair: Glabrous
Stem wings: Absent
Stipules: Sagittate
Leaflet number: Absent
Tendril: Present
Flowers per raceme: 1-2
Peduncle or pedicel length: 2-6cm
Calyx teeth: Subequal, longer than the tube
Standard width: 8-15mm
Petal colour: Golden yellow to pale cream
Style: Not contorted
Fruit size: 20-40mm
Fruit shape: Linear, often upcurved
Fruit features: Glabrous
Number of seeds: 6-8
Wild flowering period: April–July
Habitat: Open scrub, field margins, rocky areas; sea level to 1,500m
Distribution: Widespread throughout Europe, and possibly native in southern Britain. Widely introduced elsewhere as a weed

This is a very distinctive, widespread and weedy species, albeit an attractive one. The whole plant is often glaucous-grey, and the leaves are almost completely lost – persisting only as a tendril. The main photosynthetic surface is the large stipules. There is considerable variation in the shape of the stipules, which can be rotund to narrowly ovate and sometimes with a narrowing in the middle. Flower number, size and colour can also vary, and these traits tend to be stable across populations, especially in Turkey where the bulk of the diversity is to be found.

These variants have been pulled off as distinct species,

subspecies or varieties by different authors. Davis's (1970) treatment is eminently sensible:

- *Lathyrus aphaca* var. *aphaca*: peduncle with a single large (10–15mm) flower, petals bright yellow
- *Lathyrus aphaca* var. *affinis*: peduncle with a single large (10–13mm) flower, petals pale creamy yellow
- *Lathyrus aphaca* var. *biflorus*: peduncle with two large (10–13mm) flowers, petals bright yellow
- *Lathyrus aphaca* var. *floribundus*: peduncle with two large (10–13mm) flowers, petals pale creamy yellow;
- *Lathyrus aphaca* var. *pseudoaphaca*: peduncle with one small (8–10mm) flower, petals pale creamy yellow with violet veins on the standard and calyx teeth 2–3 times as long as the tube
- *Lathyrus aphaca* var. *modestus*: peduncle with one small (8–10mm) flower, petals bright uniform yellow and calyx teeth 1.5–2 times as long as the tube.

Specific epithet origin: aphaca was a vetch or lentil-like plant mentioned by Pliny.

Lathyrus binatus

Lathyrus binatus Pančić, *Fl. Serbiae*: 256 **(1874)**
Syn. *L. pratensis* var. *binatus* (Pančić) Ascherson & Kanitz

Habitat: Grassland, rocky areas; around 1,000m
Distribution: Bosnia, Serbia

This very small species has tendrils reduced to an arista and the stipules are a similar size to the leaflets. There is little to distinguish it, other than the reduced tendrils, from other small individuals of *L. pratensis*.
Specific epithet origin: twin-birth, or paired, referring to the comparable size of leaflets and stipules.

Lathyrus czeczottianus

Lathyrus czeczottianus Bässler, *Feddes Repert.* 72: 91, in adnot. (1966)
Syn. *Orobus sericeus* Boiss. & Balansa

Habitat: Spruce and broadleaved forests, meadows
Distribution: Central and eastern Turkey and neighbouring areas

Very similar to *L. laxiflorus*, this species differs in its relatively slender leaflets and stipules, lack of any tendril, and always being pubescent throughout the plant. The racemes bear 2–6 flowers that pale to dark purple. Specific epithet origin: named for Polish botanist Hanna Czeczott (1888–1982).

Lathyrus hallersteinii

Lathyrus hallersteinii Baumg., *Enum. Stirp. Transsilv.* 2: 333 (1816)
Syn. *L. pratensis* f. *grandistipulus* Roch.

Habitat: Scrubland, open hornbeam and oak woodlands; 500-1,000m
Distribution: Hungary, Romania, north Balkan region

This robust species is much like, and difficult to reliably distinguish from, a large individual of *L. pratensis*. The leaflets and stipules are around 6cm long and 1.8cm wide. The leaflets are usually smaller than the stipules, or around the same size in this species, but in *L. pratensis* the leaflets and stipules are usually shorter than 40mm, with the stipules more often smaller than the leaflets. Specific epithet origin: named for Johann Georg Haller von Hallerstein, Baumgarten's patron and sponsor of the publication.

Lathyrus layardii

Lathyrus layardii Ball ex Boiss., *Fl. Orient.* [Boissier]
suppl.: 195 (1888)

Habitat: Wet meadows
Distribution: Central Turkey, Iran

This species differs from *L. czeczottianus* and
L. laxiflorus as it is robust and erect, reaching 70cm in
height, whereas the other two are sprawling. The leaflets,
in a single pair, are about the same length as the large
stipules (each to 60mm), although the stipules are
broader (to 20mm), and the leaves are tipped with a
branching tendril. The whole plant is villously hairy.
Specific epithet origin: named for archaeologist Austen
Henry Layard (1817–1894).

Lathyrus laxiflorus

Lathyrus laxiflorus (Desf.) Kuntze, *Trudy Imp.
S.-Peterburgsk. Bot. Sada* 10: 185 (1887)
Syns. *L. inermis* Friv., *Orobus hirsutus* L., *O. laxiflorus*
Desf.

Lifecycle: Perennial
Habit: Sprawling or clambering
Height: 30cm, but spreading to 1m
Hair: Present, densely pubescent
Stem wings: Absent
Stipules: Sagittate, occasionally semisagittate, the upper
lobe ovate
Leaflet number: 1 pair
Leaflet length: 20-40mm
Leaflet width: 10-20mm
Leaflet shape: Lanceolate to ovate
Tendril: Sometimes
Flowers per raceme: 2-6
Peduncle/Pedicel: 3-12cm
Calyx teeth: Subequal, longer than the tube
Standard width: 12-18mm

Petal colour: Pink-violet to blue-violet, sometimes with white wings and keel
Style: Not contorted
Fruit size: 25–40mm
Fruit shape: Oblong, slightly upcurving
Fruit features: Pubescent or glabrous, but glands in almost all specimens
Number of seeds: 5–8
Wild flowering period: April–June
Habitat: Woodlands; sea level to 2,000m
Distribution: Throughout much of southeast Europe (the Balkan region), eastern Mediterranean, Turkey, the Caucasus and Zagros Mountains, and the Black and western Caspian Sea regions

An attractive perennial, this species sprawls, forming a patch to around 1m across, but the stems do not root. Most plants are densely and villously pubescent, although the degree of hairiness varies. Plants from the west of its range are usually assigned to *L. laxiflorus* subsp. *laxiflorus*, and tend to have broad leaflets, no tendril and pubescent fruits. Those from the east of the range, from central Turkey eastwards, have lanceolate leaflets, often have simple tendrils and can have hairless fruits. These eastern individuals have been treated as *L. laxiflorus* subsp. *angustifolius* and approach *L. czeczottianus* in overall appearance.

Grown in semi-shade in cool-temperate gardens, the plants currently available in the UK are seemingly very hardy. They retain green stems throughout the winter. Flowering begins in late May or June and typically lasts through until November. With its often bicoloured flowers, this is a very handsome garden plant, and a white-flowered selection has been offered commercially. Specific epithet origin: loose-flowered

Lathyrus pratensis

Lathyrus pratensis L., *Sp. Pl.* 2: 733 (1753)
Meadow vetchling, common vetchling

Lifecycle: Perennial
Habit: Sprawling or clambering
Height/spread: 60cm
Hair: Variable, glabrous to pubescent
Stem wings: Slight
Stipules: Sagittate, the upper part
Leaflet number: 1 pair
Leaflet length: 8-40mm
Leaflet width: 2-10mm
Leaflet shape: Linear-lanceolate
Tendril: Present, simple or branching
Flowers per raceme: 2-12, rarely to 16
Peduncle or pedicel length: 3-16cm
Calyx teeth: Unequal, about the same, or slightly longer than, the tube
Standard width: 10-14mm
Petal colour: Yellow, sometimes with fine black lines on the standard
Style: Not contorted
Fruit size: 20-40mm
Fruit shape: Oblong, slightly upcurving
Fruit features: Smooth, often drying black
Number of seeds: 3-15
Wild flowering period: May-September
Habitat: Meadows, roadsides; sea level to 2,200m
Distribution: Throughout Eurasia as far as China. Introduced to North and South America and Australia

This is a common, widespread and variable species in temperate grassland habitats where it climbs up surrounding vegetation or forms a mass of tangled stems with tendrils, clinging on to itself. It ranges from Spain to China, and from Scandinavia to Nepal. It is unclear if the Chinese populations are truly native, as there is an apparent break in distribution through parts of central Asia.

Plants can vary considerably in size, with larger plants having all their parts correspondingly larger. Although this is one of the few species from which polyploidy is known (Leitch *et al.* 2019), this condition does not appear to be responsible for the more robust individuals. Plants can also show varying degrees of pubescence. Size and pubescence have been used to recognise subspecies and varieties but *L. pratensis* has a very plastic phenotype, and these characters are among the most variable traits within an individual. For example, specimens

grown at Royal Botanic Garden Edinburgh from wild-collected Albanian seed have reduced in size and increased in pubescence within a decade in the same individuals. For instance, the leaflets and stipules have reduced from around 40mm long to 20mm long. For this reason, we are not recognising any infraspecific taxa here as there is evidently much research to be done to understand this fascinating species.

In cultivation, this species is a valuable component of meadow plantings, where its later flowering brings an attractive splash of colour and a useful resource for pollinators.

Specific epithet origin: of meadows.

Lathyrus stenolobus

Lathyrus stenolobus Boiss., *Diagn. Pl. Orient.* ser. 1, 9: 124 (1849)

Habitat: Disturbed ground, grassland, field margins
Distribution: Nur (Amanus) mountains of southeastern Turkey and neighbouring Syria

This is a small species that reaches 30cm. It can be distinguished from the much more common and widespread *L. aphaca* on the basis of its narrow stipules (to 8mm wide), very small flowers (standard to 8mm across) and shorter calyx teeth (as long as the tube). As with *L. aphaca*, the flowers are yellow.

Specific epithet origin: narrow-lobed, referring to the stipule width.

Oddities

Members of sections:
Clymenum (Mill.) DC ex Ser., *Prodr.* [A.P. de Candolle] 2: 375 (1825)
Neurolobus Bässler, *Feddes Repert.* 72: 91 (1966)
Nissolia (Mill.) Dumort., *Fl. Belg.*: 103 (1827)
Number of species: 9

This mixed group includes several species with odd morphologies that are closely related to the species traditionally placed in *Pisum* (peas) and *Vavilovia* (perennial mountain pea). Indeed, DNA evidence (Kenicer *et al.* 2009, Schaefer *et al.* 2012, Oskoueiyan *et al.* 2014) suggests that *Pisum* and *Vavilovia* are closer to other species of *Lathyrus* than at least four species, including *L. neurolobus* and most members of section *Clymenum* (*L. articulatus*, *L. clymenum* and *L. ochrus*). This has led to a recircumscription of the genus to include *Pisum* and *Vavilovia* in *Lathyrus* (Schaefer *et al.* 2012, Coulout & Rabaute 2016) that is now gaining wider acceptance (e.g. Stace 2019).

Lathyrus gloeosperma, which was formerly in section *Clymenum*, is closer to the rest of *Lathyrus* in spite of its morphological similarities to *L. clymenum* and allies. The final member of this disparate group is *L. nissolia* (grass vetchling), its phyllodic leaves being reminiscent of the young leaves of *L. clymenum* and allies.

The lineages leading to all of these species appear to have branched off relatively early in the history of this revised *Lathyrus*. The species in this group are very varied in appearance and habitat, and each may represent the remnants of old lineages that have specialised to particular niches and have not diversified into many species, or were formerly diverse, but have since lost species to extinction. This is a pattern that is typical of many plant genera – the basal groups (i.e. those from the earliest diverging lineages) have few species, but they are morphologically diverse. Essentially, we can think of peas and vavilovia as just another lineage of early-evolved *Lathyrus*, in which one of the species (garden pea) was adopted as a major crop plant. This familiarity perhaps accentuated its distinctness, leading to it being traditionally treated as a genus in formal taxonomy.

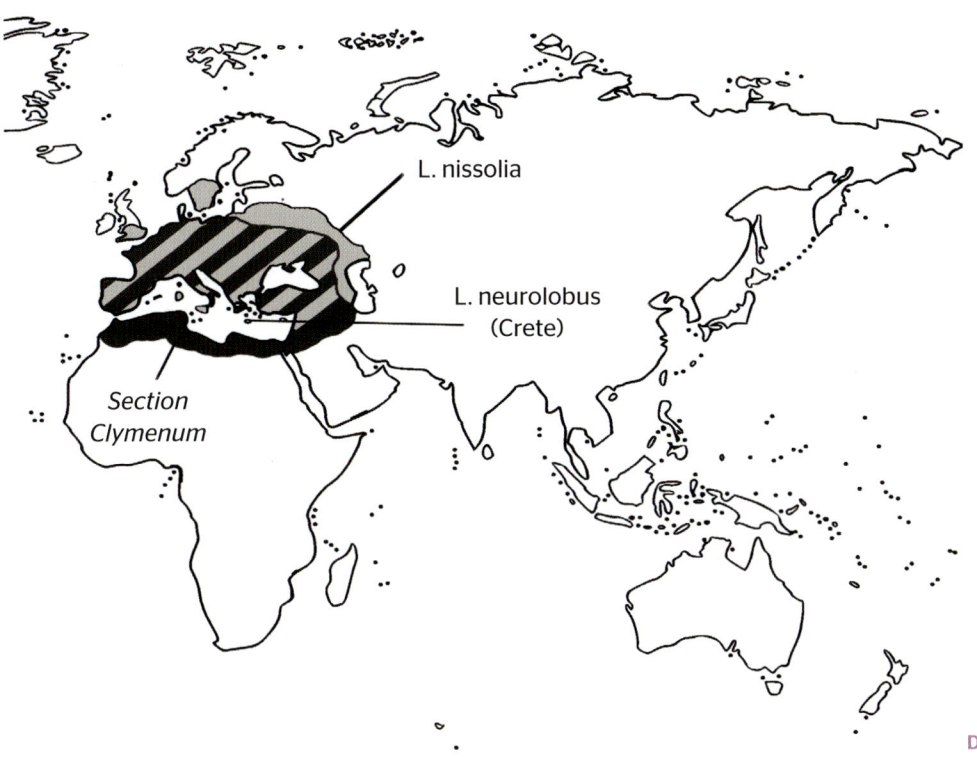

L. nissolia

L. neurolobus
(Crete)

Section
Clymenum

Distribution of section
Clymenum, Lathyrus
neurolobus and *L. nissolia.*

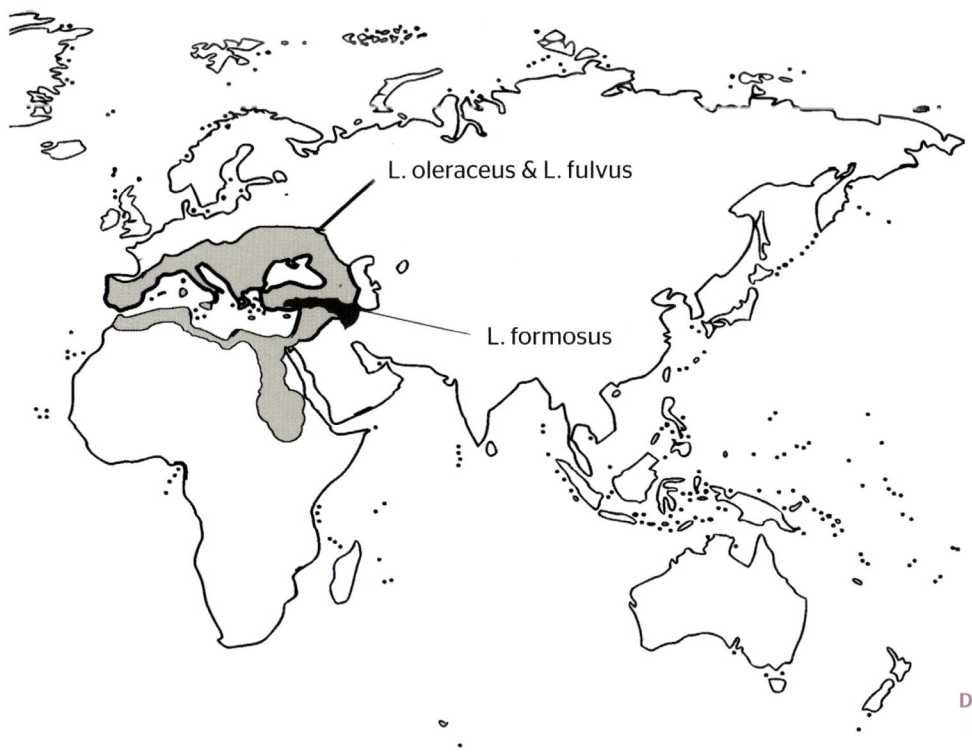

L. oleraceus & L. fulvus

L. formosus

Distribution of *Lathyrus*
formosus, L. fulvus and
L. oleraceus.

Lathyrus articulatus

Lathyrus articulatus L., *Sp. Pl.* 2: 731 (1753)
Syn. *L. clymenum* subsp. *articulatus* (L.) Ball
Joint-podded pea

Habitat: Open areas, grassland and scrub
Distribution: Throughout the middle and western Mediterranean

A sprawling or clambering annual, this species is very similar in overall appearance to *L. clymenum*, to which it is clearly allied. *Lathyrus articulatus* can be distinguished on the basis of its consistently narrower leaflets (up to 11mm), white or pink wing petals, and narrower, slightly upcurving fruit. The walls of the fruits follow the contours of the seeds closely, making the fruit appear jointed. It is also the more western element of the pair.

The two species are undoubtedly ancient domesticates or weeds of early agriculture, and are still used as fodder crops. They may have been transported and selected by humans to a degree that makes their wild taxonomy and biogeography difficult to interpret without extensive genetic analysis.

Specific epithet origin: articulated, referring to the pods.

Lathyrus clymenum

Lathyrus clymenum L., *Sp. Pl.* 2: 732 (1753)
Spanish vetchling

Lifecycle: Annual
Habit: Sprawling or clambering
Height: 30-100cm
Hair: Glabrous
Stem wings: Present, broad
Stipules: Semisagittate, linear to ovate
Leaflet number: 2-5, paired, from a winged rachis
Leaflet length: 20-70mm
Leaflet width: 5-15mm
Leaflet shape: Linear to lanceolate
Tendril: Present, branching
Flowers per raceme: 1-3, rarely up to 5
Peduncle or pedicel length: 1.5-13cm
Calyx teeth: Equal, short, and shorter than the tube
Standard width: 10-20mm
Petal colour: Pale pink to crimson, sometimes with pale or white wings and keel
Style: Not contorted, aristate at the tip
Fruit size: 30-70mm
Fruit shape: Elliptic
Fruit features: Channels in upper surface, sometimes with purple markings on the valves
Number of seeds: 5-7
Wild flowering period: April-June
Habitat: Field margins, roadsides and open ground; sea level to 1,500m
Distribution: Widespread and common throughout the central and western Mediterranean from Tunisia through much of North Africa, and Portugal to Turkey, becoming somewhat rarer in the east

Intriguingly, both this species and *L. articulatus* have young leaves with no leaflets – the leaf is reduced to a simple, strap-like, phyllodic structure. This is only otherwise seen in *L. gloeosperma* and *L. nissolia* – two of the other Oddity lineages that diverged early in the evolution of the genus. Older leaves have leaflets that branch off the main winged rachis of the leaf, and the leaf is usually tipped with a tendril. The leaflets can be in opposite pairs or very strongly alternating down the rachis. The phyllode remains as wings running up the rachis of the leaf, which is a distinct character for *L. articulatus*, *L. gloeosperma* and *L. ochrus* as well.

The morphologically very similar *L. articulatus* has been included in *L. clymenum*. However, the genetic information we have (Schaefer *et al.* 2012) suggests that *L. ochrus*, which is morphologically very distinct from *L. articulatus* and *L. clymenum*, is actually derived from inside the pair. This essentially means they cannot be treated as one species.

The flowers show up nicely against the tangle of bright green foliage, the crimson standard petals contrasting strongly with the paler violet or white wings and keel. The seeds are used in various traditional porridges and dhals, particularly in southern and insular Greece and other parts of the eastern Mediterranean.
Specific epithet origin: probably from periclymenum of Dioscorides, a twining plant.

Lathyrus formosus

Lathyrus formosus (Steven) Kenicer, *Lathyrus: The complete guide*: 419 (2021)
Syns. *Alophotrophis aucheri* (Jaub. & Spach) Grossh., *Alophotrophis formosa* (Steven) Grossh., *Orobus formosus* Steven, *Pisum aucheri* Jaub. & Spach, *Pisum formosum* (Steven) Alef., *Vavilovia formosa* (Steven) Fed., *Vicia aucheri* Boiss.
Perennial mountain pea, beautiful vavilovia

Habitat: High alpine scree; 1,800–3,400m
Distribution: Armenia, Georgia, Iran, northern Iraq, Lebanon, Turkey, Syria

This small, spreading perennial to 40cm roots from running rhizomes, and its aerial parts are sometimes purple or brown-tinged rather than green. The stipules are small and semisagittate and the leaves have one pair of leaflets and end in a bristle-like arista. With a standard petal to 2.5cm across, the pink flowers are large for the size of the plant. With *L. oleraceus* (previously *Pisum sativum*) it shares the same broad stigma with recurved margins. In the past, a variant showing different leaflet size and stipule form was separated off as *Vavilovia aucheri* (the name has not been combined in *Lathyrus*), but there is no basis for this as the differences fit within a continuum of variation.

This is an intriguing outlier in *Lathyrus*, being a perennial among many annual relatives, but it illustrates the adaptability of the genus. Similar shifts to perenniality have happened many times in the more derived temperate groups.

Unfortunately, this alpine species has proven challenging to cultivate, because of the cold, dry climate it favours.

Specific epithet origin: beautiful.

Lathyrus fulvus

Lathyrus fulvus (Sm) Kosterin, *Vavilov J. Genet. Breed.* 21(2): 168 (2017)
Syn. *Pisum fulvum* Sm.
Tawny pea

Habitat: Woodlands, woodland margins in rocky areas
Distribution: Eastern Mediterranean (southeast Turkey through Syria, Lebanon and Israel to Jordan)

A slender species to around 40cm in height, the leaves have a tendril and a single pair of leaflets to 2.5cm long. The larger stipules are 4cm long, and broad with toothed margins at least in the lower half. The flowers are solitary, or rarely up to 3, held on a peduncle 3–8cm long and are deep peach to rust-coloured.

In some individuals, some of the flowers and fruits are borne underground, a variant named as *Pisum fulvum* var. *amphicarpum*, but recognition of this under *Lathyrus* awaits a detailed revision of the group.
Specific epithet origin: tawny-orange, referring to the flower colour.

Lathyrus gloeosperma

Lathyrus gloeosperma Warb. & Eig, *Repert. Spec. Nov. Regni Veg.* 25: 351 (1928)
Glue-seeded vetchling

Habitat: Grassland, scrub and field margins
Distribution: Eastern Mediterranean (Israel, Jordan, Syria)

A sprawling and clambering annual, this reaches about 70cm, and the leaves have 4–5 pairs of lanceolate leaflets and a tendril. The creamy white flowers are very small, to 5mm across, and have a standard petal that lies flush with the wings and keel, never sitting erect. This makes it very difficult for insect visitors to get in. Because of this, some flowers of *L. gloeosperma* are thought to be cleistogamous, so may be very largely self-fertile and self-pollinating. The fruits are relatively large and inflated, with prominent raised veins all over the surface, and each contains 4–7 large, beautifully marbled seeds coated in a sticky substance.

Clearly the wild ecology of this species requires further study. However, its merits in the garden are a bit limited, other than as a curiosity.

Specific epithet origin: glue-seeded, referring to the sticky seeds.

Lathyrus neurolobus

Lathyrus neurolobus Boiss. & Heldr., *Diagn. Pl. Orient.* ser. 1, 9: 125 (1849)
Veiny-podded vetchling

Habitat: Wetland margins and areas of ground-water seepage in moist, shaded, north-facing valleys; 160–800m
Distribution: Western Crete

A low-growing, spreading, perennial species, this has slightly winged stems to 40cm. The leaves have single pairs of small, elliptic leaflets and an unbranched tendril. The flowers are small (less than 1cm across the standard), solitary and sessile, arising at the base of the leaf, and are varied shades of purple, but usually violet. The fruits are 2–3cm long, dark brown and covered in a network of prominent veins.

It is an oddity in the genus because it is very similar to several *Vicia* species. This is not surprising as the genetic evidence suggests that *L. neurolobus* is an isolated species on an early-branching lineage, so is closely allied to the vetches. It also sits in an isolated niche, endemic to the north-facing slopes of western Crete, which suggests it is a relict species trapped there from a time when its ancestors were freely able to cross between Crete and mainland Europe during periods of lower sea level. As such, it thrives in cooler, temperate, oceanic climates, like that of the UK.

Although unremarkable as a garden plant, it has merit as a novelty and works well in trough plantings or in scree beds (Kenicer & Norton 2008). It has a long flowering season in temperate areas, and the very small purple flowers are cheerful against the mat of green. Specific epithet origin: nerve-lobed, referring to the fruits.

Lathyrus nissolia

Lathyrus nissolia L., *Sp. Pl.* 2: 729 (**1753**)
Syn. *Orobus nissolia* Döll
Grass vetchling

Lifecycle: Annual
Habit: Erect
Height: 30cm
Hair: Glabrous
Stem wings: Absent
Stipules: 2mm, filiform
Leaflet number: Absent , the leaf is a phyllodic blade
Tendril: Absent
Flowers per raceme: 1–2
Peduncle or pedicel: 30–150mm
Calyx teeth: Equal, shorter than the tube
Standard width: 8–15mm
Petal colour: Crimson to pink
Style: Not contorted
Fruit size: 30–60cm
Fruit shape: Linear
Fruit features: Glabrous to densely pubescent, chestnut-brown
Number of seeds: 12–20
Wild flowering period: April–July
Habitat: Meadows; sea level to 2,000m
Distribution: Throughout much of western Eurasia (Portugal to Caucasus)

This intriguing species can be difficult to distinguish from grass when in habitat, unless the small flowers or pods are present. The leaves are phyllodes, appearing as long blades, like those of a grass but not sheathing, and with tiny stipules at the base. It grows in grasslands, which suggests a strong convergence of form with grasses

What the selective advantage of this structure might be is unclear. It could be camouflage, or it might facilitate competition with neighbouring grasses for light or other resources. The developmental origin of the phyllode is not known either, whether it be a winged rachis, an extension of the petiole, a modified tendril, a single leaflet, or some combination of these. Similar phyllodes are seen in the young stages of allied species such as *L. clymenum* and *L. ochrus*, so the phenomenon can be interpreted as neoteny. Deeper ecological, genetic and developmental research is required.

Several infraspecific taxa, including a forma, a variety and several subspecies have been proposed on the basis of habit, pubescence and flower number. The combination of these characteristics is complex and has little consistent geographical basis, so the species is treated as a single entity here.

In horticultural situations this is a valuable addition to meadow plantings, adding scattered spots of colour throughout species-rich grassland.

Specific epithet origin: named for French botanist Guillaume Nissole (1647–1735).

Lathyrus ochrus

Lathyrus ochrus (L.) DC., *Fl. Franc.* [de Candolle & Lamarck], ed. 3, **4**: 578 (1805)
Syn. *Pisum ochrus* L.
Cyprus vetch, winged vetchling, ochre-flowered pea

Habitat: Fields, meadows, roadsides and open, dry ground; sea level to 1,000m
Distribution: Mediterranean, central and southern Europe

This is a distinctive annual species because of its winged stems, and leaflets arising directly from the tips of the broad, oblong, winged rachises. Only the youngest leaves at the top of a mature plant have leaflets, so the main part of the plant looks like it has broad, simple leaves. The 1–2 flowers per raceme are pale yellow. Reminiscent of *L. oleraceus* (previously *Pisum sativum*), to which it is closely related, it was originally classified under *Pisum*.

Although the seeds contain a neurotoxin, it is grown as a fodder crop without ill-effect because the volume of seeds eaten is small compared to the overall bulk. The young leaves are also eaten as a salad in Greece.

Specific epithet origin: ochre-coloured, referring to the flowers.

Lathyrus oleraceus

Lathyrus oleraceus Lam., *Fl. Franç.* 2: 580 (1779)
Syns. *Pisum abyssinicum* A. Braun, *P. arvense* L., *P. elatius* M. Bieb.,
P. sativum L.
Garden pea, edible pea

Lifecycle: Annual
Habit: Climbing or scrambling
Height: 150cm
Hair: Glabrous
Stem wings: Absent
Stipules: Large, ovate, toothed, larger than neighbouring leaflets
Leaflet number: 2-4 pairs
Leaflet length: 20-60mm
Leaflet width: 10-40mm
Leaflet shape: Ovate to elliptical, sometimes toothed
Tendril: Present, robust and much-branched
Flowers per raceme: 1-2
Peduncle or pedicel length: 5-200mm, usually shorter than leaves
Calyx teeth: Equal, spreading, as long or longer than tube
Standard width: 25-50mm, emarginate
Petal colour: White, pink or maroon
Style: Not contorted, stigma broad with slightly curved margin
Fruit size: 50-150mm
Fruit shape: Elliptic
Fruit features: Glabrous, olive to dark brown depending on cultivar
Number of seeds: 5-12
Wild flowering period: April-June
Habitat: Woodlands, woodland margins, grasslands, on moist to dry soils. Widely cultivated in gardens and fields
Distribution: Mediterranean and Near East (Iberia to Afghanistan). Widely introduced as a crop, and naturalised almost worldwide

This was one of the earliest plant species to be domesticated, in the eastern Mediterranean. It is now widely cultivated, both commercially and in gardens, with around 35 million tonnes of peas produced annually across the globe (FAO 2021). It is most often grown for its edible seeds, for both human and animal consumption, with much of the world's production going into processed foods.

The taxonomy of *L. oleraceus* and its close relatives is complex, not least because up until recently it was contained in the small genus *Pisum*, and widely known as *Pisum sativum*. DNA studies (Smýkal *et al.* 2017) suggest that there were two closely related species (now *L. fulvus* and *L. oleraceus*) in the former

Pisum, with probably a wild subspecies and a domesticated subspecies in *L. oleraceus*.

The wild subspecies is *L. oleraceus* subsp. *biflorus* which is found as a native throughout the Mediterranean region. It typically has bicoloured flowers borne on relatively long peduncles, often longer than the leaf, with rough seeds (Coulot & Rabaute 2016).

The domesticated subspecies is *L. oleraceus* subsp. *oleraceus*, which has smooth seeds, relatively short peduncles and is almost always associated with cultivation. This latter subspecies contains numerous cultivars grown for their edible seeds (garden peas, marrowfat peas, field peas), for their whole edible pods (mangetout, snow pea, sugarsnap), and cultivars grown for whole young shoots (pea sprouts, toumyou). As well as dwarf cultivars, there are also curious ones where the leaflets have been replaced with tendrils, forming leaves that are completely tendrillous that support the plant in a tangled mass.

Specific epithet origin: of the vegetable garden.

Lathyrus oleraceus, garden pea, can be grown for its edible seeds (ABOVE) or its edible pods (RIGHT).

Cultivars

This chapter contains a selection of cultivars that demonstrates the diversity of form and colour found in *Lathyrus*. At least 7,200 cultivar epithets have been published for the genus but only about 1,400 cultivars are thought to currently exist. The selection in this chapter is of those likely to be encountered in cultivation, although at least 10 new cultivars of sweet pea are introduced each year.

Cultivars of species other than *L. odoratus* are presented first. Following that are the cultivars of *L. odoratus*, first the Grandiflora and Semi-grandiflora types, and then the Spencer types. The table (pp272–284) lists all the cultivars from this chapter in alphabetical order, along with the species they belong to and various other characters of use to gardeners.

Cultivars of *L. odoratus* classed as Grandiflora or Old-fashioned Grandiflora (sometimes also called normal, plain or typical) have a plain standard and a clamped keel. Semi-grandiflora cultivars have a waved standard and a clamped keel. Spencer types have a waved standard and an open keel. Although the open keel is definitive, Spencer types almost always have the largest flowers on the longest racemes, and are the most popular type of sweet pea.

LEFT | A selection of sweet peas. The bottom four are Grandiflora types and the rest are Spencers.
TOP ROW
LEFT to RIGHT
'Alan Titchmarsh', 'Cathy Wright', 'Dynasty', 'Kim Wilde'
SECOND ROW
LEFT to RIGHT
'Air Warden', 'Royal Wedding', 'Charlie's Angel', 'North Shore'
THIRD ROW
LEFT to RIGHT
'Noel Sutton', 'Gwendoline', 'Lizbeth'
BOTTOM ROW
LEFT to RIGHT
'America', 'Black Knight', 'Dorothy Eckford', 'Cupani'.

RIGHT TOP
Grandiflora and Semi-grandiflora types have a clamped keel.

RIGHT BOTTOM
Spencer types have an open keel.

Old-fashioned Grandifloras have the vigour, raceme length, flower number and flower size of cultivars with the Grandiflora flower form which prevailed up to 1910. There are also a few cultivars of more recent origin which fit the definition of Old-fashioned Grandiflora. Modern Grandifloras have Grandiflora flower form but have one or more characters which indicate Spencer ancestry. These characters are size of flower, length of raceme and the number of flowers on the raceme.

Some cultivars are sold as series, which generally means they share similar characteristics but differ from one another in flower colour. They often share the same prefix, or have names that link to a subject, but this is not always so. For cultivars that belong to a series, the name of the series is given in brackets. Cultivars are also sold as mixtures of colours, which are frequently given the suffix 'Mixed'.

With no International Cultivar Registration Authority currently designated for *Lathyrus*, cultivar names in the genus are frequently problematic. This is mainly because many are not published with good descriptions in dated nursery catalogues, which is a minimum requirement for establishment of a cultivar name stipulated by the *International Code of Nomenclature for Cultivated Plants* (ICNCP). The reuse of names, the changing of names for commercial purposes, and the use of names that are unacceptable from the perspective of the ICNCP are common problems. The names used here are as correct as possible, and further information can be found in the 'Checklist of cultivar epithets' chapter. Where a name is a duplicate of an earlier use, the name of the raiser or introducer is given after the name to distinguish it from the original, correct use.

The data provided for each cultivar has been extracted primarily from seed catalogues and the annuals of the National Sweet Pea Society.

INTRODUCER

For each cultivar an indication of its origin is given by citing the name of the nursery or individual responsible for its introduction. Where the raiser is known and is independent of the introducer this is shown by citing the raiser's name first, and then the introducer. For example, Albutt / Eagle indicates the raiser was Harvey Albutt but the introducer was Eagle Sweet Peas. The references to raisers and introducers are condensed, with further details of the individuals, the location of relevant nurseries, and years of activity given in the 'Checklist of raisers and companies' chapter.

DATE

The date attributed to the cultivar is the year that it was first offered for sale to the general public. Catalogues published after 1 July are often dated for the following year, the first season in general cultivation.

COMPARABLE CHARACTERS

Characters that are helpful for comparing the traits of each cultivar are given in a standardised form for every entry. The abbreviations used are:
H: Height; T = tall (1.8–2.4m), SD = semi-dwarf (0.6–1.2m), D = dwarf (up to 0.4m). Heights are dependent on cultivation conditions.
L: Leaf type; U = unijugate (leaf consists of one pair of leaflets and tendrils), M = multijugate (leaf consists of multiple pairs of leaflets and no tendrils).
N: Number of flowers; P = pauciflora (up to 4–5 flowers), M = multiflora (5–6 flowers or more).

P: Number of petals; S = simplex (typical flower form of one standard petal, two wing petals and a keel), D = duplex (two standard petals and sometimes extra wing petals), T = triplex (three standard petals and sometimes extra wing petals).
C: Colour of flowers; c.g. (cream ground), w.g. (white ground), two colours cited = bicolour.
S: Flowering season; summer (flower initiation begins when day length reaches 12 hours or longer), spring (flower initiation begins when day length reaches 11 hours or longer), winter = (flower initiation begins when day length reaches 10 hours or longer). Day length is not the only factor affecting flower initiation but it does affect seasonality.

SCENT

The strength of each cultivar's fragrance is of great interest to gardeners but we have not classified this here. We all perceive scent differently. In addition, the fragrance from a flower can vary considerably from one hour to another. It is strongest in warm, sultry conditions and weakest in cool, windy conditions. It is, however, generally recognised that sweet peas with the strongest fragrance are clamped-keel cultivars such as Grandiflora and Semi-grandiflora types, while the weakest fragrance is found in dwarf cultivars and Spencer cultivars with orange, scarlet
and dark maroon flowers.

RHS AWARD OF GARDEN MERIT

The RHS Award of Garden Merit (AGM) is given to plants considered excellent for ordinary use in appropriate garden conditions. The award is currently held by 62 *Lathyrus* cultivars. Cultivars with the AGM are indicated in the headings, alongside an RHS hardiness rating. Hardiness ratings in the RHS system range from H1 to H7 and a key is given at the end of the table.

TABLE OF CHARACTERS

The table on the following pages is intended as a quick guide to locating cultivars with particular characteristics for the garden. As well as cultivar name and species attribution it gives flower type, whether a non-tendril type, flower colour, whether dwarf, and flowering season. It also indicates whether they hold an RHS AGM.

Table of *Lathyrus* cultivars, including AGM

Cultivar	AGM	Species	Flower type	Non-tendril leaves	Flower colour	Dwarf	Flowering time
'Adorabel'		L. odoratus	Grandiflora		lavender, turning mauve blue		summer
'Aileen Walton'		L. odoratus	Spencer		mauve		
'Alan Titchmarsh'		L. odoratus	Spencer		almond pink, c.g.		summer
'Alaska Blue'		L. odoratus	Spencer		blue flush, w.g.		summer
'Alboroseus'	H6	L. vernus		Non-tendril	white & pink		spring
'Albus'		L. sativus			white	Semi	summer
'Albutt Blue'		L. odoratus	Semi-grandiflora		blue picotee, w.g.		summer
'Alice Hardwicke'		L. odoratus	Spencer		orange red, w.g.		summer
'Alisa'		L. odoratus	Semi-grandiflora		salmon pink, c.g.		summer
'Alison Valentini'		L. odoratus	Spencer	Non-tendril	crimson		summer
'Almost Black'		L. odoratus	Grandiflora		darkest maroon violet		summer
'America'	H3	L. odoratus	Grandiflora		red flake, w.g.		summer
'Andrea Robertson'		L. odoratus	Spencer		dark violet/blue		summer
'Andrew Cavendish'		L. odoratus	Spencer		lavender		summer
'Angel Kiss'		L. odoratus	Spencer		light pink		winter
'Annabelle'		L. odoratus	Spencer		lavender		summer
'Anne Barron'		L. odoratus	Spencer		warm rose pink, c.g.		summer
'Anne Hathaway'		L. odoratus	Grandiflora		pale blue flake		summer
'Anniversary'		L. odoratus	Spencer		white with pink edge		summer
'Aphrodite'	H3	L. odoratus	Spencer		white		summer
'Apple Blossom' Beane		L. odoratus	Spencer		pink stripe, w.g.		summer
'Apricot Queen'		L. odoratus	Spencer		orange pink		summer
'Apricot Sprite'		L. odoratus	Spencer		almond pink		summer
'Aquarius'		L. odoratus	Spencer	Non-tendril	mauve		summer
'Aries'		L. odoratus	Spencer	Non-tendril	salmon pink, w.g.	Semi	summer
'Ascot' Unwins		L. odoratus	Spencer		salmon pink, c.g.		summer
'Astronaut Lavender'		L. odoratus	Spencer	Non-tendril	lavender		summer
'Astronaut White'		L. odoratus	Spencer	Non-tendril	white		summer
'Atlantis'		L. odoratus	Spencer		blue stripe, w.g.		summer
'Audrey Kirkman'		L. odoratus	Spencer		marbled pink, w.g.		summer
'Aunt Jane'		L. odoratus	Spencer		magenta		summer
'Aurora Borealis' Place	H3	L. odoratus	Spencer		maroon stripe, w.g.	Semi	summer
'Azureus'		L. sativus			blue	Semi	summer
'Baby's Blush'		L. odoratus	Grandiflora		blush pink / white		summer
'Balcony Bride'		L. odoratus	Spencer		pink stripe, w.g.	Semi	summer
'Ballerina Blue'	H3	L. odoratus	Spencer		mid blue		summer
'Balmoral' Brackley		L. odoratus	Spencer		dark maroon		summer
'Banty'		L. odoratus	Spencer		rose pink, w.g.		summer
'Baronscourt'		L. odoratus	Spencer		deep mauve		summer
'Barry Dare'		L. odoratus	Spencer		cerise		summer
'Batheaston'		L. odoratus	Spencer		pale pink, w.g.		summer
'Beaujolais'		L. odoratus	Spencer		burgundy		summer
'Beth Chatto'		L. odoratus	Spencer		pale pink, c.g.		summer

Cultivar	AGM	Species	Flower type	Non-tendril leaves	Flower colour	Dwarf	Flowering time
'Beverley Kaye'		L. odoratus	Spencer		pale salmon pink		winter
'Big Blue'		L. odoratus	Spencer		mid blue		summer
'Bill's Choice'		L. odoratus	Spencer		deep rose pink, w.g.		summer
'Black Knight'		L. odoratus	Grandiflora		dark maroon		summer
'Blue Danube' Morris		L. odoratus	Spencer		mid blue		summer
'Blue Ripple' Unwins		L. odoratus	Spencer		blue flake, w.g.		summer
'Blue Shift'		L. odoratus	Spencer		purple, becoming mauve blue		summer
'Blue Stripe'		L. sativus			white with blue blotch	Semi	summer
'Blue Vein' Hammett		L. odoratus	Spencer		marbled apricot		summer
'Blue Wonder'		L. odoratus	Spencer		mid blue		early spring
'Bobby Chisholm'		L. odoratus	Spencer		rosy lavender		summer
'Bobby's Girl'	H3	L. odoratus	Spencer		pale salmon pink, c.g.		summer
'Border Beauty'		L. odoratus	Spencer		pale lavender flush		summer
'Bounce Mid Blue'	H3	L. odoratus	Semi-grandiflora		mid blue	Semi	spring
'Bounce Navy Blue'	H3	L. odoratus	Spencer		navy blue	Semi	summer
'Bouquet Crimson'		L. odoratus	Spencer		crimson		summer
'Bouquet Lavender'		L. odoratus	Spencer		lavender		summer
'Bouquet Mid Blue'		L. odoratus	Spencer		mid blue		summer
'Bouquet Pink'		L. odoratus	Spencer		pale pink		summer
'Bouquet Scarlet'		L. odoratus	Spencer		scarlet		summer
'Bouquet Violet'		L. odoratus	Spencer		violet		summer
'Bouquet White'		L. odoratus	Spencer		white		summer
'Bramdean'	H3	L. odoratus	Grandiflora		white		summer
'Brenda Bridger'		L. odoratus	Spencer		pink bicolour		summer
'Brian Clough'		L. odoratus	Spencer		salmon orange, w.g.		summer
'Brian Haynes'		L. odoratus	Spencer		light purple flake, w.g.		summer
'Bridget McAleer'		L. odoratus	Spencer		dark mauve		summer
'Bristol'	H3	L. odoratus	Spencer		pale blue		summer
'Bristol Cream'		L. odoratus	Spencer		cream		summer
'Brook Hall'	H3	L. odoratus	Spencer		white		summer
'Buccaneer'		L. odoratus	Spencer		crimsons		summer
'Burlesque'		L. odoratus	Spencer		mauve-blue flake, w.g.		summer
'Burnished Bronze'		L. odoratus	Spencer		maroon		summer
'Candy' Beane		L. odoratus	Spencer		light maroon stripe, w.g.		summer
'Carlotta'		L. odoratus	Spencer		carmine		summer
'Captain of the Blues'		L. odoratus	Grandiflora		mauve / blue		summer
'Carmel' Ferry Morse		L. odoratus	Spencer		light lavender	Semi	late spring
'Carminette'		L. odoratus	Spencer		carmine rose		spring
'Castle of Mey'		L. odoratus	Spencer		cream		summer
'Castlewellan'		L. odoratus	Spencer		pale pink, c.g.		summer
'Cathy'	H3	L. odoratus	Semi-grandiflora		deep cream		summer
'Cathy Wright'		L. odoratus	Spencer		white		summer

Table of *Lathyrus* cultivars, including AGM

Cultivar	AGM	Species	Flower type	Non-tendril leaves	Flower colour	Dwarf	Flowering time
'CCC'		L. odoratus	Grandiflora		white		summer
'Cerise Carpet'		L. odoratus	Grandiflora		orange cerise	▨	summer
'Champagne Bubbles'		L. odoratus	Spencer		pale salmon pink, c.g.		summer
'Chance'		L. odoratus	Spencer		red / pink		summer
'Charles Unwin' Colledge		L. odoratus	Spencer		salmon pink, c.g.		summer
'Charlie Bear'		L. odoratus	Spencer		mauve-pink / white		summer
'Charlie's Angel'	H3	L. odoratus	Spencer		pale blue		summer
'Charlotte Emma'		L. odoratus	Spencer		appleblossom pink, w.g.		summer
'Chatsworth'		L. odoratus	Spencer		pale blue		summer
'Chelsea'		L. clymenum			lavender / mauve	Semi	summer
'Chelsea Centenary'		L. odoratus	Spencer		pale blue		summer
'Cherub Lady T'	H3	L. odoratus	Grandiflora		cerise / lavender	▨	summer
'Cherub Northern Lights'		L. odoratus	Grandiflora		crimson flush, w.g. / blue flush, w.g.	▨	summer
'Cherub Penny Black'		L. odoratus	Grandiflora		dark maroon	▨	summer
'Cherub Pink'		L. odoratus	Grandiflora		pale pink, w.g.	▨	summer
'Cheryl Rainey'		L. odoratus	Spencer		orange salmon		summer
'Choc Stripe'		L. odoratus	Spencer		maroon stripe, w.g.		summer
'Chocolate Flake'		L. odoratus	Spencer		chocolate maroon flake, w.g.		
'Chris Harrod'	H3	L. odoratus	Spencer		pale blue		summer
'Clotted Cream' Brewer		L. odoratus	Spencer		cream		summer
'Cocktail' Hammett		L. odoratus	Spencer		maroon / violet		summer
Continental Mixed		L. odoratus	Spencer		mixed colours		summer
'Coraleena'		L. odoratus	Spencer		coral scarlet		late spring
'Countess Cadogan'		L. odoratus	Grandiflora		violet/light blue		summer
'Cream Eggs'		L. odoratus	Grandiflora		cream with violet edge		summer
'Cream Southbourne'		L. odoratus	Spencer		cream		summer
'Crescent Moon'		L. sativus			pink stripe / mauve	Semi	summer
'Crimson Purple'		L. odoratus	Spencer		red stripe, w.g.		summer
Crown Princess of Prussia		L. odoratus	Grandiflora		lilac pink / pale pink		summer
'Cupani'		L. odoratus	Grandiflora		maroon / violet		summer
'Cupid Bright Violet'		L. odoratus	Grandiflora		bright violet	▨	summer
'Cyaneus'		L. sativus			purple-blue	Semi	summer
'Cyril Plater'		L. odoratus	Spencer		rosy mauve		summer
'Dalesman'		L. odoratus	Spencer		mid blue		summer
'Dama Duet'		L. vernus		▨	mauve / lavender		spring
'Dama Emily'		L. vernus		▨	palest pink		spring
'Dancing Queen' Bolton		L. odoratus	Spencer		white		summer
'Daphne' Unwins		L. odoratus	Spencer		lavender		summer
'Darcey Bussell'		L. odoratus	Spencer		purple stripe, c.g.		summer
'Dark Passion'		L. odoratus	Spencer		deep violet		summer
'Dark Sprite'		L. odoratus	Grandiflora		maroon / violet	▨	winter
'David Unwin'		L. odoratus	Spencer		scarlet		summer
'Dawn'		L. odoratus	Spencer		blue flush, w.g.		summer

Cultivar	AGM	Species	Non-tendril leaves	Flower colour	Dwarf	Flowering time
'Deborah Devonshire'		L. odoratus	Spencer	white with pink edge		summer
'Denis Compton'		L. odoratus	Spencer	salmon pink, c.g.		summer
'Diamond Wedding'		L. odoratus	Grandiflora	white		summer
'Dolly Varden' Grayson		L. odoratus	Grandiflora	pale purple/white		summer
'Doreen' Beane		L. odoratus	Spencer	cream		summer
'Dorothy Eckford'	H3	L. odoratus	Grandiflora	white		summer
'Dr Robery Uvedale'		L. odoratus	Grandiflora	dark purple		summer
'Dragonfly' Taylor		L. odoratus	Semi-grandiflora	cream marbled with lavender		summer
'Dream Girl'		L. odoratus	Spencer	rose pink, c.g.		summer
'Duke of York'		L. odoratus	Grandiflora	rose pink/cream		summer
'Duo Salmon'	H3	L. odoratus	Spencer	cerise/pink		summer
'Dusty Springfield'		L. odoratus	Spencer	orange red		summer
'Duvet Cherry'		L. odoratus	Spencer	carmine/pink	■	winter
'Dynasty'		L. odoratus	Spencer	magenta		summer
'Earl Grey'		L. odoratus	Spencer	maroon, w.g. / violet, w.g.		summer
'Eclipse' Laidlaw		L. odoratus	Spencer	deep mauve		summer
'Edd Fincham'		L. odoratus	Spencer	maroon		summer
'Edish Flanagan'		L. odoratus	Spencer	orange red		summer
'Elegance Cranberry'		L. odoratus	Spencer	purple		summer
'Ella Maria'		L. odoratus	Spencer	pink stripe, c.g.		summer
'Emily' Unwins		L. odoratus	Grandiflora	rose pink, w.g.		summer
'Emma'		L. odoratus	Spencer	salmon pink, c.g.		summer
'Ena Margaret'		L. odoratus	Spencer	lavender flush on ivory		summer
'Enchanté'		L. odoratus	Spencer	cerise flush, w.g. / mauve flush		summer
'Erewhon'		L. odoratus	Semi-grandiflora	mauve/lavender		summer
'Esther Rantzen'		L. odoratus	Spencer	pale blue		summer
'Ethel Grace'		L. odoratus	Spencer	lavender		summer
'Evelyn' Ferry Morse 1944		L. odoratus	Spencer	salmon pink, c.g.		late spring
'Evening Glow'	H3	L. odoratus	Spencer	orange pink		summer
'Explorer Crimson'		L. odoratus	Spencer	crimson	Semi	summer
'Explorer Rose Pink'		L. odoratus	Spencer	rose pink	Semi	summer
'Explorer Scarlet'		L. odoratus	Spencer	scarlet	Semi	summer
'Fields of Fire'		L. odoratus	Spencer	scarlet		summer
'Fire and Ice'		L. odoratus	Grandiflora	crimson flake/blue		summer
'Firecrest'		L. odoratus	Spencer	cerise scarlet		summer
'First Flame'	H3	L. odoratus	Spencer	salmon cerise, w.g.		summer
'First Lady' Zvolanek		L. odoratus	Spencer	deep salmon pink		summer
'Flame'		L. odoratus	Spencer			
'Flora Norton'		L. odoratus	Grandiflora	pale blue		summer
'Florencecourt' Harrod		L. odoratus	Spencer	salmon cerise, w.g.		summer
'Flying Visit'		L. odoratus	Spencer	white flushed deep violet		summer
'Frances Kate'		L. odoratus	Spencer	navy stripe		summer

Table of *Lathyrus* cultivars, including AGM

Cultivar	AGM	Species	Non-tendril leaves	Flower colour	Dwarf	Flowering time
'Frank G' Ferry Morse 1940		*L. odoratus*	Spencer	rosy lavender		late spring
'Future Shock'		*L. odoratus*	Spencer	marbled orange, turning brown		summer
'Garnette'		*L. odoratus*	Spencer	maroon		spring
'Garry Kirkman'		*L. odoratus*	Spencer	orange red		summer
'Gawler Cerise'		*L. odoratus*	Spencer	cerise orange		winter
'Gawler Marion'		*L. odoratus*	Spencer	pale salmon pink, c.g.		late spring
'Gawler Shell Pink'		*L. odoratus*	Spencer	shell pink		winter
'Geoff Amos'		*L. odoratus*	Spencer	red stripe, w.g.		summer
'Geoff Hughes'		*L. odoratus*	Spencer	orange flake, w.g.		summer
'George Priestly'		*L. odoratus*	Spencer	light mauve, c.g.		summer
'Gerry Cullinan'		*L. odoratus*	Spencer	lavender, c.g.		summer
'Glasnevin'		*L. odoratus*	Spencer	white		summer
'Gloria' Denholm		*L. odoratus*	Spencer	carmine rose		early spring
'Glow' Unwins		*L. odoratus*	Spencer	orange pink, w.g. / cerise pink, w.g.		summer
'Grandma Butt'		*L. odoratus*	Spencer	carmine rose		summer
'Great Britain'		*L. odoratus*	Spencer	rose pink, c.g.		summer
'Greenfingers'		*L. odoratus*	Grandiflora	violet flush, c.g.		summer
'Gwendoline' Unwins	H3	*L. odoratus*	Spencer	white flushed lilac pink		summer
'Gypsy Queen'		*L. odoratus*	Spencer	crimson		summer
'Hampton Court'		*L. odoratus*	Spencer	mid blue		summer
'Hannah Dale' Grayson		*L. odoratus*	Grandiflora	maroon		winter
'Hannah Magovern'		*L. odoratus*	Spencer	scarlet		summer
'Hannah's Harmony'	H3	*L. odoratus*	Spencer	white flushed deep violet	Semi	summer
'Heartbeat'		*L. odoratus*	Spencer	cerise		summer
'Heathcliff'	H3	*L. odoratus*	Grandiflora	mauve blue		summer
'Heaven Scent'		*L. odoratus*	Spencer	pale pink, c.g.		summer
'Henry Eckford'		*L. odoratus*	Grandiflora	orange scarlet		summer
'Hero' Unwins		*L. odoratus*	Spencer	dark violet		summer
'High Scent'	H3	*L. odoratus*	Semi-grandiflora	cream with violet edge		summer
'High Society' Hammett		*L. odoratus*	Spencer	white with pink edge		early
'Hikari'		*L. odoratus*	Spencer	orange pink		winter
'Honeymoon'		*L. odoratus*	Spencer	lavender flush		summer
'Hotham Red'		*L. annuus*		red	Semi	summer
'Ida King'		*L. odoratus*	Spencer	lavender		summer
'Imogen'		*L. odoratus*	Spencer	rose pink, c.g.		summer
'Invicta' Christmas		*L. odoratus*	Spencer	white		summer
'Isabella Cochrane'		*L. odoratus*	Spencer	lavender flush, w.g.		summer
'Jack Bridger'		*L. odoratus*	Spencer	pale blush pink		summer
'Jack Ellis'		*L. odoratus*	Grandiflora	maroon / purple		summer
'Jack Eveleigh'		*L. odoratus*	Spencer	pale blue flush, w.g.		summer
'Jacko'		*L. odoratus*	Spencer	red stripe, w.g.		summer
'Jacqueline Ann'		*L. odoratus*	Spencer	deep lavender		summer
'Jaqueline Heather'	H3	*L. odoratus*	Spencer	white with pink edge		summer

Cultivar	AGM	Species	Non-tendril leaves	Flower colour	Dwarf	Flowering time
'Janet' Parsons		L. odoratus	Semi-grandiflora	white		late spring
'Janet Scott'	H3	L. odoratus	Grandiflora	appleblossom pink / pale pink		summer
'Janey'		L. odoratus	Spencer	red flake, w.g.		summer
'Janine Martin'		L. odoratus	Spencer	cream		winter
'Jayne Amanda'		L. odoratus	Spencer	magenta		summer
'Jeannie'		L. odoratus	Spencer	cream		summer
'Jemima'		L. odoratus	Spencer	cerise rose pink, w.g.		summer
'Jill Walton'		L. odoratus	Spencer	salmon pink, c.g.		summer
'Jilly'	H3	L. odoratus	Spencer	cream		summer
'Jimmy'		L. odoratus	Spencer	deep scarlet		late spring
'Joan Elizabeth Child'		L. odoratus	Spencer	cerise pink		summer
'Joejess'		L. odoratus	Spencer	orange red		summer
'John Gray'	H3	L. odoratus	Spencer	pale pink, w.g.		summer
'Joyce Stanton'		L. odoratus	Spencer	dark blue		summer
'Judith Martin'		L. odoratus	Spencer	pale mauve		winter
'Judith Wilkinson'		L. odoratus	Spencer	deep carmine		summer
'Julie Ann'		L. odoratus	Spencer	carmine		summer
'Juliet' Unwins		L. odoratus	Grandiflora	cream		summer
'Just Janet'		L. odoratus	Spencer	coral pink, w.g.		summer
'Just Jenny'		L. odoratus	Spencer	dark blue		summer
'Just Julia'	H3	L. odoratus	Spencer	mid blue		summer
'Karen Harrod'		L. odoratus	Spencer	mid blue		summer
'Karen Louise'		L. odoratus	Spencer	lavender		summer
'Karen Tremewan'		L. odoratus	Spencer	orange pink		summer
'Katie Alice'		L. odoratus	Spencer	mauve violet		summer
'Kiera Madeline'		L. odoratus	Spencer	pink picotee, c.g.		summer
'Killarney'		L. odoratus	Spencer	salmon cream pink	Semi	summer
'King Edward VII'	H3	L. odoratus	Grandiflora	scarlet		summer
'King Size Navy Blue'		L. odoratus	Semi-grandiflora	dark blue		summer
'Kingfisher'		L. odoratus	Semi-grandiflora	violet flush, c.g.		summer
'Kippen Cream'		L. odoratus	Spencer	cream		summer
'Knee-Hi Cream Pink'		L. odoratus	Spencer	salmon cream pink	Semi	spring/summer
'Knee-Hi Rose Crimson'		L. odoratus	Spencer	rose crimson	Semi	summer
'Knee-Hi White'		L. odoratus	Spencer	white	Semi	summer
'Lady Grisel Hamilton'		L. odoratus	Grandiflora	lavender		summer
'Lady Nicholson'		L. odoratus	Spencer	mauve stripe, w.g.		summer
'Lady Turral'		L. odoratus	Grandiflora	cerise / deep lilac		summer
'Laila K'		L. odoratus	Spencer	pink		summer
'Lakeland Blizzard'		L. odoratus	Spencer	white		summer
'Lamorna's Love'		L. vernus		bright mauve-blue		spring
'Laura Webster'		L. odoratus	Spencer	white-flushed warm pink		summer
'Lauren Landy'	H3	L. odoratus	Spencer	warm rose pink, w.g.		summer
'Lavender Flake'		L. odoratus	Spencer	flake		summer

Table of *Lathyrus* cultivars, including AGM

Cultivar	AGM	Species	Non-tendril leaves	Flower colour	Dwarf	Flowering time
'Lavender Sprite'	H3	L. odoratus	Grandiflora	lavender	■	winter
'Leading Light'		L. odoratus	Spencer	lavender/mauve		summer
'Leamington'		L. odoratus	Spencer	deep lavender		summer
'Lemonade'		L. chloranthus	Tall	yellow-green		summer
'Len Harrod'		L. odoratus	Spencer	orange pink, w.g.		summer
'Lilac Ripple'		L. odoratus	Spencer	lilac stripe, w.g.		summer
'Lilac Romance'		L. odoratus	Spencer	light lilac		summer
'Linda C'		L. odoratus	Spencer	mid blue		summer
'Linda Carole'		L. odoratus	Spencer	■ carmine stripe, w.g.		early spring
'Linda Mary'		L. odoratus	Spencer	pink stripe, c.g.		summer
'Linda Richards'		L. odoratus	Spencer	lilac pink flush, c.g.		summer
'Lipstick' Hammett		L. odoratus	Spencer	mid red		summer
'Lipstick' Unwins	H3	L. odoratus	Spencer	vibrant carmine		summer
'Lisa Marie'		L. odoratus	Spencer	plum stripe, w.g.		summer
'Little Red Riding Hood'		L. odoratus	Grandiflora	red/white		summer
'Lizbeth'		L. odoratus	Spencer	orange pink		summer
'Lois' Ferry Morse 1940		L. odoratus	Spencer	rose pink, w.g.		late spring
'Lord Nelson'		L. odoratus	Grandiflora	navy blue		summer
'Lovejoy'		L. odoratus	Spencer	maroon		summer
'Lucy Hawthorn'		L. odoratus	Spencer	white		summer
'Lunar Sea'		L. odoratus	Spencer	cream		early spring
'Madison'	H3	L. odoratus	Grandiflora	scarlet		summer
'Madrid'		L. odoratus	Spencer	scarlet	Semi	summer
'Maestro'		L. odoratus	Spencer	lavender		summer
'Magnificent Maroon'		L. odoratus	Spencer	maroon		summer
'Maloy'		L. odoratus	Spencer	orange-pink		summer
'Mammoth Cream Pink'		L. odoratus	Spencer	appleblossom pink, c.g.		early spring
'Mammoth Navy'		L. odoratus	Spencer	dark blue		winter
'Margaret's Delight'		L. odoratus	Spencer	rose pink		summer
'Marie's Melody'		L. odoratus	Spencer	red strip, w.g.	Semi	summer
'Marion' Walker		L. odoratus	Spencer	lavender		summer
'Marjorie Carrier'		L. odoratus	Spencer	salmon pink, c.g.		summer
'Mark Harrod'		L. odoratus	Spencer	scarlet		summer
'Mars' Unwins		L. odoratus	Spencer	red stripe, w.g.		summer
'Martha Mary'	H3	L. odoratus	Spencer	cream		summer
'Mary Mac'	H3	L. odoratus	Spencer	cream		summer
'Mary Pannell'		L. odoratus	Spencer	cerise pink		summer
'Mary Priestley'		L. odoratus	Spencer	white		summer
'Matterhorn'		L. odoratus	Spencer	white	Semi	summer
'Matucana'	H3	L. odoratus	Grandiflora	mauve	■	spring
'Mauve Queen' Eckford		L. odoratus	Grandiflora	mauve		summer
'Mauvette'		L. odoratus	Spencer	mauve	■	spring

Cultivar	AGM	Species	Non-tendril leaves	Flower colour	Dwarf	Flowering time
'Maxeen Martin'		L. odoratus	Spencer	bluish pink, c.g.		winter
'Memorial Flight'		L. odoratus	Spencer	white		summer
'Memories' Unwins		L. odoratus	Grandiflora	purple or mauve		summer
'Midnight' Jones		L. odoratus	Spencer	dark maroon		summer
'Milestone'		L. odoratus	Spencer	maroon		summer
'Millennium'		L. odoratus	Spencer	crimson		summer
'Milly'		L. odoratus	Spencer	vibrant magenta		summer
'Minmaroon'		L. odoratus	Grandiflora	maroon stripe, w.g.		summer
'Minuet Blue Splash'		L. odoratus	Spencer	blue stripe, w.g.	Semi	summer
'Minuet Orange'		L. odoratus	Spencer	orange stripe, w.g.	Semi	summer
'Minuet Orange-pink Splash'		L. odoratus	Spencer	orange stripe, w.g. / pink stripe, w.g.	Semi	summer
'Minuet Purple'		L. odoratus	Spencer	purple stripe, w.g.	Semi	summer
'Minuet Red'		L. odoratus	Spencer	red stripe, w.g.	Semi	summer
'Miss Willmott'		L. odoratus	Grandiflora	orange / pink		summer
'Misty'		L. odoratus	Spencer			
'Misty Mountain'		L. odoratus	Spencer	lavender on ivory ground		summer
'Mollie Rilstone'		L. odoratus	Spencer	pink picotee, c.g.		summer
'Monty Don'		L. odoratus	Grandiflora	dark maroon		summer
'Moorland Beauty'		L. odoratus	Spencer	deep mauve		summer
'More Scent'		L. odoratus	Semi-grandiflora	purple flush, w.g.		summer
'Morven'		L. odoratus	Spencer	orange red		summer
'Mount Stewart'		L. odoratus	Spencer	mauve		summer
'Mr P.'		L. odoratus	Spencer	dark blue flake, w.g.		summer
'Mrs Bernard Jones'	H3	L. odoratus	Spencer	candy pink flush, w.g.		summer
'Mrs Collier'		L. odoratus	Grandiflora	cream		summer
'Mrs R. Bolton'		L. odoratus	Spencer	rose pink, w.g.		summer
'Mrs R. Chisholm'		L. odoratus	Spencer	white		summer
'Mrs R. Penney'		L. annuus		orange	Semi	summer
'Mrs Walter Wright'		L. odoratus	Grandiflora	mauve / blue		summer
'Mumsie'		L. odoratus	Spencer	crimson		summer
'My Navy'		L. odoratus	Grandiflora	navy blue		summer
'Naomi Nazareth'		L. odoratus	Spencer	pale blue		summer
'Naples'		L. odoratus	Spencer	mid blue	Semi	summer
'New Dawn'		L. odoratus	Spencer	pink flake, c.g.	Semi	late spring
'Night Sky'		L. odoratus	Spencer	dark blue stripe, w.g.		summer
'Nimbus'		L. odoratus	Spencer	dark purple stripe on grey		summer
'Noel Sutton'	H3	L. odoratus	Spencer	mid blue		summer
'Nora Holman'		L. odoratus	Spencer	pale salmon pink, c.g.		summer
'North Shore'		L. odoratus	Spencer	navy blue / violet		summer
'Nuance'		L. odoratus	Spencer	pale two-tone bicolour		early spring
'Oban Bay'		L. odoratus	Spencer	silver blue		summer
'Oklahoma'	H3	L. odoratus	Spencer	red flake, w.g.		summer

Table of *Lathyrus* cultivars, including AGM

Cultivar	AGM	Species	Non-tendril leaves	Flower colour	Dwarf	Flowering time
'Olive D.'		*L. odoratus*	Spencer	maroon stripe, w.g.		summer
'Ollie Clarke'		*L. odoratus*	Spencer	orange salmon		summer
'Omay'		*L. odoratus*	Spencer	orange red, w.g.		summer
'Opalette'		*L. odoratus*	Spencer	rose pink, w.g.	▓	spring
'Orchid' Unwins		*L. odoratus*	Spencer	deep lavender		summer
'Our Colin'		*L. odoratus*	Spencer	mid blue		summer
'Our Harry'		*L. odoratus*	Spencer	mid blue		summer
'Oyama Aphrodite'		*L. odoratus*	Spencer	orange pink		winter
'Oyama Bicolour'		*L. odoratus*	Spencer	mauve / lavender		early spring
'Oyama Millennium'		*L. odoratus*	Spencer	dark pink		early spring or winter
'Oyama Russian Blue'		*L. odoratus*	Spencer	lavender-purple		early spring
'Painted Lady'		*L. odoratus*	Grandiflora	rose / white, tinted pink		summer
'Pandemonium'	H3	*L. odoratus*	Spencer	purple flake		summer
'Pansy Lavender Flush'		*L. odoratus*	Grandiflora	lavender flush, w.g.	Semi	summer
'Patio Deep Rose'		*L. odoratus*	Spencer	magenta	▓	spring
'Patio Pink/White Bicolour'		*L. odoratus*	Spencer	pink / white	▓	spring
'Patio Red/Pink Bicolour'		*L. odoratus*	Spencer	red / pink	▓	spring
'Patricia Anne'	H3	*L. odoratus*	Spencer	lavender flush		summer
'Peacock' Unwins		*L. odoratus*	Spencer	deep lavender on ivory		summer
'Pearl Anniversary'		*L. odoratus*	Spencer	pale pink flake, w.g.		summer
'Percy Thrower'		*L. odoratus*	Spencer	lavender flush, w.g.		summer
'Phoebe' Bolton		*L. odoratus*	Spencer	orange flake, w.g.		summer
'Piggy Sue'		*L. odoratus*	Spencer	cream with pink edge		early spring
'Picolino'		*L. odoratus*	Grandiflora	blue picotee, w.g.		summer
'Pink Cupid'	H3	*L. odoratus*	Grandiflora	pink / white	▓	summer
'Pink Nines'		*L. odoratus*	Spencer	mid pink		early spring
'Pip Tremewan'		*L. odoratus*	Spencer	purple		summer
'Pip's Cornish Cream'		*L. odoratus*	Spencer	cream		summer
'Pip's Maroon'		*L. odoratus*	Spencer	dark maroon		summer
'Pirate Gold'		*L. odoratus*	Spencer	orange		summer
'Pisces'		*L. odoratus*	Spencer ▓	pale pink, w.g.		summer
'Pocahontas'	H3	*L. odoratus*	Spencer	geranium red		summer
'Polar Star'		*L. odoratus*	Spencer	white		early spring
'Polyanna'		*L. odoratus*	Grandiflora	lilac pink / white		summer
'Porlock'		*L. odoratus*	Spencer	maroon / violet, marbled		summer
'Precious' Unwins		*L. odoratus*	Spencer	rose pink, w.g.		summer
'Prima Donna' Eckford		*L. odoratus*	Grandiflora	pure pink		summer
'Prince Edward of York'		*L. odoratus*	Grandiflora	red / pink		summer
'Prince of Orange' Morse		*L. odoratus*	Spencer	orange		summer
'Princess' Zvolanek		*L. odoratus*	Spencer	light salmon		winter
'Princess Elizabeth' Bolton		*L. odoratus*	Spencer	salmon pink, c.g.		summer

Cultivar	AGM	Species	Non-tendril leaves	Flower colour	Dwarf	Flowering time
'Princess of Wales' Grayson		*L. odoratus*	Grandiflora	purple flake, w.g.		summer
'Promise'		*L. odoratus*	Spencer	pink / white		summer
'Purple Pimpernel'		*L. odoratus*	Spencer	maroon / violet		summer
'Purple Prince'		*L. odoratus*	Grandiflora	purple maroon/deep violet		summer
'Queen Alexandra'		*L. odoratus*	Grandiflora	scarlet		summer
'Queen Mother' Richardson		*L. odoratus*	Spencer	orange pink		summer
'Queen of Hearts'		*L. odoratus*	Spencer	pink stripe, w.g.		summer
'Raspberry Flake'		*L. odoratus*	Spencer	crimson flake on grey		summer
'Red Arrow'		*L. odoratus*	Spencer	scarlet		summer
'Renown' Harrod		*L. odoratus*	Spencer	crimson		summer
'Restormel'		*L. odoratus*	Spencer	orange cerise		summer
'Rhineland'		*L. odoratus*	Spencer	rose crimson	Semi	summer
'Richard and Judy'		*L. odoratus*	Spencer	purple mauve		summer
'Romeo' Unwins		*L. odoratus*	Grandiflora	white with delicate blue edge		summer
'Ron Entwistle'		*L. odoratus*	Spencer	scarlet		summer
'Ronnie'		*L. odoratus*	Spencer	mid orange		late spring
'Roosterville'		*L. odoratus*	Grandiflora	purple		summer
'Rosa Perle'	H7	*L. latifolius*		pink		summer
'Rosemary Padley'		*L. odoratus*	Spencer	crimson		summer
'Roseus'		*L. tingitanus*		pink		
'Rosie' Truslove		*L. odoratus*	Spencer	cerise		summer
'Rosina' James		*L. odoratus*	Spencer	lavender		summer
'Rosy Dawn'		*L. odoratus*	Spencer	orange flake, w.g.		summer
'Rosy Salmon'		*L. odoratus*	Spencer	salmon		summer
'Roubeena'		*L. odoratus*	Spencer	ruby red		late spring
'Route 66'		*L. odoratus*	Spencer	red/white		summer
'Royal Pink' Ferry Morse		*L. odoratus*	Spencer	pink		late spring
'Royal Wedding'		*L. odoratus*	Spencer	white		summer
'Ruby Anniversary'		*L. odoratus*	Spencer	crimson		summer
'Ruby Tuesday'		*L. odoratus*	Spencer	crimson		summer
'Rubyette'		*L. odoratus*	Spencer	crimson	■	spring
'Sagittarius'		*L. odoratus*	Spencer ■	orange red		summer
'Sally Ann'		*L. odoratus*	Spencer	rose pink, w.g.		summer
'Sally Maitland'		*L. odoratus*	Spencer	carmine		summer
'Salmon Beauty'		*L. odoratus*	Semi-grandiflora	salmon pink, c.g.		winter
'Sapphire' Burpee 1966		*L. odoratus*	Spencer	mid blue	Semi	spring
'Sarah Kennedy'		*L. odoratus*	Spencer	pale pink, w.g.		summer
'Scarlett'		*L. odoratus*	Grandiflora	crimson		summer
'Scarlette'		*L. odoratus*	Spencer	scarlet	■	spring
'Scorpio'		*L. odoratus*	Spencer ■	mid blue		summer
'Selene'		*L. odoratus*	Spencer	cream		winter

Table of *Lathyrus* cultivars, including AGM

Cultivar	AGM	Species	Non-tendril leaves	Flower colour	Dwarf	Flowering time
'Senator'		*L. odoratus*	Grandiflora	dark maroon and violet flake, w.g.		summer
'Sheila Roy'		*L. odoratus*	Spencer	salmon pink		summer
'Sicilian Pink'	H3	*L. odoratus*	Grandiflora	pink bicolour		summer
'Signpost'		*L. odoratus*	Spencer	lavender pink / white		summer
'Sir Jimmy Shand'		*L. odoratus*	Spencer	lilac stripe, w.g.		summer
'Sir Max Hastings'		*L. odoratus*	Spencer	aubergine		summer
'Skywalker'		*L. odoratus*	Spencer	mid blue		summer
'Snowlight'		*L. odoratus*	Spencer	white		summer
'Solar Flare'		*L. odoratus*	Spencer	orange scarlet		summer
'Solitude'		*L. odoratus*	Spencer	pale blue		summer
'Solstice Crimson'		*L. odoratus*	Spencer	crimson		winter
'Solstice Lavender'		*L. odoratus*	Spencer	lavender		winter
'Solstice Light Blue'		*L. odoratus*	Spencer	pale blue		winter
'Solstice Orchid'		*L. odoratus*	Spencer	purple / violet		winter
'Solstice Salmon'		*L. odoratus*	Spencer	salmon pink, c.g.		winter
'Solstice Scarlet'		*L. odoratus*	Spencer	scarlet		winter
'Solstice White'		*L. odoratus*	Spencer	white		early spring
'Solway Ballerina'	H3	*L. odoratus*	Spencer ●	pale pink, w.g.	Semi	summer
'Solway Fanfare'		*L. odoratus*	Spencer ●	cerise	Semi	summer
'Solway Charm'	H3	*L. odoratus*	Grandiflora ●	pink stripe, w.g.	Semi	summer
'Solway Classic'	H3	*L. odoratus*	Grandiflora ●	red stripe, w.g.	Semi	summer
'Solway Lullaby'		*L. odoratus*	Semi-grandiflora ●	dark blue	Semi	summer
'Solway Minstrel'		*L. odoratus*	Grandiflora ●	blue stripe, w.g.	Semi	summer
'Solway Minuet'		*L. odoratus*	Grandiflora ●	white veined pink / white with blue edge	Semi	summer
'Solway Serenade'	H3	*L. odoratus*	Grandiflora ●	red/pink	Semi	summer
'Solway Shimmer'		*L. odoratus*	Spencer ●	lavender flush, c.g.	Semi	summer
'Solway Snowflake'	H3	*L. odoratus*	Grandiflora ●	pink splash, w.g.	Semi	summer
'Solway Splendour'	H3	*L. odoratus*	Grandiflora ●	red / deep pink	Semi	summer
'Solway Sunset'		*L. odoratus*	Spencer	orange cerise stripe, w.g.		summer
'Solway Symphony'		*L. odoratus*	Spencer ●	mauve		summer
'Solway Velvet'		*L. odoratus*	Grandiflora ●	maroon	Semi	summer
'Somerset Lady'	H3	*L. odoratus*	Spencer	carmine pink		summer
'Somewhere'		*L. odoratus*	Spencer	pink/mauve		summer
'Sonia'		*L. odoratus*	Spencer	carmine-veined pink		summer
'Sophisticated Lady'		*L. odoratus*	Spencer	cool rose pink		summer
'Southbourne'		*L. odoratus*	Spencer	pale pink, w.g.		summer
'Spanish Dancer'		*L. odoratus*	Grandiflora	pink on cream / blue flush or cream	Semi	summer
'Spring Sunshine Champagne'		*L. odoratus*	Spencer	pale salmon pink, c.g.		spring
'Starlight' Walker	H3	*L. odoratus*	Spencer	magenta, w.g.		summer
'Stella Denholm'		*L. odoratus*	Spencer	cream		early spring
'Strawberry Fields'		*L. odoratus*	Spencer	cerise / pink		late spring

Cultivar	AGM	Species		Non-tendril leaves	Flower colour	Dwarf	Flowering time
'Streamer Orange'		L. odoratus	Spencer		orange flake, w.g.		summer
'Su Pollard'		L. odoratus	Spencer		purple		summer
'Subtle Hints'		L. vernus		■	pale blue / pale mauve		spring
'Sunset' Marshall	H3	L. odoratus	Spencer		cerise stripe, w.g.		summer
'Supersnoop Cream Pink'		L. odoratus	Spencer	■	rose pink, c.g.	Semi	summer
'Supersnoop Magenta'		L. odoratus	Spencer	■	deep rose	Semi	summer
'Supersnoop Navy Blue'		L. odoratus	Spencer	■	navy blue	Semi	summer
'Supersnoop White'		L. odoratus	Spencer	■	white	Semi	summer
'Susan Burgess'		L. odoratus	Spencer		deep blush pink		summer
'Susan Thomas'		L. odoratus	Spencer		blue flake		summer
'Susie'		L. odoratus	Spencer		shrimp pink, c.g.		early spring
'Suzy Z'		L. odoratus	Spencer		maroon flake on grey		summer
'Sweetie Carmine Rose'		L. odoratus	Grandiflora		carmine/rose flaked	■	summer
'Sylvia Ann'		L. odoratus	Spencer		white		summer
'Sylvia Moore'		L. odoratus	Spencer		warm rose pink, w.g.		summer
'Sylvia Norton'		L. vernus			white		spring
'Tahiti Sunrise'	H3	L. odoratus	Spencer		bright orange pink, w.g.		summer
'Tara'		L. odoratus	Spencer		cerise pink		summer
'Tartan Mac'		L. odoratus	Spencer		maroon flake, w.g.		early spring
'Tell Tale'		L. odoratus	Spencer		pink picotee, w.g.		summer
'Teresa Maureen'	H3	L. odoratus	Grandiflora		mauve/white	Semi	summer
'Terry Wogan'		L. odoratus	Spencer		salmon pink, c.g.		summer
'The Doctor' Jones		L. odoratus	Spencer		mauve		summer
'The Princess Royal'		L. odoratus	Spencer		white		summer
'Theia Bella'		L. odoratus	Spencer		chocolate flake, w.g.		summer
'Thomas and Linda'		L. odoratus	Spencer		deep salmon, c.g.		summer
'Tommy' Parsons		L. odoratus	Semi-grandiflora		mid blue		late spring
'Tony Bates'		L. odoratus	Spencer		blue flush, c.g.		summer
'Topsy' Denholm		L. odoratus	Spencer		chocolate maroon		early spring
'Tranquillity' Wells	H3	L. odoratus	Spencer		salmon pink, c.g.		summer
'Trelawny'		L. odoratus	Spencer		lavender		summer
'Turquoise'		L. odoratus	Spencer		turquoise	Semi	summer
'Tubro'		Lathyrus		■	deep pink		summer
'Unique' Stark		L. odoratus	Grandiflora		pale blue flake, w.g.		summer
'Valerie Harrod'	H3	L. odoratus	Spencer		orange pink		summer
'Variety Club'		L. odoratus	Spencer		purple flake on grey		summer
'Vaudeville'		L. odoratus	Spencer		pink flake		summer
'Vera Lynn'		L. odoratus	Spencer		cerise		summer
'Vienna'		L. odoratus	Spencer		mauve	Semi	summer
'Villa Roma Raspberry'		L. odoratus	Spencer		pale purple	■	spring

Table of *Lathyrus* cultivars, including AGM

Cultivar	AGM	Species	Non-tendril leaves	Flower colour	Dwarf	Flowering time
'Villa Roma Rose'		*L. odoratus*	Spencer	rose pink	■	spring
'Villa Roma White'		*L. odoratus*	Spencer	cream	■	spring
'Villa Roma White / Rose'		*L. odoratus*	Spencer	pink / white	■	spring
'Vincent'		*L. odoratus*	Spencer	salmon orange		summer
'Violet Queen' Grayson		*L. odoratus*	Grandiflora	violet		summer
'Violette'		*L. odoratus*	Spencer	dark blue	■	spring
'Vulcan' Parsons		*L. odoratus*	Semi-grandiflora	scarlet		winter
'Wedding Belle'		*L. odoratus*	Spencer	pale pink, c.g.		summer
'Wedding Day'	H3	*L. odoratus*	Spencer	white		summer
'Wendy's Joy'		*L. latifolius*	Tall	mauve		summer
'Westminster'		*L. odoratus*	Spencer	crimson	Semi	summer
'White Frills'		*L. odoratus*	Spencer	white		summer
'White Pearl'	H7	*L. latifolius*		white		summer
'White Supreme' Jones	H3	*L. odoratus*	Spencer	white		summer
'Wild Swan'		*L. odoratus*	Spencer	white		summer
'William and Catherine'		*L. odoratus*	Spencer	salmon pink		summer
'William Willson'	H3	*L. odoratus*	Spencer	orange pink		summer
'Windsor' Brewer		*L. odoratus*	Spencer	dark maroon		summer
'Winston Churchill'		*L. odoratus*	Spencer	crimson		summer
'Winter Elegance Pink Diana'		*L. odoratus*	Spencer	appleblossom pink, w.g.		winter
'Winter Elegance Salmon Rose'		*L. odoratus*	Spencer	salmon rose pink		winter
'Winter Sunshine Lavender'		*L. odoratus*	Spencer	lavender, w.g.		winter
'Yankee Doodle'		*L. odoratus*	Spencer	brilliant rosy red		summer
'Yasmin Khan'		*L. odoratus*	Spencer	orange pink		summer
'Yvette Ann'		*L. odoratus*	Spencer	pale salmon pink, c.g.		summer
'Zillah Harrod'		*L. odoratus*	Spencer	lavender		summer
'Zorija Rose'		*L. odoratus*	Grandiflora	deep carmine		summer

Abbreviations

c.g. = cream ground

w.g. = white ground

Hardiness ratings relevant to *Lathyrus*

H3 = half-hardy, grown as an annual or in an unheated glasshouse, to -5°C

H4 = hardy in average UK winter, to -10°C

H5 = hardy in cold UK winter, to -15°C

H6 = hardy in very cold UK winter, to -20°C

H7 = very hardy, lower than -20°C

CULTIVARS FOR CUTTING

There is frequent reference in the cultivar descriptions to cultivars being good for cut-flower production, good for exhibition and good for garden decoration. These refer to the qualities that gardeners and growers are generally looking for when choosing cultivars for particular purposes.

The qualities required for commercial cut-flower production include maintaining long flower stems through the season, a long season of flowering, prolific flower production, good colour and a long vase life. Stem length is paramount. Cut-flower growers are less concerned with the size or quality of individual flowers or their even placement along the raceme. For this reason, many growers prefer Multiflora cultivars for their longer vase life, but there is a limited colour range in these so Spencers are also grown.

Those growing for exhibition at flower shows require different qualities. They want four flowers per raceme, of uniform large size, and evenly spaced on long racemes. The colour must be uniform and the racemes must be long. Each flower must have classic pea flower form with no deformities or disfigurement.

Most gardeners growing sweet peas simply want good garden decoration, coupled with the ability to cut a few for the house. The racemes need to be long enough for this purpose, but qualities such as good fragrance and decorative effect in the garden are more important. The quality, size and uniformity of individual blooms is less important than for exhibition. More important is the ready production of side shoots to give prolific flowering all over the plant and over a long season.

Lathyrus annuus

'Hotham Red'

A brightly coloured cultivar that was initially grown in the UK around 1991 when it was incorrectly named as *Lathyrus hierosolymitanus.*

Grayson, 2000

H: SD L: U N: P P: S C: red S: summer

'Mrs R. Penney'

This probably arose as a hybrid between yellow *L. annuus* **and** *L. annuus* **'Hotham Red'.**

Grayson, 1997

H: SD L: U N: P P: S C: orange S: summer

Lathyrus chloranthus

'Lemonade'

This lacks any of the red or orange shades often found in the standard petals of the typical species.
Thompson & Morgan, 1993
H: T L: U N: P P: S C: yellow-green
S: summer

Lathyrus clymenum

'Chelsea'

Following a trial by Roger Parsons in 1995 of various accessions of *L. clymenum*, this was found to be the most gardenworthy and was selected for its improved vigour, more leaflets per leaf, and longer racemes with 3 or 4 flowers, although the colour is the same as the typical species. It originated from Chelsea Physic Garden and was introduced by Grayson in 1997.

R. Parsons / Grayson, 1997

H: SD L: M N: P P: S C: lavender / mauve S: summer

Lathyrus latifolius

'Wendy's Joy'
Of all the cultivars of *L. latifolius*, this one has the most unusual flower colour.
Robert Bolton & Son, 1999
H: T L: U N: P P: S C: mauve
S: summer

'Rosa Perle' AGM H7
One of the several pale pink cultivars, this was awarded its AGM under what is thought to be its original German name. Pink Pearl is simply a translation, and 'Appleblossom' and 'Bishop's Pink' are very similar.
Raiser and date unknown
H: T L: U N: P P: S C: pink S: summer

'White Pearl' AGM H7
This and 'Albus' may have originally been distinct from each other, with 'White Pearl' having larger flowers. However, both have subsequently been raised from seed so the distinctions have blurred. Neither are as robust as the other colours.
Raiser unknown, before 1936
H: T L: U N: P P: S C: white S: summer

Lathyrus sativus

'Azureus'
This ancient cultivar with azure blue flowers is likely to be the entity referred to by Gerard (1636) as *Lathyrus aegyptiacus*. Dean (1882) referred to it as *Lathyrus azureus* and it is sometimes recognised as *L. sativus* f. *azureus*.
Raiser and date unknown
H: SD L: U N: P P: S C: blue S: summer

'Albus'
Along with 'Azureus', this is an old cultivar and is sometimes recognised as *L. sativus* f. *albus*.
Raiser and date unknow
H: SD L: U N: P P: S C: white
S: summer

'Blue Stripe'
This cultivar has larger flowers than the older colour selections. It was raised from a cultivated population of mixed colours.
Grayson, 1999
H: SD L: U N: P P: S C: white with blue blotch S: summer

'Crescent Moon'

This was selected from an ancient agricultural cultivar originating in Pakistan. The name refers to the flag of that country and the shape of the colouring.
R. Parsons, 2020
H: SD L: U N: P P: S C: pink stripe / mauve S: summer:

'Cyaneus'

This is another old cultivar and is sometimes recognised as *L. sativus* var. *cyaneus*.
Raiser and date unknown
H: SD L: U N: P P: S C: purple-blue
S: summer

Lathyrus tingitanus

'Roseus'

The delightful two-toned pink of this cultivar is more popular than the darker flowered type, but of obscure origin. It possibly arose in the 20th century and the name may have been first published in a Grayson catalogue of 1997–98.

Raiser and date unknown

H: T L: U N: P P: S C: pink S: summer

Lathyrus vernus

'Dama Duet'

Although this has the typical mauve-blue flowers of the species, it has narrow leaflets. Cultivars with the Dama prefix were selected by David Matthewman.

Matthewman, date unknown
H: D L: M N: M P: S C: mauve / lavender S: spring

'Dama Emily'

Tall for the species, this cultivar is vigorous with pale pink, almost white flowers. The leaflets are of normal width.

Matthewman, date unknown
H: D L: M N: M P: S C: palest pink
S: spring

'Alboroseus' AGM H6

With its pretty pink and white bicoloured flowers, this cultivar has more white than 'Roseus'. The leaflets are of normal width. Plants sold as 'Rosenelfe', 'Spring Melody' and 'Winter Blush' are identical to 'Alboroseus'.

Raiser and date unknown
H: D L: M N: M P: S C: pink / white S: spring

'Lamorna's Love'

With its bright bluish flowers, this is also distinguished by having narrow leaflets.

Marsh, 1990s

H: D L: M N: M P: S C: bright mauve-blue S: spring

'Roseus'

Probably of wild origin, and its name based on *L. vernus* f. *roseus*, this cultivar has more pink than 'Alboroseus'.

Raiser and date unknown

H: D L: M N: M P: S C: pink / white S: spring

'Subtle Hints'

This cultivar has distinctly bicoloured flowers, making it particularly bright and noticeable in the garden. The leaflets are of normal width.

Matthewman, c.2015

H: D L: M N: M P: S C: pale blue / pale mauve S: spring

Hybrids

'Sylvia Norton'

A cultivar with pure white flowers and narrow leaflets, this was raised from seed by Joe Sharman from a plant with the same characters given to him by Sylvia Norton. He found her plant to difficult to grow but this subsequent seedling was much more robust.

Sharman, c.2017
H: D L: M N: M P: S C: white S: spring

'Tubro'

A hybrid between *L. rotundifolius* and *L. tuberosus*, this perennial is most similar to the former parent. However, it has purple-pink instead of brick-red flowers, it flowers for longer, and is more vigorous. 'Tillyperone' is similar, but both cultivars are propagated by seed, so variation from that process blurs any differences between them.

For origin and dates, see 'Checklist of cultivar epithets' chapter
H: T L: U N: M P: S C: purple-pink S: summer

Cultivars of *Lathyrus odoratus* Grandiflora

'Almost Black'

This has the darkest flowers of all cultivars.
Hammett / Denny, 2009
H: T L: U N: P P: S C: dark maroon / dark violet S: summer

'Adorabel'

A Modern cultivar, this has flowers that open lavender and turn mauve-blue.
Grayson, 2013
H: T L: U N: P P: S C: lavender to mauve-blue S: summer

'America' AGM H3

This is an Old-fashioned cultivar.
C.C. Morse & Co. / Vaughan Seed Store, 1896
H: T L: U N: P P: S C: red flake, w.g. S: summer

'Anne Hathaway'

This is an Old-fashioned cultivar.

Grayson, 2003
H: T L: U N: P P: S C: pale blue flake, w.g. S: summer

'Baby's Blush'

With bicoloured flowers that fade to white, this Modern cultivar was originally found growing feral in Italy.

R. Parsons, 2014
H: T L: U N: P P: S C: blush pink / white
S: summer

'Black Knight'

This is an Old-fashioned cultivar.

H. Eckford, 1898
H: T L: U N: P P: S C: dark maroon
S: summer

'Bramdean' AGM H3

Arising from feral material with wild-type colouring collected in southern Italy, this Old-fashioned cultivar was named after the Hampshire garden of its discoverer.

Wakefield / R. Parsons, 2007
H: T L: U N: P P: S C: white S: summer

'Captain of the Blues' Grayson

A Modern cultivar, this appears to be a re-creation of an Eckford raising.

Grayson, 1993
H: T L: U N: P P: S C: mauve / blue
S: summer

'CCC'

With white flowers, this cultivar was named for the tercentenary of the sweet pea's introduction to cultivation.

Grayson, 1999
H: T L: U N: P P: S C: white S: summer

'Cerise Carpet'

Dwarf and trailing, this is an Old-fashioned cultivar.

Ferry Morse Seed Co., 1958
H: D L: U N: P P: S C: orange cerise
S: summer

'Cherub Lady T' AGM H3

Dwarf and trailing, this is an Old-fashioned bicoloured cultivar.

Owl's Acre Sweet Peas, 2008
H: D L: U N: P P: S C: cerise / lavender
S: summer

'Cherub Northern Lights'

A dwarf, trailing, Old-fashioned cultivar, this has crimson-flushed and blue-flushed bicoloured flowers.

Owl's Acre Sweet Peas, 2012
H: D L: U N: P P: S C: crimson flush, w.g. / blue flush, w.g. S: summer

'Cherub Penny Black'

Dwarf and trailing, this is an Old-fashioned cultivar.

Owl's Acre Sweet Peas, 2008
H: D L: U N: P P: S C: dark maroon
S: summer

'Cherub Pink'

Dwarf and trailing, this is an Old-fashioned cultivar.

Owl's Acre Sweet Peas, 2005
H: D L: U N: P P: S C: pale pink, w.g.
S: summer

'Countess Cadogan'

This is an Old-fashioned bicoloured cultivar.

H. Eckford, 1899
H: T L: U N: P P: S C: violet / light blue
S: summer

'Cream Eggs'

This is a Modern cultivar.

Seedlynx / Mr Fothergills Seeds Ltd, 2016
H: T L: U N: P P: S C: cream with violet edge S: summer

Crown Princess of Prussia

With pink bicoloured flowers, this Old-fashioned cultivar was introduced as 'Kronprinzessin von Preussen'.

Haage & Schmidt, 1868
H: T L: U N: P P: S C: lilac pink / pale pink S: summer

'Cupani'

Bearing maroon and violet flowers, this Old-fashioned cultivar was selected by Peter Grayson from wild plants on the basis of its improved vigour and larger size.

Grayson, 1992
H: T L: U N: P P: S C: maroon / violet
S: summer

'Cupid Bright Violet'

Dwarf and trailing, this is an Old-fashioned bicoloured cultivar.

E.W. King & Co., 2008
H: D L: U N: P P: S C: maroon / violet
S: summer

'Dark Sprite'

Dwarf and trailing, this has bicoloured bicoloured flowers.

Owl's Acre Sweet Peas, 2013
H: D L: U N: P P: S C: maroon / violet
S: winter

'Diamond Wedding'

This multiflora cultivar was introduced as a Spencer but has reverted to Modern Grandiflora form.

Colledge / Unwins Seeds, 1980
H: T L: U N: M P: S C: white S: summer

'Dolly Varden' Grayson

With pale purple and white bicolour flowers, this Modern sweet pea is a recreation of the cultivar of this name introduced in 1898.

Grayson, 1996
H: T L: U N: P P: S C: pale purple / white S: summer

'Dorothy Eckford' AGM H3

With white flowers, this Old-fashioned cultivar differs from 'Bramdean' in its pale seeds, which are dark in the latter.

H. Eckford, 1903
H: T L: U N: P P: S C: white S: summer

'Dr Robert Uvedale'

With dark purple flowers, this Modern cultivar is sometimes listed as 'Doctor Uvedale'.

Grayson, 1999
H: T L: U N: P P: S C: dark purple
S: summer

'Duke of York'

With pink and ivory bicoloured flowers, this Old-fashioned cultivar might be a re-creation with paler wings of the 1894 original.

H Eckford, 1894
H: T L: U N: P P: S C: rose pink / cream
S: summer

'Emily' Unwins

This is a Modern cultivar.

Unwins Seeds, 2010
H: T L: U N: P P: S C: rose pink, w.g.
S: summer

'Fire and Ice'

A Modern cultivar, if grown under polythene the crimson of the bicoloured flowers fades, giving a striking reverse bicolour effect.

Owl's Acre Sweet Peas, 2005
H: T L: U N: P P: S C: crimson flake / blue S: summer

'Flora Norton'

A pale blue, Old-fashioned cultivar with excellent provenance.

C.C. Morse & Co. / Vaughan Seed Store, 1904
H: T L: U N: P P: S C: pale blue
S: summer

'Greenfingers'

This is a Modern cultivar with flowers flushed and edged in violet.

Seedlynx / Mr Fothergills Seeds Ltd, 2017
H: T L: U N: P P: S C: violet flush, c.g.
S: summer

'Heathcliff' AGM H3

This is a Modern cultivar.
Unwins Seeds, 2003
H: T L: U N: P P: S C: mauve-blue
S: summer

'Henry Eckford'

This is an Old-fashioned cultivar.
H. Eckford, 1906
H: T L: U N: P P: S C: orange-scarlet
S: summer

'Hannah Dale' Grayson

A winter-flowering, Modern cultivar, this is possibly a re-creation of a summer-flowering cultivar of the same name introduced by Dobbie & Co. in 1907.
Grayson, 1998
H: T L: U N: P P: S C: maroon S: winter

'Janet Scott' AGM H3

This is an Old-fashioned cultivar with bicoloured flowers. The more recently named 'Wretham Pink' is now considered a synonym of 'Janet Scott'.

C.C. Morse & Co. / Burpee Seeds, 1903
H: T L: U N: P P: S C: appleblossom pink / pale pink S: summer

'Juliet' Unwins

A Modern cultivar, the name originally applied to an apricot Spencer from 1911.

Unwins Seeds, 2002
H: T L: U N: P P: S C: cream S: summer

'Jack Ellis'

A Modern cultivar, this has bicoloured flowers.

Ellis / R. Parsons, 2018
H: T L: U N: P P: S C: maroon / purple S: summer

'Lady Grisel Hamilton'

With lavender, Old-fashioned flowers, this cultivar has excellent provenance.

H. Eckford, 1898
H: T L: U N: P P: S C: lavender
S: summer

'King Edward VII' AGM H3

This is an Old-fashioned cultivar.
H. Eckford, 1903
H: T L: U N: P P: S C: scarlet S: summer

'Lady Turral'

This is an Old-fashioned cultivar with bicoloured flowers. It was raised three decades before appearing in a catalogue.
Turral / Grayson, 1962 / 1993
H: T L: U N: P P: S C: cerise / deep lilac
S: summer

'Lavender Sprite' AGM H3

A winter-flowering cultivar, this is dwarf and trailing.

Owl's Acre Sweet Peas, 2013
H: D L: U N: P P: S C: lavender S: winter

'Little Red Riding Hood'

A striking and decorative Modern cultivar, this has bicoloured flowers.

Hammett / Somerset, date unknown
H: T L: U N: P P: S C: red / white
S: summer

'Lord Nelson'

An Old-fashioned selection with navy blue flowers.

Isaac House & Son, 1907
H: T L: U N: P P: S C: navy blue
S: summer

'Madison' AGM H3

This is a Modern cultivar.

Unwins Seeds, 2014
H: T L: U N: P P: S C: scarlet S: summer

'Matucana' AGM H3

This Modern cultivar has a wonderful fragrance and it was collected from a garden in Peru in about 1955 by Harland.

Harland / Turral, c.1955
H: T L: U N: P P: S C: maroon / violet
S: summer

'Mauve Queen' Eckford

The name of this Old-fashioned cultivar dates from 1887 but the current plant may be a new raising by Grayson.

H. Eckford, 1887
H: T L: U N: P P: D C: mauve
S: summer

'Minmaroon'

A dwarf, trailing, Old-fashioned cultivar, this is sometimes sold as part of Rockery Mixed.
Beane / Plants of Distinction, 1998
H: D L: U N: P P: S C: maroon stripe, w.g. S: summer

'Miss Willmott'

An Old-fashioned cultivar, this is sometimes incorrectly listed as 'Wilmot or 'Wilmott'
H. Eckford, 1901
H: T L: U N: P P: S C: orange / pink
S: summer

'Memories' Unwins

A Modern cultivar, this is very similar to 'Violet Queen'.
Unwins Seeds, 2005
H: T L: U N: P P: S C: purple or mauve
S: summer

'Mrs Collier'

This is an Old-fashioned cultivar.
Dobbie & Co., 1907
H: T L: U N: P P: S C: cream S: summer

'Mrs Walter Wright'

An Old-fashioned cultivar, tis has hooded, bicoloured flowers.
H. Eckford, 1903
H: T L: U N: P P: S C: mauve / purple
S: summer

'Monty Don'

This is a Modern cultivar.
R. Parsons, 2008
H: T L: U N: P P: S C: dark maroon
S: summer

'Painted Lady'

An Old-fashioned cultivar, this was named and described by Philip Miller in 1752. Linnaeus had named it *Lathyrus zeylanica* in 1737.
Raiser unknown, 1752
H: T L: U N: P P: S C: rose / white, tinted pink S: summer

'Pansy Lavender Flush'

This is a semi-dwarf, Old-fashioned cultivar.
Thompson & Morgan, 2004
H: SD L: U N: P P: S C: lavender flush, w.g. S: summer

'Picolino'

This is a Modern cultivar.
Grayson, c.2004
H: T L: U N: P P: S C: blue picotee, w.g. S: summer

'Pink Cupid' AGM H3

A dwarf, trailing, Old-fashioned cultivar, this has bicoloured flowers.
Burpee Seeds, 1898
H: D L: U N: P P: S C: pink / white S: summer

'Polyanna'

A Modern cultivar, this has bicoloured flowers.
Just Sweet Peas, 2011
H: T L: U N: P P: S C: lilac pink / white S: summer

'Prima Donna' Eckford

An Old-fashioned cultivar, this has hooded flowers. The name was later applied to a pre-1962, salmon-pink cultivar.
H. Eckford, 1896
H: T L: U N: P P: S C: pure pink S: summer

'Prince Edward of York'

An Old-fashioned cultivar, this has bicoloured flowers.

H. Eckford, 1897
H: T L: U N: P P: S C: red / pink
S: summer

'Princess of Wales' Grayson

A Modern cultivar, the name originally applied to a mauve-flaked Spencer from 1885.

Grayson, 1995
H: T L: U N: P P: S C: purple flake, w.g.
S: summer

'Purple Prince'

With dark maroon and deep violet bicoloured flowers, the origin of the stock currently grown under this name is uncertain.

H. Eckford, 1886
H: T L: U N: P P: S C: purple maroon / deep violet S: summer

'Queen Alexandra'

The first truly scarlet sweet pea, this is an Old-fashioned cultivar.

H. Eckford, 1906
H: T L: U N: P P: S C: scarlet S: summer

'Romeo' Unwins

This Modern cultivar has a wonderful fragrance but the name originally applied to an orange Spencer from 1946.

Unwins Seeds, 2000
H: T L: U N: P P: S C: white with delicate blue edge. S: summer

'Roosterville'

This is a Modern cultivar.
Hammett, 2009
H: T L: U N: P P: S C: purple S: summer

'Senator'
This is an Old-fashioned cultivar.
H. Eckford, 1891
H: T L: U N: P P: S C: dark maroon and violet flake, w.g. S: summer

'Sicilian Pink' AGM H3
Despite its name, this Old-fashioned bicolour was collected from a garden in Peru.
Harland, c.1955
H: T L: U N: P P: S C: dark pink / pale pink S: summer

'Scarlett'
This is a Modern cultivar.
Unwins Seeds, 2006
H: T L: U N: P P: S C: crimson
S: summer

'Solway Classic' AGM H3

A semi-dwarf, Old-fashioned cultivar this has non-tendril leaves.

J.D. Place / R. Parsons, 2013
H: SD L: M N: P P: S C: red stripe, w.g.
S: summer

'Solway Charm' AGM H3

A semi-dwarf, Old-fashioned cultivar this has non-tendril leaves.

J.D. Place / R. Parsons, 2015
H: SD L: M N: P P: S C: pink stripe, w.g.
S: summer

'Solway Minstrel'

A semi-dwarf, Old-fashioned cultivar, this has non-tendril leaves.

J.D. Place / R. Parsons, 2015
H: SD L: M N: P P: S C: blue stripe, w.g.
S: summer

'Solway Serenade' AGM H3

A semi-dwarf, Old-fashioned cultivar, this has non-tendril leaves.

J.D. Place / Mr Fothergills Seeds Ltd, 2013
H: SD L: M N: P P: S C: red / pink
S: summer

'Solway Snowflake' AGM H3

A semi-dwarf, Old-fashioned cultivar, this has non-tendril leaves.

J.D. Place / R. Parsons, 2013
H: SD L: M N: P P: S C: pink splash, w.g.
S: summer

'Solway Minuet'

This semi-dwarf, Old-fashioned cultivar with bicoloured flowers has its standard veined pink and the wings edged with blue.

J.D. Place / Mr Fothergills Seeds Ltd, 2013
H: SD L: U N: P P: S C: white veined pink / white with blue edge S: summer

'Solway Splendour'
AGM H3

A semi-dwarf, Old-fashioned cultivar this has non-tendril leaves and is in two shades of red.

J.D. Place / R. Parsons, 2013
H: SD L: M N: P P: S C: red / deep pink
S: summer

'Solway Velvet'

A semi-dwarf, Old-fashioned cultivar, this has non-tendril leaves.

J.D. Place / Mr Fothergills Seeds Ltd, 2013
H: SD L: M N: P P: S C: maroon
S: summer

'Sweetie Carmine Rose'

A dwarf, trailing, Old-fashioned cultivar, this is part of the Sweetie Series.
Suttons, 2001
H: D L: U N: P P: S C: carmine / rose flaked S: summer

'Teresa Maureen'
AGM H3

A semi-dwarf, Old-fashioned cultivar, this has bicoloured flowers.
Cave / E.W. King & Co., 2002
H: SD L: U N: P P: S C: mauve / white S: summer

'Spanish Dancer'

With *L. × hammettii* ancestry, this Old-fashioned cultivar has deep pink and blue-flushed bicoloured flowers. It is sometimes sold as 'Painted Porcelain'.
Hammett / Burpee Seeds, 2011
H: SD L: U N: P P: S C: deep pink on cream / blue flush, c.g. S: summer

'Violet Queen' Grayson

This appears to be a reverted form of a Spencer cultivar introduced by Carters before 1930. The name originally applied to a bicoloured Grandiflora from 1877.

Grayson, 1993

H: T L: U N: P P: S C: violet S: summer

'Zorija Rose'

An Old-fashioned cultivar, the flowers vary slightly in colour.

E.W. King & Co., 2000

H: T L: U N: P P: S C: deep carmine S: summer

'Unique'

An Old-fashioned cultivar, this has white, blue flaked flowers. Ironically, three later cultivars have also carried this name.

G. Stark & Son, 1905

H: T L: U N: P P: S C: pale blue flake, w.g. S: summer

Semi-grandiflora

'Albutt Blue'

With white, blue-edged flowers, this cultivar is a contender for having the strongest fragrance of all sweet peas.

Albutt / Eagle Sweet Peas, 1999
H: T L: U N: P P: S C: blue picotee, w.g.
S: summer

'Alisa'

This is a borderline Modern Grandiflora cultivar.

Levko / R. Parsons, 2015
H: T L: U N: P P: S C: salmon pink, c.g.
S: summer

'Bounce Mid Blue' AGM H3

A good blue and with uniformly short habit, this is an improvement on the much earlier 'Sapphire' of Burpee from 1966.

Hem Zaden, 2012
H: SD L: U N: P P: S C: mid blue
S: spring

'Cathy' AGM H3

This is a superbly fragrant cultivar.

Unwins Seeds, 2003
H: T L: U N: P P: S C: deep cream
S: summer

'Dragonfly' Taylor

This cultivar may be a reversion of the Spencer cultivar with this name and colour introduced in 1912.

Taylor / Grayson, 1993
H: T L: U N: P P: S C: cream marbled with lavender S: summer

'Erewhon'

From *L. × hammettii*, this reverse bicolour is named after a novel with a title derived from 'nowhere' back-wards but with two letters swapped.

Hammett, 2008
H: T L: U N: P P: S C: mauve / lavender
S: summer

'High Scent' AGM H3

A deep cream-flowered cultivar with lavender-edged petals and a strong scent, this has also been sold as 'Hi Scent' and 'April in Paris'.

Hammett / Suttons, 2002
H: T L: U N: P P: S C: cream with violet edge S: summer

'Janet' Parsons

A long-stemmed cultivar, this is reverted from the Spencer type of the same name introduced by Ferry Morse Seed Co. in 1941.

R. Parsons, 2010
H: T L: U N: P P: S C: white S: late spring

'King Size Navy Blue'

With dark blue flowers, this is the only member of the King Size Series remaining in cultivation.

Thompson & Morgan, 1998
H: T L: U N: M P: S C: dark blue
S: summer

'Kingfisher'

An old cultivar, this is of obscure origin but reportedly raised by Taylor.

J. Taylor / Grayson, 1993
H: T L: U N: P P: S C: violet flush, c.g.
S: summer

'My Navy'

With dark blue flowers, this Modern cultivar flowers a little earlier than other summer-flowering sweet peas. It was originally sold as 'Navy' but changed to avoid confusion with earlier cultivars called 'Navy'.

Hammett, 2008
H: T L: U N: P P: S C: navy blue
S: summer

'More Scent'

With a scent reputedly stronger than 'High Scent', this cultivar has white flowers flushed with purple.

Hammett, 2012
H: T L: U N: P P: S C: purple flush, w.g.
S: summer

'Salmon Beauty'

A winter-flowering cultivar, this was sent to India in the 1940s with Spencer flower form but it has since reverted to clamped keel form.

Raiser unknown, 2010
H: T L: U N: P P: S C: salmon pink, c.g.
S: winter

'Solway Lullaby'

This is a semi-dwarf cultivar.

J.D. Place / R. Parsons, 2013
H: SD L: U N: P P: S C: dark blue
S: summer

'Tommy' Parsons

A long-stemmed cultivar with mid blue flowers, it blooms little earlier than most. It is a reverted form of the Spencer cultivar introduced as part of the Cuthbertson Series by the Ferry Morse Seed Co. in 1940.
R. Parsons, 2012
H: T L: U N: P P: S C: mid blue S: late spring

'Vulcan' Parsons

A winter-flowering cultivar with scarlet flowers, this is a reverted form of the Spencer cultivar of this name introduced by C.C. Morse & Co. in 1925.
R. Parsons, 2009
H: T L: U N: P P: S C: scarlet S: winter

Spencer

'Alan Titchmarsh'
A long-stemmed cultivar, this has rich pink flowers.

B.R. Jones / Robert Bolton & Son, 1986

H: T L: U N: P P: S C: almond pink, c.g
S: summer

'Aileen Walton'
With unusual coloured flowers, this cultivar is good for exhibition but rarely seen in seed catalogues.

Fleming Robertson / Kerton Sweet Peas, 2005

H: T L: U N: P P: S C: mauve S: summer

'Alaska Blue'
With large, ice-blue flowers, this cultivar has long stems.

Wells / Kerton Sweet Peas, 2000

H: T L: U N: P P: S C: blue flush, w.g.
S: summer

'Alice Hardwicke'

Once popular for exhibition, this cultivar has now been superseded.
B.R. Jones / Suttons, 1971
H: T L: U N: P P: S C: orange-red, w.g.
S: summer

'Alison Valentini'

This cultivar has a strong colour and non-tendril leaves.
R. Place / R. Parsons, 2016
H: T L: M N: P P: S C: crimson
S: summer

'Andrea Robertson'

A vigorous, semi-multiflora cultivar, this has bicoloured flowers on long stems.
Brackley, 2000
H: T L: U N: M P: S C: dark violet / blue
S: summer

'Andrew Cavendish'

With lavender flowers, this cultivar was named for the late Duke of Devonshire.
Hubbuck / R. Parsons, 2007
H: T L: U N: P P: S C: lavender
S: summer

'Angel Kiss'

This cultivar was received in the UK from Nozaki in Japan but its exact origin is unknown.
Nozaki, date unknown
H: T L: U N: M P: S C: pale pink
S: winter

'Annabelle'

This cultivar has slightly darker flowers than 'Andrew Cavendish'.
Robert Bolton & Son, 1990
H: T L: U N: P P: S C: lavender
S: summer

'Anne Barron'

The pink of this cultivar is verging on salmon, over a cream ground.

Entwistle / Robert Bolton & Son, 1999
H: T L: U N: P P: S C: warm rose pink,
c.g. S: summer

'Anniversary'

With its striking pink edges, this remains one of the most popular cultivars.

Truslove / Marchant, 1986
H: T L: U N: P P: S C: white with pink edge S: summer

'Aphrodite' AGM H3

This vigorous cultivar can have up to 15 flowers per stem.

Unwins Seeds, 2011
H: T L: U N: M P: S C: white S: summer

'Apple Blossom' Beane

All with similar colours, there are older cultivars also named 'Apple Blossom' and 'Appleblossom'.

Beane / Thompson & Morgan, 2002
H: T L: U N: P P: S C: pink stripe, w.g. S: summer

'Apricot Queen'

This cultivar requires shading to bring out its full apricot colour.

E.W. King & Co., 1973
H: T L: U N: P P: S C: apricot pink S: summer

'Apricot Sprite'

As with 'Apricot Queen', this cultivar requires shading to bring out its full colour.

Bailey, 1980
H: T L: U N: P P: S C: orange-pink S: summer

'Aquarius'

This has non-tendril leaves, but the same raiser released a later, blue-flowered cultivar with tendrils and the same name.

J.D. Place / E.W. King & Co., 1999
H: T L: M N: P P: S C: mauve S: summer

'Aries'

The pink of this cultivar is a deep salmon and it has non-tendril leaves.

J.D. Place / E.W. King & Co., 1999
H: SD L: M N: P P: S C: salmon pink, w.g. S: summer

'Ascot' Unwins

An earlier cultivar with the same name had rose-pink flowers.

Unwins Seeds, 1981
H: T L: U N: P P: D C: salmon pink, c.g.
S: summer

'Astronaut Lavender'

This is a selection from Astronaut Mixed and retains the non-tendril leaves.

R. Parsons, 2016
H: T L: M N: P P: S C: lavender
S: summer

'Astronaut White'

This is another selection from Astronaut Mixed but 'Lakeland Blizzard' may have better flower placement.

R. Parsons, 2016
H: T L: M N: P P: S C: white S: summer

'Atlantis'

Better than the similar 'Blue Ripple', this is widely grown as 'Betty Maiden', a later name.

Beane / Matthewman, 2008
H: T L: U N: P P: S C: blue stripe, w.g.
S: summer

'Audrey Kirkman'

This cultivar has longer stems and is more reliable for showing than the similarly coloured 'Sonia'.

R. Parsons, 2012
H: T L: U N: P P: S C: marbled pink, w.g.
S: summer

'Aunt Jane'

With its well-placed blooms this cultivar is good for exhibition and garden use.

Matthewman, 2000
H: T L: U N: P P: S C: magenta
S: summer

'Aurora Borealis' Place AGM H3

An earlier cultivar with this name is probably extinct.

J.D. Place / R. Parsons, 2017
H: SD L: U N: P P: S C: maroon stripe, w.g. S: summer

'Balcony Bride'

Although not confirmed, this is likely to have been raised by J.D. Place because of its twin stems and flower form and placement.

Plants of Distinction, 1998
H: SD L: U N: P P: S C: pink stripe, w.g.
S: summer

'Ballerina Blue' AGM H3

With its large flowers on long stems this cultivar is good for exhibition and garden use.

Welch / Thompson & Morgan, 2011
H: T L: U N: P P: S C: mid blue
S: summer

'Balmoral' Brackley

An earlier cultivar with the same name had orange flowers.

Brackley, 1994
H: T L: U N: P P: S C: dark maroon
S: summer

'Banty'

The raiser of this cultivar also bred 'Misty'.

Leese / Eagle Sweet Peas, 2008
H: T L: U N: P P: S C: rose pink, w.g.
S: summer

'Baronscourt'

With its large flowers and strong stems this is suitable for exhibition and garden use.

Harrod / Kerton Sweet Peas, 1999
H: T L: U N: P P: S C: deep mauve
S: summer

'Barry Dare'

This cultivar is a prolific bloomer.

Unwins Seeds, 1997
H: T L: U N: P P: S C: cerise S: summer

'Batheaston'

With relatively large flowers, the white ground of this cultivar is prominent at the petal bases.

James / Marchant, 1983
H: T L: U N: P P: S C: pale pink, w.g.
S: summer

'Beaujolais'

The stems of this cultivar have a tendency to become shorter early in the season.

Suttons, 1972
H: T L: U N: M P: S C: burgundy
S: summer

'Beth Chatto'

A cultivar with well-formed flowers.

Matthewman, 2009
H: T L: U N: P P: S C: pale pink, c.g.
S: summer

'Beverley Kaye'

The pink of this cultivar is very delicate.

Harkness, before 1962
H: T L: U N: P P: D C: pale salmon pink, c.g. S: winter

'Big Blue'

An exhibition quality cultivar with large, mid blue flowers.

Hammett, 2009

H: T L: U N: P P: S C: mid blue

S: summer

'Bill's Choice'

With its strong, long stems, this is good for exhibition and garden use.

Truslove / R. Parsons, 2008

H: T L: U N: P P: S C: deep rose pink w.g. S: summer

'Blue Ripple' Unwins

Although this cultivar has flaked flowers, all others with a Ripple suffix are striped.

Unwins Seeds, 2012
H: T L: U N: P P: S C: blue flake, w.g.
S: summer

'Blue Danube' Morris

Although a good colour, the top flower of this cultivar has a tendency to hang. Two earlier cultivars have this name.

Morris / Unwins Seeds, 1981
H: T L: U N: P P: S C: mid blue S: summer

'Blue Shift'

With *L. × hammettii* ancestry, the flowers of this cultivar open purple then change to mauve-blue.

Hammett / Thompson & Morgan, 2013
H: T L: U N: P P: S C: purple, becoming mauve-blue S: summer

'Blue Vein' Hammett

With *L. × hammettii* ancestry, the small, often duplex flowers of this cultivar open apricot-orange and then develop blue-brown marbling.
Hammett / Denny, 2008
H: T L: U N: P P: D C: marbled apricot
S: summer

'Blue Wonder'

An early spring-flowering cultivar with mid blue flowers.
A. Zvolanek & Sons., 1923
H: T L: U N: M P: S C: mid blue S: early spring

'Bobby Chisholm'

This cultivar has relatively large frilly flowers on strong stems.
Chisholm / Kerton Sweet Peas, 2011
H: T L: U N: P P: S C: rosy lavender
S: summer

'Bobby's Girl' AGM H3

The long stems are a good feature of this cultivar.
Robert Bolton & Son, 2000
H: T L: U N: P P: S C: pale salmon pink, c.g. S: summer

'Border Beauty'

Although genetically striped, the colouring of this cultivar is so subtle its looks almost white in full sun.
R. Parsons, 2011
H: T L: U N: P P: S C: pale lavender flush S: summer

'Bounce Navy Blue' AGM H3

This is a particularly bushy and sturdy cultivar with strong stems.
Hem Zaden, 2012
H: SD L: U N: P P: S C: navy blue
S: summer

'Bouquet Crimson'

All cultivars in the Bouquet Series usually have four to six flowers per stem.
Denholm Seeds, 1998
H: T L: U N: M P: S C: crimson
S: summer

'Bouquet Lavender'

All cultivars in the Bouquet Series usually have four to six flowers per stem.
Denholm Seeds, 1998
H: T L: U N: M P: S C: lavender
S: summer

'Bouquet Mid Blue'

All cultivars in the Bouquet Series usually have four to six flowers per stem.
Denholm Seeds, 1998
H: T L: U N: M P: S C: mid blue
S: summer

'Bouquet Pink'

All cultivars in the Bouquet Series usually have four to six flowers per stem. Denholm Seeds, 1998
H: T L: U N: M P: S C: pale pink
S: summer

'Bouquet Scarlet'

All cultivars in the Bouquet Series usually have four to six flowers per stem.
Denholm Seeds, 1998
H: T L: U N: M P: S C: scarlet
S: summer

'Bouquet Violet'

This is the only member of the Bouquet Series not raised by Denholm Seeds.
R. Parsons, 2013
H: T L: U N: M P: S C: violet S: summer

'Bouquet White'

This cultivar blooms slightly earlier than most others in the Bouquet Series.

Denholm Seeds, 1998
H: T L: U N: M P: S C: white S: summer

'Brenda Bridger'

This striking bicolour is similar to 'Chance'

Hammett / Thompson & Morgan, 1987
H: T L: U N: P P: S C: dark pink / pale pink S: summer

'Brian Clough'

Although still good for garden use, this cultivar has now been superseded for exhibition.

B.R. Jones / Unwins Seeds, 1982
H: T L: U N: P P: S C: salmon orange, w.g. S: summer

'Brian Haynes'

This is one of the best flaked Spencer cultivars.

Beane / E.W. King & Co., 2007
H: T L: U N: P P: S C: light purple flake, w.g. S: summer

'Bridget McAleer'

This strong mauve cultivar has now superseded Laidlaw's 'Eclipse'.

McAleer / Harrod, 2013
H: T L: U N: P P: S C: dark mauve S: summer

'Bristol' AGM H3

Good for exhibition and garden use, this cultivar has long, strong stems.

Kerton Sweet Peas, 1994
H: T L: U N: P P: S C: pale blue S: summer

'Bristol Cream'

The yellowish white flowers of this cultivar are particularly wavy.

Albutt / E.W. King & Co., 1990
H: T L: U N: P P: S C: cream S: summer

'Brook Hall' AGM H3

This cultivar is superb for the garden and cutting but there are better whites for exhibition.

Harrod / E.W. King & Co., 2006
H: T L: U N: P P: S C: white S: summer

'Buccaneer'

Producing a prolific display of flowers, this cultivar is good for garden use and cutting.

Albutt / E.W. King & Co., 1987
H: T L: U N: P P: S C: crimson S: summer

'Burlesque'

This is a strong-growing cultivar with heavily flaked flowers.

Hammett, 2009
H: T L: U N: P P: S C: mauve-blue flake, w.g. S: summer

'Burnished Bronze'

The colour of this long-stemmed cultivar deepens as the flowers age.

Harrod / Kerton Sweet Peas, 1994
H: T L: U N: P P: S C: maroon
S: summer

'Candy' Beane

This cultivar is still good for garden use and cutting but it has been supersed by the larger flowered 'Olive D.'.

Beane / Unwins Seeds, 1991
H: T L: U N: P P: S C: pale maroon stripe, w.g. S: summer

'Carlotta'

An older cultivar that is still good for garden use and cutting.

Carters Tested Seeds, 1937
H: T L: U N: P P: S C: carmine
S: summer

'Carmel' Ferry Morse

Flowering from late spring, this cultivar is part of the Knee-Hi Series.

Ferry Morse Seed Co., 1967
H: SD L: U N: M P: S C: pale lavender
S: late spring

'Carminette'

This cultivar is is part of the Bijou Series.

Burpee Seeds, 1968
H: D L: U N: P P: S C: carmine-rose
S: spring

'Castle of Mey'

This cultivar is suitable for
exhibition and garden use.

Unwins Seeds, 2001
H: T L: U N: P P: S C: cream S: summer

'Castlewellan'

This cultivar is also sold as 'Harlow
Carr'.

Harrod / Unwins Seeds, 2005
H: T L: U N: P P: S C: pale pink, c.g.
S: summer

'Cathy Wright'

With strong stems and suitable for exhibition, this cultivar also has pale seeds.

Eagle Sweet Peas, 2000
H: T L: U N: P P: S C: white S: summer

'Champagne Bubbles'

This cultivar sometimes has duplex flowers.

Unwins Seeds, 1986
H: T L: U N: P P: D C: pale salmon pink, c.g. S: summer

'Chance'

This bicolour is similar to 'Brenda Bridger'.

R. Parsons, 2006
H: T L: U N: P P: S C: dark pink / pale pink S: summer

'Charles Unwin' Colledge

The long stems make this a good exhibition cultivar.

Colledge / Unwins Seeds, 1985
H: T L: U N: P P: S C: salmon pink, c.g. S: summer

'Charlie Bear'

The wing petals of this bicolour are often pure white.

Kerton Sweet Peas, 2015
H: T L: U N: P P: S C: mauve pink / white S: summer

'Charlie's Angel' AGM H3

With its long stems making it good for cutting, this is one of the best pale blues.

Hanmer / Unwins Seeds, 1990
H: T L: U N: P P: S C: pale blue S: summer

'Charlotte Emma'

The strong stems make this a good exhibition cultivar.

Kerton Sweet Peas, 2009
H: T L: U N: P P: S C: appleblossom pink, w.g. S: summer

'Chatsworth'

This cultivar has long stems and a delicate colour.

Albutt / Thompson & Morgan, 1998
H: T L: U N: P P: S C: pale blue
S: summer

'Chelsea Centenary'

With up to 15 flowers per stem, this very vigorous cultivar is suitable for commercial cut-flower growing.

Hammett / Mr Fothergills Seeds Ltd, 2013
H: T L: U N: M P: S C: pale blue
S: summer

'Cheryl Rainey'

Large flowers on long stems make this cultivar suitable for exhibiting.

Harrod / R. Parsons, 2019
H: T L: U N: P P: S C: salmon-orange
S: summer

'Choc Stripe'

Although a pretty cultivar, this has been superseded by 'Lisa Marie'.

Kerton Sweet Peas, 2015
H: T L: U N: P P: S C: maroon stripe, w.g. S: summer

'Chocolate Flake'

This cultivar is also sold as 'Sir Henry Cecil'.

Hammett, 2012
H: T L: N: P: C: chocolate-maroon flake, w.g. S: summer

'Chris Harrod' AGM H3

Large flowers on long stems characterise this cultivar.

Harrod / Kerton Sweet Peas, 2008
H: T L: U N: P P: S C: pale blue
S: summer

'Clotted Cream' Brewer

This is a prolifically blooming cultivar with rather plain-edged petals.

K. Brewer / Matthewman, 2015
H: T L: U N: P P: S C: cream S: summer

'Cocktail' Hammett

This bicolour has good-sized flowers and long stems.

Hammett, c. 1977
H: T L: U N: P P: S C: maroon / violet
S: summer

Continental Mixed

The colours in this mixture include deep rose, rose pink, ruby and scarlet.

Brackley, date unknown
H: SD L: U N: P P: S C: mixed
S: summer

'Coraleena'

This cultivar blooms slightly earlier than most.

Harrod, 2009
H: T L: U N: P P: S C: coral-scarlet
S: late spring

'Cream Southbourne'

A long-stemmed cultivar, this is popular with some cut-flower growers.

Colledge / Unwins Seeds, 1982
H: T L: U N: P P: S C: cream S: summer

'Crimson Ripple'

The large blooms of this cultivar are borne on long stems.

Thompson & Morgan, 2002
H: T L: U N: P P: S C: red stripe, w.g.
S: summer

'Cyril Plater'

The strong stems make this a good exhibition cultivar.

Kerton Sweet Peas, 2011
H: T L: U N: P P: S C: rosy mauve
S: summer

'Dalesman'

This cultivar has long stems and is good as a cut flower and for exhibition.

Beane / Myers, 2013
H: T L: U N: P P: S C: mid-blue
S: summer

'Dancing Queen'

Athough this cultivar readily produces long stems, there are better whites for exhibition.

Robert Bolton & Son, 2001
H: T L: U N: P P: S C: white S: summer

'Daphne' Unwins

There are three older cultivars with this name.

Unwins Seeds, 1993
H: T L: U N: P P: S C: lavender
S: summer

'Darcey Bussell'

With long stems and distinctive colouring, this cultivar is popular with some cut-flower growers.

Unwins Seeds, 2001
H: T L: U N: P P: S C: purple stripe, c.g.
S: summer

'Dark Passion'

The flowers of this cultivar are well-placed and have a silky sheen.
Beane / Matthewman, 2006
H: T L: U N: P P: S C: deep violet
S: summer

'David Unwin'

This is a good exhibition cultivar.
Unwins Seeds, 2003
H: T L: U N: P P: S C: scarlet S: summer

'Dawn' Beane

A vigorous cultivar, this is good for exhibition. Six earlier cultivars, all of dfferent colours, have also used this name.
Beane / Matthewman, 1996
H: T L: U N: P P: S C: blue flush, w.g.
S: summer

'Deborah Devonshire'

Good for garden use and as a cut flower, this cultivar is not suitable for exhibition.
Beane / Myers, 2014
H: T L: U N: P P: S C: white with pink edge S: summer

'Denis Compton'

An excellent cultivar, this is rarely offered because it produces seed reluctantly.
Robert Bolton & Son, 1988
H: T L: U N: P P: S C: salmon pink, c.g.
S: summer

'Doreen' Beane

This cultivar has well-placed blooms on long stems.
Beane / Eagle Sweet Peas, 2013
H: T L: U N: P P: S C: cream S: summer

'Dream Girl'

This is possibly the best pink Spencer cultivar produced by this prolific raiser.

Harrod, 2009
H: T L: U N: P P: S C: rose pink, c.g.
S: summer

'Duo Salmon' AGM H3

The blooms of this cultivar are relatively small but it produces numerous flower stems.

Unwins Seeds, 2009
H: T L: U N: P P: S C: cerise / pink
S: summer

'Dusty Springfield'

This excellent cultivar is only held back by its reluctance to produce seed.

Priestley / Unwins Seeds, 2002
H: T L: U N: P P: S C: orange-red
S: summer

'Duvet Cherry'

This dwarf cultivar makes a good, bushy plant.

Seedlynx, 2016
H: D L: U N: P P: S C: carmine / pink
S: winter

'Dynasty'

This is a vigorous cultivr with long stems.

Ford Robertson / Unwins Seeds, 1986
H: T L: U N: P P: S C: magenta
S: summer

'Earl Grey'

This was the first bicoloured and flaked cultivar to be raised.

Hammett / R. Parsons, 2014
H: T L: U N: P P: S C: maroon, w.g. /
violet, w.g. S: summer

'Eclipse' Laidlaw

Although still a good mauve, this cultivar has been supersed by 'Bridget McAleer'.

Laidlaw / Unwins Seeds, 1975
H: T L: U N: P P: S C: deep mauve
S: summer

'Edd Fincham'

This cultivar is sometimes seen incorrectly listed as 'Ed Fincham'.

Harrod / Samuel Dobie & Sons Ltd, 1994
H: T L: U N: P P: S C: maroon
S: summer

'Edith Flanagan'

Bearing large flowers, this cultivar also has long stems.

Beane / R. Parsons, 2017
H: T L: U N: P P: S C: orange-red
S: summer

'Elegance Cranberry'

This summer-flowering cultivar was originally in the Winter Elegance Series.

Hem Zaden, 2012
H: T L: U N: M P: S C: purple
S: summer

'Ella Maria'

The strong stems and large flowers make this suitable for exhibition, cutting and grden use.

Kerton Sweet Peas, 2003
H: T L: U N: P P: S C: pink stripe, c.g.
S: summer

'Emma'

Some flowers of this highly frilly cultivar are duplex.

Brackley, 2001
H: T L: U N: P P: D C: salmon pink, c.g.
S: summer

'Enchanté'

With cerise, mauve and white, this tricoloured cultivar is very striking.

Hammett / Denny, 2009

H: T L: U N: P P: S C: cerise flush, w.g. / mauve flush, w.g. S: summer

'Esther Rantzen'

Although good for cut-flower production, others in this colour are better for exhibition.

Brackley, 1989

H: T L: U N: P P: S C: pale blue S: summer

'Ena Margaret'

An older cultivar, this is good for garden use and cutting for the house.

Everitt, 1976

H: T L: U N: P P: S C: lavender flush on ivory S: summer

'Ethel Grace'

This is vigorous and good for exhibition and, like several other lavender cultivars, has small seeds.

B.R. Jones / Robert Bolton & Son, 1994
H: T L: U N: P P: S C: lavender
S: summer

'Evelyn' Ferry Morse 1944

This early-flowering cultivar is part of the Cuthbertson Series.

Ferry Morse Seed Co., 1944
H: T L: U N: M P: S C: salmon pink, c.g.
S: late spring

'Evening Glow' AGM H3

Although a good exhibition cultivar, for this colour it has been superseded by the more uniform 'Valerie Harrod'.

Beane / E.W. King & Co., 1997
H: T L: U N: P P: S C: orange-pink
S: summer

'Explorer Crimson'

This semi-dwarf cultivar has non-tendril leaves.

Bodger Seeds Ltd, 1992
H: SD L: M N: P P: S C: crimson
S: summer

'Explorer Rose Pink'

This semi-dwarf cultivar has non-tendril leaves.

Bodger Seeds Ltd, 1992
H: SD L: M N: P P: S C: rose pink
S: summer

'Explorer Scarlet'

This semi-dwarf cultivar has non-tendril leaves.

Bodger Seeds Ltd, 1992
H: SD L: M N: P P: S C: scarlet
S: summer

'Fields of Fire'

This was probably the first scarlet-flowered cultivar to have scent.

Robson / Eagle Sweet Peas, 2008
H: T L: U N: P P: S C: scarlet S: summer

'Firecrest'

With long stems, this cultivar flowers prolifically.

Robert Bolton & Son, 1987
H: T L: U N: P P: S C: cerise-scarlet
S: summer

'First Flame' AGM H3

This is still a good cultivar for garden use but has been superseded for exhibition.

Harrod / E.W. King & Co., 2006
H: T L: U N: P P: S C: salmon-cerise,
w.g. S: summer

'First Lady' Zvolanek

A winter-bloomer, there have been two subsequent cultivars with the same name.

W. Zvolanek & Co., pre-1974
H: T L: U N: M P: S C: deep salmon
pink S: winter

'Flame' Unwins

The original name 'Olympic Flame' was not permitted under the London Olympic Games Act 2006, but 'Flame' has been used before for three other cultivars.

Harrod / Unwins Seeds, 2012
H: T L: U N: P P: S C: salmon-cerise,
w.g. S: summer

'Florencecourt'

This cultivar has well-placed, large, frilly flowers on long stems,

Harrod, 2008
H: T L: U N: P P: S C: salmon-cerise,
w.g. S: summer

'Flying Visit'

With well-placed flowers, this is a good garden cultivar.

Hammett / Maishman, 1981
H: T L: U N: P P: S C: white flushed deep violet S: summer

'Frances Kate'

This cultivar has consistently long, strong stems. It makes a good alternative to the similarly coloured but rarely available 'Leilani Bluebell'.

R. Parsons, 2011
H: T L: U N: P P: S C: navy blue stripe S: summer

'Frank G' Ferry Morse 1940

Part of Cuthbertson Series, this cultivar blooms earlier than most.

Ferry Morse Seed Co., 1940
H: T L: U N: P P: S C: rosy lavender S: late spring

'Future Shock'

With *L. × hammettii* ancestry, the flowers open marbled orange but quickly turn brown – definitely an acquired taste.

Hammett, 2019
H: T L: U N: P P: S C: marbled orange, turning brown S: summer

'Garnette'

Part of the Bijou Series, this is a dwarf, trailing cultivar that flowers in spring.

Burpee Seeds, 1968
H: D L: U N: P P: S C: maroon S: spring

'Garry Kirkman'

This is a good exhibition cultivar.

R. Parsons, 2012
H: T L: U N: P P: S C: orange-red S: summer

'Gawler Cerise'

A winter-flowering cultivar, like most of the Gawler types it tends to have only three flowers per stem in the northern hemisphere.

Harkness, before 1971
H: T L: U N: P P: D C: cerise-orange
S: winter

'Gawler Marion'

This is a strong-growing cultivar with sturdy stems.

Austalia, 1920s
H: T L: U N: P P: D C: pale salmon pink, c.g. S: late spring

'Gawler Shell Pink'

A winter-flowering cultivar with very frilly, duplex flowers.

Harkness, 1949
H: T L: U N: P P: S C: shell pink
S: winter

'Geoff Amos'

A long-stemmed cultivar, the red intensifies as the flowers age.

Thompson & Morgan, 2001
H: T L: U N: P P: S C: red stripe, w.g.
S: summer

'Geoff Hughes'

This cultivar is one of the best flaked Spencers.

Sarrer / Eagle Sweet Peas, 2010
H: T L: U N: P P: S C: orange flake, w.g.
S: summer

'George Priestley'

With large flowers, this is a good exhibition cultivar.

Hubbuck / Matthewman, 2008
H: T L: U N: P P: S C: light mauve, c.g.
S: summer

'Gerry Cullinan'

With large, frilly flowers on strong stems this is suitable for exhibition, garden use and as a cut flowers.
Kerton Sweet Peas, 2007
H: T L: U N: P P: S C: lavender, c.g.
S: summer

'Glasnevin'

The large flowers of this cultivar gain slight hints of pink as they age.
Harrod, 2006
H: T L: U N: P P: S C: white S: summer

'Gloria' Denholm

This cultivar belongs to the Early Multiflora Gigantea Series.

Denholm Seeds, 1960
H: T L: U N: M P: S C: carmine-rose
S: early spring

'Glow' Unwins

A tricoloured cultivar, this has a white ground flushed with orange-red and pink.

Unwins Seeds, 1997
H: T L: U N: P P: S C: orange-pink, w.g. / cerise pink, w.g. S: summer

'Grandma Butt'

With large flowers on long stems, this is a good all-round cultivar.

Beane / R. Parsons, 2006
H: T L: U N: P P: S C: carmine-rose
S: summer

'Great Britain'

Part of the Galaxy Series, this has multiflora flowers.

Burpee Seeds, 1966
H: T L: U N: M P: S C: rose pink, c.g.
S: summer

'Gwendoline' Unwins AGM H3

This cultivar has good resistance to bud drop.

Unwins Seeds, 1999
H: T L: U N: P P: S C: white flushed lilac pink S: summer

'Gypsy Queen'

This cultivar is popular for its uniform colour and is good for garden use and cutting.

Robert Bolton & Son, 1965
H: T L: U N: P P: S C: crimson
S: summer

'Hampton Court'

A multipurpose cultivar, this is good for exhibition, garden use and cutting.
Brackley, 1991
H: T L: U N: P P: S C: mid-blue
S: summer

'Hannah Magovern'

This is one of the few scarlet-flowered cultivars with good scent.
R. Parsons, 2010
H: T L: U N: P P: S C: scarlet S: summer

'Hannah's Harmony' AGM H3

A semi-dwarf cultivar, this may be the same as 'Minuet Magenta'.
J.D. Place / R. Parsons, 2013
H: SD L: U N: P P: S C: magenta stripe, w.g. S: summer

'Heartbeat'

With long stems and a distinct colour, this cultivar is good for cut-flower growers.
Sewell, 2001
H: T L: U N: P P: S C: cerise S: summer

'Heaven Scent'

Large frilly flowers are borne on long, straight stems in this cultivar.
Harrod, 2007
H: T L: U N: P P: S C: pale pink, c.g.
S: summer

'Hero' Unwins

This is a good cut-flower cultivar with large blooms on long stems.
Unwins Seeds, 2010
H: T L: U N: P P: S C: dark violet
S: summer

'High Society' Hammett

This is an early spring-flowering, multiflora cultivar.

Hammett / Somerset, 2015
H: T L: U N: M P: S C: white with pink edge S: winter

'Hikari'

A multiflora cultivar, this is winter-flowering.

Nozaki, date unknown
H: T L: U N: P P: S C: orange-pink
S: winter

'Honeymoon'

The flowers of this cultivar open white and then turn pale lavender.

Kershaw / Maishman, 1972
H: T L: U N: P P: S C: lavender flush
S: summer

'Ida King'

Although still good for garden use, this cultivar has been superseded for exhibition.

G. King / Eagle Sweet Peas, 2007
H: T L: U N: P P: S C: lavender
S: summer

'Imogen'

From the same cross as 'Evening Glow', this cultivar is good for exhibition and as a cut flower.

Beane / E.W. King & Co., 2001
H: T L: U N: P P: S C: rose pink, c.g.
S: summer

'Invicta' Christmas

With frilly flowers on long stems, this exhibition and cut-flower cultivar is resistant to bud drop.

Christmas / P. Johnson, 2015
H: T L: U N: P P: S C: white S: summer

'Isabella Cochrane'

This makes a good exhibition cultivar.

Chisholm / Kerton Sweet Peas, 2001
H: T L: U N: P P: S C: lavender flush, w.g. S: summer

'Jack Bridger'

Although having small flowers by modern standards, this cultivar has good colour.

Hammett / Maishman, 1981
H: T L: U N: P P: S C: pale blush-pink S: summer

'Jack Eveleigh'

This cultivar has good flower form and placement.

R. Parsons, 2017
H: T L: U N: P P: S C: pale blue flush, w.g. S: summer

'Jacko'

This is a non-tendril cultivar.

R. Place / R. Parsons, 2016
H: T L: M N: P P: S C: red stripe, w.g. S: summer

'Jacqueline Ann'

A good all-round cultivar, this is suitable for exhibition, garden use and cutting.

R. Parsons, 2008
H: T L: U N: P P: S C: deep lavender S: summer

'Jacqueline Heather' AGM H3

The flowers of this cultivar are occasionally duplex.

R. Parsons, 2012
H: T L: U N: P P: D C: white with pink edge S: summer

'Janey'

Flowering prolifically, this cultivar gives a good garden display.

Hammett / R. Parsons, 2016
H: T L: U N: P P: S C: red flake, w.g.
S: summer

'Janine Martin'

This cultivar has the same fault as other Gawlers of producing fewer flowers per stem in the northern hemisphere.

Martin, 1960s
H: T L: U N: P P: D C: cream S: winter

'Jayne Amanda'

An excellent cultivar, this is just as good as the ubiquitous 'Gwendoline'.

Truslove / Marchant, 1985
H: T L: U N: P P: S C: pale magenta, w.g. S: summer

'Jeannie'

This is the best cream-coloured Spencer from this prolific raiser.

Harrod, 2007
H: T L: U N: P P: S C: cream S: summer

'Jemima'

The large frilly flowers on strong stems make this cultivar suitable for exhibition, garden use and cutting.

Beane / Kerton Sweet Peas, 2010
H: T L: U N: P P: S C: cerise rose pink, w.g. S: summer

'Jill Walton'

This cultivar has ood clean colour right down to the base of the petals.

Gubb / Kerton Sweet Peas, 1993
H: T L: U N: P P: S C: salmon pink, c.g. S: summer

'Jilly' AGM H3

The young flowers of this cultivar
are quite yellow and it is popular for
exhibition.

Harriss / Unwins Seeds, 1988
H: T L: U N: P P: S C: cream S: summer

'Jimmy'

A long-stemmed sweet pea that
flowers a little earlier than others.
Some stocks of this cultivar are
Grandiflora types.

Ferry Morse Seed Co., 1951
H: T L: U N: P P: S C: deep scarlet
S: late spring

'Joan Elizabeth Child'

This cultivar is similar to 'Mary
Pannell' (syn. 'Daily Mail') but lacks
the purple base to the petals.

R. Parsons, 2012
H: T L: U N: P P: S C: cerise pink
S: summer

'Joejess'

Some orange cultivars suffer
bleaching of their colour in full
sun, but not this one.

Hubbuck / McDonald, 2014
H: T L: U N: P P: S C: orange-red
S: summer

'John Gray' AGM H3

With its large frilly flowers on long
stems, this cultivar is good for
exhibition and cut-flower use.

R. Parsons, 2009
H: T L: U N: P P: S C: pale pink, w.g.
S: summer

'Joyce Stanton'

With weather-resistant colour, this
makes a good cut-flower cultivar.

Manston, 2009
H: T L: U N: P P: S C: dark blue
S: summer

'Judith Martin'

A winter-flowering cultivar, this has particularly frilly flowers.

Martin, 1960s
H: T L: U N: P P: D C: pale mauve
S: winter

'Judith Wilkinson'

With saturated colour, this popular cultivar is good for cutting.

Truslove / R. Parsons, 2008
H: T L: U N: P P: S C: deep carmine
S: summer

'Julie Ann'

This cultivar is good for cutting and exhibition.

Eagle Sweet Peas, 2011
H: T L: U N: P P: S C: carmine
S: summer

'Just Janet'

The large, frilly flowers of this cultivar are produced over a long period.

Harrod / Unwins Seeds, 2014
H: T L: U N: P P: S C: coral pink, w.g.
S: summer

'Just Jenny'

This cultivar flowers prolifically and is good for exhibition and garden use.

Eagle Sweet Peas, 2005
H: T L: U N: P P: S C: dark blue
S: summer

'Just Julia' AGM H3

This makes a good exhibition cultivar.

R. Parsons, 2011
H: T L: U N: P P: S C: mid blue
S: summer

'Karen Harrod'

With large, frilly flowers on strong stems this is suitable for exhibition, garden use and cutting.

Harrod / Kerton Sweet Peas, 2011
H: T L: U N: P P: S C: mid blue
S: summer

'Karen Louise'

One of the most reliable cultivars for exhibition, this is also good for garden use.

Beane / E.W. King & Co., 1998
H: T L: U N: P P: S C: lavender
S: summer

'Karen Tremewan'

This cultivar flowers prolifically but the blooms are slightly smaller than more recent cultivars.

Tremewan / Marchant, 1984
H: T L: U N: P P: S C: orange-pink
S: summer

'Katie Alice'

This cultivar is a popular colour, but it has been superseded by other mauves.

Eagle Sweet Peas, 2006
H: T L: U N: P P: S C: mauve
S: summer

'Kiera Madeline'

This cultivar is excellent for cut flowers but 'Anniversary' is preferred for exhibition.

Eagle Sweet Peas, 2010
H: T L: U N: P P: S C: pink picotee, c.g.
S: summer

'Killarney'

This multiflora cultivar is part of the Jet Set Series.

Ferry Morse Seed Co., 1973
H: SD L: U N: P P: S C: cream and salmon pink S: summer

'Kippen Cream'

With large frilly flowers on long, strong stems this is suitable for exhibition, garden use and cutting.

Chisholm / Kerton Sweet Peas, 1998
H: T L: U N: P P: S C: cream S: summer

'Knee-Hi Cream Pink'

This multiflora cultivar, sometimes with duplex flowers, is part of the Knee-Hi Series and is also sold as 'San Francisco'.

Ferry Morse Seed Co., 1966
H: SD L: U N: M P: S C: cream and salmon pink S: spring / summer

'Knee-Hi Rose Crimson'

This multiflora cultivar is part of the Knee-Hi Series and is also sold as 'San Jose'.

Ferry Morse Seed Co., 1966
H: SD L: U N: M P: S C: rose-crimson S: summer

'Laila K'

This reliable cultivar competes well with others of this colour.

Kerton Sweet Peas, 2013
H: T L: U N: P P: S C: pink S: summer

'Lakeland Blizzard'

With non-tendril leaves, the flowers of this cultivar have good placement.

R. Place / R. Parsons, 2016
H: T L: M N: P P: S C: white S: summer

'Laura Webster'

With its large flowers on long stems this cultivar is good for cut-flower growers.

Hammett / Denny, 2009
H: T L: U N: P P: S C: warm pink S: summer

'Lavender Flake'

Excellent for garden use, this cultivar produces a mass of flowers.
Owl's Acre Sweet Peas, date unknown
H: T L: U N: P P: S C: lavender flake, w.g. S: summer

'Leading Light'

This cultivar was the first reverse bicolour so the flowers are relatively small by modern standards.
Hammett / Arthur Yates & Co., date unknown
H: T L: U N: P P: S C: lavender / mauve
S: summer

'Lauren Landy' AGM H3

Stocks of this previously excellent cultivar have deteriorated in quality but it is currently being reselected.
Harrod, 2010
H: T L: U N: P P: S C: warm rose-pink, w.g. S: summer

'Leamington'

Once supremely popular for its quality and long season of flowering, this cultivar has deteriorated, so is currently being reselected.
Colledge / Unwins Seeds, 1961
H: T L: U N: P P: S C: deep lavender
S: summ

'Len Harrod'

This cultivar flowers prolifically with blooms of exhibition quality..
Harrod, 2012
H: T L: U N: P P: S C: orange-pink, w.g.
S: summer

'Lilac Romance'

A delightful colour, this cultivar has long stems.

Wells / Kerton Sweet Peas, 2010
H: T L: U N: P P: S C: light lilac
S: summer

'Linda C'

A popular exhibition cultivar, this has long, sturdy stems.

Chisholm / Kerton Sweet Peas, 2001
H: T L: U N: P P: S C: mid blue
S: summer

'Lilac Ripple'

Although still good for garden use, as an exhibition stripe this cultivar has been superseded by 'Sir Jimmy Shand'. It is also sold as 'Pulsar'.

W. Thomas / Thompson & Morgan, 1989
H: T L: U N: P P: S C: lilac stripe, w.g. S: summer

'Linda Carole'

This early-flowering multiflora cultivar has non-tendril leaves.

J.D. Place / Eagle Sweet Peas, 2004
H: T L: M N: M P: S C: carmine stripe, w.g. S: early spring

'Linda Mary'

Although bearing duplex flowers the stems of this cultivar are too short for cut-flower sales.

R. Parsons, 2007
H: T L: U N: P P: D C: pink stripe, c.g.
S: summer

'Linda Richards'

The distinctive shade of this cultivar is loved by some cut-flower growers.

R. Parsons, 2011
H: T L: U N: P P: S C: lilac-pink flush, c.g.
S: summer

'Lipstick'

With large wavy blooms on long stems, this cultivar is suitable for exhibition and as a cut flower.

Hammett / Shepherd, 2003
H: T L: U N: P P: S C: mid red
S: summer

'Lipstick' Unwins AGM H3

This carmine-pink cultivar should not be confused with the crimson Hammett-raised cultivar also called 'Lipstick' that was named first.

Unwins Seeds, 2008
H: T L: U N: P P: S C: vibrant carmine
S: summer

'Lisa Marie'

With long stems this cultivar is similar in colour to 'Choc Stripe' and 'Wiltshire Ripple' but an improvement in size and vigour.

J.D. Place / Eagle Sweet Peas, 2004
H: T L: U N: P P: S C: plum stripe, w.g.
S: summer

'Lizbeth'

With large blooms, this is a popular exhibition cultivar, and the petals are more frilly than the similar 'Valerie Harrod'.

Tremewan, 1993
H: T L: U N: P P: S C: orange-pink
S: summer

'Lois'

This early-flowering cultivar is part of the Cuthbertson Series.

Ferry Morse Seed Co., 1940
H: T L: U N: P P: S C: rose pink, w.g.
S: late spring

'Lovejoy'

A shade paler than some dark maroon cultivars, this is popular with some cut-flower growers.

Robert Bolton & Son, 1992
H: T L: U N: P P: S C: maroon
S: summer

'Lucy Hawthorne'

Like white-flowered 'Cathy Wright', this cultivar also has pale seeds.

Eagle Sweet Peas, 2011
H: T L: U N: P P: S C: white S: summer

'Lunar Sea'

This is an early spring-flowering, multiflora cultivar.

Hammett, 2009
H: T L: U N: M P: S C: cream S: early spring

'Madrid'

A multiflora cultivar, this is part of the Jet Set Series.

Ferry Morse Seed Co., 1973
H: SD L: U N: P P: S C: scarlet
S: summer

'Maestro'

With large flowers on long stems, this is suitable for exhibition.

B.R. Jones / Eagle Sweet Peas, 2009
H: T L: U N: P P: S C: lavender
S: summer

'Magnificent Maroon'

Although 'Windsor' is preferred for exhibition, this cultivar is likely to be better for cut-flower growers.

Harrod / R. Parsons, 2016
H: T L: U N: P P: S C: maroon
S: summer

'Maloy'

A multiflora cultivar good for cut-flower production, this was the first reverse bicolour in red shades.

Hammett, 2015
H: T L: U N: M P: S C: orange-pink
S: summer

'Mammoth Cream Pink'

This is a multiflora cultivar flowering in early spring.

Denholm Seeds, 1982
H: T L: U N: M P: S C: appleblossom pink, c.g. S: early spring

'Mammoth Navy'

This is a multiflora cultivar flowering in winter or early spring.

Denholm Seeds, around 1982
H: T L: U N: M P: S C: dark blue
S: winter

'Margaret's Delight'

Although good for cut flowers, others in this colour are better for exhibition.

Fleming Robertson / Kerton Sweet Peas, 2012
H: T L: U N: P P: S C: rose-pink
S: summer

'Marie's Melody'

With two flower stems per leaf node, a clump of this semi-dwarf cultivar is completely smothered in blooms.

J.D. Place / R. Parsons, 2013
H: SD L: U N: P P: S C: red stripe, w.g.
S: summer

'Marion' Walker

The lavender flowers of this cultivar are enhanced by dark veins and it is resistant to bud-drop. The name has been used five times before.

W. Walker / Marchant, 1983
H: T L: U N: P P: S C: lavender
S: summer

'Marjorie Carrier'

This cultivar has frilly flowers on long, strong stems.

R. Parsons, 2016
H: T L: U N: P P: S C: salmon pink, c.g.
S: summer

'Mark Harrod'

This cultivar has large flowers on long, strong stems.

Harrod, 2007
H: T L: U N: P P: S C: scarlet S: summer

'Mars' Unwins

This name has been used twice before, the original being a red Grandiflora from 1896.

Unwins Seeds, 1996
H: T L: U N: P P: S C: red stripe, w.g.
S: summer

'Martha Mary' AGM H3

The large frilly flowers of this cultivar are borne on long, strong stems.

Kerton Sweet Peas, 2016
H: T L: U N: P P: S C: cream S: summer

'Mary Priestley'

This is a good exhibition cultivar with strong stems, regarded by some as better than 'White Frills'.
Priestley / Myers, 2015
H: T L: U N: P P: S C: white S: summer

'Mary Pannell'

With purple splashes at the base of the petals, this is good for cutting. It is widely sold as 'Daily Mail'.
Beane / Unwins Seeds, 1997
H: T L: U N: P P: S C: cerise pink
S: summer

'Mary Mac' AGM H3

The deep colour and very frilly flowers distinguish this cultivar from other cream Spencers.
McDonald, 2015
H: T L: U N: P P: S C: cream S: summer

'Maxeen Martin'

This is one of the better Gawler cultivars for the northern hemisphere.

Martin, date unknown
H: T L: U N: P P: S C: blush pink, c.g.
S: winter

'Matterhorn'

This multiflora cultivar sometimes has duplex flowers and is part of the Jet Set Series.

Ferry Morse Seed Co., 1973
H: SD L: U N: P P: S C: white
S: summer

'Memorial Flight'

With frilly flowers and strong stems, this is a good exhibition cultivar.

R.D. King / Kerton Sweet Peas, 1998
H: T L: U N: P P: S C: white S: summer

'Midnight' Jones

Although having little scent, this is
a vigorous cultivar. The original use
of the name was for a Grandiflora.
B.R. Jones / Unwins Seeds, 1986
H: T L: U N: P P: S C: dark maroon
S: summer

'Milestone'

Although not as dark as some,
and good for cut-flower growers,
'Lovejoy' may be better.
Unwins Seeds, 1971
H: T L: U N: P P: D C: maroon
S: summer

'Millennium'

With strong stems, this is a good
exhibition cultivar.
D.M. Jones / Unwins Seeds, 2000
H: T L: U N: P P: S C: crimson
S: summer

'Milly'

With well-placed flowers, this is
a good exhibition cultivar.
Matthewman, 2007
H: T L: U N: P P: S C: vibrant magenta
S: summer

'Minuet Blue Splash'

This cultivar was selected by Roger
Parsons from Minuet Mixed raised
by Unwins.
Unwins Seeds, n/k
H: SD L: U N: P P: S C: blue stripe, w.g.
S: summer

'Minuet Orange'

This cultivar was selected by Roger
Parsons from Minuet Mixed raised
by Unwins.
Unwins Seeds, n/k
H: SD L: U N: P P: S C: orange stripe,
w.g. S: summer

'Minuet Orange-pink Splash'

This cultivar combines two colours of stripe in its bicoloured flowers.

Unwins Seeds, n/k
H: SD L: U N: P P: S C: orange stripe, w.g. / pink stripe, w.g. S: summer

'Minuet Purple'

This cultivar was selected by Roger Parsons from Minuet Mixed raised by Unwins.

Unwins Seeds, n/k
H: SD L: U N: P P: S C: purple stripe, w.g. S: summer

'Minuet Red'

This cultivar was selected by Roger Parsons from Minuet Mixed raised by Unwins.

Unwins Seeds, n/k
H: SD L: U N: P P: S C: red stripe, w.g. S: summer

'Misty'

Almost lavender in colour, this cultivar has good flower form and placement.

Leese / Eagle Sweet Peas, 2008
H: T L: U N: P P: S C: pale mauve flush, w.g. S: summer

'Misty Mountain'

The flushing on this cultivar is a clear shade of lavender.

Evans / Matthewman, 2004
H: T L: U N: P P: S C: lavender on ivory ground S: summer

'Mollie Rilstone'

Extremely popular for garden use, time will tell if the recently introduced 'Gwawr Cymru' replaces it.

Tremewan, 1993
H: T L: U N: P P: S C: pink picotee, c.g. S: summer

'Morven'

Although this cultivar has long stems and flowers prolifically, it is not suitable for exhibition.
Chisholm / Kerton Sweet Peas, 1998
H: T L: U N: P P: S C: orange red
S: summer

'Mount Stewart'

This cultivar has also been sold as 'Wisley'.
Harrod / Unwins Seeds, 2005
H: T L: U N: P P: S C: mauve
S: summer

'Moorland Beauty'

This cultivar has large flowers that are well-placed on long stems.
Albutt / Eagle Sweet Peas, 1995
H: T L: U N: P P: S C: deep mauve
S: summer

'Mrs Bernard Jones' AGM H3

A reliable cultivar, this has long stems and makes a good cut flower.
B.R. Jones / Unwins Seeds, 1981
H: T L: U N: P P: S C: candy-pink flush, w.g. S: summer

'Mrs R. Bolton'

Once supremely popular, this cultivar has now been superseded by others with larger flowers on longer stems.
Robert Bolton & Son, 1945
H: T L: U N: P P: S C: rose pink, w.g. S: summer

'Mr P.'

This cultivar has darker blue flaking than the popular 'Susan Thomas'.
McDonald / R. Parsons, 2017
H: T L: U N: P P: S C: dark blue flake, w.g. S: summer

'Mrs R. Chisholm'

With large frilly flowers on strong stems this is good for exhibition, garden use and cutting.
Chisholm / Kerton Sweet Peas, 2009
H: T L: U N: P P: S C: white S: summer

'Mumsie'

A vigorous cultivar, this has a particularly bold colour.
Eagle Sweet Peas, 1993
H: T L: U N: P P: S C: crimson
S: summer

'Naomi Nazareth'

With its excellent stem length, this is a good exhibition and cut-flower cultivar.

R. Parsons, 2009
H: T L: U N: P P: S C: pale blue
S: summer

'Naples'

This multiflora cultivar is part of the Jet Set Series.

Ferry Morse Seed Co., 1973
H: SD L: U N: P P: S C: mid blue
S: summer

'New Dawn' Harkness or Martin

A spring-flowering cultivar, the name originally applied to a pale pink Spencer from 1937.

Raiser unknown, before 1968
H: SD L: U N: P P: D C: pink flake, c.g.
S: late spring

'Night Sky'

Although a good cultivar, this is very similar to the earlier 'Frances Kate'.

Matthewman, 2017
H: T L: U N: P P: S C: dark blue stripe, w.g. S: summer

'Nimbus'

With its unusual colouring, this cultivar is popular with cut-flower growers.

Unwins Seeds, 1996
H: T L: U N: P P: S C: dark purple stripe on grey S: summer

'Noel Sutton' AGM H3

This all-purpose cultivar performs reliably for the whole flowering season.

Suttons, 1968
H: T L: U N: P P: S C: mid blue
S: summer

'Nora Holman'

This large-flowered cultivar has been popular for exhibition since its introduction.
Tremewan, 1991
H: T L: U N: P P: S C: pale salmon pink, c.g. S: summer

'North Shore'

A striking bicolour, this was one of Keith Hammett's early raisings and is still popular.
Hammett / Thompson & Morgan, 1987
H: T L: U N: P P: S C: navy blue / violet S: summer

'Nuance'

This multiflora bicoloured cultivar has well-spaced flowers.
Hammett, 2012
H: T L: U N: P P: S C: mid pink / pale pink S: early spring

'Oban Bay'

A vigorous and reliable cultivar, this is good for exhibition.
Chisholm / Robert Bolton & Son, 1997
H: T L: U N: P P: S C: silver blue S: summer

'Oklahoma' AGM H3

Flowering prolifically, this gives a striking display.
Unwins Seeds, 2002
H: T L: U N: P P: S C: red flake, w.g. S: summer

'Olive D.'

This cultivar has supersed 'Candy' because of its larger flowers.
Owl's Acre Sweet Peas, 2008
H: T L: U N: P P: S C: maroon stripe, w.g. S: summer

'Omay'

This long-stemmed cultivar wth large and frilly flowers is also sold as 'Happy Birthday' but 'Omay' was published first.
K. Brewer / Matthewman, 2003
H: T L: U N: P P: S C: orange red, w.g.
S: summer

'Opalette'

This dwarf, trailing cultivar is part of the Bijou Series.
Burpee Seeds, 1967
H: D L: U N: P P: S C: rose pink, w.g.
S: spring

'Ollie Clarke'

A good all-rounder, this is also likely to become more popular for exhibition.
Harrod / R. Parsons, 2018
H: T L: U N: P P: S C: orange salmon
S: summer

'Orchid' Unwins

This is a good lavender-coloured cultivar, but the name has been used five times before, all for similar colours.

Unwins Seeds, 2008
H: T L: U N: P P: S C: deep lavender
S: summer

'Our Colin'

With its large, frilly flowers on strong stems, this is suitable for exhibition, garden use and cutting.

Chisholm / Kerton Sweet Peas, 2009
H: T L: U N: P P: S C: mid blue
S: summer

'Our Harry'

The strong stems of this cultivar make it good for exhibition as well as garden use.

F.G. Davis / Marchant, 1987
H: T L: U N: P P: S C: mid blue
S: summer

'Oyama Aphrodite'

This is a multiflora cultivar.

Oyama, 1991 / 97
H: T L: U N: M P: S C: orange-pink
S: winter

'Oyama Bicolour'

Although a bicolour, this multiflora cultivar appears to be mauve.

Oyama, before 1984
H: T L: U N: P P: S C: mauve / lavender
S: early spring

'Oyama Millennium'

This is a multiflora cultivar.

Fujisawa, before 2012
H: T L: U N: P P: S C: dark pink
S: winter

'Oyama Russian Blue'

This is a multiflora cultivar.
Oyama, before 1984
H: T L: U N: P P: S C: lavender purple
S: early spring

'Pandemonium' AGM H3

The long stems and long flowering period make this cultivar suitable for cut-flower growers.
Hammett, 2009
H: T L: U N: P P: S C: purple flake, w.g.
S: summer

'Patio Deep Rose'

This is a dwarf, bush cultivar flowering from late spring.
Burpee Seeds, before 1979
H: D L: U N: P P: S C: magenta
S: spring

'Patio Pink / White Bicolour'

A dwarf, bush bicoloured cultivar, this flowers from late spring.
Burpee Seeds, before 1979
H: D L: U N: P P: S C: pink / white
S: spring

'Patio Red / Pink Bicolour'

This is a dwarf, bush bicoloured cultivar that flowers from late spring.
Burpee Seeds, before 1979
H: D L: U N: P P: S C: red / pink
S: spring

'Patricia Anne' AGM H3

A reliable cultivar that is easy to grow, this deserves to be more popular.
W. Sutton / Kerton Sweet Peas, 2006
H: T L: U N: P P: S C: lavender flush
S: summer

'Peacock' Unwins

The flowers of this cultivar darken significantly as they mature. The name originally applied to a Grandiflora from 1908.

Unwins Seeds, 2003

H: T L: U N: P P: S C: deep lavender on ivory S: summer

'Pearl Anniversary'

This cultivar was selected by Roger Parsons from material sent to him by Keith Hammett.

R. Parsons, 2016

H: T L: U N: P P: S C: pale pink flake, w.g. S: summer

'Percy Thrower'

The flowers of this cultivar are large and frilly.

B.R. Jones / Robert Bolton & Son, 1984

H: T L: U N: P P: S C: lavender flush, w.g. S: summer

'Phoebe' Bolton

This has a striking colour but is not the most robust cultivar. The name originally applied to a winter-flowering Spencer from 1916.

Robert Bolton & Son, 1998

H: T L: U N: P P: S C: orange flake, w.g. S: summer

'Piggy Sue'

This is an early-flowering, multiflora cultivar that starts off picotee then develops a pink flush.

Hammett, 2012

H: T L: U N: P P: S C: cream with pink edge and flush S: early spring

'Pink Nines'

This early-flowering, multiflora cultivar is named for the fact that it often has nine flowers per stem .

Hammett, 2010

H: T L: U N: M P: S C: mid pink S: early spring

'Pip Tremewan'

With its long, sturdy stems, this cultivar is good for cutting.

Tremewan / Thompson & Morgan, 1999

H: T L: U N: P P: S C: purple S: summer

'Pip's Cornish Cream'

A good exhibition cultivar, this was raised by Mike Carr from material sent to him by Pip Tremewan's widow.

Tremewan / Carr / R. Parsons, 2014

H: T L: U N: P P: S C: cream S: summer

'Pip's Maroon'

Making a good replacement for 'Windsor' as an exhibition cultivar, this was raised by Mike Carr from material sent to him by Pip Tremewan's widow.

Tremewan / Carr / R. Parsons, 2008

H: T L: U N: P P: S C: dark maroon S: summer

'Pirate Gold'

This has good colour but the flowers are small by modern standards. It is not sunproof, so needs to be grown under cover.

Waller-Franklin Seed Co., 1932

H: T L: U N: P P: S C: orange S: summer

'Pisces'

This cultivar has non-tendril leaves.

J.D. Place / E.W. King & Co., 1999

H: T L: M N: P P: S C: pale pink, w.g. S: summer

'Pocahontas' AGM H3

This makes a good cut-flower cultivar when grown under glass but develops better colour outside.

Harrod, 2005

H: T L: U N: P P: S C: geranium red S: summer

'Polar Star'

This early-flowering multiflora cultivar of Japanese origin opens with a hint of pink and also has dark seeds.

Raiser unknown, 1991 / 97 or earlier
H: T L: U N: M P: S C: white S: early spring

'Porlock'

This cultivar has strikingly veined flowers and a broadly rounded standard petal.

Hammett, 2015
H: T L: U N: P P: S C: maroon / violet, marbled S: summer

'Precious' Unwins

There are several cultivars in this colour and others may be better. The name originally applied to a carmine Spencer from 1993.

Unwins Seeds, 2014
H: T L: U N: P P: S C: rose pink, w.g. S: summer

'Prince of Orange' Morse

This cultivar requires shading to bring out the full colour. Three earlier sweet peas have borne the same name.

C.C. Morse & Co., 1928
H: T L: U N: P P: S C: orange S: summer

'Princess' Zvolanek

This is an early-flowering, multiflora cultivar.

A. Zvolanek & Sons, date unknown
H: T L: U N: M P: S C: light salmon S: winter

'Princess Elizabeth' Bolton

The top flower of this cultivar has a tendency to hang. The name originally applied to a 1946 cultivar.

Robert Bolton & Son, 1950
H: T L: U N: P P: S C: salmon pink, c.g. S: summer

'Promise'

This popular bicoloured cultivar makes a good cut flower.
R. Parsons, 2006
H: T L: U N: P P: S C: pink / white
S: summer

'Purple Pimpernel'

With large flowers on long, strong stems, this bicolour makes a good exhibition and cut-flower cultivar.
Hunt / Thompson & Morgan, 2014
H: T L: U N: P P: S C: maroon / violet
S: summer

'Queen Mother' Richardson

This cultivar sometimes has duplex flowers. The name originally applied to a lilac Spencer from 1913.

B. Richardson / Unwins Seeds, 1991
H: T L: U N: P P: D C: orange-pink
S: summer

'Queen of Hearts'

Suitable for exhibition and garden use, this cultivar has a long flowering season. It has also been sold as 'Cirrus'.

Tullett / Unwins Seeds, 2004
H: T L: U N: P P: S C: pink stripe, w.g.
S: summer

'Raspberry Flake'

With its unusual background colour of grey, this appears to be derived from Keith Hammett material.

Unwins Seeds, 2009
H: T L: U N: P P: S C: crimson flake on grey S: summer

'Red Arrow'

With stiffer petals than most reds, this cultivar has good weather resistance.

B.R. Jones / Unwins Seeds, 1983
H: T L: U N: P P: S C: scarlet S: summer

'Renown' Harrod

This has a good deep colour. The name originally applied to a pink Spencer from 1922.

Harrod, 2012
H: T L: U N: P P: S C: crimson
S: summer

'Restormel'

With large flowers on strong stems, this makes a good exhibition cultivar.

Tremewan, 1989
H: T L: U N: P P: S C: orange-cerise
S: summer

'Rhineland'

This semi-dwarf, multiflora cultivar is part of the Jet Set Series.

Ferry Morse Seed Co., 1973
H: SD L: U N: P P: S C: rose crimson
S: summer

'Richard and Judy'

The strong stems of this bicoloured cultivar support neatly arranged flowers.

Matthewman, 2002
H: T L: U N: P P: S C: purple / mauve
S: summer

'Ron Entwistle'

This is a free-blooming cultivar that was introduced after the raiser's death.

Entwistle / Grayson, 1999
H: T L: U N: P P: S C: scarlet S: summer

'Ronnie'

This early-flowering cultivar is part of the Cuthbertson Series.

Ferry Morse Seed Co., 1953
H: T L: U N: P P: S C: mid orange S: late spring

'Rosemary Padley'

Excellent for garden use, this also makes a good cut flower.

Tullett / Robert Bolton & Son, 1995
H: T L: U N: P P: S C: crimson
S: summer

'Rosie' Truslove

Good for garden use, this was raised by Andrew Beane from material sent to him by Bill Truslove's widow. The original name applied to a pink Spencer from 1932.

Truslove / Beane / E.W. King & Co., 2011
H: T L: U N: P P: S C: cerise S: summer

'Rosina' James

This is still a good cultivar, but has been superseded by others in this colour. The name originally applied to a Spencer from 1914.

A.J. James / Matthewman, 1994
H: T L: U N: P P: S C: lavender
S: summer

'Rosy Dawn'

Introduced around the same time as Bolton's similarly coloured 'Phoebe', this Unwins cultivar seems more robust.

Unwins Seeds, 1999
H: T L: U N: P P: S C: orange flake, w.g.
S: summer

'Rosy Salmon'

A prolific bloomer, this cultivar is good for garden use and cutting for the house.

Brackley / E.W. King & Co., 2015
H: T L: U N: P P: S C: cerise pink
S: summer

'Roubeena'

This cultivar has uniform colour throughout the petals.

Harrod, 2010
H: T L: U N: P P: S C: ruby red S: late spring

'Route 66'

This bicoloured cultivar is good for cutting and some stems have five flowers.

Hammett, 2015
H: T L: U N: P P: S C: red / white
S: summer

'Royal Pink' Ferry Morse

Earlier flowering than most, this cultivar is part of the Royal Series. The name originally applied to a cultivar from 1926.

Ferry Morse Seed Co., 1968
H: T L: U N: P P: S C: pink S: late spring

'Royal Wedding'

This long-stemmed cultivar is one of the best whites and is popular for exhibiition.

Unwins Seeds, 1982
H: T L: U N: P P: S C: white S: summer

'Ruby Anniversary'

A good exhibition cultivar, this has long stems.

Sewell, 2001
H: T L: U N: P P: S C: crimson
S: summer

'Ruby Tuesday'

With flowers slightly larger than most, this cultivar is widely grown as 'Rouge Parfum' but 'Ruby Tuesday' is the earlier name.

Beane / E.W. King & Co., 2005
H: T L: U N: P P: S C: crimson
S: summer

'Rubyette'

A dwarf, trailing cultivar, this is part of the Bijou Series.

Burpee Seeds, 1966
H: D L: U N: P P: S C: crimson S: spring

'Sagittarius'

This cultivar has non-tendril leaves.

J.D. Place / E.W. King & Co., 1999
H: T L: M N: P P: S C: orange-red
S: summer

'Sally Ann'

With its frilly blooms, this makes a good exhibition cultivar.

K. Brewer / Matthewman, 1998
H: T L: U N: P P: S C: rose pink, w.g.
S: summer

'Sally Maitland'

This relatively new cultivar is already proving itself for exhibition.

G. King / R. Parsons, 2020
H: T L: U N: P P: S C: carmine
S: summer

'Sapphire' Burpee 1966

A dwarf, trailing cultivar, this is part of the Bijou Series. The name was originally used for a 1910 Grandiflora.

Burpee Seeds, 1966
H: SD L: U N: P P: S C: mid blue
S: spring

'Scarlette'

This dwarf, trailing cultivar is part of the Bijou Series. 'Villa Roma Scarlet' appears to be a reselection of this.
Burpee Seeds, 1966
H: D L: U N: P P: S C: scarlet S: spring

'Scorpio'

This cultivar has non-tendril leaves.
J.D. Place / E.W. King & Co., 1999
H: T L: M N: P P: S C: mid blue
S: summer

'Sarah Kennedy'

This vigorous cultivar was good for exhibition but is currently being reselected.
Sewell, 2002
H: T L: U N: P P: S C: pale pink, w.g.
S: summer

'Selene'

A multiflora cultivar, this is winter-flowering.

Oyama, date unknown
H: T L: U N: M P: S C: cream S: winter

'Sheila Roy'

This makes a good exhibition cultivar.

Silvester / R. Parsons, 2013
H: T L: U N: P P: S C: salmon pink
S: summer

'Signpost'

This is a striking bicolour with five flowers per stem.

Hammett, before 1977
H: T L: U N: P P: S C: lavender pink / white S: summer

'Sir Jimmy Shand'

This is the most popular striped cultivar for exhibition.

Chisholm / Kerton Sweet Peas, 2008
H: T L: U N: P P: S C: lilac stripe, w.g.
S: summer

'Sir Max Hastings'

With its large frilly flowers on strong stems, this is good for exhibition.

Kerton Sweet Peas, 2009
H: T L: U N: P P: S C: aubergine
S: summer

'Skywalker'

With well-placed flowers on long stems, this makes a good cut flower. It is also sold as 'Anna's Hope'.

Beane / E.W. King & Co., 2012
H: T L: U N: P P: S C: mid blue
S: summer

'Solar Flare'

The flowers of this multiflora
cultivar are sometimes duplex.
Hammett / R. Parsons, 2009
H: T L: U N: P P: D C: orange-scarlet
S: summer

'Solitude'

The frilly flowers of this cultivar
are well-placed on long stems.
Harrod / Unwins Seeds, 2014
H: T L: U N: P P: S C: pale blue
S: summer

'Snowlight'

This may supersede 'White Frills'
as an exhibition cultivar.
Harrod / R. Parsons, 2016
H: T L: U N: P P: S C: white S: summer

'Solstice Lavender'
Cultivars in the Solstice Series are all early-flowering multifloras with wavy flowers.
Lemon, 2008
H: T L: U N: M P: S C: lavender
S: winter

'Solstice Crimson'
Cultivars in the Solstice Series are all early-flowering multifloras with wavy flowers.
Lemon, 2008
H: T L: U N: M P: S C: crimson S: winter

'Solstice Light Blue'
Cultivars in the Solstice Series are all early-flowering multifloras with wavy flowers.
Lemon, 2008
H: T L: U N: M P: S C: pale blue
S: winter

'Solstice Salmon'

Cultivars in the Solstice Series are all early-flowering multifloras with wavy flowers.
Lemon, 2008
H: T L: U N: M P: S C: salmon pink, c.g.
S: winter

'Solstice Scarlet'

Cultivars in the Solstice Series are all early-flowering multifloras with wavy flowers.
Lemon, 2008
H: T L: U N: M P: S C: scarlet S: winter

'Solstice Orchid'

This Solstice Series cultivar is a bicolour although it can appear mauve at first glance.
Lemon, 2008
H: T L: U N: M P: S C: purple / violet S: winter

'Solstice White'

Cultivars in the Solstice Series are all early-flowering multifloras with wavy flowers.

Lemon, 2008
H: T L: U N: M P: S C: white
S: early spring

'Solway Ballerina' AGM H3

This semi-dwarf cultivar has non-tendril leaves.

J.D. Place / R. Parsons, date unknown
H: SD L: M N: P P: S C: pale pink, w.g.
S: summer

'Solway Fanfare'

A semi-dwarf, multiflora cultivar with non-tendril leaves, this flowers early in the summer.

J.D. Place / R. Parsons, 2015
H: SD L: M N: M P: S C: cerise
S: summer

'Solway Shimmer'

This semi-dwarf cultivar has non-tendril leaves.

J.D. Place / R. Parsons, 2017
H: SD L: M N: P P: S C: lavender flush, c.g. S: summer

'Solway Sunset'

A tall cultivar with non-tendril leaves, this was raised by J.D. Place from material sent to him by Andrew Beane.

J.D. Place / Unwins Seeds, 2000
H: T L: U N: P P: S C: orange-cerise stripe, w.g. S: summer

'Solway Symphony'

This is a tall cultivar with non-tendril leaves.

J.D. Place / R. Parsons, 2017
H: T L: M N: P P: S C: mauve
S: summer

'Somerset Lady' AGM H3

The large blooms on long stems make this cultivar good for exhibition, garden use and cutting.

Somerset, 2012
H: T L: U N: P P: S C: carmine pink
S: summer

'Somewhere'

With *L. × hammettii* ancestry, this cultivar is an improvement on 'Erewhon', having larger, better shaped flowers.

Hammett, 2019
H: T L: U N: P P: S C: pink / mauve
S: summer

'Sonia'

Although having attractively marbled flowers, this cultivar has been superseded by 'Audrey Kirkman' which has longer stems.

Hunt / Robert Bolton & Son, 1985
H: T L: U N: P P: S C: carmine-veined pink S: summer

'Sophisticated Lady'

With large frilly flowers on strong stems, this cultivar is suitable for exhibition, garden use and cutting.

Harrod / Kerton Sweet Peas, 2012
H: T L: U N: P P: S C: cool rose pink
S: summer

'Southbourne'

This is a reliable and prolifically flowering cultivar.

Colledge / Unwins Seeds, 1973
H: T L: U N: P P: S C: pale pink, w.g.
S: summer

'Spring Sunshine Champagne'

Flowering in early spring, this is a multiflora cultivar.

Owl's Acre Sweet Peas, 2008
H: T L: U N: M P: S C: pale salmon pink, c.g. S: early spring

'Starlight' Walker AGM H3

This cultivar is good for exhibition. The name has been used before for lavender and white cultivars.
W. Walker / Kerton Sweet Peas, 2004
H: T L: U N: P P: S C: magenta, w.g. S: summer

'Stella' Denholm

This early-flowering multiflora cultivar has dark seeds and is part of the Early Multiflora Gigantea Series.
Denholm Seeds, 1960
H: T L: U N: M P: S C: cream S: early spring

'Strawberry Fields'

An early-flowering bicoloured cultivar, this has long stems.
Hammett, 2005
H: T L: U N: P P: S C: cerise / pink S: late spring

'Streamer Orange'

This cultivar is one of a range of flakes sold as Streamer Series and Fandango Series.
Hammett / Arthur Yates & Co., before 2002
H: T L: U N: P P: S C: orange flake, w.g. S: summer

'Su Pollard'

Of all purple Spencers, this is the best for all purposes.
Brackley, 1991
H: T L: U N: P P: S C: purple S: summer

'Sunset' Marshall AGM H3

Although this cultivar has good flower placement, the wings furl so it is best avoided for exhibition. This name has been used for seven other cultivars.
S.E. Marshall & Co., 2002
H: T L: U N: P P: S C: cerise stripe, w.g. S: summer

'Supersnoop Cream Pink'

This semi-dwarf cultivar with non-tendril leaves is part of the Supersnoop Series.

Denholm Seeds, 1984

H: SD L: M N: P P: S C: rose pink, c.g.

S: summer

'Supersnoop Magenta'

This semi-dwarf cultivar with non-tendril leaves is part of the Supersnoop Series.

Denholm Seeds, 1984

H: SD L: M N: P P: S C: deep rose

S: summer

'Supersnoop Navy Blue'

This semi-dwarf cultivar with non-tendril leaves is part of the Supersnoop Series.

Denholm Seeds, 1985

H: SD L: M N: P P: S C: navy blue

S: summer

'Supersnoop White'

This semi-dwarf cultivar with non-tendril leaves is part of the Supersnoop Series.

Denholm Seeds, 1984

H: SD L: M N: P P: S C: white

S: summer

'Susan Burgess'

The flower colour of this cultivar is slightly richer when grown under glass or polythene.

Beane / R. Parsons, 2015

H: T L: U N: P P: S C: deep blush pink, c.g. S: summer

'Susan Thomas'

This cultivar is good for garden use but is not exhibition quality.

R. Parsons, 2013

H: T L: U N: P P: S C: blue flake

S: summer

'Susie'

The colour of this cultivar is uniform throughout the petals. It was raised as a multiflora, but no longer has those characteristics.
Denholm Seeds, 1960
H: T L: U N: P P: S C: shrimp pink, c.g. S: early spring

'Suzy Z'

Good for the garden and cutting, this cultivar is too variable for exhibition use.
Owl's Acre Sweet Peas, 2004
H: T L: U N: P P: S C: maroon flake on grey S: summer

'Sylvia Ann'

Although a good white for general use, the flowers are a bit small by modern standards for exhibition.
Tullett / Kerton Sweet Peas, 1997
H: T L: U N: P P: S C: white S: summer

'Sylvia Moore'

This cultivar is good for garden use and cutting.
Albutt / Eagle Sweet Peas, 2000
H: T L: U N: P P: S C: warm rose pink, w.g. S: summer

'Tahiti Sunrise' AGM H3

Although this is a decorative cultivar, it is not as robust as others of the same colour.
Harrod, 2005
H: T L: U N: P P: S C: bright orange pink, w.g. S: summer

'Tara'

This is a good exhibition cultivar.
Harrod / E.W. King & Co., 2003
H: T L: U N: P P: S C: cerise pink, w.g. S: summer

'Tartan Mac'

This cultivar is an improvement on 'Gawler Warrior' and better in the northern hemisphere.

McDougall, late 1970s

H: T L: U N: P P: D C: maroon flake, w.g.

S: early spring

'Tell Tale'

As well as good stocks being available from seed sellers, there is a deteriorated form sometimes offered.

Robert Bolton & Son, 1946

H: T L: U N: P P: S C: pink picotee, w.g.

S: summer

'Terry Wogan'

Some flowers of this cultivar are duplex.
Colledge / Unwins Seeds, 1983
H: T L: U N: P P: D C: salmon pink, c.g.
S: summer

'The Doctor' Jones

The veining on the petals of this cultivar is conspicuous.
B.R. Jones / Unwins Seeds, 1979
H: T L: U N: P P: S C: mauve
S: summer

'The Princess Royal'

This excellent cultivar is as good as the several best white Spencers currently available. It is also sold as 'Gardener's Jubilee'.
Beane / Simply Sweet Peas, 2012
H: T L: U N: P P: S C: white S: summer

'Theia-Bella'

Long flower stems are borne on strong plants in this cultivar.
R. Parsons, 2017
H: T L: U N: P P: S C: chocolate flake, w.g. S: summer

'Thomas and Linda'

With good colour and stem length, this cultivar should prove popular with flower arrangers.
Harrod / R. Parsons, 2018
H: T L: U N: P P: S C: deep salmon, c.g.
S: summer

'Tony Bates'

Although a good cultivar, those with a similar colour on a white ground always seem to be preferred.
R. Parsons, 2008
H: T L: U N: P P: S C: blue flush, c.g.
S: summer

'Topsy'

This early-flowering multiflora cultivar is part of the Early Multiflora Gigantea Series.

Denholm Seeds, 1960
H: T L: U N: M P: S C: chocolate maroon S: early spring

'Tranquillity' Wells AGM H3

This cultivar should not be confused with the crimson Unwins cultivar of the same name.

Wells / R. Parsons, 2015
H: T L: U N: P P: S C: salmon pink, c.g. S: summer

'Trelawny'

With small flowers by modern standards, this cultivar has excellent flower form and placement.

Tremewan, 1989
H: T L: U N: P P: S C: lavender S: summer

'Turquoise'

With *L. × hammettii* ancestry, this semi-dwarf selection has small flowers that open mauve-blue and turn turquoise with age.

Hammett / R. Parsons, 2012
H: SD L: U N: P P: S C: turquoise S: summer

'Valerie Harrod' AGM H3

With its more uniform colour, this has superseded 'Evening Glow' as an exhibition cultivar. Its petals are not as frilly as those of 'Lizbeth'.

Harrod / Kerton Sweet Peas, 2001
H: T L: U N: P P: S C: orange-pink S: summer

'Variety Club'

The bright flowers of this cultivar are large and frilly.

Beane / Unwins Seeds, 2004
H: T L: U N: P P: S C: purple flake on grey S: summer

'Vaudeville'

This is one of the best flaked cultivars for garden use and cut-flower production.

Hammett, 2009
H: T L: U N: P P: S C: pink flake, w.g.
S: summer

'Vera Lynn'

This has well-placed flowers and is good for exhibition.

Colledge / Unwins Seeds, 1990
H: T L: U N: P P: S C: cerise S: summer

'Vienna'

This semi-dwarf multiflora cultivar is part of the Jet Set Series.
Ferry Morse Seed Co., 1973
H: SD L: U N: P P: S C: mauve
S: summer

'Villa Roma Raspberry'

The Villa Roma Series of dwarf, trailing cultivars is ideal for containers, hanging baskets and groundcover.
Hem Zaden, 2012
H: D L: U N: P P: S C: pale purple
S: spring

'Villa Roma Rose'

This is one of two bicolours in the Villa Roma Series.
Hem Zaden, 2012
H: D L: U N: P P: S C: carmine / rose pink S: spring

'Villa Roma White'

As with many white-flowered cultivars, this has pale seeds.
Hem Zaden, 2012
H: D L: U N: P P: S C: cream S: spring

'Villa Roma White / Rose'

This is one of two bicolours in the Villa Roma Series.
Hem Zaden, 2012
H: D L: U N: P P: S C: pink / white
S: spring

'Vincent'

Excellent flower form, size and placement are features of this cultivar. It is widely grown as 'Leominster Boy' but 'Vincent' has priority.
Beane / Eagle Sweet Peas, 2010
H: T L: U N: P P: S C: salmon-orange
S: summer

'Violette'

This dwarf, trailing cultivar is part of the Bijou Series.

Burpee Seeds, 1971

H: D L: U N: P P: S C: dark blue
S: spring

'Wedding Belle'

This cultivar is a popular colour with flower arrangers but is not suitable for exhibition.

Unwins Seeds, 2007

H: T L: U N: P P: S C: pale pink, c.g.
S: summer

'Wedding Day' AGM H3

This cultivar usually has some duplex blooms.

Matthewman, 2001

H: T L: U N: P P: D C: white S: summe

'Westminster'

This semi-dwarf multiflora cultivar is part of the Jet Set Series.

Ferry Morse Seed Co., 1973

H: SD L: U N: P P: S C: crimson
S: summer

'White Frills'

This is one of the best pure white cultivars, especially for exhibition.

Truslove / Kerton Sweet Peas, 2002

H: T L: U N: P P: S C: white S: summer

'White Supreme' AGM H3

One of the best whites for garden use, this is also a good exhibition cultivar.

B.R. Jones / Robert Bolton & Son, 1990

H: T L: U N: P P: S C: white S: summer

'Wild Swan'

This multiflora has large, well-spaced flowers on long stems.

Hammett, 2010
H: T L: U N: P P: S C: white S: summer

'William and Catherine'

A reliable and vigorous cultivar, this is good for garden use and exhibition.

Eagle Sweet Peas, 2011
H: T L: U N: P P: S C: salmon pink
S: summer

'William Willson' AGM H3

This has everything you could want in a cultivar except the ability to set seed prolifically.

Beane / E.W. King & Co., 2011
H: T L: U N: P P: S C: orange-pink
S: summer

'Windsor' Brewer

Still a good dark colour, this has been superseded by 'Pip's Maroon' for exhibition. The name originally applied to a blue Spencer from 1951.

K. Brewer / Unwins Seeds, 1998
H: T L: U N: P P: S C: dark maroon
S: summer

'Winston Churchill'

Still popular for garden use, this cultivar is no longer good enough for exhibition.

Thomas Cullen & Sons, 1956
H: T L: U N: P P: S C: crimson
S: summer

'Winter Elegance Pink Diana'

This is a winter-flowering, multiflora cultivar.

Bodger Seeds Ltd, 1992
H: T L: U N: M P: S C: appleblossom pink, w.g. S: winter

'Winter Elegance Salmon Rose'

This winter-flowering multiflora cultivar has flowers that bleach, even under polythene.

Hem Zaden, 2012
H: T L: U N: M P: S C: salmon pink
S: winter

'Winter Sunshine Lavender'

This is a winter-flowering,multiflora cultivar that is also sold as 'Sunshine Lavender'.

Owl's Acre Sweet Peas, 2002
H: T L: U N: M P: S C: lavender, w.g.
S: winter

'Yankee Doodle'

This multiflora has some duplex flowers and is slightly earlier to bloom than most summer-flowering cultivars. It is part of the Galaxy Series.

Burpee Seeds, 1966
H: T L: U N: M P: S C: brilliant rosy red
S: summer

'Yasmin Khan'

This cultivar bears large flowers on long stems.

Khan / Robert Bolton & Son, 1992
H: T L: U N: P P: S C: orange-pink
S: summer

'Yvette Ann'

This is a good cultivar for exhibition
and cutting
R. Parsons, 2009
H: T L: U N: P P: S C: pale salmon pink
c.g. S: summer

'Zillah Harrod'

Good for exhibition, this cultivar is
also suitable for garden use
Harrod / Kerton Sweet Peas, 2007
H: T L: U N: P P: S C: lavender
S: summer

Checklist of botanical epithets

The accounts of *Lathyrus* in the Species chapter include some of the more commonly encountered synonyms. This Checklist is more extensive, containing the majority of the botanical epithets in *Lathyrus* and associated genera. It is not completely exhaustive (for example, in infraspecific taxa), and the taxonomy is constantly changing in response to evidence from DNA.

Name in **bold:** Currently accepted name and its place of publication.
Name in roman: Synonym, followed by an equals (=) sign and the accepted name.

acutifolius Vogel   *Linnaea* 13: 27 (1839)
aegyptiacus Hasselq. (1757)   = *L. tingitanus*
affinis Guss. (1845)   = *L. aphaca* var. *affinis*
alatus (Maxim.) Kom. (1904)   = *L. komarovii*
albidus Aikin ex Eaton (1833)   = *L. ochroleucus*
albus (L. f.) Kitt. (1844)   = *L. pannonicus*
albus S. Watson (1880)   = *L. rigidus*
alefeldii T.G. White (1894)   = *L. vestitus* var. *alefeldii*
aleuticus (Greene) Pobed. (1959)   = *L. japonicus*
alpestris (Waldst. & Kit.) Kit. ex Reichb.   *Icon. Fl. Germ. Helv.* 22: t. 219 (1886)
altaicus Ledeb. (1831)   = *L. humilis*
amoenus Fenzl (1843)   = *L. gorgoni*
amoenus var. *stenophyllus* Post (1896)   = *L. gorgoni*
amphicarpos Gouan, non L. (1762)   = *L. setifolius*
amphicarpos L.   *Sp. Pl.* 2: 729 (1753)
andicola Gand. (1913)   = *L. pubescens*
andicolus Gand. (1913)   = *L. pubescens*
angulatus L.   *Sp. Pl.* 2: 731 (1753)
angulatus var. *angustifolius* Rouy (1899)   = *L. angulatus*
angulatus var. *brachycarpus* Rouy (1899)   = *L. angulatus*
angulatus var. *genuinus* Rouy, nom. inval. (1899)   = *L. angulatus*
angulatus subsp. *sphaericus* (Retz.) Mateo & Figuerola (1987)   = *L. sphaericus*
anhuiensis Y.J. Zhu & R.X. Meng   *Acta Phytotax. Sin.* 24(5): 402 (1986)
annuus L.   *Demonstr. Pl.* 1753: 20 (1753)
annuus subsp. *cassius* (Boiss.) Holmboe (1914)   = *L. annuus*
annuus var. *cassius* (Boiss.) Post (1896)   = *L. annuus*
annuus var. *hierosolymitanus* Post (1896)   = *L. hierosolymitanus*
annuus var. *genuinus* Rouy nom. inval. (1899)   = *L. annuus*
annuus var. *latifolius* Rouy (1899)   = *L. annuus*
anuus var. *angustifolius* Rouy (1899)   = *L. annuus*
aphaca L.   *Sp. Pl.* 2: 729 (1753).
aphaca var. affinis (Guss.) Arcang.   *Comp. Fl. Ital.* [Arcangeli]: 195 (1882)
aphaca var. biflorus Post   *Fl. Syria*: 292 (1896)
aphaca var. floribundus (Velen.) K. Malý   *Verh. K. K. Zool.-Bot. Ges. Wien* 55: 227 (1904)
aphaca var. *marmoratus* (Alef.) Post (1896)   = *L. aphaca*
aphaca var. modestus P.H. Davis   *Notes Roy. Bot. Gard. Edinburgh* 29: 319 (1969)
aphaca var. pseudoaphaca (Boiss.) P.H. Davis   *Fl. Turkey* 3: 368 (1970)
aphaca f. *subbiflora* Azn. (1897)   = *L. aphaca* var. *biforus*
appeninus F. Conti   *Pl. Biosystems* 144: 814 (2010) (status uncertain, allied to *L. linifolius* (Reichard) Bässler)
arizonicus Britton (1894)   = *L. lanszwertii*
armenus (Boiss. & A. Huet) Čelak.   *Oesterr. Bot. Z.* 38: 85 (1888)
armitageanus Westc. ex Loudon (1835)   = *L. nervosus*

articulatus **L.**   *Sp. Pl.* 2: 731 (1753)

articulatus subsp. *climenum* (L.) Maire (1932)
    = *L. articulatus*

articulatus var. *clymenum* (L.) Maire (1932)
    = *L. articulatus*

articulatus var. *latifolius* Rouy (1899)   = *L. clymenum*

articulatus var. *tenuifolius* (Desf.) Rouy (1899)
    = *L. articulatus*

articulatus subsp. *typicus* Maire, nom. inval. (1931)
    = *L. articulatus*

arvensis Phil. (1857)   = *L. crassipes*

asiaticus (Zalkind) Kudr. (1955)   = *L. sativus*

asphodeloides (Gouan) Gren. & Godr. (1848)
    = *L. pannonicus*

asphodeloides subsp. *varius* (Hill) Arcang. (1882)
    = *L. pannonicus*

atropatanus (Grossh.) Širj. (1934)   = *L. nivalis* subsp.
    atropatanus

aureus **(G. Lodd. ex Drapiez) D. Brândză**   *Prodr. Fl.*
    Románe 1883: 546 (1883)

austriacus (Crantz) Wissjul. (1954)   = *L. pannonicus*

axillaris Lam. (1785)   = *L. sphaericus*

basalticus **Rech. f.**   *Arkiv för Botanik n.s.* 1: 511
    (1952).

bauhinii **P.A. Genty**   *Bull. Soc. Dauphin. Échange Pl.*
    ser. 2. 3: 90 (1892)

belinensis **Maxted & Goyder**   *Kew Bull.* 43(4): 711
    (1988).

berteroanus **Colla ex Savi**   *Mem. Reale Accad. Sci.*
    Torino 37: 61 (1834)

berteroi Phil. (1872)   = *L. magellanicus*

biflorus **T.W. Nelson & J.P. Nelson**   *Brittonia* 35: 183
    (1983)

bijugatus T.G. White (1894)   = *L. lanszwertii* var.
    sandbergii

binatus **Pančić**   *Fl. Serbiae* 1874: 256 (1874)

blepharicarpus **Boiss.**   *Diagn. Pl. Orient.* ser. 1, 9: 126
    (1849).

boissieri **Širj.**   = *Izv. Bulg. Bot. Druzh.* 6: 62 (1934)

bolanderi S. Watson (1885)   = *L. vestitus*

bolanderi var. *barbarae* (T.G. White) Jeps. (1936)
    = *L. vestitus*

bolanderi subsp. *quercetorum* (A. Heller) Bradshaw
    (1925)   = *L. vestitus*

bolanderi var. *quercetorum* (A. Heller) Jeps. (1936)
    = *L. vestitus*

bolanderi var. *tracyi* (Bradshaw) Jeps. (1936)

    = *L. lanszwertii*

bolanderi subsp. *violaceus* (Greene) Bradshaw
    (1925)   = *L. vestitus*

bolanderi var. *violaceus* (Greene) Jeps. (1936)
    = *L. vestitus*

brachycalyx **Rydb.**   *Bull. Torrey Bot. Club* 34: 425
    (1907)

brachycalyx subsp. *eucosmus* (Butters & H. St. John)
    S.L. Welsh (1965)   = *L. eucosmus*

brachycalyx var. *eucosmus* (Butters & H. St. John)
    S.L. Welsh (1978)   = *L. eucosmus*

brachycalyx subsp. *zionis* (C.L. Hitchc.) S.L. Welsh
    (1965)   = *L. brachycalyx* var. *zionis*

brachycalyx **var. *zionis* (C.L. Hitchc.) S.L. Welsh**
    (1978)

brachyodon Murb. (1897)   = *L. brachyodus*

brachyodus **Murb. & Murb.**   *Contr. Fl. Nord-Oest Afr.*
    ser. 2: 44 (1905)

brachypterus Alef. (1861)   = *L. latifolius*

brachypterus **Čelak.**   *Oesterr. Bot. Z.* 38: 47 (1888)

brachypterus **var. *hausknechtii* (Širj.) P.H. Davis**
    Fl. Turkey vol. 3: 338 (1970)

brachypterus subsp. *hausknechtii* (Širj.) Ponert
    (1972)   = *L. brachypterus* var. *hausknechtii*

bradfieldianus A. Nelson (1912)   = *L. pauciflorus*

broteroi Mariz (1889)   = *L. amphicarpos*

brownii Eastw. (1903)   = *L. lanszwertii*

brutius Ten. (1825)   = *L. grandiflorus*

cabrerianus **Burkart**   *Darwiniana* 6: 14 (1942)

californicus Douglas (1828)   = *L. japonicus*

campestris **Phil.**   *Linnaea* 28(5): 626 (1857)

canescens (L. f.) Gren. & Godr. (1848)   = *L. filiformis*

cassius **Boiss.**   *Diagn. Pl. Orient.*, ser. 1, 9: 128 (1849)

caudatus **Z. Wei & H.P. Tsui**   *Bull. Bot. Res., Harbin*
    4(1): 49 (1984)

chilensis Steud. (1841)   = *L. magellanicus*

chius Boiss. & Orph. (1859)   = *L. annuus*

chloranthus **Boiss. & balansa**   *Diagn. Pl. Orient.* ser
    2. 6: 67 (1856)

chrysanthus **Boiss.**   *Diagn. Pl. Orient.* ser. 1, 6: 46
    (1846)

cicera **L.**   *Sp. Pl.* 2: 730 (1753)

cicera var. *angustifolius* Rouy (1899)   = *L. cicera*

cicera f. *ciliata* Gomez Hern. (1977)   = *L. cicera*

cicera var. *genuinus* Rouy, nom. inval. (1899)
    = *L. cicera*

cicera var. *latifolius* Rouy (1899)   = *L. cicera*

cicera var. *patagonica* Speg. (1897) = *L. crassipes*

cicera var. *sub-bijugus* Cout. (1939) = *L. cicera*

ciliatidentatus Czefr. *Novosti Sist. Vyssh. Rast.* 1964: 220 (1964) (status uncertain)

ciliatus Guss. (1826) = *L. saxatilis* (this species has recently been shown to be a *Vicia*)

cilicicus Hayek & Siehe *Ann. Nat. Hofmus. Wien* 28: 164 (1914)

ciliolatus Sam. ex Rech. f. *Ark. Bot. n.s.* 1: 311 (1950)

cirrhosus Ser. *Prodr.* [A.P. de Candolle] 2: 374 (1825)

cirpicii Güneş *Biol. Diversity Conservation* 12(2): 162 (2019)

cirrhosus var. *elongatus* Sennen (1927) = *L. cirrhosus*

clymenum L. *Sp. Pl.* 2: 732 (1753)

clymenum var. *angustifolius* Rouy (1899) = *L. articulatus*

clymenum var. *articulatus* (L.) Pérez Lara (1892) = *L. clymenum*

clymenum subsp. *articulatus* (L.) Ball (1878) = *L. articulatus*

clymenum subvar. *latifolius* (Godr.) Pérez Lara (1892) = *L. clymenum*

clymenum var. *latifolius* Godr. (1848) = *L. clymenum*

clymenum var. *tenuifolius* (Desf.) Godr. (1848) = *L. articulatus*

coccineus All. (1785) = *L. sphaericus*

collinus (J. Ortmann) Landolt (2010) = *L. pannonicus*

coriaceus T.G. White (1894) = *L. lanszwertii* var. *aridus*

coriaceus subsp. *aridus* Piper (1918) = *L. lanszwertii* var. *aridus*

coruscans Emb. & Maire (1929) = *L. tingitanus*

crassipes Gillies ex Hook. & Arn. *Bot. Misc.* 3(8): 198 (1833)

crassipes var. *brevipes* Griseb. (1879) = *L. crassipes*

crassipes var. *montevidensis* (Vogel) Griseb. (1879) = *L. crassipes*

currentifolius Lam., nom. illeg. (1778) = *L. ochrus*

cusickii S. Watson (1882) = *L. nevadensis* var. *cusickii*

cyaneus (Steven) K. Koch *Linnaea* 15(6): 723 (1841)

cyaneus subsp. *digitatus* (M. Bieb.) Ponert (1973) = *L. digitatus*

cyaneus subsp. pinnatus (P.H.Davis) Ponert *Feddes Repert.* 83(9-10): 635 (1973)

czeczottianus Bässler *Feddes Repert.* 72: 91 (1966)

davidii Hance *J. Bot.* 9: 130 (1871)

davidii var. *roseus* C.W. Chang (1981) = *L. dielsianus*

debilis Vogel (1839) = *L. subulatus*

debilis Clos (1847) = *L. berterianus*

debilis var. *arvensis* (Phil.) Reiche (1898) = *L. crassipes*

debilis var. *berterianus* (Colla) Reiche (1897) = *L. berterianus*

debilis var. *campestris* (Phil.) Reiche (1897) = *L. campestris*

delnorticus C.L. Hitchc. *Univ. Wash. Publ. Biol.* 15: 30 (1952)

dicirrhus Clos (1847) = *L. crassipes*

dielsianus Harms *Bot. Jahrb. Syst.* 29(3-4): 417 (1900)

digitatus (M. Bieb.) Fiori *Fl. Italia* 2: 105 (1900)

dominianus Litv. (1910) = *L. humilis*

dubius Ten. (1825) = *L. cicera*

dumetorum Burkart (1942) = *L. cabrerianus*

dumetorum Phil. (1857) = *L. pubescens*

dumetorum var. *longipes* (Phil.) Reiche (1897) = *L. magellanicus*

ecirrhosus Phil. (1892) = *L. multiceps*

ecirrhosus A. Heller (1904) = *L. polyphyllus*

egirdiricus Genç & Sahin (2008) = *L. stenophyllus*

elegans Porta & Rigo (1891, 1893) = *L. pulcher*

elegans Vogel *Linnaea* 13: 30 (1839).

eliasii Sennen (1928) = *L. palustris* subsp. *nudicaulis*

elongatus (Bornm.) Širj. (1936) = *L. spathulatus* subsp. *elongatus*

emodi (Wall. ex Fritsch) Fritsch *Sitzungsber. Akad. Wiss. Wien* 104: 516 (1895)

ensifolius (Lapeyr.) J. Gay (1857) = *L. bauhinii*

ensifolius Badarò (1824) = *L. latifolius*

epetiolaris Clos (1847) = *L. magellanicus*

epetiolaris var. *litoralis* (Phil.) Reiche (1898) = *L. magellanicus*

erectus Lag. (1816) = *L. inconspicuus*

erectus var. *stenophyllus* Boiss. (1872) = *L. inconspicuus*

eucosmus Butters & H. St. John *Rhodora* 19: 160 (1917)

eurypetalus Phil. (1893) = *L. multiceps*

filiformis (Lam.) J. Gay *Ann. Sci. Nat., Bot., sér. 4* 8: 315 (1857)

filiformis subsp. *ensifolius* (Lapeyr.) Gams (1924) = *L. bauhinii*

flaccidus (Kit. ex Rchb.) Dalla Torre & Sarnth. (1909) = *L. vernus* subsp. *flaccidus floribundus* Velen. (1891) = L. *aphaca* var. *floribundus*

formosus (Steven) Kenicer *Lathyrus: The complete guide*: 419 (2021)

friedrichsthalii (Griseb.) K. Malý = L. *alpestris* var. *friedrichsthalii*

frolovii Fisch ex Rupr. *Fl. Ingrica* 1860: 290 (1860).

fulvus (Sm.) Kosterin *Vavilov J. Genet. Breed.* 21(2): 168 (2017).

furtivus Woronow (1914) = L. *woronowii*

gladiatus Hook. (1837) = L. *magellanicus* var. *gladiatus*

glandulosus Broich *Madroño* 33: 136 (1986).

glaucifolius L.C. Beck (1833) = L. *ochroleucus*

gloeosperma Warb. & Eig *Repert. Spec. Nov. Regni Veg.* 25: 351 (1928).

gloeosperma var. *aaronsohnianus* Opphr. (1931) = L. *gloeosperma*

gloeosperma var. *pilosus* Warb. & Eig (1928) = L. *gloeosperma*

gmelinii (Fisch. ex DC.) Fritsch *Sitzungsber. Kaiserl. Akad. Wiss., Math.-Naturwiss. Cl., Abt. 1* 104: 516 (1895).

gmelinii var. *angustifolius* Krylov (status uncertain)

goldsteiniae Eastw. (1905) – L. *lanszwertii*

gorgoni Parl. *Giorn. Sci. Sicilia* 62 (184–185): 3(–4) (1838).

gorgoni var. lineatus (Post) C.C. Towns. *Kew Bull.* 25: 471 (1971)

gorgoni var. *pilosus* C.C. Towns. (1968) = L. *gorgoni*

gorgoni var. *stenophyllus* (Post) Dinsmore = L. *gorgoni*

gorgoni var. *variegatus* Evenari = L. *gorgoni*

gracilis Phil. (1857) = L. *berterianus*

gracillimus Reiche (1898) = L. *campestris*

gramineus Gray, nom. illeg. (1821) = L. *nissolia*

gramineus Kern.,nom. illeg. (1863) = L. *nissolia*

graminifolius (S. Watson) T.G. White *Bull. Torrey Bot. Club* 21(10): 454 (1894)

grandiflorus Sm. *Fl. Graec. Prodr.* 2: 67 (1813).

grandifolius (Boiss. ex Fritsch) Fritsch (1900) = L. *laevigatus* subsp. *occidentalis*

grimesii Barneby *Intermount. Fl.* [Cronquist et al.] 3(B): 208 (1989)

guaraniticus Hassl. (1919) = L. *crassipes*

hallersteinii Baumg. *Enum. Stirp. Transsilv.* 2: 333 (1816)

× **hammettii Dawn Edwards (L. belinensis ×**
L. odoratus) *The Plantsman* n.s. 13(4): 253 (2014)

hasslerianus Burkart *Revista Fac. Agron. Veterin.* 8: 100, figs. 16c & 17r (1935)

haussknechtii Širj. (1934) = L. *brachypterus* var. *hausknechtii*

henanensis S.Y. Wang (1988) = L. *anhuiensis*

heterocirrus Phil. (1893) = L. *magellanicus*

heterophyllus L. *Sp. Pl.*: 733 (1753)

hexaedrus Bory & Chaub. (1832) = L. *angulatus*

hierosolymitanus Boiss. *Diagn. Pl. Orient.* 9: 127 (1849)

hierosolymitanus var. amphicarpos Plitmann *Fl. Palaestina* 2: 457 (1972)

hierosolymitanus var. *grandiflorus* Boiss. (1872) = L. *annuus*

hierosolymitanus var. luteus Plitmann *Fl. Palaestina* 2: 457 (1972)

hirsutus L. *Sp. Pl.*: 732 (1753).

hirsutus f. *brevipedunculatus* Cout (1939) = L. *hirsutus*

hirticarpus Mattatia & Heyn *Israel J. Bot.* 25(3–4): 216 (1976)

hispidulus Boiss. (1846) = L. *inconspicuus*

hitchcockianus Barneby & Reveal *Aliso* 7: 362 (1971)

holochlorus (Piper) C.L. Hitchc. *Univ. Wash. Publ. Biol.* 15: 31 (1952)

hookeri G. Don (1832) = L. *magellanicus*

hookeri var. *trichocalyx* (Phil.) Burkart (1942) = L. *magellanicus*

hookerianus Gillies ex Hook. & Arn. (1833) = L. *subulatus*

hultenii J. Rousseau & Raymond (1969) = L. *japonicus*

humilis (Ser.) Fisch. ex Spreng. *Syst. Veg.* 3: 263 (1826)

hupehensis (Pamp.) E. Peter (1940) = L. *dielsianus*

hygrophilus Taub. *Pflanzenw. Ost-Afrikas* C: 219 (1895)

hygrophilus var. *angustifolius* Baker f. (1924) = L. *hygrophilus*

ibicuiensis Abruzzi de Oliveira (2015) = L. *nitens*

incanus (J.G. Sm. & Rydb.) Rydb. (1906) = L. *polymorphus* var. *incanus*

inconspicuus L. *Sp. Pl.* 2: 730 (1753)

inconspicuus var. *erectus* (Lag.) Fiori et Beg. (1901–

1902) = *L. inconspicuus*

inconspicuus var. *erectus* (Lag.) H. Lindb. (1932)
  = *L. inconspicuus*

inconspicuus subvar. *grandiflorus* Rouy (1899)
  = *L. inconspicuus*

inconspicuus subvar. *leiocarpus* Rouy (1899)
  = *L. inconspicuus*

inconspicuus var. *oblongus* Ser. (1825)
  = *L. inconspicuus*

inconspicuus var. *stans* (Vis.) Vis. (1852)
  = *L. inconspicuus*

incurvus Rchb. (1832) = *L. palustris*

incurvus (Roth) Willd. *Sp. Pl.* [Willdenow], ed. 4,
  3(2): 1091 (1802)

inermis Rochel ex Friv. (1835) = *L. laxiflorus*

intricatus Baker (1897) = *L. hygrophilus*

japonicus Willd. *Sp. Pl.* [Willdenow], ed. 4, 3(2):
  1092 (1802)

japonicus var. *acutifolius* (Bab.) Bässler (1973)
  = *L. japonicus*

japonicus var. *aleuticus* (T.G. White) Fernald (1932)
  = *L. japonicus*

japonicus var. *glaber* (Ser.) Fernald (1932)
  = *L. japonicus*

japonicus subsp. maritimus (L.) P.W. Ball *Feddes*
  Repert. 79: 45 (1968)

japonicus var. *pellitus* Fernald (1932) = *L. japonicus*
  subsp. *maritimus*

japonicus var. *pilosiusculus* Pobed. (1959)
  = *L. japonicus* subsp. *maritimus*

japonicus f. *pubescens* (Hartm.) H. Ohashi & Tateishi
  (1977) = *L. japonicus* subsp. *maritimus*

japonicus subsp. *pubescens* (Hartm.) Korobkov
  (1986) = *L. japonicus* subsp. *maritimus*

japonicus var. *typicus* Fernald (1932) = *L. japonicus*

jepsonii Greene *Pittonia* 2(9): 158 (1890)

jepsonii var. californicus (S. Watson) Hoover *Leafl.*
  W. Bot. 10: 349 (1966)

karsianus P.H. Davis *Notes Roy. Bot. Gard.*
  Edinburgh 24: 19 (1962)

kilimandscharicus Taub. (1895) = *L. hygrophilus*

komarovii Ohwi *J. Jap. Bot.* 12: 329 (1936)

krylovii Serg. – discussed under *L. gmelinii*; status
  uncertain

lacaitae Czefr. (1965) = *L. pannonicus* subsp.
  longestipulatus

laetiflorus Greene (1893) = *L. vestitus*

laetiflorus subsp. *alefeldii* (T.G. White) Bradshaw (1952
  or 25?) = *L. vestitus* var. *alefeldii*

laetiflorus var. *alefeldii* (T.G. White) Jeps. (1936)
  = *L. vestitus* var. *alefeldii*

laetiflorus subsp. *barbarae* (T.G. White) C.L. Hitchc.
  (1952) = *L. vestitus* var. *vestitus*

laetiflorus subsp. *glaber* C.L. Hitchc. = *L. vestitus*

laetivirens Greene ex Rydb. = *L. lanszwertii*

laevigatus (Waldst. & Kit.) Gren. *Mém. Soc. Émul.*
  Doubs, sér. 3 10: 193 (1865)

laevigatus subsp. *emodi* (Wall. ex Fritsch) Breistoffer
  (1940) = *L. emodi*

laevigatus subsp. *gmelinii* (Fisch. ex DC) Hendrych
  (1959) = *L. gmelinii*

laevigatus var. *grandifolius* (Boiss. ex Fritsch) Breistr.
  (1940) = *L. laevigatus* subsp. *occidentalis*

laevigatus subsp. *grandifolius* (Boiss. ex Fritsch)
  M. Gruber (1973) = *L. laevigatus* subsp.
  occidentalis

laevigatus subsp. *hispanicus* (Rouy) Kerguelen
  (1987) = *L. laevigatus* subsp. *occidentalis*

laevigatus subsp. *krylovii* (Serg.) Hendrych (1959)
  – discussed under *L. gmelinii*; status uncertain

laevigatus subsp. occidentalis (Fisch. & C.A. Mey.)
  Breistr. *Bull. Soc. Bot. France* 87: 53 (1940)

laevigatus subsp. *transsylvanicus* (Spreng.) Soo
  (1964) = *L. transsilvanicus*

lanceolatus Howell (1898) = *L. nevadensis*

lancifolius Reiche (1898) = *L. campestris*

lanszwertii Kellogg *Proc. Calif. Acad. Sci.* 2: 150
  (1863)

lanszwertii subsp. *aridus* (Piper) Bradshaw (1925)
  = *L. lanszwertii* var. *aridus*

lanszwertii var. aridus (Piper) Jeps. *Fl. Calif.* 2: 389
  (1936)

lanszwertii var. *arizonicus* (Britton) S.L. Welsh
  (1978) = *L. lanszwertii* var. *leucanthus*

lanszwertii var. *brownii* (Eastw.) Jeps. (1936)
  = *L. lanszwertii*

lanszwertii var. *laetivirens* (Rydb.) S.L. Welsh (1978)
  = *L. laetivirens*

lanszwertii var. leucanthus (Rydb.) Dorn *Vasc. Pl.*
  Wyoming: 297 (1988)

lanszwertii var. *pallescens* Barneby (1989)
  = *L. laetivirens*

lanszwertii var. sandbergii (T.G. White) Broich
  Madroño 54: 65 (2007)

lanszwertii var. *tracyi* (Bradshaw) Isely (1992)
= L. *lanszwertii*

latifolius L. *Sp. Pl.* 2: 733 (1753)

latifolius f. albiflorus Moldenke *Phytologia* 26: 355 (1973)

latifolius var. *angustifolius* Roth, nom. illeg. (1788)
= L. *latifolius*

latifolius var. *angustifolius* Godr. (1848) = L. *latifolius*

latifolius var. *genuinus* Godr., nom. inval. (1848)
= L. *latifolius*

latifolius var. *neglectus* Puel ex Rouy, nom. illeg. (1899) = L. *latifolius*

latifolius f. rubicundus Moldenke *Phytologia* 29: 75 (1974)

laxiflorus (Desf.) Kuntze *Trudy Imp. S.-Peterburgsk. Bot. Sada* 10: 185 (1887)

laxiflorus var. *angustifolius* Post ex Dinsm. (1932)
= L. *laxiflorus* subsp. *angustifolius*

laxiflorus subsp. angustifolius (Post ex Dinsm.) P.H. Davis *Fl. Turkey* 3: 348 (1970)

layardii Ball ex Boiss. *Fl. Orient. Suppl.* 1888: 195 (1888)

ledebourii Trautv. (1874) = L. *pannonicus*

lentiformis Plitmann *Israel J. Bot.* 14: 90 (1965)

leucanthus Rydb. (1901) = L. *lanszwertii* var. *leucanthus*

leucanthus var. *laetivirens* (Rydb.) C.L. Hitchc. (1952)
= L. *laetivirens*

libani Fritsch *Sitzungsber. Kaiserl. Akad. Wiss., Math.-Naturwiss. Cl.*, Abt. 1, 104: 517 (1895)

linearifolius Nyman (1878) = L. *palustris*

linearifolius Vogel *Linnaea* 13: 28 (1839)

linifolius (Reichard) Bässler *Feddes Repert.* 82(6): 434 (1971)

linifolius var. *montanus* (Bernh.) Bässler (1971)
= L. *linifolius*

linifolius f. *montanus* Bässler (1973) = L. *linifolius*

linifolius f. *pubescens* (Beck) Bässler (1973)
= L. *linifolius*

linifolius f. *pyrenaicus* (L.) Bässler (1973)
= L. *linifolius*

linnaei subsp. *tournefortii* (Lapeyr.) Rouy (1899)
= L. *vivantii*

litoralis Phil. (1856) = L. *magellanicus*

littoralis (Nutt.) Endl. ex Walp. *Repert. Bot. Syst.* 1: 722 (1842)

litvinovii Iljin (1922) = L. *rotundifolius*

lomanus I.M. Johnst. *J. Arnold Arbor.* 19: 250 (1938)

longipes Phil. (1856) = L. *tropicalandinus*

longipes T.G. White (1894) = L. *whitei*

luteus Baker (1879) = L. *emodi*

luteus var. *gmelinii* (Fisch. ex DC) Rchb. (1903)
= L. *gmelinii*

luteus subsp. *hispanicus* (Rouy) V. Allorge & P. Allorge (1941) = L. *laevigatus* subsp. *occidentalis*

luteus subsp. *occidentalis* (Fisch. & C.A. Mey.) Gams (1924) = L. *laevigatus* subsp. *occidentalis*

lycius Boiss. & Heldr. *Diagn. Pl. Orient.* 9: 128 (1849)

macropus Gillies ex Hook. & Arn. *Bot. Misc.* 3: 198 (1833)

macrorrhizus Wimm. (1840) = L. *linifolius*

macrorrhizus var. *angustissimus* Rouy (1899)
= L. *linifolius*

macrorrhizus var. *divaricatus* (Lapeyr.) Godr. (1848) = L. *linifolius*

macrorrhizus var. *pyrenaicus* (L.) Godr. (1848)
= L. *linifolius*

macrorrhizus var. *tenuifolius* (Roth) Godr. (1848)
= L. *linifolius*

macrostachys Vogel *Linnaea* 13: 23 (1839)

magellanicus Lam. *Encycl.* [J. Lamarck *et al.*] 2(2): 708 (1788)

magellanicus f. albiflorus Kuntze *Revis. Gen. Pl.* 3(3): 65 (1898)

magellanicus var. *araucanus* Phil. (1893)
= L. *magellanicus*

magellanicus var. *campestris* Dusén (1914)
= L. *magellanicus* var. *glaucescens*

magellanicus var. gladiatus (Hook.) Kuntze *Revis. Gen. Pl.* 3(3): 65 (1898)

magellanicus var. glaucescens Speg. *Anales Mus. Nac. Buenos Aires* 7: 279 (1902)

magellanicus var. *heterocirrus* (Phil.) Reiche (1897) = L. *magellanicus*

magellanicus f. *longepetiolatus* Hassl. (1919)
= L. *magellanicus*

magellanicus var. *ovalifolius* Reiche (1898)
= L. *magellanicus*

magellanicus var. *oxyphylla* Speg. (1902)
= L. *magellanicus* var. *glaucescens*

magellanicus var. *pterocaulos* (Phil.) Kenicer (2007) = L. *magellanicus*

magellanicus var. *subsessilifolius* Kuntze (1898)
= L. *magellanicus*

magellanicus var. *tucumanensis* Burkart (1935)
= *L. magellanicus* var. *gladiatus*

maritimus (L.) Fr. (1835)   = *L. japonicus* subsp. *maritimus*

maritimus var. *acutifolius* Bab. (1843)   = *L. japonicus* subsp. *maritimus*

maritimus subsp. *acutifolius* (Bab.) Pedersen (1966)   = *L. japonicus* subsp. *maritimus*

maritimus var. *aleuticus* Greene (1832)
= *L. japonicus* subsp. *maritimus*

maritimus var. *aleuticus* T.G. White (1894)
= *L. japonicus* subsp. *maritimus*

maritimus var. *glaber* (Ser.) Eames (1909)
= *L. japonicus* subsp. *maritimus*

maritimus subsp. *glaber* (Ser.) C. Regel (1935)
= *L. japonicus* subsp. *maritimus*

maritimus f. *pubescens* (Hartm.) Saelan (1889)
= *L. japonicus* subsp. *maritimus*

maritimus var. *pubescens* (Hartm.) X.Y. Zhu (2007)
= *L. japonicus* subsp. *maritimus*

maritimus var. *velutinus* Fr. (1846)   = *L. japonicus* subsp. *maritimus*

marmoratus Boiss. & Balansa ex Boiss.   *Fl. Orient.* [Boissier] 2: 606 (1872 0r 1873)

megalanthos Steud., nom. illeg. (1841)   = *L. latifolius*

membranaceus C. Presl (1822)   = *L. latifolius*

meridensis Pittier   *Bol. Soc. Venez. Ci. Nat.* 4: 345 (1938)

mexicanus Wender. (1837)   = *L. tingitanus*

micranthus Gerard ex Loisel. (1809)
= *L. inconspicuus*

miniatus M. Bieb. ex Steven (1856)   = *L. rotundifolius* subsp. *miniatus*

miniatus P. Candargy (1897)   = *L. annuus*

missionum Hassl. (1919)   = *L. subulatus*

miyabei Matsum. (1902)   = *L. palustris*

montanus Bernh. (1800)   = *L. linifolius*

montanus Godr. (1848)   = *L. laevigatus* subsp. *occidentalis*

montanus [f.] *angustissimus* (Rouy) Asch. & Graebn. (1910)   = *L. linifolius*

montanus subsp. *divaricatus* (Lapeyr.) Arcang. (1882)   = *L. linifolius*

montanus var. *divaricatus* (Lapeyr.) Fiori (1900)
= *L. linifolius*

montanus [β] *linifolius* (Reichard) Asch. (1864)   = *L. linifolius*

montanus var. *pubescens* Beck (1927)   = *L. linifolius*

montanus subsp. *pyrenaicus* (L.) Arcang. (1882)
= *L. linifolius*

montanus [f.] *pyrenaicus* (L.) Asch. & Graebn. (1910)   = *L. linifolius*

montanus var. *tenuifolius* (Roth) Garcke (1848)
= *L. linifolius*

montanus subsp. *tenuifolius* (Roth) Arcang. (1882)
= *L. linifolius*

montevidensis Vogel (1839)   = *L. crassipes*

mulkak Lipsky   *Trudy Imp. S.-Peterburgsk. Bot. Sada* 18: 49 (1900).

multiceps Clos   *Fl. Chil.* [Gay] 2: 149 (1847).

multiceps var. *normalis* Burkart (1942)
= *L. multiceps*

multiceps var. *pastorei* Burkart (1942)   = *L. multiceps*

multiceps var. *peruviana* Burkart (1942)
= *L. tropicalandinus*

multiceps var. *setiger* (Phil.) Acevedo (1928)
= *L. multiceps*

multiflorus Peterm. (1849)   = *L. venetus*

multijugus (Ledeb.) Czefr. (1965)   = *L. pannonicus*

myrtifolius Muhl. ex Willd. (1802)   = *L. palustris*

myrtifolius var. *macranthus* T.G. White (1894)
= *L. palustris*

neglectus Puel (1852)   = *L. latifolius*

nervosus Lam.   *Encycl.* [J. Lamarck *et al.*] 2: 708 (1788)

neurolobus Boiss. & Heldr.   *Diagn. Pl. Orient.* 9: 125 (1849).

nevadensis S. Watson   *Proc. Amer. Acad. Arts* 11: 133 (1876)

nevadensis subsp. *cusickii* (S. Watson) C.L. Hitchc. (1952)   = *L. nevadensis* var. *cusickii*

nevadensis var. cusickii (S. Watson) Broich *Madroño* 54(1): 64 (2007)

nevadensis subsp. *lanceolatus* (Howell) C.L. Hitchc. (1961)   = *L. nevadensis*

nevadensis var. parkeri (H. St. John) C.L. Hitchc. *Univ. Wash. Publ. Biol.* 15: 45 (1952)

nevadensis var. *pilosellus* (M. Peck) C.L. Hitchc. & Ownbey (1961)   = *L. nevadensis*

niger (L.) Bernh.   *Syst. Verz.* (Bernhardi): 248 (1800)

niger var. *angustifolius* Rouy (1899)   = *L. niger*

niger var. *genuinus* Rouy, nom. inval. (1899)
= *L. niger*

niger var. *latifolius* Rouy (1899)   = *L. niger*

***nigrivalvis* Burkart**   *Revista Fac. Agron. Veterin.* 8: 68 (1935)

nigrivalvis f. *puberulus* Burkart (1935)   = *L. nigrivalvis*

***nissolia* L.**   *Sp. Pl.* 2: 729 (1753)

nissolia subsp. *futakii* Chrtková (1983) = *L. nissolia*

nissolia var. *glabrescens* Freyn (1878)   = *L. nissolia*

nissolia var. *gramineus* (A. Kern.) G. Beck (1903)   = *L. nissolia*

nissolia var. *gramineus* (A. Kern.) Aschers. & Graebn. (1898)   = *L. nissolia*

nissolia var. *lanceolatus* Rouy (1899)   = *L. nissolia*

nissolia var. *linearis* Rouy (1899)   = *L. nissolia*

nissolia subsp. *pubescens* (Beck) Soják (1980)   = *L. nissolia*

nissolia var. *pubescens* Beck (1903)   = *L. nissolia*

***nitens* Vogel**   *Linnaea* 13: 25 (1839).

***nivalis* Hand.-Mazz.**   *Ann. Nat. Hofmus. Wien* 27: 80 (1913)

***nivalis* subsp. *atropatanus* (Grossh.) Ponert**   *Feddes Repert.* 83(9–10): 635 (1973)

***nivalis* subsp. *sahinii* Genç**   *Nordic J. Bot.* 27: 402 (2009).

nudicaulis (Willk.) Amo (1861)   = *L. palustris* subsp. *nudicaulis*

nudicaulis f. *angustifolius* Cout. (1939)   = *L. palustris* subsp. *nudicaulis*

nuttallii S. Watson (1886)   = *L. nevadensis*

nuttallii subsp. *lanceolatus* (Howell) Piper (1918)   = *L. nevadensis*

occidentalis Torr. & A. Gray (1837)   = *L. palustris*

occidentalis (Fisch. & C.A. Mey.) Fritsch (1895)   = *L. laevigatus* subsp. *occidentalis*

occidentalis var. *grandiflorus* Boiss. ex Fritsch (1895)   = *L. laevigatus* subsp. *occidentalis*

occidentalis subsp. *grandifolius* (Boiss. ex Fritsch) Bässler (1973)   = *L. laevigatus* subsp. *occidentalis*

occidentalis subsp. *hispanicus* (Rouy) M. Laínz & Loriente (1982)   = *L. laevigatus* subsp. *occidentalis*

occidentalis f. *lanceolatus* (Rouy) Bässler (1973)   = *L. laevigatus* subsp. *occidentalis*

ochraceus Kitt. (1844)   = *L. laevigatus* subsp. *occidentalis*

ochraceus subsp. *hispanicus* (Rouy) M. Laínz (1976)   = *L. laevigatus* subsp. *occidentalis*

ochraceus subsp. *occidentalis* (Fisch. & C.A. Mey.) Bässler (1977)   = *L. laevigatus* subsp. *occidentalis*

***ochroleucus* Hook**.   *Fl. Bor.-Amer.* 1(3): 159 (1831)

ochropetalus Piper (1918)   = *L. vestitus* subsp. *ochropetalus*

ochropetalus subsp. *holochlorus* Piper (1918)   = *L. holochlorus*

***ochrus* (L.) DC.**   *Fl. Franc.* [de Candolle & Lamarck], ed. 3, 4: 578 (1805)

ochrus var. *petiolaris* Rouy (1899)   = *L. ochrus*

***odoratus* L.**   *Sp. Pl.* 2: 732 (1753)

***oleraceus* Lam.**   *Fl. Franç.* 2: 580 (1779)

***oleraceus* subsp. *biflorus* (Raf.) H. Schaef., Coulot & Rabaute**   *Bull. Soc. Bot. Centre-Ouest. Numero Special* 46(4): 180 (2016)

oregonensis T.G. White (1894)   = *L. lanszwertii*

ornatus Nutt. (1838)   = *L. polymorphus* var. *incanus*

ornatus var. *incanus* J.G. Sm. & Rydb. (1895)   = *L. polymorphus* var. *incanus*

ovalifolius Phil. (1872)   = *L. magellanicus*

ovalifolius var. *mucronatus* Phil. (1893)   = *L. nervosus*

***pallescens* (M. Bieb.) K. Koch**   *Linnaea* 15(6): 723 (1842)

***palustris* L.**   *Sp. Pl.* 2: 733 (1753)

palustris subsp. *exalatus* H.B. Cui (1984)   = *L. palustris*

palustris var. *graminifolius* S. Watson (1888)   = *L. graminifolius*

***palustris* subsp. *nudicaulis* (Willk.) P.W. Ball**   *Feddes Repert.* 79: 47 (1968)

palustris subsp. *pilosus* (Cham.) Hultén (1837)   = *L. palustris*

palustris var. *nudicaulis* Willk (1851)   = *L. palustris* subsp. *nudicaulis*

palustris var. *sericea* Franch.   = *L. quinquenervius*

***pancicii* (Jurišić) Adamovic**   *Prosv. Glasn.* 22(9): 1246(–1247) (1901)

***pannonicus* (Jacq.) Garcke**   *Fl. N. Mitt.-Deutschland*, ed. 6: 112 (1863).

***pannonicus* subsp. *asphodeloides* (Gouan) Bässler**   *Feddes Repert.* 72: 89 (1966)

***pannonicus* subsp. *collinus* (J. Ortmann) Soó**   *Scripta Bot. Mus. Transsilv.* 1: 46 (1942)

pannonicus var. *hispanicus* (E. Rev.) Sirj. (1937)   = *L. pannonicus* subsp. *longestipulatus*

pannonicus subsp. *hispanicus* (Lacaita) Bässler   = *L. pannonicus* subsp. *longestipulatus*

pannonicus subsp. *ledebourii* (Trautv.) Bässler   = *L. pannonicus*

***pannonicus* subsp. *longestipulatus* M. Laínz**   *Bol.*

Inst. Estud. Astur., Suppl. CI. 3: 166 (1961)

pannonicus subsp. *multijugus* (Ledeb.) Bässler *Feddes Repert.* 82(6): 438 (1971)

pannonicus subsp. *varius* (Hill) P.W. Ball (1968) = L. pannonicus

paraguariensis Hassl. *Repert. Spec. Nov. Regni Veg.* 16: 224 (1919)

paranensis Burkart *Revista Fac. Agron. Veterin.* 8: 71 (1935)

paranensis f. *albiflorus* Burkart *Revista Fac. Agron. Veterin.* 8: 74 (1935)

parkeri H. St. John (1937) = L. nevadensis var. parkeri

parodii Burkart *Revista Fac. Agron. Veterin.* 8: 100 (1935)

parviflorus Roth (1797) = L. inconspicuus

parvifolius S. Watson *Proc. Amer. Acad. Arts* 17: 345 (1882)

parvifolius var. *tenuior* Piper (1901) = L. pauciflorus

pastorei (Burkart) Rossow (1982) = L. multiceps

patagonicus Hauman (1913) = L. magellanicus

pauciflorus Fernald *Bot. Gaz.* 19: 335 (1894)

pauciflorus var. *brownii* (Eastw.) Piper (1918) = L. lanszwertii

pauciflorus var. *schaffneri* (Rydb.) Jeps. (1936) = L. pauciflorus

pauciflorus subsp. *schaffneri* (Rydb.) Piper (1918) = L. pauciflorus

pauciflorus var. *tenuior* (Piper) H. St.John (1937) = L. pauciflorus

pauciflorus var. *utahensis* Piper (1918) = L. pauciflorus var. utahensis

pauciflorus var. *utahensis* (M.E. Jones) R.J. Davis (1951) *Madroño* 11: 144 (1951)

peckii Piper (1918) = L. vestitus var. bolanderi

petiolaris Vogel (1839) = L. pubescens

phaselitanus Hub.-Mor. & P.H. Davis (1969) = L. lycicus

philippi Alef. ex Phil. (1872) = L. magellanicus

phillipianus Speg. (1902) = L. magellanicus

phlloideus St.-Lag. (1889) = L. nissolia

pilosus Cham. (1831) = L. palustris

pisiformis L. *Sp. Pl.* 2: 734 (1753)

platyphyllus Retz. (1795) = L. sylvestris

polyanthus Boiss. & Blanche (1856) = L. aphaca

polymorphus Nutt. *Gen. N. Amer. Pl.* [Nuttall] 2: 96–97 (1818)

polymorphus subsp. *incanus* (J.G. Sm. & Rydb.) C.L.

Hitchc. (1952) = L. polymorphus. var. incanus

polymorphus var. *incanus* (J.G. Sm. & Rydb.) Dorn *Vasc. Pl. Wyoming* 1988: 297 (1988)

polyphyllus Nutt. *Fl. N. Amer.* [Torr. & A. Gray] 1(2): 274 (1838).

pratensis L. *Sp. Pl.* 2: 733 (1753)

pratensis var. *binatus* (Pančić) Ascherson & Kanitz (1877) = L. binatus

pratensis subsp. *hallersteinii* (Baumg.) Nyman (1889) = L. hallersteinii

pratensis subsp. *lusseri* (Heer. ex W.D.J. Koch) Soják (1983) = L. pratensis

pratensis subsp. *velutinus* (DC.) Soják (1983) = L. pratensis

pratensis var. *velutinus* DC. (1815) = L. pratensis

prostratus Brign. (1810) = L. subandinus

pseudoaphaca Boiss. (1843) = L. aphaca var. pseudoaphaca

pseudocicera Pamp. *Nuovo Giorn. Bot. Ital.*, n.s. 31: 213, 214 (1924)

pseudocicera subsp. *negevensis* (Plitmann) Plitmann & Heyn *Willdenowia* 19(1): 32 (1989)

pterocaulos Phil. (1872) = L. magellanicus

pubescens Hook. & Arn. *Bot. Beechey Voy.* 1: 21 (1830)

pubescens Clos = L. cabrerianus

pubescens var. *acutifolius* Griseb. (1879) = L. pubescens var. monticola

pubescens var. *monticola* Burkart *Darwiniana* 6: 17 (1942)

pulcher J. Gay *Ann. Sci. Nat., Bot.*, sér. 4 8: 311 (1857)

purpureo-coeruleus Knowles & Westc. (1838) = L. pubescens

purpureus Gilib. (1782) nom. inval. = L. latifolius

purpureus Desf. (1808) = L. articulatus

pusillus Elliott *Sketch Bot. S. Carolina* 2: 223 (1823)

pyrenaicus Jord. (1848) = L. sylvestris

quadrimarginatus Bory & Chaub. (1832) = L. amphicarpos

quadrimarginatus var. *amphicarpos* Pérez Lara (1892) = L. amphicarpos

quadrimarginatus subsp. *tetrapterus* (Pomel) Maire (1931) = L. amphicarpos

quinquenervius (Miq.) Litv. *Kom. & Aliss. Opred. Rast. Dal'nevost. Kraia* 2: 683 (1932)

rigidus T.G. White *Bull. Torrey Bot. Club* 21: 455 (1894) *rigidus* var. *pilosellus* M. Peck (1928) = L. *nevadensis*

roseus Phil. (1856) = L. *magellanicus*

roseus Steven *Mém. Soc. Imp. Naturalistes Moscou* 4: 92 (1813)

rotundifolius Willd. *Sp. Pl.* ed. 4 [Willdenow] 3: 1088 (1802)

rotundifolius subsp. *miniatus* (M. Bieb. ex Steven) P.H. Davis *Fl. Turkey* 3: 350 (1970)

rotundifolius subsp. *undulatus* ((Boiss.) Ponert *Feddes Repert.* 83(9–10): 635 (1973)

sandbergii (T.G. White) Howell (1898) = L. *lanszwertii* var. *sandbergii*

sargentianus W.G. Craib (1914) = L. *dielsianus*

satdaghensis P.H. Davis *Notes Roy. Bot. Gard. Edinburgh* 29: 317 (1969)

sativus L. *Sp. Pl.* 2: 730 (1753).

sativus f. *albus* Smekalova *Sborn. Nauchn. Trudov Prikl. Bot. Genet. Selekts.* 139: 69 (1991)

sativus subsp. *asiaticus* Zalkind (1955) = L. *sativus*

sativus f. *azureus* Smekalova *Sborn. Nauchn. Trudov Prikl. Bot. Genet. Selekts.* 139: 67 (1991)

sativus var. *cyaneus* A. Howard & Khan *Mem. Dep. Agri. India Botany* 15(2) (1928)

sativus var. *stipulaceus* Willk. (1880) = L. *amphicarpos*

sativus f. *violascens* Smekalova *Sborn. Nauchn. Trudov Prikl. Bot. Genet. Selekts.* 139: 66 (1991)

saxatilis (Vent.) Vis. (1852) = Vicia *saxatilis* (Vent.) Tropea

schaffneri Rydb. (1917) = L. *parvifolius*

segetum Lam., nom. illeg. (1779) = L. *aphaca*

sericeus Lam. (1788) = L. *tomentosus*

sericeus (Boiss. & Balansa) Czeczott (1939) = L. *czeczottianus*

sessilifolius (Sm.) Ten. (1826) = L. *digitatus*

sessilifolius Hook. & Arn. (1831) = L. *magellanicus*

sessilifolius f. *trichocalyx* (Phil.) Burkart (1935) = L. *magellanicus*

setifolius L. *Sp. Pl.* 2: 731 (1753)

setifolius var. *amphicarpos* Godr., nom. inval. (1848) = L. *setifolius*

setifolius var. *angustissimus* Rouy (1899) = L. *setifolius*

setifolius var. *genuinus* Godr., nom. inval. (1848) = L. *setifolius*

setifolius var. *genuinus* Rouy, nom. inval. (1899) = L. *setifolius*

setifolius [f.] *gouanii* Rouy, nom. inval. (1899) = L. *setifolius*

setifolius var. *heterocarpus* Loret & Barrandon (1876) = L. *setifolius*

setifolius var. *sharonensis* Zohary & Plitmann *Fl. Palaestina* 2: 458 (1972)

setiger Phil. (1864) = L. *multiceps*

setiger var. *eurypetalus* (Phil.) Reiche (1897) = L. *multiceps*

spathulatus Čelak. *F:Oesterr. Bot. Z.* 38: 6 (1888)

spathulatus subsp. *elongatus* (Bornm.) Ponert *Feddes Repert.* 83: 635 (1972)

sphaericus Retz. *Observ. Bot.* 3: 39 (1783)

sphaericus var. *genuinus* Rouy, nom. inval. (1899) = L. *sphaericus*

sphaericus var. *longearistatus* Rigual, nom. illeg. (1972) = L. *sphaericus*

sphaericus var. *pilosus* Ser. (1825) = L. *sphaericus*

sphaericus var. *stenophyllus* Boiss. (1872) = L. *sphaericus*

splendens Kellogg *Proc. Calif. Acad. Sci.* 7: 90 (1877)

stans Vic. (1829) = L. *inconspicuus*

stenolobus Boiss. *Diagn. Pl. Orient.* 9: 124 (1849).

stenophyllus Boiss. & Heldr. *Diagn. Pl. Orient.* ser. 1, 9: 126 (1849)

stipularis Tamamsch. (1927) = L. *aphaca* var. *floribundus*

strictus var. *alefeldii* (T.G. White) Jeps. (1936) = L. *vestitus* subsp. *alefeldii*

subandinus Phil. *Linnaea* 33(1): 52 (1864)

subulatus Lam. *Encycl.* [J. Lamarck et al.] 2: 707 (1788)

subulatus var. *longifolius* Hassl. (1919) = L. *subulatus*

sulphureus W.H. Brewer ex A.Gray *Proc. Amer. Acad. Arts* 7: 399 (1868)

sulphureus var. *argillaceus* Jeps. *Fl. Calif.* [Jepson] 2: 393 (1936)

sylvestris [f.] *pyrenaicus* (Jord.) Rouy, nom. inval. (1899) = L. *sylvestris*

sylvestris L. *Sp. Pl.* 2: 733 (1753)

sylvestris subsp. *cirrhosus* (Ser.) P. Fourn. (1936) = L. *cirrhosus*

sylvestris subsp. *heterophyllus* (L.) Bonnier & Layens (1894) = L. *heterophyllus*

sylvestris subsp. *latifolius* (L.) Arcang. (1882) = L. *latifolius*

sylvestris subsp. *pyrenaicus* (Jord.) O. Bolòs & Vigo

(1974)   = L. sylvestris

szowitsii Boiss.   Fl. Orient. [Boissier] 2: 605 (1872)
(status uncertain)

tauricola P.H. Davis   Notes Roy. Bot. Gard.
Edinburgh 29: 318 (1969)

tefennicus Genç & Sahin   J. Syst. Evol. 49(5): 505
(2011)

tenuifolius Desf. (1799)   = L. articulatus

tenuior (Piper) Rydb. (1917)   = L. pauciflorus

tetrapterus Pomel (1874)   = L. amphicarpos

thirkaenus K. Koch (1847)   = L. ochrus

tingitanus L.   Sp. Pl. 2: 732 (1753)

tingitanus f. granatensis Pau ex Lacaita (1928)
= L. tingitanus

tomentosus Lam.   Encycl. [J. Lamarck et al.] 2(2):
709 (1788)

torreyi A. Gray   Proc. Amer. Acad. Arts 7: 337 (1868).

tournefortii (Lapeyr.) A.W. Hill (1926)   = L. vivantii

trachycarpus (Boiss.) Boiss.   Fl. Orient. [Boissier] 2:
608 (1872)

trachyspermus Webb ex J.J. Rodr. (1878)   = L. annuus

tracyi Bradshaw (1925)   = L. lanszwertii

transsylvanicus (Spreng.) Rchb.   Icon. Fl. Germ.
Helv. 22: t. 220, f. IV (1886)

tremolsianus Pau (1891)   = L. pulcher

trichocalyx Phil. (1872)   = L. magellanicus

trigonus Vogel (1839)   = L. nervosus

tropicalandinus Burkart   Darwiniana 6: 16 (1942)

tuberosus L.   Sp. Pl. 2: 732 (1753).

tukhtensis Czeczott   Acta Soc. Bot. Polon. 9: 36
(1932)

undulatus Boiss. (1856)   = L. rotundifolius subsp.
undulatus

utahensis M.E. Jones (1895)   = L. pauciflorus

vaniotii H. Lév.   Repert. Spec. Nov. Regni Veg. 7: 230
(1909)

variabilis (Boiss. & Kotschy) Čelak.   Oesterr. Bot. Z.
38: 46 (1888)

variegatus (Ten.) Gren. & Godr. (1848)   = L. venetus

varius (Hill) K. Koch (1841)   = L. pannonicus

venetus (Mill.) Wohlf. ex Koch   Syn. Deut. Schweiz.
Fl. ed. 3: 714 (1892)

venosus Muhl. ex Willd.   Sp. Pl. [Willdenow], ed. 4,
3(2): 1092 (1802)

venosus var. arkansanus Fassett   Rhodora 39: 377
(1937)

venosus var. intonsus Butters & H. St. John

Rhodora 19: 158 (1917)

venosus var. meridionalis Butters & H. St. John
(1917)   = L. venosus

vernus (L.) Bernh. (1800)   Syst. Verz.: 248 (1800)

vernus var. alatus Maxim. (1873)   = L. komarovii

**vernus subsp. vernus f. angustifolius Asch. &
Graebn.**   Syn. Mitteleur. Fl. [Ascherson & Graebner]
6(2): 1048 (1910)

vernus subsp. flaccidus (Kit.) Arcang.   Comp. Fl. Ital.
edn. 2: 522 (1894)

**vernus subsp. flaccidus f. gracilis (Gaud.) Asch. &
Graebn.**   Syn. Mitteleur. Fl. [Ascherson & Graebner]
6(2): 1049 (1910)

vernus f. roseus Beck   Flora von Nieder-Österreich
1: 886 (1892)

vernus f. variegatus (Schuster) Bässler   Feddes
Repert. 84(5-6): 382 (1973)

vestitus Nutt.   Fl. N. Amer. [Torr. & A. Gray] 1: 276
(1838)

vestitus subsp. alefeldii (T.G. White) Broich
= L. vestitus var. alefeldii

vestitus var. alefeldii (T.G. White) Isely   Madroño
39: 96 (1992)

vestitus subsp. bolanderi (S. Watson) C.L. Hitchc.
= L. vestitus

vestitus subsp. laetiflorus (Greene) Broich
= L. vestitus

vestitus subsp. ochropetalus (Piper) C.L. Hitchc.
(1952)   = L. vestitus var. ochropetalus

vestitus var. ochropetalus (Piper) Isely   Madroño
39: 96 (1992)

vestitus var. puberulus (T.G. White ex Greene) Jeps.
(1901)   = L. vestitus var. vestitus

vestitus subsp. puberulus (Greene) C.L. Hitchc.
= L. vestitus var. vestitus

viciaeformis Wallr. (1782)   = L. palustris

vinealis Boiss. & Noë   Diagn. Pl. Orient. ser. 2, 2: 42
(1856)

violaceus Greene (1893)   = L. vestitus

violaceus var. barbarae T.G. White (1894)
= L. vestitus

vivantii P. Monts.   Bull. Soc. Bot. France, Lett. Bot.
127: 517 (1981)

volckmanni Phil. (1862)   = ?L. campestris

whitei Kupicha   Notes Roy. Bot. Gard. Edinburgh
41(2): 226 (1983)

wilsonii Craib (1914)   = L. dielsianus

woronowii Bornm.   *Vestn. Tiflissk. Bot. Sada* 26: 2
    (1912)
zionis C.L. Hitchc. (1952)   = *L. brachycalyx* var. *zionis*

Synonyms in genera other than *Lathyrus*

Alophotrophis aucheri (Jaub. & Spach) Grossh.
    (1949)   = *L. formosus*
Alophotrophis formosa (Steven) Grossh. (1949)
    = *L. formosus*
Anurus linifolius C. Presl., nom. illeg. (1837)
    = *L. nissolia*
Anurus nissolia (L.) Fourr. (1868)   = *L. nissolia*
Aphaca marmorata Alef. (1861)   = *L. aphaca*
Aphaca vulgaris C. Presl. (1837)   = *L. aphaca*
Astrophia littoralis Nutt. (1838)   = *L. littoralis*
Cicercula alata Moench. (1794)   = *L. sativus*
Cicercula cicera (L.) Alef. (1861)   = *L. cicera*
Cicercula sativa (L.) Medik. (1789)   = *L. sativus*
Clymenum bicolor Moench, nom. illeg. (1794)
    = *L. clymenum*
Clymenum ochrus (L.) Link (1831)   = *L. ochrus*
Clymenum uncinatum Moench (1794)
    = *L. clymenum*
Ervum woronowii (Bornm.) Stank. (1999)
    = *L. woronowii*
Graphiosa inconspicua (L.) Alef. (1861)
    = *L. inconspicuus*
Lastila hirsuta (L.) Alef. (1861)   = *L. hirsutus*
Lastila hirsuta var. *annua* Alef. (1861)   = *L. hirsutus*
Lastila hirsuta var. *biennis* Alef. (1861)   = *L. hirsutus*
Navidura tingitana (L.) Alef. (1861)   = *L. tingitanus*
Nissolia uniflora Moench (1794)   = *L. nissolia*
Ochrus pallida Pers. (1807), nom. illeg.   = *L. ochrus*
Ochrus uniflorus Moench (1794)   = *L. ochrus*
Orobus alatus Maxim. (1859)   = *L. komarovii*
Orobus albus L. f. (1782)   = *L. pannonicus*
Orobus alpestris Waldst. & Kit. (1804)   = *L. alpestris*
Orobus angustifolius L. (1753)   = *L. pallescens*
Orobus angustifolius Vill. (1786)   = *L. filiformis*
Orobus armenus Boiss. & A. Huet (1856)
    = *L. armenus*
Orobus articulatus A. Braun (1853)   = *L. articulatus*
Orobus asphodeloides Gouan (1773)   = *L. pannonicus*
Orobus atropatanus Grossh. (1930)   = *L. nivalis* subsp.
    atropatanus

Orobus aureus G. Lodd. ex Drapiez (1833)   = *L. aureus*
Orobus austriacus Crantz (1769)   = *L. pannonicus*
Orobus bauhinii Genty (1892)   = *L. bauhinii*
Orobus californicus Alef. (1861)   = *L. japonicus*
Orobus canescens L. f. (1782)   = *L. filiformis*
Orobus canescens var. *filiformis* (Lam.) Porta & Rigo
    (1891)   = *L. filiformis*
Orobus clymenum (L.) A. Braun (1853)
    = *L. clymenum*
Orobus cyaneus Steven (1813)   = *L. cyaneus*
Orobus davidii (Hance) Stank. & Roskov (1998)
    = *L. davidii*
Orobus digitatus M. Bieb. (1808)   = *L. digitatus*
Orobus dissitifolius Alef. (1861)   = *L. graminifolius*
Orobus divaricatus Lapeyr. (1815)   = *L. linifolius*
Orobus emodi Wall. ex Fritsch (1895)   = *L. emodi*
Orobus ensifolius Lapeyr. (1815)   = *L. bauhinii*
Orobus ewaldii Meinsh. (1868)   = *L. laevigatus*
Orobus filiformis Lam. (1778)   = *L. filiformis*
Orobus formosus Steven (1813)   = *L. formosus*
Orobus friedrichsthalii Griseb. (1846)   = *L. alpestris*
Orobus gmelinii Fisch. ex DC. (1825)   = *L. gmelinii*
Orobus gracilis Gaudin (1829)   = *L. vernus* subsp.
    flaccidus f. *gracilis*
Orobus graminifolius Becker (1827)   = *L. linifolius*
Orobus grandiflorus Boiss. (1872)   = *L. libani*
Orobus hirsutus L. (1753)   = *L. laxiflorus*
Orobus hispanicus (E. Rev.) Lacaita (1928)
    = *L. pannonicus* subsp. *longestipulatus*
Orobus humilis Ser. (1825)   = *L. humilis*
Orobus hupehensis (Pamp.) Stank. (1999)
    = *L. dielsianus*
Orobus incurvus (Roth) A. Braun (1853)   = *L. incurvus*
Orobus intermedius C.A. Mey. (1831)   = *L. ledebourii*
Orobus kolenatii K. Koch (1851)   = *L. aureus*
Orobus komarovii (Ohwi) Stank. & Roskov (1998)
    – *L. komarovii*
Orobus krylovii (Serg.) Stank. & Roskov (1998)
    = *L. krylovii*
Orobus lacaitae (Cefr.) Stank. & Roskov (1998)
    = *L. pannonicus*
Orobus lacteus M. Bieb. (1808)   = *L. pannonicus*
Orobus lacteus f. *hispanicus* E. Rev. (1895)
    = *L. pannonicus* subsp. *longestipulatus*
Orobus laevigatus Waldst. & Kit. (1812)
    = *L. laevigatus*
Orobus laxiflorus Desf. (1808)   = *L. laxiflorus*

Orobus ledebourii (Trautv.) Roldugin (1961)
  = *L. pannonicus*
Orobus linifolius Reichard (1782)   = *L. linifolius*
Orobus littoralis (Nutt.) A.Gray (1860)   = *L. littoralis*
Orobus luteus [β] *occidentalis* (Fisch & C.A. Mey.) Beck
  (1903)   = *L. laevigatus* subsp. *occidentalis*
Orobus luteus L. (1753)   = *L. gmelinii* Fritsch
Orobus luteus var. *occidentalis* Fisch. & C.A. Mey.
  (1837)   = *L. laevigatus* subsp. *occidentalis*
Orobus macrorrhizus Dulac (1867)   = *L. linifolius*
Orobus maritimus (L.) Rchb. (1832)   = *L. japonicus*
Orobus montanus Scop. (1772)   = *L. linifolius*
Orobus muhlenbergii Alef. (1861)   = *L. venosus*
Orobus multijugus (Ledeb.) Stank. & Roskov (1998)
  = *L. pannonicus*
Orobus myrtifolius Alef. (1861)   = *L. palustris*
Orobus niger L. (1753)   = *L. niger*
Orobus nissolia (L.) Döll (1843)   = *L. nissolia*
Orobus ochroleucus Waldst. & Kit. (1803)
  = *L. ochroleucus*
Orobus ochrus (L.) A. Braun (1853)   = *L. ochrus*
Orobus orientalis Boiss. (1843)   = *L. aureus*
Orobus pallescens M. Bieb. (1808)   = *L. pallescens*
Orobus palustris (L.) Rchb. (1832)   = *L. palustris*
Orobus pannonicus Jacq. (1762)   = *L. pannonicus*
Orobus pannonicus var. *collinus* J. Ortmann (1852)
  = *L. pannonicus*
Orobus philippi Alef. (1861)   = *L. magellanicus*
Orobus pluckenetii Lapeyr. (1815)   = *L. linifolius*
Orobus polymorphus (Nutt.) Alef. (1861)
  = *L. polymorphus*
Orobus pratensis (L.) Stokes (1812)   = *L. pratensis*
Orobus pubescens (Hook. & Arn.) Alef. (1861)
  = *L. pubescens*
Orobus pyrenaicus L. (1753)   = *L. linifolius*
Orobus roseus (Steven) Ledeb. (1843)   = *L. roseus*
Orobus saxatilis Vent. (1803)   = *L. saxatilis*
Orobus sericeus Boiss. & Balansa (1872)
  = *L. czeczottianus*
Orobus sessilifolius Sm. (1813)   = *L. digitatus*
Orobus sessilifolius subsp. *elongatus* Bornm.
  (1906)   = *L. spathulatus* subsp. *elongatus*
Orobus setifolius (L.) Philippe (1859)   = *L. setifolius*
Orobus skorpilii Velen. (1890)   = *L. friedrichsthalii*
Orobus speciosus Hausskn. ex Širj. (1934)
  = *L. brachypterus*
Orobus sphaericus (Retz.) Philippe (1859)

= *L. sphaericus*
Orobus subalpinus Herbich (1853)   = *L. laevigatus*
Orobus tenuifolius Roth (1782)   = *L. linifolius*
Orobus tournefortii Lapeyr. (1815)   = *L. vivantii*
Orobus trachycarpus Boiss. (1846)   = *L. trachycarpus*
Orobus transsylvanicus Spreng. (1826)
  = *L. transsilvanicus*
Orobus tuberosus L. (1753)   = *L. linifolius*
Orobus tuberosus var. *divaricatus* (Lapeyr.) Ser.
  (1825)   = *L. linifolius*
Orobus tuberosus var. *pyrenaicus* (L.) Ser. (1825)
  = *L. linifolius*
Orobus tuberosus var. *tenuifolius* (Roth) Willd.
  (1802)   = *L. linifolius*
Orobus tuberosus [β] *unijugus* Willk. (1877)
  = *L. linifolius*
Orobus variabilis Boiss. & Kotschy (1872)
  = *L. variabilis*
Orobus variegatus Ten. (1820)   = *L. venetus*
Orobus venetus Mill. (1768)   = *L. venetus*
Orobus vernus L. (1753)   = *L. vernus*
Orobus vernus var. *alatus* (Maxim.) Regel (1861)
  = *L. komarovii*
Orobus versicolor J.F. Gmel. (1792)   = *L. pannonicus*
Orobus vestitus (Nutt.) Alef. (1861)   = *L. vestitus*
Orobus villosus Torr. (1874)   = *L. torreyi*
Pisum abyssinicum A. Braun (1841)   = *L. oleraceus*
Pisum americanum Mill. (1768)   = *L. nervosus*
Pisum arvense L. (1753)   = *L. oleraceus*
Pisum aucheri Jaub. & Spach (1842)   = *L. formosus*
Pisum clymenum (L.) E.H.L. Krause (1901)
  = *L. articulatus*
Pisum elatius M. Bieb.. (1808)   = *L. oleraceus*
Pisum flavum E.H.L. Krause (1901)   = *L. annuus*
Pisum formosum (Steven) Alef. (1861)   = *L. formosus*
Pisum fulvum Sm. (1813)   = *L. fulvus*
Pisum fulvum var. *amphicarpum* Warb. & Eig   *Agric.
  Rec. Inst. Agric. Nat. Hist.* 1: 2, t.1 (1926) – status
  uncertain
Pisum heterophyllum (L.) E.H.L. Krause (1901)
  = *L. heterophyllus*
Pisum hirsutum (L.) E.H.L. Krause (1901)
  = *L. hirsutus*
Pisum maritimum L. (1753)   = *L. japonicus*
Pisum maritimum var. *glabrum* Ser. (1825)
  = *L. japonicus*
Pisum maritimum var. *pubescens* Hartm. (1832)

= *L. japonicus*

Pisum ochrus L. (1753) = *L. ochrus*

Pisum sativum L. (1753) = *L. oleraceus*

Vavilovia aucheri Fed. (1939) = *L. formosus*

Vavilovia formosa (Steven) Fed. (1939) = *L. formosus*

Vicia aucheri Boiss. (1856) = *L. formosus*

Vicia incurva Roth (1783) = *L. incurvus*

Vicia quinquenervia Miq. (1867) = *L. quinquenervius*

Vicia saxatilis (Vent.) Tropea (1907) = *Vicia saxatilis*

Vicia venosa var. *willdenowiana* Miura (1926)

= *L. vaniotii*

Appendix
Recombination

Lathyrus formosus (Steven) Kenicer, comb. nov.

Basionym: *Orobus formosus* Steven, *Mém. Soc. Imp. Naturalistes Moscou* 4: 50 (1813).

Synonyms: *Alophotrophis aucheri* (Jaub. & Spach) Grossh., *Opred. Rast. Kavk.*: 162 (1949); *Alophotrophis formosa* (Steven) Grossh., *Opred. Rast. Kavk.*: 162 (1949); *Pisum aucheri* Jaub. & Spach, *Ill. Pl. Orient.* 1: 91 (1842); *Pisum formosum* (Steven) Alef., *Bonplandia* 9: 237 (1861); *Vavilovia aucheri* Fed., *Trud. Biol. Inst. Arm. Fil. Akad. Nauk URSS* 1: 53 (1939); *Vavilovia formosa* (Steven) Fed., *Trud. Biol. Inst. Arm. Fil. Akad. Nauk URSS* 1: 52 (1939); *Vicia aucheri* Boiss., *Diagn. Pl. Orient.* ser. 2, 3: 166 (1856).

Checklist of cultivar epithets

There are around 7,200 recorded cultivar epithets in the genus *Lathyrus*, with the vast majority belonging to *L. odoratus* (sweet pea). Roger Parsons has compiled a full checklist, but because of its size it cannot all be included in this book. The checklist published here of about 1,200 epithets is a subset of his work. It includes all cultivars mentioned in this book plus the majority of those that have been offered for sale in the UK in the past five years. The full checklist of 7,200 entries is available at: www.rpsweetpeas.com/epithets

Where a cultivar name has been used more than once, the raiser's name is given after later, unacceptable uses of the epithet. If the same raiser has developed more than one cultivar with the same name, the date of introduction of each repeated cultivar epithet is given. Some of the sources used for the names need further verification. For example, many names published by Kelsey & Dayton (1942) duplicate existing names but list a different raiser. Similarly, colour descriptions in Rowntree catalogues may simply be incorrect. Also, there are many more published sources to explore, especially older seed catalogues where cultivars were first named and described. The checklist presented here, and the larger one it is a subset of, should therefore be viewed with some caution, but it is better than anything that has previously existed.

Comparable characters, such as plant height, flower number and, for *L. odoratus* cultivars, flower form, are given for each entry in a standardised form (see key below). More detailed descriptions of the most commonly grown cultivars can be found in the Cultivars chapter. Where known, information regarding the discovery, introduction and earliest known publication details of cultivars is given.

Name in **bold:** Currently accepted name, with the species it is attributed to in brackets. Name in roman: Synonym or unacceptable name. In the case of synonyms, the species it is attributed to (or was attributed to when first published) is in brackets, followed by an equals (=) sign and the accepted name. Names are regarded as unacceptable if they are duplicates of earlier names, in which case the raiser is cited as well.

Forms of *L. odoratus* flowers: Grandiflora – plain petals and a clamped keel; Semi-grandiflora – waved petals and a clamped keel; Spencer – waved petals and an open keel.

RHS Details of RHS awards: AGM = Award of Garden Merit; AM = Award of Merit; FCC = First Class Certificate.

F Earliest identified publication of the cultivar name with a description (ad. = advertisement; cat. = catalogue; n/k = not known).

R The name of the raiser or seed supplier who introduced it. Where two are given, the last name is the supplier who may or may not be the raiser.

I Year when first offered for sale.

A Notes giving additional information about the cultivar, including reference to the name where the earliest reference has not been located.

H Height: T = tall (plants usually make 1.8–2.4m, depending on cultivation); SD = semi-dwarf (plants usually make 0.6–1.2m, depending on cultivation); D = dwarf (plants usually make up to 0.4m, depending on cultivation).

L Leaf type: U = unijugate (leaf consists of one pair of leaflets and tendrils); M = multijugate (leaf consists of multiple pairs of leaflets and no tendrils).

N Number of flowers: P = pauciflora (4–5 flowers or fewer); M = multiflora (5–6 flowers or more).

P Number of petals: S = simplex (typical flower form of one standard petal, two wing petals and a keel); D = duplex (two standard petals and sometimes extra wings); T = triplex (three standard petals and sometimes extra wings).

C Colour of flowers: c.g. = cream ground; w.g. = white ground; / = bicolour (standard petal / wing and keel petals)

S Flowering season (day length is not the only factor affecting flower initiation but affects seasonality): summer = flower initiation begins when day length reaches 12 hours or longer; spring = flower initiation begins when day length reaches 11 hours or longer; winter = flower initiation begins when day length reaches 10 hours or longer.

'Adorabel' (*L. odoratus*) Grandiflora   **F:** R. Parsons cat. 2016/17. **R:** Grayson. **I:** 2013. **D:** see Cultivars chapter.

'Aerospace' (*L. odoratus*) Spencer   **F:** *NSPS Annual* 1983: 81. **R:** Manning / Suttons. **I:** 1987. **H:** T. **L:** U. **N:** P. **P:** S. **C:** white. **S:** summer.

'Aileen Christina' (*L. odoratus*) Spencer   **F:** McDougall cat. 1998. **R:** McDougall. **I:** n/k. **H:** T. **L:** U. **N:** P. **P:** S. **C:** deep blue / red throat. **S:** winter.

'Aileen Walton' (*L. odoratus*) Spencer   **F:** Kerton Sweet Peas cat. 2005. **R:** Fleming Robertson / Kerton Sweet Peas. **I:** 2005. **D:** see Cultivars chapter.

'Air Warden' (*L. odoratus*) Spencer   **F:** G. Stark & Son cat. 1950/51. **R:** Thomas Cullen & Sons. **I:** 1942. **H:** T. **L:** U. **N:** P. **P:** S. **C:** scarlet. **S:** summer.

'Airan' (*L. odoratus*) Spencer   **F:** *NSPS Annual* 1997:

74. **R:** Kerton Sweet Peas. **I:** 2002. **H:** T. **L:** U. **N:** P. **P:** S. **C:** light blue flush, w.g. **S:** summer.

'Alan Roberts' (*L. odoratus*) Spencer   **F:** n/k. **R:** Truslove / Beane / Simply Sweet Peas. **I:** 2010. **H:** T. **L:** U. **N:** P. **P:** D. **C:** pink stripe, w.g. **S:** summer.

'Alan Titchmarsh' (*L. odoratus*) Spencer   **F:** Robert Bolton & Son cat. 1985/86. **R:** B.R. Jones / Robert Bolton & Son. **I:** 1986. **D:** see Cultivars chapter.

'Alan Williams' (*L. odoratus*) Spencer   **F:** Suttons cat. 1986. **R:** Williams / Suttons. **I:** 1986. **H:** T. **L:** U. **N:** P. **P:** S. **C:** mid blue. **S:** summer.

'Alaska Blue' (*L. odoratus*) Spencer   **F:** Kerton Sweet Peas cat. 2000. **R:** Wells / Kerton Sweet Peas. **I:** 2000. **D:** see Cultivars chapter.

'Alberta' (*L. odoratus*) Spencer   **F:** *Australian Garden Lover* (1963). **R:** Harkness. **I:** 1963. **H:** T. **L:** U. **N:** P. **P:** D. **C:** dark red, w.g. **S:** winter.

'Alboroseus' (*L. vernus*)   **RHS:** AGM (H6) 1997. **F:** Rice (2006). **R:** n/k. **I:** n/k. **A:** The flowers are of f. *variegatus* type and the leaflets are of f. *vernus* type (30–100mm wide). **D:** see Cultivars chapter.

'Albus' (*L. latifolius*)   **F:** n/k. **R:** n/k. **I:** Early 19th century. **D:** see Cultivars chapter under 'White Pearl'.

'Albus' (*L. sativus*)   **A:** Sometimes recognised as f. *albus*. **D:** see Cultivars chapter.

'Albutt Blue' (*L. odoratus*) Semi-grandiflora   **F:** Eagle Sweet Peas cat. 1998/99. **R:** Albutt / Eagle Sweet Peas. **I:** 1999. **D:** see Cultivars chapter.

'Alice' (*L. odoratus*) Spencer   **F:** Ferry Morse Seed Co. cat. 1953. **R:** Ferry Morse Seed Co. **I:** 1953. **H:** T. **L:** U. **N:** P. **P:** S. **C:** blush pink, c.g. **S:** late spring.

'Alice' n/k (*L. odoratus*) Spencer   **F:** R. Parsons cat. 2017/18. **R:** n/k. **I:** n/k. **H:** T. **L:** U. **N:** M. **P:** S. **C:** deep salmon, c.g. **S:** winter.

'Alice Hardwicke' (*L. odoratus*) Spencer   **F:** Malin cat. 1971/72. **R:** B.R. Jones / Suttons. **I:** 1971. **D:** see Cultivars chapter.

'Alicia Jade' (*L. odoratus*) Spencer   **F:** McDougall cat. 2015. **R:** McDougall. **I:** 1980s. **H:** T. **L:** U. **N:** P. **P:** S. **C:** deep mauve / blue. **S:** winter.

'Alisa' (*L. odoratus*) Semi-grandiflora   **F:** R. Parsons cat. 2015. **R:** Levko / R. Parsons. **I:** 2015. **D:** see Cultivars chapter.

'Alison' (*L. odoratus*) Spencer   **F:** Kerton Sweet Peas cat. 1991. **R:** F.G. Davis / Kerton Sweet Peas. **I:** 1991. **H:** T. **L:** U. **N:** P. **P:** S. **C:** pink picotee, c.g. **S:** summer.

'Alison Louise' (*L. odoratus*) Spencer   **F:** R. Parsons cat. 2019/20. **R:** R. Parsons. **I:** 2020. **H:** T. **L:** U. **N:** M. **P:** S. **C:** bright blue, w.g. **S:** summer.

'**Alison Valentini**' (*L. odoratus*) Spencer **F:** R. Parsons cat. 2016. **R:** R. Place / R. Parsons. **I:** 2016. **D:** see Cultivars chapter.

'**Almost Black**' (*L. odoratus*) Grandiflora **F:** n/k. **R:** Hammett / Denny. **I:** 2009. **A:** Name first appeared on the Seedngrow website (seen 19 Feb 2009) and was mentioned in the 2014 *NSPS Classification List*. **D:** see Cultivars chapter.

'**Ambition**' (*L. odoratus*) Spencer **F:** Burpee Seeds cat. 1932, Ball cat. 1932. **R:** Thomas Cullen & Sons / Burpee Seeds. **I:** 1932. **H:** T. **L:** U. **N:** P. **P:** S. **C:** rosy lavender. **S:** summer.

'**America**' (*L. odoratus*) Grandiflora **RHS:** AGM (H3) 1995. **F:** Vaughan Seed Store cat. autumn 1895. **R:** C.C. Morse & Co. / Vaughan Seed Store. **I:** 1896. **D:** see Cultivars chapter.

'**American Beauty**' (*L. odoratus*) Spencer **F:** Elliott cat. 1927. **R:** Elliott. **I:** 1927. **H:** T. **L:** U. **N:** P. **P:** S. **C:** salmon rose. **S:** summer.

'American Beauty' Ferry Morse (*L. odoratus*) Spencer **F:** Burpee Seeds cat. 1937. **R:** Ferry Morse Seed Co. **I:** 1930/1937. **H:** T. **L:** U. **N:** P. **P:** S. **C:** crimson rose. **S:** winter.

'**Andrea Robertson**' (*L. odoratus*) Spencer **F:** Brackley cat. 1999/2000. **R:** Brackley. **I:** 2000. **D:** see Cultivars chapter.

'**Andrew Cavendish**' (*L. odoratus*) Spencer **F:** *NSPS Annual* 2006: 135. **R:** Hubbuck / R. Parsons. **I:** 2007. **D:** see Cultivars chapter.

'**Angel Kiss**' (*L. odoratus*) Spencer **F:** n/k. **R:** Nozaki. **I:** n/k. **D:** see Cultivars chapter.

'**Angela Ann**' (*L. odoratus*) Spencer **F:** *NSPS Annual* 1985: 30. **R:** Albutt / E.W. King & Co. **I:** 1987. **H:** T. **L:** U. **N:** P. **P:** S. **C:** warm rose pink, w.g. **S:** summer.

'**Angel's Blush**' (*L. odoratus*) Spencer **F:** Samuel Dobie & Sons Ltd cat. 2005. **R:** Mr Fothergills Seeds Ltd. **I:** before 1999. **H:** SD. **L:** M. **N:** P. **P:** S. **C:** rose pink, w.g. **S:** spring.

'Anna's Hope' = 'Skywalker'

'**Annie B. Gilroy**' (*L. odoratus*) Grandiflora **F:** *NSPS Annual* 1909: xi ad / H. Eckford cat. 1909. **R:** H. Eckford. **I:** 1907. **H:** T. **L:** U. **N:** P. **P:** S. **C:** deep cerise. **S:** summer.

'Annie B. Gilroy' Grayson (*L. odoratus*) Grandiflora **F:** Grayson cat. autumn 1994. **R:** Grayson. **I:** 1995.

H: T. **L:** U. **N:** P. **P:** S. **C:** carmine / rose pink. **S:** summer.

'**Annie Edith**' (*L. odoratus*) Spencer **F:** McDougall cat. 1998. **R:** McDougall. **I:** post-1984. **H:** T. **L:** U. **N:** P. **P:** S. **C:** lilac. **S:** early spring.

'**Annie Good**' (*L. odoratus*) Spencer **F:** *NSPS Annual* 1979: 88. **R:** Tasker. **I:** 1983. **H:** T. **L:** U. **N:** P. **P:** S. **C:** magenta. **S:** summer.

'**Annie Wilson**' (*L. odoratus*) Spencer **F:** McDougall cat. 2011. **R:** McDougall. **I:** n/k. **H:** T. **L:** U. **N:** P. **P:** S. **C:** soft mauve. **S:** winter.

'**Anniversary**' (*L. odoratus*) Spencer **F:** Marchant cat. 1986. **R:** Truslove / Marchant. **I:** 1986. **D:** see Cultivars chapter.

'**Anthea Turner**' (*L. odoratus*) Spencer **F:** Thompson & Morgan cat. 1998. **R:** Beane / Thompson & Morgan. **I:** 1995. **H:** T. **L:** U. **N:** P. **P:** S. **C:** salmon pink, c.g. **S:** summer.

'**Aoraki**' (*L. odoratus*) Spencer **F:** n/k. **R:** Hammett. **I:** 2017. **H:** T. **L:** U. **N:** P. **P:** S. **C:** white. **S:** early spring.

'**Aphrodite**' (*L. odoratus*) Spencer **RHS:** AGM (H3) 2012. **F:** Unwins Seeds cat. 2011. **R:** Unwins Seeds. **I:** 2011. **D:** see Cultivars chapter.

''**Appeal**' (*L. odoratus*) Spencer **F:** Sewell cat. 1998/99. **R:** Sewell. **I:** 1999. **H:** T. **L:** U. **N:** P. **P:** S. **C:** cerise rose. **S:** summer.

'**Apple Blossom**' (*L. odoratus*) Grandiflora **F:** R.D. (1887). **R:** H. Eckford. **I:** 1888. **H:** T. **L:** U. **N:** P. **P:** S. **C:** rose pink / pale pink, w.g. **S:** summer.

'Apple Blossom' Beane (*L. odoratus*) Spencer **F:** Thompson & Morgan cat. 2002. **R:** Beane / Thompson & Morgan. **I:** 2002. **D:** see Cultivars chapter.

'**Appleblossom**' (*L. latifolius*) **F:** Grayson cat. 1993. **R:** Grayson. **I:** 1993. **H:** T. **L:** U. **N:** P. **P:** S. **C:** pale pink. **S:** summer.

'**Apricot Queen**' (*L. odoratus*) Spencer **F:** *NSPS Annual* 1968: 55. **R:** E.W. King & Co. **I:** 1973. **D:** see Cultivars chapter.

'**Apricot Sprite**' (*L. odoratus*) Spencer **F:** Bailey cat. 1981/82. **R:** Bailey. **I:** 1980. **D:** see Cultivars chapter.

'April in Paris' = 'High Scent'

'**April Louise**' (*L. odoratus*) Spencer **F:** *NSPS Annual* 2006: 56. **R:** Kerton Sweet Peas. **I:** 2007. **H:** T. **L:** U. **N:** P. **P:** S. **C:** crimson. **S:** summer.

'**Aquarius**' (*L. odoratus*) Spencer **F:** E.W. King & Co. cat. autumn 1999. **R:** J.D. Place / E.W. King & Co.

I: 1999. **D:** see Cultivars chapter.

'Aquarius' Place 2001 (*L. odoratus*) Spencer
F: Unwins Seeds cat. autumn 2000. **R:** J.D. Place /
Unwins Seeds. **I:** 2001. **H:** T. **L:** U. **N:** P. **P:** S. **C:** blue
stripe, w.g. **S:** summer.

'**Aries**' (*L. odoratus*) Spencer   **F:** E.W. King & Co. cat.
autumn 1999. **R:** J.D. Place / E.W. King & Co. **I:** 1999.
D: see Cultivars chapter.

'**Ascot**' (*L. odoratus*) Spencer   **F:** H. Eckford cat. 1932.
R: Thomas Cullen & Sons. **I:** n/k. **H:** T. **L:** U. **N:** M. **P:** S.
C: rose pink, w.g. **S:** summer.

'Ascot' Unwins (*L. odoratus*) Spencer   **F:** Unwins
Seeds cat. autumn 1980. **R:** Unwins Seeds. **I:** 1981.
D: see Cultivars chapter.

'**Astrid**' (*L. odoratus*) Spencer   **F:** E.W. King & Co. cat.
1955/56. **R:** Ferry Morse Seed Co. **I:** 1955. **H:** T. **L:** U.
N: M. **P:** S. **C:** lavender. **S:** late spring.

'Astrid' Parsons (*L. odoratus*) Grandiflora
F: R. Parsons cat. 2009/10. **R:** R. Parsons. **I:** 2010.
H: T. **L:** U. **N:** P. **P:** S. **C:** lavender. **S:** late spring.

'**Astronaut**' (*L. odoratus*) Spencer   **RHS:** AM 1989.
F: *NSPS Annual* 1990: 16. **R:** Albutt. **I:** n/k. **H:** T. **L:** M.
N: P. **P:** S. **C:** sky blue. **S:** summer.

'**Astronaut Lavender**' (*L. odoratus*) Spencer
F: R. Parsons cat. 2016. **R:** R. Parsons. **I:** 2016. **D:** see
Cultivars chapter.

Astronaut Mixed (*L. odoratus*) Spencer   **F:** Thompson
& Morgan cat. 2002. **R:** Albutt / Thompson &
Morgan. **I:** 2002. **H:** T. **L:** M. **N:** P. **P:** S. **C:** mixed
colours. **S:** summer.

'**Astronaut White**' (*L. odoratus*) Spencer
F: R. Parsons cat. 2016. **R:** R. Parsons. **I:** 2016. **D:** see
Cultivars chapter.

'**Atlantis**' (*L. odoratus*) Spencer   **F:** *NSPS Annual*
2002: 33. **R:** Beane / Matthewman. **I:** 2008. **A:** This
name, then agreed by the raiser, was published in
2002 following an award in 2001 at an RHS trial. It
was introduced as 'Betty Maiden' in Matthewman's
2007–8 catalogue. **D:** see Cultivars chapter.

'**Audrey Kirkman**' (*L. odoratus*) Spencer
F: R. Parsons cat. 2011/12. **R:** R. Parsons. **I:** 2012.
D: see Cultivars chapter.

'**Aunt Jane**' (*L. odoratus*) Spencer   **F:** *NSPS Annual*
1998: 57. **R:** Matthewman. **I:** 2000. **D:** see Cultivars
chapter.

'**Aurora Borealis**' (*L. odoratus*) Spencer   **F:** *NSPS
Catalogue of Variety Names* 1912: 4. **R:** L Smith.

I: n/k. **H:** T. **L:** U. **N:** P. **P:** S. **C:** brown rose flush on
blue. **S:** summer.

'Aurora Borealis' Place (*L. odoratus*) Spencer
RHS: AGM (H3) 2007. **F:** *NSPS Annual* 2007: 63.
R: J.D. Place / R. Parsons. **I:** 2017. **D:** see Cultivars
chapter.

'**Azureus**' (*L. sativus*)   **A:** Sometimes recognised as
f. *azureus*. **D:** see Cultivars chapter.

'**Baby's Blush**' (*L. odoratus*) Grandiflora   **F:** R. Parsons
cat. 2013/14. **R:** R. Parsons. **I:** 2014. **D:** see Cultivars
chapter.

'**Baerbel Mac**' (*L. odoratus*) Spencer   **F:** n/k.
R: McDougall. **I:** 1990s. **H:** T. **L:** U. **N:** P. **P:** D.
C: maroon / mauve flake, w.g. **S:** winter.

'**Balcony Bride**' (*L. odoratus*) Spencer   **F:** Plants of
Distinction cat. 1998. **R:** Plants of Distinction.
I: 1998. **D:** see Cultivars chapter.

'**Ballerina Blue**' (*L. odoratus*) Spencer   **RHS:** AM
(after trial) 2003, AGM (H3) 2003. **F:** *NSPS Annual*
2004: 56. **R:** Welch / Thompson & Morgan. **I:** 2011.
D: see Cultivars chapter.

'**Balmoral**' (*L. odoratus*) Spencer   **F:** Carters Tested
Seeds cat. 1936. **R:** Carters Tested Seeds. **I:** 1936. **H:** T.
L: U. **N:** P. **P:** S. **C:** salmon-orange. **S:** summer.

'Balmoral' Brackley (*L. odoratus*) Spencer
F: Brackley cat. 1997. **R:** Brackley. **I:** 1994. **D:** see
Cultivars chapter.

'**Band Aid**' (*L. odoratus*) Spencer   **F:** Unwins Seeds
cat. autumn 1986. **R:** Harriss / Unwins Seeds. **I:** 1987.
H: T. **L:** U. **N:** P. **P:** S. **C:** salmon pink, c.g. **S:** summer.

'**Banty**' (*L. odoratus*) Spencer   **F:** *NSPS Annual* 2002:
33. **R:** Leese / Eagle Sweet Peas. **I:** 2008. **D:** see
Cultivars chapter.

'**Baronscourt**' (*L. odoratus*) Spencer   **F:** Kerton Sweet
Peas cat. 1999. **R:** Harrod/Kerton Sweet Peas. **I:** 1999.
D: see Cultivars chapter.

'**Barry Dare**' (*L. odoratus*) Spencer   **F:** Unwins Seeds
cat. autumn 1996. **R:** Unwins Seeds. **I:** 1997. **D:** see
Cultivars chapter.

'**Bateman Scarlet**' (*L. odoratus*) Spencer   **F:** n/k.
R: Bateman. **I:** before 1984. **H:** T. **L:** U. **N:** P. **P:** S.
C: scarlet. **S:** early spring.

'Bath's Crimson'   = 'Queen Alexandra'

'**Batheaston**' (*L. odoratus*) Spencer   **F:** *NSPS Annual*
1983: 5. **R:** C.F. James / Marchant. **I:** 1983. **D:** see
Cultivars chapter.

'**Beaujolais**' (*L. odoratus*) Spencer   **F:** *NSPS Annual*

1968: 55. **R:** Suttons. **I:** 1972. **D:** see Cultivars chapter.

'Benishikibu' (*L. odoratus*) Spencer   **F:** n/k. **R:** Miyazaki prefecture. **I:** 2010. **A:** Name first appeared on the Japanese Plant Variety Protection website (seen 22 Apr 2009). **H:** T. **L:** U. **N:** M. **P:** S. **C:** maroon / lavender. **S:** winter.

'Benjamin Townsend' (*L. odoratus*) Grandiflora   **F:** Grayson cat. 1997/98. **R:** Grayson. **I:** 1998. **H:** T. **L:** U. **N:** P. **P:** S. **C:** white. **S:** summer.

'Bert Boucher' (*L. odoratus*) Spencer   **F:** Kerton Sweet Peas cat. 1995. **R:** K Brewer / Kerton Sweet Peas. **I:** 1996. **H:** T. **L:** U. **N:** P. **P:** S. **C:** white. **S:** summer.

'Beth Chatto' (*L. odoratus*) Spencer   **F:** *NSPS Annual* 2009: 162. **R:** Matthewman. **I:** 2009. **D:** see Cultivars chapter.

'Betsy Ross' Burpee 1933 (*L. odoratus*) Spencer   **F:** Burpee Seeds cat. 1932. **R:** Burpee Seeds. **I:** 1933. **H:** T. **L:** U. **N:** P. **P:** S. **C:** rose pink, c.g. **S:** winter.

'Betty Maiden'   = 'Atlantis'

'Beverley Kaye' (*L. odoratus*) Spencer   **F:** *Australian Garden Lover* (1963). **R:** Harkness. **I:** before 1962. **D:** see Cultivars chapter.

'Big Blue' (*L. odoratus*) Spencer   **F:** Somerset cat. 2012. **R:** Hammett. **I:** 2009. **D:** see Cultivars chapter.

'Bill's Choice' (*L. odoratus*) Spencer   **F:** *NSPS Annual* 2007: 154. **R:** Truslove / R. Parsons. **I:** 2008. **D:** see Cultivars chapter.

'Bishop's Pink' (*L. latifolius*)   **F:** Grayson cat. 1997/98. **R:** J. Bishop / Grayson. **I:** 1998. **H:** T. **L:** U. **N:** P. **P:** S. **C:** pale pink. **S:** summer.

'Bix' (*L. odoratus*) Spencer   **F:** n/k. **R:** Hammett. **I:** 2017. **H:** T. **L:** U. **N:** M. **P:** S. **C:** white with pink edge. **S:** summer.

'Black Knight' (*L. odoratus*) Grandiflora   **F:** Joseph Breck & Co. cat. 1899. **R:** H. Eckford. **I:** 1898. **D:** see Cultivars chapter.

'Blackberry' (*L. odoratus*) Grandiflora   **F:** Unwins Seeds cat. autumn 2008. **R:** Unwins Seeds. **I:** 2009. **H:** T. **L:** U. **N:** P. **P:** S. **C:** dark maroon. **S:** summer.

'Blackberry Ice' (*L. odoratus*) Grandiflora   **F:** E.W. King & Co. cat. autumn 2001. **R:** E.W. King & Co. **I:** 2002. **H:** T. **L:** U. **N:** P. **P:** S. **C:** mid blue. **S:** summer.

'Blackcurrant Mousse' (*L. odoratus*) Spencer   **F:** E.W. King & Co. cat. autumn 1999. **R:** E.W. King & Co. **I:** 1999. **H:** T. **L:** U. **N:** P. **P:** S. **C:** mauve. **S:** summer.

'Blanche Ferry' (*L. odoratus*) Grandiflora   **F:** Benary cat 1893. **R:** DM Ferry & Co. **I:** 1889. **H:** T. **L:** U. **N:** P. **P:** S. **C:** rose pink / pale pink. **S:** spring.

'Blanche Ferry' Bailey (*L. odoratus*) Grandiflora   **F:** *NSPS Annual* 1990: 60. **R:** Bailey. **I:** 1990. **H:** T. **L:** U. **N:** P. **P:** S. **C:** rose pink / pale pink. **S:** summer.

'Blanche Ferry' Waller-Franklin   = 'Early Blanche Ferry Spencer'

'Blue Danube' (*L. odoratus*) Spencer   **F:** E.W. King & Co. cat. 1951/52. **R:** Ryders Seeds. **I:** 1937. **H:** T. **L:** U. **N:** P. **P:** S. **C:** rich blue. **S:** summer.

'Blue Danube' Macdonald (*L. odoratus*) Spencer   **F:** n/k. **R:** Macdonald. **I:** before 1942. **H:** T. **L:** U. **N:** P. **P:** S. **C:** n/k. **S:** winter.

'Blue Danube' Morris (*L. odoratus*) Spencer   **F:** Unwins Seeds cat. autumn 1980. **R:** Morris / Unwins Seeds. **I:** 1981. **D:** see Cultivars chapter.

'Blue Ripple' (*L. odoratus*) Spencer   **F:** Thompson & Morgan cat. 1989. **R:** W. Thomas / Thompson & Morgan. **I:** 1989. **H:** T. **L:** U. **N:** P. **P:** S. **C:** blue stripe, w.g. **S:** summer.

'Blue Ripple' Unwins (*L. odoratus*) Spencer   **F:** Unwins Seeds cat. autumn 2012. **R:** Unwins Seeds. **I:** 2012. **D:** see Cultivars chapter.

'Blue Shift' (*L. odoratus*) Spencer   **F:** Somerset cat. 2012. **R:** Hammett / Thompson & Morgan. **I:** 2013. **D:** see Cultivars chapter.

'Blue Stripe' (*L. sativus*)   **F:** Grayson cat. 1998/99. **R:** Grayson. **I:** 1999. **D:** see Cultivars chapter.

'Blue Vein' (*L. odoratus*) Spencer   **F:** *NSPS Annual* 1965: 33. **R:** Carters Tested Seeds. **I:** n/k. **H:** T. **L:** U. **N:** P. **P:** S. **C:** blue stripe, w.g. **S:** summer.

'Blue Vein' Hammett (*L. odoratus*) Spencer   **F:** n/k. **R:** Hammett / Denny. **I:** 2008. **A:** Name first appeared on the Seedngrow website (seen 19 Feb 2009). **D:** see Cultivars chapter.

'Blue Velvet' (*L. odoratus*) Spencer   **F:** Unwins Seeds cat. autumn 1971. **R:** Unwins Seeds. **I:** 1972. **H:** T. **L:** U. **N:** P. **P:** S. **C:** dark blue. **S:** summer.

'Blue Wonder' (*L. odoratus*) Spencer   **F:** A. Zvolanek & Sons cat. 1922/23. **R:** A. Zvolanek & Sons. **I:** 1923. **D:** see Cultivars chapter.

'Blush Strokes' (*L. odoratus*) Spencer   **F:** Unwins Seeds cat. autumn 2003. **R:** Unwins Seeds. **I:** 2004. **H:** T. **L:** U. **N:** P. **P:** S. **C:** orange flake, c.g. **S:** summer.

'Blushing Bride' (*L. odoratus*) Grandiflora   **F:** Joseph Breck & Co. cat. 1896, Sunset Seed and Plant Co. cat. 1896. **R:** Joseph Breck & Co. **I:** 1891. **H:** T. **L:** U. **N:** P.

P: S. **C:** pink / white. **S:** summer.

'Blushing Bride' Metcalf (*L. latifolius*) **F:** n/k. **R:** n/k. **I:** R.J. Metcalf. **H:** T. **L:** U. **N:** M. **P:** S. **C:** pale pink. **S:** summer.

'Blushing Bride' Albutt (*L. odoratus*) Spencer **F:** E.W. King & Co. cat. autumn 1989. **R:** Albutt / E.W. King & Co. **I:** 1989. **H:** T. **L:** U. **N:** P. **P:** S. **C:** rose pink, c.g. **S:** summer.

'Bobby Bolton' (*L. odoratus*) Spencer **F:** Robert Bolton & Son cat. 2002. **R:** Robert Bolton & Son. **I:** 2002. **H:** T. **L:** U. **N:** P. **P:** S. **C:** cerise. **S:** summer.

'Bobby Chisholm' (*L. odoratus*) Spencer **F:** Kerton Sweet Peas cat. 2011. **R:** Chisholm / Kerton Sweet Peas. **I:** 2011. **D:** see Cultivars chapter.

'Bobby's Girl' (*L. odoratus*) Spencer **RHS:** AGM (H3) 2000. **F:** Robert Bolton & Son cat. 1999. **R:** Robert Bolton & Son. **I:** 2000. **D:** see Cultivars chapter.

'Border Beauty' (*L. odoratus*) Spencer **F:** R. Parsons cat. 2010/11. **R:** R. Parsons. **I:** 2011. **D:** see Cultivars chapter.

'Borderline' (*L. odoratus*) Spencer **F:** *NSPS Annual* 1995: 76. **R:** Albutt / Thompson & Morgan. **I:** 2004. **H:** T. **L:** U. **N:** P. **P:** S. **C:** magenta stripe, w.g. **S:** summer.

'Bounce Light Salmon' (*L. odoratus*) Spencer **F:** Hem Zaden cat. 2011/12. **R:** Hem Zaden. **I:** 2012. **H:** SD. **L:** U. **N:** P. **P:** S. **C:** light salmon. **S:** winter.

'Bounce Mid Blue' (*L. odoratus*) Semi-grandiflora **RHS:** AGM (H3) 2014. **F:** Hem Zaden cat. 2011/12. **R:** Hem Zaden. **I:** 2012. **D:** see Cultivars chapter.

'Bounce Navy Blue' (*L. odoratus*) Spencer **RHS:** AGM (H3) 2014. **F:** Hem Zaden cat. 2011/12. **R:** Hem Zaden. **I:** 2012. **D:** see Cultivars chapter.

'Bouquet' (*L. odoratus*) Grandiflora **F:** *NSPS Catalogue of Variety Names* 1912: 5. **R:** Deal. **I:** 1911. **H:** T. **L:** U. **N:** P. **P:** S. **C:** rosy salmon flake, c.g. **S:** summer.

'Bouquet' n/k (*L. odoratus*) Spencer **F:** Suttons cat. 1939. **R:** n/k. **I:** 1939. **H:** T. **L:** U. **N:** P. **P:** S. **C:** salmon rose, c.g. **S:** summer.

'Bouquet' Unwins (*L. odoratus*) Spencer **F:** *NSPS Annual* 1960: 83. **R:** Unwins Seeds. **I:** 1962. **H:** T. **L:** U. **N:** P. **P:** S. **C:** mauve. **S:** summer.

'Bouquet Crimson' (*L. odoratus*) Spencer **F:** R. Parsons cat. 2012/13. **R:** Denholm Seeds. **I:** 1998. **D:** see Cultivars chapter.

'Bouquet Lavender' (*L. odoratus*) Spencer **F:** E.W.

King & Co. cat. autumn 1997. **R:** Denholm Seeds. **I:** 1998. **D:** see Cultivars chapter.

'Bouquet Mauve' (*L. odoratus*) Spencer **F:** n/k. **R:** Denholm Seeds. **I:** 1998. **H:** T. **L:** U. **N:** M. **P:** S. **C:** mauve. **S:** summer.

'Bouquet Mid Blue' (*L. odoratus*) Spencer **F:** R. Parsons cat. 2012/13. **R:** Denholm Seeds. **I:** 1998. **D:** see Cultivars chapter.

'Bouquet Navy' (*L. odoratus*) Spencer **F:** E.W. King & Co. cat. autumn 1997. **R:** Denholm Seeds. **I:** 1998. **H:** T. **L:** U. **N:** M. **P:** S. **C:** navy blue. **S:** summer.

'Bouquet Pink' (*L. odoratus*) Spencer **F:** E.W. King & Co. cat. autumn 1997. **R:** Denholm Seeds. **I:** 1998. **D:** see Cultivars chapter.

'Bouquet Purple' (*L. odoratus*) Spencer **F:** n/k. **R:** Denholm Seeds. **I:** 1998. **H:** T. **L:** U. **N:** M. **P:** S. **C:** purple. **S:** summer.

'Bouquet Rose' (*L. odoratus*) Spencer **F:** E.W. King & Co. cat. autumn 1997. **R:** Denholm Seeds. **I:** 1998. **H:** T. **L:** U. **N:** M. **P:** S. **C:** rose pink, w.g. **S:** early spring.

'Bouquet Salmon Cream Pink' (*L. odoratus*) Spencer **F:** E.W. King & Co. cat. autumn 1997. **R:** Denholm Seeds. **I:** 1998. **H:** T. **L:** U. **N:** M. **P:** S. **C:** salmon cream pink. **S:** summer.

'Bouquet Salmon Pink' (*L. odoratus*) Spencer **F:** n/k. **R:** Denholm Seeds. **I:** 1998. **H:** T. **L:** U. **N:** M. **P:** S. **C:** salmon pink, c.g. **S:** summer.

'Bouquet Scarlet' (*L. odoratus*) Spencer **F:** E.W. King & Co. cat. autumn 1997. **R:** Denholm Seeds. **I:** 1998. **D:** see Cultivars chapter.

Bouquet Series (*L. odoratus*) Spencer **R:** Denholm Seeds. **I:** 1998. **D:** Summer-flowering, semi-multiflora, Spencer cultivars, all with a Bouquet prefix.

'Bouquet Violet' (*L. odoratus*) Spencer **F:** R. Parsons cat. 2012/13. **R:** R. Parsons. **I:** 2013. **D:** see Cultivars chapter.

'Bouquet White' (*L. odoratus*) Spencer **F:** E.W. King & Co. cat. autumn 1997. **R:** Denholm Seeds. **I:** 1998. **D:** see Cultivars chapter.

'Brad's Cream' (*L. odoratus*) Spencer **F:** McDougall cat. 2011. **R:** Brad McDougall. **I:** late 1990s. **H:** T. **L:** U. **N:** P. **P:** S. **C:** pale cream. **S:** winter.

'Bramdean' (*L. odoratus*) Grandiflora **RHS:** AGM (H3) 2008. **F:** R. Parsons cat. 2006/07. **R:** Wakefield / R. Parsons. **I:** 2007. **D:** see Cultivars chapter.

'Brenda Bridger' (*L. odoratus*) Spencer **F:** *NSPS*

Annual 1983: 81. **R**: Hammett / Thompson & Morgan. **I**: 1987. **D**: see Cultivars chapter.

'Brian Clough' (*L. odoratus*) Spencer   **F**: Unwins Seeds cat. autumn 1981. **R**: B.R. Jones / Unwins Seeds. **I**: 1982. **D**: see Cultivars chapter.

'Brian Haynes' (*L. odoratus*) Spencer   **RHS**: AM 2002. **F**: *NSPS Annual* 2003: 42. **R**: Beane / E.W. King & Co. **I**: 2007. **D**: see Cultivars chapter.

'Bridget McAleer' (*L. odoratus*) Spencer   **F**: Cooltonagh cat. 2012/13. **R**: McAleer / Harrod. **I**: 2013. **D**: see Cultivars chapter.

'Brightness' (*L. odoratus*) Spencer   **F**: Suttons cat. 1939. **R**: Suttons. **I**: 1927. **H**: T. **L**: U. **N**: P. **P**: S. **C**: cerise flushed orange scarlet. **S**: summer.

'Brightness' n/k (*L. odoratus*) Spencer   **F**: *Australian Garden Lover* (1935). **R**: n/k. **I**: n/k. **H**: T. **L**: U. **N**: P. **P**: n/k. **C**: crimson. **S**: winter.

'Brightness' Ferry Morse (*L. odoratus*) Spencer   **F**: G. Stark & Son cat. 1950/51. **R**: Ferry Morse Seed Co. **I**: 1947. **H**: T. **L**: U. **N**: P. **P**: S. **C**: salmon, c.g. **S**: summer.

'Bristol' (*L. odoratus*) Spencer   **RHS**: AM 1993, AGM (H3) 1999. **F**: Kerton Sweet Peas cat. 1994. **R**: Kerton Sweet Peas. **I**: 1994. **D**: see Cultivars chapter.

'Bristol Cream' (*L. odoratus*) Spencer   **RHS**: AM 1989. **F**: E.W. King & Co. cat. autumn 1989. **R**: Albutt / E.W. King & Co. **I**: 1990. **D**: see Cultivars chapter.

'Bronwyn Dorothy' (*L. odoratus*) Spencer   **F**: McDougall cat. 1998. **R**: McDougall. **I**: 1980s. **H**: T. **L**: U. **N**: P. **P**: S. **C**: cerise. **S**: early spring.

'Brook Hall' (*L. odoratus*) Spencer   **RHS**: AGM (H3) 2002. **F**: *NSPS Annual* 2003: 41. **R**: Harrod / E.W. King & Co. **I**: 2006. **D**: see Cultivars chapter.

'Buccaneer' (*L. odoratus*) Spencer   **F**: *NSPS Annual* 1986: 79. **R**: Albutt / E.W. King & Co. **I**: 1987. **D**: see Cultivars chapter.

'Burlesque' (*L. odoratus*) Spencer   **F**: Somerset cat. 2013/14. **R**: Hammett. **I**: 2009. **D**: see Cultivars chapter.

'Burnished Bronze' (*L. odoratus*) Spencer   **F**: Kerton Sweet Peas cat. 1994. **R**: Harrod / Kerton Sweet Peas. **I**: 1994. **D**: see Cultivars chapter.

'Busby'   = 'The Busby Pea'

'Bush Blanche Ferry' (*L. odoratus*) Grandiflora   **F**: Vaughan Seed Store cat. 1903. **R**: n/k. **I**: 1903. **H**: SD. **L**: U. **N**: P. **P**: S. **C**: pink /white. **S**: summer.

'Butterfly' (*L. odoratus*) Grandiflora   **F**: Peter Henderson & Co. cat. 1882. **R**: Suttons. **I**: 1878. **D**: Flowers hooded with side notches. **H**: T. **L**: U. **N**: P. **P**: S. **C**: mauve marble, w.g. **S**: summer.

'Butterfly' Smith (*L. odoratus*) Spencer   **F**: Cuthbertson (1916). **R**: Smith. **I**: before 1916. **H**: T. **L**: U. **N**: P. **P**: S. **C**: bright blue marble c.g. **S**: summer.

'Butterfly' Simons (*L. odoratus*) Spencer   **F**: n/k. **R**: Simons. **I**: 1957. **H**: T. **L**: U. **N**: P. **P**: S. **C**: deep pink/ cream. **S**: summer.

'Butterfly' Grayson (*L. odoratus*) Grandiflora   **F**: Grayson cat. autumn 1996. **R**: Grayson. **I**: 1997. **H**: T. **L**: U. **N**: P. **P**: S. **C**: white with purple veins. **S**: summer.

Butterfly Hybrids Mixed   = Unwins Stripes Mixed

'Caeruleus' (*L. vernus*)   = *L. vernus*. **A**: This name, along with 'Cyaneus', has traditionally been used for selections with more blue flowers, but propagation from seed has resulted in plants being offered with inconsistent colours.

'Candy' (*L. odoratus*) Spencer   **F**: *NSPS Annual* 1954: 52. **R**: Thomas Cullen & Sons. **I**: 1956. **H**: T. **L**: U. **N**: P. **P**: S. **C**: salmon pink, c.g. **S**: summer.

'Candy' Beane (*L. odoratus*) Spencer   **F**: Unwins Seeds cat. autumn 1990. **R**: Beane / Unwins Seeds. **I**: 1991. **D**: see Cultivars chapter.

'Candy King' (*L. odoratus*) Spencer   **F**: E.W. King & Co. cat. 2014/15. **R**: Brackley / E.W. King & Co. **I**: 2015. **H**: T. **L**: U. **N**: P. **P**: S. **C**: deep pink, w.g. **S**: summer.

'Candyfloss' (*L. odoratus*) Spencer   **F**: R. Parsons cat. 2019/20. **R**: Hammett. **I**: 2018. **A**: Name first appeared on the Hammett website (seen 4 Aug. 2018). **H**: T. **L**: U. **N**: P. **P**: S. **C**: soft orange-pink. **S**: summer.

'Capel Manor' (*L. odoratus*) Spencer   **F**: Mr Fothergills Seeds Ltd cat. 2019. **R**: Seedlynx / Mr Fothergills Seeds Ltd. **I**: 2019. **H**: T. **L**: U. **N**: P. **P**: S. **C**: purple bicolour. **S**: summer.

'Capri' (*L. odoratus*) Spencer   **F**: Ferry Morse Seed Co. cat. 1936, Dobbie & Co. cat. 1936, Carters Tested Seeds cat. 1936. **R**: Ferry Morse Seed Co. **I**: 1936. **H**: T. **L**: U. **N**: P. **P**: S. **C**: lavender blue. **S**: summer.

'Captain of the Blues' (*L. odoratus*) Grandiflora   **F**: R.D. (1893). **R**: H. Eckford. **I**: 1889. **H**: T. **L**: U. **N**: P. **P**: S. **C**: purple blue/pale blue. **S**: summer.

'Captain of the Blues' Grayson (*L. odoratus*) Grandiflora   **F**: Grayson cat. 1992/93. **R**: Grayson. **I**: 1993. **D**: see Cultivars chapter.

'Carlotta' (*L. odoratus*) Spencer **F:** Unwins Seeds cat. 1941. **R:** Carters Tested Seeds. **I:** 1937. **D:** see Cultivars chapter.

'Carmel' (*L. odoratus*) Spencer **F:** n/k. **R:** Macdonald. **I:** 1951. **H:** T. **L:** U. **N:** P. **P:** S. **C:** mid blue. **S:** early.

'Carmel' Ferry Morse (*L. odoratus*) Spencer **F:** *NSPS Annual* 1967: 108. **R:** Ferry Morse Seed Co. **I:** 1967. **D:** see Cultivars chapter.

'Carminette' (*L. odoratus*) Spencer **F:** *NSPS Annual* 1968: ii. **R:** Burpee Seeds. **I:** 1968. **D:** see Cultivars chapter.

Carnival Parade Mixed (*L. odoratus*) Spencer **F:** R. Parsons cat. 2017/18. **R:** R. Parsons. **I:** 2018. **H:** SD. **L:** U. **N:** P. **P:** S. **C:** mixed colours. **S:** summer.

'Carol Klein' (*L. odoratus*) Spencer **F:** *NSPS Annual* 2012: i. **R:** Eagle Sweet Peas. **I:** 2013. **H:** T. **L:** U. **N:** P. **P:** S. **C:** dark mauve. **S:** summer.

'Cascade' (*L. odoratus*) Spencer **F:** Buckman cat. 1940. **R:** William Zvolanek & Co. **I:** n/k. **A:** Pale seeds. **H:** T. **L:** U. **N:** P. **P:** S. **C:** white. **S:** winter.

'Cascade' Cullen (*L. odoratus*) Spencer **F:** *NSPS Annual* 1956: 51. **R:** Thomas Cullen & Sons. **I:** 1957. **A:** Pale seeds. **H:** T. **L:** U. **N:** P. **P:** S. **C:** white. **S:** summer.

'Castle of Mey' (*L. odoratus*) Spencer **F:** Unwins Seeds cat. autumn 2000. **R:** Unwins Seeds. **I:** 2001. **D:** see Cultivars chapter.

'Castlewellan' (*L. odoratus*) Spencer **F:** Cooltonagh cat. 2004/05. **R:** Harrod / Unwins Seeds. **I:** 2005. **D:** see Cultivars chapter.

'Cathy' (*L. odoratus*) Semi-grandiflora **RHS:** AGM (H3) 2002. **F:** Unwins Seeds cat. autumn 2002. **R:** Unwins Seeds. **I:** 2003. **D:** see Cultivars chapter.

'Cathy Wright' (*L. odoratus*) Spencer **F:** Eagle Sweet Peas cat. 1999/2000. **R:** Eagle Sweet Peas. **I:** 2000. **D:** see Cultivars chapter.

'CCC' (*L. odoratus*) Grandiflora **F:** Grayson cat. 1998/99. **R:** Grayson. **I:** 1999. **D:** see Cultivars chapter.

Celeste Series = Solstice Series

'Cerise Carpet' (*L. odoratus*) Grandiflora **F:** *NSPS Annual* 1958: 49. **R:** Ferry Morse Seed Co. **I:** n/k. **D:** see Cultivars chapter.

'Champagne Bubbles' (*L. odoratus*) Spencer **F:** Unwins Seeds cat. autumn 1985. **R:** Unwins Seeds. **I:** 1986. **D:** see Cultivars chapter.

'Chance' (*L. odoratus*) Spencer **F:** R. Parsons cat. 2004/05. **R:** R. Parsons. **I:** 2006. **D:** see Cultivars chapter.

'Charles Unwin' (*L. odoratus*) Grandiflora **F:** Cuthbertson (1916). **R:** Unwins Seeds. **I:** 1907. **H:** T. **L:** U. **N:** P. **P:** S. **C:** cream, hooded. **S:** summer.

'Charles Unwin' Colledge (*L. odoratus*) Spencer **F:** *NSPS Annual* 1984: 69. **R:** Colledge / Unwins Seeds. **I:** 1985. **D:** see Cultivars chapter.

'Charlie Bear' (*L. odoratus*) Spencer **F:** *NSPS Annual* 2016: 64. **R:** Kerton Sweet Peas. **I:** 2015. **D:** see Cultivars chapter.

'Charlie's Angel' (*L. odoratus*) Spencer **RHS:** FCC 1987, AGM (H3) 1993. **F:** *NSPS Annual* 1988: 17. **R:** Hanmer / Unwins Seeds. **I:** 1990. **D:** see Cultivars chapter.

'Charlotte Emma' (*L. odoratus*) Spencer **RHS:** AM 2007. **F:** *NSPS Annual* 2008: 53. **R:** Kerton Sweet Peas. **I:** 2009. **D:** see Cultivars chapter.

'Charlotte Ryley' (*L. odoratus*) Grandiflora **F:** Grayson cat. 1997/98. **R:** Grayson. **I:** 1998. **H:** T. **L:** U. **N:** P. **P:** S. **C:** dark blue. **S:** summer.

'Chatsworth' (*L. odoratus*) Spencer **F:** Thompson & Morgan cat. 1998. **R:** Albutt / Thompson & Morgan. **I:** 1998. **D:** see Cultivars chapter.

'Chelsea' (*L. odoratus*) Spencer **F:** *NSPS Annual* 1922: iii, Elliott cat. 1922. **R:** Robert Bolton & Son. **I:** 1922. **H:** T. **L:** U. **N:** P. **P:** S. **C:** buff salmon. **S:** summer.

'Chelsea' King (*L. odoratus*) Spencer **F:** E.W. King cat. 1938. **R:** n/k. **I:** 1938. **H:** T. **L:** U. **N:** P. **P:** S. **C:** n/k. **S:** summer.

'Chelsea' Parsons (*L. clymenum*) **F:** Grayson cat. autumn 1996. **R:** R. Parsons / Grayson. **I:** 1997. **D:** see Cultivars chapter.

'Chelsea Centenary' (*L. odoratus*) Spencer **F:** Mr Fothergills Seeds Ltd cat. 2013. **R:** Hammett / Mr Fothergills Seeds Ltd. **I:** 2013. **D:** see Cultivars chapter.

'Cherub' (*L. odoratus*) Spencer **F:** *NSPS Annual* 1915: 79. **R:** Malcolm / Burpee Seeds. **I:** 1916. **H:** T. **L:** U. **N:** P. **P:** S. **C:** rose picotee, c.g. **S:** summer.

'Cherub' Carters (*L. odoratus*) Spencer **F:** *NSPS Annual* 1960: viii. **R:** Carters Tested Seeds. **I:** 1959. **H:** T. **L:** U. **N:** P. **P:** S. **C:** clear pink c.g. **S:** summer.

'Cherub Cherry' (*L. odoratus*) Grandiflora **F:** Owl's Acre Sweet Peas cat. 2004/05. **R:** Owl's Acre Sweet Peas. **I:** 2005. **H:** SD. **L:** U. **N:** P. **P:** S. **C:** cerise. **S:** summer.

'Cherub Crimson' (*L. odoratus*) Grandiflora
RHS: AGM (H3) 2010. **F:** Owl's Acre Sweet Peas cat.
2004/05. **R:** Owl's Acre Sweet Peas. **I:** 2005. **H:** SD.
L: U. **N:** P. **P:** S. **C:** crimson. **S:** summer.

'Cherub Lady T' (*L. odoratus*) Grandiflora   **RHS:** AGM
(H3) 2011. **F:** Owl's Acre Sweet Peas cat. 2008/09.
R: Owl's Acre Sweet Peas. **I:** 2008. **D:** see Cultivars
chapter.

'Cherub Lavender' (*L. odoratus*) Grandiflora
F: Owl's Acre Sweet Peas cat. 2004/05. **R:** Owl's Acre
Sweet Peas. **I:** 2005. **H:** SD. **L:** U. **N:** P. **P:** S. **C:** lavender.
S: summer.

'Cherub Light Purple' (*L. odoratus*) Grandiflora
F: Owl's Acre Sweet Peas cat. 2004/05. **R:** Owl's Acre
Sweet Peas. **I:** 2005. **H:** SD. **L:** U. **N:** P. **P:** S. **C:** purple.
S: summer.

'Cherub Matty' (*L. odoratus*) Grandiflora   **F:** Owl's
Acre Sweet Peas cat. 2008/09. **R:** Owl's Acre Sweet
Peas. **I:** 2008. **H:** SD. **L:** U. **N:** P. **P:** S. **C:** maroon/
purple. **S:** summer.

'Cherub Northern Lights' (*L. odoratus*) Grandiflora
RHS: AGM (H3) 2014. **F:** *NSPS Annual* 2013: 89.
R: Owl's Acre Sweet Peas. **I:** 2012. **D:** see Cultivars
chapter.

'Cherub Penny Black' (*L. odoratus*) Grandiflora
F: Owl's Acre Sweet Peas cat. 2008/09. **R:** Owl's Acre
Sweet Peas. **I:** 2008. **D:** see Cultivars chapter.

'Cherub Pink' (*L. odoratus*) Grandiflora   **F:** Owl's
Acre Sweet Peas cat. 2004/05. **R:** Owl's Acre Sweet
Peas. **I:** 2005. **D:** see Cultivars chapter.

'Cherub Pink Bicolour' (*L. odoratus*) Grandiflora
F: Owl's Acre Sweet Peas cat. 2004/05. **R:** Owl's Acre
Sweet Peas. **I:** 2005. **H:** SD. **L:** U. **N:** P. **P:** S. **C:** pink
bicolour. **S:** summer.

'Cherub Royal Mauve' (*L. odoratus*) Grandiflora
F: Owl's Acre Sweet Peas cat. 2004/05. **R:** Owl's Acre
Sweet Peas. **I:** 2005. **H:** SD. **L:** U. **N:** P. **P:** S. **C:** mauve.
S: summer.

'Cherub Salmon' (*L. odoratus*) Grandiflora   **F:** Owl's
Acre Sweet Peas cat. 2004/05. **R:** Owl's Acre Sweet
Peas. **I:** 2005. **H:** SD. **L:** U. **N:** P. **P:** S. **C:** salmon pink
w.g. **S:** summer.

'Cherub Scarlet Stripe' (*L. odoratus*) Grandiflora
F: Owl's Acre Sweet Peas cat. 2004/05. **R:** Owl's Acre
Sweet Peas. **I:** 2005. **H:** SD. **L:** U. **N:** P. **P:** S. **C:** scarlet
stripe, w.g. **S:** summer.

Cherub Series (*L. odoratus*) Grandiflora   **R:** Owl's

Acre Sweet Peas. **D:** Dwarf Grandiflora cultivars that
are procumbent and trailing.

'Cherub White' (*L. odoratus*) Grandiflora   **F:** Owl's
Acre Sweet Peas cat. 2004/05. **R:** Owl's Acre Sweet
Peas. **I:** 2005. **H:** SD. **L:** U. **N:** P. **P:** S. **C:** white.
S: summer.

'Cheryl Rainey' (*L. odoratus*) Spencer   **F:** R. Parsons
cat. 2018/19. **R:** Harrod / R. Parsons. **I:** 2019. **D:** see
Cultivars chapter.

'Cheshire Dark Blue' (*L. odoratus*) Grandiflora
F: Turral cat. 1964. **R:** Synge. **I:** before 1964. **H:** T. **L:** U.
N: P. **P:** S. **C:** mauve blue. **S:** summer.

'Chigasaki Deep Pink' (*L. odoratus*) Spencer   **F:** *NSPS
Annual* 2006: 63. **R:** Chigasaki. **I:** before 1984. **H:** T.
L: U. **N:** M. **P:** S. **C:** magenta. **S:** winter.

'Chigasaki no. 11' (*L. odoratus*) Spencer   **F:** *NSPS
Annual* 2006: 62. **R:** Chigasaki. **I:** before 1984. **H:** T.
L: U. **N:** M. **P:** S. **C:** magenta w.g. **S:** early spring.

'Choc Stripe' (*L. odoratus*) Spencer   **F:** Kerton Sweet
Peas cat. 2017. **R:** Kerton Sweet Peas. **I:** 2015. **D:** see
Cultivars chapter.

'Chocolate Flake' (*L. odoratus*) Spencer   **F:** *NSPS
Classification List* 2013. **R:** Hammett. **I:** 2012. **D:** see
Cultivars chapter.

'Chris Harrod' (*L. odoratus*) Spencer   **RHS:** AGM (H3)
2006. **F:** *NSPS Annual* 2006: 54. **R:** Harrod / Kerton
Sweet Peas. **I:** 2008. **D:** see Cultivars chapter.

'Cilla' (*L. odoratus*) Spencer   **F:** R. Parsons cat.
2019/20. **R:** K. Bell / R. Parsons. **I:** 2020. **H:** T. **L:** U.
N: P. **P:** S. **C:** pale blue flush, w.g. **S:** summer.

'Cirrus'   = 'Queen of Hearts'

'Claire Elizabeth' (*L. odoratus*) Spencer   **F:** *NSPS
Annual* 1986: 35. **R:** RA Hunt / Robert Bolton & Son.
I: 1988. **H:** T. **L:** U. **N:** P. **P:** S. **C:** pink picotee, w.g.
S: summer.

'Clementine Kiss' (*L. odoratus*) Spencer   **F:** *NSPS
Annual* 2011: 159. **R:** Matthewman. **I:** 2012. **H:** T. **L:** U.
N: P. **P:** S. **C:** orange. **S:** summer.

'Clotted Cream' (*L. odoratus*) Spencer   **F:** *NSPS
Annual* 1965: vi. **R:** Carters Tested Seeds. **I:** 1965.
H: T. **L:** U. **N:** P. **P:** S. **C:** cream. **S:** summer.

'Clotted Cream' K. Brewer (*L. odoratus*) Spencer
F: *NSPS Annual* 2014: 193. **R:** K. Brewer /
Matthewman. **I:** 2015. **D:** see Cultivars chapter.

'Cocktail' (*L. odoratus*) Spencer   **F:** n/k. **R:** Hammett.
I: n/k. **D:** see Cultivars chapter

'Coconut Ice' (*L. odoratus*) Spencer   **F:** Hem Zaden

cat. 2011/12. **R:** n/k. **I:** 2012. **H:** T. **L:** U. **N:** P. **P:** S. **C:** pink flake, w.g. **S:** summer.

'Cold Steel' (*L. odoratus*) Spencer **F:** *NSPS Classification List* 2019. **R:** Hammett. **I:** 2019. **H:** T. **L:** U. **N:** P. **P:** S. **C:** blue / white. **S:** summer.

'Comet' (*L. odoratus*) Spencer **F:** Cuthbertson (1916). **R:** Hemus. **I:** 1912. **H:** T. **L:** U. **N:** P. **P:** S. **C:** rose pink, c.g. **S:** summer.

'Comet' Zvolanek (*L. odoratus*) Spencer **F:** A. Zvolanek & Sons cat. 1922/23. **R:** A. Zvolanek & Sons. **I:** 1923. **H:** T. **L:** U. **N:** P. **P:** S. **C:** salmon, c.g. **S:** winter.

'Comet' Walker (*L. odoratus*) Spencer **F:** SNSPCRS 1960/61. **R:** W. Walker / Dobbie & Co. **I:** 1964. **H:** T. **L:** U. **N:** P. **P:** S. **C:** carmine. **S:** summer.

'Comet' Unwins (*L. odoratus*) Spencer **F:** Unwins Seeds cat. autumn 1997. **R:** Unwins Seeds. **I:** 1998. **H:** T. **L:** U. **N:** P. **P:** S. **C:** cerise-pink stripe. **S:** summer.

'Constance Hinton' (*L. odoratus*) Spencer **F:** E.W. King & Co. cat. 1914. **R:** H.T. Hinton / Wheeler. **I:** 1914. **A:** dark seeds. **H:** T. **L:** U. **N:** P. **P:** S. **C:** white. **S:** summer.

Continental Mixed (*L. odoratus*) Spencer **F:** E.W. King & Co. cat. autumn 1997. **R:** Brackley. **I:** n/k. **H:** SD. **L:** U. **N:** P. **P:** S. **C:** mixed colours. **S:** summer.

'Coraleena' (*L. odoratus*) Spencer **F:** Cooltonagh cat. 2008/09. **R:** Harrod. **I:** 2009. **D:** see Cultivars chapter.

'Corinne' (*L. odoratus*) Spencer **F:** Robert Bolton & Son cat. 1975/76. **R:** Robert Bolton & Son. **I:** 1976. **H:** T. **L:** U. **N:** P. **P:** S. **C:** magenta. **S:** summer.

'Countess Cadogan' (*L. odoratus*) Grandiflora **F:** Anon. (1897/98). **R:** H. Eckford. **I:** 1899. **D:** see Cultivars chapter.

'Cream Cracker' (*L. odoratus*) Spencer **F:** *NSPS Annual* 2001: 57. **R:** Wells / Kerton Sweet Peas. **I:** 2005. **H:** T. **L:** U. **N:** P. **P:** S. **C:** cream. **S:** summer.

'Cream Eggs' (*L. odoratus*) Grandiflora **F:** Mr Fothergills Seeds Ltd cat. 2016. **R:** Seedlynx / Mr Fothergills Seeds Ltd. **I:** 2016. **D:** see Cultivars chapter.

'Cream Ripple' (*L. odoratus*) Spencer **F:** Kerton Sweet Peas cat. 1997. **R:** Kerton Sweet Peas. **I:** 1997. **H:** T. **L:** U. **N:** P. **P:** S. **C:** lilac stripe, c.g. **S:** summer.

'Cream Southbourne' (*L. odoratus*) Spencer **F:** *NSPS Annual* 1979: 89. **R:** Colledge / Unwins Seeds. **I:** 1982. **D:** see Cultivars chapter.

'Crescent Moon' (*L. sativus*) **F:** R. Parsons cat. 2019/20. **R:** R. Parsons. **I:** 2020. **D:** see Cultivars chapter.

'Crimson Ripple' (*L. odoratus*) Spencer **F:** Thompson & Morgan cat. 2008/09. **R:** Thompson & Morgan. **I:** 2002. **D:** see Cultivars chapter.

Crown Princess of Prussia (*L. odoratus*) Grandiflora **F:** Carters Tested Seeds cat. 1888. **R:** Haage & Schmidt. **I:** 1868. **D:** see Cultivars chapter.

'Cupani' (*L. odoratus*) Grandiflora **F:** Grayson cat. 1993. **R:** Grayson. **I:** 1992. **D:** see Cultivars chapter.

'Cupani's Original' = 'Cupani'

'Cupid' (*L. odoratus*) Grandiflora **F:** Burpee Seeds cat. 1895. **R:** C.C. Morse & Co. / Burpee Seeds. **I:** 1896. **H:** SD. **L:** U. **N:** P. **P:** S. **C:** pure white, red tinted, waved. **S:** summer.

'Cupid Bright Violet' (*L. odoratus*) Grandiflora **F:** n/k. **R:** E.W. King & Co. **I:** 2008. **D:** see Cultivars chapter.

'Cupid Cherry' (*L. odoratus*) Grandiflora **F:** Hem Zaden cat. 2011/12. **R:** n/k. **I:** n/k. **H:** SD. **L:** U. **N:** P. **P:** S. **C:** n/k. **S:** summer.

'Cupid Lavender' = 'Lavender Cupid'

'Cupid Mahogany' (*L. odoratus*) Grandiflora **F:** E.W. King & Co. cat. autumn 2007. **R:** E.W. King & Co. **I:** 2008. **H:** SD. **L:** U. **N:** P. **P:** S. **C:** maroon. **S:** summer.

Cupid Mixed (*L. odoratus*) **F:** E.W. King & Co. cat. autumn 1997

'Cupid Navy Blue' (*L. odoratus*) Grandiflora **F:** n/k. **R:** n/k. **I:** n/k. **H:** SD. **L:** U. **N:** P. **P:** S. **C:** navy blue. **S:** summer.

'Cupid Pink' = 'Pink Cupid'

'Cupid Purple' (*L. odoratus*) Grandiflora **F:** Hem Zaden cat. 2011/12. **R:** n/k. **I:** n/k. **H:** SD. **L:** U. **N:** P. **P:** S. **C:** n/k. **S:** summer.

'Cupid Rose' (*L. odoratus*) Grandiflora **F:** Hem Zaden cat. 2011/12. **R:** n/k. **I:** n/k. **H:** SD. **L:** U. **N:** P. **P:** S. **C:** n/k. **S:** summer.

Cupid Series (*L. odoratus*) **D:** Dwarf trailing cultivars with Old-fashioned Grandiflora flowers. **A:** The original 'Cupid' introduced in 1896 was followed by 'Pink Cupid' and 'Primrose Cupid'. Within 20 years a considerable number of cultivars with this habit and form were named but quickly disappeared. Cultivars sold today as Cupid Series are thought to mostly belong to the Cuthbertson Cupid Series, introduced by Ferry Morse in 1958. This includes:

'Blossom Carpet', 'Blush Carpet', 'Carmine Carpet', 'Cerise Carpet', 'Cream Carpet', 'Crimson Carpet', 'Lavender Carpet', 'Pink Carpet', 'Rose Carpet' and 'White Carpet'.

'Cupid Violet' (*L. odoratus*) Grandiflora **F:** E.W. King & Co. cat. autumn 2007. **R:** E.W. King & Co. **I:** 2008. **H:** SD. **L:** U. **N:** P. **P:** S. **C:** violet. **S:** summer.

'Cupid White' = 'White Cupid'

Cuthbertson Mixed (*L. odoratus*) Spencer **F:** n/k. **R:** n/k. **I:** n/k. **H:** T. **L:** U. **N:** P. **P:** S. **C:** mixed colours. **S:** late spring.

Cuthbertson Cupid Mixed (*L. odoratus*) Grandiflora **F:** Unwins Seeds cat. 1958. **R:** Ferry Morse Seed Co. **I:** 1959. **H:** SD. **L:** U. **N:** P. **P:** S. **C:** mixed colours. **S:** late spring.

Cuthbertson Floribunda Mixed (*L. odoratus*) **F:** Moles cat. 1961.

Cuthbertson Series (*L. odoratus*) **R:** Frank Cuthbertson / Ferry Morse Seed Co. **I:** from 1940 but unnamed, named from 1947. **N:** A later Cuthbertson Floribunda Series consisted of Multiflora Spencers. Some names were used for both series and were sold in the trade interchangeably, making it difficult to allocate cultivar names to each series with certainty. The two series included 'Alice', 'Ann', 'Astrid', 'Billy', 'Carol', 'Catherine', 'Coline', 'Connie', 'Daisy', 'Danny', 'David', 'Doris', 'Eileen', 'Evelyn', 'Flora', 'Francis', 'Frank G.', 'Hazel', 'Helen', 'Janet', 'Jenny', 'Jessie', 'Jimmy', 'Joan', 'Joy', 'Katie', 'Kenneth', 'Liza', 'Lois', 'Mac', 'Marion', 'Nancy', 'Robert', 'Ronnie', 'Ruth', 'Tommy', 'Waneta' and 'William'. In addition, other cultivars of the Cuthbertson Floribunda Series were raised by others, notably Denholm Seeds. These include 'Dawn', 'Dolores', 'Drummer Boy', 'Richard' and 'Sandra'. **D:** Spring-flowering Spencer cultivars.

'Cyaneus' (*L. sativus*) **A:** Sometimes recognised as var. *cyaneus*. **D:** see Cultivars chapter.

'Cyaneus' (*L. vernus*) = *L. vernus*. **A:** This name, along with 'Caeruleus', has traditionally been used for selections with more blue flowers, but propagation from seed has resulted in plants being offered with inconsistent colours.

'Cyril Plater' (*L. odoratus*) Spencer **F:** *NSPS Annual* 2009: 56. **R:** Kerton Sweet Peas. **I:** 2011. **D:** see Cultivars chapter.

'Daily Mail' = 'Mary Pannell'

'Dalesman' (*L. odoratus*) Spencer **F:** *NSPS Annual* 2012: 165. **R:** Beane / Myers. **I:** 2013. **D:** see Cultivars chapter.

'Dama Duet' (*L. vernus*) **F:** n/k. **R:** Matthewman. **I:** n/k. **A:** Cultivars with thee Dama prefix were selected by David Matthewman. The leaflets are of f. *angustifolius* type (15–30mm wide). **D:** see Cultivars chapter.

'Dama Emily' (*L. vernus*) **F:** n/k. **R:** Matthewman. **I:** n/k. **A:** The leaflets are of f. *vernus* type (30–100mm wide). **D:** see Cultivars chapter.

'Dama Little Elf' (*L. vernus*) **F:** n/k. **R:** Matthewman. **I:** n/k. **A:** Shorter than most *L. vernus*. **H:** SD. **L:** M. **N:** M. **P:** S. **C:** palest pink. **S:** spring.

'Dama Rosa' (*L. vernus*) **F:** n/k. **R:** Matthewman. **I:** n/k. **H:** SD. **L:** M. **N:** M. **P:** S. **C:** deep pink. **S:** spring.

'Dama Violetta' (*L. vernus*) = *L. vernus* subsp. *vernus*

'Dancing Queen' (*L. odoratus*) Spencer **F:** Robert Bolton & Son cat. 2000/01. **R:** Robert Bolton & Son. **I:** 2001. **D:** see Cultivars chapter.

'Dancing Queen' Grayson (*L. odoratus*) Grandiflora **F:** Grayson cat. autumn 2005. **R:** Grayson. **I:** 2005. **H:** T. **L:** U. **N:** P. **P:** S. **C:** cream with purple edge. **S:** summer.

'Daphne' (*L. odoratus*) Spencer **F:** Ferry Morse Seed Co. cat. 1938. **R:** Ferry Morse Seed Co. **I:** 1938. **H:** T. **L:** U. **N:** P. **P:** S. **C:** light salmon pink. **S:** winter.

'Daphne' Simons (*L. odoratus*) Spencer **F:** *NSPS Annual* 1946: 95. **R:** Simons. **I:** 1945. **H:** T. **L:** U. **N:** P. **P:** S. **C:** mauve. **S:** summer.

'Daphne' King (*L. odoratus*) Spencer **F:** E.W. King & Co. cat. 1946. **R:** E.W. King & Co. **I:** 1946. **H:** T. **L:** M. **N:** P. **P:** S. **C:** cream pink. **S:** summer.

'Daphne' Unwins (*L. odoratus*) Spencer **F:** Unwins Seeds cat. autumn 1992. **R:** Unwins Seeds. **I:** 1993. **D:** see Cultivars chapter.

'Darcey Bussell' (*L. odoratus*) Spencer **F:** Unwins Seeds cat. autumn 2000. **R:** Unwins Seeds. **I:** 2001. **D:** see Cultivars chapter.

'Dark Passion' (*L. odoratus*) Spencer **F:** Matthewman cat. 2005/06. **R:** Beane / Matthewman. **I:** 2006. **D:** see Cultivars chapter.

'Dark Sprite' (*L. odoratus*) Grandiflora **F:** Owls Acre cat. 2013/14. **R:** Owl's Acre Sweet Peas. **I:** 2013. **D:** see Cultivars chapter.

'Dave R' (*L. odoratus*) Grandiflora **F:** *NSPS Classification List* 2020. **R:** Rollinson / P Johnson.

I: 2020. **H**: T. **L**: U. **N**: P. **P**: S. **C**: cerise-red. **S**: summer.

'Dave Thomas' (*L. odoratus*) Spencer   **RHS**: AM 1997. **F**: *NSPS Annual* 1998: 57. **R**: Harrod / Kerton Sweet Peas. **I**: 2000. **H**: T. **L**: U. **N**: P. **P**: S. **C**: scarlet. **S**: summer.

'David Unwin' (*L. odoratus*) Spencer   **F**: Unwins Seeds cat. autumn 2002. **R**: Unwins Seeds. **I**: 2003. **D**: see Cultivars chapter.

'Dawn' (*L. odoratus*) Grandiflora   **F**: ST Walker cat. 1898. **R**: ST Walker. **I**: 1898. **H**: T. **L**: U. **N**: P. **P**: D. **C**: mauve & purple flake, w.g. **S**: summer.

'Dawn' Stark (*L. odoratus*) Grandiflora   **F**: *NSPS Annual* 1908: 64. **R**: G. Stark & Son. **I**: c.1906. **H**: T. **L**: U. **N**: P. **P**: S. **C**: crimson bicolour. **S**: summer.

'Dawn' Damerum (*L. odoratus*) Spencer   **F**: *NSPS Annual* 1950: 50. **R**: Damerum / Suttons. **I**: 1929. **H**: T. **L**: U. **N**: P. **P**: S. **C**: salmon-orange. **S**: summer.

'Dawn' Stevenson (*L. odoratus*) Spencer   **F**: *NSPS Annual* 1936: 71. **R**: J. Stevenson. **I**: 1936. **H**: T. **L**: U. **N**: P. **P**: S. **C**: buff pink, c.g. **S**: summer.

'Dawn' Law Somner (*L. odoratus*) Spencer   **F**: Law Somner Pty Ltd cat. 1938. **R**: n/k. **I**: n/k. **H**: T. **L**: U. **N**: P. **P**: S. **C**: pink, w.g. **S**: early.

'Dawn' Denholm (*L. odoratus*) Spencer   **F**: Denholm Seeds cat. 1964. **R**: Denholm Seeds. **I**: n/k. **H**: T. **L**: U. **N**: M. **P**: S. **C**: lilac, w.g. **S**: late spring.

'Dawn' Beane (*L. odoratus*) Spencer   **F**: *NSPS Annual* 1996: 131. **R**: Beane / Matthewman. **I**: 1996. **D**: see Cultivars chapter.

'Deborah Devonshire' (*L. odoratus*) Spencer   **F**: *NSPS Annual* 2013: 169. **R**: Beane / Myers. **I**: 2014. **D**: see Cultivars chapter.

'Denis Compton' (*L. odoratus*) Spencer   **F**: Robert Bolton & Son cat. 1987/88. **R**: Robert Bolton & Son. **I**: 1988. **D**: see Cultivars chapter.

'Denise Tanner' (*L. odoratus*) Grandiflora   **F**: Grayson cat. autumn 1996. **R**: Grayson. **I**: 1997. **H**: T. **L**: U. **N**: P. **P**: S. **C**: bicolour. **S**: summer.

'Diamond Wedding' (*L. odoratus*) Grandiflora **F**: Unwins Seeds cat. autumn 1979. **R**: Colledge / Unwins Seeds. **I**: 1980. **A**: A Spencer cultivar that has reverted to Grandiflora. **D**: see Cultivars chapter.

'Doctor Uvedale'   = 'Dr Robert Uvedale'

'Dolly Varden' (*L. odoratus*) Grandiflora   **F**: Anon. (1898/99). **R**: C.C. Morse & Co. / Burpee Seeds. **I**: 1898. **D**: Flowers hooded. **H**: T. **L**: U. **N**: P. **P**: S. **C**: light purple bicolour. **S**: summer.

'Dolly Varden' Grayson (*L. odoratus*) Grandiflora **F**: Grayson cat. autumn 1995. **R**: Grayson. **I**: 1996. **D**: see Cultivars chapter.

'Don Mac' (*L. odoratus*) Spencer   **F**: McDougall cat. 1998. **R**: McDougall. **I**: n/k. **H**: T. **L**: U. **N**: P. **P**: n/k. **C**: dark maroon. **S**: winter.

'Donna Jones' (*L. odoratus*) Grandiflora   **F**: Grayson cat. 1997/98. **R**: Grayson. **I**: 1998. **H**: T. **L**: U. **N**: P. **P**: S. **C**: scarlet. **S**: summer.

'Doreen' Morse (*L. odoratus*) Spencer   **F**: C.C. Morse & Co. cat. 1925, Edward Webb & Sons cat. 1925. **R**: C.C. Morse & Co. **I**: 1925. **H**: T. **L**: U. **N**: P. **P**: S. **C**: bright carmine. **S**: summer.

'Doreen' Beane (*L. odoratus*) Spencer   **F**: *NSPS Annual* 2012: i. **R**: Beane / Eagle Sweet Peas. **I**: 2013. **D**: see Cultivars chapter.

'Dorothy Eckford' (*L. odoratus*) Grandiflora   **RHS**: AGM (H3) 1995. **F**: Wright (1902). **R**: H. Eckford. **I**: 1903. **D**: see Cultivars chapter.

'Dot.Com' (*L. odoratus*) Spencer   **F**: Eagle Sweet Peas cat. 2001/02. **R**: Albutt / Eagle Sweet Peas. **I**: 2002. **H**: T. **L**: U. **N**: P. **P**: S. **C**: blue stripe, w.g. **S**: summer.

'Dr Robert Uvedale' (*L. odoratus*) Grandiflora **F**: Grayson cat. 1998/99. **R**: Grayson. **I**: 1999. **D**: see Cultivars chapter.

'Dragon Fly' (*L. odoratus*) Spencer   **F**: Cuthbertson (1916). **R**: Alex Dickson & Sons. **I**: before 1915. **H**: T. **L**: U. **N**: P. **P**: S. **C**: magenta pink / mauve, c.g. **S**: summer.

'Dragonfly' (*L. odoratus*) Spencer   **F**: *NSPS Catalogue of Variety Names* 1912: 8. **R**: Aldersey. **I**: 1912. **H**: T. **L**: U. **N**: P. **P**: S. **C**: lavender marble, c.g. **S**: summer.

'Dragonfly' Taylor (*L. odoratus*) Semi-grandiflora **F**: Grayson cat. 1993. **R**: J. Taylor / Grayson. **I**: 1993. **D**: see Cultivars chapter.

'Dream Girl' (*L. odoratus*) Spencer   **F**: Cooltonagh cat. 2008/09. **R**: Harrod. **I**: 2009. **D**: see Cultivars chapter.

'Duchess of Roxburghe' (*L. odoratus*) Spencer **F**: Unwins Seeds cat. autumn 1983. **R**: Harriss / Unwins Seeds. **I**: 1984. **H**: T. **L**: U. **N**: P. **P**: S. **C**: pale blue. **S**: summer.

'Duke of York' (*L. odoratus*) Grandiflora   **F**: Anon. (1893c). **R**: H. Eckford. **I**: 1894. **D**: see Cultivars chapter.

'Dunollie Coline' (*L. odoratus*) Spencer   **F**: McDougall cat. 1998. **R**: McDougall. **I**: n/k. **H**: T. **L**: U. **N**: P. **P**: S.

C: lilac pink marble. **S:** early spring.

'Duo Magenta' (*L. odoratus*) Spencer   **F:** Unwins
Seeds cat. autumn 2006. **R:** Unwins Seeds. **I:** 2007.
H: T. **L:** U. **N:** P. **P:** S. **C:** maroon / violet. **S:** summer.

'Duo Salmon' (*L. odoratus*) Spencer   **RHS:** AGM (H3)
2010. **F:** Unwins Seeds cat. autumn 2008. **R:** Unwins
Seeds. **I:** 2009. **D:** see Cultivars chapter.

'Dusty Springfield' (*L. odoratus*) Spencer   **F:** Unwins
cat. autumn 2001. **R:** Priestley / Unwins Seeds.
I: 2002. **D:** see Cultivars chapter.

'Duvet Cherry' (*L. odoratus*) Spencer   **F:** n/k.
R: Seedlynx. **I:** n/k. **D:** see Cultivars chapter.

'Duvet White' (*L. odoratus*) Spencer   **F:** n/k.
R: Seedlynx. **I:** n/k. **H:** SD. **L:** U. **N:** P. **P:** S. **C:** white.
S: winter.

'Dynasty' (*L. odoratus*) Spencer   **F:** Unwins Seeds cat.
autumn 1985. **R:** Ford Robertson / Unwins Seeds.
I: 1986. **D:** see Cultivars chapter.

'Dzintra' (*L. odoratus*) Spencer   **F:** n/k. **R:** Maltenieks.
I: n/k. **H:** T. **L:** U. **N:** P. **P:** D. **C:** cream picotee.
S: summer.

'Earl Grey' (*L. odoratus*) Spencer   **F:** R. Parsons cat.
2013/14. **R:** Hammett / R. Parsons. **I:** 2014. **D:** see
Cultivars chapter.

'Early Blanche Ferry Spencer' (*L. odoratus*) Spencer
F: Arthur Yates & Co. cat. 1920. **R:** L.D. Waller Seed
Co. **I:** n/k. **H:** T. **L:** U. **N:** P. **P:** S. **C:** pink / white.
S: winter.

Early Multiflora Gigantea Series (*L. odoratus*) Spencer
F: *NSPS Annual* 1965: 57. **R:** Denholm Seeds. **I:** from
1960. **A:** This series includes 'Carmen', 'Celeste',
'Chloe', 'Coquette', 'Diana', 'Dinah', 'Eleanor', 'Gloria',
'Grace', 'June', 'Lily', 'Louise', 'Mamie', 'Margaret',
'Marilyn', 'Minnie', 'Miranda', 'Patti', 'Peaches', 'Pearl',
'Ramona', 'Rhoda', 'Rosie', 'Stella', 'Susie', 'Sylvia',
'Topsy' and 'Vicki'. **H:** T. **L:** U. **N:** M. **P:** S. **C:** various
colours. **S:** winter.

'Eclipse' (*L. odoratus*) Spencer   **F:** Cuthbertson
(1916). **R:** Robert Bolton & Son. **I:** 1916. **H:** T. **L:** U.
N: P. **P:** S. **C:** deep sky blue. **S:** summer.

'Eclipse' Bland (*L. odoratus*) Spencer   **F:** n/k.
R: Bland. **I:** 1940. **H:** T. **L:** U. **N:** P. **P:** S. **C:** white ground
picotee. **S:** summer.

'Eclipse' Laidlaw (*L. odoratus*) Spencer   **F:** Unwins
Seeds cat. autumn 1974. **R:** Laidlaw / Unwins Seeds.
I: 1975. **D:** see Cultivars chapter.

'Ed Fincham'   = 'Edd Fincham'

'Edd Fincham' (*L. odoratus*) Spencer   **F:** *NSPS Annual*
1986: 35. **R:** Harrod / Samuel Dobie & Sons Ltd.
I: 1994. **D:** see Cultivars chapter.

'Edith Flanagan' (*L. odoratus*) Spencer   **F:** R. Parsons
cat. 2016/17. **R:** Beane / R. Parsons. **I:** 2017. **D:** see
Cultivars chapter.

'Electric Blue'   = *L. sativus* f. *azureus*

'Elegance' (*L. odoratus*) Grandiflora   **F:** *NSPS Annual*
1910: 79. **R:** G. Stark & Son. **I:** 1909. **H:** T. **L:** U. **N:** P.
P: S. **C:** orange scarlet flake, w.g. **S:** summer.

'Elegance' Dickson (*L. odoratus*) Spencer   **F:** *NSPS
Annual* 1918: 57. **R:** Alex Dickson & Sons. **I:** 1920.
H: T. **L:** U. **N:** P. **P:** S. **C:** soft lilac pink with silver
sheen, c.g. **S:** summer.

'Elegance' Zvolanek (*L. odoratus*) Spencer
F: William Zvolanek & Co. cat. 1974. **R:** William
Zvolanek & Co. **I:** n/k. **H:** T. **L:** U. **N:** M. **P:** S. **C:** salmon
pink. **S:** spring.

'Elegance' Brackley (*L. odoratus*) Spencer   **F:** *NSPS
Annual* 1996: 127. **R:** Brackley. **I:** 1997. **H:** T. **L:** U. **N:** P.
P: S. **C:** white. **S:** summer.

'Elegance Cranberry' (*L. odoratus*) Spencer
F: R. Parsons cat. 2017/18. **R:** Hem Zaden. **I:** n/k.
D: see Cultivars chapter.

'Elegance Cream' (*L. odoratus*) Spencer   **F:** R. Parsons
cat. 2016/17. **R:** R. Parsons. **I:** 2017. **H:** T. **L:** U. **N:** M.
P: S. **C:** cream. **S:** winter.

'Elegance Lipstick'   = 'Lipstick' Unwins

'Elegance Maroon'   = 'Winter Elegance Burgundy'

Elegance Series   = Winter Elegance Mixed

'Elizabeth' (*L. odoratus*) Spencer   **F:** Cuthbertson
(1916). **R:** Cross. **I:** 1913. **H:** T. **L:** U. **N:** P. **P:** S. **C:** brick
red. **S:** summer.

'Elizabeth' Woodcock (*L. odoratus*) Spencer
F: Dobbie & Co. cat. 1936. **R:** Woodcock. **I:** 1928. **H:** T.
L: U. **N:** P. **P:** S. **C:** lilac pink, c.g. **S:** summer.

'Elizabeth' Australia (*L. odoratus*) Spencer
F: *Australian Garden Lover* (1955). **R:** n/k. **I:** n/k.
H: T. **L:** U. **N:** P. **P:** D. **C:** rosy lavender. **S:** winter.

'Elizabeth' Japan (*L. odoratus*) Spencer   **F:** Inoue
(2007). **R:** n/k. **I:** before 2002. **H:** T. **L:** U. **N:** P. **P:** D.
C: rose pink, w.g. **S:** winter.

'Elizabeth Shorthouse' (*L. odoratus*) Spencer
F: Kerton Sweet Peas cat. 2004. **R:** Kerton Sweet
Peas. **I:** 2004. **H:** T. **L:** U. **N:** P. **P:** S. **C:** rose pink, c.g.
S: summer.

'Elizabeth Taylor' (*L. odoratus*) Spencer   **F:** *NSPS*

Annual 1949: 65. **R:** J. Taylor / Unwins Seeds. **I:** 1951. **H:** T. **L:** U. **N:** P. **P:** D. **C:** mauve. **S:** summer.

'Ella Maria' (*L. odoratus*) Spencer   **F:** *NSPS Annual* 2001: 57. **R:** Kerton Sweet Peas. **I:** 2003. **D:** see Cultivars chapter.

'Elsie Pearl' (*L. odoratus*) Spencer   **F:** McDougall cat. 1998. **R:** McDougall. **I:** n/k. **H:** T. **L:** U. **N:** P. **P:** n/k. **C:** pale pink, w.g. **S:** winter.

'Emily' (*L. odoratus*) Spencer   **F:** Cuthbertson (1916). **R:** Isaac House & Son. **I:** 1912. **H:** T. **L:** U. **N:** P. **P:** S. **C:** rosy mauve. **S:** summer.

'Emily' Harriss (*L. odoratus*) Spencer   **F:** *NSPS Annual* 1988: 16. **R:** Harriss. **I:** n/k. **H:** T. **L:** U. **N:** P. **P:** S. **C:** light blue. **S:** summer.

'Emily' Sakata (*L. odoratus*) Spencer   **F:** n/k. **R:** Sakata Seed Co. **I:** 1991. **A:** Name first appeared on the Japanese Plant Variety Protection website (seen 18 Jul 1991) **H:** T. **L:** U. **N:** P. **P:** S. **C:** rose pink, w.g. **S:** early.

'Emily' Sakata, n/k (*L. odoratus*) Spencer   **F:** n/k. **R:** Sakata Seed Co. **I:** n/k. **A:** Name first appeared on the Japanese Plant Variety Protection website (seen 18 Jul 1991) **H:** T. **L:** U. **N:** P. **P:** S. **C:** rose pink. **S:** winter.

'Emily' Unwins (*L. odoratus*) Grandiflora   **F:** Unwins Seeds cat. autumn 2009. **R:** Unwins Seeds. **I:** 2010. **D:** see Cultivars chapter.

'Emma' (*L. odoratus*) Spencer   **F:** Brackley cat. 2000/01. **R:** Brackley. **I:** 2001. **D:** see Cultivars chapter.

'Ena Margaret' (*L. odoratus*) Spencer   **F:** Everitt cat. 1975/76. **R:** Everitt. **I:** 1976. **D:** see Cultivars chapter.

'Enchanté' (*L. odoratus*) Spencer   **F:** R. Parsons cat. 2011/12. **R:** Hammett / Denny. **I:** 2009. **A:** Name first appeared on the Seedngrow website (seen 19 Feb 2009). **D:** see Cultivars chapter.

'Enchanted'   = 'Enchanté'

'Erewhon' (*L. odoratus*) Semi-grandiflora   **F:** Somerset cat. 2011. **R:** Hammett. **I:** 2008. **D:** see Cultivars chapter.

'Ernest Ireland' (*L. odoratus*) Spencer   **F:** R. Parsons cat. 2008/09. **R:** R. Parsons. **I:** 2009. **H:** T. **L:** U. **N:** P. **P:** S. **C:** crimson. **S:** summer.

'Ernest William' (*L. odoratus*) Spencer   **F:** Kerton Sweet Peas cat. 2011. **R:** Robson/Kerton Sweet Peas. **I:** 2011. **H:** T. **L:** U. **N:** P. **P:** S. **C:** purple. **S:** summer.

'Esther Rantzen' (*L. odoratus*) Spencer   **F:** Brackley cat. 1998/99. **R:** Brackley. **I:** 1989. **D:** see Cultivars chapter.

'Ethel Grace' (*L. odoratus*) Spencer   **RHS:** AM 1990. **F:** *NSPS Annual* 1991: 35. **R:** B.R. Jones / Robert Bolton & Son. **I:** 1994. **D:** see Cultivars chapter.

'Eveleena' (*L. odoratus*) Spencer   **F:** Cooltonagh cat. 2008/09. **R:** Harrod. **I:** 2009. **H:** T. **L:** U. **N:** P. **P:** S. **C:** salmon pink, c.g. **S:** late spring.

'Evelyn' (*L. odoratus*) Spencer   **F:** Cuthbertson (1916). **R:** Anderson & Co. **I:** 1916. **H:** T. **L:** U. **N:** P. **P:** S. **C:** light red. **S:** winter.

'Evelyn' Ferry Morse 1944 (*L. odoratus*) Spencer   **F:** Ferry Morse Seed Co. cat. 1947. **R:** Ferry Morse Seed Co. **I:** 1944. **D:** see Cultivars chapter.

'Evelyn' Ferry Morse 1955 (*L. odoratus*) Spencer   **F:** Ferry Morse Seed Co. cat. 1956. **R:** Ferry Morse Seed Co. **I:** 1955. **H:** T. **L:** U. **N:** M. **P:** S. **C:** deep salmon pink, c.g. **S:** late spring.

'Evelyn's Delight' (*L. odoratus*) Spencer   **F:** Kerton Sweet Peas cat. 2020. **R:** Fleming Robertson / Kerton Sweet Peas. **I:** 2020. **H:** T. **L:** U. **N:** P. **P:** S. **C:** pink. **S:** summer.

'Evening Glow' (*L. odoratus*) Spencer   **RHS:** AM 1996, AGM (H3) 1996. **F:** E.W. King & Co. cat. 1996/97. **R:** Beane / E.W. King & Co. **I:** 1997. **D:** see Cultivars chapter.

'Evie Jones' (*L. odoratus*) Spencer   **F:** 2018 Classification list. **R:** Eagle Sweet Peas. **I:** 2018. **H:** T. **L:** U. **N:** P. **P:** S. **C:** magenta. **S:** summer.

'Explorer Crimson' (*L. odoratus*) Spencer   **F:** NSPS Annual 1992: 49. **R:** Bodger Seeds Ltd. **I:** 1992. **D:** see Cultivars chapter.

'Explorer Mid-Blue' (*L. odoratus*) Spencer   **F:** *NSPS Annual* 1992: 49. **R:** Bodger Seeds Ltd. **I:** 1992. **H:** SD. **L:** M. **N:** P. **P:** S. **C:** mid blue. **S:** summer.

'Explorer Rose Pink' (*L. odoratus*) Spencer   **F:** *NSPS Annual* 1992: 49. **R:** Bodger Seeds Ltd. **I:**1992. **D:** see Cultivars chapter.

'Explorer Scarlet' (*L. odoratus*) Spencer   **F:** *NSPS Annual* 1992: 49. **R:** Bodger Seeds Ltd. **I:**1992. **D:** see Cultivars chapter.

Explorer Series (*L. odoratus*)   **F:** *NSPS Annual* 1922: 49. **R:** Bodger Seeds Ltd. **I:** from 1992. **A:** Introduced as an improvement on Supersnoop Series. **D:** Eight colours, the selections all have an 'Explorer' prefix.

'Far Gough' (*L. odoratus*) Spencer   **F:** *NSPS Classification List* 2020. **R:** Somerset Sweet Peas.

I: 2020. **H:** T. **L:** U. **N:** P. **P:** S. **C:** dark blue flake.
S: summer.

'Fields of Fire' (*L. odoratus*) Spencer　**F:** Eagle Sweet
Peas cat. 2009/10. **R:** Robson / Eagle Sweet Peas.
I: 2008. **D:** see Cultivars chapter.

'Fiery Cross' (*L. odoratus*) Spencer　**F:** Burpee Seeds
cat. 1916. **R:** Malcolm / Burpee Seeds. **I:** 1916. **H:** T.
L: U. **N:** P. **P:** S. **C:** orange cerise. **S:** summer.

'Fire and Ice' (*L. odoratus*) Grandiflora　**F:** Owl's Acre
Sweet Peas cat. 2005/06. **R:** Owl's Acre Sweet Peas.
I: 2005. **D:** see Cultivars chapter.

'Firecrest' (*L. odoratus*) Spencer　**F:** Robert Bolton &
Son cat. 1986/87. **R:** Robert Bolton & Son. **I:** 1987.
D: see Cultivars chapter.

'First Flame' (*L. odoratus*) Spencer　**RHS:** AGM (H3)
2002. **F:** *NSPS Annual* 2003: 41. **R:** Harrod / E.W.
King & Co. **I:** 2006. **D:** see Cultivars chapter.

'First Lady' (*L. odoratus*) Spencer　**F:** William
Zvolanek & Co. cat. 1974. **R:** William Zvolanek & Co.
I: n/k. **D:** see Cultivars chapter.

'First Lady' King (*L. odoratus*) Spencer　**F:** *NSPS
Annual* 1986: 36. **R:** E.W. King & Co. **I:** 1988. **H:** T.
L: U. **N:** P. **P:** S. **C:** pale rose pink, c.g. **S:** summer.

'First Lady' Hamayu (*L. odoratus*) Spencer
F: Nakamura *et al.* (2010). **R:** Hamayu. **I:** n/k. **H:** T.
L: U. **N:** P. **P:** S. **C:** rose pink. **S:** spring.

'First Love' (*L. odoratus*) Spencer　**F:** McDougall cat.
1998. **R:** McDougall. **I:** 1980s. **H:** T. **L:** U. **N:** P. **P:** S.
C: soft maroon blush, c.g. **S:** winter.

'First Love' Oyama (*L. odoratus*) Spencer　**F:** n/k.
R: Oyama. **I:** before 2012. **H:** T. **L:** U. **N:** M. **P:** S. **C:** pale
pink, w.g. **S:** winter.

'Flaccidus' (*L. vernus*)　= *L. vernus* subsp. *flaccidus*

'Flagship' (*L. odoratus*) Spencer　**F:** SNSPCRS
1934/35. **R:** Ferry Morse Seed Co. **I:** 1937. **H:** T. **L:** U.
N: P. **P:** S. **C:** dark blue. **S:** summer.

'Flame' (*L. odoratus*) Spencer　**F:** n/k. **R:** n/k. **I:** before
1922. **H:** T. **L:** U. **N:** P. **P:** S. **C:** n/k. **S:** summer.

'Flame' Simons (*L. odoratus*) Spencer　**F:** n/k.
R: Simons. **I:** 1935. **H:** T. **L:** U. **N:** P. **P:** S. **C:** orange
cerise. **S:** summer.

'Flame' Ferry Morse (*L. odoratus*) Spencer　**F:** Ferry
Morse Seed Co. cat. 1958. **R:** n/k. **I:** n/k. **H:** T. **L:** U.
N: P. **P:** S. **C:** brilliant scarlet. **S:** winter.

'Flame' Unwins (*L. odoratus*) Spencer　**F:** *NSPS
Annual* 2005: 63 (as 'Olympic Flame'). **R:** Harrod /
Unwins Seeds. **I:** 2012. **D:** see Cultivars chapter.

'Flora Cave' (*L. odoratus*) Spencer　**F:** *NSPS Annual*
1999: 63. **R:** Cave / Kerton Sweet Peas. **I:** 2005. **H:** T.
L: U. **N:** P. **P:** S. **C:** appleblossom pink, w.g. **S:** summer.

'Flora Jean' (*L. odoratus*) Spencer　**F:** McDougall cat.
1998. **R:** McDougall. **I:** n/k. **H:** T. **L:** U. **N:** P. **P:** S.
C: magenta flake, w.g. **S:** winter.

'Flora Norton' (*L. odoratus*) Grandiflora　**F:** Vaughan
Seed Store cat. 1904. **R:** C.C. Morse & Co. / Vaughan
Seed Store. **I:** 1904. **D:** see Cultivars chapter.

'Florencecourt' (*L. odoratus*) Spencer　**RHS:** AM
1999. **F:** *NSPS Annual* 2000: 69. **R:** Harrod. **I:** 2008.
D: see Cultivars chapter.

'Florencecourt' Kerton Sweet Peas (*L. odoratus*)
Spencer　**F:** Kerton Sweet Peas cat. 2008. **R:** Kerton
Sweet Peas. **I:** 2008. **H:** T. **L:** U. **N:** P. **P:** S. **C:** orange-
red. **S:** summer.

'Flying Visit' (*L. odoratus*) Spencer　**F:** *NSPS Annual*
1979: 88. **R:** Hammett / Maishman. **I:** 1981. **D:** see
Cultivars chapter.

'Fragrance' (*L. odoratus*) Spencer　**F:** Ball cat. 1932.
R: Macdonald. **I:** 1932. **H:** T. **L:** U. **N:** P. **P:** D.
C: lavender. **S:** winter.

'Fragrance' Burpee (*L. odoratus*) Spencer　**F:** Simons
cat. 1954/55, E.W. King & Co. cat. 1954/55. **R:** Burpee
Seeds. **I:** 1952. **H:** T. **L:** U. **N:** P. **P:** D. **C:** cream, tinted
pink. **S:** summer.

'Fragrant Beauty'　= *L. odoratus*

'Frances Kate' (*L. odoratus*) Spencer　**F:** R. Parsons
cat. 2010/11. **R:** R. Parsons. **I:** 2011. **D:** see Cultivars
chapter.

'Frank Dolby' (*L. odoratus*) Semi-grandiflora　**F:** *NSPS
Annual* 1906: v ad. **R:** Unwins Seeds / Sharpe /
Watkins & Simpson. **I:** 1906. **H:** T. **L:** U. **N:** P. **P:** S.
C: lavender blue. **S:** summer.

'Frank G.' (*L. odoratus*) Spencer　**F:** Ferry Morse Seed
Co. cat. 1947. **R:** Ferry Morse Seed Co. **I:** 1940. **D:** see
Cultivars chapter.

'Frank G.' Ferry Morse 1955 (*L. odoratus*)
Spencer　**F:** Ferry Morse Seed Co. cat. 1956. **R:** Ferry
Morse Seed Co. **I:** 1955. **H:** T. **L:** U. **N:** M. **P:** S. **C:** light
lavender. **S:** late spring.

'Frilly Milly' (*L. odoratus*) Spencer　**F:** n/k.
R: Hammett. **I:** 2019. **A:** Name first appeared on the
Hammett website (seen 29 May 2019). **H:** T. **L:** U.
N: P. **P:** S. **C:** pink flush, c.g. **S:** spring.

'Future Shock' (*L. odoratus*) Spencer　**F:** *NSPS
Classification List* 2019. **R:** Hammett. **I:** 2019. **D:** see

Cultivars chapter.

'Futuristic' (*L. odoratus*) Spencer **F:** n/k. **R:** Harrod.
I: n/k. **H:** T. **L:** U. **N:** P. **P:** S. **C:** white. **S:** summer.

'Gaiety' (*L. odoratus*) Grandiflora **F:** RHS trials 1894,
Peter Henderson & Co. cat. 1894. **R:** H. Eckford.
I: 1893. **H:** T. **L:** U. **N:** P. **P:** S. **C:** bright rose flake, w.g.
S: summer.

'Gaiety' Bolton (*L. odoratus*) Spencer **F:** *NSPS
Annual* 1947: 41. **R:** Robert Bolton & Son. **I:** 1946.
H: T. **L:** U. **N:** P. **P:** S. **C:** pink / white. **S:** summer.

Galaxy Series (*L. odoratus*) Spencer **F:** E.W. King &
Co. cat. 1961/62. **R:** Burpee Seeds. **I:** from 1962.
A: This series includes 'Alaska', 'Amigo', 'Angel Face',
'Blue Argo', 'Blue Sails', 'Blue Swan', 'Cerise Glow',
'Cream Whizz', 'Eskimo', 'Fireglo', 'Gigi', 'Great
Britain', 'Great Scot', 'Jupiter', 'Lavender Delight',
'Love Song', 'Mercury', 'Milky Way', 'Navy Blue',
'Neptune', 'Purity', 'Rosie', 'Sachet', Scarlet Glow',
'Scarlet Whizz', 'Tangerine', 'Venus' and 'Yankee
Doodle'. **H:** T. **L:** U. **N:** M. **P:** S. **C:** various colours.
S: summer.

'Gardener's Jubilee' = 'The Princess Royal'

'Garnette' (*L. odoratus*) Spencer **F:** *NSPS Annual*
1968: ii. **R:** Burpee Seeds. **I:** 1968. **D:** see Cultivars
chapter.

'Garry Kirkman' (*L. odoratus*) Spencer **F:** R. Parsons
cat. 2011/12. **R:** R. Parsons. **I:** 2012. **D:** see Cultivars
chapter.

'Gawler Ballerina' (*L. odoratus*) Spencer
F: *Australian Garden Lover* (1963). **R:** n/k. **I:** 1940s.
H: T. **L:** U. **N:** P. **P:** D. **C:** lilac pink, w.g. **S:** winter.

'Gawler Cerise' (*L. odoratus*) Spencer **F:** McDougall
cat. 1998. **R:** Harkness. **I:** before 1971. **D:** see Cultivars
chapter.

'Gawler Fascination' (*L. odoratus*) Spencer
F: *Australian Garden Lover* (1935). **R:** n/k. **I:** 1933.
H: T. **L:** U. **N:** P. **P:** S. **C:** light pink, w.g. **S:** winter.

'Gawler Fascination Improved' (*L. odoratus*) Spencer
F: *Australian Garden Lover* (1948). **R:** Harkness.
I: n/k. **H:** T. **L:** U. **N:** P. **P:** S. **C:** light pink. **S:** winter.

'Gawler Lavender' (*L. odoratus*) Spencer
F: *Australian Garden Lover* (1948). **R:** Harkness.
I: n/k. **H:** T. **L:** U. **N:** P. **P:** S. **C:** lavender. **S:** winter.

'Gawler Lavender Pink' (*L. odoratus*) Spencer
F: *Australian Garden Lover* (1955). **R:** n/k. **I:** n/k.
H: T. **L:** U. **N:** P. **P:** D. **C:** pink, overlaid lavender pink.
S: winter.

'Gawler Louise' (*L. odoratus*) Spencer **F:** R. Parsons
cat. 2008/09. **R:** n/k. **I:** n/k. **H:** T. **L:** U. **N:** P. **P:** D.
C: cerise / salmon. **S:** early spring.

'Gawler Margaret' (*L. odoratus*) Spencer **F:** n/k.
R: n/k. **I:** n/k. **H:** T. **L:** U. **N:** P. **P:** D. **C:** lavender blue
flake, w.g. **S:** winter.

'Gawler Marianne' (*L. odoratus*) Spencer **F:** n/k.
R: n/k. **I:** n/k. **H:** T. **L:** U. **N:** P. **P:** D. **C:** pink flake, w.g.
S: winter.

'Gawler Marion' (*L. odoratus*) Spencer **F:** McDougall
cat. 1998. **R:** Australia. **I:** 1920s. **D:** see Cultivars
chapter.

'Gawler Mauve Pink' (*L. odoratus*) Spencer
F: *Australian Garden Lover* (1948). **R:** Harkness.
I: n/k. **H:** T. **L:** U. **N:** P. **P:** S. **C:** pale pink. **S:** winter.

'Gawler Plum' (*L. odoratus*) Spencer **F:** *Australian
Garden Lover* (1948). **R:** Harkness. **I:** n/k. **H:** T. **L:** U.
N: P. **P:** S. **C:** rich plum. **S:** winter.

Gawler Mixed (*L. odoratus*) Spencer **F:** *Australian
Garden Lover* (1955). **R:** Gawler / Adelaide area of
South Australia. **I:** n/k. **A:** Some cultivars have
distinct characteristics such as hairless vegetative
parts, characteristic legumes, very frilly triplex petals
and very strong fragrance, but they are not a series.
Most of those sold with a Gawler prefix have had this
added to distinguish them from other cultivars with
the same name. **H:** T. **L:** U. **N:** P. **P:** D. **C:** mixed
colours. **S:** early.

'Gawler Shaded Pink' (*L. odoratus*) Spencer
F: *Australian Garden Lover* (1935). **R:** Harkness.
I: n/k. **H:** T. **L:** U. **N:** P. **P:** S. **C:** pink, c.g. **S:** winter.

'Gawler Shell Pink' (*L. odoratus*) Spencer
F: *Australian Garden Lover* (Feb. 1949). **R:** Harkness.
I: 1949. **D:** see Cultivars chapter.

'Gawler Violet' (*L. odoratus*) Spencer **F:** *Australian
Garden Lover* (1948). **R:** Harkness. **I:** n/k. **H:** T. **L:** U.
N: P. **P:** S. **C:** violet. **S:** winter.

'Gawler Violet Rose' (*L. odoratus*) Spencer
F: *Australian Garden Lover* (1935). **R:** Harkness.
I: n/k. **H:** T. **L:** U. **N:** P. **P:** S. **C:** violet rose. **S:** winter.

'Gawler Warrior' (*L. odoratus*) Spencer **F:** *Australian
Garden Lover* (1947). **R:** n/k. **I:** before 1948. **H:** T.
L: U. **N:** P. **P:** D. **C:** red flake, w.g. **S:** winter.

'Gawler White' (*L. odoratus*) Spencer **F:** *Australian
Garden Lover* (1948). **R:** Harkness. **I:** n/k. **H:** T. **L:** U.
N: P. **P:** S. **C:** white. **S:** winter.

'Gawler White Improved' (*L. odoratus*) Spencer

F: *Australian Garden Lover* (1935). **R:** n/k. **I:** n/k. **H:** T. **L:** U. **N:** P. **P:** S. **C:** white. **S:** winter.

'Geoff Amos' (*L. odoratus*) Spencer   **F:** Thompson & Morgan cat. 2001. **R:** Thompson & Morgan. **I:** 2001. **D:** see Cultivars chapter.

'Geoff Hughes' (*L. odoratus*) Spencer   **F:** *NSPS Annual* 2009: 169. **R:** Sarrer / Eagle Sweet Peas. **I:** 2010. **D:** see Cultivars chapter.

'George Priestley' (*L. odoratus*) Spencer   **F:** *NSPS Annual* 2005: 54. **R:** Hubbuck / Matthewman. **I:** 2008. **D:** see Cultivars chapter.

'Geranium' (*L. odoratus*) Spencer   **F:** Ferry Morse Seed Co. cat. 1958. **R:** Ferry Morse Seed Co. **I:** 1942. **H:** T. **L:** U. **N:** P. **P:** S. **C:** warm salmon cerise. **S:** winter.

'Geranium' n/k (*L. odoratus*) Spencer   **F:** n/k. **R:** n/k. **I:** before 1925. **H:** T. **L:** U. **N:** P. **P:** S. **C:** n/k. **S:** summer.

'Geranium Pink' (*L. odoratus*) Spencer   **F:** n/k. **R:** G. Stark & Son. **I:** 1953. **H:** T. **L:** U. **N:** P. **P:** S. **C:** orange-red. **S:** summer.

'Geranium Pink Improved' (*L. odoratus*) Spencer   **F:** E.W. King & Co. cat. 1954/55. **R:** G. Stark & Son. **I:** 1955. **H:** T. **L:** U. **N:** P. **P:** S. **C:** orange red. **S:** summer.

'Gerry Cullinan' (*L. odoratus*) Spencer   **F:** Kerton Sweet Peas cat. 2007. **R:** Kerton Sweet Peas. **I:** 2007. **D:** see Cultivars chapter.

'Gilly Norah' (*L. odoratus*) Spencer   **F:** R. Parsons cat. 2018/19. **R:** Harrod / R. Parsons. **I:** 2019. **H:** T. **L:** U. **N:** P. **P:** S. **C:** pale salmon pink, c.g. **S:** summer.

'Glasnevin' (*L. odoratus*) Spencer   **F:** Cooltonagh cat. 2005/06. **R:** Harrod. **I:** 2006. **D:** see Cultivars chapter.

'Glenice Percy' (*L. odoratus*) Spencer   **F:** *Australian Garden Lover* (1948). **R:** Harkness. **I:** before 1946. **H:** T. **L:** U. **N:** P. **P:** S. **C:** cerise / pink. **S:** winter.

'Glitters' Lumley (*L. odoratus*) Spencer   **F:** *NSPS Annual* 1910: 80. **R:** Lumley. **I:** 1910. **H:** T. **L:** U. **N:** P. **P:** S. **C:** scarlet orange. **S:** summer.

'Gloria' (*L. odoratus*) Spencer   **F:** Macdonald cat. 1933. **R:** Macdonald. **I:** 1932. **H:** T. **L:** U. **N:** P. **P:** S. **C:** salmon rose. **S:** winter.

'Gloria' Bland (*L. odoratus*) Spencer   **F:** Dobbie & Co. cat. 1936, Carters Tested Seeds cat. 1936, Unwin Supplement 1936. **R:** Bland. **I:** 1934. **H:** T. **L:** U. **N:** P. **P:** S. **C:** picotee, c.g. **S:** summer.

'Gloria' Denholm (*L. odoratus*) Spencer   **F:** E.W. King & Co. cat. 1963/64. **R:** Denholm Seeds. **I:** 1960. **D:** see Cultivars chapter.

'Gloria' Bolton (*L. odoratus*) Spencer   **F:** *NSPS Annual* 1966: 71. **R:** Robert Bolton & Son. **I:** 1967. **H:** T. **L:** U. **N:** P. **P:** S. **C:** salmon pink, c.g. **S:** summer.

'Glow' (*L. odoratus*) Spencer   **F:** *NSPS Annual* 1915: 89. **R:** RH Bath Ltd. **I:** 1913. **H:** T. **L:** U. **N:** P. **P:** S. **C:** light salmon orange. **S:** summer.

'Glow' Burpee (*L. odoratus*) Spencer   **F:** *NSPS Annual* 1950: 66. **R:** Burpee Seeds. **I:** n/k. **H:** T. **L:** U. **N:** P. **P:** S. **C:** salmon-cerise. **S:** summer.

'Glow' Unwins (*L. odoratus*) Spencer   **F:** Unwins Seeds cat. autumn 1996. **R:** Unwins Seeds. **I:** 1997. **D:** see Cultivars chapter.

'Grandma Butt' (*L. odoratus*) Spencer   **F:** *NSPS Annual* 1997: 75. **R:** Beane / R. Parsons. **I:** 2006. **D:** see Cultivars chapter.

'Great Britain' (*L. odoratus*) Spencer   **F:** *NSPS Annual* 1965: 33. **R:** Burpee Seeds. Sold in the UK by Samuel Dobie & Sons Ltd. **I:** 1966. **D:** see Cultivars chapter.

'Greenfingers' (*L. odoratus*) Grandiflora   **F:** Mr Fothergills Seeds Ltd cat. 2017. **R:** Seedlynx / Mr Fothergills Seeds Ltd. **I:** 2017. **D:** see Cultivars chapter.

'Gwawr Cymru' (*L. odoratus*) Spencer   **F:** R. Parsons cat. 2019/20. **R:** Harrod / R. Parsons. **I:** 2020. **H:** T. **L:** U. **N:** P. **P:** S. **C:** cream with pink edge. **S:** summer.

'Gwendoline' (*L. odoratus*) Spencer   **F:** *NSPS Annual* 1911: 87. **R:** Isaac House & Son. **I:** 1910. **H:** T. **L:** U. **N:** P. **P:** S. **C:** blue. **S:** summer.

'Gwendoline' Australia (*L. odoratus*) Spencer   **F:** *Australian Garden Lover* (1963). **R:** n/k. **I:** n/k. **H:** T. **L:** U. **N:** P. **P:** S. **C:** cherry salmon. **S:** winter.

'Gwendoline' Unwins (*L. odoratus*) Spencer   **RHS:** AM 1998, AGM (H3) 1998. **F:** Unwins Seeds cat. autumn 1998. **R:** Unwins Seeds. **I:** 1999. **D:** see Cultivars chapter.

'Gypsy Queen' (*L. odoratus*) Spencer   **F:** Robert Bolton & Son cat. autumn 1964. **R:** Robert Bolton & Son. **I:** 1965. **D:** see Cultivars chapter.

'Hampton Court' (*L. odoratus*) Spencer   **F:** Brackley cat. 1992/93. **R:** Brackley. **I:** 1991. **D:** see Cultivars chapter.

'Hannah Beth' (*L. odoratus*) Spencer   **F:** Kerton Sweet Peas cat. 2005. **R:** Harrod / Kerton Sweet Peas. **I:** 2005. **H:** T. **L:** U. **N:** P. **P:** S. **C:** lavender flush. **S:** summer.

'Hannah Dale' (*L. odoratus*) Grandiflora   **F:** *NSPS Annual* 1908: ix ad. **R:** Dobbie & Co. **I:** 1907. **H:** T.

L: U. **N:** P. **P:** S. **C:** rich maroon. **S:** summer.

'Hannah Dale' Grayson (*L. odoratus*) Grandiflora
F: Grayson cat. 1997/98. **R:** Grayson. **I:** 1998. **D:** see
Cultivars chapter.

'**Hannah Joy**' (*L. odoratus*) Spencer   **F:** Kerton Sweet
Peas cat. 2019. **R:** Fleming Robertson / Kerton Sweet
Peas. **I:** 2019. **H:** T. **L:** U. **N:** P. **P:** S. **C:** white.
S: summer.

'**Hannah Magovern**' (*L. odoratus*) Spencer
F: R. Parsons cat. 2009/10. **R:** R. Parsons. **I:** 2010.
D: see Cultivars chapter.

'**Hannah Rachel**' (*L. odoratus*) Spencer   **F:** Kerton
Sweet Peas cat. 2017. **R:** Kerton Sweet Peas. **I:** 2017.
H: T. **L:** U. **N:** P. **P:** S. **C:** coral pink. **S:** summer.

'**Hannah's Harmony**' (*L. odoratus*) Spencer
RHS: AGM (H3) 1996. **F:** *NSPS Annual* 1997: 73.
R: J.D. Place / R. Parsons. **I:** 2013. **D:** see Cultivars
chapter.

'Happy Birthday'   = 'Omay'

'**Harbinger**' (*L. odoratus*) Spencer   **F:** n/k.
R: Hammett. **I:** 2017. **H:** T. **L:** U. **N:** P. **P:** S. **C:** maroon /
violet. **S:** early.

'**Hard Times**' (*L. odoratus*) Spencer   **F:** *NSPS Annual*
1987: 17. **R:** Bailey. **I:** 1989. **H:** T. **L:** U. **N:** P. **P:** S. **C:** mid
blue. **S:** summer.

'Harlow Carr'   = 'Castlewellan'

'Harmony' (*L. tingitanus*)   = 'Roseus'

'**Harvey's Blush**' (*L. odoratus*) Spencer   **F:** R. Parsons
cat. 2004/05. **R:** Albutt / E.W. King & Co. **I:** 1996.
H: T. **L:** U. **N:** P. **P:** S. **C:** salmon pink, c.g. **S:** summer.

'**Heartbeat**' (*L. odoratus*) Spencer   **F:** Sewell cat.
2000/01. **R:** Sewell. **I:** 2001. **D:** see Cultivars chapter.

'**Heart's Delight**' (*L. odoratus*) Spencer   **F:** Unwins
Seeds cat. autumn 2006. **R:** Unwins Seeds. **I:** 2007.
H: T. **L:** U. **N:** P. **P:** S. **C:** orange-red. **S:** summer.

'**Heathcliff**' (*L. odoratus*) Grandiflora   **RHS:** AGM
(H3) 2003. **F:** Unwins Seeds cat. autumn 2002.
R: Unwins Seeds. **I:** 2003. **D:** see Cultivars chapter.

'**Heaven Scent**' (*L. odoratus*) Spencer   **F:** Cooltonagh
cat. 2006/07. **R:** Harrod. **I:** 2007. **D:** see Cultivars
chapter.

Heaven Scent Mixed (*L. odoratus*) Spencer   **F:** Hem
Zaden cat. 2011/12. **R:** n/k. **I:** n/k. **H:** T. **L:** U. **N:** P. **P:** S.
C: mixed colours. **S:** summer.

Heaven Scent Mixed, S.E. Marshall & Co. (*L. odoratus*)
Grandiflora   **F:** S.E. Marshall & Co. cat. 2004. **D:** A
mixture of Old-fashioned Grandiflora cultivars.

C: mixed colours.

'**Helen Millar**' (*L. odoratus*) Spencer   **F:** Eagle Sweet
Peas cat. 2015/16. **R:** Eagle Sweet Peas. **I:** 2014. **H:** T.
L: U. **N:** P. **P:** S. **C:** lavender flush, w.g. **S:** summer.

'**Henry Eckford**' (*L. odoratus*) Grandiflora   **F:** *NSPS
Annual* 1905: iii ad. **R:** H. Eckford. **I:** 1906. **D:** see
Cultivars chapter.

'**Henry Thomas**' (*L. odoratus*) Spencer   **F:** Eagle
Sweet Peas cat. 2009/10. **R:** Eagle Sweet Peas.
I: 2008. **H:** T. **L:** U. **N:** P. **P:** S. **C:** crimson. **S:** summer.

Here Come The Girls Mixed (*L. odoratus*) Spencer
F: Thompson & Morgan cat. 2019. **D:** A mixture of
Spencer cultivars. **C:** mixed colours.

'**Hero**' (*L. odoratus*) Spencer   **F:** C.C. Morse & Co. cat.
1928. **R:** C.C. Morse & Co. **I:** 1928. **H:** T. **L:** U. **N:** P. **P:** S.
C: cerise. **S:** summer.

'Hero' Unwins (*L. odoratus*) Spencer   **F:** Unwins
Seeds cat. autumn 2009. **R:** Unwins Seeds. **I:** 2010.
D: see Cultivars chapter.

'**Hidcote**' (*L. sylvestris*)   **F:** n/k. **R:** n/k. **I:** n/k. **H:** SD.
L: U. **N:** M. **P:** S. **C:** purple. **S:** summer.

'**High Scent**' (*L. odoratus*) Semi-grandiflora
RHS: AGM (H3) 2008. **F:** Suttons cat. 2002.
R: Hammett / Suttons. **I:** 2002. **D:** see Cultivars
chapter.

'**High Society**' (*L. odoratus*) Spencer   **F:** *NSPS Annual*
2011: 135. **R:** K. Brewer. **I:** n/k. **H:** T. **L:** U. **N:** P. **P:** S.
C: n/k. **S:** summer.

'High Society' Hammett (*L. odoratus*) Spencer
F: Somerset cat. 2014/15. **R:** Hammett / Somerset.
I: 2015. **D:** see Cultivars chapter.

'**Hikari**' (*L. odoratus*) Spencer   **F:** n/k. **R:** Nozaki.
I: n/k. **D:** see Cultivars chapter.

'Hi Scent'   = 'High Scent'

'**Hollie Adams**' (*L. odoratus*) Spencer   **F:** McDougall
cat. 2015. **R:** McDougall. **I:** n/k. **H:** T. **L:** U. **N:** P. **P:** S.
C: soft claret with blue tinge. **S:** winter.

'**Honeymoon**' (*L. odoratus*) Spencer   **F:** Brackley cat.
1974/75. **R:** Kershaw / Maishman. **I:** 1972. **D:** see
Cultivars chapter.

'**Honeypink**' (*L. odoratus*) Spencer   **F:** *NSPS Annual*
1979: 88. **R:** Kershaw / Maishman. **I:** 1977. **H:** T. **L:** U.
N: P. **P:** S. **C:** deep rose pink, w.g. **S:** summer.

'**Hotham Red**' (*L. annuus*)   **F:** Grayson cat. autumn
1999. **R:** Grayson. **I:** 2000. **D:** see Cultivars chapter.

'**Ida King**' (*L. odoratus*) Spencer   **F:** Eagle Sweet Peas
cat. 2006/07. **R:** G King / Eagle Sweet Peas. **I:** 2007.

D: see Cultivars chapter.

'**Imogen**' (*L. odoratus*) Spencer **F:** E.W. King & Co. cat. autumn 2000. **R:** Beane / E.W. King & Co. **I:** 2001. **D:** see Cultivars chapter.

'**Indigo Eyes**' (*L. vernus*) **F:** n/k. **R:** n/k. **I:** n/k. **A:** The leaflets are of f. *gracilis* type (1–2mm wide). **H:** T. **L:** M. **N:**M. **P:** S. **C:** blue. **S:** spring.

'**Indigo King**' (*L. odoratus*) Grandiflora **F:** R.D. (1883). **R:** H. Eckford. **I:** 1886. **H:** T. **L:** U. **N:** P. **P:** S. **C:** maroon shaded bronze. **S:** summer.

'**Indigo King**' Grayson (*L. odoratus*) Grandiflora **F:** Grayson cat. 1991/92. **R:** Grayson. **I:** 1992. **H:** T. **L:** U. **N:** P. **P:** S. **C:** maroon/violet. **S:** summer.

'**Invicta**' (*L. odoratus*) Spencer **F:** *NSPS Annual* 1922: xiii, Elliott cat. 1922. **R:** Woodcock. **I:** 1922. **H:** T. **L:** U. **N:** P. **P:** S. **C:** old rose. **S:** summer.

'**Invicta**' Christmas (*L. odoratus*) Spencer **F:** *NSPS Annual* 2008: 55. **R:** Christmas / P Johnson. **I:** 2015. **D:** see Cultivars chapter.

'**Isabella Cochrane**' (*L. odoratus*) Spencer **F:** Kerton Sweet Peas cat. 2001. **R:** Chisholm / Kerton Sweet Peas. **I:** 2001. **D:** see Cultivars chapter.

'**Jack Bridger**' (*L. odoratus*) Spencer **F:** Maishman cat. 1980/81. **R:** Hammett / Maishman. **I:** 1981. **D:** see Cultivars chapter.

'**Jack Ellis**' (*L. odoratus*) Grandiflora **F:** R. Parsons cat. 2017/18. **R:** Ellis / R. Parsons. **I:** 2018. **D:** see Cultivars chapter.

'**Jack Eveleigh**' (*L. odoratus*) Spencer **F:** R. Parsons cat. 2016/17. **R:** R. Parsons. **I:** 2017. **D:** see Cultivars chapter.

'**Jacko**' (*L. odoratus*) Spencer **F:** R. Parsons cat. 2016. **R:** R. Place / R. Parsons. **I:** 2016. **D:** see Cultivars chapter.

'**Jacqueline Ann**' (*L. odoratus*) Spencer **F:** R. Parsons cat. 2007/08. **R:** R. Parsons. **I:** 2008. **D:** see Cultivars chapter.

'**Jacqueline Heather**' (*L. odoratus*) Spencer **RHS:** AGM (H3) 2014. **F:** R. Parsons cat. 2011/12. **R:** R. Parsons. **I:** 2012. **D:** see Cultivars chapter.

'**Janet**' (*L. odoratus*) Spencer **F:** *NSPS Annual* 1933: x. **R:** J. Stevenson. **I:** 1933. **H:** T. **L:** U. **N:** P. **P:** S. **C:** rose pink. **S:** summer.

'**Janet**' Ferry Morse 1941 (*L. odoratus*) Spencer **F:** Ferry Morse Seed Co. cat. 1947. **R:** Ferry Morse Seed Co. **I:** 1941. **A:** Dark seeds. **H:** T. **L:** U. **N:** P. **P:** S. **C:** white. **S:** late spring.

'**Janet**' Ferry Morse 1961 (*L. odoratus*) Spencer **F:** E.W. King & Co. cat. 1961/62. **R:** Ferry Morse Seed Co. **I:** 1961. **A:** Dark seeds. **H:** T. **L:** U. **N:** M. **P:** S. **C:** white. **S:** late spring.

'**Janet**' Parsons (*L. odoratus*) Semi-grandiflora **F:** R. Parsons cat. 2009/10. **R:** R. Parsons. **I:** 2010. **D:** see Cultivars chapter.

'**Janet Scott**' (*L. odoratus*) Grandiflora **RHS:** AGM (H3) 1995. **F:** Vaughan Seed Store cat. 1904. **R:** C.C. Morse & Co. / Burpee Seeds. **I:** 1903. **D:** see Cultivars chapter.

'**Janetta Harrod**' (*L. odoratus*) Spencer **F:** Cooltonagh cat. 2004/05. **R:** Harrod. **I:** 2005. **H:** T. **L:** U. **N:** P. **P:** S. **C:** cream. **S:** summer.

'**Janey**' (*L. odoratus*) Spencer **F:** R. Parsons cat. 2015/16. **R:** Hammett / R. Parsons. **I:** 2016. **D:** see Cultivars chapter.

'**Janine Martin**' (*L. odoratus*) Spencer **F:** McDougall cat. 1998. **R:** Martin. **I:** 1960s. **D:** see Cultivars chapter.

'**Jayne Amanda**' (*L. odoratus*) Spencer **F:** Kerton Sweet Peas cat. 1990. **R:** Truslove / Marchant. **I:** 1985. **D:** see Cultivars chapter.

'**Jean Clifford**' (*L. odoratus*) Spencer **F:** n/k. **R:** n/k. **I:** n/k. **H:** T. **L:** U. **N:** P. **P:** D. **C:** purple flake, w.g. **S:** early spring.

'**Jeannie**' (*L. odoratus*) Spencer **F:** Cooltonagh cat. 2006/07. **R:** Harrod. **I:** 2007. **D:** see Cultivars chapter.

'**Jemima**' (*L. odoratus*) Spencer **F:** Kerton Sweet Peas cat. 2010. **R:** Beane / Kerton Sweet Peas. **I:** 2010. **D:** see Cultivars chapter.

Jet Set Series (*L. odoratus*) Spencer **F:** *NSPS Annual* 1973: i. **R:** Ferry Morse Seed Co. **I:** 1973. **N:** This series includes 'Amsterdam', 'Avon', 'Cologne', 'Killarney', 'Loch Lomond', 'Madrid', 'Mallorca', 'Matterhorn', 'Monte Carlo', 'Naples', 'Picotee', 'Rhineland', 'Riviera', 'Rome', 'St. Moritz', 'Tivoli', 'Venice', 'Vienna' and 'Westminster'. **H:** SD. **L:** U. **N:** P. **P:** S. **C:** various colours. **S:** summer.

'**Jill Walton**' (*L. odoratus*) Spencer **F:** *NSPS Annual* 1991: 35. **R:** Gubb / Kerton Sweet Peas. **I:** 1993. **D:** see Cultivars chapter.

'**Jilly**' (*L. odoratus*) Spencer **RHS:** AGM (H3) 1994. **F:** Unwins Seeds cat. autumn 1987. **R:** Harriss / Unwins Seeds. **I:** 1988. **D:** see Cultivars chapter.

'**Jim**' (*L. odoratus*) Spencer **F:** R. Parsons cat. 2007/08. **R:** R. Parsons. **I:** 2008. **H:** T. **L:** U. **N:** P. **P:** S.

C: cream. **S:** summer.

'Jim Mac' (*L. odoratus*) Spencer **F:** *NSPS Classification List* 2019. **R:** Beane / McDonald. **I:** 2019. **H:** T. **L:** U. **N:** P. **P:** S. **C:** pale mauve, c.g. **S:** summer.

'Jimelda' = 'Lynda's Blush'

'Jimmie MacBain' (*L. odoratus*) Spencer **F:** Kerton Sweet Peas cat. 1997. **R:** K Brewer / Kerton Sweet Peas. **I:** 1997. **H:** T. **L:** U. **N:** P. **P:** S. **C:** pale pink, w.g. **S:** summer.

'Jimmy' (*L. odoratus*) Spencer **F:** Ferry Morse Seed Co. cat. 1951. **R:** Ferry Morse Seed Co. **I:** 1951. **D:** see Cultivars chapter.

'Joan Elizabeth Child' (*L. odoratus*) Spencer **F:** R. Parsons cat. 2011/12. **R:** R. Parsons. **I:** 2012. **D:** see Cultivars chapter.

'Joejess' (*L. odoratus*) Spencer **F:** McDonald cat. 2014. **R:** Hubbuck / McDonald. **I:** 2014. **D:** see Cultivars chapter.

'John Adie' (*L. odoratus*) Spencer **F:** Kerton Sweet Peas cat. 2010. **R:** Adie / Kerton Sweet Peas. **I:** 2010. **H:** T. **L:** U. **N:** P. **P:** S. **C:** carmine. **S:** summer.

'John Gray' (*L. odoratus*) Spencer **RHS:** AM 2007, AGM (H3) 2009. **F:** *NSPS Annual* 2008: 53. **R:** R. Parsons. **I:** 2009. **D:** see Cultivars chapter.

'John William' (*L. odoratus*) Spencer **F:** Myers cat. 2015/16. **R:** Myers. **I:** 2016. **H:** T. **L:** U. **N:** P. **P:** S. **C:** rose pink, w.g. **S:** summer.

'Joker' (*L. odoratus*) Spencer **F:** Robert Bolton & Son cat. autumn 1972. **R:** Robert Bolton & Son. **I:** 1973. **H:** T. **L:** U. **N:** P. **P:** S. **C:** purple maroon. **S:** summer.

'Joyce Stanton' (*L. odoratus*) Spencer **F:** Manston cat. 2012. **R:** Manston. **I:** 2009. **D:** see Cultivars chapter.

'Judith Martin' (*L. odoratus*) Spencer **F:** McDougall cat. 1998. **R:** Martin. **I:** 1960s. **D:** see Cultivars chapter.

'Judith Wilkinson' (*L. odoratus*) Spencer **F:** *NSPS Annual* 2007: 55. **R:** Truslove / R. Parsons. **I:** 2008. **D:** see Cultivars chapter.

'Julie Ann' (*L. odoratus*) Spencer **F:** *NSPS Annual* 2010: 169. **R:** Eagle Sweet Peas. **I:** 2011. **D:** see Cultivars chapter.

'Juliet' (*L. odoratus*) Spencer **F:** *NSPS Catalogue of Names* 1912: 14. **R:** Deal. **I:** 1911. **H:** T. **L:** U. **N:** P. **P:** S. **C:** pale apricot on lemon. **S:** summer.

'Juliet' Simons (*L. odoratus*) Spencer **F:** n/k. **R:** Simons. **I:** 1938. **H:** T. **L:** U. **N:** P. **P:** S. **C:** cream pink.

S: summer.

'Juliet' Carters (*L. odoratus*) Spencer **F:** *NSPS Annual* 1946: 5. **R:** Carters Tested Seeds. **I:** 1946. **H:** T. **L:** U. **N:** P. **P:** S. **C:** blush pink with salmon edges. **S:** summer.

'Juliet' King (*L. odoratus*) Spencer **F:** *NSPS Annual* 1977: 65. **R:** E.W. King & Co. **I:** 1977. **H:** SD. **L:** M. **N:** P. **P:** S. **C:** salmon pink. **S:** summer.

'Juliet' Unwins (*L. odoratus*) Grandiflora **F:** Unwins Seeds cat autumn 2001. **R:** Unwins Seeds. **I:** 2002. **D:** see Cultivars chapter.

'Just Janet' (*L. odoratus*) Spencer **F:** Unwins Seeds cat. autumn 2013. **R:** Harrod / Unwins Seeds. **I:** 2014. **D:** see Cultivars chapter.

'Just Jenny' (*L. odoratus*) Spencer **F:** Eagle Sweet Peas cat. 2004/05. **R:** Eagle Sweet Peas. **I:** 2005. **D:** see Cultivars chapter.

'Just Julia' (*L. odoratus*) Spencer **RHS:** AGM (H3) 2012. **F:** R. Parsons cat. 2010/11. **R:** R. Parsons. **I:** 2011. **D:** see Cultivars chapter.

'Karen Harrod' (*L. odoratus*) Spencer **F:** *NSPS Annual* 2007: 55. **R:** Harrod / Kerton Sweet Peas. **I:** 2011. **D:** see Cultivars chapter.

'Karen Louise' (*L. odoratus*) Spencer **F:** E.W. King & Co. cat. autumn 1997. **R:** Beane / E.W. King & Co. **I:** 1998. **D:** see Cultivars chapter.

'Karen Lynette' (*L. odoratus*) Spencer **F:** McDougall cat. 2011. **R:** B McDougall. **I:** n/k. **H:** T. **L:** U. **N:** P. **P:** D. **C:** hot pink flake, w.g. **S:** winter.

'Karen Reeve' (*L. odoratus*) Spencer **F:** *NSPS Annual* 1981: 105. **R:** T Reeve / Marchant. **I:** 1985. **H:** T. **L:** U. **N:** P. **P:** S. **C:** dark maroon. **S:** summer.

'Karen Tremewan' (*L. odoratus*) Spencer **F:** *NSPS Annual* 1982: 80. **R:** Tremewan / Marchant. **I:** 1984. **D:** see Cultivars chapter.

'Karley' (*L. odoratus*) Spencer **F:** n/k. **R:** McDougall. **I:** 2016. **H:** T. **L:** U. **N:** P. **P:** D. **C:** n/k. **S:** winter.

'Kate Cumberpatch' (*L. odoratus*) Spencer **F:** *NSPS Annual* 2014: 63. **R:** Kerton Sweet Peas. **I:** 2015. **H:** T. **L:** U. **N:** P. **P:** S. **C:** lavender. **S:** summer.

'Katie Alice' (*L. odoratus*) Spencer **F:** Eagle Sweet Peas cat. 2005/06. **R:** Eagle Sweet Peas. **I:** 2006. **D:** see Cultivars chapter.

'Katrina Lee' (*L. odoratus*) Spencer **F:** McDougall cat. 1998. **R:** McDougall. **I:** n/k. **H:** T. **L:** U. **N:** P. **P:** D. **C:** magenta pink. **S:** early spring.

'Kenneth' (*L. odoratus*) Spencer **F:** Ferry Morse Seed

Co. cat. 1947. **R:** Ferry Morse Seed Co. **I:** 1944. **H:** T. **L:** U. **N:** P. **P:** S. **C:** deep crimson. **S:** late spring.

'Kenneth' Ferry Morse 1957 (*L. odoratus*) Spencer **F:** E.W. King & Co. cat. 1956/57. **R:** Ferry Morse Seed Co. **I:** 1957. **H:** T. **L:** U. **N:** M. **P:** S. **C:** deep crimson. **S:** late spring.

'**Kiera Madeline**' (*L. odoratus*) Spencer **F:** *NSPS Annual* 2009: 169. **R:** Eagle Sweet Peas. **I:** 2010. **D:** see Cultivars chapter.

'**Killarney**' (*L. odoratus*) Spencer **F:** *NSPS Annual* 1973: i. **R:** Ferry Morse Seed Co. **I:** 1973. **D:** see Cultivars chapter.

'**King Edward VII**' (*L. odoratus*) Grandiflora **RHS:** AGM (H3) 1995. **F:** *NSPS Annual* 1905: 28. **R:** H. Eckford. **I:** 1903. **D:** see Cultivars chapter.

'**King Size Crimson**' (*L. odoratus*) Spencer **F:** n/k. **R:** n/k. **I:** n/k. **H:** T. **L:** U. **N:** M. **P:** S. **C:** crimson. **S:** summer.

'**King Size Deep Rose**' (*L. odoratus*) Spencer **F:** R. Parsons cat. 2012/13. **R:** n/k. **I:** n/k. **H:** T. **L:** U. **N:** M. **P:** S. **C:** deep rose. **S:** early spring.

'**King Size Lavender**' (*L. odoratus*) Spencer **F:** n/k. **R:** n/k. **I:** n/k. **H:** T. **L:** U. **N:** M. **P:** S. **C:** lavender. **S:** summer.

'**King Size Light Salmon**' (*L. odoratus*) Spencer **F:** n/k. **R:** n/k. **I:** n/k. **H:** T. **L:** U. **N:** M. **P:** S. **C:** light salmon. **S:** summer.

'**King Size Mid Blue**' (*L. odoratus*) Spencer **F:** n/k. **R:** n/k. **I:** n/k. **H:** T. **L:** U. **N:** M. **P:** S. **C:** mid blue. **S:** summer.

'**King Size Navy Blue**' (*L. odoratus*) Semi-grandiflora **F:** Thompson & Morgan cat. 1998. **R:** Thompson & Morgan. **I:** 1998. **D:** see Cultivars chapter.

'**King Size Rose Pink**' (*L. odoratus*) Spencer **F:** R. Parsons cat. 2012/13. **R:** n/k. **I:** n/k. **H:** T. **L:** U. **N:** M. **P:** S. **C:** rose pink. **S:** summer.

'**King Size Salmon Cream**' (*L. odoratus*) Spencer **F:** n/k. **R:** n/k. **I:** n/k. **H:** T. **L:** U. **N:** M. **P:** S. **C:** salmon pink, c.g. **S:** summer.

'**King Size Scarlet**' (*L. odoratus*) Spencer **F:** n/k. **R:** n/k. **I:** n/k. **H:** T. **L:** U. **N:** M. **P:** S. **C:** scarlet. **S:** summer.

King Size Series **A:** Appear to be reverted early multiflora Spencer material.

'**King Size White**' (*L. odoratus*) Spencer **F:** n/k. **R:** n/k. **I:** n/k. **H:** T. **L:** U. **N:** M. **P:** S. **C:** white. **S:** summer.

'**Kingfisher**' (*L. odoratus*) Semi-grandiflora **F:** Grayson cat. 1993. **R:** J. Taylor / Grayson. **I:** 1993. **D:** see Cultivars chapter.

'**Kippen Cream**' (*L. odoratus*) Spencer **F:** Kerton Sweet Peas cat. 1998. **R:** Chisholm / Kerton Sweet Peas. **I:** 1998. **D:** see Cultivars chapter.

'**Knee-Hi Blush Pink**' (*L. odoratus*) Spencer **F:** *NSPS Annual* 1966: 70. **R:** Ferry Morse Seed Co. **I:** 1966. **H:** SD. **L:** U. **N:** M. **P:** S. **C:** blush rose pink. **S:** summer.

'Knee-Hi Bright Blue' = 'Knee-Hi Mid Blue'

'**Knee-Hi Carmine**' (*L. odoratus*) Spencer **F:** Robert Bolton & Son cat. autumn 1967. **R:** Robert Bolton & Son. **I:** 1968. **H:** SD. **L:** U. **N:** M. **P:** S. **C:** carmine. **S:** summer.

'**Knee-Hi Cerise Pink**' (*L. odoratus*) Spencer **F:** *NSPS Annual* 1968: viii. **R:** Carters Tested Seeds. **I:** 1968. **H:** SD. **L:** U. **N:** M. **P:** S. **C:** cerise pink. **S:** summer.

'**Knee-Hi Cream Pink**' (*L. odoratus*) Spencer **F:** *NSPS Annual* 1966: 70. **R:** Ferry Morse Seed Co. **I:** 1966. **D:** see Cultivars chapter.

'**Knee-Hi Crimson**' (*L. odoratus*) Spencer **F:** *NSPS Annual* 1966: 70. **R:** Ferry Morse Seed Co. **I:** 1966. **H:** SD. **L:** U. **N:** M. **P:** S. **C:** crimson. **S:** summer.

'**Knee-Hi Deep Rose Pink**' (*L. odoratus*) Spencer **F:** Everitt cat. 1973/74. **R:** Ferry Morse Seed Co. / Everitt. **I:** 1974. **H:** SD. **L:** U. **N:** M. **P:** S. **C:** deep rose. **S:** summer.

'**Knee-Hi Deep Scarlet**' (*L. odoratus*) Spencer **F:** *NSPS Annual* 1966: 70. **R:** Ferry Morse Seed Co. **I:** 1966. **H:** SD. **L:** U. **N:** M. **P:** S. **C:** deep scarlet. **S:** summer.

'**Knee-Hi Light Blue**' (*L. odoratus*) Spencer **F:** Everitt cat. 1973/74. **R:** Ferry Morse Seed Co. / Everitt. **I:** 1974. **H:** SD. **L:** U. **N:** M. **P:** S. **C:** pale blue. **S:** summer.

'**Knee-Hi Light Lavender**' (*L. odoratus*) Spencer **F:** E.W. King & Co. cat. 1966/67. **R:** Carters Tested Seeds. **I:** 1966. **H:** SD. **L:** U. **N:** M. **P:** S. **C:** lavender-mauve. **S:** summer.

'**Knee-Hi Mid Blue**' (*L. odoratus*) Spencer **F:** *NSPS Annual* 1966: 70. **R:** Ferry Morse Seed Co. **I:** 1966. **H:** SD. **L:** U. **N:** M. **P:** S. **C:** mid blue. **S:** summer.

'**Knee-Hi Pink**' (*L. odoratus*) Spencer **F:** *NSPS Annual* 1966: 70. **R:** Ferry Morse Seed Co. **I:** 1966. **H:** SD. **L:** U. **N:** M. **P:** S. **C:** clear pink. **S:** summer.

'**Knee-Hi Rose Crimson**' (*L. odoratus*) Spencer **F:** *NSPS Annual* 1966: 70. **R:** Ferry Morse Seed Co. **I:** 1966. **D:** see Cultivars chapter.

'Knee-Hi Rose Pink' (*L. odoratus*) Spencer **F:** Robert Bolton & Son cat. autumn 1967. **R:** Carters Tested Seeds. **I:** 1968. **H:** SD. **L:** U. **N:** M. **P:** S. **C:** rose pink, w.g. **S:** summer.

'Knee-Hi Salmon Pink' (*L. odoratus*) Spencer **F:** *NSPS Annual* 1966: 70. **R:** Ferry Morse Seed Co. **I:** 1966. **H:** SD. **L:** U. **N:** M. **P:** S. **C:** salmon pink. **S:** summer.

'Knee-Hi Scarlet Cerise' (*L. odoratus*) Spencer **F:** *NSPS Annual* 1966: 71. **R:** Ferry Morse Seed Co. **I:** 1966. **H:** SD. **L:** U. **N:** M. **P:** S. **C:** scarlet cerise. **S:** summer.

Knee-Hi Series (*L. odoratus*) Spencer **R:** Ferry Morse Seed Co. **I:** from 1966. **A:** Originally cultivars in this Series were given Knee-Hi prefix names but later sold under more attractive names of Californian cities. Succeeded by Jet-Set Series.

'Knee-Hi White' (*L. odoratus*) Spencer **F:** *NSPS Annual* 1966: 71. **R:** Ferry Morse Seed Co. **I:** 1966. **D:** see Cultivars chapter.

'Kronprinzessin von Preussen' = Crown Princess of Prussia

'Kyle the Clown' (*L. odoratus*) Spencer **F:** Kerton Sweet Peas cat. 2001. **R:** Chisholm / Kerton Sweet Peas. **I:** 2001. **H:** T. **L:** U. **N:** P. **P:** S. **C:** stripe. **S:** summer.

'Lady Exeter' (*L. odoratus*) Spencer **F:** *NSPS Annual* 1912. **R:** Elsom. **I:** n/k. **H:** T. **L:** U. **N:** P. **P:** S. **C:** rose. **S:** summer.

'Lady Fairbairn' (*L. odoratus*) Spencer **F:** Unwins Seeds cat. autumn 1982. **R:** Harriss / Unwins Seeds. **I:** 1983. **H:** T. **L:** U. **N:** P. **P:** S. **C:** soft lilac pink. **S:** summer.

'Lady Grisel Hamilton' (*L. odoratus*) Grandiflora **F:** Anon. (1895/96). **R:** H. Eckford. **I:** 1898. **D:** see Cultivars chapter.

'Lady Nicholson' (*L. odoratus*) Spencer **F:** R. Parsons cat. 2016. **R:** G King / R. Parsons. **I:** 2016. **D:** see Cultivars chapter.

'Lady Penny' (*L. odoratus*) Spencer **F:** Robert Bolton & Son cat. 1994/95. **R:** Robert Bolton & Son. **I:** 1995. **H:** T. **L:** U. **N:** P. **P:** S. **C:** lavender. **S:** summer.

'Lady Susan' (*L. odoratus*) Spencer **F:** *NSPS Annual* 1992: 51. **R:** Albutt / Eagle Sweet Peas. **I:** 1995. **H:** T. **L:** U. **N:** P. **P:** S. **C:** orange-pink. **S:** summer.

'Lady Turral' (*L. odoratus*) Grandiflora **F:** Grayson cat. 1993. **R:** Turral / Grayson. **I:** 1962 / 1993. **D:** see

'Laila K' (*L. odoratus*) Spencer **F:** Kerton Sweet Peas cat. 2013. **R:** Kerton Sweet Peas. **I:** 2013. **D:** see Cultivars chapter.

'Lake Windermere' (*L. odoratus*) Spencer **F:** Robert Bolton & Son cat. 2002/03. **R:** Robert Bolton & Son. **I:** 2003. **H:** T. **L:** U. **N:** P. **P:** S. **C:** mid blue. **S:** summer.

'Lakeland Blizzard' (*L. odoratus*) Spencer **F:** *NSPS Annual* 2005: 54. **R:** R. Place / R. Parsons. **I:** 2016. **D:** see Cultivars chapter.

'Lamorna's Love' (*L. vernus*) **F:** n/k. **R:** Marsh. **I:** 1990s. **A:** Anon. (2000). The leaflets are of f. *angustifolius* type (15–30mm wide). **D:** see Cultivars chapter.

'Laura Webster' (*L. odoratus*) Spencer **F:** n/k. **R:** Hammett / Denny. **I:** 2009. **A:** Name first appeared on the Seedngrow website (seen 19 Jan 2009). **D:** see Cultivars chapter.

'Lauren Landy' (*L. odoratus*) Spencer **RHS:** AGM (H3) 2011. **F:** *NSPS Annual* 2008: 54. **R:** Harrod. **I:** 2010. **D:** see Cultivars chapter.

'Lauren Louise' (*L. odoratus*) Spencer **F:** Kerton Sweet Peas cat. 2017. **R:** Kerton Sweet Peas. **I:** 2017. **H:** T. **L:** U. **N:** P. **P:** S. **C:** blue flush, w.g. **S:** summer.

'Lavender Flake' (*L. odoratus*) Spencer **F:** Owl's Acre Sweet Peas cat. 2002/03. **R:** Owl's Acre Sweet Peas. **I:** n/k. **D:** see Cultivars chapter.

'Lavender Sprite' (*L. odoratus*) Grandiflora **RHS:** AGM (H3) 2013. **F:** *NSPS Annual* 2014: 58. **R:** Owl's Acre Sweet Peas. **I:** 2013. **D:** see Cultivars chapter.

'Leading Light' (*L. odoratus*) Spencer **F:** R. Parsons cat. 2004/05. **R:** Hammett / Arthur Yates & Co. **I:** n/k. **D:** see Cultivars chapter.

'Leamington' (*L. odoratus*) Spencer **F:** *NSPS Annual* 1959: 1. **R:** Colledge / Unwins Seeds. **I:** 1961. **D:** see Cultivars chapter.

'Leilani Bluebell' (*L. odoratus*) Spencer **F:** n/k. **R:** Beane. **I:** 2017. **H:** T. **L:** U. **N:** P. **P:** S. **C:** purple / mauve stripe. **S:** summer.

'Lemon and Lime' = 'Lemonade'

'Lemonade' (*L. chloranthus*) **F:** Thompson & Morgan 1993 cat. **R:** n/k. **I:** n/k. **D:** see Cultivars chapter.

'Len Harrod' (*L. odoratus*) Spencer **F:** Cooltonagh cat. 2011/12. **R:** Harrod. **I:** 2012. **D:** see Cultivars chapter.

'Leominster Boy' = 'Vincent'

'Lilac Kiss' (*L. odoratus*) Spencer   **F:** *NSPS Annual* 2007: 54. **R:** Wells. **I:** n/k. **H:** T. **L:** U. **N:** P. **P:** S. **C:** mid lilac. **S:** summer.

'Lilac Ripple' (*L. odoratus*) Spencer   **F:** Thompson & Morgan cat. 1989. **R:** W. Thomas / Thompson & Morgan. **I:** 1989. **D:** see Cultivars chapter.

'Lilac Romance' (*L. odoratus*) Spencer   **F:** *NSPS Annual* 2007: 54. **R:** Wells / Kerton Sweet Peas. **I:** 2010. **D:** see Cultivars chapter.

'Lilac Silk' (*L. odoratus*) Spencer   **F:** *NSPS Annual* 1988: 16. **R:** Robert Bolton & Son. **I:** 1989. **H:** T. **L:** U. **N:** P. **P:** S. **C:** lilac pink, w.g. **S:** summer.

'Limelight' (*L. odoratus*) Spencer   **F:** n/k. **R:** n/k. **I:** before 1930. **H:** T. **L:** U. **N:** P. **P:** S. **C:** n/k. **S:** summer.

'Limelight' Bolton (*L. odoratus*) Spencer   **F:** *NSPS Annual* 1950: 66. **R:** Robert Bolton & Son. **I:** 1951. **H:** T. **L:** U. **N:** P. **P:** S. **C:** pale blue. **S:** summer.

'Limelight' Owl's Acre Sweet Peas (*L. odoratus*) Spencer   **F:** Owl's Acre Sweet Peas cat. 2002/03. **R:** Owl's Acre Sweet Peas. **I:** 2003. **H:** T. **L:** U. **N:** P. **P:** S. **C:** cream. **S:** summer.

'Linda C.' (*L. odoratus*) Spencer   **F:** Kerton Sweet Peas cat. 2001. **R:** Chisholm / Kerton Sweet Peas. **I:** 2001. **D:** see Cultivars chapter.

'Linda Carole' (*L. odoratus*) Spencer   **F:** Eagle Sweet Peas cat. 2003/04. **R:** J.D. Place / Eagle Sweet Peas. **I:** 2004. **D:** see Cultivars chapter.

'Linda Mary' (*L. odoratus*) Spencer   **F:** R. Parsons cat. 2006/07. **R:** R. Parsons. **I:** 2007. **D:** see Cultivars chapter.

'Linda Richards' (*L. odoratus*) Spencer   **F:** R. Parsons cat. 2010/11. **R:** R. Parsons. **I:** 2011. **D:** see Cultivars chapter.

'Lipstick' (*L. odoratus*) Spencer   **F:** *NSPS Classification List* 2015. **R:** Hammett / Shepherd. **I:** 2003. **A:** Name first appeared on the Keating website (seen 28 Dec 2002). **D:** see Cultivars chapter.

'Lipstick' Unwins (*L. odoratus*) Spencer   **RHS:** AGM (H3) 2010. **F:** Unwins Seeds cat. autumn 2007. **R:** Unwins Seeds. **I:** 2008. **D:** see Cultivars chapter.

'Lisa Marie' (*L. odoratus*) Spencer   **F:** Eagle Sweet Peas cat. 2003/04. **R:** J.D. Place / Eagle Sweet Peas. **I:** 2004. **D:** see Cultivars chapter.

'Little Red Riding Hood' (*L. odoratus*) Grandiflora   **F:** Somerset cat. 2012. **R:** Hammett / Somerset. **I:** n/k. **D:** see Cultivars chapter.

Little Sweetheart Series (*L. odoratus*) Spencer   **R:** Macdonald. **I:** 1957. **A:** Usually sold as Erect Dwarf Mixed, but includes 'Boy Blue', 'Caprice', 'Coquette', 'Heidi', 'Pansy Face', 'Pollyanna', 'Sinbad' and 'Snowflake'. **D:** Dwarf, upright plants. **H:** SD.

'Lizbeth' (*L. odoratus*) Spencer   **F:** Tremewan cat. 1992/93. **R:** Tremewan. **I:** 1993. **D:** see Cultivars chapter.

'Lois' (*L. odoratus*) Spencer   **F:** Ferry Morse Seed Co. cat. 1947. **R:** Ferry Morse Seed Co. **I:** 1940. **D:** see Cultivars chapter.

'Lois' Ferry Morse 1961 (*L. odoratus*) Spencer   **F:** E.W. King & Co. cat. 1961/62. **R:** Ferry Morse Seed Co. **I:** 1961. **H:** T. **L:** U. **N:** M. **P:** S. **C:** rose pink, w.g. **S:** late spring.

'Lord Nelson' (*L. odoratus*) Grandiflora   **F:** *NSPS Annual* 1906. **R:** Isaac House & Son. **I:** 1907. **D:** see Cultivars chapter.

'Love Song' (*L. odoratus*) Spencer   **F:** E.W. King & Co. cat. 1965/66. **R:** Burpee Seeds. **I:** 1966. **H:** T. **L:** U. **N:** M. **P:** S. **C:** salmon pink, w.g. **S:** summer.

'Lovejoy' (*L. odoratus*) Spencer   **F:** Robert Bolton & Son cat. 1991/92. **R:** Robert Bolton & Son. **I:** 1992. **D:** see Cultivars chapter.

'Lucy Hawthorne' (*L. odoratus*) Spencer   **F:** *NSPS Annual* 2010: 169. **R:** Eagle Sweet Peas. **I:** 2011. **A:** Pale seeds. **D:** see Cultivars chapter.

'Lunar Sea' (*L. odoratus*) Spencer   **F:** R. Parsons cat. 2013/14. **R:** Hammett. **I:** 2009. **D:** see Cultivars chapter.

'Lynda's Blush' (*L. odoratus*) Spencer   **F:** *NSPS Annual* 1985: 29. **R:** Hammett / Mr Fothergills Seeds Ltd. **I:** 2015. **H:** T. **L:** U. **N:** M. **P:** S. **C:** crimson. **S:** summer.

'Lynn Davey' (*L. odoratus*) Spencer   **RHS:** AM 1993. **F:** *NSPS Annual* 1994: 65. **R:** E.W. James / Sewell. **I:** 1998. **H:** T. **L:** U. **N:** P. **P:** S. **C:** lavender. **S:** summer.

'Lynn Fiona' (*L. odoratus*) Spencer   **F:** Kerton Sweet Peas cat. 2000. **R:** Fleming Robertson / Kerton Sweet Peas. **I:** 2000. **H:** T. **L:** U. **N:** P. **P:** S. **C:** pale blush pink, c.g. **S:** summer.

'Madelaine' (*L. vernus*)   **F:** n/k. **R:** Joe Sharman, Monksilver Nursery. **I:** c.2000. **A:** The leaflets are of f. *gracilis* type (1–2mm wide). **H:** T. **L:** M. **N:** M. **P:** S. **C:** pink / white. **S:** spring.

'Madison' (*L. odoratus*) Grandiflora   **RHS:** AGM (H3) 2015. **F:** Unwins Seeds cat. autumn 2013. **R:** Unwins

Seeds. **I:** 2014. **D:** see Cultivars chapter.

'**Madrid**' (*L. odoratus*) Spencer   **F:** Everitt cat. 1972/73. **R:** Ferry Morse Seed Co. **I:** 1973. **D:** see Cultivars chapter.

'**Maestro**' (*L. odoratus*) Spencer   **F:** *NSPS Annual* 2008: 153. **R:** B.R. Jones / Eagle Sweet Peas. **I:** 2009. **D:** see Cultivars chapter.

'**Magic**' (*L. odoratus*) Spencer   **F:** *NSPS Annual* 1920: 60. **R:** Robert Bolton & Son. **I:** 1919. **H:** T. **L:** U. **N:** P. **P:** S. **C:** mauve / amethyst. **S:** summer.

'Magic' Bolton 1967 (*L. odoratus*) Spencer   **F:** Robert Bolton & Son cat. autumn 1966, E.W. King & Co. cat. 1966/67. **R:** Robert Bolton & Son. **I:** 1967. **H:** T. **L:** U. **N:** P. **P:** D. **C:** deep pink, w.g. **S:** summer.

'Magic' Ferry Morse (*L. odoratus*) Spencer   **F:** n/k. **R:** Ferry Morse Seed Co. **I:** 1942. **H:** T. **L:** U. **N:** P. **P:** S. **C:** rosy lavender. **S:** early.

'Magic' Walker (*L. odoratus*) Spencer   **F:** Marchant cat. 1986. **R:** W. Walker / Marchant. **I:** 1986. **H:** T. **L:** U. **N:** P. **P:** S. **C:** pale pink, c.g. **S:** summer.

'**Magnificent Maroon**' (*L. odoratus*) Spencer   **F:** R. Parsons cat. 2016. **R:** Harrod / R. Parsons. **I:** 2016. **D:** see Cultivars chapter.

'**Mahogany**' (*L. odoratus*) Spencer   **F:** *NSPS Annual* 1934: vi. **R:** Suttons. **I:** 1934. **H:** T. **L:** U. **N:** P. **P:** S. **C:** red maroon. **S:** summer.

'Mahogany' Hammett (*L. odoratus*) Spencer   **F:** n/k. **R:** Hammett. **I:** 2017. **H:** T. **L:** U. **N:** P. **P:** S. **C:** dark maroon. **S:** spring.

'Mahogany Cupid'   = 'Cupid Mahogany'

'**Malmac Alba**' (*L. odoratus*) Spencer   **F:** McDougall cat. 1998. **R:** McDougall. **I:** n/k. **H:** T. **L:** U. **N:** P. **P:** S. **C:** white. **S:** winter.

'**Maloy**' (*L. odoratus*) Spencer   **F:** Parsons cat. 2015/16. **R:** Hammett. **I:** 2015. **A:** Name first appeared on the Hammett website (seen 23 Feb. 2015). **D:** see Cultivars chapter.

'**Mammoth Cream Pink**' (*L. odoratus*) Spencer   **F:** E.W. King & Co. cat. autumn 1989. **R:** Denholm Seeds. **I:** 1982. **D:** see Cultivars chapter.

'**Mammoth Crimson**' (*L. odoratus*) Spencer   **F:** Bailey cat. 1986. **R:** Denholm Seeds. **I:** 1982. **H:** T. **L:** U. **N:** M. **P:** n/k. **C:** crimson. **S:** winter.

'**Mammoth Deep Rose**' (*L. odoratus*) Spencer   **F:** Bailey cat. 1986. **R:** Denholm Seeds. **I:** 1982. **H:** T. **L:** U. **N:** M. **P:** n/k. **C:** rosy magenta. **S:** winter.

'**Mammoth Flag Blue**' (*L. odoratus*) Spencer   **F:** Gaisford cat. 1985. **R:** Denholm Seeds. **I:** n/k. **H:** T. **L:** U. **N:** M. **P:** n/k. **C:** flag blue. **S:** winter.

'**Mammoth Lavender**' (*L. odoratus*) Spencer   **F:** Gaisford cat. 1985. **R:** Denholm Seeds. **I:** 1982. **H:** T. **L:** U. **N:** M. **P:** n/k. **C:** lavender. **S:** winter.

'**Mammoth Light Salmon**' (*L. odoratus*) Spencer   **F:** E.W. King & Co. cat. autumn 1991. **R:** Denholm Seeds. **I:** 1982. **H:** T. **L:** U. **N:** M. **P:** n/k. **C:** light salmon. **S:** winter.

'**Mammoth Mid Blue**' (*L. odoratus*) Spencer   **F:** Gaisford cat. 1985. **R:** Denholm Seeds. **I:** 1982. **H:** T. **L:** U. **N:** M. **P:** n/k. **C:** mid blue. **S:** winter.

'**Mammoth Navy**' (*L. odoratus*) Spencer   **F:** E.W. King & Co. cat. autumn 1989. **R:** Denholm Seeds. **I:** around 1982. **D:** see Cultivars chapter.

'**Mammoth Orchid**' (*L. odoratus*) Spencer   **F:** E.W. King & Co. cat. autumn 1989. **R:** Denholm Seeds. **I:** n/k. **H:** T. **L:** U. **N:** M. **P:** S. **C:** mauve. **S:** early spring.

'**Mammoth Rose Pink**' (*L. odoratus*) Spencer   **F:** Bailey cat. 1986. **R:** Denholm Seeds. **I:** 1982. **H:** T. **L:** U. **N:** M. **P:** S. **C:** rose pink, w.g. **S:** early spring.

'**Mammoth Salmon Cream Pink**' (*L. odoratus*) Spencer   **F:** Bailey cat. 1986. **R:** Denholm Seeds. **I:** 1982. **H:** T. **L:** U. **N:** M. **P:** n/k. **C:** pale salmon pink, c.g. **S:** winter.

'**Mammoth Salmon Pink**' (*L. odoratus*) Spencer   **F:** Gaisford cat. 1985. **R:** Denholm Seeds. **I:** 1982. **H:** T. **L:** U. **N:** M. **P:** S. **C:** salmon pink, c.g. **S:** early spring.

'**Mammoth Scarlet**' (*L. odoratus*) Spencer   **F:** Gaisford cat. 1985. **R:** Denholm Seeds. **I:** 1982. **H:** T. **L:** U. **N:** M. **P:** n/k. **C:** scarlet. **S:** winter.

Mammoth Series (*L. odoratus*) Spencer   **R:** Denholm Seeds. **D:** Early-flowering, multiflora sweet peas.

'**Mammoth White**' (*L. odoratus*) Spencer   **F:** Gaisford cat. 1985. **R:** Denholm Seeds. **I:** 1982. **A:** Dark seeds. **H:** T. **L:** U. **N:** M. **P:** n/k. **C:** white. **S:** winter.

'**Margaret**' (*L. odoratus*) Spencer   **F:** Cuthbertson (1916). **R:** R. Wright. **I:** before 1916. **H:** T. **L:** U. **N:** P. **P:** S. **C:** orange salmon. **S:** summer.

'Margaret' King (*L. odoratus*) Spencer   **F:** n/k. **R:** E.W. King & Co. **I:** 1948. **H:** T. **L:** U. **N:** P. **P:** S. **C:** mauve. **S:** summer.

'Margaret' Denholm (*L. odoratus*) Spencer   **F:** E.W. King & Co. cat. 1963/64. **R:** Denholm Seeds. **I:** 1960. **H:** T. **L:** U. **N:** M. **P:** S. **C:** rose pink, w.g. **S:** early spring.

'Margaret' Pettipher (*L. odoratus*) Spencer   **F:** Eagle Sweet Peas cat. 2003/04. **R:** Pettipher / Eagle Sweet

Peas. **I:** 2004. **H:** T. **L:** U. **N:** P. **P:** S. **C:** orange red.
S: summer.

'Margaret' UK (*L. odoratus*) Spencer **F:** *NSPS Annual*
2006: 63. **R:** n/k. **I:** 2008. **H:** T. **L:** U. **N:** M. **P:** S.
C: scarlet. **S:** winter.

'Margaret Hastie' (*L. odoratus*) Spencer **F:** R. Parsons
cat. 2010/11. **R:** R. Parsons. **I:** 2011. **H:** T. **L:** U. **N:** P.
P: S. **C:** lavender stripe, w.g. **S:** summer.

'Margaret Hughson' (*L. odoratus*) Spencer **F:** Kerton
Sweet Peas cat. 2008. **R:** Chisholm / Kerton Sweet
Peas. **I:** 2008. **H:** T. **L:** U. **N:** P. **P:** S. **C:** white with pink
flush on wings. **S:** summer.

'Margaret Joyce' (*L. odoratus*) Spencer **RHS:** AGM
(H3) 1997. **F:** Kerton Sweet Peas cat. 1996.
R: Fleming Robertson / Kerton Sweet Peas. **I:** 1996.
H: T. **L:** U. **N:** P. **P:** S. **C:** mid blue. **S:** summer.

'Margaret's Delight' (*L. odoratus*) Spencer **F:** Kerton
Sweet Peas cat. 2012. **R:** Fleming Robertson / Kerton
Sweet Peas. **I:** 2012. **D:** see Cultivars chapter.

'Margret Joy' (*L. odoratus*) Spencer **F:** McDougall cat.
1998. **R:** McDougall. **I:** n/k. **H:** T. **L:** U. **N:** P. **P:** D.
C: purple. **S:** early spring.

'Marie's Melody' (*L. odoratus*) Spencer **F:** *NSPS
Annual* 1997: 73. **R:** J.D. Place / R. Parsons. **I:** 2013.
D: see Cultivars chapter.

'Marilyn Jean' (*L. odoratus*) Spencer **F:** McDougall
cat. 1998. **R:** McDougall. **I:** 1980s. **H:** T. **L:** U. **N:** P.
P: n/k. **C:** mid blue. **S:** winter.

'Marion' (*L. odoratus*) Spencer **F:** *NSPS Catalogue of
Names* 1912: 17. **R:** Dobbie & Co. **I:** 1910. **H:** T. **L:** U.
N: P. **P:** S. **C:** pale lilac, rose pink. **S:** summer.

'Marion' Dipnall (*L. odoratus*) Spencer
F: Cuthbertson (1916). **R:** Dipnall. **I:** 1914. **H:** T. **L:** U.
N: P. **P:** S. **C:** clear salmon rose. **S:** summer.

'Marion' Unwins (*L. odoratus*) Spencer **F:** Robert
Bolton & Son cat. 1935. **R:** Unwins Seeds. **I:** 1932.
H: T. **L:** U. **N:** P. **P:** S. **C:** rich salmon pink. **S:** summer.

'Marion' Ferry Morse (*L. odoratus*) Spencer **F:** Ferry
Morse Seed Co. cat. 1947. **R:** Ferry Morse Seed Co.
I: 1942. **A:** Dark seeds. **H:** T. **L:** U. **N:** P. **P:** S. **C:** cream.
S: late spring.

'Marion' Walker (*L. odoratus*) Spencer **F:** *NSPS
Annual* 1983: 5. **R:** W. Walker / Marchant. **I:** 1983.
D: see Cultivars chapter.

'Marjorie Carrier' (*L. odoratus*) Spencer **F:** R. Parsons
cat. 2016. **R:** R. Parsons. **I:** 2016. **D:** see Cultivars
chapter.

'Mark Harrod' (*L. odoratus*) Spencer **F:** Cooltonagh
cat. 2006/07. **R:** Harrod. **I:** 2007. **D:** see Cultivars
chapter.

'Mark Williams' (*L. odoratus*) Spencer **F:** *NSPS
Classification List* 2018. **R:** Eagle Sweet Peas. **I:** 2018.
H: T. **L:** U. **N:** P. **P:** S. **C:** maroon. **S:** summer.

'Mars' (*L. odoratus*) Grandiflora **F:** Anon. (1895/96).
R: H. Eckford. **I:** 1896. **H:** T. **L:** U. **N:** P. **P:** S. **C:** mid red,
hooded. **S:** summer.

'Mars' Ferry Morse (*L. odoratus*) Spencer **F:** Ferry
Morse Seed Co. cat. 1938. **R:** Ferry Morse Seed Co.
I: 1938. **H:** T. **L:** U. **N:** P. **P:** S. **C:** deep crimson.
S: winter.

'Mars' Unwins (*L. odoratus*) Spencer **F:** Unwins
Seeds cat. autumn 1995. **R:** Unwins Seeds. **I:** 1996.
D: see Cultivars chapter.

'Martha Lane Fox' (*L. odoratus*) Spencer **F:** Brackley
cat. 2000/01. **R:** Brackley. **I:** 2001. **H:** T. **L:** U. **N:** P. **P:** S.
C: scarlet. **S:** summer.

'Martha Mary' (*L. odoratus*) Spencer **RHS:** AGM (H3)
2015. **F:** *NSPS Annual* 2015: 70. **R:** Kerton Sweet
Peas. **I:** 2016. **D:** see Cultivars chapter.

'Marti Caine' (*L. odoratus*) Spencer **F:** Matthewman
cat. 1995/96. **R:** Beane / Matthewman. **I:** 1996. **H:** T.
L: U. **N:** P. **P:** S. **C:** crimson. **S:** summer.

'Mary' (*L. odoratus*) Spencer **F:** n/k. **R:** n/k. **I:** before
1927. **H:** T. **L:** U. **N:** P. **P:** S. **C:** n/k. **S:** summer.

'Mary' King (*L. odoratus*) Spencer **F:** E.W. King & Co.
cat. 1951/52. **R:** E.W. King & Co. **I:** 1948. **H:** T. **L:** M.
N: P. **P:** S. **C:** rose pink. **S:** summer.

'Mary' Sakata (*L. odoratus*) Spencer **F:** n/k. **R:** Sakata
Seed Co. **I:** 1994. **A:** Name first appeared on the
Japanese Plant Variety Protection website (seen 5
Dec 1994). **H:** T. **L:** U. **N:** M. **P:** D. **C:** salmon pink, c.g.
S: winter.

'Mary Cynthia' (*L. odoratus*) Spencer **F:** *NSPS
Annual* 2008: 55. **R:** Hunt / E.W. King & Co. **I:** 2010.
H: T. **L:** U. **N:** P. **P:** S. **C:** salmon pink, c.g. **S:** summer.

'Mary Lou Heard' (*L. odoratus*) Spencer **F:** n/k.
R: Hammett / Shepherd. **I:** 2004. **H:** T. **L:** U. **N:** P. **P:** S.
C: mauve / lavender. **S:** summer.

'Mary Mac' (*L. odoratus*) Spencer **RHS:** AGM (H3)
2012. **F:** *NSPS Annual* 2013: 55. **R:** McDonald. **I:** 2015.
D: see Cultivars chapter.

'Mary Malcolm' (*L. odoratus*) Spencer **F:** E.W. King &
Co. cat. 1956/57. **R:** Robert Bolton & Son. **I:** 1957. **H:** T.
L: U. **N:** P. **P:** D. **C:** peach, c.g. **S:** summer.

'Mary Pannell' (*L. odoratus*) Spencer   **RHS:** AM 1996 as 'Daily Mail'. **F:** *NSPS Annual* 1991: 36. **R:** Beane / Unwins Seeds. **I:** 1997. **D:** see Cultivars chapter.

'Mary Priestley' (*L. odoratus*) Spencer   **F:** *NSPS Annual* 2014: 194. **R:** Priestley / Myers. **I:** 2015. **D:** see Cultivars chapter.

'Matterhorn' (*L. odoratus*) Spencer   **F:** *NSPS Annual* 1973: i. **R:** Ferry Morse Seed Co. **I:** 1973. **D:** see Cultivars chapter.

'Matucana' (*L. odoratus*) Grandiflora   **RHS:** AGM (H3) 2014. **F:** Turral cat. 1964. **R:** Harland / Turral. **I:** 1955. **D:** see Cultivars chapter.

'Maudie Best' (*L. odoratus*) Spencer   **F:** Malin cat. 1971/72. **R:** Malin. **I:** 1972. **H:** T. **L:** U. **N:** P. **P:** S. **C:** maroon. **S:** summer.

'Mauve Queen' (*L. odoratus*) Grandiflora   **F:** R.D. (1887). **R:** H. Eckford. **I:** 1887. **D:** see Cultivars chapter.

'Mauve Queen' Heslington (*L. odoratus*) Spencer   **F:** Beal (1914). **R:** Heslington / Dobbie & Co. **I:** 1911. **H:** T. **L:** U. **N:** P. **P:** S. **C:** bright mauve. **S:** summer.

'Mauve Queen' Simons (*L. odoratus*) Spencer   **F:** n/k. **R:** Simons. **I:** 1938. **H:** T. **L:** U. **N:** P. **P:** S. **C:** soft mauve. **S:** summer.

'Mauve Queen Cupid' (*L. odoratus*) Grandiflora   **F:** C.C. Morse & Co. cat. 1906. **R:** n/k. **I:** n/k. **H:** SD. **L:** U. **N:** P. **P:** D. **C:** mauve. **S:** summer.

'Mauvette' (*L. odoratus*) Spencer   **F:** *NSPS Annual* 1963: 46. **R:** Burpee Seeds. **I:** 1966. **A:** Belongs to the Bijou Series. **H:** D. **L:** U. **N:** P. **P:** S. **C:** mauve. **S:** spring.

'Maxeen Martin' (*L. odoratus*) Spencer   **F:** McDougall cat. 2011. **R:** Martin. **I:** n/k. **D:** see Cultivars chapter.

'Mayflower 400' (*L. odoratus*) Spencer   **F:** Fothergills cat. 2019/20. **R:** Hammett / Mr Fothergills Seeds Ltd. **I:** 2020. **H:** T. **L:** U. **N:** P. **P:** S. **C:** pink flake, c.g. **S:** summer.

'Melanie Ann' (*L. odoratus*) Spencer   **F:** *NSPS Annual* 1991: 36. **R:** Albutt / R. Parsons. **I:** 2014. **H:** T. **L:** U. **N:** P. **P:** S. **C:** salmon pink, c.g. **S:** summer.

'Memorial Flight' (*L. odoratus*) Spencer   **F:** Kerton Sweet Peas cat. 1998. **R:** RD King / Kerton Sweet Peas. **I:** 1998. **D:** see Cultivars chapter.

'Memories' (*L. odoratus*) Spencer   **F:** Dobbie & Co. cat. 1936. **R:** n/k. **I:** n/k. **H:** T. **L:** U. **N:** P. **P:** S. **C:** pale rose cerise. **S:** summer.

'Memories' Davis (*L. odoratus*) Spencer   **F:** Kerton Sweet Peas cat. 1990. **R:** F.G. Davis / Kerton Sweet Peas. **I:** 1990. **H:** T. **L:** U. **N:** P. **P:** S. **C:** rose pink, w.g. **S:** summer.

'Memories' Unwins (*L. odoratus*) Grandiflora   **F:** Unwins Seeds cat. autumn 2004. **R:** Unwins Seeds. **I:** 2005. **D:** see Cultivars chapter.

Memories Mixed (*L. odoratus*) Grandiflora   **F:** Plants of Distinction cat. 2013. **D:** A mixture of Old-fashioned Grandiflora cultivars with flaked flowers. **C:** mixed flakes.

'Midnight' (*L. odoratus*) Grandiflora   **F:** Burpee Seeds cat. 1909. **R:** Burpee Seeds. **I:** 1908. **H:** T. **L:** U. **N:** P. **P:** S. **C:** deep maroon & indigo, hooded. **S:** summer.

'Midnight' Jones (*L. odoratus*) Spencer   **F:** Unwins Seeds cat. autumn 1985. **R:** B.R. Jones / Unwins Seeds. **I:** 1986. **D:** see Cultivars chapter.

'Midnight' Unwins (*L. odoratus*) Spencer   **F:** Unwins Seeds cat. 1957. **R:** Unwins Seeds. **I:** 1957. **H:** T. **L:** U. **N:** P. **P:** S. **C:** chocolate maroon. **S:** summer.

'Milestone' (*L. odoratus*) Spencer   **F:** Unwins Seeds cat. autumn 1970, E.W. King & Co. cat. 1970/71. **R:** Unwins Seeds. **I:** 1971. **D:** see Cultivars chapter.

'Millennium' (*L. odoratus*) Spencer   **RHS:** AM 1997. **F:** *NSPS Annual* 1998: 58. **R:** D.M. Jones / Unwins Seeds. **I:** 2000. **D:** see Cultivars chapter.

'Milly' (*L. odoratus*) Spencer   **F:** Matthewman cat. 2006/07. **R:** Matthewman. **I:** 2007. **D:** see Cultivars chapter.

'Minmaroon' (*L. odoratus*) Grandiflora   **F:** R. Parsons cat. 2010/11. **R:** Beane / Plants of Distinction. **I:** 1998. **D:** see Cultivars chapter.

'Minuet' (*L. odoratus*) Spencer   **F:** Unwins Seeds cat. 1941. **R:** Unwins Seeds. **I:** 1940. **H:** T. **L:** U. **N:** P. **P:** S. **C:** salmon pink, w.g. **S:** summer.

'Minuet Blue Splash' (*L. odoratus*) Spencer   **F:** *NSPS Annual* 2014: 61. **R:** Unwins Seeds. **I:** n/k. **D:** see Cultivars chapter.

'Minuet Magenta' (*L. odoratus*) Spencer   **F:** n/k. **R:** Unwins Seeds. **I:** n/k. **A:** This may be the same as 'Hannah's Harmony'. **H:** SD. **L:** U. **N:** P. **P:** S. **C:** magenta stripe, c.g. **S:** summer.

Minuet Mixed (*L. odoratus*) Spencer   **F:** Unwins Seeds cat. autumn 2003. **R:** Unwins Seeds. **I:** 2004. **H:** SD. **L:** U. **N:** P. **P:** S. **C:** mixed colours. **S:** summer.

'Minuet Orange' (*L. odoratus*) Spencer   **F:** R. Parsons cat. 2012/13. **R:** Unwins Seeds. **I:** n/k. **D:** see Cultivars chapter.

'Minuet Orange-pink Splash' (*L. odoratus*) Spencer

F: *NSPS Annual* 2014: 60. **R:** Unwins Seeds. **I:** n/k.
D: see Cultivars chapter.

'Minuet Purple' (*L. odoratus*) Spencer **F:** R. Parsons
cat. 2014/15. **R:** Unwins Seeds. **I:** n/k. **D:** see Cultivars
chapter.

'Minuet Red' (*L. odoratus*) Spencer **F:** R. Parsons cat.
2012/13. **R:** Unwins Seeds. **I:** n/k. **D:** see Cultivars
chapter.

'Miss Truslove' (*L. odoratus*) Spencer **F:** Kerton
Sweet Peas cat. 1991. **R:** Truslove / Kerton Sweet
Peas. **I:** 1991. **H:** T. **L:** U. **N:** P. **P:** S. **C:** pale mauve.
S: summer.

'Miss Willmott' (*L. odoratus*) Grandiflora **F:** Anon.
(1900b) / *Gard. Mag.* (1900). **R:** H. Eckford. **I:** 1901.
D: see Cultivars chapter.

'Miss Willmott Improved' (*L. odoratus*) Grandiflora
F: *NSPS Annual* 1910: iv ad. **R:** Watkins & Simpson.
I: 1910. **H:** T. **L:** U. **N:** P. **P:** S. **C:** orange-pink, shaded
rose. **S:** summer.

'Misty' (*L. odoratus*) Spencer **F:** *NSPS Annual* 2004:
74. **R:** Leese / Eagle Sweet Peas. **I:** 2008. **D:** see
Cultivars chapter.

'Misty Mountain' (*L. odoratus*) Spencer **F:** *NSPS
Annual* 2004: 167. **R:** Evans / Matthewman. **I:** 2004.
D: see Cultivars chapter.

'MM' (*L. odoratus*) Spencer **F:** Grayson cat. spring
2002. **R:** Grayson. **I:** 2000. **H:** T. **L:** U. **N:** P. **P:** S.
C: cerise. **S:** summer.

'Mollie Rilstone' (*L. odoratus*) Spencer **F:** *NSPS
Annual* 1992: 50. **R:** Tremewan. **I:** 1993. **D:** see
Cultivars chapter.

'Monty Don' (*L. odoratus*) Grandiflora **F:** R. Parsons
cat. 2008/09. **R:** R. Parsons. **I:** 2008. **D:** see Cultivars
chapter.

'Moorland Beauty' (*L. odoratus*) Spencer **F:** *NSPS
Annual* 1995: 78. **R:** Albutt / Eagle Sweet Peas.
I: 1995. **D:** see Cultivars chapter.

'More Scent' (*L. odoratus*) Semi-grandiflora
F: Somerset cat. 2013/14. **R:** Hammett. **I:** 2012. **D:** see
Cultivars chapter.

'Morven' (*L. odoratus*) Spencer **F:** Kerton Sweet Peas
cat. 1998. **R:** Chisholm / Kerton Sweet Peas. **I:** 1998.
D: see Cultivars chapter.

'Mount Stewart' (*L. odoratus*) Spencer **F:** Cooltonagh
cat. 2004/05. **R:** Harrod / Unwins Seeds. **I:** 2005.
D: see Cultivars chapter.

'Mr P.' (*L. odoratus*) Spencer **F:** R. Parsons cat.

2016/17. **R:** R. Parsons. **I:** 2017. **D:** see Cultivars
chapter.

'Mrs Bernard Jones' (*L. odoratus*) Spencer **RHS:** AGM
(H3) 1994. **F:** Unwins Seeds cat. autumn 1980.
R: B.R. Jones / Unwins Seeds. **I:** 1981. **D:** see Cultivars
chapter.

'Mrs Collier' (*L. odoratus*) Grandiflora **F:** *NSPS
Annual* 1906: ix ad. **R:** Dobbie & Co. **I:** 1907. **D:** see
Cultivars chapter.

'Mrs Douglas MacArthur' (*L. odoratus*) Spencer
F: Burpee Seeds cat. 1947. **R:** Burpee Seeds. **I:** 1944.
H: T. **L:** U. **N:** P. **P:** S. **C:** deep salmon pink, c.g.
S: winter.

'Mrs R. Bolton' (*L. odoratus*) Spencer **F:** G. Stark &
Son cat. 1950/51. **R:** Robert Bolton & Son. **I:** 1945.
D: see Cultivars chapter.

'Mrs R. Chisholm' (*L. odoratus*) Spencer **F:** *NSPS
Annual* 2005: 54. **R:** Chisholm / Kerton Sweet Peas.
I: 2009. **D:** see Cultivars chapter.

'Mrs R. Penney' (*L. annuus*) **F:** Grayson cat. autumn
1996. **R:** Grayson. **I:** 1997. **D:** see Cultivars chapter.

'Mrs T.' (*L. odoratus*) Spencer **F:** *NSPS Annual* 2016:
187. **R:** Fleming Robertson / Kerton Sweet Peas.
I: 2016. **H:** T. **L:** U. **N:** P. **P:** S. **C:** mid blue. **S:** summer.

'Mrs Walter Wright' (*L. odoratus*) Grandiflora
F: *NSPS Annual* 1905: iii ad. **R:** H. Eckford. **I:** 1903.
D: see Cultivars chapter.

'Mumsie' (*L. odoratus*) Spencer **F:** Eagle Sweet Peas
cat. 1994. **R:** Eagle Sweet Peas. **I:** 1993. **D:** see
Cultivars chapter.

'My Navy' (*L. odoratus*) Semi-grandiflora **F:** Hem
Zaden cat. 2011/12. **R:** Hammett. **I:** 2008. **D:** see
Cultivars chapter.

'Nanna K.' (*L. odoratus*) Spencer **F:** Owl's Acre Sweet
Peas cat. 2004/05. **R:** Owl's Acre Sweet Peas. **I:** 2004.
H: T. **L:** U. **N:** P. **P:** S. **C:** lavender flake, w.g. **S:** summer.

'Naomi Nazareth' (*L. odoratus*) Spencer **RHS:** AM
2008. **F:** R. Parsons cat. 2008/09. **R:** R. Parsons.
I: 2009. **D:** see Cultivars chapter.

'Naples' (*L. odoratus*) Spencer **F:** *NSPS Annual*
1973: i. **R:** Ferry Morse Seed Co. **I:** 1973. **D:** see
Cultivars chapter.

'Natalie Joy' (*L. odoratus*) Spencer **F:** McDougall cat.
1998. **R:** McDougall. **I:** n/k. **H:** T. **L:** U. **N:** P. **P:** n/k.
C: dark blue. **S:** winter.

'Navy' (*L. odoratus*) Grandiflora **F:** Hemus cat., 1906.
R: n/k. **I:** n/k. **H:** T. **L:** U. **N:** P. **P:** S. **C:** dark blue.

S: summer.

'Navy' Hammett   = 'My Navy'

'Navy' Ireland & Hitchcock (*L. odoratus*) Spencer
F: RHS Trials 1921. **R:** Ireland & Hitchcock. **I:** n/k.
H: T. **L:** U. **N:** P. **P:** S. **C:** navy blue. **S:** summer.

'**Nelly Viner**' (*L. odoratus*) Grandiflora   **F:** Grayson
cat. 1997/98. **R:** Grayson. **I:** 1998. **H:** T. **L:** U. **N:** P. **P:** S.
C: pale pink, w.g. **S:** summer.

'**New Dawn**' (*L. odoratus*) Spencer   **F:** *NSPS Annual*
1947: i. **R:** Simons. **I:** 1937. **H:** T. **L:** U. **N:** P. **P:** S.
C: salmon pink, w.g. **S:** summer.

'New Dawn' Harkness or Martin (*L. odoratus*) Spencer
F: Martin cat. 1968. **R:** Harkness or Martin. **I:** before
1968. **D:** see Cultivars chapter.

'New Dawn' Wiltshire (*L. odoratus*) Spencer   **F:** *NSPS
Annual* 1986: 79. **R:** Wiltshire. **I:** n/k. **H:** T. **L:** U. **N:** P.
P: S. **C:** pink. **S:** summer.

'**Niamh Mae**' (*L. odoratus*) Spencer   **F:** *NSPS Annual*
2008: 55. **R:** Chisholm / Kerton Sweet Peas. **I:** 2011.
H: T. **L:** U. **N:** P. **P:** S. **C:** lavender flush. **S:** summer.

'**Night Sky**' (*L. odoratus*) Spencer   **F:** Matthewman
cat. 2016/17. **R:** Matthewman. **I:** 2017. **D:** see
Cultivars chapter.

'**Nimbus**' (*L. odoratus*) Spencer   **F:** Unwins Seeds cat.
autumn 1995. **R:** Unwins Seeds. **I:** 1996. **D:** see
Cultivars chapter.

'**Noel Sutton**' (*L. odoratus*) Spencer   **RHS:** AGM (H3)
1994. **F:** *NSPS Annual* 1966: 71. **R:** Suttons. **I:** 1968.
D: see Cultivars chapter.

'**Nora Holman**' (*L. odoratus*) Spencer   **F:** Tremewan
cat. 1990/91. **R:** Tremewan. **I:** 1991. **D:** see Cultivars
chapter.

'**Nora Unwin**' (*L. odoratus*) Semi-grandiflora   **F:** *NSPS
Annual* 1906: v ad. **R:** Unwins Seeds / Sharpe /
Watkins & Simpson. **I:** 1906. **A:** Pale seeds. **H:** T. **L:** U.
N: P. **P:** S. **C:** white. **S:** summer.

'**Norman Wisdom**' (*L. odoratus*) Spencer   **F:** Unwins
Seeds cat. autumn 2002. **R:** Unwins Seeds. **I:** 2003.
H: T. **L:** U. **N:** P. **P:** S. **C:** white. **S:** summer.

'**North Shore**' (*L. odoratus*) Spencer   **F:** *NSPS Annual*
1984: 67. **R:** Hammett / Thompson & Morgan. **I:** 1987.
D: see Cultivars chapter.

'**Northern Lights**' (*L. odoratus*) Grandiflora   **F:** *NSPS
Annual* 2014: 61. **R:** Owl's Acre Sweet Peas. **I:** 2014.
H: SD. **L:** U. **N:** P. **P:** S. **C:** crimson flake / blue flush,
w.g. **S:** early.

'**Nozaki Cerise**' (*L. odoratus*) Spencer   **F:** R. Parsons

cat. 2017/18. **R:** Nozaki. **I:** n/k. **H:** T. **L:** U. **N:** M. **P:** S.
C: salmon cerise. **S:** winter.

'**Nozaki Viola**' (*L. odoratus*) Spencer   **F:** n/k.
R: Nozaki. **I:** n/k. **H:** T. **L:** U. **N:** P. **P:** S. **C:** deep purple.
S: early spring.

'**Nuance**' (*L. odoratus*) Spencer   **F:** R. Parsons cat.
2013/14. **R:** Hammett. **I:** 2012. **D:** see Cultivars
chapter.

'**NZ Gardener**' (*L. odoratus*) Semi-grandiflora   **F:** n/k.
R: Hammett. **I:** 2020. **H:** T. **L:** U. **N:** M. **P:** S. **C:** mid
blue. **S:** summer.

'**Oban Bay**' (*L. odoratus*) Spencer   **F:** Robert Bolton &
Son cat. 1997/98. **R:** Chisholm / Robert Bolton & Son.
I: 1997. **D:** see Cultivars chapter.

'**Oklahoma**' (*L. odoratus*) Spencer   **RHS:** AGM (H3)
2000. **F:** *NSPS Annual* 2001: 56. **R:** Unwins Seeds.
I: 2002. **D:** see Cultivars chapter.

'**Old Times**' (*L. odoratus*) Spencer   **F:** Unwins Seeds
cat. autumn 1975. **R:** Unwins Seeds. **I:** 1976. **H:** T. **L:** U.
N: P. **P:** D. **C:** blue flush, c.g. **S:** summer.

'**Olive D.**' (*L. odoratus*) Spencer   **F:** Owl's Acre Sweet
Peas cat. 2009/10. **R:** Owl's Acre Sweet Peas. **I:** 2008.
D: see Cultivars chapter.

'**Olivia**' (*L. odoratus*) Spencer   **F:** McDonald cat. 2014.
R: Chisholm / McDonald. **I:** 2014. **H:** T. **L:** U. **N:** P. **P:** S.
C: pink stripe, w.g. **S:** summer.

'**Ollie Clarke**' (*L. odoratus*) Spencer   **F:** R. Parsons cat.
2017/18. **R:** Harrod / R. Parsons. **I:** 2018. **D:** see
Cultivars chapter.

'Olympic Flame'   = 'Flame' Unwins

'**Omay**' (*L. odoratus*) Spencer   **RHS:** AM 1997. **F:** *NSPS
Annual* 1998: 58. **R:** K. Brewer / Matthewman.
I: 2003. **D:** see Cultivars chapter.

'**Opalette**' (*L. odoratus*) Spencer   **F:** *NSPS Annual*
1967: 112. **R:** Burpee Seeds. **I:** 1967. **D:** see Cultivars
chapter.

'**Orange Dragon**' (*L. odoratus*) Spencer   **F:** Robert
Bolton & Son cat. autumn 1959. **R:** Robert Bolton &
Son. **I:** 1958. **H:** T. **L:** U. **N:** P. **P:** S. **C:** orange.
S: summer.

'**Orchid**' (*L. odoratus*) Spencer   **F:** *NSPS Annual* 1912:
22. **R:** Malcolm / Burpee Seeds. **I:** 1913. **H:** T. **L:** U.
N: P. **P:** S. **C:** lilac. **S:** summer.

'Orchid' Dickson (*L. odoratus*) Spencer
F: Cuthbertson (1916). **R:** Alex Dickson & Sons.
I: before 1916. **H:** T. **L:** U. **N:** P. **P:** S. **C:** rosy lavender.
S: summer.

'Orchid' Malcolm 1921 (*L. odoratus*) Spencer **F:** *NSPS Annual* 1921: vii, RHS Trials 1921. **R:** Malcolm / Dobbie & Co. **I:** 1921. **H:** T. **L:** U. **N:** P. **P:** S. **C:** rosy lavender. **S:** summer.

'Orchid' Zvolanek 1962 (*L. odoratus*) Spencer **F:** *Australian Garden Lover* (1962). **R:** William Zvolanek & Co. **I:** n/k. **H:** T. **L:** U. **N:** M. **P:** S. **C:** orchid-mauve. **S:** winter.

'Orchid' Zvolanek 1974 (*L. odoratus*) Spencer **F:** William Zvolanek & Co. cat. 1974. **R:** William Zvolanek & Co. **I:** n/k. **H:** T. **L:** U. **N:** M. **P:** S. **C:** orchid-mauve. **S:** summer.

'Orchid' Unwins (*L. odoratus*) Spencer **F:** Unwins Seeds cat. autumn 2007. **R:** Unwins Seeds. **I:** 2008. **D:** see Cultivars chapter.

'Our Colin' (*L. odoratus*) Spencer **F:** *NSPS Annual* 2005: 54. **R:** Chisholm / Kerton Sweet Peas. **I:** 2009. **D:** see Cultivars chapter.

'Our Harry' (*L. odoratus*) Spencer **F:** Marchant cat. 1987. **R:** F.G. Davis / Marchant. **I:** 1987. **D:** see Cultivars chapter.

'Oyama Aphrodite' (*L. odoratus*) Spencer **F:** n/k. **R:** Oyama. **I:** 1991/97. **D:** see Cultivars chapter.

'Oyama Bicolour' (*L. odoratus*) Spencer **F:** n/k. **R:** Oyama. **I:** before 1984. **D:** see Cultivars chapter.

'Oyama Mauve' (*L. odoratus*) Spencer **F:** n/k. **R:** Oyama. **I:** n/k. **H:** T. **L:** U. **N:** P. **P:** S. **C:** mauve bicolour. **S:** early spring.

'Oyama Millennium' (*L. odoratus*) Spencer **F:** n/k. **R:** Fujisawa. **I:** before 2012. **D:** see Cultivars chapter.

'Oyama Russian Blue' (*L. odoratus*) Spencer **F:** n/k. **R:** Oyama. **I:** before 1984. **D:** see Cultivars chapter.

'Oyama Violet' (*L. odoratus*) Spencer **F:** R. Parsons cat. 2013/14. **R:** Oyama. **I:** n/k. **H:** T. **L:** U. **N:** M. **P:** S. **C:** violet. **S:** early spring.

'Painted Lady' (*L. odoratus*) Grandiflora **F:** Russell cat. 1827. **R:** n/k. **I:** 1752. **D:** see Cultivars chapter.

'Painted Porcelain' = 'Spanish Dancer'

'Pandemonium' (*L. odoratus*) Spencer **RHS:** AGM (H3) 2014. **F:** Mr Fothergills Seeds Ltd cat. 2012. **R:** Hammett. **I:** 2009. **D:** see Cultivars chapter.

'Pansy Lavender Flush' (*L. odoratus*) Grandiflora **F:** Thompson & Morgan cat. 2004. **R:** Thompson & Morgan. **I:** 2004. **D:** see Cultivars chapter.

'Parsifal' (*L. odoratus*) Spencer **F:** *NSPS Annual* 2005: 55. **R:** Hargreaves / Myers. **I:** 2015. **H:** T. **L:** U. **N:** P. **P:** S. **C:** pale lavender-blue flush, w.g. **S:** summer.

'Patio Crimson' (*L. odoratus*) Spencer **F:** n/k. **R:** Burpee Seeds. **I:** before 1979. **H:** SD. **L:** U. **N:** P. **P:** S. **C:** crimson. **S:** spring.

'Patio Dark Blue' (*L. odoratus*) Spencer **F:** n/k. **R:** Burpee Seeds. **I:** before 1979. **H:** SD. **L:** U. **N:** P. **P:** S. **C:** dark blue. **S:** spring.

'Patio Deep Purple' (*L. odoratus*) Spencer **F:** Nakamura *et al.* (2010). **R:** n/k. **I:** n/k. **H:** SD. **L:** U. **N:** P. **P:** S. **C:** dark grey-purple. **S:** spring.

'Patio Deep Rose' (*L. odoratus*) Spencer **F:** n/k. **R:** Burpee Seeds. **I:** before 1979. **D:** see Cultivars chapter.

'Patio Pink / White Bicolour' (*L. odoratus*) Spencer **F:** n/k. **R:** Burpee Seeds. **I:** before 1979. **D:** see Cultivars chapter.

'Patio Red / Pink Bicolour' (*L. odoratus*) Spencer **F:** n/k. **R:** Burpee Seeds. **I:** before 1979. **D:** see Cultivars chapter.

'Patio Salmon Pink' (*L. odoratus*) Spencer **F:** n/k. **R:** Burpee Seeds. **I:** before 1979. **H:** SD. **L:** U. **N:** P. **P:** S. **C:** salmon pink, w.g. **S:** spring.

'Patio Scarlet' (*L. odoratus*) Spencer **F:** n/k. **R:** Burpee Seeds. **I:** before 1979. **H:** SD. **L:** U. **N:** P. **P:** S. **C:** scarlet. **S:** spring.

Patio Series (*L. odoratus*) Spencer **F:** Unwins Seedsa autumn cat. 1979. **R:** Burpee Seeds. **I:** before 1979. **A:** Eight colours are known, each named with a Patio prefix. **D:** Dwarf, upright cultivars. **H:** SD. **L:** U. **N:** P. **P:** S. **C:** various colours. **S:** spring.

'Patricia Anne' (*L. odoratus*) Spencer **RHS:** AGM (H3) 1999. **F:** *NSPS Annual* 2000: 69. **R:** W. Sutton / Kerton Sweet Peas. **I:** 2006. **D:** see Cultivars chapter.

'Patricia Marilyn' (*L. odoratus*) Spencer **F:** *NSPS Classification List* 2018. **R:** Eagle Sweet Peas. **I:** 2018. **H:** T. **L:** U. **N:** P. **P:** S. **C:** pale pink. **S:** summer.

'Patti' (*L. odoratus*) Spencer **F:** Bodger Seeds Ltd cat. 1965. **R:** Denholm Seeds. **I:** 1960. **H:** T. **L:** U. **N:** M. **P:** S. **C:** salmon pink. **S:** early spring.

'Pauline May' (*L. odoratus*) Spencer **F:** McDougall cat. 2015. **R:** n/k. **I:** 1986. **H:** T. **L:** U. **N:** P. **P:** S. **C:** cyclamen pink. **S:** winter.

'Peacock' (*L. odoratus*) Grandiflora **F:** *NSPS Annual* 1910: 86. **R:** H.J. Jones. **I:** 1908. **H:** T. **L:** U. **N:** P. **P:** S. **C:** red / blue. **S:** summer.

'Peacock' Unwins (*L. odoratus*) Spencer **F:** Unwins Seeds cat., autumn 2002. **R:** Unwins Seeds. **I:** 2003. **D:** see Cultivars chapter.

'Pearl Anniversary' (*L. odoratus*) Spencer
F: R. Parsons cat. 2016. R: R. Parsons. I: 2016. D: see Cultivars chapter.

'Pearl Buck' (*L. odoratus*) Spencer   F: Burpee Seeds cat. 1941. R: Burpee Seeds. I: 1937. H: T. L: U. N: P. P: S. C: orange-pink / magenta. S: early spring.

'Peggy' (*L. odoratus*) Spencer   F: *NSPS Annual* 1912: 24. R: Lumley. I: 1912. H: T. L: U. N: P. P: S. C: blush. S: summer.

'Peggy' Bolton (*L. odoratus*) Spencer   F: Elliott cat. 1926. R: Robert Bolton & Son. I: 1926. H: T. L: U. N: P. P: S. C: cerise flushed orange. S: summer.

'Peggy' King (*L. odoratus*) Spencer   F: E.W. King & Co. cat. 1946. R: E.W. King & Co. I: 1946. H: T. L: M. N: P. P: S. C: scarlet cerise. S: summer.

'Peggy' Ferry Morse (*L. odoratus*) Spencer   F: E.W. King & Co. cat. 1955/56. R: Ferry Morse Seed Co. I: 1955. H: T. L: U. N: M. P: S. C: mauve. S: late spring.

'Peggy' Parsons (*L. odoratus*) Grandiflora   F: R Parsons cat. 2009/10. R: R. Parsons. I: 2010. H: T. L: U. N: P. P: S. C: mauve. S: late spring.

'Pendulous' (*L. vernus*)   F: *RHS Plant Finder 2013*. R: Hardy's Cottage Garden Plants. I: 2013. H: SD. L: U. N: M. P: S. C: pink / white. S: spring.

'Percy Thrower' (*L. odoratus*) Spencer   F: Robert Bolton & Son cat. 1983/84. R: B.R. Jones / Robert Bolton & Son. I: 1984. D: see Cultivars chapter.

'Peter George Wale' (*L. odoratus*) Spencer   F: R. Parsons cat. 2016. R: R. Parsons. I: 2016. H: T. L: U. N: P. P: S. C: lavender, paler wings. S: summer.

'Philip Miller' (*L. odoratus*) Grandiflora   F: Grayson cat. autumn 1996. R: Grayson. I: 1997. H: T. L: U. N: P. P: S. C: scarlet. S: summer.

'Phoebe' (*L. odoratus*) Spencer   F: Cuthbertson (1916). R: Anderson & Co. I: 1916. H: T. L: U. N: P. P: S. C: white with pink edge. S: winter.

'Phoebe' Bolton (*L. odoratus*) Spencer   F: Robert Bolton & Son cat. 1997/98. R: Robert Bolton & Son. I: 1998. D: see Cultivars chapter.

'Picolino' (*L. odoratus*) Grandiflora   F: n/k. R: Grayson. I: Around 2004. D: see Cultivars chapter.

'Piggy Sue' (*L. odoratus*) Spencer   F: n/k. R: Hammett. I: 2012. D: see Cultivars chapter.

'Pink Cupid' (*L. odoratus*) Grandiflora   RHS: AGM (H3) 1995. F: Anon. (1898/99). R: Burpee Seeds. I: 1898. D: see Cultivars chapter.

'Pink Nines' (*L. odoratus*) Spencer   F: R. Parsons cat. 2013/14. R: Hammett. I: 2010. D: see Cultivars chapter.

'Pink Panther' (*L. odoratus*) Spencer   F: *NSPS Annual* 2005: 54. R: Beane / E.W. King & Co. I: 2007. H: T. L: U. N: P. P: S. C: pale pink, w.g. S: summer.

Pink Pearl (*L. latifolius*)   = 'Rosa Perle'

'Pip Tremewan' (*L. odoratus*) Spencer   F: Thompson & Morgan cat. 1999. R: Tremewan / Thompson & Morgan. I: 1999. D: see Cultivars chapter.

'Pip's Cornish Cream' (*L. odoratus*) Spencer   F: R. Parsons cat. 2013/14. R: Tremewan / Carr / R. Parsons. I: 2014. D: see Cultivars chapter.

'Pip's Maroon' (*L. odoratus*) Spencer   F: R. Parsons cat. 2007/08. R: Tremewan / Carr / R. Parsons. I: 2008. D: see Cultivars chapter.

'Piralilla Cream' (*L. odoratus*) Spencer   F: McDougall cat. 1998. R: Bennett. I: early 1970s. A: Pale seeds. H: T. L: U. N: P. P: D. C: cream. S: early spring.

'Piralilla Fay' (*L. odoratus*) Spencer   F: n/k. R: Bennett. I: n/k. H: T. L: U. N: P. P: D. C: salmon pink, c.g. S: early spring.

'Piralilla Joy' (*L. odoratus*) Spencer   F: R. Parsons cat. 2012/13. R: Bennett. I: n/k. H: T. L: U. N: P. P: D. C: lilac-pink picotee, w.g. S: early spring.

'Piralilla Margaret' (*L. odoratus*) Spencer   F: McDougall cat. 1998. R: Bennett. I: early 1970s. H: T. L: U. N: P. P: D. C: lavender flake, w.g. S: early spring.

'Piralilla Marianne' (*L. odoratus*) Spencer   F: McDougall cat. 1998. R: Bennett. I: early 1970s. H: T. L: U. N: P. P: D. C: pink flake, w.g. S: early spring.

'Pirate Gold' (*L. odoratus*) Spencer   F: Waller-Franklin Seed Co. cat. 1932. R: Waller-Franklin Seed Co. I: 1932. D: see Cultivars chapter.

'Pisces' (*L. odoratus*) Spencer   F: E.W. King & Co. cat. autumn 1999. R: J.D. Place / E.W. King & Co. I: 1999. D: see Cultivars chapter.

'Plum Bob' (*L. odoratus*) Spencer   F: McDougall cat. 1998. R: Bennett. I: early 1970s. H: T. L: U. N: P. P: S. C: plum red. S: winter.

'Pluto' (*L. odoratus*) Spencer   F: *NSPS Annual* 1915: 89. R: Robert Bolton & Son. I: 1914. H: T. L: U. N: P. P: S. C: purple carmine / blue magenta. S: summer.

'Pluto' Bolton 1977 (*L. odoratus*) Spencer   F: Robert Bolton & Son cat. 1976/77. R: Robert Bolton & Son. I: 1977. H: T. L: U. N: P. P: S. C: dark blue. S: summer.

'Pocahontas' (*L. odoratus*) Spencer   RHS: AGM (H3)

1996. **F:** *NSPS Annual* 1997: 74. **R:** Harrod. **I:** 2005. **D:** see Cultivars chapter.

'Polar Star' (*L. odoratus*) Spencer **F:** *NSPS Annual* 2006: 62. **R:** n/k. **I:** 1991/97 or earlier. **D:** see Cultivars chapter.

'Pollyanna' (*L. odoratus*) Spencer **F:** Waller-Franklin Seed Co. cat. 1965. **R:** Macdonald. **I:** n/k. **H:** SD. **L:** U. **N:** P. **P:** S. **C:** cream. **S:** summer.

'Polyanna' (*L. odoratus*) Grandiflora **F:** n/k. **R:** Just Sweet Peas. **I:** 2011. **D:** see Cultivars chapter.

'Porlock' (*L. odoratus*) Spencer **F:** *The Plantsman* 13(4): 254. **R:** Hammett. **I:** 2015. **D:** see Cultivars chapter.

'Precious' (*L. odoratus*) Spencer **F:** *NSPS Annual* 1993: 51. **R:** K Brewer. **I:** n/k. **H:** T. **L:** U. **N:** P. **P:** S. **C:** carmine. **S:** summer.

'Precious' Unwins (*L. odoratus*) Spencer **F:** Unwins Seeds cat. autumn 2013. **R:** Unwins Seeds. **I:** 2014. **D:** see Cultivars chapter.

'Prima Donna' (*L. odoratus*) Grandiflora **F:** Sunset Seed and Plant Co. cat. 1896. **R:** H. Eckford. **I:** 1896. **D:** see Cultivars chapter.

'Prima Donna' Australia (*L. odoratus*) Spencer **F:** *Australian Garden Lover* (1963). **R:** n/k. **I:** 1910–1962. **H:** T. **L:** U. **N:** P. **P:** D. **C:** salmon pink, c.g. **S:** early spring.

'Prince Edward of York' (*L. odoratus*) Grandiflora **F:** ST Walker cat. 1898, Peter Henderson & Co. cat. 1898. **R:** H. Eckford. **I:** 1897. **D:** see Cultivars chapter.

'Prince of Orange' (*L. odoratus*) Grandiflora **F:** RHS Trials 1894. **R:** H. Eckford. **I:** n/k. **H:** T. **L:** U. **N:** P. **P:** S. **C:** orange-salmon. **S:** summer.

'Prince of Orange' Hemus 1910a (*L. odoratus*) Spencer **F:** *NSPS Annual* 1910: 87. **R:** Hemus. **I:** 1910. **H:** T. **L:** U. **N:** P. **P:** S. **C:** orange-scarlet. **S:** summer.

'Prince of Orange' Hemus 1910b (*L. odoratus*) Grandiflora **F:** *NSPS Catalogue of Names* 1912: 25. **R:** Hemus. **I:** 1910. **H:** T. **L:** U. **N:** P. **P:** S. **C:** orange / rose. **S:** summer.

'Prince of Orange' Morse (*L. odoratus*) Spencer **F:** Semences Davy 1935. **R:** C.C. Morse & Co. **I:** 1928. **D:** see Cultivars chapter.

'Princess' (*L. odoratus*) Grandiflora **F:** R.D. (1882) **R:** H. Eckford. **I:** n/k. **H:** T. **L:** U. **N:** P. **P:** S. **C:** purple / blue flaked. **S:** summer.

'Princess' Burpee (*L. odoratus*) Spencer **F:** Burpee Seeds cat. 1920. **R:** Burpee Seeds. **I:** n/k. **H:** T. **L:** U.

N: P. **P:** S. **C:** deep lavender. **S:** winter.

'Princess' Suttons (*L. odoratus*) Spencer **F:** *NSPS Annual* 1934: 62. **R:** Suttons. **I:** 1935. **H:** T. **L:** U. **N:** P. **P:** S. **C:** cerise salmon, c.g. **S:** summer.

'Princess' Zvolanek (*L. odoratus*) Spencer **F:** A. Zvolanek & Sons cat. 1925/26. **R:** A. Zvolanek & Sons. **I:** n/k. **D:** see Cultivars chapter.

'Princess Elizabeth' (*L. odoratus*) Spencer **F:** E.W. King & Co. cat. 1946. **R:** E.W. King & Co. **I:** 1946. **H:** T. **L:** M. **N:** P. **P:** S. **C:** lavender. **S:** summer.

'Princess Elizabeth' Bolton (*L. odoratus*) Spencer **F:** *NSPS Annual* 1949: 65. **R:** Robert Bolton & Son. **I:** 1950. **D:** see Cultivars chapter.

'Princess Elizabeth' n/k (*L. odoratus*) Spencer **F:** n/k.. **R:** n/k. **I:** before 1929. **H:** T. **L:** U. **N:** P. **P:** S. **C:** n/k. **S:** summer.

'Princess of Prussia' = Crown Princess of Prussia

'Princess of Wales' (*L. odoratus*) Grandiflora **F:** Anon. (1884). **R:** H. Eckford. **I:** 1886. **H:** T. **L:** U. **N:** P. **P:** S. **C:** mauve blue flake, w.g., hooded. **S:** summer.

'Princess of Wales' Grayson (*L. odoratus*) Grandiflora **F:** Grayson cat. autumn 1994. **R:** Grayson. **I:** 1995. **D:** see Cultivars chapter.

'Promise' (*L. odoratus*) Spencer **F:** R. Parsons cat. 2004/05. **R:** R. Parsons. **I:** 2006. **D:** see Cultivars chapter.

'Prospect' (*L. odoratus*) Spencer **F:** *Australian Garden Lover* (1947). **R:** Steward / Gellatly. **I:** 1941. **H:** T. **L:** U. **N:** P. **P:** D. **C:** bright mauve / light heliotrope. **S:** winter.

'Pulsar' = 'Lilac Ripple'

'Purple Pimpernel' (*L. odoratus*) Spencer **F:** n/k. **R:** Hunt / Thompson & Morgan. **I:** 2014. **D:** see Cultivars chapter.

'Purple Prince' (*L. odoratus*) Grandiflora **F:** Markham (1891). **R:** H. Eckford. **I:** 1886. **D:** see Cultivars chapter.

'Queen Alexandra' (*L. odoratus*) Grandiflora **F:** *NSPS Annual* 1905: iii ad.. **R:** H. Eckford. **I:** 1906. **D:** see Cultivars chapter.

'Queen Mother' (*L. odoratus*) Spencer **F:** Cuthbertson (1916). **R:** Breadmore. **I:** 1913. **H:** T. **L:** U. **N:** P. **P:** S. **C:** deep lilac. **S:** summer.

'Queen Mother' Richardson (*L. odoratus*) Spencer **F:** Unwins Seeds cat. autumn 1990. **R:** B Richardson/ Unwins Seeds. **I:** 1991. **D:** see Cultivars chapter.

'Queen of Hearts' (*L. odoratus*) Spencer **F:** *NSPS*

Annual 2001: 57. **R:** Tullett / Unwins Seeds. **I:** 2004.
D: see Cultivars chapter.

Queen of Hearts Mixed   **D:** A mixture of cultivars.
C: mixed colours.

'Queen of the Isles' (*L. odoratus*) Grandiflora
F: Anon. (1884). **R:** H. Eckford. **I:** 1885. **H:** T. **L:** U. **N:** P.
P: S. **C:** crimson flake, w.g. **S:** summer.

'Quito' (*L. odoratus*) Grandiflora   **F:** E.W. King & Co.
cat. autumn 1989. **R:** Harland / E.W. King & Co.
I: 1990. **H:** T. **L:** U. **N:** P. **P:** S. **C:** bicolour. **S:** summer.

'Rainbow' (*L. odoratus*) Spencer   **F:** C.C. Morse & Co.
cat. 1912, Burpee Seeds cat. 1912. **R:** C.C. Morse & Co.
/ Burpee Seeds. **I:** 1912. **H:** T. **L:** U. **N:** P. **P:** S. **C:** rose
pink flake on ivory. **S:** summer.

Rainbow Mixed (*L. odoratus*)   **D:** A mixture of
cultivars. **C:** mixed colours.

'Rainbow' (*L. vernus*)   = *L. vernus* mixed. **A:** 'Rainbow'
is a name used by Matthewmans for mixed *L. vernus*
seedlings pricked out as a clump to form what looks
like a single plant.

'R. Veale' (*L. odoratus*) Spencer   **F:** McDougall cat.
1998. **R:** C.R. Veale **I:** 1920s. **H:** T. **L:** U. **N:** P. **P:** S.
C: pink / blue hue. **S:** winter.

'Raspberry Flake' (*L. odoratus*) Spencer   **F:** Unwins
Seeds cat. autumn 2008. **R:** Unwins Seeds. **I:** 2009.
D: see Cultivars chapter.

'Reconnaissance' (*L. odoratus*) Spencer   **F:** *NSPS
Annual* 1945: 57. **R:** Dobbie & Co. **I:** 1942. **H:** T. **L:** U.
N: P. **P:** S. **C:** pink picotee, c.g. **S:** summer.

'Red Ace' (*L. odoratus*) Spencer   **F:** Kerton Sweet Peas
cat. 1997. **R:** W. Walker / Kerton Sweet Peas. **I:** 1997.
H: T. **L:** U. **N:** P. **P:** S. **C:** scarlet. **S:** summer.

'Red Arrow' (*L. odoratus*) Spencer   **F:** Unwins Seeds
cat. autumn 1982. **R:** B.R. Jones / Unwins Seeds.
I: 1983. **D:** see Cultivars chapter.

'Red Ensign' (*L. odoratus*) Spencer   **F:** *NSPS Annual*
1919: 61. **R:** J. Stevenson. **I:** 1920. **H:** T. **L:** U. **N:** P. **P:** S.
C: red cerise. **S:** summer.

'Red Ensign' Jones (*L. odoratus*) Spencer   **F:** *NSPS
Annual* 1975: 57. **R:** B.R. Jones / Suttons. **I:** 1981. **H:** T.
L: U. **N:** P. **P:** S. **C:** scarlet. **S:** summer.

'Regal Reflection' (*L. odoratus*) Spencer   **F:** Suttons
cat. 2001. **R:** Suttons. **I:** 2001. **H:** T. **L:** U. **N:** P. **P:** S.
C: mauve / lavender. **S:** late spring.

'Renown' (*L. odoratus*) Spencer   **F:** *NSPS Annual*
1922: v, Elliott cat. 1922. **R:** Dobbie & Co. **I:** 1922. **H:** T.
L: U. **N:** P. **P:** S. **C:** carmine-rose. **S:** summer.

'Renown' Harrod (*L. odoratus*) Spencer
F: Cooltonagh cat. 2011/12. **R:** Harrod. **I:** 2012. **D:** see
Cultivars chapter.

'Restormel' (*L. odoratus*) Spencer   **F:** *Proc. Roy. Hort.
Soc. London* 1987: 155. **R:** Tremewan. **I:** 1989. **D:** see
Cultivars chapter.

'Rhineland' (*L. odoratus*) Spencer   **F:** Everitt cat.
1972/73. **R:** Ferry Morse Seed Co. **I:** 1973. **D:** see
Cultivars chapter.

'Richard and Judy' (*L. odoratus*) Spencer
F: Matthewman cat. 2001/02. **R:** Matthewman.
I: 2002. **D:** see Cultivars chapter.

'Riga 800' (*L. odoratus*) Spencer   **F:** n/k. **R:** Dubovkis.
I: 2001. **H:** T. **L:** U. **N:** P. **P:** S. **C:** stripe. **S:** summer.

Rockery Mixed (*L. odoratus*) Grandiflora   **F:** Plants of
Dist. 1998. **R:** Plants of Distinction. **I:** n/k. **H:** SD. **L:** U.
N: P. **P:** S. **C:** mixed colours. **S:** summer.

'Romeo' (*L. odoratus*) Spencer   **F:** *NSPS Annual*
1946: 5. **R:** Carters Tested Seeds. **I:** 1946. **H:** T. **L:** U.
N: P. **P:** S. **C:** rich orange-scarlet. **S:** summer.

'Romeo' Simons (*L. odoratus*) Spencer   **F:** Simons cat.
1961/62, E.W. King & Co. cat. 1961/62. **R:** Simons.
I: 1962. **H:** T. **L:** U. **N:** P. **P:** S. **C:** rose picotee, w.g.
S: summer.

'Romeo' Unwins (*L. odoratus*) Grandiflora   **F:** Unwins
Seeds cat. autumn 1999. **R:** Unwins Seeds. **I:** 2000.
D: see Cultivars chapter.

'Ron Entwistle' (*L. odoratus*) Spencer   **F:** Grayson cat.
1998/99. **R:** Entwistle / Grayson. **I:** 1999. **D:** see
Cultivars chapter.

'Ronnie' (*L. odoratus*) Spencer   **F:** Ferry Morse Seed
Co. cat. 1953. **R:** Ferry Morse Seed Co. **I:** 1953. **D:** see
Cultivars chapter.

'Roosterville' (*L. odoratus*) Grandiflora   **F:** n/k.
R: Hammett. **I:** 2009. **D:** see Cultivars chapter.

'Rory K.' (*L. odoratus*) Spencer   **F:** *NSPS Annual*
2008: 55. **R:** Kerton Sweet Peas. **I:** 2009. **H:** T. **L:** U.
N: P. **P:** S. **C:** lavender. **S:** summer.

'Rosa Perle' (*L. latifolius*)   **RHS:** AGM (H7) 1997.
F: n/k. **R:** n/k. **I:** n/k. **D:** see Cultivars chapter.

'Rosay' (*L. odoratus*) Grandiflora   **F:** Unwins Seeds
cat. autumn 2011. **R:** Unwins Seeds. **I:** 2012. **H:** T. **L:** U.
N: P. **P:** S. **C:** pink. **S:** summer.

'Rosemary Padley' (*L. odoratus*) Spencer   **F:** Robert
Bolton & Son cat. 1994/95. **R:** Tullett / Robert Bolton
& Son. **I:** 1995. **D:** see Cultivars chapter.

'Rosenelfe' (*L. vernus*)   = 'Alboroseus'

'Roseus' (*L. tingitanus*)   **D:** see Cultivars chapter.

'Roseus' (*L.vernus*)   **D:** see Cultivars chapter.

'**Rosie**' (*L. odoratus*) Spencer   **F:** Ball cat. 1932. **R:** Unwins Seeds. **I:** 1932. **H:** T. **L:** U. **N:** P. **P:** S. **C:** rose. **S:** summer.

'Rosie' Bodger Seeds (*L. odoratus*) Spencer   **F:** Bodger Seeds Ltd cat. 1978. **R:** n/k. **I:** n/k. **H:** T. **L:** U. **N:** M. **P:** S. **C:** rose, w.g. **S:** early.

'Rosie' Burpee (*L. odoratus*) Spencer   **F:** *NSPS Annual* 1971: v. **R:** Burpee Seeds. **I:** 1971. **H:** T. **L:** U. **N:** M. **P:** S. **C:** deep rose pink. **S:** summer.

'Rosie' Parker (*L. odoratus*) Spencer   **F:** Kerton Sweet Peas cat. 1992. **R:** Parker / Kerton Sweet Peas. **I:** 1992. **H:** T. **L:** U. **N:** P. **P:** S. **C:** bright carmine. **S:** summer.

'Rosie' Truslove (*L. odoratus*) Spencer   **F:** E.W. King & Co. cat. autumn 2011. **R:** Truslove / Beane / E.W. King & Co. **I:** 2011. **D:** see Cultivars chapter.

'Rosie' Waller-Franklin (*L. odoratus*) Spencer   **F:** Waller-Franklin Seed Co. cat. 1932. **R:** Waller-Franklin Seed Co. **I:** 1931. **H:** T. **L:** U. **N:** P. **P:** S. **C:** deep rose pink. **S:** summer.

'**Rosina**' (*L. odoratus*) Spencer   **F:** *NSPS Annual* 1917: 95, Cuthbertson (1916). **R:** Robert Bolton & Son. **I:** 1914. **H:** T. **L:** U. **N:** P. **P:** S. **C:** rosy heliotrope, c.g. **S:** summer.

'Rosina' James (*L. odoratus*) Spencer   **F:** *NSPS Annual* 1993: 129. **R:** A.J. James / Matthewman. **I:** 1994. **D:** see Cultivars chapter.

'Rosina' Simons (*L. odoratus*) Spencer   **F:** n/k. **R:** Simons. **I:** 1936. **H:** T. **L:** U. **N:** P. **P:** S. **C:** rose, c.g. **S:** summer.

'**Rosy Dawn**' (*L. odoratus*) Spencer   **F:** Unwins Seeds cat. autumn 1998. **R:** Unwins Seeds. **I:** 1999. **D:** see Cultivars chapter.

'**Rosy Frills**' (*L. odoratus*) Spencer   **F:** *NSPS Annual* 1956: 7. **R:** Unwins Seeds. **I:** 1956. **H:** T. **L:** U. **N:** P. **P:** S. **C:** pink picotee, w.g. **S:** summer.

'**Rosy Salmon**' (*L. odoratus*) Spencer   **F:** E.W. King & Co. cat. 2014/15. **R:** Brackley / E.W. King & Co. **I:** 2015. **D:** see Cultivars chapter.

'**Roubeena**' (*L. odoratus*) Spencer   **F:** Cooltonagh cat. 2009/10. **R:** Harrod. **I:** 2010. **D:** see Cultivars chapter.

'Rouge Parfum'   = 'Ruby Tuesday'

'**Route 66**' (*L. odoratus*) Spencer   **F:** *NSPS Annual* 2016: 65. **R:** Hammett. **I:** 2015. **D:** see Cultivars chapter.

'**Rowallane**' (*L. odoratus*) Spencer   **F:** *NSPS Annual*

2002: 33. **R:** Harrod / Unwins Seeds. **I:** 2006. **H:** T. **L:** U. **N:** P. **P:** S. **C:** cerise. **S:** summer.

'**Royal Blue**' (*L. odoratus*) Spencer   **F:** Suttons cat. 1917. **R:** Suttons. **I:** n/k. **H:** T. **L:** U. **N:** P. **P:** S. **C:** n/k. **S:** summer.

'Royal Blue' Burpee (*L. odoratus*) Spencer   **F:** *NSPS Annual* 1927: xi. **R:** Burpee Seeds. **I:** 1927. **H:** T. **L:** U. **N:** P. **P:** S. **C:** royal blue. **S:** summer.

'Royal Blue' Ferry Morse (*L. odoratus*) Spencer   **F:** E.W. King & Co. cat. 1970/71. **R:** Ferry Morse Seed Co. **I:** 1968. **H:** T. **L:** U. **N:** P. **P:** S. **C:** mid blue. **S:** late spring.

'**Royal Navy Blue**' (*L. odoratus*) Spencer   **F:** E.W. King & Co. cat. 1970/71. **R:** Ferry Morse Seed Co. **I:** 1968. **H:** T. **L:** U. **N:** P. **P:** S. **C:** dark blue. **S:** late spring.

'**Royal Pink**' (*L. odoratus*) Spencer   **F:** Elliott cat., 1926. **R:** Robert Bolton & Son. **I:** 1926. **H:** T. **L:** U. **N:** P. **P:** S. **C:** orange-pink. **S:** summer.

'Royal Pink' Ferry Morse (*L. odoratus*) Spencer   **F:** n/k. **R:** Ferry Morse Seed Co. **I:** 1968. **D:** see Cultivars chapter.

'**Royal Wedding**' (*L. odoratus*) Spencer   **F:** Unwins Seeds cat. autumn 1981. **R:** Unwins Seeds. **I:** 1982. **D:** see Cultivars chapter.

'**Royal White**' (*L. odoratus*) Spencer   **F:** E.W. King & Co. cat. 1970/71. **R:** Ferry Morse Seed Co. **I:** 1968. **H:** T. **L:** U. **N:** P. **P:** S. **C:** white. **S:** late spring.

'Royal White' Parsons (*L. odoratus*) Grandiflora   **F:** R. Parsons cat. 2013/14. **R:** R. Parsons. **I:** 2014. **H:** T. **L:** U. **N:** P. **P:** S. **C:** white. **S:** late spring.

'**Ruby Anniversary**' (*L. odoratus*) Spencer   **F:** *NSPS Annual* 2000: 135. **R:** Sewell. **I:** 2001. **D:** see Cultivars chapter.

'**Ruby Charm**' (*L. odoratus*) Spencer   **F:** *NSPS Annual* 2013: 169. **R:** Matthewman. **I:** 2014. **H:** T. **L:** U. **N:** P. **P:** S. **C:** crimson. **S:** summer.

'**Ruby Tuesday**' (*L. odoratus*) Spencer   **F:** *NSPS Annual* 2001: 57. **R:** Beane / E.W. King & Co. **I:** 2005. **D:** see Cultivars chapter.

'**Rubyette**' (*L. odoratus*) Spencer   **F:** *NSPS Annual* 1968: ii. **R:** Burpee Seeds. **I:** 1966. **D:** see Cultivars chapter.

'**Ruth Ellen**' (*L. odoratus*) Spencer   **F:** Kerton Sweet Peas cat. 2006. **R:** Cave / Kerton Sweet Peas. **I:** 2006. **H:** T. **L:** U. **N:** P. **P:** S. **C:** salmon pink, c.g. **S:** summer.

'**Sagittarius**' (*L. odoratus*) Spencer   **F:** E.W. King & Co. cat. autumn 1999. **R:** J.D. Place / E.W. King & Co.

I: 1999. **D**: see Cultivars chapter.

'Saint Anne' (*L. odoratus*) Spencer　**F**: Cooltonagh cat. 2004/05. **R**: Harrod. **I**: 2005. **H**: T. **L**: U. **N**: P. **P**: S. **C**: white. **S**: summer.

'Sally Ann' (*L. odoratus*) Spencer　**F**: *NSPS Annual* 1992: 49. **R**: K Brewer / Matthewman. **I**: 1998. **D**: see Cultivars chapter.

'Sally Maitland' (*L. odoratus*) Spencer　**F**: R. Parsons cat. 2019/20. **R**: G. King / R. Parsons. **I**: 2020. **D**: see Cultivars chapter.

'Salmon Beauty' (*L. odoratus*) Semi-grandiflora **F**: R. Parsons cat. 2009/10. **R**: n/k. **I**: 2010. **D**: see Cultivars chapter.

'San Diego'　= 'Knee-Hi Salmon Pink'

'San Francisco'　= 'Knee-Hi Cream Pink'

'San Jose'　= 'Knee-Hi Rose Crimson'

'San Juan'　= 'Knee-Hi White'

'Sandi Jones' (*L. odoratus*) Spencer　**F**: Eagle Sweet Peas cat. 2002/03. **R**: Albutt / Eagle Sweet Peas. **I**: 2003. **H**: T. **L**: U. **N**: P. **P**: S. **C**: orange red. **S**: summer.

'Sapphire' (*L. odoratus*) Grandiflora　**F**: *NSPS Annual* 1911: 98. **R**: Aldersey. **I**: 1910. **H**: T. **L**: U. **N**: P. **P**: S. **C**: indigo blue. **S**: summer.

'Sapphire' Burpee 1924 (*L. odoratus*) Spencer **F**: Burpee Seeds cat. 1924, Arthur Yates & Co. cat. 1924, Elliot cat. 1924. **R**: Burpee Seeds. **I**: 1924. **H**: T. **L**: U. **N**: P. **P**: S. **C**: mid blue. **S**: summer.

'Sapphire' Burpee 1966 (*L. odoratus*) Spencer　**F**: E.W. King & Co. cat. 1965/66. **R**: Burpee Seeds. **I**: 1966. **D**: see Cultivars chapter.

'Sapphire' Damerum (*L. odoratus*) Spencer **F**: H. Eckford cat. 1932. **R**: Damerum. **I**: c.1932. **H**: T. **L**: U. **N**: P. **P**: S. **C**: blue. **S**: summer.

'Sapphire' Dobbie (*L. odoratus*) Spencer　**F**: G. Stark & Son cat. 1950/51. **R**: Dobbie & Co. **I**: 1951. **H**: T. **L**: U. **N**: P. **P**: S. **C**: blue. **S**: summer.

'Sapphire' Yates　= 'My Navy'

'Sarah Kennedy' (*L. odoratus*) Spencer　**F**: Sewell cat. 2001/02. **R**: Sewell. **I**: 2002. **D**: see Cultivars chapter.

'Scarlett' (*L. odoratus*) Grandiflora　**F**: Unwins Seeds cat. autumn 2005. **R**: Unwins Seeds. **I**: 2006. **D**: see Cultivars chapter.

'Scarlette' (*L. odoratus*) Spencer　**F**: *NSPS Annual* 1963: 47. **R**: Burpee Seeds. **I**: 1966. **D**: see Cultivars chapter.

'Scorpio' (*L. odoratus*) Spencer　**F**: E.W. King & Co. cat. autumn 1999. **R**: J.D. Place / E.W. King & Co. **I**: 1999.

D: see Cultivars chapter.

'Sea Wolf' (*L. odoratus*) Spencer　**F**: Marchant cat. 1985. **R**: Tebby / Marchant. **I**: 1985. **H**: T. **L**: U. **N**: P. **P**: S. **C**: lavender flush, w.g. **S**: summer.

'Second Honeymoon' (*L. odoratus*) Spencer **F**: Cooltonagh cat. 2004/05. **R**: Harrod. **I**: 2005. **H**: T. **L**: U. **N**: P. **P**: S. **C**: lavender. **S**: summer.

'Selene' (*L. odoratus*) Spencer　**F**: n/k. **R**: Oyama. **I**: n/k. **D**: see Cultivars chapter.

'Senator' (*L. odoratus*) Grandiflora　**F**: R.D. (1893). **R**: H. Eckford. **I**: 1891. **D**: see Cultivars chapter.

'Serendipity' (*L. odoratus*) Spencer　**F**: *NSPS Classification List* 2018. **R**: McDonald. **I**: 2018. **H**: T. **L**: U. **N**: P. **P**: S. **C**: white with blue edge. **S**: summer.

'Serenity' (*L. odoratus*) Spencer　**F**: Matthewman cat. 2019/20. **R**: Matthewman. **I**: 2020. **H**: T. **L**: U. **N**: P. **P**: S. **C**: lavender. **S**: summer.

'Sgt. Blott' (*L. odoratus*) Spencer　**F**: Kerton Sweet Peas cat. 2014. **R**: Chisholm / Kerton Sweet Peas. **I**: 2014. **H**: T. **L**: U. **N**: P. **P**: S. **C**: scarlet. **S**: summer.

'Shee's Pink' (*L. odoratus*) Spencer　**F**: *NSPS Annual* 2006: 63. **R**: n/k. **I**: n/k. **H**: T. **L**: U. **N**: P. **P**: D. **C**: magenta, w.g. **S**: winter.

'Sheila Macqueen' (*L. odoratus*) Spencer　**F**: Unwins Seeds cat. autumn 1979. **R**: Unwins Seeds. **I**: 1980. **H**: T. **L**: U. **N**: P. **P**: S. **C**: salmon pink, c.g. **S**: summer.

'Sheila Murray' (*L. odoratus*) Spencer　**F**: R. Parsons cat. 2012/13. **R**: Murray / R. Parsons. **I**: 2013. **H**: T. **L**: U. **N**: P. **P**: S. **C**: deep carmine. **S**: summer.

'Sheila Roy' (*L. odoratus*) Spencer　**F**: R. Parsons cat. 2012/13. **R**: Silvester / R. Parsons. **I**: 2013. **D**: see Cultivars chapter.

'Sicilian Fuchsia'　= 'Sicilian Pink'

'Sicilian Pink' (*L. odoratus*) Grandiflora　**RHS**: AGM (H3) 1995. **F**: Turral cat. 1964. **R**: Harland. **I**: Around 1955. **D**: see Cultivars chapter.

'Signpost' (*L. odoratus*) Spencer　**F**: Somerset cat. 2013/14. **R**: Hammett. **I**: before 1977. **D**: see Cultivars chapter.

'Silvia Simonetti' (*L. odoratus*) Spencer　**F**: Kerton Sweet Peas cat. 2006. **R**: Chisholm / Kerton Sweet Peas. **I**: 2006. **H**: T. **L**: U. **N**: P. **P**: S. **C**: orange red. **S**: summer.

'Sir Cliff' (*L. odoratus*) Spencer　**F**: Unwins Seeds cat. autumn 1998. **R**: Unwins Seeds. **I**: 1999. **H**: T. **L**: U. **N**: P. **P**: S. **C**: deep mauve. **S**: summer.

'Sir Henry Cecil'　= 'Chocolate Flake'

'**Sir Jimmy Shand**' (*L. odoratus*) Spencer **F:** Kerton Sweet Peas cat. 2008. **R:** Chisholm / Kerton Sweet Peas. **I:** 2008. **D:** see Cultivars chapter.

'**Sir Max Hastings**' (*L. odoratus*) Spencer **F:** Kerton Sweet Peas cat. 2009. **R:** Kerton Sweet Peas. **I:** 2009. **D:** see Cultivars chapter.

'**Skywalker**' (*L. odoratus*) Spencer **F:** *NSPS Annual* 2007: 54. **R:** Beane / E.W. King & Co. **I:** 2012. **D:** see Cultivars chapter.

'**Snoopea Scarlet**' (*L. odoratus*) Spencer **F:** Thompson & Morgan cat. 1989. **R:** n/k. **I:** n/k. **H:** SD. **L:** M. **N:** P. **P:** S. **C:** scarlet. **S:** summer.

Snoopea Series (*L. odoratus*) Spencer **F:** *NSPS Annual* 1980: v. **R:** E.W. King & Co. / Thompson & Morgan. **I:** 1980. **A:** Includes 'Beatrice', 'Bianca', 'Desdemona', 'Jessica', 'Juliet', 'Ophelia', 'Phebe', 'Rosalind' and 'Silvia'. **H:** SD. **L:** M. **N:** P. **P:** S. **C:** various colours. **S:** summer.

'**Snowlight**' (*L. odoratus*) Spencer **F:** *NSPS Annual* 2007: 55. **R:** Harrod / R. Parsons. **I:** 2016. **D:** see Cultivars chapter.

'**Snowy Rau**' (*L. odoratus*) Spencer **F:** McDougall cat. 2011. **R:** n/k. **I:** 1970s. **H:** T. **L:** U. **N:** P. **P:** S. **C:** white. **S:** winter.

'**Solar Flare**' (*L. odoratus*) Spencer **F:** R. Parsons cat. 2008/09. **R:** Hammett / R. Parsons. **I:** 2009. **D:** see Cultivars chapter.

'**Solitude**' (*L. odoratus*) Spencer **F:** Unwins Seeds cat autumn 2013. **R:** Harrod / Unwins Seeds. **I:** 2014. **D:** see Cultivars chapter.

'**Solstice Crimson**' (*L. odoratus*) Spencer **F:** The Sweet Pea Co. cat. 2009. **R:** Lemon. **I:** 2008. **D:** see Cultivars chapter.

'**Solstice Deep Rose**' (*L. odoratus*) Spencer **F:** n/k. **R:** Lemon. **I:** 2008. **H:** T. **L:** U. **N:** M. **P:** n/k. **C:** rosy magenta. **S:** winter.

'**Solstice Lavender**' (*L. odoratus*) Spencer **F:** The Sweet Pea Co. cat. 2009. **R:** Lemon. **I:** 2008. **D:** see Cultivars chapter.

'**Solstice Light Blue**' (*L. odoratus*) Spencer **F:** The Sweet Pea Co. cat. 2009. **R:** Lemon. **I:** 2008. **D:** see Cultivars chapter.

'**Solstice Light Pink**' (*L. odoratus*) Spencer **F:** The Sweet Pea Co. cat. 2009. **R:** Lemon. **I:** 2008. **H:** T. **L:** U. **N:** M. **P:** S. **C:** pale pink, w.g. **S:** early spring.

'**Solstice Maroon**' (*L. odoratus*) Spencer **F:** The Sweet Pea Co. cat. 2009. **R:** Lemon. **I:** 2008. **H:** T. **L:** U. **N:** M. **P:** n/k. **C:** dark maroon. **S:** winter.

'**Solstice Mid Blue**' (*L. odoratus*) Spencer **F:** The Sweet Pea Co. cat. 2009. **R:** Lemon. **I:** 2008. **H:** T. **L:** U. **N:** M. **P:** n/k. **C:** mid blue. **S:** winter.

'**Solstice Orchid**' (*L. odoratus*) Spencer **F:** The Sweet Pea Co. cat. 2009. **R:** Lemon. **I:** 2008. **D:** see Cultivars chapter.

'**Solstice Rose**' (*L. odoratus*) Spencer **F:** R. Parsons cat. 2013/14. **R:** Lemon. **I:** 2008. **H:** T. **L:** U. **N:** M. **P:** S. **C:** rose pink. **S:** winter.

'Solstice Ruby Red Hat' = 'Solstice Scarlet'

'**Solstice Salmon**' (*L. odoratus*) Spencer **F:** The Sweet Pea Co. cat. 2009. **R:** Lemon. **I:** 2008. **D:** see Cultivars chapter.

'**Solstice Scarlet**' (*L. odoratus*) Spencer **F:** The Sweet Pea Co. cat. 2009. **R:** Lemon. **I:** 2008. **D:** see Cultivars chapter.

Solstice Series (*L. odoratus*) Spencer **R:** Lemon. **I:** 2008. **A:** The latest development of winter-flowering early multiflora Spencer material. All names have a Solstice prefix. Sold in Australia as Celeste Series. **H:** T. **L:** U. **N:** M. **C:** various colours. **S:** winter.

'**Solstice Soft Pink**' (*L. odoratus*) Spencer **F:** A reselection of Solstice Salmon. **R:** Hammett. **I:** 2019. **H:** T. **L:** U. **N:** M. **P:** n/k. **C:** salmon pink, c.g. **S:** winter.

'**Solstice White**' (*L. odoratus*) Spencer **F:** The Sweet Pea Co. cat. 2009. **R:** Lemon. **I:** 2008. **D:** see Cultivars chapter.

'**Solway Ballerina**' (*L. odoratus*) Spencer **RHS:** AGM (H3) 2006. **F:** *NSPS Annual* 2006: 54. **R:** J.D. Place / R. Parsons. **I:** n/k. **D:** see Cultivars chapter.

'Solway Blue Vein' = 'Solway Sapphire'

'**Solway Charm**' (*L. odoratus*) Grandiflora **RHS:** AGM (H3) 2004. **F:** *NSPS Annual* 2005: 53. **R:** J.D. Place / R. Parsons. **I:** 2015. **D:** see Cultivars chapter.

'**Solway Classic**' (*L. odoratus*) Grandiflora **RHS:** AGM (H3) 2006. **F:** *NSPS Annual* 2006: 46. **R:** J.D. Place / R. Parsons. **I:** 2013. **D:** see Cultivars chapter.

'**Solway Duet**' (*L. odoratus*) Grandiflora **F:** n/k. **R:** J.D. Place. **I:** n/k. **H:** SD. **L:** M. **N:** P. **P:** S. **C:** pink stripe. **S:** summer.

'**Solway Fanfare**' (*L. odoratus*) Spencer **F:** *NSPS Annual* 1997: 73. **R:** J.D. Place / R. Parsons. **I:** 2015. **D:** see Cultivars chapter.

'**Solway Lullaby**' (*L. odoratus*) Semi-grandiflora **F:** *NSPS Annual* 2005: 53. **R:** J.D. Place / R. Parsons.

I: 2013. **D:** see Cultivars chapter.

'Solway Minstrel' (*L. odoratus*) Grandiflora **F:** *NSPS Annual* 2005: 53. **R:** J.D. Place / R. Parsons. **I:** 2015. **D:** see Cultivars chapter.

'Solway Minuet' (*L. odoratus*) Grandiflora **F:** *NSPS Annual* 2004: 56. **R:** J.D. Place / Mr Fothergills Seeds Ltd. **I:** 2013. **D:** see Cultivars chapter.

'Solway Sapphire' (*L. odoratus*) Grandiflora **RHS:** AGM (H3) 2006. **F:** *NSPS Annual* 2006: 46. **R:** J.D. Place / Mr Fothergills Seeds Ltd. **I:** 2013. **H:** SD. **L:** M. **N:** P. **P:** S. **C:** blue stripe, w.g. **S:** summer.

'Solway Serenade' (*L. odoratus*) Grandiflora **RHS:** AGM (H3) 2002. **F:** *NSPS Annual* 2003: 41. **R:** J.D. Place / Mr Fothergills Seeds Ltd. **I:** 2013. **D:** see Cultivars chapter.

'Solway Shimmer' (*L. odoratus*) Spencer **F:** *NSPS Annual* 2006: 46. **R:** J.D. Place / R. Parsons. **I:** 2017. **D:** see Cultivars chapter.

'Solway Snowflake' (*L. odoratus*) Grandiflora **RHS:** AGM (H3) 2003. **F:** *NSPS Annual* 2004: 57. **R:** J.D. Place / R. Parsons. **I:** 2013. **D:** see Cultivars chapter.

'Solway Spectrum' (*L. odoratus*) Spencer **F:** *NSPS Annual* 2007: 63. **R:** J.D. Place. **I:** n/k. **H:** SD. **L:** U. **N:** P. **P:** S. **C:** claret stripe, w.g. **S:** summer.

'Solway Splendour' (*L. odoratus*) Grandiflora **RHS:** AGM (H3) 2004. **F:** *NSPS Annual* 2005: 53. **R:** J.D. Place / R. Parsons. **I:** 2013. **D:** see Cultivars chapter.

'Solway Sunset' (*L. odoratus*) Spencer **F:** *NSPS Annual* 1991: 40. **R:** J.D. Place / Unwins Seeds. **I:** 2000. **D:** see Cultivars chapter.

'Solway Symphony' (*L. odoratus*) Spencer **F:** *NSPS Annual* 2003: 45. **R:** J.D. Place / R. Parsons. **I:** 2017. **D:** see Cultivars chapter.

'Solway Velvet' (*L. odoratus*) Grandiflora **F:** Mr Fothergills Seeds Ltd cat. 2013. **R:** J.D. Place / Mr Fothergills Seeds Ltd. **I:** 2013. **D:** see Cultivars chapter.

'Solway Vintage' (*L. odoratus*) Grandiflora **F:** n/k. **R:** J.D. Place. **I:** n/k. **H:** SD. **L:** M. **N:** P. **P:** S. **C:** claret stripe. **S:** summer.

'Somerset Lady' (*L. odoratus*) Spencer **RHS:** AGM (H3) 2014. **F:** Somerset cat. 2011. **R:** Somerset. **I:** 2012. **D:** see Cultivars chapter.

'Somerset Ripple' (*L. odoratus*) Spencer **F:** Somerset cat. 2012. **R:** Somerset. **I:** 2013. **H:** T. **L:** U. **N:** P. **P:** S.

C: raspberry stripe, w.g. **S:** summer.

'Somewhere' (*L. odoratus*) Spencer **F:** n/k. **R:** Hammett. **I:** 2019. **A:** Name first appeared on the Hammett website (seen 4 Aug 2018). **D:** see Cultivars chapter.

'Sonia' (*L. odoratus*) Spencer **F:** *NSPS Annual* 1983: 82. **R:** Hunt / Robert Bolton & Son. **I:** 1985. **D:** see Cultivars chapter.

'Sophisticated Lady' (*L. odoratus*) Spencer **F:** *NSPS Annual* 2008: 56. **R:** Harrod / Kerton Sweet Peas. **I:** 2012. **D:** see Cultivars chapter.

'Southbourne' (*L. odoratus*) Spencer **F:** Unwins Seeds cat. autumn 1972. **R:** Colledge / Unwins Seeds. **I:** 1973. **D:** see Cultivars chapter.

'Spanish Dancer' (*L. odoratus*) Grandiflora **F:** Mr Fothergills Seeds Ltd cat. 2017. **R:** Hammett / Burpee Seeds. **I:** 2011. **A:** Name first appeared on the Burpee Seeds website (seen Dec. 2010). **D:** see Cultivars chapter.

'Spring Beauty' (*L. vernus*) = 'Alboroseus'

'Spring Coquette' (*L. odoratus*) Spencer **F:** n/k. **R:** Hammett / R. Parsons. **I:** 2019. **H:** T. **L:** U. **N:** M. **P:** S. **C:** soft orange-pink. **S:** spring.

'Spring Delight' (*L. vernus*) = *L. vernus* subsp. *vernus*

'Spring Melody' (*L. vernus*) = 'Alboroseus'

'Spring Sunshine Blush' (*L. odoratus*) Spencer **F:** Owl's Acre Sweet Peas cat. 2018/19. **R:** Owl's Acre Sweet Peas. **I:** 2019. **H:** T. **L:** U. **N:** M. **P:** S. **C:** cream pink. **S:** early spring.

'Spring Sunshine Burgundy' (*L. odoratus*) Spencer **F:** Owl's Acre Sweet Peas cat. 2017/18. **R:** Owl's Acre Sweet Peas. **I:** 2018. **H:** T. **L:** U. **N:** M. **P:** S. **C:** maroon. **S:** early spring.

'Spring Sunshine Cerise' (*L. odoratus*) Spencer **F:** Owl's Acre Sweet Peas cat. 2017/18. **R:** Owl's Acre Sweet Peas. **I:** 2018. **H:** T. **L:** U. **N:** M. **P:** S. **C:** cerise. **S:** early spring.

'Spring Sunshine Champagne' (*L. odoratus*) Spencer **F:** Owl's Acre Sweet Peas cat. 2017/18. **R:** Owl's Acre Sweet Peas. **I:** 2008. **D:** see Cultivars chapter.

'Spring Sunshine Cream' (*L. odoratus*) Spencer **F:** Owl's Acre Sweet Peas cat. 2017/18. **R:** Owl's Acre Sweet Peas. **I:** 2018. **H:** T. **L:** U. **N:** M. **P:** S. **C:** cream. **S:** early spring.

'Spring Sunshine Light Blue' (*L. odoratus*) Spencer **F:** n/k. **R:** Owl's Acre Sweet Peas. **I:** 2002. **H:** T. **L:** U. **N:** M. **P:** S. **C:** pale blue. **S:** early spring.

'**Spring Sunshine Mauve**' (*L. odoratus*) Spencer
    F: n/k. **R:** Owl's Acre Sweet Peas. **I:** 2002. **H:** T. **L:** U.
    N: M. **P:** S. **C:** mauve. **S:** early spring.

'**Spring Sunshine Peach**' (*L. odoratus*) Spencer
    F: Owl's Acre Sweet Peas cat. 2018/19. **R:** Owl's Acre
    Sweet Peas. **I:** 2002. **H:** T. **L:** U. **N:** M. **P:** S. **C:** peach.
    S: early spring.

'**Spring Sunshine White**' (*L. odoratus*) Spencer
    F: Owl's Acre Sweet Peas cat. 2017/18. **R:** Owl's Acre
    Sweet Peas. **I:** 2018. **H:** T. **L:** U. **N:** M. **P:** S. **C:** white.
    S: early spring.

'**Starlight**' (*L. odoratus*) Spencer   **F:** A. Zvolanek &
    Sons cat. 1925/26. **R:** Waller-Franklin Seed Co. **I:** n/k.
    H: T. **L:** U. **N:** P. **P:** S. **C:** pale lavender. **S:** winter.

'Starlight' Walker (*L. odoratus*) Spencer   **RHS:** AGM
    (H3) 2004. **F:** *NSPS Annual* 2001: 57. **R:** W. Walker /
    Kerton Sweet Peas. **I:** 2004. **D:** see Cultivars chapter.

'Starlight' Welch (*L. odoratus*) Spencer   **F:** *NSPS
    Annual* 1999: 63. **R:** Welch. **I:** n/k. **H:** T. **L:** U. **N:** P.
    P: S. **C:** white. **S:** summer.

'Starlight' Unwins   = 'Starlight Sonata'

'**Starlight Sonata**' (*L. odoratus*) Spencer   **F:** *NSPS
    Annual* 2001: 57. **R:** J.D. Place / Unwins Seeds.
    I: 2012. **H:** SD. **L:** U. **N:** P. **P:** S. **C:** navy blue stripe, w.g.
    S: summer.

'**Stella**' (*L. odoratus*) Spencer   **F:** n/k. **R:** Sands.
    I: before 1925. **H:** T. **L:** U. **N:** P. **P:** S. **C:** n/k. **S:** summer.

'Stella' Bolton (*L. odoratus*) Spencer   **F:** Robert Bolton
    & Son cat. autumn 1953. **R:** Robert Bolton & Son.
    I: 1939. **H:** T. **L:** U. **N:** P. **P:** S. **C:** deep blue. **S:** summer.

'Stella' Denholm (*L. odoratus*) Spencer   **F:** E.W. King
    & Co. cat. 1963/64. **R:** Denholm Seeds. **I:** 1960. **D:** see
    Cultivars chapter.

'**Strawberry Fields**' (*L. odoratus*) Spencer
    F: R. Parsons cat. 2013/14. **R:** Hammett. **I:** 2005.
    A: Name first appeared on the Seedngrow website
    (seen 19 Feb 2009). **D:** see Cultivars chapter.

Strawberry Fields Mixed (*L. odoratus*) Spencer
    F: Hem Zaden cat. 2011/12. **R:** n/k. **I:** n/k. **H:** T. **L:** U.
    N: P. **P:** S. **C:** mixed colours. **S:** summer.

'**Streamer Blue**' (*L. odoratus*) Spencer   **F:** Suttons cat.
    2002. **R:** Hammett / Arthur Yates & Co. **I:** before
    2002. **H:** T. **L:** U. **N:** P. **P:** S. **C:** flake. **S:** summer.

'**Streamer Lavender**' (*L. odoratus*) Spencer   **F:** Hem
    Zaden cat. 2011/12. **R:** Hem Zaden. **I:** 2012. **H:** T. **L:** U.
    N: P. **P:** S. **C:** lavender flake. **S:** summer.

'**Streamer Maroon**' (*L. odoratus*) Spencer   **F:** Suttons
cat. 2002. **R:** Hammett / Arthur Yates & Co. **I:** before
    2002. **H:** T. **L:** U. **N:** P. **P:** S. **C:** flake. **S:** summer.

'**Streamer Orange**' (*L. odoratus*) Spencer   **F:** Suttons
    cat. 2002. **R:** Hammett / Arthur Yates & Co. **I:** before
    2002. **D:** see Cultivars chapter.

'**Streamer Pink**' (*L. odoratus*) Spencer   **F:** Suttons cat.
    2002. **R:** Hammett / Arthur Yates & Co. **I:** before
    2002. **H:** T. **L:** U. **N:** P. **P:** S. **C:** flake. **S:** summer.

'**Streamer Scarlet**' (*L. odoratus*) Spencer   **F:** Hem
    Zaden cat. 2011/12. **R:** Hem Zaden. **I:** 2012. **H:** T. **L:** U.
    N: P. **P:** S. **C:** scarlet flake. **S:** summer.

Streamer Series (*L. odoratus*) Spencer   **F:** Suttons cat.
    2002. **R:** Hammett / Suttons. **I:** 2002. **H:** T. **L:** U. **N:** P.
    P: S. **C:** various flakes. **S:** summer.

'**Su Pollard**' (*L. odoratus*) Spencer   **F:** Brackley cat.
    1992/93. **R:** Brackley. **I:** 1991. **D:** see Cultivars
    chapter.

'**Subtle Charm**' (*L. odoratus*) Spencer   **RHS:** AM 1990.
    F: *NSPS Annual* 1991: 35. **R:** Albutt / Eagle Sweet
    Peas. **I:** 1995. **H:** T. **L:** U. **N:** P. **P:** S. **C:** pale pink, w.g.
    S: summer.

'**Subtle Hints**' (*L. vernus*)   **F:** Matthewman (2015).
    R: n/k. **I:** n/k. **A:** The leaflets are of f. *vernus* type
    (30–100mm wide). **D:** see Cultivars chapter.

'**Sunset**' (*L. odoratus*) Grandiflora   **F:** Vaughan Seed
    Store cat. 1904. **R:** C.C. Morse & Co. / Vaughan Seed
    Store. **I:** 1904. **H:** T. **L:** U. **N:** P. **P:** S. **C:** rose flake, c.g.,
    hooded. **S:** summer.

'Sunset' Bolton (*L. odoratus*) Spencer   **F:** Elliott cat.
    1922. **R:** Robert Bolton & Son. **I:** 1922. **H:** T. **L:** U. **N:** P.
    P: S. **C:** cherry-red, c.g. **S:** summer.

'Sunset' Ferry Morse (*L. odoratus*) Spencer   **F:** n/k.
    R: Ferry Morse Seed Co. **I:** before 1942. **H:** T. **L:** U. **N:** P.
    P: S. **C:** n/k. **S:** summer.

'Sunset' Harriss (*L. odoratus*) Spencer   **F:** *NSPS
    Annual* 1988: 16. **R:** Harriss / E.W. King & Co. **I:** 1993.
    H: T. **L:** U. **N:** P. **P:** S. **C:** orange-cerise. **S:** summer.

'Sunset' Marshall (*L. odoratus*) Spencer   **RHS:** AGM
    (H3) 2002. **F:** S.E. Marshall & Co. cat. 2002.
    R: S.E. Marshall & Co.. **I:** 2002. **D:** see Cultivars
    chapter.

'Sunset' n/k (*L. odoratus*) Spencer   **F:** Gill & Searle cat.
    1934. **R:** n/k. **I:** n/k. **H:** T. **L:** U. **N:** P. **P:** S. **C:** poppy-
    scarlet. **S:** winter.

'Sunset' Stevenson (*L. odoratus*) Spencer   **F:** *NSPS
    Annual* 1922: vii, Elliott cat. 1922. **R:** J. Stevenson.
    I: 1922. **H:** T. **L:** U. **N:** P. **P:** S. **C:** salmon-orange.

S: summer.

'Sunset' Unwins (*L. odoratus*) Spencer **F:** Unwins Seeds cat. autumn 1971. **R:** Unwins Seeds. **I:** 1972. **H:** T. **L:** U. **N:** P. **P:** S. **C:** salmon-cerise. **S:** summer.

Sunset Pastel Mixed (*L. odoratus*) Spencer **I:** Suttons, 2007. **D:** A mixture of cultivars. **C:** mixed colours.

'Sunshine Light Pink' = 'Winter Sunshine Light Pink'

'Supersnoop Cream Pink' (*L. odoratus*) Spencer **F:** n/k. **R:** Denholm Seeds. **I:** 1984. **D:** see Cultivars chapter.

'Supersnoop Magenta' (*L. odoratus*) Spencer **F:** n/k. **R:** Denholm Seeds. **I:** 1984. **D:** see Cultivars chapter.

'Supersnoop Mid Pink' (*L. odoratus*) Spencer **F:** n/k. **R:** Seedlynx. **I:** n/k. **A:** Selected out of Supersnoop mixture. Although there is seed under this name in circulation, the name does not appear to have been published. **H:** SD. **L:** M. **N:** P. **P:** S. **C:** pink. **S:** summer.

'Supersnoop Navy Blue' (*L. odoratus*) Spencer **F:** *NSPS Annual* 1983: 80. **R:** Denholm Seeds. **I:** 1985. **D:** see Cultivars chapter.

'Supersnoop Pale Purple' (*L. odoratus*) Spencer **F:** Nakamura *et al.* (2010). **R:** Miyazaki prefecture. **I:** n/k. **H:** T. **L:** M. **N:** n/k. **P:** S. **C:** mid blue. **S:** summer.

'Supersnoop Pink' = 'Supersnoop Light Rose Pink'

'Supersnoop Purple' (*L. odoratus*) Spencer **F:** Nakamura *et al.* (2010). **R:** Denholm Seeds. **I:** 1984. **H:** SD. **L:** M. **N:** P. **P:** S. **C:** purple. **S:** spring.

'Supersnoop Red' = 'Supersnoop Crimson'

Supersnoop Series (*L. odoratus*) Spencer **F:** *NSPS Annual* 1984: 36. **R:** Denholm. **I:** 1985. **H:** SD. **L:** M. **N:** P. **P:** S. **C:** various colours **S:** summer

'Supersnoop White' (*L. odoratus*) Spencer **F:** *NSPS Annual* 1983: 80. **R:** Denholm Seeds. **I:** 1984. **D:** see Cultivars chapter.

'Susan Burgess' (*L. odoratus*) Spencer **F:** R. Parsons cat. 2014/15. **R:** Beane / R. Parsons. **I:** 2015. **D:** see Cultivars chapter.

'Susan Thomas' (*L. odoratus*) Spencer **F:** R. Parsons cat. 2012/13. **R:** R. Parsons. **I:** 2013. **D:** see Cultivars chapter.

'Susie' (*L. odoratus*) Spencer **F:** n/k. **R:** Denholm Seeds. **I:** 1960. **D:** see Cultivars chapter.

'Suzy Z' (*L. odoratus*) Spencer **F:** Owl's Acre Sweet Peas cat. 2006/07. **R:** Owl's Acre Sweet Peas. **I:** 2004. **D:** see Cultivars chapter.

'Swan Lake' (*L. odoratus*) Spencer **F:** *NSPS Annual* 1954: 101. **R:** Carters Tested Seeds. **I:** 1954. **H:** T. **L:** U.

N: P. **P:** S. **C:** white. **S:** summer.

'Sweetie Carmine Rose' (*L. odoratus*) Grandiflora **F:** Suttons cat. 2001. **R:** Suttons. **I:** 2001. **D:** see Cultivars chapter.

'Sylvia Ann' (*L. odoratus*) Spencer **F:** NSPS Annual 1991: 36. **R:** Tullett / Kerton Sweet Peas. **I:** 1997. **D:** see Cultivars chapter.

'Sylvia Mary' (*L. odoratus*) Spencer **F:** Robert Bolton & Son cat. 1990/91. **R:** B.R. Jones / Robert Bolton & Son. **I:** 1991. **H:** T. **L:** U. **N:** P. **P:** S. **C:** orange-red. **S:** summer.

'Sylvia Moore' (*L. odoratus*) Spencer **F:** Eagle Sweet Peas cat. 1999/2000. **R:** Albutt / Eagle Sweet Peas. **I:** 2000. **D:** see Cultivars chapter.

'Sylvia Norton' (*L. vernus*) **F:** n/k. **R:** Joe Sharman, Monksilver Nursery. **I:** c.2017. **A:** The leaflets are of f. *angustifolius* type (15–30mm wide). **D:** see Cultivars chapter.

'Symphony' (*L. odoratus*) Spencer **F:** *NSPS Annual* 2006: 63. **R:** n/k. **I:** n/k. **H:** T. **L:** U. **N:** M. **P:** D. **C:** pale pink, w.g. **S:** winter.

'Tahiti Sunrise' (*L. odoratus*) Spencer **RHS:** AGM (H3) 1996. **F:** *NSPS Annual* 1997: 74. **R:** Harrod. **I:** 2005. **D:** see Cultivars chapter.

'Tara' (*L. odoratus*) Spencer **F:** *NSPS Annual* 2002: 32. **R:** Harrod / E.W. King & Co. **I:** 2003. **D:** see Cultivars chapter.

'Tartan Mac' (*L. odoratus*) Spencer **F:** McDougall cat. 1998. **R:** McDougall. **I:** late 1970s. **D:** see Cultivars chapter.

'Tell Tale' (*L. odoratus*) Spencer **F:** E.W. King & Co. cat. 1951/52. **R:** Robert Bolton & Son. **I:** 1946. **D:** see Cultivars chapter.

'Teresa Maureen' (*L. odoratus*) Grandiflora **RHS:** AGM (H3) 1996. **F:** *NSPS Annual* 1997: 73. **R:** Cave / E.W. King & Co. **I:** 2002. **D:** see Cultivars chapter.

'Terry Wogan' (*L. odoratus*) Spencer **F:** Unwins Seeds cat. autumn 1982. **R:** Colledge / Unwins Seeds. **I:** 1983. **D:** see Cultivars chapter.

'The Busby Pea' (*L. odoratus*) Grandiflora **F:** Grayson cat. 1993. **R:** n/k. **I:** 1823. **H:** T. **L:** U. **N:** P. **P:** S. **C:** pink / white. **S:** summer.

'The Doctor' (*L. odoratus*) Grandiflora **F:** *J. Hort. Cottage Gard.* (1894) **R:** H. Eckford. **I:** n/k. **H:** T. **L:** U. **N:** P. **P:** S. **C:** scarlet. **S:** summer.

'The Doctor' Jones (*L. odoratus*) Spencer **F:** *NSPS*

Annual 1976: 30. **R:** B.R. Jones / Unwins Seeds.
I: 1979. **D:** see Cultivars chapter.

'The Major' (*L. odoratus*) Spencer **F:** Simons cat.
1954/55. **R:** Simons. **I:** before 1950. **H:** T. **L:** U. **N:** P.
P: S. **C:** deep red cerise. **S:** summer.

'The Major' Turral (*L. odoratus*) Grandiflora **F:** Owl's
Acre Sweet Peas cat. 2008/09. **R:** Turral. **I:** 1960s.
H: T. **L:** U. **N:** P. **P:** S. **C:** flake. **S:** summer.

'The Princess Royal' (*L. odoratus*) Spencer **F:** n/k.
R: Beane / Simply Sweet Peas. **I:** 2012. **D:** see
Cultivars chapter.

'Theia-Bella' (*L. odoratus*) Spencer **F:** R. Parsons cat.
2016/17, *NSPS Annual* 2016: 198. **R:** R. Parsons.
I: 2017. **D:** see Cultivars chapter.

'Thelma May' (*L. odoratus*) Spencer **F:** McDougall
cat. 1998. **R:** McDougall. **I:** late 1970s. **H:** T. **L:** U. **N:** P.
P: n/k. **C:** deep violet. **S:** winter.

'Thomas and Linda' (*L. odoratus*) Spencer
F: R. Parsons cat. 2017/18. **R:** Harrod / R. Parsons.
I: 2018. **D:** see Cultivars chapter.

'Tillyperone' (*L. rotundifolius* × *L. tuberosus*)
RHS: AGM (H7) 2012. **F:** Norton (1994). **R:** n/k.
Donated in 1985 to University of Oxford Botanic
Garden by a Mrs Clutterbuck of Wootton,
Oxfordshire, who obtained it from a garden in Wales,
presumably called Tillyperone. **I:** Distributed by
Sylvia Norton after 1991. **A:** See notes under 'Tubro'.
H: T. **L:** U. **N:** P. **P:** S. **C:** purple-pink. **S:** summer.

'Tommy' (*L. odoratus*) Spencer **F:** Ferry Morse Seed
Co. cat. 1947. **R:** Ferry Morse Seed Co. **I:** 1940. **H:** T.
L: U. **N:** P. **P:** S. **C:** mid blue. **S:** late spring.

'Tommy' Parsons (*L. odoratus*) Semi-grandiflora
F: R. Parsons cat. 2011/12. **R:** R. Parsons. **I:** 2012.
D: see Cultivars chapter.

'Tony Bates' (*L. odoratus*) Spencer **F:** R. Parsons cat.
2007/08. **R:** R. Parsons. **I:** 2008. **D:** see Cultivars
chapter.

'Top Hat' (*L. odoratus*) Spencer **F:** Peter Henderson
& Co. cat. 1940, Gill & Searle cat. c.1939.
R: Macdonald. **I:** 1936. **H:** T. **L:** U. **N:** P. **P:** S. **C:** dark
blue. **S:** winter.

'Top Hat' Parsons (*L. odoratus*) Semi-grandiflora
F: n/k. **R:** R. Parsons. **I:** n/k. **H:** T. **L:** U. **N:** P. **P:** S. **C:**
dark blue. **S:** summer.

'Topsy' (*L. odoratus*) Spencer **F:** Denholm Seeds cat.
1964. **R:** Denholm Seeds. **I:** 1960. **D:** see Cultivars
chapter.

'Topsy' Bolton (*L. odoratus*) Spencer **F:** Robert
Bolton & Son cat. autumn 1963, E.W. King & Co. cat.
1963/64. **R:** Robert Bolton & Son. **I:** 1964. **H:** T. **L:** U.
N: P. **P:** S. **C:** picotee, w.g. **S:** summer.

'Tracy Ann' (*L. odoratus*) Spencer **F:** *NSPS Annual*
2002: 32. **R:** Tierney / Eagle Sweet Peas. **I:** 2007. **H:** T.
L: U. **N:** P. **P:** S. **C:** white. **S:** summer.

'Tranquility' (*L. odoratus*) Spencer **F:** n/k. **R:** n/k.
I: before 1933. **H:** T. **L:** U. **N:** P. **P:** S. **C:** n/k. **S:** summer.

'Tranquillity' Ferry Morse (*L. odoratus*) Spencer
F: Ferry Morse Seed Co. cat. 1932. **R:** Ferry Morse
Seed Co. **I:** 1932. **H:** T. **L:** U. **N:** P. **P:** D. **C:** rosy mauve,
c.g. **S:** summer.

'Tranquility' Unwins (*L. odoratus*) Spencer
F: Unwins Seeds cat. 2011. **R:** Unwins Seeds. **I:** 2011.
H: T. **L:** U. **N:** P. **P:** S. **C:** crimson. **S:** summer.

'Tranquillity' Wells (*L. odoratus*) Spencer **RHS:** AGM
(H3) 2003. **F:** *NSPS Annual* 2004: 57. **R:** Wells /
R Parsons. **I:** 2015. **D:** see Cultivars chapter.

'Trelawny' (*L. odoratus*) Spencer **F:** *NSPS Annual*
1988: vii. **R:** Tremewan. **I:** 1989. **D:** see Cultivars
chapter.

'True Blue' (*L. odoratus*) Spencer **F:** *NSPS Annual*
1912: 29. **R:** Aldersey. **I:** 1912. **H:** T. **L:** U. **N:** P. **P:** S.
C: indigo. **S:** summer.

'True Blue' Burpee (*L. odoratus*) Spencer **F:** Burpee
Seeds cat. 1920. **R:** Burpee Seeds. **I:** n/k. **H:** T. **L:** U.
N: P. **P:** S. **C:** light violet blue. **S:** winter.

'True Blue' Zvolanek (*L. odoratus*) Spencer
F: William Zvolanek & Co. cat. 1932/33. **R:** William
Zvolanek & Co. **I:** before 1933. **H:** T. **L:** U. **N:** P. **P:** S.
C: blue / mauve. **S:** winter.

'Tubro' (*L. rotundifolius* × *L. tuberosus*) **F:** Norton
(1994). **R:** n/k. **I:** Distributed by Sylvia Norton after
1991. **A:** The name is a condensation of the two
species names involved in this hybrid. The initial
hybrids that may have given rise to 'Tubro' are
described by Marsden-Jones (1920). He exhibited a
plant from this cross at an RHS show in July 1957
where it won an award (Norton 2008). Two plants of
the cross obtained by Norton, although not directly
traced back to the Marsden-Jones crosses (Turrill
1962, Norton 2008), have the form of *L. rotundifolius*
but with purple-pink instead of brick-red flowers
(Norton 1994). Both remain in cultivation under the
names *L.* 'Tubro' and *L.* 'Tillyperone'. DNA testing
supports their hybrid origin (Kenicer, unpublished).

Norton regarded them as different to each other, with 'Tillyperone' having slightly larger flowers of a more intense colour. However, they are both propagated by seed that has caused variation which blurs these differences. **D:** see Cultivars chapter.

'Turquoise' (*L. odoratus*) Spencer   **F:** R. Parsons cat. 2011/12. **R:** Hammett / R. Parsons. **I:** 2012. **D:** see Cultivars chapter.

'Turquoise Lagoon'   = 'Turquoise'

'Tutankhamun'   = *L. sativus* f. *azureus*

'Tutti Frutti' (*L. odoratus*) Spencer   **F:** R. Parsons cat. 2019/20. **R:** R. Parsons. **I:** 2020. **H:** T. **L:** M. **N:** P. **P:** S. **C:** orange stripe, w.g. **S:** summer.

'Una Scobie' (*L. odoratus*) Spencer   **F:** *Australian Garden Lover* (1947). **R:** J.F. Scobie. **I:** 1948. **H:** T. **L:** U. **N:** P. **P:** D. **C:** mid blue. **S:** early spring.

'Unique' (*L. odoratus*) Grandiflora   **F:** *NSPS Annual* 1906: xi ad. **R:** G. Stark & Son. **I:** 1905. **D:** see Cultivars chapter.

'Unique' Harkness (*L. odoratus*) Spencer   **F:** Bunyip 17 Oct 1952. **R:** Harkness. **I:** 1953. **H:** T. **L:** U. **N:** P. **P:** S. **C:** salmon rose, c.g. / cream. **S:** winter.

'Unique' Stevenson (*L. odoratus*) Spencer   **F:** *NSPS Annual* 1936: 71. **R:** J. Stevenson. **I:** 1936. **H:** T. **L:** U. **N:** P. **P:** S. **C:** crushed strawberry, c.g. **S:** summer.

'Unique' Unwins (*L. odoratus*) Spencer   **F:** Unwins Seeds cat. autumn 1977. **R:** Unwins Seeds. **I:** 1978. **H:** T. **L:** U. **N:** P. **P:** S. **C:** lilac pink. **S:** summer.

Unwins Stripes Mixed (*L. odoratus*) Spencer   **F:** Moles cat. 1961. **R:** Unwins Seeds. **I:** 1951. **H:** T. **L:** U. **N:** P. **P:** S. **C:** mixed striped. **S:** summer.

'Valentine' (*L. odoratus*) Spencer   **F:** *NSPS Annual* 1918: 57. **R:** Robert Bolton & Son. **I:** 1917. **H:** T. **L:** U. **N:** P. **P:** S. **C:** pale pink, c.g. **S:** summer.

'Valentine' Semences Davy (*L. odoratus*) Spencer   **F:** Semences Davy 1935. **R:** n/k. **I:** n/k. **H:** T. **L:** U. **N:** P. **P:** S. **C:** red flushed with pink. **S:** summer.

'Valentine' Unwins (*L. odoratus*) Grandiflora   **F:** Unwins Seeds cat. autumn 2000. **R:** Unwins Seeds. **I:** 2001. **H:** T. **L:** U. **N:** P. **P:** S. **C:** white. **S:** summer.

'Valentine' Zvolanek (*L. odoratus*) Spencer   **F:** Bodger Seeds Ltd cat. 1965. **R:** William Zvolanek & Co. **I:** n/k. **H:** T. **L:** U. **N:** M. **P:** S. **C:** salmon cerise, c.g. **S:** winter.

'Valerie Harrod' (*L. odoratus*) Spencer   **RHS:** AGM (H3) 2001. **F:** Kerton Sweet Peas cat. 2001. **R:** Harrod / Kerton Sweet Peas. **I:** 2001. **D:** see Cultivars chapter.

'Vanilla Ice' (*L. odoratus*) Grandiflora   **F:** E.W. King & Co. cat. 1996/97. **R:** E.W. King & Co. **I:** 1997. **H:** T. **L:** U. **N:** P. **P:** S. **C:** white. **S:** summer.

'Variegatus' (*L. vernus*)   = 'Alboroseus'

'Variety Club' (*L. odoratus*) Spencer   **F:** Unwins Seeds cat. autumn 2003. **R:** Beane / Unwins Seeds. **I:** 2004. **D:** see Cultivars chapter.

'Vaudeville' (*L. odoratus*) Spencer   **F:** n/k. **R:** Hammett. **I:** 2009. **D:** see Cultivars chapter.

'Vera Lynn' (*L. odoratus*) Spencer   **F:** Unwins Seeds cat. autumn 1989. **R:** Colledge / Unwins Seeds. **I:** 1990. **D:** see Cultivars chapter.

'Vienna' (*L. odoratus*) Spencer   **F:** *NSPS Annual* 1973: i. **R:** Ferry Morse Seed Co. **I:** 1973. **D:** see Cultivars chapter.

'Villa Roma Carmine' (*L. odoratus*) Spencer   **F:** Hem Zaden cat. 2011/12. **R:** Hem Zaden. **I:** 2012. **H:** SD. **L:** U. **N:** P. **P:** S. **C:** carmine. **S:** spring.

'Villa Roma Navy Blue' (*L. odoratus*) Spencer   **F:** Hem Zaden cat. 2011/12. **R:** Hem Zaden. **I:** 2012. **H:** SD. **L:** U. **N:** P. **P:** S. **C:** navy blue. **S:** spring.

'Villa Roma Pink' (*L. odoratus*) Spencer   **F:** Hem Zaden cat. 2011/12. **R:** Hem Zaden. **I:** 2012. **H:** SD. **L:** U. **N:** P. **P:** S. **C:** salmon pink. **S:** spring.

'Villa Roma Raspberry' (*L. odoratus*) Spencer   **F:** Hem Zaden cat. 2011/12. **R:** Hem Zaden. **I:** 2012. **D:** see Cultivars chapter.

'Villa Roma Rose' (*L. odoratus*) Spencer   **F:** Hem Zaden cat. 2011/12. **R:** Hem Zaden. **I:** 2012. **D:** see Cultivars chapter.

'Villa Roma Scarlet' (*L. odoratus*) Spencer   **F:** Hem Zaden cat. 2011/12. **R:** n/k. **I:** n/k. **A:** This appears to be a reselection of 'Scarlette'. **H:** SD. **L:** U. **N:** P. **P:** S. **C:** scarlet. **S:** spring.

'Villa Roma White' (*L. odoratus*) Spencer   **F:** Hem Zaden cat. 2011/12. **R:** Hem Zaden. **I:** 2012. **D:** see Cultivars chapter.

'Villa Roma White / Rose' (*L. odoratus*) Spencer   **F:** Hem Zaden cat. 2011/12. **R:** Hem Zaden. **I:** 2012. **D:** see Cultivars chapter.

'Vincent' (*L. odoratus*) Spencer   **F:** *NSPS Annual* 2008: 56. **R:** Beane / Eagle Sweet Peas. **I:** 2010. **D:** see Cultivars chapter.

'Violet Queen' (*L. odoratus*) Grandiflora   **F:** Anon. (1877). **R:** Carters Tested Seeds. **I:** 1877. **H:** T. **L:** U. **N:** P. **P:** S. **C:** light magenta / violet. **S:** summer.

'Violet Queen' Carters 1936 (*L. odoratus*)

Spencer **F:** Dobbie & Co. cat. 1936, Carters Tested Seeds cat. 1936. **R:** Carters Tested Seeds. **I:** before 1930. **H:** T. **L:** U. **N:** P. **P:** S. **C:** light violet. **S:** summer.

'Violet Queen' Grayson (*L. odoratus*) Grandiflora **F:** Grayson cat. 1993. **R:** Grayson. **I:** 1993. **D:** see Cultivars chapter.

'Violet Wings' (*L. odoratus*) Semi-grandiflora **F:** R. Parsons cat. 2006/07. **R:** Beautiful Gardens. **I:** 2002. **H:** T. **L:** U. **N:** P. **P:** S. **C:** dark blue. **S:** summer.

'Violette' (*L. odoratus*) Spencer **F:** *NSPS Annual* 1971: vii. **R:** Burpee Seeds. **I:** 1971. **D:** see Cultivars chapter.

'Virgo' (*L. odoratus*) Spencer **RHS:** AM 1999. **F:** E.W. King & Co. cat. autumn 1999. **R:** J.D. Place / E.W. King & Co. **I:** 2000. **H:** T. **L:** M. **N:** P. **P:** S. **C:** white. **S:** summer.

'Vulcan' (*L. odoratus*) Spencer **F:** Ball cat. 1925. **R:** C.C. Morse & Co. **I:** 1925. **H:** T. **L:** U. **N:** P. **P:** n/k. **C:** scarlet cerise. **S:** winter.

'Vulcan' Parsons (*L. odoratus*) Semi-grandiflora **F:** R. Parsons cat. 2008/09. **R:** R. Parsons. **I:** 2009. **D:** see Cultivars chapter.

'Watermelon' (*L. odoratus*) Semi-grandiflora **F:** R. Parsons cat. 2006/07. **R:** Renee's Garden. **I:** 2005. **H:** T. **L:** U. **N:** P. **P:** S. **C:** orange-pink. **S:** summer.

'Wedding Belle' (*L. odoratus*) Spencer **F:** Unwins Seeds cat. autumn 2006. **R:** Unwins Seeds. **I:** 2007. **D:** see Cultivars chapter.

'Wedding Day' (*L. odoratus*) Spencer **RHS:** AGM (H3) 2001. **F:** Matthewman cat. 2000/01. **R:** Matthewman. **I:** 2001. **D:** see Cultivars chapter.

Weisse Perle (*L. latifolius*) = 'White Pearl'

'Welcome to Yorkshire' (*L. odoratus*) Spencer **F:** Matthewman cat. 2012/13. **R:** Matthewman. **I:** 2013. **H:** T. **L:** U. **N:** P. **P:** S. **C:** dark mauve. **S:** summer.

'Wendy's Joy' (*L. latifolius*) **F:** Robert Bolton & Son cat. autumn 1998. **R:** Robert Bolton & Son. **I:** 1999. **D:** see Cultivars chapter.

'Wenvoe Beauty' (*L. odoratus*) Spencer **F:** *NSPS Annual* 1915: 73. **R:** Wheeler. **I:** n/k. **H:** T. **L:** U. **N:** P. **P:** S. **C:** deep pink. **S:** summer.

'Wenvoe Castle' (*L. odoratus*) Spencer **F:** *NSPS Annual* 1911: 100. **R:** Gerhold / Crossling. **I:** 1910. **H:** T. **L:** U. **N:** P. **P:** S. **C:** rosy mauve. **S:** summer.

'Westminster' (*L. odoratus*) Spencer **F:** *NSPS Annual* 1973: i. **R:** Ferry Morse Seed Co. **I:** 1973. **D:** see

Cultivars chapter.

'White Cupid' (*L. odoratus*) Grandiflora **F:** A. Zvolanek & Sons cat. 1925/26. **R:** A. Zvolanek & Sons. **I:** 1926. **A:** Pale seeds. **H:** SD. **L:** U. **N:** P. **P:** S. **C:** white. **S:** winter.

'White Cupid' Eagle Sweet Peas (*L. odoratus*) Grandiflora **F:** Eagle Sweet Peas cat. 2005. **R:** Eagle Sweet Peas. **I:** 2005. **H:** SD. **L:** U. **N:** P. **P:** S. **C:** white. **S:** summer.

'White Fragrance' (*L. odoratus*) Spencer **F:** n/k. **R:** n/k. **I:** n/k. **H:** T. **L:** U. **N:** P. **P:** D. **C:** white. **S:** winter.

'White Frills' (*L. odoratus*) Spencer **F:** Kerton Sweet Peas cat. 2002. **R:** Truslove / Kerton Sweet Peas. **I:** 2002. **D:** see Cultivars chapter.

'White Gawler' (*L. odoratus*) Spencer **F:** R. Parsons cat. 2009/10. **R:** n/k. **I:** 2010. **A:** Pale seeds. **H:** T. **L:** U. **N:** P. **P:** D. **C:** white. **S:** winter.

'White Gem' (*L. odoratus*) Spencer **F:** NSPS (1912). **R:** Holmes. **I:** 1909. **H:** T. **L:** U. **N:** P. **P:** S. **C:** white. **S:** summer.

'White Gem' McDougall (*L. odoratus*) Spencer **F:** McDougall cat. 1998. **R:** n/k. **I:** before 1969. **H:** T. **L:** U. **N:** P. **P:** n/k. **C:** white. **S:** winter.

'White Giant' (*L. odoratus*) Spencer **F:** Law Somner Pty Ltd cat. 1938. **R:** n/k. **I:** n/k. **A:** Pale seeds. **H:** T. **L:** U. **N:** P. **P:** S. **C:** white. **S:** winter.

'White Pearl' (*L. latifolius* f. *albiflorus*) **RHS:** FCC 1955 after trial, AGM (H7) 1993. **F:** Peter Henderson & Co. cat. 1910. **R:** n/k. **I:** n/k. **D:** see Cultivars chapter.

'White Pearl' (*L. odoratus*) Spencer **F:** *NSPS Annual* 1915: 90. **R:** n/k. **I:** n/k. **H:** T. **L:** U. **N:** P. **P:** S. **C:** white. **S:** summer.

'White Pearl' Burpee (*L. odoratus*) Spencer **F:** *NSPS Annual* 1963: 47. **R:** Burpee Seeds. **I:** 1966. **H:** SD. **L:** U. **N:** P. **P:** S. **C:** white. **S:** spring.

'White Supreme' (*L. odoratus*) Spencer **RHS:** AGM (H3) 1994. **F:** *NSPS Annual* 1988: 17. **R:** B.R. Jones / Robert Bolton & Son. **I:** 1990. **D:** see Cultivars chapter.

'White Wisps' (*L. vernus*) **F:** n/k. **R:** n/k. **I:** n/k. **A:** The leaflets are of f. *gracilis* type (1–2mm wide). **H:** T. **L:** M. **N:** M. **P:** S. **C:** white. **S:** spring.

'Wild Swan' (*L. odoratus*) Spencer **F:** Somerset cat. 2012. **R:** Hammett. **I:** 2010. **D:** see Cultivars chapter.

'William and Catherine' (*L. odoratus*) Spencer **F:** *NSPS Annual* 2011: 162. **R:** Eagle Sweet Peas.

I: 2011. **D:** see Cultivars chapter.

'William Willson' (*L. odoratus*) Spencer   **RHS:** AGM
(H3) 2004. **F:** *NSPS Annual* 2005: 54. **R:** Beane /
E.W. King & Co. **I:** 2011. **D:** see Cultivars chapter.

'Willie's Red' (*L. odoratus*) Spencer   **F:** Robert Bolton
& Son cat. 1988/89. **R:** Milne / Robert Bolton & Son.
I: 1989. **H:** T. **L:** U. **N:** P. **P:** S. **C:** scarlet. **S:** summer.

'Willmot'   = 'Miss Willmott'

'Wilmot'   = 'Miss Willmott'

'Wiltshire Ripple' (*L. odoratus*) Spencer   **F:** *NSPS
Annual* 1983: 81. **R:** Wiltshire / Beane / Thompson &
Morgan. **I:** n/k. **H:** T. **L:** U. **N:** P. **P:** S. **C:** chocolate
stripe, w.g. **S:** summer.

'Windsor' (*L. odoratus*) Spencer   **F:** n/k. **R:** Suttons.
I: 1951. **H:** T. **L:** U. **N:** P. **P:** S. **C:** light blue. **S:** summer.

'Windsor' Brewer (*L. odoratus*) Spencer   **F:** Unwins
Seeds cat. autumn 1997. **R:** K Brewer / Unwins Seeds.
I: 1998. **D:** see Cultivars chapter.

'Winner' (*L. odoratus*) Spencer   **F:** E.W. King & Co.
cat. autumn 1989. **R:** Albutt / E.W. King & Co. **I:** 1989.
H: T. **L:** U. **N:** P. **P:** S. **C:** scarlet. **S:** summer.

'Winston Churchill' (*L. odoratus*) Spencer   **F:** *NSPS
Annual* 1956: 51. **R:** Thomas Cullen & Sons. **I:** 1956.
D: see Cultivars chapter.

'Winter Blush' (*L. vernus*)   – 'Alboroseus'

'Winter Elegance Burgundy' (*L. odoratus*) Spencer
F: R. Parsons cat. 2008/09. **R:** Fragrant Garden.
I: 2007. **H:** T. **L:** U. **N:** M. **P:** S. **C:** dark maroon. **S:** late
spring.

'Winter Elegance Cranberry' (*L. odoratus*) Spencer
F: Hem Zaden cat. 2011/12. **R:** Hem Zaden. **I:** 2012.
H: T. **L:** U. **N:** M. **P:** n/k. **C:** n/k. **S:** winter.

'Winter Elegance Deep Red' (*L. odoratus*) Spencer
F: Hem Zaden cat. 2011/12. **R:** Hem Zaden. **I:** 2012.
H: T. **L:** U. **N:** M. **P:** n/k. **C:** crimson. **S:** winter.

'Winter Elegance Deep Rose' (*L. odoratus*) Spencer
F: Nakamura *et al.* (2010). **R:** Bodger Seeds Ltd.
I: 1992. **H:** T. **L:** U. **N:** M. **P:** S. **C:** deep rose. **S:** winter.

'Winter Elegance Lavender' (*L. odoratus*) Spencer
F: Nakamura *et al.* (2010). **R:** Bodger Seeds Ltd.
I: 1992. **H:** T. **L:** U. **N:** M. **P:** S. **C:** lavender. **S:** winter.

'Winter Elegance Mid Blue' (*L. odoratus*) Spencer
F: R. Parsons cat. 2008/09. **R:** Fragrant Garden.
I: 2007. **H:** T. **L:** U. **N:** M. **P:** S. **C:** mid blue. **S:** winter.

Winter Elegance Mixed (*L. odoratus*) Spencer
F: E.W. King & Co. cat. autumn 1997. **R:** Bodger Seeds
Ltd. **I:** 1992. **A:** All cultivars have a Winter Elegance

prefix. **H:** T. **L:** U. **N:** M. **P:** S. **C:** mixed colours.
S: winter.

'Winter Elegance Pink Diana' (*L. odoratus*) Spencer
F: Nakamura *et al.* (2010). **R:** Bodger Seeds Ltd.
I: 1992. **D:** see Cultivars chapter.

'Winter Elegance Purple' (*L. odoratus*) Spencer
F: Hem Zaden cat. 2011/12. **R:** Hem Zaden. **I:** 2012.
H: T. **L:** U. **N:** M. **P:** n/k. **C:** purple. **S:** winter.

'Winter Elegance Rose' (*L. odoratus*) Spencer
F: R. Parsons cat. 2008/09. **R:** Bodger Seeds Ltd.
I: 1992. **H:** T. **L:** U. **N:** M. **P:** n/k. **C:** rose pink, w.g.
S: winter.

'Winter Elegance Salmon Cream Pink' (*L. odoratus*)
Spencer   **F:** Hem Zaden cat. 2011/12. **R:** Bodger
Seeds Ltd. **I:** 1992. **H:** T. **L:** U. **N:** M. **P:** S. **C:** shrimp
pink, c.g. **S:** early spring.

'Winter Elegance Salmon Rose' (*L. odoratus*) Spencer
F: Hem Zaden cat. 2011/12. **R:** Hem Zaden. **I:** 2012.
D: see Cultivars chapter.

'Winter Elegance Scarlet' (*L. odoratus*) Spencer
F: Nakamura *et al.* (2010). **R:** Bodger Seeds Ltd.
I: 1992. **H:** T. **L:** U. **N:** M. **P:** n/k. **C:** scarlet. **S:** winter.

Winter Elegance Series (*L. odoratus*) Spencer   **F:**
E.W. King cat. autumn 1997. **R:** Bodger. **I:** 1992. **H:** T.
L: U. **N:** M. **P:** S. **C:** various colours. **S:** winter

'Winter Elegance Velvet' (*L. odoratus*) Spencer
F: Hem Zaden cat. 2011/12. **R:** Hem Zaden. **I:** 2012.
H: T. **L:** U. **N:** M. **P:** n/k. **C:** n/k. **S:** winter.

'Winter Elegance White' (*L. odoratus*) Spencer
F: Hem Zaden cat. 2011/12. **R:** Bodger Seeds Ltd.
I: 1992. **H:** T. **L:** U. **N:** M. **P:** n/k. **C:** white. **S:** winter.

'Winter Sunshine Cream' (*L. odoratus*) Spencer
F: Owl's Acre Sweet Peas cat. 2009/10. **R:** Owl's Acre
Sweet Peas. **I:** 2008. **A:** Pale seeds. **H:** T. **L:** U. **N:** M.
P: S. **C:** cream. **S:** winter.

'Winter Sunshine Deep Rose' (*L. odoratus*) Spencer
F: Owl's Acre Sweet Peas cat. 2004/05. **R:** Owl's Acre
Sweet Peas. **I:** 2002. **H:** T. **L:** U. **N:** M. **P:** S. **C:** deep
magenta pink. **S:** winter.

'Winter Sunshine Lavender' (*L. odoratus*) Spencer
F: Owl's Acre Sweet Peas cat. 2004/05. **R:** Owl's Acre
Sweet Peas. **I:** 2002. **D:** see Cultivars chapter.

'Winter Sunshine Light Blue' (*L. odoratus*) Spencer
F: Owl's Acre Sweet Peas cat. 2009/10. **R:** Owl's Acre
Sweet Peas. **I:** 2009. **H:** T. **L:** U. **N:** M. **P:** S. **C:** pale blue.
S: winter.

'Winter Sunshine Light Pink' (*L. odoratus*) Spencer

F: Owl's Acre Sweet Peas cat. 2004/05. **R:** Owl's Acre Sweet Peas. **I:** 2002. **I:** 2002. **H:** T. **L:** U. **N:** M. **P:** S. **C:** pale pink. **S:** winter.

'Winter Sunshine Mauve' (*L. odoratus*) Spencer
F: Owl's Acre Sweet Peas cat. 2009/10. **R:** Owl's Acre Sweet Peas. **I:** 2009. **H:** T. **L:** U. **N:** M. **P:** S. **C:** mauve. **S:** winter.

'Winter Sunshine Mid Blue' (*L. odoratus*) Spencer
F: Owl's Acre Sweet Peas cat. 2004/05. **R:** Owl's Acre Sweet Peas. **I:** 2002. **H:** T. **L:** U. **N:** M. **P:** S. **C:** mid blue. **S:** winter.

'Winter Sunshine Navy' (*L. odoratus*) Spencer
F: Owl's Acre Sweet Peas cat. 2006/07. **R:** Owl's Acre Sweet Peas. **I:** 2002. **H:** T. **L:** U. **N:** M. **P:** S. **C:** dark blue. **S:** winter.

'Winter Sunshine Opal' (*L. odoratus*) Spencer
F: Owl's Acre Sweet Peas cat. 2009/10. **R:** Owl's Acre Sweet Peas. **I:** 2009. **H:** T. **L:** U. **N:** M. **P:** S. **C:** white flushed lilac pink. **S:** early spring.

'Winter Sunshine Pink' (*L. odoratus*) Spencer
F: Owl's Acre Sweet Peas cat. 2004/05. **R:** Owl's Acre Sweet Peas. **I:** 2005. **H:** T. **L:** U. **N:** M. **P:** S. **C:** pink. **S:** winter.

'Winter Sunshine Rose' (*L. odoratus*) Spencer
F: Owl's Acre Sweet Peas cat. 2006/07. **R:** Owl's Acre Sweet Peas. **I:** 2002. **H:** T. **L:** U. **N:** M. **P:** S. **C:** rose pink w.g. **S:** winter.

'Winter Sunshine Salmon' (*L. odoratus*) Spencer
F: R. Parsons cat. 2010/11. **R:** Owl's Acre Sweet Peas. **I:** 2002. **H:** T. **L:** U. **N:** M. **P:** S. **C:** salmon pink, c.g. **S:** winter.

'Winter Sunshine Scarlet' (*L. odoratus*) Spencer
F: Owl's Acre Sweet Peas cat. 2004/05. **R:** Owl's Acre Sweet Peas. **I:** 2002. **H:** T. **L:** U. **N:** M. **P:** S. **C:** scarlet. **S:** winter.

Winter Sunshine Series (*L. odoratus*) Spencer
R: Owl's Acre Sweet Peas. **I:** between 2002 and 2009. **A:** The 14 colours all have a Winter Sunshine prefix. **H:** T. **L:** U. **N:** M. **P:** S. **C:** various colours. **S:** winter.

'Winter Sunshine White' (*L. odoratus*) Spencer
F: Owl's Acre Sweet Peas cat. 2004/05. **R:** Owl's Acre Sweet Peas. **I:** 2002. **H:** T. **L:** U. **N:** M. **P:** S. **C:** white. **S:** early spring.

'Wisley'   = 'Mount Stewart'

'Wretham Pink'   = 'Janet Scott'

'Yankee Doodle' (*L. odoratus*) Spencer   **F:** *NSPS*

Annual 1966: xi. **R:** Burpee Seeds. **I:** 1966. **D:** see Cultivars chapter.

'Yasmin Khan' (*L. odoratus*) Spencer   **F:** Robert Bolton & Son cat. 1991/92. **R:** Khan / Robert Bolton & Son. **I:** 1992. **D:** see Cultivars chapter.

'Yvette Ann' (*L. odoratus*) Spencer   **RHS:** AM 2008. **F:** R. Parsons cat. 2008/09. **R:** R. Parsons. **I:** 2009. **D:** see Cultivars chapter.

'Yvonne Johns' (*L. odoratus*) Spencer   **F:** Kerton Sweet Peas cat. 2007. **R:** Kerton Sweet Peas. **I:** 2007. **H:** T. **L:** U. **N:** P. **P:** S. **C:** white. **S:** summer.

'Zillah Harrod' (*L. odoratus*) Spencer   **F:** *NSPS Annual* 2006: 56. **R:** Harrod / Kerton Sweet Peas. **I:** 2007. **D:** see Cultivars chapter.

'Zinfadel' (*L. odoratus*) Spencer   **F:** n/k. **R:** Renee's Garden. **I:** 2009. **H:** T. **L:** U. **N:** P. **P:** S. **C:** maroon. **S:** late spring.

'Zorija Rose' (*L. odoratus*) Grandiflora   **F:** Thompson & Morgan cat. 2001. **R:** E.W. King & Co. **I:** 2000. **D:** see Cultivars chapter.

Directory of raisers and companies

All those who have raised new cultivars, or have introduced into commerce cultivars raised by others, are listed in this directory. This includes cultivars that are not mentioned in this book. All cultivar names referred to are of *Lathyrus odoratus* (sweet pea) unless stated otherwise. Biographical information is given where known, but the authors would welcome any further information where this is missing.

Adie, John, (d. c.2008), Callander, Stirling, Scotland. An amateur grower who raised two cultivars, introduced by Kerton Sweet Peas in 2008 and 2010.

Agate, James, Sea View Nurseries, Havant, Hampshire. Raised at least 15 cultivars introduced between 1908 and 1915. A firm named Agate and Conway was trading as a florists and fruiterers and a seed company at East Street, Havant, in 1890.

Aitkens, George (name also frequently found as Aitken and Aitkin). Head gardener at Erddig Park, Wrexham, Denbighshire, until 1911. Went into partnership with S. Faulkner and Co., trading as Faulkner & Aitkens. Raised about 10 cultivars introduced between 1912 and 1916.

Albutt, Harvey, (d. 1994), Mickleover, Derbyshire. Amateur raiser of at least 25 cultivars, introduced by various seed companies between 1987 and 2014. These include the non-tendril 'Astronaut'. After his death, his stock went to Eagle Sweet Peas who introduced a number of his cultivars.

Aldersey, Hugh, Aldersey Hall, Chester, Cheshire. Raiser of more than 40 cultivars introduced between 1906 and 1914. Some were introduced by other seed companies. In partnership with Marsden Jones from 1913.

Alexander, Dr M.K., Warwick. Amateur raiser of 'Alastair' introduced by Unwins in 1988.

Allan, Donald (d. c.1956). Employed by Dobbies to manage their seed farm at Marks Tey, Essex, from 1919 to 1953. He raised many Spencer cultivars including 'Gleneagles', 'Springtime' and 'Reconnaissance'. He was made an RHS Associate of Honour in 1934.

Alsen, Wilhelm Emil (1879–1931), Denmead Nursery, Waterlooville, Hampshire. Introduced 4 cultivars between 1910 and 1913. Of Danish and Scottish extraction, he set up the nursery in 1906 but the business folded in late 1912.

Anderson & Co., George Street, Sydney, New South Wales, Australia. Introduced 16 cultivars in 1916, mostly early-flowering Spencer types.

Angus. Credited with introducing 'British Queen' in 1898 but no other information has been traced.

Arkwright, Revd Edwyn (1839–1922) Télemy, Algiers, presumably there as a Christian missionary (Jacob 1911).Raised a strain of winter-flowering cultivars, none of which were named.

Avondale Nursery, Mill Hill, Baginton, Coventry. Owned by Brian Ellis. Introduced *L. vernus* 'Sky' in 2019.

Bailey, Ron (d. 1993) Midway Lane, Mardy, Abergavenny, 1980–82, then of Preston Wynne, Hereford. An amateur who turned professional, he introduced at least 6 cultivars.

Baines, Thomas (1887–1950). Worked for Dobbies until 1934 and had nurseries at different locations until 1946, when he moved to South House Farm Nurseries, Billingshurst, West Sussex. In 1948 the NSPS trials were held there. Traded as T. Baines & Sons.

Baines, Thomas Campbell (1920–1985). Son of Thomas Baines (1887–1950). Managed T. Baines & Sons on his father's death but by 1954 had succeeded George Burt at E.W. King & Co. In 1955, Jim Tandy (1914–1989) replaced Baines who went to work for Atlee Burpee Seed Co. at Lompoc, California. Baines later joined Charles Sharpe & Co.

Ltd. of Sleaford, Lincolnshire, and Denholm Seeds before taking charge at Suttons Seeds in 1970. The family business continued throughout his career.

Messrs Bakers, Codsall, Wolverhampton. Introduced at least 13 cultivars between 1906 and 1910. J.S. Baker was a vice president of the NSPS at this time.

Ball, George Jacob (1874–1949), of Chicago. He formed George J. Ball Inc. in 1905 who specialised in cut flower production and introduced at least 8 cultivars between 1918 and 1928, all early Spencer types. After his death the company was managed by his four sons. There had been a longstanding relationship with W. Atlee Burpee & Co. and in 1991 the two merged. In 1995, Ball's granddaughter, Anna Caroline Ball, became president and divided the business into Ball Horticultural and W. Atlee Burpee & Co., run by her brother, George Ball Jr.

Barnes, Thomas, Leeds. Recorded as a gardener c.1758, in 1773 he announced a new seed business from Park Lane, Leeds. He sold seeds in 1782 of scarlet, white, 'Painted Lady' and purple to Edwin Lascelles of Harewood House. Shortly after, he entered into partnership with Ebenezer Romain Callender. Barnes & Callender produced a catalogue c.1785–90 from The Orange Tree, Briggate, Leeds, and were still there in 1795.

Bateman, Australia. Presumed raiser of 'Bateman Scarlet'.

R.H. Bath Ltd, Floral Farms, Wisbech, Cambridgeshire. Introduced more than 20 cultivars between 1908 and 1913. Their manager, G.W. Leak, was awarded the RHS Victoria Medal of Honour in 1930 and was president of the NSPS in 1937.

Bathurst, R., Dean Lodge, Iron Acton, Gloucestershire 1904–05, and Lawell House, Chudleigh, Devon, 1906 onwards. Raised two cultivars introduced by Mackereth, 'Devonshire Cream' in 1906 and 'Finetta Bathurst' in 1908.

Beale, Edward John (1835–1902) FLS, VMH. A partner of James Carter & Co. and a vice president of the NSPS Bicentenary Committee.

Beale, Harold. President of the NSPS in 1929 and in 1937 was awarded their Henry Eckford Gold Memorial Medal. See James Carter & Co.

Beane, Charles Andrew (b. 1949), Kippax, Leeds. An amateur raiser who is still active, he has raised around 50 cultivars introduced by various seed companies since 1989. He has specialised in bringing Spencer cultivars with fancy colour patterns up to exhibition quality and is also a raiser of dwarf cultivars.

Beautiful Gardens, Ipswich. Short-lived and possibly a trading name of a larger enterprise. Introduced 'Pastel Pink' and 'Violet Wings' in 2002, which may be other cultivars renamed.

Belham, F.H. Raised at least three cultivars around 1973 of which 'Hanslope Gem' may be the only one to come into commerce.

Bell, Karen, Liverpool. Raiser of 'Cilla', introduced in 2020.

Bell & Bieberstedt, Leith, Edinburgh. Raised 'Mrs Bieberstedt', introduced in 1908, and 'Northumbrian Crimson', introduced in 1910. David Bell and August Bieberstedt were partners until 1914. The latter was a German who moved to the Netherlands in September 1914. David Bell's business may have been wound up following prosecution by the Inland Revenue in 1930. There was an August Bieberstedt living in London in the 1930s.

Bennett, Richard (Dick) F. Raiser of Piralilla cultivars and 'Plum Bob'.

Benary, Ernst (1819–1893), Erfut, Germany. Served his apprenticeship at Haage & Schmidt and began his business in 1843. He raised a dwarf sweet pea in the 1890s which he named 'Tom Thumb White' but Lester Morse in California, USA, had already named this selection 'Cupid'. Benary introduced 'Dunkelroth' (Dark Red) before 1893 and 'Mont Blanc' in 1900. Frederick (Fritz) Benary entered the business in 1880 and was an NSPS vice president from 1899 to 1914. The business was moved to Hann, Munden, Lower Saxony, in 1946, and continues trading in the sixth generation of the family.

S. Bide & Sons, Alma Nurseries, Farnham, Surrey. Introduced about 25 cultivars between 1909 and 1915. H.E. Bide of Farnham was an NSPS member at this time.

Biffen, Sir Rowland (1874–1949). The first Professor of Agricultural Botany at Cambridge in 1908 and an early proponent of using genetics to improve crop plants. Biffen is credited with at least seven new sweet peas during the Edwardian era, all introduced by his sister-in-law, Miss (Hilda) Hemus. Mary

Biffen, Rowland's wife and sister to Hilda Hemus, is known to have made his crosses but it is not clear whether this was under his direction or using her own initiative.

Birtles, E.W., Frodsham, Warrington, Cheshire. Raiser of 'Cottage Rose' (c.1922).

Bishop, Frank A., Windsor. Raised at least 3 cultivars around 1915.

Bishop, John Roland Frank (1932–2019), Stokenchurch, Buckinghamshire. Finder of *L. latifolius* 'Bishop's Pink' as wild material. He received the NSPS Henry Eckford Gold Memorial Medal in 1998 and was president of the NSPS from 1998 to 2015.

Blades, A.F., Reigate, Surrey. Raiser of 'Yvonne' (c.1909).

Bland, James Allan, Victoria, British Columbia, Canada. Introduced at least 8 cultivars between 1911 and 1951. Secretary of the Victoria Horticultural Society in 1906, and later became a seed retailer.

Boddington, Arthur T., New York, USA. Seed retailer who introduced some Zvolanek cultivars between 1906 and 1912.

Bodger Seeds Ltd, California, USA. See 'Breeding and selection' chapter.

Robert Bolton & Son, Halstead, Essex. The Bolton family contained several generations of sweet pea specialists who made introductions of their own and other raisers over more than 100 years.. Robert Bolton (1871–1949) was originally based at Carnforth, Lancashire, and in 1909 the business advertised its 75th year. Around 1908 they bought land at Birdbrook, Essex, for better seed production and moved the business there in 1916. His son, Tom Bolton (1899–1972), joined the business in 1921 (Curtis 1922). Tom's son, Robert Bleasdale Bolton (1924–2001), joined the business in 1949 and maintained the family's passion for raising new cultivars (Bishop 2002). All three received the NSPS Henry Eckford Gold Memorial Medal. Robert Bolton & Son was bought out by Unwins in 2001–02.

Boucher, Albert (Bert) (d. 1987), West Street Nursery, Newport, Isle of Wight. Raised 'Ellen Mary' (c.1982).

Bowness, George, Scotland. Raised 'Saint Mungo' (c.1932).

Box, James, Haywards Heath, West Sussex. Raiser of at least 12 cultivars introduced between 1911 and 1914.

Brackley, Norman Peter Thomas (1926–2016) Aylesbury, Buckinghamshire. Active between 1974 and 2001 and raiser of at least 26 cultivars. After his retirement his stock went to E.W. King & Co.

Brande, Jeff (1925–2018), Guildford, Surrey. Raiser of 'Peerless Pink', introduced by Unwins in 1974. Received the NSPS Henry Eckford Gold Memorial Medal in 1994.

Breadmore, Major Charles W. (1869–1960). A corn merchant with offices in High Street, Winchester, and a nursery and trial grounds at Sutton Scotney, Hampshire. Raised at least 70 cultivars introduced between 1901 and 1913. George Herbert did the hybridising for 11 years. Also introduced two cultivars raised by Lumley. He served in the Army throughout the First World War.

Joseph Breck & Co., later Joseph Breck and Sons, Boston, Massachusetts, USA. Founded in 1818 by Joseph Breck (1794–1873). Introduced 'Blushing Bride' in 1891, 'Harvard' in 1894 and 'Snowflake' in 1897. The business still trades as an importer of Dutch bulbs.

Brewer, Frank, Richmond, Surrey. Raiser of 'Mrs F. Brewer', introduced in 1901.

Brewer, Keith, Ventnor, Isle of Wight. Raised at least 17 cultivars, introduced by various seed companies.

Brown, Chris. Raiser of *L. vernus* 'Indigo Eyes' in 2001–02.

Brown, Steven, Sudbury, Suffolk. Raiser of 'Scarlet Invincible', which, in 1867, became the first sweet pea to be recognised for an award, receiving an RHS First Class Certificate. It was introduced by Carters.

Browne, Dodwell Francis (1841–1921) Co. Mayo, Ireland. Appears to be the raiser of 'Dodwell F. Browne', introduced by Eckfords in 1909.

F.H. Brunning Pty. Ltd, Melbourne, Victoria, Australia. Raiser of 'Radiance' Brunning (before 1939). In 1874, Frederick Hamilton Brunning acquired William Adamson's seed store in Elizabeth Street. In 1926 the retail business was transferred to two former employees, Gill and Searle, while the Brunning family retained the wholesale business.

Buckman, Denholm & Holden Seed Co., Lompoc, California, USA. See 'Breeding and selection' chapter.

William Bull & Sons, King's Road, Chelsea, London.

Introduced the first cultivar raised by Eckford, 'Bronze Prince', in 1882. William Bull (1818–c.1902) acquired the nursery of John Weeks in 1861. On his death he left the business to his sons and it had ceased trading by 1920.

G.A. Bunting & Co., Bucknall Street, London. Introduced 'Mrs Walter Carter' in 1909 and 'Waterwitch' in 1911.

Burpee, Washington Atlee (1858–1915), Philadelphia, USA. See 'Breeding and selection' chapter. See also George J. Ball.

Burt, George H. (1886–1949). Worked for Unwins and then spent a period in the USA. In 1912 he moved to E.W. King and Co. where he was an active raiser of new Spencer cultivars. He was awarded the NSPS Henry Eckford Gold Memorial Medal in 1930. In the 1930s and 1940s he raised an improved series of tall, non-tendril cultivars with Spencer flower form. These did not prove popular, possibly because for garden decoration they are not self-supporting and perhaps because the flowers were still not as good as tendril cultivars.

Burton, L.F., Wolverhampton. Amateur raiser of 'Blue Mist' (c.1978).

Button, Howard S., Northwood, Middlesex. Raiser of 'Palestine', introduced in 1918.

Busby, Mrs John. Brought 'Painted Lady' into New South Wales, Australia, in 1823, although the species may have been introduced into Australia earlier. The Busby family maintained this stock through many generations so that it remains in cultivation today (Pockley 1983).

H. Cannell & Sons, The Nurseries, Swanley, Kent. Introduced at least five cultivars around 1908. Henry Rumsby Cannell (1834–1914) started a nursery in Woolwich (c.1864) but moved to Swanley in 1880.

Carr, Michael (Mike) George Trevor (d. 2009), Helston, Cornwall. See Tremewan.

Carter, Eric C.A., trading in 1947/48 as Carter Brothers of Fort Road, Woodville, South Australia, and in 1955 as Eric Carter of Galway Avenue, Broadview, South Australia.

James Carter & Co., High Holborn, London, until 1910, then Raynes Park, London, until 1970. See 'Breeding and selection' chapter.

Carters Tested Seeds. See 'Breeding and selection' chapter.

Castle, F.R., Foxcombe Hill, Oxford. Raiser of 'F.R. Castle', introduced in 1907.

Cattell, High Street, Westerham, Kent. A nursery founded in 1799. John Cattell (1786/87–1860), florist, nurseryman and seedsman, is in the 1851 census. His son is John Cattell (1819/20–1869) florist, nurseryman and seedsman. John James Cattell (1853/54–1920), nurseryman and seedsman, is in the 1881 census. Introduced 'The Queen' prior to 1881. Supplied seeds to Charles Darwin for his experimental hybridising work. The nursery may have closed soon after 1883.

Cautley, W.H., Mary Tavy, Devon. Introduced at least seven cultivars between 1910 and 1914.

Cave, Alec, Markeaton Park, Derby. Raiser of at least four cultivars, including the semi-dwarf 'Teresa Maureen', named for his wife.

Chandler, Allen, Haslemere, Surrey. Raiser of three cultivars introduced around 1908.

Chapman, Frederick Herbert (b. 1863), Rye, East Sussex. Raiser of six cultivars introduced between 1908 and 1915. Traded as Herbert Chapman Ltd.

Chigasaki, Japan. Presumed raiser of at least two cultivars known to predate 1984. As one is named 'Chigasaki no. 11', perhaps there were more.

Chisholm, Robert (Bob), MBE (c.1922–2008), Falkirk, Scotland. Raiser of more than 20 cultivars introduced between 1994 and 2014, mostly by Kerton Sweet Peas. Awarded an MBE in 1980.

Chivers, Gerald T, Chippenham, Wiltshire. Raiser of 'Bowden Hill', introduced in 1975.

Christmas, Philip (d. c.2010–2013), Pembury, Tunbridge Wells, Kent. Raiser of 'Invicta' Christmas and 'Kentish Maiden'. Last entry was in the 2011 RHS trials.

Churchman, H.W., Cambridge. Raiser of at least five cultivars in around 1911.

Clark, Henry (c.1702–1778), Chipping Campden, Gloucestershire. In 1750 he supplied "2 sorts sented pease" and in 1751 "two sorts sweet pease" to Powell Snell of Guiting Grange, Gloucestershire (Harvey 1974).

G. & A. Clark Ltd., Maison Dieu Nursery, Dover, Kent. Introduced at least 16 cultivars between 1906 and 1910.

Clarke, Major Trevor (1813–1897) Daventry,

Northamptonshire. Introduced 'Blue Edged' in 1860 and claimed that the cultivar was the result of crossing a white sweet pea with *Lathyrus nervosus*.

Cole, Silas (1866–1939), head gardener to Earl Spencer at Althorp, Northamptonshire. Raiser of at least 24 cultivars introduced between 1902 and 1912. Most famously, he raised 'Countess Spencer'.

Coleman, C., Deal, Kent. Raiser of 'Sunny Jim' (*Sweet Pea Annual 2005*) but it does not appear to have gone on general sale.

Colledge, Revd T. Kenneth (1911–1990), Leamington Spa (to 1960), then Southbourne, Bournemouth (1961–1977), then Christchurch, Dorset (from 1978). Raiser of at least 26 cultivars introduced between 1961 and 1994.

Comstock, Ferre & Co., Wethersfield, Connecticut, USA. Established in 1820 by James Lockwood Belden as the Wethersfield Seed Co. The company expanded in the 19th century when Franklin Comstock and his son William succeeded Belden, and they were later joined by William Ferre. Incorporated as Comstock, Ferre & Co in 1853. Stephen F. Willard was the company president between 1898 and 1924, later succeeded by three more generations of Willards. They were wholesale seed producers until beginning a retail arm in 1958. In 2010 the business was sold to Baker Creek Heirloom Seed Co. of Mansfield, Missouri, USA, and is still trading.

Cooltonagh Irish Sweet Peas. See Sydney Harrod.

Cooper, Taber & Co. Ltd, Southwark Street, London, with trial grounds at Witham, Essex. Wholesale seed producer founded in 1887, and very active before 1914 when H.T. Huggins and H. Simpson were prominent Introduced 'Witham Blaze' in 1951 and 'Pink Champagne' in 1957. Merged with Hurst & Son in 1962.

Cordery, Ron, East Clandon, Guildford, Surrey. Raised several cultivars around 1995 but none have yet entered commerce.

Cotswold Garden Flowers, Badsey, Evesham, Worcestershire. Owned by Bob Brown. Introduced *Lathyrus tuberosus* 'Baby Pink'.

Cross, Thomas, Bury St. Edmunds, Suffolk. Raiser of five cultivars introduced in 1913.

Crossling, John, Penarth Nurseries, Penarth, Glamorgan, Wales. Raiser of three cultivars

introduced before 1915, and introduced those raised by H.A. Gerhold.

Thomas Cullen & Sons, Braintree Road, Witham, Essex. Founded around 1894 by Thomas Cullen (1846–1935). His oldest son Frank Cullen took control in 1909 and in 1921 they employed Hugh Dickson. Employed John Ness (1877–1955), who raised their sweet peas before moving to Carters in 1927 or 1929. Introduced at least 50 cultivars between 1921 and 1966. The business later became part of ASMER Seeds.

Cupani, Franciscus (d. 1711) Panormi, Sicily. First described the sweet pea in 1696 when he included it in his *Hortus Catholicus* as *Lathyrus distoplatyphylos, hirsutus, mollis, magno et peramoena, flore odoro*. In 1699, Cupani sent seeds to Robert Uvedale at Enfield, UK, and Casper Commellin at Amsterdam, the Netherlands.

Curtis, Charles Henry OBE (d. 1958), Brentford, Middlesex. Editor of *Gardeners' Chronicle* from 1919 to 1950, and a founder of the NSPS of which he held every office and was president in 1932. He introduced two sweet pea cultivars in 1922. He was awarded the NSPS Henry Eckford Gold Memorial Medal in 1923, the RHS Victoria Medal of Honour in 1933 and an OBE in 1950.

Curtis, S.F., Fairfield, Lancaster. Introduced at least four cultivars around 1918.

Curtis, William (1746–1799) Lambeth, London. A botanist, seedsman and publisher, who wrote in 1788: 'There is scarcely a plant more generally cultivated than the sweet pea. [...] Several varieties of this plant are enumerated by authors, but general cultivation extends to two only. The one with blossoms perfectly white and the other white and rose-coloured, commonly called the Painted Lady Pea'.

Cuthbertson, Frank Goodwin (d. 1973), USA. A step-son of William Cuthbertson, he joined C.C. Morse & Co. in 1911 and quickly began to breed sweet peas, but worked on many other genera during his career. He retired from Ferry Morse in 1956 and received the NSPS Henry Eckford Gold Memorial Medal in 1964.

Cuthbertson, William (1859–1934) Rothesay, Bute, Scotland to 1908, then Edinburgh. He bought Dobbie & Co. in 1887, was president of the NSPS in

1907, received the RHS Victoria Medal of Honour in 1914 and the NSPS Henry Eckford Gold Memorial Medal in 1926.

Damerum, Henry J. (d. c.1956), South Hayling Nurseries, Hayling Island, Hampshire. In 1910 he joined W. Lumley before becoming independent in 1912. He introduced more than 30 cultivars between 1914 and 1939.

Darbishire. Raiser of 'Dorothy Darbishire' in c.1906 but nothing further is known.

Darlington, Thomas W., Carnforth, Lancashire. Raiser of three cultivars introduced in 1909–10.

Davies, Frederick S., Farnham, Surry. Raiser of three cultivars introduced around 1910–12.

Davis, A.J., Spencer Road Nursery, Seven Kings, Redbridge, Essex. Raised three cultivars introduced in 1916.

Davis, F.G., Burnham-on-Sea, Somerset. Raiser of five cultivars introduced between 1987 and 1991, initially by Marchant and later by Kerton Sweet Peas.

Day. Raiser of 'Bride of Niagara', introduced by Vick in 1895, possibly the earliest cultivar with duplex blooms. Nothing more about the raiser is known.

Deal, Bertrand William (d. c.1920), Kelvedon, Essex. Introduced more than 20 cultivars between 1907 and 1914. William Deal and Sons, seed producers, was established at Inworth, Essex, in 1892 by William Deal Snr. (1832–1905). He retired in 1901 and was succeeded by his second son, John. His older son William Deal Jnr. (d. c.1911) set up a business at an estate called Brooklands, in Kelvedon, specialising in sweet peas and was succeeded after his death by his son Bertrand.

Denholm, David S. See 'Breeding and selection' chapter.

Denney, Peter Clifford (b. 1964). Established Seed N Grow Ltd in 2008 and for a short time retailed sweet pea seeds online. He now specialises in sunflowers.

Dew, Hedley, Gawler, South Australia, Australia. Active by 1926, he raised at least three early Spencer cultivars around 1945–46, introduced by Tunia Service.

Alex Dickson & Sons, Royal Nurseries, Newtownards, Co. Down, Northern Ireland (with offices in Belfast). Introduced at least 45 cultivars between 1908 and 1926, including their Hawlmark Series. By 1913 they had bought land at Marks Tey, Essex, for seed production. A family business, the hybridiser was Hugh Dickson who was president of the NSPS in 1914 and awarded its Henry Eckford Gold Memorial Medal in 1929. He left Northern Ireland in 1921 and joined Thomas Cullen & Sons of Witham until his retirement in 1945.

Dipnall, Thomas Heath (d. 1925), Overbury Hall, Hadleigh, Suffolk. Introduced more than ten cultivars between 1911 and 1916.

Dobbie & Co., Rothesay, Bute, Scotland, until 1908, then Edinburgh. See 'Breeding and selection' chapter.

Samuel Dobie & Sons Ltd, Chester, Cheshire. Founded in 1881 and introduced Galaxy Series to the UK around 1960. Other introductions include 'Edd Fincham' in 1994. Dobies is now part of the same group as Suttons Seeds.

Dreer, Henry Augustus (1818–1873), Pennsylvania, Philadelphia, USA. The son of a German immigrant, he started his seed business in 1838. His son, William F. Dreer (1849–1918), joined the business at an early age and worked in Germany with Benary in 1868–69. William took control on his father's death. The business was incorporated in 1892 and in 1924 moved to Spring Garden Street, Philadelphia. Their nurseries closed in 1944. They were a general nursery and retailer whose interest in *Lathyrus* was purely as retailers.

Dubovkis, Riga, Latvia. Raiser of 'Riga 800'. Business partner of Martins Maltenieks and may have raised all their cultivars.

Eagle Sweet Peas, Stowe-by-Chartley, Stafford, Staffordshire. See 'Breeding and selection' chapter.

Eckford, Henry (1823–1905) Wem, Shropshire. Raised at least 190 cultivars. See 'Breeding and selection' chapter.

Eckford, John Stainer (1864–1944). See 'Breeding and selection' chapter.

Edds, H.G. Raiser of 'Dolphin', introduced in 1963.

Edwards. Raiser of 'Gladys Edwards', introduced in 1910. Possibly G.M. Edwards of Addlestone, Surrey.

Edwards, H.P., Overton Bridge, Wrexham. Raised at least three cultivars around 1949–53.

Elliott, Charles, Park Ridge, Illinois, USA. Introduced at least 20 Spencer cultivars between 1921 and 1927.

Ellis, Jack R. (d. c.2016), Halesworth, Suffolk. Raiser of 'Jack Ellis', introduced by Parsons in 2018. Worked with S.C. Harland at University of Manchester in the 1950s.

Elsom, George (c.1887–1957), Spalding, Lincolnshire. Isaac Elsom had established a family seed business by 1885, which was handed over to son George (c.1860–1901) in 1886. His eldest son, George (born c.1887), started work at the company in 1901 and raised 'Lady Exeter' around 1912. The company continues as Elsoms Seeds Ltd.

Engelmann, Carl Gustav (1874–1941) Saffron Walden, Essex. A German by birth, his business began in 1897 and was most noted for breeding pansies and as a cut-flower grower. He was most active with sweet peas between 1906 and 1913. C. Engelmann Ltd was continued by his son Eric Engelmann until 1975.

English Sweet Peas. See Seedlynx.

Entwistle, Ron (c.1912–1996) Chesterfield, Derbyshire. Raised about 12 cultivars introduced between 1992 and 2001. Most were introduced after his death by Grayson.

Errington, George J. (1878–1960) Dunedin, New Zealand. Born in London, he was an active breeder of new cultivars from 1907 until his death.

Evans, M. Neil, Bryn Crescent, Rhuddlan, Rhyl, Denbighshire. Raiser of 'Misty Mountain', introduced by Matthewman in 2004.

Everitt, L Joe (1903–1996), Little Clacton, Clacton-on-Sea, Essex. Born at Chappel, Essex, he worked at Dobbies, Marks Tey, and then another nursery before starting his own nursery in 1928 as a cut-flower grower and seed retailer. He introduced at least seven sweet pea cultivars between 1954 and 1976.

Fairchild, Thomas (1667–1729) Hoxton, London. He started his London nursery in about 1691. It was reported in July 1722 that he had flowers of 'Sweet Peas, Scarlet and Common' as well as 'Everlasting Pease' (Harvey 1974). In 1717 he made the first artificial plant hybrid, 'Fairchild's Mule', a cross between a sweet William and a carnation. In later years his nursery was run by his nephew Stephen Bacon (1709–1734) who inherited the nursery on Fairchild's death. It was then owned by John Simpson (d. 1740) but ceased on Simpson's death (Harvey 1974).

Fallick, Charles (c.1907–1993), Newport, Isle of Wight. An amateur raiser of 'Fair Charm', introduced in 1973 as 'Sally Unwin'.

Farmen, Naples, Italy. Introduced Fantasia Series of dwarf cultivars around 2002.

R. & J. Farquar & Co., Boston, Massachusetts, USA. Robert Farquar established the business in 1884 and they introduced 'Nellie Janes' in 1892. It was still trading in 1924, perhaps later.

S. Faulkner & Co., Tarvin, Chester, Cheshire. Raised at least 20 cultivars introduced between 1910 and 1914. In partnership with George Aitkens from 1912 and trading as Faulkner & Aitkens.

D.M. Ferry & Co., Detroit, Michigan, USA. See 'Breeding and selection' chapter.

Ferry Morse Seed Co., San Francisco, California, USA. This was formed in 1930 as a merger of D.M. Ferry & Co. and C.C. Morse & Co. See 'Breeding and selection' chapter.

Fidge, Ernest Lewis (d. 1925), Pedlers Creek, Aldinga, South Australia. Active from 1913 and developed the Elfin Series of early Spencers, the name being derived from his initials.

Fisher, S. Raiser of 'Snowflake', introduced by Breck in 1897.

Floragran B.V., Lochem, the Netherlands. Founded in 1977 as a wholesale supplier of F1 seeds.

Fogwills Ltd, Guildford, Surrey. Retailers of sweet pea seeds who were active from the 1920s to the 1960s, possibly longer.

Forward, Ron J. (1915–2000), St Albans, Hertfordshire. Raiser of 'Fergie' (1986).

Foster, F.G., Brockhampton Nurseries, Havant, Hampshire. Raiser of two cultivars, 'Aurora' Foster in 1898 and 'Cream of Brockhampton' in 1902.

Mr Fothergills Seeds Ltd, Kentford, Newmarket, Suffolk. A business founded in 1978 that has become more active in introducing new sweet pea cultivars in the 21st century.

Fragrant Garden Nursery, Brookings, Oregon, USA. The source of two Winter Elegance Series colours, but unlikely to have raised them.

Francis, Roy W. (c.1921–1992), New Milton, Hampshire. Active in the 1980s and raised at least two cultivars, 'Blue Pearl' Francis and 'Bright Dawn'.

Franklin, John Henry (1880–1934), Waller-Franklin Seed Co. See Lionel D. Waller.

Fujisawa, Japan. Raiser of 'Oyama Millennium' before 2012.

Fukuda, Akira (Fukuda Hikari), Miyazaki, Japan. Raiser of 'Kitago Pink', introduced in 2008.

Furber, Robert (c.1674–1756) Kensington Gore, London. Founded a nursery c.1700. Dicks (1900) says Furber lists purple, white, and 'variegated or Painted Lady sweet-scented pea' in a 1730s seed catalogue (Parsons 2011) but the reference is for 1780s by a different author. On his death, Furber's nursery was left to his assistant, John Williamson, and continued under a succession of owners until the mid-19th century.

S.E. Gaisford & Sons, Colerne, Wiltshire. Specialist retailers of young plants and cut flowers who invariably offered all the new season's novelties. In 1911 Ernest George Gaisford (1868–1966) was a 'mason journeyman' at Elm Cottage, Colerne, and had three children including Samuel Ernest (b. 1903). By 1939, E.G. Gaisford and Son were at West End nurseries, but they ceased trading in 1987.

Gellatly, George L., Sydney, New South Wales, Australia. He sold cultivars raised by W. Steward from c.1933 to 1961.

Gentle, Arthur George, Little Gaddesden, Berkhamsted, Hertfordshire. Gardener to Mrs Denison and raiser of 'Mrs E.H. Denison' before 1916.

Gerhold, H.A., Penarth, Glamorgan, Wales. Raiser of two cultivars introduced in 1909 by Crossling. There remains today a pharmacy at 36 Windsor Road, Penarth, trading as H.A. Gerhold Ltd.

Gibbs. Raiser of 'White Queen' Gibbs.

J.T. Gilbert & Son, Anemone Nursery, Dyke, Bourne, Lincolnshire. Introduced at least 17 cultivars between 1907 and 1911.

Gill & Searle, Melbourne, Victoria, Australia. See Searle.

Godfrey, W.J., Exmouth, Devon. Raiser of 'Mrs W.J. Godfrey', introduced in 1908.

Gould, Thomas, California, USA. Raiser of two early-flowering cultivars, 'Extreme Early, Earliest of All' and 'Earliest White', introduced by Burpee in 1902 and 1906 respectively.

Gower, A.W. (d. 1958), Reading, Berkshire. Raiser of 'Joan Krabbé', introduced by Boltons in 1951. A professional gardener in private service, becoming head gardener to Colonel Krabbé of Calcot Grange for 48 years. Received the NSPS Henry Eckford Gold Memorial Medal in 1938 and made an RHS Associate of Honour in 1948.

Grayson, Peter (d. 2013), Chesterfield, Derbyshire. Introduced at least 46 cultivars of his own raising between 1992 and 2013, plus others from Entwistle.

Greig, Dr Robert M., Stevenston, Ayrshire. Raiser of 'Katherine Margaret' in c.1934 but there is no evidence it ever entered commerce.

Gubb, Den, Bridgend, Glamorgan, Wales. Raised at least four cultivars introduced between 1983 and 1995, of which 'Jill Walton' has been the most successful.

Haage & Schmidt Erfurt, Germany. See 'Breeding and selection' chapter.

E. & W. Hackett Ltd, Adelaide, South Australia. Sold the Karkoo strain in the 1930s, raised before 1918 by F.A. Joyner of Bridgewater, South Australia.

Hallam, F.E., Moseley, Birmingham. Raiser of 'Kitty Lea', introduced in 1908.

Hallawell Seed Co., San Francisco, California, USA. Gardening retailers active from the 1910s to 1960s, possibly longer.

Hamayu, Japan. Raiser of at least three cultivars prior to 2010.

Hammett, Dr Keith Richard William (b. 1942), Massey, Auckland, New Zealand. Worked for the New Zealand Department of Scientific and Industrial Research, Auckland, but is now an independent plant breeder in Auckland. Hammett has a global reputation for his work, not just on *Lathyrus* but on other genera including *Clivia*, *Dahlia* and *Dianthus*. He was raised in Surrey, UK, but moved to New Zealand in 1967 to work as a plant pathologist. Among other honours he has received the NSPS Henry Eckford Gold Memorial Medal in 1996, the Queen's Service Medal in 2008, and the RHS Gold Veitch Memorial Medal in 2013. He has raised at least 68 sweet pea cultivars.

Hammond. Raiser of two or three cultivars introduced around 1910. Probably W.R. Hammond of Grovelands, Burgess Hill, West Sussex.

Hanmer, Charles (d. c.1991), Butterbusk,

Conisbrough, South Yorkshire. Raiser of 'Charlie's Angel', introduced by Unwins in 1990.

Hannam, Alfred Derrick (1920–1997) Freshwater, Isle of Wight. Raiser of 'Mrs E. Hannam', introduced in 1970.

Harada, Noriyasu, Okayama, Japan. Raiser of 'Kurione', introduced in 2001.

Hardy's Cottage Garden Plants, Priory Lane Nursery, Freefolk Priors, Whitchurch, Hampshire. A business started by Rosy Hardy in 1988. Introduced *L. vernus* 'Pendulous', claimed to be a more pendulous form of *L. vernus* var. *variegatus*, and they stock a wide range of *L. vernus* selections.

Hargreaves, Michael (Mike), Guiseley, Leeds. Raiser of 'Parsifal', introduced by Myers in 2015.

Harkness, James, King Street, Willaston, South Australia. Among the leading growers from the Adelaide area from 1926, he was working for Harris Scarfe Ltd in 1928. In a letter of 1980 to Keith Hammett, Dick Bennett of Willaston, South Australia, explained the extreme frilliness of the Gawler strain was developed by a Mr Pengilly who took 13 years to produce this character in 'Athol Pearl Pink'. This cultivar was then used by Harkness in his breeding work. 'Elfin White' was used by Harkness when producing his first cultivar in 1926. He raised over 20 cultivars including 'Alberta', introduced in 1963.

Harland, Prof. Stephen Cross (1891–1982). A professor of botany at the University of Manchester from 1950 to 1958. He collected and introduced to cultivation wild sweet peas from Sicily and feral sweet peas from South America, such as 'Matucana', 'Quito' and 'Sicilian Pink'.

Harris Scarfe Ltd, Adelaide, South Australia. They sold 'Invincible varieties raised by J. Harkness, well-known exhibitor' under the heading Gawler sweet peas, which included 'Gladys Harkness'. Started as an ironmongery store in 1849, the business is now a large chain of department stores.

Harrison, Arthur (c.1916–c.2001), Hinckley, Leicestershire. Raiser of 'Claire', introduced in 1980.

Harrison, F.J., Rosedene, Ulverston, Cumbria. Raiser of two cultivars before 1916, 'Mrs F.J. Harrison' and 'G.H. Mackereth'.

Harriss, Fred C. (d. c.1987), Christchurch, Dorset. Active from 1980 and raised at least 20 cultivars.

Harrod, Sydney (b. 1933) Londonderry, Northern Ireland. See 'Breeding and selection' chapter.

Hatcher, Charles, Sydney, New South Wales, Australia. Son of W.H. Hatcher and a leading exhibitor in the 1930s.

Hatcher, W.H., Sydney, New South Wales, Australia. He developed the Zyris strain and raised at least eight cultivars, initially selling through Anderson & Co. from 1916.

Hatting, LH, Hornchurch, Essex. Raiser of 'Mrs A. Hatting', introduced in 1905.

Heathcote, Derek (b. 1947). See 'Breeding and selection' chapter.

Hem Zaden. Introduced the Bounce, Matchmaker and Villa Roma Series' in 2012. See 'Breeding and selection' chapter.

Hemus, Hilda (1874–1954) Holdfast Hall, Upton-on-Severn, Worcestershire. See 'Breeding and selection' chapter.

Peter Henderson & Co., Cortlandt Street, New York, USA. Founded by Peter Henderson (1822–1890) in 1871 and they introduced at least 10 sweet pea cultivars between 1888 and 1910. The business was continued after his death by his sons, Alfred Henderson and Charles Henderson.

Herbert, George (d. 1954). Colden Common, Hampshire, while working for Breadmore at Winchester, probably 1901–1912, then worked at John Piper & Son. He introduced three cultivars in his own name in 1919, when at Northwood, Middlesex. He raised more than 40 cultivars in total but these are usually credited to his employer.

Heslington, W.S., Yore Garth, Ripon, North Yorkshire. Introduced three cultivars in 1910–11.

Hill, Vernon T., Mendip Nurseries, Langford, Bristol. Raiser of 'White Hercules' in about 1915.

Hinton Brothers, Coventry Road, Guys Cliffe, Warwickshire. Raisers of three cultivars between 1895 and 1904. Hintons Nursery still exists at this site.

Hinton, Dr H.T., Heytesbury, Wiltshire. Raiser of four or more cultivars in around 1912–15, including 'Constance Hinton', introduced by Wheeler.

Hitchcock, Arnold (1874–1933), Tiptree, Essex. Raiser of three cultivars from 1916 to 1921. Then in partnership with Andrew Ireland, trading as Ireland and Hitchcock.

Hobbies Ltd, Norfolk Nurseries, Dereham, Norfolk. Introduced at least 17 cultivars between 1907 and 1916. John Green represented them in 1905.

Hodgson, Allan (1937–2014), Merrybent, Darlington, Co. Durham. Raiser of 'Phyllis Elizabeth', recorded at an RHS trial in 1996.

Hodson, Victor C. (c.1919–1993), Coventry. Raiser of 'Coombe Park', introduced by Malin in 1972, and 'Tom Bufton', introduced by Marchant in 1988.

Holden, Ted. Initially worked for Bodger Seeds, then joined the Buckman, Denholm & Holden Seed Co., formed in 1939, as their hybridiser. The company went into the sole ownership of David Denholm in 1945.

Holden. The raiser of 'Lord Aberconway', introduced in 1914, so presumably a gardener at Bodnant in Conwy, Wales.

Holmes, Robert, Tuckswood Farm, Norwich. Raiser of at least 30 cultivars introduced between 1908 and 1915. Some appear to be introduced by him and some by other seed companies, mostly Sydenham.

Isaac House & Son, Westbury-on-Trym, Bristol. They introduced at least 19 cultivars between 1902 and 1912. They were represented by James C. House in 1907.

Hubbuck, Andrew A., Somersall, Chesterfield, Derbyshire. Raised at least five cultivars, three introduced between 2007 and 2014.

Hughes, John, Gresford, Wrexham, Denbighshire, Wales. Raiser of 'Hillbury', introduced in 1959.

Humphrey. Raiser of 'Susan Hawes', introduced in 1909. Possibly E.W. Humphrey of The Cottage, Greenford, Ealing, Essex.

Humphreys Bros, The Nurseries, Coggeshall, Essex. R.H. Humphreys worked for more than seven years under George Burt at E.W. King & Co. before joining this firm. He raised at least three cultivars introduced between 1949 and 1954.

Hunt, J.H., Harpenden, Hertfordshire. Raiser of 'Lynda Jane' in 1986.

Hunt, R.A. (Toby), Birdbrook, Halstead, Essex. Raiser of at least six cultivars introduced between 1985 and 2019.

Hurst & Son, Houndsditch, London, and land at Kelvedon, Essex, for trials and seed production from about 1890. William Hurst Snr. (d. 1864) formed Hurst & McMullen in 1843. In 1857, W.G.

McMullen left, so Hurst's son, William Hurst Jnr (d. 1871) joined to form Hurst and Son. Nathaniel Newman Sherwood VMH (1846–1916) had married into the family and took charge of the business in 1871. In 1895, his sons William Henry Charles Sherwood and John Edward Newman Sherwood (1876–1939) became partners. After 1939 the business continued under a succession of managers, becoming a limited company in 1944. They had introduced at least nine sweet pea cultivars. Following a merger they became Hurst Gunson from 1954 to 1962, then merging with Cooper Taber to become, from 1962 to 1986, Hurst, Gunson, Cooper, Taber. In 1984 the business became a division of Booker McConnell plc and was joined by Charles Sharpe plc in 1985. The Booker group merged with Tesco in 2018.

Hutchins, Revd William Tucker (1849–1917) Indian Orchard, Massachusetts, USA. Best known as a writer and lecturer, he is credited more than anyone for the early popularity of sweet peas in the USA. He raised at least two cultivars introduced by Burpee, 'Daybreak' in 1895 and 'Columbia' in 1897.

Hutt, G., Eynsford, Kent. Raiser of 'Lady Emily Dyke' in 1912.

IAANAAFRC (Incorporated Administrative Agency, National Agriculture and Food Research Organisation), Kannondai, Tsukuba-shi, Ibaraki, Japan. Registered two cultivars in 2005. Breeders listed are Kyosuke Yamamoto and Yoshimi Yagashita (see Kanagawa prefecture).

Inoue, Dr Tomoaki, Japan. A researcher at the University of Tokyo and raiser of at least three cultivars.

Ireland, Andrew, Marks Tey, Essex. Working for Dobbies from before 1901 until 1918, he then entered a partnership with Arnold Hitchcock, trading as Ireland & Hitchcock. He was awarded the NSPS Henry Eckford Gold Memorial Medal in 1925. Recorded as living in St Albans in 1934, so may have moved to Ryders Seeds.

Ireland & Hitchcock, Marks Tey, Essex. Raised more than 20 cultivars introduced between 1921 and 1931. See Arnold Hitchcock and Andrew Ireland.

James, Anthony J., Oxford, Oxfordshire. Raised at least three cultivars from around 1986 to 1993.

James, Chris F. (c.1906–c.1995), Batheaston,

Somerset. Raised at least three cultivars introduced in 1983 and 1991.

James, Edward (Ted) W. (d. 1997). Raiser of 'Lynn Davey', introduced by Sewell in 1998.

Jarman & Co., Chard, Somerset. Raised at least 12 cultivars between 1908 and 1915.

Jelitto Staudensamen GmbH, Schwarmestedt, Germany. A wholesale supplier of hardy perennial seeds that started trading in 1957 and now has offices in the UK, USA and Japan.

Jenkins, P.G., Newport, Isle of Wight. Raised 'Queen Eira', introduced by Parsons in 1912. He may have been her gardener.

Johnson, Philip (b. 1966), Borden, Sittingbourne, Kent. Introduced 'Invicta' Christmas in 2015. Bought Seedlynx in 2017 but still also trades as Johnson Sweet Peas.

W.W. Johnson & Sons Ltd, Boston, Lincolnshire. Introduced nine cultivars between 1904 and 1911.

Johnstone. Raiser of 'Mrs E.J. Johnstone', introduced in 1910. Possibly V.B. Johnstone of Ryhall Hall, Stamford, Lincolnshire.

Jones & Sons, Shoplatch, Shrewsbury, Shropshire. Trading by 1900 and introduced five or more cultivars between 1901 and 1911. Herbert Jones represented the company in 1905.

Jones, Bernard Rees (1906–1996), Warwick, Warwickshire. See 'Breeding and selection' chapter.

Jones, DH, St Osyth, Clacton-on-Sea, Essex. Raiser of 'Alison Elizabeth' in 1986.

Jones, David Morlais (d. 1998), Waters Upton, Telford, Shropshire. Raised at least three cultivars, but only 'Millennium', introduced by Unwins, appears to have come into commerce.

Jones, G. Raiser of 'Dorothy Tapscott' in about 1915. Possibly George Jones of Heswall, Wirral, Cheshire.

Jones, H.J., Rycroft Nursery, Hither Green, Lewisham, London. Trading by 1900 and introduced at least 18 cultivars between 1907 and 1909.

Joy, Harry. Worked for Ferry Morse Seed Co. from 1930 until 1968, and succeeded Frank G. Cuthbertson when he retired. He moved to Denholm Seeds from 1968 until 1972.

Joyner, F.A., Bridgewater, South Australia. Raiser of the Karkoo strain sold by Hackett, but no cultivar names have been identified to date.

Just Sweet Peas. A short-lived online business, which introduced 'Polyanna' in 2011.

Kanagawa prefecture, Japan. A region in Japan from which nine new cultivars were registered between 2002 and 2017. Breeders are listed as Kyosuke Yamamoto (1994–2003), Yoshimi Yagashita (2001–17) and Tomoko Hisatsune (2017). See also IAANAAFRC.

Keating, Susan, Sweet Pea Gardens, Surry, Maine, USA. Retailer of sweet pea seeds. In 2015 the business was sold to Rebecca Bell.

Kelway and Son, Langport, Somerset. Best known nowadays for their delphiniums and tuberous begonias, this business introduced at least four sweet pea cultivars from 1910 to 1912.

Kerr, George W. (1865–1930). Originally from Scotland, he migrated to the USA in about 1908 and worked for Burpee. He was president of the short-lived American Sweet Pea Society.

Kershaw, Edwin (d. c.2001), Southport, Lancashire, later the Isle of Man. Raised at least three cultivars introduced between 1972 and 1980.

Kerton Sweet Peas, Bridgwater, Somerset. See 'Breeding and selection' chapter.

Khan, Dr M. Sadiq, Leamington Spa, Warwickshire. Raiser of 'Yasmin Khan', introduced by Boltons in 1992.

E.W. King & Co., Coggeshall, Essex. See 'Breeding and selection' chapter.

J.K. King & Sons, Coggeshall, Essex. John King founded the business in 1793. His descendant John Kemp King (d. pre-1895) had retired by 1885 handing over the business to his sons Herbert T. King (1865–1918) and Leonard G. King (d. c.1903). They introduced at least eight cultivars between 1907 and 1916. There was acrimonious rivalry with E.W. King & Co. but following several misadventures, including Herbert's death in London during the First World War, Ernest William King (1869–1930) took control in 1920 and in 1925 J.K. King & Sons stopped selling sweet pea seeds.

King, Ron D., Cheltenham, Gloucestershire. Raiser of 'Memorial Flight', introduced by Kerton Sweet Peas in 1998.

Kinoshita, Shigenobu, Saga, Japan. Raiser of 'Yurika' in 1991.

Knight. Raiser of 'Joan Knight' before 1971.

Kosuga, Akiyoshi, Kanagawa, Japan. Raiser of four

cultivars registered between 1991 and 1999.

Laidlaw, William (Bill) (d. 1983), Bournemouth, Dorset. Raiser of 'Eclipse' Laidlaw, introduced by Unwins in 1975.

Lanchbury, Robert, Gotherington, Cheltenham, Gloucestershire. A retailer of sweet pea seeds in the 1970s.

Law Somner Pty Ltd, Elizabeth Street, Melbourne, Australia. A seed company and nursery since 1850, originally at Swanston Street, Melbourne.

Laxton, Thomas (1830–1893), Bedford. See 'Breeding and selection' chapter.

Lees, H.H., Warblington, Havant, Hampshire. Raiser of at least three cultivars introduced between 1913 and 1917.

Leese, Cecil (c.1926–2011), Tittensor, Stoke-on-Trent, Staffordshire. Raiser of two cultivars introduced by Eagle Sweet Peas in 2008.

Legutko, W., Smolice, Poland, to 2008, then Jutrosin, Poland. A general seed business established in 1992.

Lemon, David (b. 1934), born in Dublin, Ireland, and worked at Watkins and Simpson, London, from 1955 to 1964. This included two years training at RHS Garden Wisley from 1956 to 1958. He then spent a year at Denholm Seeds before joining Ferry Morse from 1965 to 1973, where he worked on producing Jet Set Series. In 1973 he returned to Denholm Seeds where he produced the Supersnoop Series. He also worked on the early multiflora type, creating the Mammoth Series introduced in 1982. In 1984 he moved to Bodger Seeds where he created the Winter Elegance Series, introduced in 1992. He also produced the Explorer Series, as an improved Supersnoop. After leaving Bodger in 1994 he continued to work on early multifloras at Oglevee Ltd, producing for Pan American (Waller). His final evolution of the type is Solstice Series, introduced in 2009. From 2007 to 2015 he worked for Floranova as an independent breeder. He worked on many other genera and is perhaps best known for marigolds.

Levko, Gennadiy, Vniissok, Lesnoy Gorodok, Moscow, Russia. Raised at least seven cultivars.

Liggit, C.U., Philadelphia, Pennsylvania, USA. A plant, seed and bulb broker active in the 1920s and 30s.

Linnaeus, Carl (1707–1778). Swedish naturalist, best known for formalising the system of binomial nomenclature. He listed an early pink/white bicoloured form of sweet pea in 1737 as *Lathyrus zeylanica* (Linnaeus 1753), now better known as 'Painted Lady'. It may predate the white form, since it is only one mutation removed from the wild type, whereas it takes two mutations to produce a pure white flower.

Lorenz, Chr., Erfurt, Germany. Introduced 'Celestial' in 1896 and 'Striped Celestial' in 1897.

Loudon, Jane C. (1807–1858). Her 1840 book, *Ladies' Flower Garden of Ornamental Plants*, includes the purple wild type, New Painted Lady, Old Painted Lady, blue ('which has the wings and keel a pale blue and the standard dark bluish-purple') and violet ('which has the keel a pale violet, the wings a deep violet and the standard a dark reddish-purple'). Violet appears to be what earlier writers referred to as black or black-purple.

Lowe. Raiser of 'Mrs H. Lowe', introduced in 1910. Possibly W. Lowe of Shrewsbury, Shropshire.

Lumley, W., Dawn Nurseries, Hayling Island, Hampshire. Raised at least 19 cultivars, introduced between 1908 and 1912, with the first two introduced by Breadmore. His business was possibly transferred to Damerum in 1912.

Lynch, James T., California, USA. Raised three cultivars introduced in 1897.

Macdonald, William (1883–1955). See 'Breeding and selection' chapter.

Mackereth, G.H., Ulverston, Cumbria. Introduced about 10 cultivars for himself and other raisers between 1906 and 1914. Appears to have traded as H.W. Mackereth. Henry Whittaker Mackereth of Ulverston appears in the 1881 census.

Madeleines Floral Farms, Johannesburg, South Africa. Raised 'Harlequin' Madeleines Floral Farms before 1942.

Maishman, William (Bill) (1913–1995), Reigate, Surrey. See 'Breeding and selection' chapter.

Malcolm, Alexander, Duns, Scotland. Raised at least 38 cultivars introduced between 1909 and 1921.

Malin, Charles (d. 1993), Leamington Spa, Warwickshire. Introduced at least eight cultivars, including some for other raisers, between 1969 and 1976.

Maltenieks, Martins, Riga, Latvia. See Dubovkis.

Mamitsch, Herman, Rockville Centre, New York, USA. Raiser of 'Jeanne Mamitsch', introduced in 1926.

Manning, Jack T. (d. 2001), Weybridge, Surrey. Raised at least four cultivars introduced between 1977 and 1987.

Manston, David, Fordingbridge, Hampshire. Introduced three cultivars between 2006 and 2009.

Marchant, Les (d. 1989), Bridgwater, Somerset. Raised five cultivars, introduced between 1983 and 1985, and introduced some from other amateur raisers. Was succeeded by Kerton Sweet Peas following his death.

Marple. Raiser of 'Herbert Marple', introduced in 1907. Possibly William Marple of Summer House, Penkridge, Stafford, Staffordshire.

Marsden-Jones, Eric Marsden (1887–1960), Tilston, Malpas, Cheshire. In partnership with Hugh Aldersey in 1913, trading as Aldersey & Marsden Jones. See 'Breeding and selection' chapter.

Marsh, Viv, Hunkington Nurseries, Walford Heath, Shrewsbury, Shropshire. Raiser of *L. vernus* 'Lamorna's Love'.

Marshall, Leonard F., Addiscombe, Surrey. Raiser of 'Vivienne Corfield', introduced in 1915.

S.E. Marshall & Co. Ltd, Alconbury Hill, Huntingdon, Cambridgeshire. Primarily known for vegetable seeds, but introduced 'Ethel Marshall' and 'Wisbech Fairy' in 1975, 'Blue Ice' Colledge in 1994 and 'Sunset' Marshall in 2002 when based at Wisbech. Now a division of Westlands, along with Unwins.

Martin, Fred C., Gawler South, South Australia, Australia. Introduced his first cultivar in 1956 and was still alive in 1980.

Martyn, Thomas (1735–1825). Professor of botany at the University of Cambridge. In 1807 he described the New Painted Lady pea, with red standards and pink wings (Parsons 2011).

Mason, John. A seedsman named at the sign of the Orange Tree, Fleet Street, London, listed five sweet peas in 1793: black, purple, scarlet, white and 'Painted Lady' amd a black-purple is mentioned in 1800 (Curtis & Eckford 1900), presumably the same as Mason's black. 'Black' may be the colour we now see in 'Purple Prince'. Mason was trading from 1781–1827 and following many changes of ownership the business became Cooper Taber in 1887.

Matthewman, David (b. 1948) Pontefract, West Yorkshire. A raiser and nurseryman who started trading in 1993 and raised his first sweet pea cultivar in 2000. He is still actively raising cultivars but Matthewman Sweet Peas are now sold from Solihull, West Midlands.

L.L. May & Co., St Paul, Minnesota, USA. Introduced 12 cultivars in 1894 and 1895.

McAleer, Chris, Balbriggan, Co. Dublin, Ireland. Raiser of 'Bridget McAleer', introduced by Cooltonagh in 2013, and 'Josie' McAleer.

McDonald, D.J. (b. 1941), Stockbridge, Hampshire. With his wife Mary he has recently introduced several late Spencer cultivars and is the raiser of 'Mary Mac', introduced in 2015, and 'Serendipity', introduced in 2018.

McDougall family. Malcolm McDougall (d. 2018) of Meadows, South Australia, his brother Barry McDougall of Gawler South, South Australia, together with Barry & Bronwyn's son, Brad McDougall of Evanston, South Australia, have raised many Gawler sweet pea cultivars between them.

McMahon, Bernard (c.1775–1816) Philadelphia, Pennsylvania, USA. He included purple, white, 'Painted Lady', blue and scarlet in an 1804 seed list. The blue may be *Lathyrus sativus* var. *azureus*.

Miller, S., Newport, Isle of Wight. Raised four cultivars introduced between 1908 and 1916.

Milne, William T. (c.1921–1987) Swindon, Wiltshire, but spent most of his life in Scotland. Raiser of 'Willie's Red', introduced by Boltons in 1989.

Miyazaki prefecture, Japan. A region in Japan from where the cultivars raised are guarded to prevent growers elsewhere from obtaining them. One of the most noted breeders is Kaoru Nakamura who has developed at least 25 distinct early-flowering cultivars since 2004, which include winter-flowering, multiflora, non-tendril cultivars, known as Musica Series. Breeders are listed as Hiroshi Tominaga (2002–07), Hirotoshi Hino (2002–07), Sadao Gunji (2002–17), Toshio Murata (2002–07), Kazumi Shibata (2002–03), Norio Hattanda (2003–12), Kaoru Nakamura (2003–17), Hideo Tagahashi (2003–05), Hiroaki Nagatomo (2004–17), Koichi Fukumoto (2007–12), Naoshi Nakaoka (2011–15), Toru Nakamura (2012–13) and Yasuyo

Kuranaga (2015–17).

Moa Seed Farm, Dumbarton, Otago, New Zealand. Founded in 1918 and operated between 1922 and 1966. Raiser of 'His Majesty', introduced by Burpee in 1939. The manager was J.W. Hadfield.

Moles, J.W., Turkey Cock Lane, Stanway, Colchester, Essex. A wholesale seed supplier that became Moles Seeds (UK) Ltd in 2007 as part of a management buyout from Michael Moles.

Moody, Leslie John (d. c.2012), Twyford, Reading, Berkshire. Raiser of 'Jeanne', introduced in 1981.

Moon, Wilfred J. (1903–1976), Braunton, Devon. Raiser of 'Marion Moon' in 1954 and 'Lorna Doone' Moon in 1961.

Moring, A., Goring-on-Thames, Oxfordshire. Raiser of at least four cultivars introduced in around 1914.

Morris, Tom (1913–1998), Marston Green, Birmingham. Raiser of 'Lily Morris', introduced in 1975, and 'Blue Danube' Morris, introduced in 1981.

C.C. Morse & Co., California, USA. See 'Breeding and selection' chapter.

Mott, Hamilton Charnock (1871–1963) Albury, New South Wales, Australia. A newspaper proprietor who was an amateur raiser of early-flowering cultivars in the early 20th century. He raised at least 16 cultivars, mostly introduced by Anderson & Co.

Mount Iris Nursery, Dee Why, New South Wales, Australia. Introduced at least four cultivars prior to 1949.

Murakami, Japan. Possibly raised at least four cultivars.

Murray, Jack, Glasgow, Scotland. Raiser of 'Sheila Murray', introduced by Parsons in 2013.

Muskett & Sons. Raiser of 'Carmine Rose', introduced by Hurst in 1883.

Myers, Darren, Wakefield, West Yorkshire. Introduced 'Parsifal' and 'Just William', both in 2015–16.

NAFRO (National Agriculture and Food Research Organisation), Kannondai, Tsukuba-shi, Ibaraki, Japan. Registered two cultivars in 2005. Breeders listed are Kyosuke Yamamoto and Yoshimi Yagashita. See Kanagawa prefecture.

Ness, John (1877–1955). A raiser of sweet peas for Thomas Cullen & Sons of Witham, Essex. In 1927 or 1929 he moved to Carters. He was awarded the NSPS Henry Eckford Gold Memorial Medal in 1954.

Noble, Cooper & Bolton. Introduced 'Dark' in 1850.

This may simply have been an improved form of the earlier 'Black' or 'Black/Purple' (see John Mason). The firm later became Cooper, Taber & Co.

Nozaki, Tomomitzu, Miyazaki, Japan. Nurseryman and supplier of at least six early multiflora cultivars.

Okayama prefecture, Japan. A region in Japan from which at least six early multiflora cultivars have been registered. Breeders are listed as Norihide Doi (1992–2017), Shinsuke Kono (1992), Takao Kawai (1992), Hideaki Kimoto (1992), Yasuhiro Okamoto (1992), Shintaro Fujii (1992), Yoshio Mori (2008–17), Katsuhiko Kishida (2008) and Yasushi Morimoto (2017).

Osuzu, Japan. Raiser of 'Grace' Osuzu and 'Rosé' before 2010.

Otter. Raiser of two cultivars introduced in 1910. No details are known.

Owls Acre Sweet Peas. A business begun by Mark Rowland and his wife Maggie Goodsell at Spalding, Lincolnshire. They were initially cut flower producers but produced Winter Sunshine, Spring Sunshine, Cherub and Sprite Series of sweet peas. They have now transferred the retail seed business to Elizabeth Crawford at Driffield, East Yorkshire, and their wholesale sweet pea production to EconSeeds BV of Enkhuizen, the Netherlands.

Oyama, Yukimitsu, Kanagawa, Japan. Raiser of at least seven early multiflora cultivars.

Page, William Bridgewater. Page (1818) lists white, scarlet 'Painted Lady', purple, black and striped all grown at Southampton Botanic Garden. References in the 19th century to striped colouring describe what we now call flaked colouring. Modern use of the term 'striped' refers to a mutation first seen in the 1925 cultivar 'Lady Gay'.

Parker, Sidney A. (d. 2002), West Portishead, Bristol. Raiser of 'Rosie' Parker introduced by Kerton Sweet Peas in 1992.

Parsons. Introduced 'Queen Eira' in 1912, raised by Jenkins. Possibly Frank or Emily Parsons, Channel View, Shanklin, Isle of Wight. The address is a hotel but "Parsons' Sweet Peas" were being traded by Mrs E. Parsons of Channel View in the 1930s.

Parsons, Roger (b. 1953), Bracklesham Bay, Chichester, West Sussex. Co-author of this book and Chairman of the National Sweet Pea Society from 2017 to 2020. He started a seedbank in 1998 to conserve *Lathyrus* species and cultivars and holds a National Plant Collection (Scientific) of the genus. He started trading in 2005 as Roger Parsons Sweet Peas and has raised at least 40 cultivars. He received the NSPS Henry Eckford Gold Memorial Medal in 2012 and the Plant Heritage Brickell Award in 2019.

Parsons, R.G., Leighton Buzzard, Bedfordshire. Raiser of 'Nimrod', introduced in 1975.

Pauling, R.F.M., Bradfield, Reading, Berkshire. Raiser of 'Susan Bristow', introduced in 1970.

J.R. Pearson & Sons, Chilwell Nurseries, Lowdham, Nottinghamshire. Raiser of 'T.S. Dodd' in 1909 and 'Elfrida Pearson' in 1911.

Pengilly. See J. Harkness.

Perkin, H.A., Reigate, Surrey. Raiser of 'Biddy Perkin' in 1905 and 'Nancy Perkin' in 1910.

Petit, Indianapolis, Indiana, USA. Raiser of 'Rose Queen' Petit, introduced in 1918.

Pettipher, Frank (c.1920–2003), Radford, Coventry, Warwickshire. Raiser of 'Margaret' Pettipher, introduced by Eagle Sweet Peas in 2004.

John Piper & Son Ltd, Bayswater, London. Introducer of at least three cultivars in around 1915–17. Their raiser was George Herbert.

Pitcher, Mrs J., Christchurch, Dorset. Raiser of 'Beauty of Dorset' in about 1990. This may be a cultivar raised by F.C. Harriss and submitted for trial by a family member.

Pitts. Raiser of 'Ellen' in about 1975.

Place, Joseph Dickson (1929–2007) Wigton, Cumbria. An amateur raiser of more than 35 cultivars introduced since 1999. His tall cultivars include many non-tendril ones, introduced by E.W. King & Co. See 'Breeding and selection' chapter.

Place, Richard (b. 1953), Wigton, Cumbria. Son of J.D. Place. Raiser of three non-tendril cultivars introduced by Parsons in 2016.

Plants of Distinction, Needham Market, Suffolk. A nursery that has introduced at least 15 sweet pea cultivars since 1998, including the dwarf Pinnochio Series.

Pope, George. Raiser of at least six cultivars introduced in 1915.

Pratt, E. John, Broadfern Road, Knowle, Solihull, Warwickshire. Raiser of 'Samantha Jane' in about 1994. He was NSPS treasurer for more than 40 years and received their Henry Eckford Gold Memorial Medal in 1989.

Priestley, George (1926–2001), Craiseland, Haxey, Doncaster, Yorkshire. Raiser of 'Dusty Springfield', introduced by Unwins in 2002, and 'Mary Priestley', introduced by Myers in 2015.

Rawnsley. Raiser of 'Alice Goodman', introduced in 1909.

Reeve, Tom (1922–1983), High Street, Ravensthorpe, Northamptonshire. Raiser of 'Karen Reeve', introduced by Marchant in 1985.

Renee's Garden, Graham Hill Road, Felton, California, USA. A business started by Renee Shepherd. They introduced at least two new cultivars but these may simply be other cultivars renamed.

Richards, A.W. (c.1878–c.1961), Swainston, Isle of Wight. Raiser of 'Island Queen', introduced in 1953.

John Richards & Co., The Nurseries, Dursley, Gloucestershire. Raiser of 'Giant Maroon' John Richards & Co., introduced in around 1915.

Richardson, Bridget (b. 1966), Gisborne, New Zealand. Granddaughter of Charles William John Unwin and raiser of 'Queen Mother' B. Richardson, introduced by Unwins in 1991.

F.B. Richardson & Son, Colwyn Bay, Conwy, Wales. A seed company in the 1980s that co-introduced 'Roy Phillips' in 1986.

Roberts, Revd F. Page (d. 1927), Strathfieldsaye Rectory, Mortimer, Berkshire. Raiser of 'Audrey', introduced in 1915.

Robertson, A. Fleming, Scone, Perthshire, Scotland. Raiser of at least eight cultivars since 1996, all introduced by Kerton Sweet Peas. The son of A. Ford Robertson.

Robertson, A. Ford, Scone, Perthshire, Scotland. Amateur raiser of 'Dynasty', introduced by Unwins in 1986.

Robson, John M., Castle Douglas, Dumfries, Scotland. Possibly the raiser of at least three cultivars.

Rollinson, David, Offenham, Evesham, Worcestershire. Raiser of 'Dave R', introduced in 2020.

T. Rothera & Co., The Gardens, Burton Joyce, Nottinghamshire. H. Rothera was the raiser of 'Mrs Rothera', introduced by Suttons in 1908.

Routzahn, Revd Louis (Lewis) C. (1859–1936), Arroyo Grande, California, USA. Owner of a wholesale seed-producing business that began in 1893 and the raiser of several cultivars introduced around 1910. These seem to be reselections from his production of existing cultivars.

Rowland, Mark (b. 1947) see Owls Acre Sweet Peas.

Rowles, W.F., Ellisfield Manor Gardens, Basingstoke, Hampshire. Raiser of 'Lady Geraldine Hoare', introduced around 1915. Lady Geraldine Hoare and her husband owned the manor, so it is presumed that Rowles was their gardener.

Rowntree Bros, St Albans, Hertfordshire. Credited with at least 30 cultivars but they may simply be renamings. Their undated catalogues are from the 1930s.

Rupp, Heinrich Bernhard (1688–1719). Rupp (1718) says of the sweet pea: 'Sometimes it varies with a white flower', the earliest reference to white-flowered *Lathyrus odoratus*.

Ryders Seeds. A company active in the mid-20th century and owned by Samuel Ryder (1858–1936) of St Albans, Hertfordshire. It is credited with introducing 70 or more cultivars, but some may have been reselections or renamings of existing cultivars.

Sakata Seed Co., Kanagawa, Japan. Raiser of at least 10 cultivars, including the Ceremony Series of non-tendril, early multiflora cultivars. Breeders are listed as Takao Nakamura (1990), Akira Moriyama (1990–94), Masahiro Nakagawa (1994–97) and Hitoshi Kojima (1997).

Sands, W.E., Lisburn, Northern Ireland. Raiser of at least four cultivars around 1930.

Sarrer. Raiser of 'Geoff Hughes', introduced by Eagle Sweet Peas in 2010.

Savage. Raiser of at least 14 cultivars introduced from 1909 to 1914. Several cultivars have the names Boleyn, Manor Park and Plashet as prefixes, suggesting a connection with Newham, London, but nothing is known of this grower.

Schmidt, J.C. Raiser of 'Vesuvius', introduced in 1886 and may have a connection to Haage & Schmidt.

Scobie, J.F., New Lambton, New South Wales, Australia. Raiser of 'Gawler Warrior' before 1948, 'Una Scobie' introduced in 1948, and 'Margaret Scobie'.

Searle, Alec W. Introduced at least 19 cultivars in 1915–16. He had previously worked for Brunnings

and in 1926 formed Gill & Searle of Elizabeth Street, Melbourne, Victoria, with Herbert Fitzmaurice Gill (c.1871–1957), who had been a director of Brunnings since 1906.

Seedlynx, Woodham Mortimer, Maldon, Essex. A wholesale seed producer supplying major packet-seed retail companies, with a retail arm called English Sweet Peas. They have raised at least four cultivars and are still very active. The company was founded by John Macefield (b. 1949) in 2000 as a division of Agrifusion Ltd. and sold to Philip Johnson in 2017.

Semences Davy, France. Seed wholesaler active in the 1930s.

Sewell, Diane (b. 1945) Over, Cambridgeshire. Introducer of at least six cultivars raised by her husband, Terry. She took over the business of Bill Maishman on his retirement in 1988, and she retired following Terry's death in 2003, at which point her business ceased.

Sharman, Joe, Monksilver Nursery, Oakington Road, Cottenham, Cambridge. Introducer of *Lathyrus vernus* cultivars selected by Sylvia Norton from material in general circulation.

Charles Sharpe & Co., Sleaford, Lincolnshire. A business started by Charles Sharpe (d. 1897) in 1888. They introduced four Bolton cultivars in 1908 and Bolton introduced a Sharpe novelty in 1908. This suggests Sharpe may have been Bolton's seed producer until Boltons bought their own land in around 1908. They raised and introduced new sweet peas in the early 1960s when Thomas Campbell Baines worked for them. In 1986 the business was acquired by Advanta Seeds.

Silvester, Roy, Market Drayton, Shropshire (c.1934–2009). Raiser of 'Sheila Roy', introduced by Parsons in 2013.

Simmonds, J., Turners Hill, Crawley, West Sussex. Raiser of 'Fay Simmonds' in about 1975.

Simons, Philip (1903–1968), Lyndhurst Nurseries, Ardleigh, Colchester, Essex. Raised more than 80 cultivars introduced between 1933 and 1968. He received the NSPS Henry Eckford Gold Memorial Medal in 1966.

Simply Sweet Peas. A partnership between Geoff Freeman and Richard Massey. Primarily a producer of young plants for retail sales who introduced at least five cultivars between 2006 and 2012 via online sales.

W.H. Simpson & Sons, Monument Road, Birmingham. Raiser of 'Doris Palmer', introduced by 1916.

Slater, J.E. Raiser of at least two cultivars between 1978 and 1981.

Smellie, J., Helensburgh, Dunbartonshire, Scotland. Raiser of at least two cultivars around 1918 to 1932.

Smith, E.J. Raiser of multiflora Spencer 'Sextet Queen', introduced by Suttons in 1931.

Smith, Lewis, Norwich until 1911, then Cadland, Southampton, from 1912. Raiser of eight cultivars introduced around 1912. This may be the same Smith listed as raiser of a further five cultivars in this era.

Smith, R.S., Burbage, Hinckley, Leicestershire. Submitted 'Bill Truslove' to the 2003 RHS trials but this is sure to be a cultivar raised by Truslove.

Somerset Sweet Peas, Minehead, Somerset. A trading name of Peter King who introduced at least three cultivars between 2011 and 2014.

Somerville, Adam, Fleetwood, Lancashire. Raiser of 'Fleetwood Blue' around 1968.

Southfield Nurseries. Raiser of 'Michael' around 1930. There are currently nurseries with this name at Broughton Gifford, Wiltshire, and one also known as Cactus Land in Bourne, Lincolnshire.

Sproule, James, San Francisco, California, USA. Raiser of 'Navy Blue', introduced by Burpee in 1899.

G. Stark & Son, Great Ryburgh, Norfolk, until c.1926, then Fakenham, Norfolk. Arthur George Stark (c.1870–c.1956) raised at least 120 cultivars introduced between 1905 and 1964. In 1935 he was awarded the NSPS Henry Eckford Gold Memorial Medal.

Stevenson, Joseph (d. 1940), Wimborne, Dorset. Raiser of at least 83 cultivars introduced between 1907 and 1938. Awarded the NSPS Henry Eckford Gold Memorial Medal in 1930.

Stevenson, Thomas, Addlestone, Surrey. Brother of Joseph Stevenson and raiser of 'Rosie Adams', introduced by H.J. Wright in 1908. Around 1917, he became a nurseryman and in 1934 was awarded the NSPS Henry Eckford Gold Memorial Medal.

Steward, W., New South Wales, Australia. Raised at least eight cultivars introduced by Gallatly from around 1933 to 1961.

Strong. Raiser of 'Blue Bird' Strong before 1914.

Sunset Seed and Plant Co., Sansome Street, San Francisco, California, USA. Prior to 1895 this business was called Sherwood Hall Nursery. They were still trading in around 1937. They introduced 'Red Riding Hood' in 1897, the first of the Snapdragon type of sweet pea in which the standard petal is undeveloped and folds down to form a hood over the wings. Further introductions followed over the following five years but the type was never popular and died out within 10 years.

Suttons, Reading, Berkshire, now Paignton, Devon. John Sutton (1777–1863) founded an agricultural seed shop in Reading in 1806 and ownership remained in the family for generations. They introduced 'Butterfly' in 1878 and were very active with sweet peas in the early 20th century, introducing at least 115 cultivars. In recent decades they continued to introduce new cultivars from amateur raisers, such as Alan Williams of Leamington Spa, Warwickshire. Suttons was part of Vilmorin Clause & Co. until a management buyout in 2014.

Sutton, William (Bill) (d. 2015), Southport, Lancashire. Raiser of 'Patricia Anne', named for his wife.

The Sweet Pea Co., Gazeley Road, Kentford, Newmarket, Suffolk. A short-lived marketing vehicle for Mr Fothergills Seeds Ltd used around 2006 to 2009.

Robert Sydenham Ltd, Tenby Street, Birmingham. Robert Sydenham (1848–1913) was a diamond merchant who started Sydenham Bros. in 1875 as a jewellery company, and the business ceased in 1930. He became a seed and bulb merchant by 1885 and introduced four Aldersey sweet pea cultivars in 1909 and at least 17 for Robert Holmes between 1908 and 1915. He introduced at least six other cultivars during this period. The seed business still appeared in the *NSPS Annual* up to 1932.

Synge, Katherine C. (Mrs Laurence) (1885–1972). Supplied 'Cheshire Dark Blue' to J.F. Turral prior to 1964, although the cultivar's original name had been lost. Her son shared a Nobel Prize in Chemistry in 1952.

Takachiho, Japan. Raiser of 'Spring Fair'.

Takeda, Tadakazu, Hokkaido, Japan. Raiser of

'Takedanosakurako'.

Takeda, Tadayuki, Hokkaido, Japan. Raiser of 'Takedanoayaka' and 'Takedanoharukaze'.

Tandy, Jim (1914–1989). In 1955 he replaced T.C. Baines at E.W. King & Co. and is perhaps best remembered for developing the Snoopea Series (Jones 1986, 1990).

Tasker, Doug, Harrold, Bedfordshire. Raiser of at least four cultivars introduced by him from 1983 to 1986, although only 'Annie Good' has endured.

Taylor, George Morrison, Midlothian. Wrote to the *Gardeners' Chronicle* in 1916 claiming to have crossed *L. odoratus* with *L. pratensis*. Better known as an author of several books on garden flowers.

Taylor, J.H. (d. 1950), Cambridge, Cambridgeshire. Raiser of 'Elizabeth Taylor', introduced by Unwins in 1951. It was named for his daughter but, to his irritation, the general public assumed it was named for the actress.

Taylor, Reginald G., Market Lavington, Wiltshire. Raiser of 'Olive Dunn' in about 1956. He started working for Suttons in 1917 and retired to Jersey in 1968.

Tebby, Raymond (Ray) Edgar (1936–2002), Winton, Eccles, Manchester. Raised three cultivars introduced by Marchant in 1985-86.

Tesselaar, Sylvan, Victoria, Australia. Business established in 1945 by Cees and Johanna Tesselaar. They introduced eight cultivars in 2019 but these are existing early multiflora cultivars renamed.

Thomas, Revd D. Gourlay (c.1896–1962), Exeter, Devon. Writer, amateur hybridist and raiser of at least five cultivars introduced between 1938 and 1951.

Thomas, William (Bill), Farncombe, Surrey. Raiser of at least 10 cultivars introduced between 1976 and 1989.

Thompson & Morgan, Ipswich, Suffolk. A business founded in 1855 by William Thompson (1833–1903), later to be joined by John Morgan (d. 1921), although not active with sweet peas until recent years. They introduced three cultivars from Bill Thomas in 1988–89, then 14 other introductions from 1993. They employed Charles Valin (b. 1978) as their plant breeder from 2004 to 2018 who worked on sweet peas and interspecific *Lathyrus* hybrids as well as many other genera.

Thomson, W.G., Dover, Kent. Raiser of 'Margaret Thomson', introduced around 1946–48.

Tibbets, J.E., Suffolk. Raiser of at least two cultivars in about 1985, but there is no evidence they became commercially available.

Tierney, Peter, Whitmore Park, Coventry, Warwickshire. Raiser of two cultivars introduced by Eagle Sweet Peas in 2007–08.

Tigwell, Mrs A., Greenford, Southall, London. Raiser of 'Dorothy Tigwell' in 1907 and 'Mrs H.D. Tigwell' in 1911.

Tilby, H.R. Submitted 'Vair Rosa' to the 1954 RHS trial, but nothing more is known.

Toogood & Sons, Southampton, Hampshire. Raiser of 'Minnie Toogood', introduced in 1909. The business was acquired by Finneys Seeds Ltd in 1955.

Tremewan, Pip (1919–1994), St Austell, Cornwall. See 'Breeding and selection' chapter.

Trevethick, Charles (1854–1928), Lower Hutt, Wellington, New Zealand. An exhibitor, breeder and seedsman who raised at least five cultivars introduced into the UK in 1911 by Mackereth.

Truslove, William (Bill), Burbage, Hinckley, Leicestershire. Raiser of at least 13 cultivars introduced between 1980 and 2011.

Tullett, Roy, Northgate, Crawley, West Sussex, now living in Lincolnshire. Raiser of at least six cultivars introduced between 1995 and 2006.

Tunia Service, Adelaide, South Australia. Introduced 'Our Elizabeth' and two cultivars from C.R. Veale in 1948

Turral, Major John F. (d. 1967), Farnley, Otley, West Yorkshire. Originator of at least two Old-fashioned Grandiflora cultivars in the early 1960s.

Tuttle. Raiser of 'Coral Gem', introduced by Vaughan in 1907.

Unwins Seeds, Histon, Cambridgeshire. Sweet peas were the mainstay for William James Unwin (1872–1947) to develop his general seed business. He was a general cut-flower grower at Histon who was a friend of pioneer geneticist Sir Rowland Biffen and had access to the findings of early geneticists. His son, Charles William James Unwin (1895–1986), also produced numerous sweet pea cultivars. Both received the NSPS Henry Eckford Gold Memorial Medal. The company has raised at least 322 cultivars and introduced others from amateur raisers. In 2001–02 they bought out Robert Bolton & Son of Birdbrook, Halstead, Essex, and the family sold Unwins to Westland in 2004.

Uprising Seeds, Bellingham, Washington, USA. Raiser of 'Lunar Blue', introduced in 2019.

Usher. Raiser of 'Bertie Usher' in 1910 and 'Doris Usher' in 1911. Probably A.E. Usher of Ranston House, Blandford, Dorset, gardener to Sir Randolph Baker Bt.

Uvedale, Revd Dr Robert (1642–1722), Enfield, Middlesex. A teacher and horticulturist who was Master of Enfield Grammar School. He received seeds of wild sweet pea in 1699 from Franciscus Cupani and from there distributed it to other growers. James Petiver said in 1713: 'This elegant sweet-flowered plant I first observed with Dr Plukenet in Dr Uvedale's most curious garden at Enfield, and since at Chelsea and elsewhere' (Parsons 2011). The colour was described as 'purple' but we can be certain this refers to the maroon/violet bicolour we know as typical *Lathyrus odoratus*. Uvedale is also known for having stolen, as a schoolboy, the satin coat-of-arms from Oliver Cromwell's funeral procession.

Vaughan Seed Store, West Randolph Street, Chicago, Illinois, USA. Founded in 1876 by John Charles Vaughan (1851–1924) and now part of Novartis Seeds. Between 1896 and 1904 they introduced nine cultivars raised by Morse.

Veale, CR, Australia. Raiser of at least two cultivars introduced by Tunia Service in 1948.

Verge, Frank, Sevenoaks, Kent. Raiser of at least three cultivars in about 1985.

Vick, James (1818–1882), Rochester, New York, USA. Established a seed business in 1855 that was continued by his sons. They changed the name in 1891 to James Vick's Sons, thereby including Charles Vick (1858–1952). It was sold to Burpee early in the 20th century. By 1870 they were offering nine colours, including 'Black', described as 'very dark, brownish purple', and 'black with light blue', described as 'brownish purple and light blue'. They also introduced 'Bride of Niagara' in 1895 and 'Dorothy Vick' in 1897.

Vickers. Raiser of two cultivars around 1909–10. Possibly T. Vickers of The Gardens, Well Vale, Alford, Lincolnshire.

Wakayama prefecture, Japan. A region in Japan from which at least seven cultivars have been registered. since 1999. Breeders listed are Kazundo Kato (1995), Yoshiki Miyamoto (1995–2003), Tadashi Fujioki (1995–2007), Hiromi Hanada (1995–2007), Masayoshi Fujita (1995), Yoshinari Ito (1995), Masaaki Fukui (1995), Akitsugu Shiba (1995), Hidenobu Fujiwara (1995), Masamich Okada (1995), Yutaka Mori (2002–04), Toshiteru Kabata (2002–03), Ayaka Yamamoto (2002–03), Satoshi Nakanishi (2004), Takahiro Marakami (2007) and Takayuki Furuya (2007).

Wakefield, Victoria, Bramdean House, Alresford, Hampshire. Raiser of 'Bramdean', introduced by Parsons in 2007.

Walker, S.T., Forest Grove, Oregon, USA. Raiser of at least 10 cultivars introduced between 1894 and 1899.

Walker, Wilfred E. (1921–2001), Pawlett, Bridgwater, Somerset. Raiser of at least 12 cultivars introduced between 1983 and 2004.

Waller, Lionel D. (1882–1940). See 'Breeding and selection' chapter.

Waller-Franklin Seed Co. See 'Breeding and selection' chapter.

Ward, Howard E., Cartref, Vicar's Cross, Chester, Cheshire. Raiser of at least nine cultivars introduced between 1907 and 1916.

Ward, F.W. Raiser of two cultivars introduced by Woodcock in 1996 and 2004.

Watanabe, Hiroaki, Agatanishi, Nichinan-shi, Miyazaki, Japan. Raiser of 'Nichinan Natural Green', introduced in 2015.

Waterer, Percy, Fawkham, Kent. Raiser of 'Begorra', introduced by 1905, and president of the NSPS in 1905.

Watkins & Simpson, Tavistock Street, Covent Garden, London, with a trial ground at Twickenham, Middlesex. This company introduced at least 18 cultivars between 1905 and 1916. Alfred Watkins was president of the NSPS in 1906 and was awarded the NSPS Henry Eckford Gold Memorial Medal in 1927.

Watson, J., The Gardens, Orford House, Ham Common, Richmond-upon-Thames, Surrey. Raiser of 'Helen Lewis', introduced by Breadmore in 1904.

Weardon, FM, Norton, Mawdesley, Ormskirk,

Lancashire. Raiser of 'Alicia' in 1972, Nora in 1975, and 'Ella' in 1975.

Edward Webb & Sons, Wordsley, Stourbridge, West Midlands. Edward Webb started his business around 1850 and by 1910 his grandson, Colonel William G. Webb MP, was running it. They were recorded as raising 'Giant Lavender' Webb in 1925. The business merged with Bees Seeds in the 1960s and is now part of Unwins. The business was involved in the foundation of the NSPS.

Welch, C.W., Carbrooke, Thetford, Norfolk. Raiser of at least three cultivars from around 1999 to 2005.

Wellesley, Francis, Woking, Surrey. Raiser of 'Mrs F. Wellesley', introduced in 1910. He employed W. Hopkins as his gardener.

Wells, Graham, BEM, Didcot, Oxfordshire, later at Sutton Courtenay, Abingdon. Raiser of at least 12 cultivars introduced between 1979 and 2015.

Weston, Richard (1733–1806) His vol. 1 of *Flora Anglicana* (1775) included the first reference to scarlet sweet pea, listed as *Lathyrus odoratus coccineus* (Wright 1912).

Wheeler, H.J., Warminster, Wiltshire. Introduced 'Constance Hinton' for H.T. Hinton in 1914. 'Wenvoe Beauty' is attributed to Wheeler but the name suggests it may have been raised by Gerhold, so Wheeler may have been the seed seller.

Whitelegg & Page, Chislehurst, Kent. Introduced at least five cultivars in 1910–11. George G. Whitelegg (1877–1957) was in partnership with Page until 1915.

Wilkinson's Seeds, Leamington, Warwickshire. Introduced 'Herald' for Colledge in 1962. Alexander Wilkinson (d. 1978) and May Wilkinson (1900–1991) ran a floristry shop from 1946 to 1983.

Williams, Alan J., Leamington Spa, Warwickshire. An amateur breeder who raised at least three cultivars around 1983 to 1986.

Wiltshire, Ronald Francis Morey (1901–1981), Netley Abbey, Hampshire, until 1942, then Fawley, Hampshire, from 1943, then Fair Oak, Eastleigh, Hampshire, from 1975. Raiser of 'Kathleen Wiltshire' around 1932, 'Wiltshire Ripple' around 1982 and 'New Dawn' Wiltshire around 1986.

Winn, George H., Duffield, Derbyshire. Raiser of 'Mrs George Winn', recorded at the 1921 RHS trials.

Woodcock, Walmer, Deal, Kent. Over three generations the Woodcock family raised and introduced at least 50 cultivars between 1910 and 2003. Frederick C. Woodcock established the nursery in 1892, was succeeded by his son Austin Frederick Woodcock (1902–1988), and finally his daughter Frances Woodcock (1939–2018).

Woodman, Henry (c.1698–1758) Strand-on-the-Green, Chiswick, London. Son of Henry & Esther Woodman of Chiswick, his nursery was established by 1727. In 1729 he supplied 2oz of 'Sweet sented Pease' to Henry Ellison of Gateshead Park, Co. Durham. On his death, the nursery continued under his wife, Eleanor, until her death in 1780 (Harvey 1974).

Jacob Wrench & Sons, London Bridge, London. Raiser of 'Princess Mary' around 1894. The business was started in 1750 by Jacob Wrench. They were trading as Jacob Wrench and Sons by 1830 and were taken over by Howcroft Watkins in 1905, which became part of Cooper Taber in 1912.

Wright, Horace John (1868–1925) Wandsworth, London. A seedsman from 1906 to 1910 and perhaps longer. He introduced 'Rosie Adams' in 1908, raised by T. Stevenson.

Wright, Robert, Formby, Liverpool. Raiser of at least seven cultivars introduced between 1913 and 1915.

Wright, A.V., Gloucester, Gloucestershire. Raiser of 'Mrs B.W. Price', introduced in 1916.

Yamamoto, Kyosuke, Kanagawa, Japan. Raiser of 'Artemis' in 1994 and 'Shonan Orion' in 2002. In 2008 he registered two cultivars raised with Yagashita Yoshimi. See Kanagawa prefecture.

Arthur Yates & Co. Arthur Yates (d. 1926) emigrated in 1879 from England to New Zealand and set up a seed business in Auckland in 1883. In 1887 he set up a new seed business in Sydney, Australia, leaving his brother Ernest to run the New Zealand one. He introduced at least 35 winter-flowering cultivars between 1912 and 1922.

Yoshimi, Yagashita. See Kyosuke Yamamoto and Kanagawa prefecture.

Young, James, Sydney, New South Wales, Australia. The cultivar 'Yarrawa' arose in his garden in 1908. It was introduced in 1912 by Arthur Yates & Co. and was used extensively in the USA and Australia to improve the quality of early Spencer cut-flower cultivars.

Zvolanek, Anton (1878–1958), Bound Brook, New Jersey, USA, then to Lompoc, California around 1912–15. He was a sole trader until about 1918 when his son William joined to form A. Zvolanek & Son. The other son, Edward, joined them in 1920 to form A. Zvolanek & Sons. Anton retired in 1929 and William started his own business, William Zvolanek & Co., but the original business reverted to A. Zvolanek & Son and continued trading. Edward ran the latter business but did no hybridising, relying on his retired father for new cultivars.

Zvolanek, William (1892–1979), Lompoc, California, USA. Started working for his father after 1918 when the business became A. Zvolanek & Son. He traded as William Zvolanek & Co. after his father retired. He was a pioneer developer of the Duplex and Early Multiflora types and also did considerable innovation on semi-dwarf types. In 1971 he received the NSPS Henry Eckford Gold Memorial Medal, and he retired in 1975 when he sold the business to Denholm Seeds (Christensen 2006). Father and son raised at least 410 cultivars introduced between 1902 and 1977, but it is not easy to distinguish which Zvolanek raised which cultivars. Many were simply reselections of existing cultivars.

Glossary

Adaxial – a surface directed towards the axis, such as the inner edge of a style.

Amphicarpic – having two types of fruit; in the case of some *Lathyrus*, usually above and below ground.

Androecium – a collection of stamens forming the male reproductive organs.

Anther – the pollen-producing part of the stamen.

Arista – a short, soft bristle, usually at the tip of a leaf.

Blade – the 'free' portion of a petal, usually the visible part when looking at a flower, held in place by the claw. Also, the main part of a leaf or leaflet, distinct from its stalk.

Chipping – mechanical abrasion of the seed coat to assist penetration of water into the seed and initiate germination.

Chitting – pre-germination of seeds in a warm, moist environment.

Calyx teeth – the free parts of the calyx.

Calyx tube – the fused bell-shaped basal portion of the calyx.

Claw – the basal part of a petal, usually tucked into the flower and not visible.

Cleistogamous – having flowers that do not open, which therefore self-pollinate

Cordon – plant training that involves the cultivation of a single haulm and the removal of all other shoots.

Diadelphous – stamens in which the filaments are fused to form to two groups.

Dominant – a gene that produces a character when just one of its two forms (alleles) is present in a single dose, as it does with a double dose.

Duplex – flowers with two standard petals instead of the typical one standard.

Echinate – covered with small points or spines.

Emarginate – a leaf, petal or sepal that has a notch at its apex.

Endosperm – tissue inside seeds that surrounds the embryo and provides nutrition to enable germination.

Filiform – thread-like, long and slender

Grandiflora – sweet peas with the typical flower form of a clamped keel and plain petals.

Haulm – the main structural stem of the plant.

Hilum – scar on the seed coat from where the seed was attached to the seed pod.

Hybrid – an individual that has arisen from a cross between two different parents, usually of separate species.

Hypogeal – a type of seed germination where the seed leaves stay below ground.

Indehiscent – fruits that do not open to release seeds.

Interspecific hybridisation – the crossing of two different species.

Keel – the lowest part of a *Lathyrus* flower, formed by the fusion of two small petals to create a structure like a boat hull. Typically, the end is clamped around the pistil and stamen but in Spencer sweet peas the top is more open and there is no clamping. It is also known as the carina.

Lomentose – a seed pod that breaks open at constrictions between the seeds.

Mesotrophic – an environment with a moderate amount of nutrients.

Monophyletic – a group of species (or other taxonomic grouping) that shares a common ancestor.

Multiflora – refers to cultivars usually having five or more florets per raceme.

Neoteny – the retention of juvenile features in an adult.

Non-perennating – not persisting from year to year.

Old-fashioned – sweet peas with typical flower form that pre-date the advent of Spencer flower form.

Ovary – the part of a flower that holds the ovules and develops into the seed pod.

Paripinnate – a pinnate leaf in which all the leaflets are in pairs.

Pauciflora – cultivars usually having four or fewer florets per raceme.

Pedicel – the stalk of one flower in an inflorescence.

Peduncle – the stalk of an inflorescence.

Petiole – leaf stalk.

Phyllode – a leaf-like petiole.

Pistil – the female part of a flower, consisting of ovary, style and stigma.

Pollen tube – a tube that emerges from a pollen grain and grows down the style to enable male gamete cells to pass along and achieve fertilisation.

Polyploidy – having more than the usual two sets of chromosomes found in diploid organisms.

Raceme – a type of inflorescence in which the main axis continues to grow and produces flowers laterally.

Recessive – a gene that produces a character only when both its two forms (alleles) are present, but which is masked if a dominant allele is present.

Rhizome – a horizontally creeping underground stem, usually producing aerial stems that emerge from the ground at some distance from one another.

Sagittate – shaped like an arrow head, usually in reference to stipules in *Lathyrus*.

Semi-grandiflora – sweet peas with the wavy petals of the Spencer type but with clamped keels of the Grandiflora type.

Semisagittate – shaped like half an arrow head, with one triangular upper part and a single basal spur, usually in reference to stipules in *Lathyrus*.

Spathulate – having an apex that is broad and flattened, like a spoon.

Spencer – a flower form found in sweet peas with open keels and wavy petals.

Stamen – the male part of a flower consisting of filaments supporting anthers that produce pollen.

Standard – the vertical petal on a *Lathyrus* flower, and more commonly known as the banner in the US, or botanically as the vexillum.

Stigma – the area at the top of the style that receives the pollen.

Stipule – paired leafy structures near the base of a leaf petiole.

Stolon – a modified stem with long internodes, usually creeping at, or just below, ground level.

Stylar amputation – reduction of the length of the style during artificial hybridisation to assist a species that has shorter pollen tubes than those of the female species.

Style – the stalk above the carpel that supports the stigma.

Suture – the weak part of a pod, where the two halves (valves) join together.

Tendril – part of a stem, leaf or petiole that is modified into a delicate, thread-like, twisting appendage that aids climbing.

Terete – circular in cross section.

Sweet pea – the common name of *Lathyrus odoratus*, but also used for cultivars with *L. × hammettii* in their origin that resemble *L. odoratus*.

Valves – the two halves of a seed pod.

Vernalisation – the induction of growth by cold treatment.

Villous – covered with long, soft hairs.

Wings – the two horizontal petals on a *Lathyrus* flower, botanically known as alae.

References

Anon. (1866/67) Awards. *J. Roy. Hort. Soc.* 1(3): xx

Anon. (1868/70) Annuals. *J. Roy. Hort. Soc.* 2(7/8): cxxv

Anon. (1877) Extract from Carter's list of novelties for 1877. *Gard. Chron.* n.s. 8: 635

Anon. (1882) Reports on societies. Royal Horticultural. *Gard. Chron.* n.s. 18: 215

Anon. (1884) Mr Eckford's sweet peas. *Gard. Chron.* n.s. 22: 114

Anon. (1890) Awards recommended. *J. Roy. Hort. Soc.* 12: xcvii

Anon. (1891) Awards recommended. *J. Roy. Hort. Soc.* 13: cxxvii

Anon. (1893a) Societies; Royal Horticultural, Floral Committee. *Gard. Chron.* Ser. 3, 14: 70

Anon. (1893b) Notices to correspondents. *Gard. Chron.* Ser. 3, 14: 75

Anon. (1893c) Eckford's new peas. *Gard. Chron.* Ser. 3, 14: 566

Anon. (1895/6) Awards recommended. *J. Roy. Hort. Soc.* 19: clxxiv

Anon. (1897/98) Other exhibits. *J. Roy. Hort. Soc.* 21: cl, cxlvii

Anon. (1898) Sweet peas. *Gard. Chron.* Ser. 3, 24: 56

Anon. (1898/99) Report on annuals at Chiswick, 1898. Sweet peas. *J. Roy. Hort. Soc.* 22: 393, 394

Anon. (1900a) Sweet pea. *Gard. Chron.* Ser. 3, 28: 50

Anon. (1900b) The sweet pea bi-centenary celebration. *Gard. Chron.* Ser. 3, 28: 70

Anon. (1900c) Sweet pea 'Mont Blanc'. *Gard. Chron.* Ser. 3, 28: 341

Anon. (1901/02) Report on miscellaneous flowering plants at Chiswick, 1901. Sweet pea. *J. Roy. Hort. Soc.* 26: 612

Anon. (1905) Sweet peas. *Sweet Pea Annual*: iii

Anon. (1907) Awards recommended. *J. Roy. Hort. Soc.* 32: cxx

Anon. (1908) Wolverhampton floral fête. Sweet peas. *Gard. Chron.* Ser. 3, 44: 57

Anon. (1909/10) Awards recommended. *J. Roy. Hort. Soc.* 35: cxlvii

Anon. (1919/20) Awards recommended. *J. Roy. Hort. Soc.* 45: cxi

Anon. (2000) Old and new share stage. *The Garden* 125(7): 498

Anon. (2006) Plant Forum. Scented plants to satisfy demand. *The Garden* 131(1): 11

Arcangeli, G. (1894) *Compendio della Flora Italiano.* 2nd edn. Ermanno Loescher, Rome, Turin

Asmussen, C. & Liston, A. (1998) Chloroplast DNA characters, phylogeny and classification of *Lathyrus* (*Fabaceae*). *Am. J. Bot.* 85: 387–401

Bal, A.K. & Khetmalas, M.B. (1996) Pre- and postwinter changes in the root nodules of *Lathyrus maritimus* (L.) Bigel. with special reference to storage organelles. *Int. J. Pl. Sci.* 157: 432–439

Bailey, R. (1990) Rogues. *NSPS Annual* 1990: 59–60

Ball, G.J. (1930) *Better Sweet Peas ed.* 2. Florists' Publishing Co., Chicago

Ball, P.W. (1968) *Lathyrus.* In: Tutin, T.G., Heywood, V.H., Burgess, N.A., Moore, D.M., Valentine, D.H., Walters, S.M. & Webb, D.A. (eds.) *Flora Europaea.* Cambridge University Press, Cambridge

Bao, B. & Kenicer, G. (2010) *Lathyrus.* In: Flora of China Editorial Committee (eds.) *Flora of China. Vol. 10.* Science Press, Beijing, & Missouri Botanical garden press, St Louis

Barker, B.T.P. (1916) Sweet pea hybrids. *Gard. Chron.* Ser. 3, 60: 156–157

Barrington, D. & Schmitz, S. (2013) Quaternary divergence and Holocene secondary contact via the Northwest Passage in the circumpolar *Lathyrus japonicus* (*Leguminosae*) *Rhodora* 115: 133–157

Bassler, M. (1973) Revision der Eurisatischen arten von *Lathyrus* L. sect. *Orobus* (L.) Gren. et. Godr. *Feddes Repert.* 84: 329–447

Bateson, W. (1909) *Mendel's Principles of Heredity.* Cambridge University Press, Cambridge

Bässler, M. (1966) Die stellung des subgen. *Orobus* (L.) Baker in der gattung *Lathyrus* L. und seinesystem-atische gliederung. *Feddes Repert.* 72: 69–97

Bässler, M. (1971) Beitrage zur nomenklatur der gattung *Lathyrus* L. *Feddes Repert.* 82: 433–439

Bässler, M. (1973) Revision der Eurasiatischen arten von *Lathyrus* L. sect. *Orobus.* (L.) Gren. et Godr.

Feddes Repert. 84(5–6): 329–447

Bässler, M. (1981) Revision von *Lathyrus* L. sect. *Lathyrostylis* (Griseb.) Bassler (*Fabaceae*). *Feddes Repert.* 92: 179–254

Bauhin, J. (1650) *Historia Plantarum Universalis* Ebroduni, Yverdon

Beal, A.C. (1912) Sweet pea studies III: culture of the sweet pea. *Cornell Univ. Agric. Exp. Sta. Bull.* No. 320, Ithaca, New York

Beal, A.C. (1914) Classification of garden varieties of the sweet pea. *Cornell Univ. Agric. Exp. Sta. Bull.* No. 342, Ithaca, New York

Beale, G.H., Robinson, G.M., Robinson, R. & Scott-Moncrieff, R. (1939) Genetics and chemistry of flower colour variation in *Lathyrus odoratus*. *J. Genet.* 37(3): 375–388

Bell, E.A. (1962a) Associations of ninhydrin-reacting compounds in the seeds of 49 species of *Lathyrus*. *Biochem. J.* 83 225–229

Bell, E.A. (1962b) The isolation of L-homoarginine from seeds of *Lathyrus cicera*. *Biochem. J.* 85(10): 91-93

Bell, E.A., Lackey, J.A. & Polhill, R.M. (1978) Systematic significance of canavanine in the *Papilionoideae*. *Biochem. Syst. Ecol.* 6: 201–212

Bishop, J.R.F. (2002) Robert Bleasdale Bolton. *NSPS Annual* 2002: 113–114

Bodger Whitman, L. (1981) *The House of Bodger*. Whitman, California

Brickell, C. & Sharman, F. (1986) *The Vanishing Garden*. John Murray, London

Broich, S.J. (in press) *Lathyrus*. In: Flora of North America Editorial Committee (eds). *Flora of North America*. New York & Oxford

Buchan, U. (1999) Sweet smell of success. *The Garden* 124(2): 86–89

Burkart, A. (1935) Revision de las especies de *Lathyrus* de la República Argentina. *Revista Fac. Agron. Veterin.* 8(1): 41–133

Burton, M.A. (1956) *Genetical Studies in the Genus Lathyrus*. MSc thesis, University of Manchester

Campbell, C.G. (1997) *Grass pea, Lathyrus sativus L. Promoting the Conservation and Use of Underutilized and Neglected Crops*. Institute of Plant Genetics and Crop Plant Research, Gatersleben / International Plant Genetic Resources Institute, Rome

Chapman, G.T.L. & Tweddle M. (1995) *A New Herbal by Wiliam Turner (1551), Vol. 1*. Cambridge

University Press, Cambridge

Chittenden, F.J. & Synge, P.M. (1956) *The Royal Horticultural Society Dictionary of Gardening*. 2nd edn. Clarendon Press, Oxford

Christensen, B.G. (2006) *Acres of Loveliness: The Flower-Seed Industry of the Lompoc Valley*. Lompoc Valley Botanical and Horticultural Society, Lompoc, California

Clos, D. (1846) *Lathyrus*. In: Gay, C. (ed.) *Flora Chilena. Botanica* 2: 142–149

Colborn, N. (2006) Vernal vetchlings. *The Garden* 131(3): 169–171

Commelin, C. (1701) *Horti-Medici Amstelodamensis Rariorum* 2: 159–160, t.80. Amsterdam

Connelly, K. (1993) Pride of California. *Pacific Horticulture* 54(4): 58–9

Coulot, P. & Rabaute, P. (2016) *Monographie des Leguminosae de France. Tome 4. Tribus des Fabeae, des Cicereae et des Genisteae*. Societe Botanique du Centre-Ouest, Jarnac

Crane, M.B. & Lawrence, W.J.C. (1947) *The Genetics of Garden Plants*. Edn. 3 Macmillan & Co., London

Cupani, F. (1696) *Hortus Catholicus*. Palermo, Sicily

Curtis, C.H. (1905) The newer sweet pea. *NSPS Annual* 1905: 27–32

Curtis, C.H. (1922) Mr Robert Bolton. *NSPS Annual* 1922: 12

Curtis, C.H. & Eckford, J.S. (1900) The evolution of the sweet pea. In: Dean, R. (ed.) *The Sweet Pea Bicentenary Celebration* 1900: 23–31

Curtis, W. (1788) *Lathyrus odoratus*. Sweet pea, or vetchling. *Bot. Mag.* 2: t.60

Cuthbertson, F. (1916) *Field Notes on Sweet Peas* (edited by Morse, L.L.). C.C. Morse & Co., San Francisco

Czefranova, Z.V. (1971) Summary of the taxonomy of the genus *Lathyrus* L. *Novitiates Sys. Pl. Vasc.* 8: 205–213

Davies, A.J.S. (1957) Successful crossing in the genus *Lathyrus* through stylar amputation. *Nature* 180: 612

Davies, A.J.S. (1958) *A Cytogenetic Study in the Genus Lathyrus*. PhD thesis. University of Manchester

Davis, J.C.P.M. (1965) Post War Henry Eckford Memorial Medallists. *NSPS Annual* 1965: 79–83

Davis, P.H. 1970. *Lathyrus* L. In: Davis, P.H. (ed.) *Flora of Turkey and East Aegean Islands*. Vol. 3. Edinburgh University Press, Edinburgh

Dean, R. (1882) *Lathyrus azureus*. *The Florist and Pomologist* 1882: 22

Edwards, D. (2014) Developing a yellow sweet pea. *The Plantsman* n.s. 13(4): 252–254

Ehrlen, J. (1992) Proximate limits to seed production in a herbaceous perennial legume, *Lathyrus vernus*. *Ecol.* 73: 1820–1830

Ehrlen, J. (1995a) Demography of the perennial herb *Lathyrus vernus* I. Herbivory and individual performance. *J. Ecol.* 83: 287–295

Ehrlen, J. (1995b) Demography of the perennial herb *Lathyrus vernus* II. Herbivory and population dynamics. *J. Ecol.* 83: 297–308

FAO (2021) Food and Agriculture Organization of the United Nations FAOSTAT database. www.fao.org/faostat/en (accessed 23 March 2021)

Fairbairn, A., Martinoli, D., Butler, A. & Hillman, G. (2007) Wild plant seed storage at Neolithic Çatalhöyük East, Turkey. *Veget. Hist. Archaeobot.* 16: 467–479

Fedchenko, B.A. (1948) *Lathyrus*. In: Komarov, V.L., Shishkin, B.K. & Bobrov, E.G. (eds) *Flora of the USSR. Vol. 13.* 1972 translation by the Israeli Program for Scientific Translation, Jerusalem

Fuchs, L. (1542) *De Historia Stirpium*. Basel

Gallego, M.J. (1999) *Lathyrus*. In: Talavera, S., Aedo, C., Castroviejo, S., Romero Zarco, C., Sáez, L., Salgueiro, F.J. & Velayos, M. (eds.). *Flora Iberica. Vol. VII.* Real Jardín Botánico, CSIC, Madrid

Genc, H. & Sahin, A. (2008) A new species of *Lathyrus* L. (section *Cicercula; Fabaceae*) from Turkey. *Bot. J. Linn. Soc.* 158: 301–305

Gerard, J. (1597) *The Herball or Generall Historie of Plantes*. John Norton, London.

Gerard, J. (1636) *The Herball* or *Generall Historie of Plantes*. Rev. ed. by Thomas Johnson. Adam Islip, Joice Norton & Richard Whitakers, London

Gorer, R., Harvey, J.H. & Vickery, R. (1991) The mysteries of Lord Anson's pea. *The Plantsman* 13(3): 129–139

Gunn, C.R. & Kluve, J. (1976) Androecium and pistil characters for the tribe *Vicieae (Fabaceae)*. *Taxon* 25: 563–575

Gutiérez, J.F., Vaquero, F. & Vences, F.J. (1994) Allopolyploid vs. autopolyploid origins in the genus *Lathyrus (Leguminosae)*. *Heredity* 73: 29–40

Hambidge, C. (2002) *The Unwins Century 1903–2003.* Unwins Seeds, Cambridge

Hammett, K.R.W. (2000) Early flowering sweet pea strains. In: Ball, C. (ed.) *National Sweet Pea Society Centenary Celebration 1900–2000.* NSPS, Stockbridge, Hampshire

Hammett, K.R.W., Murray, B.G., Markham, K.R. & Hallett, I.C. (1994) Interspecific hybridization between *Lathyrus odoratus* and *L. belinensis*. *Int. J. Pl. Sci.* 155(6): 763–771

Hammett, K.R.W., Murray, B.G., Markham, K.R., Hallett, I.C. & Osterloh, I. (1996) New interspecific hybrids in *Lathyrus*: *L. annuus* × *L. hierosolymitanus*. *Bot. J. Linn. Soc.* 122: 89–101

Harvey, J.H. (1974) *Early Nurserymen*. Phillimore, West Sussex

Haughton, C.S. (1978) *Green Immigrants: the Plants that Transformed America*. Harcourt Brace Jovanovich, New York

Henderson, D.M. & Dickson, J.H. (1994) *A Naturalist in the Highlands. James Robertson; His Life and Travels in Scotland, 1767–1771.* Scottish Academic Press, Edinburgh

Herrick, J.F., Murray, B.G., & Hammett, K.R.W. (1993) Barriers preventing hybridisation of *Lathyrus odoratus* with *L. chloranthus* and *L. chrysanthus*. *New Zeal. J. Crop. Hort.* 21: 115–121

Hibberd, F.K. (2011) *Lathyrus*. In: Cullen, J., Knees, S.G. & Cubey, H.S. (eds) *European Garden Flora. Vol. 3.* 2nd edn. Cambridge University Press, Cambridge

Holm, L., Pancho J.V., Herberger, J.P & Plucknett D.L. (1979) *A Geographical Atlas of World Weeds.* Wiley Interscience, New York.

Hull, E.F. (1994) My ways of growing sweet peas for garden decoration. *NSPS Annual* 1994: 75–77

Inoue, T. (2007) *Suitopi* [sweet peas, in Japanese]. Nosan Gyson Bunka Kyokai (Rural Culture Association of Japan), Japan

Jackson, M.T. & Yunus, A.G. (1984) Variation in the grass pea (*Lathyrus sativus*) and wild species. *Euphytica* 33: 549–559

Jacob, J. (1911) The Télemly sweet peas. *NSPS Annual* 1911: 33–34

Johnson, C.P. & Sowerby, J.E. (1862) *The Useful Plants of Great Britain*. W. Kent, London

Jones, B.R. (1986) Thomas Campbell Baines. *NSPS Annual* 1986: 6–7

Jones, B.R. (1990) James O. Tandy. *NSPS Annual* 1990:

108–109

Jones, F.R. (1924) A mycorrhizal fungus in the roots of legumes and some other plants. *J. Agric. Res.* 29: 459–470

Jones, W.H.S. & Andrews, A.C. (trans.) (1956) Pliny, Natural History, Volume VII: Books 24–27. Loeb Classical Library 393. Harvard University Press, Massachusetts

Kelsey, H.P. & Dayton, W.A. (1942) *Standardised Plant Names.* 2nd edn. Harrisburg, Pennsylvania

Kenicer, G.J. (2007) *Systematics and Biogeography of Lathyrus L. (Leguminosae), Papilionoideae.* PhD thesis, University of Edinburgh

Kenicer, G.J., Kajita, T., Pennington, R.T. & Murata, J. (2005) Systematics and biogeography of *Lathyrus* (*Leguminosae*) based on ITS and cpDNA sequence data. *Am. J. Bot.* 92: 1199–1209

Kenicer, G., Nieto-Blásques, E.M., Mikic, A. & Smýkal, P. (2009) *Lathyrus* – diversity and phylogeny in the genus. *Grain Legum.* 54: 16–18

Kenicer, G. & Norton, S. (2008) *Lathyrus neurolobus. Curtis's Bot. Mag.* 25(4): 310–316

Kerr, G.W. (1910) *All About Sweet Peas.* W. Atlee Burpee & Co., Philadelphia

Kerr, G.W. (1914) *Sweet Peas Up-to-Date.* W. Atlee Burpee & Co., Philadelphia.

Khawaja, H.I.T. (1988a) A new interspecific *Lathyrus* hybrid to introduce the yellow flower character into the sweet pea. *Euphytica* 37: 69–75

Khawaja, H.I.T. (1988b) New interspecific hybrids in the genus *Lathyrus. Genome* 30(suppl. 1): 263

Kislev, M.E. (1989) Origins of the cultivation of *Lathyrus sativus* and *L. cicera. Econ. Bot.* 43: 262–270

Kupicha, F.K. (1976) The infrageneric structure of *Vicia. Notes Roy. Bot. Gard. Edinburgh* 34: 287–326

Kupicha, F.K. (1983) The infrageneric structure of *Lathyrus. Notes Roy. Bot. Gard. Edinburgh* 41: 209–244

Lambein, F., Chaudhury, B. & Kuo, Y.-H. (1999) Biochemistry of the *Lathyrus* toxins. In: Mathur, P.N., Ramanantha Rao, V. & Arora, R.K. (eds) *Lathyrus Genetic Resources Network Proceedings of an IPGRI–ICARDA–ICAR Regional Working Group Meeting.* International Plant Genetic Resources Institute, New Delhi.

Lawson, P. (1852) *Synopsis of the Vegetable Products of Scotland.* Peter Lawson, Edinburgh

Leitch, I.J., Johnstone, E., Pellicer, J., Hidalgo, O. & Bennett, M.D. (2019) Plant DNA C-values Database. Release 7.1. https://cvalues.science.kew.org (accessed 22 March 2021)

Lemon, D. (1974) Frank G. Cuthbertson. *NSPS Annual* 1974: 105

Linnaeus, C. (1753) *Species Plantarum. Vol. 2.* Laurentius Salvius, Stockholm

Loudon, J.W. (1840) *The Ladies Flower Garden of Ornamental Annuals.* William Smith, London

Lwin, S. (1956) *Studies in the Genus Lathyrus.* MSc thesis, University of Manchester

Markham, H. (1891) Eckford's sweet peas. *Gard. Chron.* Ser. 3, 10: 284

Marsden-Jones, E.M. (1920) Hybrids of *Lathyrus. J. Roy. Hort. Soc.* 45: xcii–xciii

Martin, G. (2017) *The Sweet Pea Man.* Scotland Street Press, Edinburgh

Martin, M. (2014) *A Description of the Western Islands of Scotland, circa 1695, and a Late Voyage of St. Kilda.* Birlinn, Edinburgh

Matthewman, D. (2015) *Lathyrus vernus. NSPS Spring Bulletin* 2015: 6–8

Maxted, N. (1993) Notes on *Lathyrus hirticarpus* from Syria. *Edinburgh J. Bot.* 50(1): 83–87

Miller, P. (1768) *Gardener's Dictionary.* 8th edn. London

Miller, P. & Martyn, T. (1807) *The Gardener's and Botanist's Dictionary.* F.C. & J. Rivington, London

Mitchell, S. (2016) *Diversity of Floral Traits within the Genus Lathyrus and their Impacts on Pollinator Attraction.* BSc thesis, University of St Andrews

Moldenke, H.N. (1973) Notes on new and noteworthy plants. LXI. *Phytologia* 26: 355

Moldenke, H.N. (1974) Notes on new and noteworthy plants. LXXI. *Phytologia* 29: 75–78

Molyneux, E. (1895) Sweet peas. *Gard. Chron.* Ser. 3, 17: 392

Motoyama, T. (1914) Sweet peas in Japan. *NSPS Annual* 1914: 34

Murray, B.G. & Hammett, K.R.W. (1989) *Lathyrus chloranthus × L. chrysanthus*: a new interspecific hybrid. *Bot. Gaz.* 150(4): 469–476

Nakamura, K., Fukumoto, K. & Akashi, R. (2010) Genetic variability of morphological and cultural characteristics in sweetpea (*Lathyrus odoratus* L.).

J. Japan. Soc. Hort. Sci. 79(2): 179–191

Nandini, A.V., Hammett, K.R.W. & Murray, B.G. (1999) Interspecific hybridization in perennial species of *Lathyrus*. *Agronomie* 19: 521–529

Narayan, R.K.J. (1982) Discontinuous variation in the evolution of plant species: the genus *Lathyrus*. *Evol.* 36: 877–891

National Sweet Pea Society (1912) *The National Sweet Pea Society Catalogue of Variety Names*. NSPS, Brentford

National Sweet Pea Society (2020) *The National Sweet Pea Society Classification List*. NSPS, UK

Nelson, E.C. (2000) *Sea Beans and Nickar Nuts*. Botanical Society of The British Isles, London

Neubert, E.E. & Miotto, S.T.S. (2001) O gênero *Lathyrus* L. (*Leguminosae-Faboideae*) no Brasil. *Iheringia, Bot.* 56: 51–114

Norton, S. (1994) Some observations on *Lathyrus rotundifolius*. *The New Plantsman* 1(2): 78–83

Norton, S. (1996) *Lathyrus, Cousins of the Sweet Pea*. National Council for the Conservation of Plants and Gardens, Surrey

Norton, S. (2008) *Lathyrus* at Weaver's Cottage, West Wickham, Cambridge, and the species illustrated in *Curtis's Botanical Magazine*. *Curtis's Bot. Mag.* 25(4): 350–360

Ohashi, H. (1979) *Leguminosae*. In: Hara, H. & Williams, L.H.J (eds) *An Enumeration of the Flowering Plants of Nepal. Vol. 2*. Trustees of the Natural History Museum, London

Oskoueiyan, R., Kazempour Osaloo, S. & Amirahmadi, A. (2014) Molecular phylogeny of the genus *Lathyrus* (Fabaceae-Fabeae) based on cpDNA matK sequence in Iran. *Iranian J. Biotech.* 12: 41–48

Page, W.B. (1818) *Prodromus*. John Murray, London

Parsons, R. (2000) Early history of the sweet pea. In: Ball, C. (ed.) *National Sweet Pea Society Centenary Celebration 1900–2000*. National Sweet Pea Society, Stockbridge, Hampshire

Parsons, R. (2002) A history of sweet pea trials in England. *NSPS Annual* 2002: 52–60

Parsons, R. (2011) *Sweet Peas: An Essential Guide*. Crowood Press, Marlborough

Parsons, R. (2014) Old-fashioned sweet peas: how authentic are they? *The Plantsman* n.s. 13(1): 10–15

Parsons, R. (2016) Gawler sweet peas. *NSPS Annual* 2016: 107–111

Pecket, R.C. (1960) The nature of the variation in flower colour in the genus *Lathyrus*. *New Phytol.* 59(2): 138–144

Peña-Chocarro, L. & Peña, L.Z. (1999) History and traditional cultivation of *Lathyrus sativus* L. and *Lathyrus cicera* L. in the Iberian peninsula. *Vegetation History and Archaeobotany* 8: 49–52

Pennant, T. (1774) *A Tour in Scotland and Voyage to the Hebrides*. John Monk, Chester

Petiver, J (1713) Botanicum hortense. III. XX. Giving an account of divers rare plants, observed this summer, A.D. 1713, in several curious gardens about London, and particularly the Society of Apothecaries Physick Garden at Chelsea. *Philos. Trans. Roy. Soc. London* 28(337): 177–221

Plitmann, U. (1972) *Lathyrus*. In: Zohary, M (ed.) *Flora Palaestina. Vol. 2*. Jerusalem Academy of Sciences, Jerusalem.

Pockley, D. (1983) The Busby sweet peas. *Australian Garden J.* 2(7): 123

R.D. (1882) Pedigree sweet peas. *Gard. Chron.* n.s. 18: 298

R.D. (1883) Eckford's new sweet peas. *Gard. Chron.* n.s. 20: 264

R.D. (1885) Sweet peas from Boreatton Park. *Gard. Chron.* n.s. 24: 150

R.D. (1887) New sweet peas. *Gard. Chron.* Ser. 3, 2: 170

R.D. (1893) Sweet peas. *Gard. Chron.* Ser. 3, 14: 182, 183

Rees, H. & Narayan, R.K.J. (1989) Biological implications of genome evolution. In: Stirton, C.H. & Zarrucchi, J.L. (eds) *Advances in Legume Biology*. Missouri Botanical Gardens, St Louis

Renfrew, J.M. (1969) The archaeological evidence for the domestication of plants: methods and problems. In: Ucko, P.J. & Dimbleby, G.W. (eds) *The Domestication and Exploitation of Plants and Animals*. Duckworth, London

Rice, G. (2002) *The Sweet Pea Book*. B.T. Batsford, London

Rice, G. (ed.) (2006) *RHS Encyclopedia of Perennials*. Dorling Kindersley, London

Riehl, S. (2008) Climate and agriculture in the ancient Near East: a synthesis of the archaeobotanical and stable carbon isotope evidence. *Veget. Hist. Archaeobot.* 17(suppl. 1): S43–S51

Ritchie, M. & Tilman, D. (1995) Responses of legumes

to herbivores and nutrients during succession on a nitrogen-poor soil. *Ecol.* 76: 2648–2655

Roper, E.M.C. (1989) *Seedtime, the History of Essex Seeds.* Phillimore, Chichester

Rumsey, F. (2019) *Lathyrus hirsutus* L. Native or not... and should it really matter? *BSBI News* 140: 16–20

Rupp, H.B. (1718) *Flora Jenensis.* Jena, Germany

Schaefer, H., Hechenleitner, P., de Sequeira, A., Santos-Guerra, M.M., Pennington, R.T., Kenicer, G. & Carine, M.A. (2012) Systematics, biogeography, and character evolution of the legume tribe *Fabeae* with special focus on the middle-Atlantic island lineages. *BMC Evol. Biol.* 12: 250

Senn, H. (1938) Experimental data for a revision of the genus *Lathyrus. Amer. J. Bot.* 25(2): 67–78

Simola, L.K. (1966) Chemical and morphological characteristics of some endemic species of *Lathyrus* (preliminary report). *Suomen Kemistilehti: the Finnish Chemical Journal* B39: 148–150

Simola, L.K. (1968a) Comparative studies on number of leaflets, venation, and epidermal structure in the genus *Lathyrus. Canad. J. Bot.* 46: 71–84

Simola, L.K. (1968b) Comparative studies on the amino acid pools of three *Lathyrus* species. *Acta Bot. Fenn.* 81: 4–62

Smýkal, P., Hradilová, I., Trněný, O., Brus, J., Rathore, A, Bariotakis, M., Das, R.D., Bhattacharyya, D., Richards, C., Coyne, C.J. & Pirintsos, S. (2017) Genomic diversity and macroecology of the crop wild relatives of domesticated pea. *Nature Sci. Reports* 7: 17384

Sprent, J.I., Ardley, J. & James, E.K. (2017) Biogeography of nodulated legumes and their nitrogen-fixing symbionts. *New Phytol.* 215: 40–56

Stace, C. (2019) *New Flora of the British Isles.* 4th edn. C&M Floristics, Suffolk

Stearn, W.T. (1996) *Report of the Lathyrus Conference, 7–9 June 1996 at Cambridge.* Plant Heritage, Guildford

Taylor, G.M. (1916) The yellow sweet pea. *Gard. Chron.* Ser. 3, 60: 146

Taylor, J.M. (2008) *Ferry-Morse Seed Company.* Argonaut, San Francisco

Taylor, J.M. (2014) *Visions of Loveliness, Great Flower Breeders of the Past.* Swallow Press, Ohio

Teesdale, I. (2006) Growing *Lathyrus nervosus. The Plantsman* n.s. 5(3): 190–191

Thomas, P.J. (1971) Growing sweet peas in the island of St Helena. *NSPS Annual* 1971: 68–69

Townsend, C.C. (1974) *Leguminales.* In: Townsend, C.C. & Guest, E. (eds) *Flora of Iraq. Vol.* 3. Ministry of Agriculture & Agrarian Reform, Baghdad

Tsui, H.P. (1998) *Lathyrus.* In: Tsui H.-P. (ed.) *Flora of China (Flora Reipublicae Popularis Sinicae). Vol.* 42. Chinese Academy of Sciences, Beijing

Turral, J.F. (1965) The old sweet peas. *J. Roy. Hort. Soc.* 90(1): 23–29

Turrill, W.B. (1962) *Lathyrus rotundifolius* × *L. tuberosus. Curtis's Bot. Mag.* 173: t. 384

Unwin, C.W.J. (1926) *Sweet Peas: Their History, Development and Culture.* Heffer, Cambridge

Unwin, C.W.J. (1973) Thomas Henry Bolton. *NSPS Annual* 1973: 3

Unwin, P. (1964) Sweet peas in New Zealand. *NSPS Annual* 1964: 36–39

Valdés B., Rejdali, M., Achhal El Kadmiri, A., Jury, S.L. & Montserrat, J.M. (eds.) (2002) *Checklist of Vascular Plants of N Morocco with Identification Keys.* Consejo Superior de Investigaciones Científicas, Madrid

Van Zeist, W. & de Roller, G.J. (1992) Plant remains from Maadi, a Predynastic site in Lower Egypt. *Veget. Hist. Archaeobot.* 2: 2–14

Vick, J. (1871) *Vick's Illustrated Catalogue and Floral Guide.* Rochester, New York

Weston, T.A. (1920) Sulphuric acid, an aid to germination. *NSPS Annual* 1920: 23–24

Williams, T. (1878) The everlasting pea. *The Garden* 13: 546

Williamson, D.R. (1906) New sweet peas. *Gard. Chron.* Ser. 3, 40: 12–13

Wright, H.J. (1902) Sweet pea 'Dorothy Eckford'. *Gard. Chron.* Ser. 3, 32: 85

Wright, W.P. (1910) *Cassell's Dictionary of Gardening.* Cassell & Co., London

Wright, W.P. (1912) *A Book About Sweet Peas.* 2nd edn. Headley, London

W.W. (1894) Kew notes. *Gard. Chron.* Ser. 3, 16: 7

Zohary D., Hopf, M. & Weiss, E. (2012) *Domestication of Plants in the Old World: The Origin and Spread of Domesticated Plants in Southwest Asia, Europe, and the Mediterranean Basin.* 4th edn. Oxford University Press, Oxford

Index

Publisher's acknowledgements

In additon to those thanked in the authors' acknowledgements (p11) and the photography credits (pp510–511, many of whom have also helped with other aspects of the book), the publisher acknowledges the assistance of James Armitage, Rachel Bedford, Tim Berry, Matthew Cromey, John David, Alistair Griffiths, Keith Hammett, Yvette Harvey, Debora Hodgson, Julie Hollobone, Fiona Hood, Michelle Housden, Tom Howard, Hayley Jones, Jeremy Kirk, Alan Leslie, Diana Levy, Rosalyn Marshall, Anthony Masi, Simon Maughan, Brian Murray, Charlotte Olver, Ally Page, Joe Sharman, Rae Spencer-Jones, Melanie Steel, Lou Tee, Mark Timothy, Tim Upson, Julian Weigall and Chris Young.

Photography credits

AnRo / Wikimedia Commons / CCO 1.0 141
Biodiversity Heritage Library 79, 86B, 87L
Mark Bolton / GAP Photos 109TR
Anna Brockman / RHS 329BL, 335BC, 364BR, 378BR
Caroline Simpson Library and Research Collection 75
Ali Cundy / RHS 287
Peter Davis 166
Sheila Dearing / RHS 98
Heather Drake / Alamy Stock Photo 116
Sue Drew / RHS 81TR, 83L, 102L, 117, 299TL, 302TR, 307L, 324BR, 326TL, 331R, 332BC, 336TL, 338TC, 346BR, 348L, 351BR, 352BC, 354TL, 354BC, 358L, 361BC, 363BR, 367TR, 368TL, 372TL, 372BR, 373BR, 375TL, 376TC, 377TR, 378TR, 381BC, 381BR, 384BR, 386L, 387BL, 395BC, 397BR, 405L
Aleksandr Ebel 58T, 143B
Felspar13 / Wikimedia Commons / CC BY-SA 4.0 241
John Fielding 5, 8, 17, 23T, 48BR, 54, 55, 109TL, 109BL, 109BR, 110, 111BL, 162B, 163, 229, 257, 293L, 293BR, 308BL, 318TC, 400BL
Ori Fragman-Sapir / Jerusalem Botanical Gardens 132T, 142, 146, 153T, 162T, 167T, 172, 259
Martin Gardner 178
Bob Gibbons / Alamy Stock Photo 34L, 258B
Mike Grant 13, 31, 43, 53T, 60, 107, 111BR
Susan Grayer / RHS 317BC, 361TC
David Guscott 285
Andrew Halstead / RHS 111TR, 112R
Keith Hammett 29, 67B (courtesy of), 72B, 81L, 88, 90, 91R, 289BR, 327L, 379TC

Steve Hampson 107
Sydney Hac 3TC, 342TC, 345BR, 388BR, 405R
Neil Hepworth / RHS rear jacket TR, 207, 344TR, 364BC, 370TR, 380L
Heritage Image Partnership Ltd / Alamy Stock Photo 21
Andr Hospr / Wikimedia Commons / CC BY-SA 4.0 147
Colin Hughes 194, 197
Hunt Institute for Botanical Documentation 37
Greg Kenicer rear jacket BR, 2R, 15, 18T, 18C, 19L, 19R, 20T, 20B, 23BL, 23BR, 24TR, 24BR, 25L, 25R, 33, 36, 38, 40T, 40BR, 44, 45R, 46BL, 46BR, 47T, 47C, 47B, 48T, 48BL, 50, 52L, 52R, 53BL, 63BC, 53BR, 58BL, 58BR, 59, 63, 97, 99, 115L, 115R, 118, 128T, 128C, 128B, 131, 134, 135B, 138T, 139T, 139B, 140T, 140B, 143T, 152T, 152B, 153B, 157, 167, 179T, 179B, 181T, 181B, 183T, 183B, 185, 187, 190, 195T, 195B, 196, 202, 203T, 203B, 209, 211, 213T, 213B, 214, 217, 221, 222, 223, 225T, 225B, 226, 228, 232T, 232B, 233, 234B, 235, 237, 240T, 240B, 242, 245, 249, 251, 258T, 260, 262, 263
David Lemon 80
Lindley Library / RHS 1, 16, 27L, 32, 68R, 71, 86T, 87R
Bob Martin / RHS 266
J. McDonald 77
Sarah Mitchell 51
Martin Mulchinock / RHS 64
Kaome Nakamura 30
National Sweet Pea Society 70B
Roger Parsons rear jacket L, 2C, 10, 18B, 24L, 26, 27R, 45L, 46T, 49T, 49B, 65, 66, 67TL, 67TR, 68L (courtesy of), 69 (courtesy of), 70T, 72T, 73, 74 (courtesy of), 76L, 76TR, 76BR, 78T, 78B, 80T, 81BR, 82T, 82B, 83R, 86, 85L, 85R, 89, 92, 95,

102R, 103T (courtesy of), 103B, 104, 105R, 112L,
113B, 129, 132B, 133, 135T, 138B, 145, 155, 189, 193,
210, 234T, 239, 246, 256, 269T, 269B, 286L,
286R, 288, 289TR, 290L, 290TR, 290BR, 291T,
291B, 292, 294TL, 294BL, 294R, 295R, all on
pp296–405 (except 296BR, 299TL, 302TR,
304L, 307L, 308BL, 317BC, 318TC, 324BR, 326TL,
327L, 329BL, 331R, 332BC, 333TC, 335BC, 336TL,
338TC, 342TC, 344TR, 345BR, 346BR, 348L,
350BL, 351BR, 352BC, 354BC, 354TL, 355BR,
356TL, 358L, 361BC, 361TC, 363BR, 364BC,
364BR, 367TR, 368TL, 370TR, 372BR, 372TL,
373BR, 375TL, 376TC, 377TR, 378BR, 378TR,
379TC, 380L, 381BC, 381BR, 382TR, 384BR,
386L, 387BL, 388BR, 392TC, 395BC, 397BR,
400BL, 405L, 405R)

Peganum / **Wikimedia Commons** / **CC BY-SA 2.0**
100

Barry Phillips / **RHS** 355BR

Katy Prentice / **RHS** 91

RHS 108, 111TL, 113TL, 113TR, 296BR, 304L,
350BL, 382TR

Tim Sandall / **RHS** 2L, 12, 42, 94, 96, 105L, 106L,
106R, 149, 267, 268

Carol Sheppard / **RHS** 34R, 40BL, 101, 261, 265,
293TR

Trevor Sims / **GWI Images** front jacket

Mike Sleigh / **RHS** 137

Sergey Stefanov / **Wikimedia Commons** / **CC
BY-SA 3.0** 219

Steinsplitter / **Wikimedia Commons** / **CC BY-SA
3.0** 61

Graham Titchmarsh / **RHS** 289L

Tim Woodford 14, 114, 356TL, 392TC

H. Zell / **Wikimedia Commons** / **CC BY-SA 3.0**
151